# THE MOLIÈRE ENCYCLOPEDIA

# THE MOLIÈRE ENCYCLOPEDIA

*Edited by James F. Gaines*

GREENWOOD PRESS
Westport, Connecticut · London

**Library of Congress Cataloging-in-Publication Data**

The Molière Encyclopedia / edited by James F. Gaines.
   p.  cm.
  Includes bibliographical references and index.
  ISBN 0–313–31255–9 (alk. paper)
  1. Moliáre, 1622–1673—Dictionaries. I. Gaines, James F.
PQ1851.M57 2002
 842′.4—dc21   2002016082

British Library Cataloguing in Publication Data is available.

Library of Congress Catalog Card Number: 2002016082
ISBN: 0–313–31255–9

First published in 2002

Greenwood Press, 88 Post Road West, Westport, CT 06881
An imprint of Greenwood Publishing Group, Inc.
www.greenwood.com

Printed in the United States of America

The paper used in this book complies with the
Permanent Paper Standard issued by the National
Information Standards Organization (Z39.48–1984).

10 9 8 7 6 5 4 3 2 1

# Contents

# Introduction

The primary purpose of this encyclopedia is to make available to the average American reader all desirable reference information on the great French comic dramatist Molière. However, behind this simple statement lie two major matters that require further definition: what is meant by the "average American reader" and how much information is desirable? To address the first question, it must be assumed that the average American reader is not a specialist with a graduate degree, but a curious and well-trained amateur or a student at secondary or undergraduate level who has come into contact with Molière in the course of studies in French, comparative, or world literature. Though such a person may not be fluent in French, he or she must be willing to deal with some French terminology in order to satisfy the thirst for information. Since there is no standard English translation for the whole of Molière's work, it is virtually impossible not to include some French terms in this volume. However, to make them more accessible to Americans, they have been glossed and translated as frequently as possible without being too repetitious. The editor has rendered quotes from the original text into English in his own wording to give the clearest meaning in the particular context. Where feasible, efforts have been made to conserve some of the poetic quality of Molière's verse, but this has not been practical in all cases. I have chosen to retain as much of the original denotative and connotative content of Molière's French as possible. It may be argued that modern theatrical scripts of the plays that depart from some of the more dated terminology are just as enjoyable as ones that are linguistically correct, and this can be true for spectators in a theater audience. However, it must be pointed out that what is appreciated in the departure from the original is the art of Tony Harrison or John Wood or Richard Wilbur, rather than that of Molière.

Furthermore, I have decided not to create an overly simplified, "pop" version of knowledge on Molière. What is true enough to say to an undergraduate should also hold true for the most sophisticated scholar, though the latter may delve deeper into specialized interpretations and investigations. As will be clear from certain entries in this encyclopedia, Molière studies have suffered ever since the beginning from too much popularization, which has introduced a large amount of inaccurate and dubious material into a great many books in both French and English. What unfortunately is lost in appealing to such a wide Anglophone readership is the degree to which Molière's original language has permeated the mentality and culture of France, in a way that can only be compared to Shakespeare in English, Goethe in German, Tolstoy in Russian. Without a deeper knowledge of the French language, the amateur cannot appreciate how phrases, scenes, and characters from his plays leap into the consciousness of French-speakers as they deal with the problems of the universe and those of everyday life. However, no encyclopedia can hope simultaneously to bridge the gaps of language and culture at the same time as those of knowledge. Thus, while making things clear enough for the average young nonspecialist, I have tried to maintain a degree of veracity and detail worthy of higher critical levels.

The second major question, that of what constitutes the boundary of useful knowledge on the subject of Molière, also must be examined in the perspective of relativity. The wide category of possible readers for the encyclopedia ranges from people searching for single bits of specific information, to those looking for a very generalized summary of larger areas, and on to those seeking references related to the texts of whole plays or groups of them. I have sought to group knowledge succinctly under well-defined rubrics, while relying on liberal cross-references to supply related concepts, rather than trying to provide all-inclusive entries. This compromise is necessary to accommodate the interests of a general readership.

Obviously, it would be shameful to try to limit the knowledge of Molière to what is written in English. Although his plays attracted a wide audience in Britain and revolutionized the English stage even before the dramatist had died, and although English-language scholarship since the beginning of the twentieth century has added many important insights on him, it would be impossible to get even a general perspective of knowledge on Molière without including French primary sources. I have tried to organize material from French and English sources in such a way as to provide as seamless a body of data as possible. Bibliographies accompanying specific entries are limited to a small number of salient items, especially those in English. The inclusive bibliography at the end of the book will supplement those sources for persons curious to know more about the topics. Obviously, this bibliography is selective, since a complete and detailed bibliography of work on Molière would itself occupy an entire volume. For readers needing this kind of reference, I ask them to consult the fine existing bibliographies available in research libraries everywhere. I have confined the bibliography in this book to the items that are most timely and most directly related to the information in the entries.

The dimension of time is equally important to the organization of knowledge in this encyclopedia. Given the gradual disappearance of

Shakespeare, much less Restoration dramatists, from the English-language curriculum, one faces a mass of readers who have little acquaintance with the actual conditions of early modern theater and who are mainly conversant in the genres of musical comedy and cinema. It is therefore essential to provide a good deal of coverage on subjects such as the staging conditions of the plays and even the historical, economical, and social background from which they emerged. Fortunately, scholarship on the latter subjects has never been better than at the present time, when we are able to take advantage of nearly a century of revisionist research that has profoundly altered and reformed thinking about the Age of Louis XIV. With a myriad of myths dispelled and an equal quantity of lost facts restored, we are now more than ever able to appreciate the life of Molière, his colleagues, his friends and enemies, and their clients and protectors, in a high degree of detail and relevance. Rather than deal with Molière from an imaginary Victorian armchair, as have so many writers on this subject, I have attempted to present an up-to-date state of judgment on the author in a most dynamic and probing historical setting. As I preserved even the archaic elements of Molière's plays, I have framed the discussion in terms of the latest and best understanding of all features. Molière's own emphasis on timeliness demands no less.

In speaking of the dramatist and his life, I have been extremely conservative as to verifiable facts. Some readers may not be pleased that I attribute no reliability at all to the anecdotes that have peppered lives of Molière from the beginning through modern efforts, including Ariane Mnouchkine's film "biography." But romantic fiction deserves no status as information. The Molière who emerges from these pages will be less fantastical than the one painted in many books, but he will be truer and, I would argue, no less fascinating for being a common, self-made man, a hard, conscientious worker, and a careful artist.

# Chronology

| | | |
|---|---|---|
| **1621** | April 27 | Marriage of Jean Poquelin and Marie Cressé, Molière's parents. |
| **1622** | January 15 | Baptism of Jean–Baptiste Poquelin, presumably born within the previous few days at the "House of the Apes," on the corner of the rue Saint–Honoré and the rue des Vieilles–Étuves. |
| **1632** | May 11 | Death of Molière's mother. |
| **1633** | April 11 | Molière's father signs a contract to remarry with Catherine Fleurette, a neighbor. |
| **1636** | November 12 | Death of Molière's stepmother. |
| **1637** | December 14 | Earliest legal reference to Molière designated as his father's heir to the office of royal upholsterer (*tapissier et valet de chambre du roi*). The official designation of Molière as heir to the office had occurred at an earlier date and would not be overturned until 1657, when Molière transferred the office to his younger brother. |

| | | |
|---|---|---|
| **1643** | June 30 | Contract signed for the constitution of the company of the Illustre Théâtre. Along with Molière, who still signed under his birth name, the other partners include Madeleine and Geneviève Béjart and their older brother Joseph, Denis Beys, Germain Clérin, Nicolas Bonnenfant, Georges Pinel (Molière's old writing teacher), Catherine Des Urlis, and Madeleine Malingre. Molière, Joseph Béjart, and Clerin were to alternate as male leads, while Madeleine had her choice of the female roles. Most of them would continue their theatrical careers for some time after the collapse of the ill–fated company. Molière is recorded as living on his own in the rue de Thorigny, near the Béjarts. Having become an actor, Molière cedes his office as *tapissier et valet de chambre du roi* to his brother Jean. |
| **1644** | December 19 | The Illustre Théâtre company dissolves its lease at the Mestayers tennis court and creates a new one with the Black Cross tennis court, relocating from the vicinity of the Tour de Nesle in the Saint–Germain neighborhood to the less remote rue des Barrés. |
| **1645** | April and May | Beginnings of the debt proceedings against Molière and the other members of the Illustre Théâtre company, culminating in September with a 1600 *livres* judgment against them for their unpaid rent of the Black Cross. |
| | August 2 | 2 August: Having been briefly placed in prison for debts, Molière is released. |
| | Autumn | Molière leaves Paris to join Charles Dufresne's wandering troupe. |
| **1646** | | Dufresne's troupe moves back and forth between Nantes and Rennes. |
| **1647** | | Dufresne's players, sponsored now by the duc d'Épernon, are recorded in Carcassone, Albi, and Toulouse. |
| **1648** | | The wandering troupe performs at Nantes and Poitiers. |

| | | |
|---|---|---|
| | June 11 | First written evidence of Molière in Dufresne's troupe. |
| 1649 | | Dufresne's troupe plays in Toulouse and Narbonne, having been prevented from playing in Poitiers by order of the town government. |
| 1650 | | The troupe is recorded at Narbonne, Agen, and Pézenas. |
| 1652 | | Performances at Grenoble. |
| 1653 | | The troupe is at Lyon. |
| | September | Dufresne's troupe performs before the Prince de Conti at Pézenas and receives his patronage. |
| 1654 | | Performances at Montpellier and Vienne. |
| | November 2 | The troupe performs Molière's *L'Étourdi* for the first time. |
| 1655 | | The players' presence is noted at Lyon, Dijon, and Pézenas, where the Ballet des Incompatibles is performed. |
| 1656 | | Pézenasm Narbonne, Bordeaux, Agen, and Béziers record the passage of the troupe. |
| 1657 | | Apart from a summer visit to Dijon, where they are identified as the Comedians of the Prince de Conti, the troupe spends most of the year in Lyon. |
| 1658 | | Molière's troupe has relocated to Rouen for the summer, in preparation for their return to Paris. |
| | October 24 | Command performance of Corneille's *Nicomède* and the farce *Le Docteur amoureux* for Louis XIV at the Louvre. |
| | November 2 | Having become the Troupe de Monsieur, the players soon begin performances at the Petit–Bourbon theater, with the highly acclaimed Paris premiere of *L'Étourdi*. |
| | December | Paris premiere of *Dépit amoureux*. |

**1659**   April 13         Charles Dufresne retires from the troupe; Gros René and Mlle. Du Parc quit the troupe to join the Marais company, while Jodelet and his brother L'Espy do the opposite.   Young La Grange also joins.

           October 4        Du Parc and his wife sign papers to rejoin the Troupe de Monsieur, having left it together for the Marais during the Easter break.   Their contract contains an unusual four–year obligation.

           November 18      Premiere of *Les Précieuses ridicules.*

**1660**   January 13       Privilege to Guillaume de Luynes to print *Les Précieuses ridicules.*   Printing will conclude January 29.

           April 3          Death of Molière's brother Jean.   Molière resumes holding the family office of royal *tapissier.*

           March 25         Good Friday: death of Jodelet.

           May 28           Premiere of *Sganarelle.*

           May 31           Privilege to Molière to print *L'Étourdi, Dépit amoureux, Sganarelle,* and *Dom Garcie de Navarre.*

           August 12        Publication of pirate edition of *Sganarelle* by Jean Ribou.

           August
           through          Legal proceedings against the pirate bookseller Jean Ribou.
           November

           October 11       Surprise demolition of the Petit–Bourbon theater begins.

**1661**   January 20       The Palais–Royal Theater opens and the Troupe de Monsieur resumes regular performances, having given private performances since October.

           February 4       Premiere of *Dom Garcie de Navarre.*

           June 24          Premiere of *L'École des maris.*

| | | |
|---|---|---|
| | July 9 | Privilege to Molière to print *L'École des maris*, ceded to de Luynes, who will share the printing with de Sercy, Guignard, Barbin, and Quinet. |
| | August 17 | Premiere of *Les Fâcheux* in private performance at Vaux–le–Vicomte. |
| | September 2 | Molière rents an apartment in the rue Saint–Thomas–du–Louvre in the building belonging to Louis–Henry Daquin, one of the royal physicians; he will move in during the coming month. |
| | November 4 | Paris premiere of *Les Fâcheux*. |
| **1662** | January 8 | The Italian players return to France and once again share the stage with Molière, this time at the Palais–Royal. |
| | January 23 | Molière signs a marriage contract with Armande Béjart. |
| | February 5 | Privilege to *print* Les *Fâcheux*; printing was completed by February 18 by Guignard. |
| | February 20 | Marriage ceremony of Molière and Armande Béjart takes place in the church of Saint–Germain–l'Auxerrois. |
| | Easter break | Brécourt and La Thorillière join the troupe for the coming year. |
| | October 27 | Transfer of privilege for *Étourdi*, *Dépit amoureux*, *Sganarelle*, and *Dom Garcie de Navarre* to Barbin and Quinet. |
| | November 24 | Publication of *Dépit amoureux* by Quinet. |
| | December 26 | Premiere of *L'École des femmes*. |
| **1663** | February 4 | Privilege to print *L'École des femmes* to de Luynes; printing will be completed on March 17. |
| | Easter break | L'Espy retires from the troupe. |
| | June 1 | Premiere of *La Critique de l'École des femmes*. |

|              |                |                                                                                                                                                                                                                                                                                                                                                                        |
| ------------ | -------------- | ---------------------------------------------------------------------------------------------------------------------------------------------------------------------------------------------------------------------------------------------------------------------------------------------------------------------------------------------------------------------- |
|              | June 10        | Privilege to print *La Critique de l'École des femmes* to Claude de Sercy; printing will be completed August 7.                                                                                                                                                                                                                                                         |
|              | October 19     | Premiere of *L'Impromptu de Versailles*.                                                                                                                                                                                                                                                                                                                                |
| **1664**     | January 19     | Birth of Louis Poquelin, Molière's first son; he would not be baptized until February 28, perhaps because illness prevented his going to the church, and would die on November 10 of the same year. The godparents were the King and Henrietta of England, by proxy through the Duke de Créqui and the Maréchale du Plessis, two faithful members of the court.          |
|              | January 29     | Premiere of *Le Mariage forcé* at the Louvre.                                                                                                                                                                                                                                                                                                                           |
|              | Easter break   | Brécourt leaves the troupe for the Hôtel de Bourgogne, while Hubert comes from the Marais to take his place.                                                                                                                                                                                                                                                            |
|              | May            | The troupe travels to Versailles to participate in the *Plaisirs de l'Île enchantée* festival; premieres of *La Princesse d'Élide* (May 8) and *Tartuffe* (May 12). The latter, presented in a truncated three–act version, had already been denounced as early as April 17 by the Company of the Holy Sacrament.                                                        |
|              | June 20        | Molière's troupe presents Racine's first staged tragedy, *La Thébaïde*.                                                                                                                                                                                                                                                                                                 |
|              | October 28     | Death of Gros–René.                                                                                                                                                                                                                                                                                                                                                     |
|              | November 9     | Paris premiere of *La Princesse d'Élide*.                                                                                                                                                                                                                                                                                                                               |
| **1665**     | February 15    | Premiere of *Dom Juan*.                                                                                                                                                                                                                                                                                                                                                 |
|              | March 11       | Privilege to print *Dom Juan* to Louis Billaine; it will be registered May 24, along with Prades's *Arsace*, but never used.                                                                                                                                                                                                                                            |
|              | August 4       | Baptism of Esprit–Madeleine Poquelin, Molière's only daughter, who had been born, most probably, in the days just before.                                                                                                                                                                                                                                               |

August 14    Louis XIV officially adopts the troupe as his own and accords them a yearly subsidy of 7,000 *livres*.

September 14    Premiere of *L'Amour médecin* at Versailles; it opens in Paris on September 22.

October    Molière and his family move from Daquin's building to another in the rue Saint–Thomas–du–Louvre; he will make a similar move in the same street during the 1668 Easter break.

December 4    Molière's troupe stages Racine's *Alexandre le grand*; on the 18, they will be shocked to find that the author has given it to the rival Hôtel de Bourgogne troupe.

December 29    Molière falls seriously ill and the troupe suspends operations until February 21.

December 30    Privilege to print *L'Amour médecin* to Molière, transferred to Gabriel Quinet and later to other printers; printing will be completed on January 15.

**1666**    January 20    Death of the Queen Mother; official mourning period closes all theaters until the next month.

March 6    Privilege to Quinet to print a collective edition containing *Sganarelle, L'École des maris, L'École des femmes, La Critique de l'École des femmes, Dépit amoureux, L'Étourdi,* and *La Princesse d'Élide.*

June 4    Premiere of *Le Misanthrope.*

June 21    Privilege to print *Le Misanthrope*, later ceded to Ribou; printing was completed on Christmas Eve, but there was apparently a delay of over a month in the sale of the book. It has been speculated that this was due to the inclusion of the *Lettre sur le Misanthrope* as a preface.

August 6    Premiere of *Le Médecin malgré lui.*

October 8    Privilege to print *Le Médecin malgré lui*, later ceded to Ribou; the printing was finished the same day as that of *Le Misanthrope*, December 24.

| | | |
|---|---|---|
| | December 1 | Departure of the troupe for Saint–Germain, where they will perform in the Ballet des muses, beginning with *Mélicerte* on the 2nd  The festival would continue until February 20 of the subsequent year, including the premieres of the *Pastorale comique* on January 5 and *Le Sicilien* on February 14. |
| **1667** | Easter break | Mlle. Du Parc leaves the troupe for the Hôtel de Bourgogne; she will die suddenly and mysteriously on December 11, 1668. |
| | June 10 | Paris premiere of *Le Sicilien*. |
| | August 5 | The first and only presentation of *L'Imposteur*, the intermediary form of *Tartuffe*, leads to a ban by civil and religious authorities.  While La Grange and La Thorillière carry appeals to the King at the battle front in northeast France, the troupe takes a break until September 25, with Molière spending most of the vacation at his country cottage in Auteuil. |
| | October 31 | Privilege to print *Le Sicilien* obtained by Molière, later ceded to Ribou; printing concluded on November 9. |
| **1668** | January 13 | Premiere of *Amphitryon*. |
| | February 20 | Privilege to print *Amphitryon* and *Le Mariage forcé* to Molière, ceded later to Ribou; printing will conclude on March 4 and March 9, respectively. |
| | July 18 | Premiere of *George Dandin* during the *Grand divertissement royal de Versailles* festival. |
| | September 9 | Premiere of *L'Avare* in Paris. |
| | September 30 | Privilege to print *L'Avare* and *George Dandin*; printing for both probably was finished on February 18, 1669. |
| | November 9 | Paris premiere of *George Dandin*. |
| **1669** | February 27 | Death of Molière's father. |

|  | March 15 | Privilege to print *Le Tartuffe* to Molière, ceded to Barbin, and later to Ribou. Printing finished on March 23. In July, Molière will be forced to take legal action to stop a counterfeit edition by the bookseller Hénault. |
|---|---|---|
|  | April 4 | Printing of Molière's poem, "La Gloire du Val de Grâce." |
|  | October 6 | Premiere of *Monsieur de Pourceaugnac* during the royal hunts at Chambord. |
|  | November 15 | Paris premiere of *Monsieur de Pourceaugnac*. |
| **1670** | February 4 | Premiere of *Les Amants magnifiques* at Saint–Germain in command performance for the King. |
|  | February 20 | Privilege to print *Monsieur de Pourceaugnac* to Molière, later ceded to Ribou; printing completed on March 3. |
|  | April 16 | Molière's troupe creates a pension for the retiring Louis Béjart. |
|  | April 28 | Baron returns to Molière's troupe with a full share of the proceeds. |
|  | July | Beauval and Mlle. Beauval are summoned by royal letter to join the troupe, with a share and a half of the proceeds, due mainly to the wife's talents. |
|  | October 14 | Premiere of *Le Bourgeois gentilhomme* during the royal hunts at Chambord. |
|  | November 23 | Paris premiere of *Le Bourgeois gentilhomme*. |
|  | December 31 | Privilege to Molière to print *Le Bourgeois gentilhomme*, *Psyché*, and *Les Femmes savantes*, later ceded to Le Monnier and Barbin, Le Monnier, and Promé, respectively. Printing will conclude on March 17, 1671; October 6, 1671; and December 10, 1672, respectively. |
| **1671** | January 17 | Premiere of *Psyché* at the Tuileries Palace in a royal command performance. |

|             |              |                                                                                                                                                                                                                                                          |
|-------------|--------------|----------------------------------------------------------------------------------------------------------------------------------------------------------------------------------------------------------------------------------------------------------|
|             | March 18     | Privilege granted to Molière to publish *Les Fourberies de Scapin*; printing completed on August 18.                                                                                                                                                      |
|             | May 24       | Premiere of *Les Fourberies de Scapin*.                                                                                                                                                                                                                   |
|             | July 24      | Paris premiere of *Psyché*.                                                                                                                                                                                                                               |
|             | December 2   | Premiere of *La Comtesse d'Escarbagnas* at Saint–Germain Palace.                                                                                                                                                                                          |
| **1672**    | February 17  | Death of Madeleine Béjart.                                                                                                                                                                                                                                |
|             | March 11     | Premiere of *Les Femmes savantes*.                                                                                                                                                                                                                        |
|             | March 29     | Molière takes legal action against Lully after the latter had managed unilaterally to set up a royal academy of music in Paris. Lully will obtain further privileges in opera production and musical copyright over the course of the summer.              |
|             | July 8       | Paris premiere of *La Comtesse d'Escarbagnas*.                                                                                                                                                                                                            |
|             | July 26      | Molière rents a new apartment in the rue de Richelieu. He will move in in September.                                                                                                                                                                      |
|             | September 15 | Birth of Molière's second son, Pierre–Jean–Baptiste–Armand; he would be baptized two weeks later with Boileau's brother Pierre as godfather and Mignard's daughter Catherine–Marguerite as godmother. The child would only survive until October 11.      |
| **1673**    | February 10  | Premiere of *Le Malade imaginaire*.                                                                                                                                                                                                                       |
|             | February 17  | Death of Molière.                                                                                                                                                                                                                                         |
|             | February 21  | Burial of Molière at Saint–Joseph Cemetary.                                                                                                                                                                                                               |

# A

**Abominable Book**. In the fifth act of **Le Misanthrope**, **Alceste** relates that his opponent in a lawsuit, besides corrupting the justices, lying, and bringing to bear the influence of his devout friends, has circulated an "abominable book" through the salons of **Paris**, claiming that it is a product of Alceste. Some of Molière's detractors, such as **Pierre Roullé**, make vague references to unnamed texts that are shameful or dangerous. The editor Louis–Auguste Ménard in 1883 published what he believed to be the manuscript in question, an anonymous tome from the Arsenal Library entitled *L'Innocence persécutée*. However, there is no indication whatsoever that this was the work referred to by either Molière or his enemies, nor does it bear any resemblance to the author's style. Of course, he had little spare time to devote to lengthy volumes of satirical prose. There were a number of books published during the 1660s that caused scandals, political or religious, perhaps the most famous being Bussy–Rabutin's *Histoire amoureuse des Gaules*, a thinly veiled account of **Louis XIV's love** life that earned the author a stay in the Bastille and a long sentence of internal exile to his Burgundian estates. However, there was no known implication of Molière in the writing or distribution of any well known scandalous books of the period. Another hypothesis is that the abominable book referred to Molière's translation of **Lucretius**, which he apparently read in some salons. While Lucretius could be considered controversial, *De Rerum natura* does not contain anything indecent or directly challenging to religion. In fact, its pagan status acted to deflect some of the criticism that such a philosophical treatise might have incurred, had it come from an early modern pen. It seems wisest to accept Alceste's claim that rumors of such a work are total fabrications.

**Académie Française, or Academy.** Founded in 1634 by **Richelieu** and chartered in 1637, this group of forty intellectuals was given the charge to produce a dictionary and other standardized linguistic documents for the French **language.** Richelieu acted partly in order to bring within his control an unofficial group that had been organized by the Protestant Conrart, and partly to enlarge the stable of writers at his disposal for political purposes. Though the young Academy quickly was involved in the literary evaluation of **Pierre Corneille's** tragicomedy *Le Cid*, it seldom thereafter intervened directly in literary quarrels. Academicians such as **Chapelain** did watch over Molière's works and recommended him for the royal pension list. However, he was not, like his friends **Boileau** and **La Fontaine**, admitted to the Academy during his lifetime. This is perhaps because the theater was not considered a very lofty genre. Most writers had to earn their membership on the basis of translations, Classical scholarship, or, as in the case of Corneille, religious writings. Molière might have undertaken his work on **Lucretius** in hopes of eventual acceptance.

**Acante** (*Mélicerte*). Acante is in love with **Daphné**, as we learn in the first scene, but she is in love with **Myrtil**. Acante and his friend **Tyrène** present themselves to complain to Myrtil (II, 5), only to learn to their immense relief that he is in love with **Mélicerte**. It is probable that this role was taken either by **La Grange** or **Du Croisy**.

**Acaste** (*Le Misanthrope*). The noisier of the two vain, foppish aristocrats who visit **Célimène**. They first make their appearance in Act II, scene 4, where they figure as *fâcheux*, interrupting **Alceste's** private conversation with Célimène over their relationship. The lady is only too happy to welcome this break, however, for it is Alceste's ultimatums that are bothersome to her. Once together, the group launches immediately into the famous "**portrait** scene," and the two marquis take turns feeding possibilities to their hostess as she viciously skewers her acquaintences with accurate but devastating descriptions of their behavior and character. Acaste's flippancy, name dropping, and use of expressions such as "Dieu me damne!" mark him as a ridiculous fellow, an impression that was probably reinforced by typical, outlandish marquis attire. Despite Alceste's attempts to get rid of them, both Acaste and his sidekick **Clitandre** express their intention of staying at Célimène's all day long. We learn at the beginning of the third act the reason for this persistence, for they both are courting the lady and each fancies himself the stronger in her affections. It is Acaste who gives the lengthy, conceited speech about his own merit and then goes on to voice a typical view of *galant* **love** relationships. According to this standpoint, love should be casual, seeking pleasure while avoiding cumbersome commitments. He frames this discussion in ironically commercial language. After a good deal of verbal sparring with his rival to see which has proof of his preferment, the two retire to examine the evidence rather than suffer **Arsinoé's** prudish presence. Indeed, they do not reappear until the final scene of the play, where they take turns giving a dramatic reading of the **letters** where Célimène subjects each of them to the harshness of her portraiture, while at the same time promising love in the corresponding missive. Once again, it is Acaste who is the more talkative of the marquis, showing that he considers the shame of having been mistreated by Célimène to be less important than the opportunity for taking center stage in every salon, which chance is furnished by the guilty letters. He would rather be able to flaunt his importance, even if he is the victim of the criticism. This foolishness fits with many of La Rochefoucauld's maxims on *l'amour propre*, which insist on the irresistible call of vanity, even when vanity itself must pay the price for ostentation. The original casting is unknown, but one imagines **Du Croisy** or **André Hubert** in this role more readily than **Louis Béjart** or **La Thorillière**.

*Adelphi.* A **Latin** comedy by **Terence** that may have influenced Molière's *L'École des maris*, although the sex of the minors in the Roman play is different, both of Terence's youngsters being boys.

**Adraste** (*Le Sicilien*). He is the master of **Hali**, the brother of **Climène**, and the wooer of **Isidore**, the former **Greek slave** girl sequestered by **Dom Pèdre**. He first appears in scene 2 to lead a serenade beneath Isidore's window, telling Hali that the two have been communicating merely with their eyes for some weeks. After the singing, Dom Pèdre eavesdrops as he tells Hali of his plans to present himself to Isidore through "some means, some invention, some ruse" that will give him access. He gives Hali his permission to try his best, but just when the Turk is about to admit defeat in scene 9, Adraste himself says that his acquaintance with the painter Damon has given him the plan he needed. He boldly proceeds to kiss Isidore as they meet, explaining to the irritated Dom Pèdre that it is the custom of France. Knowing something of the art of painting (against the general rule that gentlemen should not know how to do anything), he uses his status to gain Isidore's full attention: "A bit more to this side, your eyes always turned towards me, please. Your gaze and mine should be constantly joined." Hali arrives **disguised** as a **duelist** just in time to avert Dom Pèdre's nosiness, as the badinage between lovers goes on. He has just had time to explain his ruse to her and perhaps to sneak a kiss, when Dom Pèdre returns, and he excuses their closeness by explaining that he was just giving her complexion a thorough inspection. When Adraste returns in scene 15, it is as the jealous husband of Climène. He explains to Dom Pèdre that the French always excel in whatever they do, and that if they take it into their heads to be jealous, they can be twenty times more so than any Sicilian. Nevertheless, he quickly promises an accommodation in order to be able to abscond with his beloved, and unlike many such elopers in Molière's comedies, they never return to beg forgiveness. **La Grange** shows himself to be craftier in this role than in any other, except perhaps that of **Dom Juan**. He manages here to surpass himself not only as a seducer, but also as something of a patriot.

**Agen**. City on the Garonne between **Bordeaux** and **Toulouse** where Molière performed as part of the itinerant troupe of **Charles Dufresne**. The troupe spent the Mardi Gras season of 1650 there and returned in the winter of 1656.

**Agénor** (*Psyché*). He is one of the two young princes who court the princess and who together make a profession of **love** in the first act of the play. It is known that **La Grange** and **Hubert** played the two roles, but it is uncertain which actor played which prince. Since **Cléomène** seems the quicker to speak of the two, we may assume it was Hubert who played Agénor. After fending off the undesired attentions of **Psyche's** sisters and presenting their feelings, the young men are rejected on the grounds that their merit is too equal and their friendship too perfect to spoil by preferring one over the other. They reappear in the second act at the scene of the sacrifice and bravely offer to defend the princess from whatever monster is sent to take her, but she dismisses them. Love leads them to their deaths, and Psyche meets them again in the underworld in Act IV.

**Aglante** (*La Princesse d'Élide*). This cousin of the **Princess** was played by the lovely **Mlle. Du Parc**. Her role is largely that of a confidante. Though often present on stage, her main contributions are confined to Act II, scene 2, where she and **Cynthie** defend the joys of love against the Princess's criticisms, and Act IV, scene 3, where she somewhat reluctantly agrees to her cousin's demand that she reject any offer of marriage by **Euryale**. In fact, we see very little of her emotional reaction to this prospect, which Euryale has raised in order to trick the Princess, and nothing of her response to the offers by **Aristomène** or **Théocle** that come in the concluding act.

**Aglaure** (*Psyché*). One of the jealous sisters of young **Psyche**, Aglaure was played by either **Mlle. Marotte**, La Grange's future wife, or **Mlle. Beauval**, but we are not sure which actress played which sister. The two are equally miserable and equally disagreeable as they spend the entire first scene moping about why their younger sibling manages to attract all the suitors. Unable to believe she is actually more beautiful than they, the pair finally attributes her superior success to her faculty of being easygoing and polite. Though they vow to try to imitate this behavior, the next scenes show how incapable they are, for they greet Psyche's attempt to deflect a couple of suitors their way with the worst possible grace. The two are rather happy to hear that their sister is to be sacrificed, and they seem to want to actually witness her destruction as they linger by her side in the second act, even though their presence is unwished. When they are brought to **Cupid's** realm in the third act, through an act of kindness by the naïve Psyche, they grow even more **jealous** of her fate. There is little difference between these two Grecian ladies and a pair of nasty, importunate aristocrats of seventeenth–century **Paris**.

**Agnès** (*L'École des femmes*). This young lady, played originally by **Mlle. de Brie**, is described as a naïve girl whom **Arnolphe** has literally purchased from a woman in the country in order to raise according to his own fantasies and eventually marry. Her name evokes lamblike innocence and the double face of that innocence dominates the dynamics of the play. Proposing to display her to his friend **Chrysalde**, Arnolphe considers her a total idiot and offers as evidence a question she asked about whether babies could be conceived by the ear. Of course, the bully misses the point of the phrase, which is much more sophisticated than he guesses, since Agnès has already discovered, even in her ignorance, that words and gestures are the first steps in the elaborate process of **love**. When she appears, knitting in hand, and tells her captor that the only news during his absence is the death of a kitten, he wrongly congratulates himself on his complete mastery of her.

In the second act, when she discloses the events of **Horace's** first appearance to her, she displays such candor that even Arnolphe accepts her implication that she did not divulge them before because she considered them unworthy of his attention. It is clear that she has failed to perceive Arnolphe's lecherous intent for her, which is more than even his evil behavior would have led her to guess. Arnolphe is not clever enough to exploit her own hesitations about the prospects of love and the unique pleasure that it seems to offer. Instead, he attempts to paint it with such a dark brush that she cannot accept the likelihood of his depiction, and she has to start thinking for herself — exactly the opposite of what the man would have intended. The shock of learning that Arnolphe intends to marry her himself, instead of opening the door to knowledge of the pleasure bearing other, the "là" that she cannot accurately describe, destroys any remaining faith she could have had in his advice. Thus, when in Act III he tries to brainwash her by making her recite the Maxims of **Marriage**, it is already too late. Beneath the enforced words of authoritarian virtue, the mind has already been working out its own view of reality, expressed in the remarkable **letter** that Horace finds attached to the rock she hurls at him from her window. Though couched in very simple **language**, Agnès's letter reveals a sentimental sophistication far beyond her years and experience. Even if her appeal to Horace were in vain, she has already evolved past the point where Arnolphe could possibly control her, even were he much more clever than he pretends to be.

So much of Agnès's development comes secondhand, through report and letter, or slipped in between words that are not completely hers, that her tête-à-tête with Horace in Act V, scene 3 and the ensuing discussion with the unveiled Arnolphe assume supreme importance. Through her understated conversation, she projects the all importance of love to the human spirit and the vanity of logical attempts to corral it or exploit it. Agnès's sympathetic plainness of speech is a necessary foil to Arnolphe's pathetic whining, once he removes the mask of brutality and tries to behave, in turn, like a human, only to produce a ridiculous simulacrum of emotion. In terms of the emotional plot, this scene is the actual conclusion of the play, for afterward the element of chance takes over, exactly as Chrysalde had earlier predicted, and Arnolphe's final precautions prove as useless as his earlier ones had been. Agnès occupies an unusually prominent position among the women in Molière's canon, since his later young lovers will be similarly beset by parental authority, the threat of misery, or the internal conflicts of **lovers' spite**, but will never have so clear a chance to present the movements and motives of their untrained, guileless hearts.

*Aimer sans savoir qui* (1646).    A comedy by **D'Ouville** that may have contributed certain elements to *Dépit amoureux*.

**Alain** (*L'École des femmes*).    A bumbling **servant** type in the tradition of **Gros–René**. Alain and his feminine counterpart, **Georgette**, enrage **Arnolphe** by their inefficiency, failing to open the door to him promptly in Act I, scene 2 and then giving ridiculous excuses for their tardiness. Presumably picked for their stupidity, they are an unlikely pair to guard his treasured ward **Agnès**. Alain prefigures such servants as **Dubois** in *Le Misanthrope*, **Sganarelle** in *Dom Juan*, and **Maître Jacques** in *L'Avare*. The character was played originally by **Brécourt**, who specialized in comic **peasant** roles. Alain's mixture of bluster and cowardice is typical of the peasant on the comic stage. He threatens to shove Georgette out of the way and later administers a true shoving to his master during a rehearsal of how he is supposed to treat the intruder, **Horace**. But when Arnolphe yells and scowls at him, he faints and cowers like Georgette, and along with her, he readily accepts a bribe. Later, when it seems the guardians have actually killed Horace in his attempt to elope with Agnès, Alain is criticized for excessive use of force, but defends himself by saying that he was only following orders. His finest moment probably comes when the two servants are alone for a moment on the stage, discussing their master's mania. In response to Georgette's inquiry about sexual **jealousy**, he reverts to the culinary metaphor that dominates peasant dialogue and describes a wife as "man's stew," which he greedily defends against all interlopers, disgusted by the idea that the dirty fingers of others may have already dipped into the source of his pleasure. The lines objectifying female sexuality as a *potage* were considered both wildly funny and quite controversial by different segments of the public, and contributed to the **Quarrel of the School for Wives**.

**Albanians**.    In *Dépit amoureux*, old **Albert** shows that, even though he has never learned enough **Latin** to make sense of his prayers, he at least knows some geography. In his conversation with **Métaphraste**, which the pedant fills with fractured **Greek**, Albert finally exclaims that he cares little what the Greeks say, or for that matter the Albanians or **Slavonians** either. These were the three main ethnic divisions of the western Balkans as far as Bourbon diplomacy was concerned.

**Albert** (*Dépit amoureux*). The elderly father of the female lead, **Lucile**, who is also pretending to be the father of **Ascagne**. However, Ascagne is actually a girl, substituted in infancy for the deceased Ascagne with the connivance of the two mothers. She is not a blood relative of Albert, and thinks that he has not found out about the switch of babies. Actually he has, and feels many qualms about it, but he only seems to know half the truth, since everyone else believes he thinks Ascagne is a boy. The ruse was necessary to keep in the family a very large inheritance from the real Ascagne's uncle, which would go to another family (**Valére's**) if it were known that the heir has died. In the early acts, Albert expresses awareness and regret for his own greed, as well as a great deal of anxiety over the well–being of his surrogate son. He is thus far more complex and interesting than the average crotchedy pantaloon figure. In the final act, the scenario becomes far more complex, though unfortunately all information is related indirectly in an account by **Frosine**. It then appears that Albert knew all along that Ascagne was a girl, in fact his own daughter! There never was a male Ascagne, and at the birth of the girl, he himself supervised the switch of his baby with a boy infant born to a local *petite bourgeoise*. It was when that boy died that Albert's wife switched the infants back so that she could live with her own daughter, albeit secretly. In summary, then, Albert was laboring under the impression that Ascagne was a boy, but not his own child. When he learns the truth in the final act, he takes it remarkably well, probably because he and **Polidore** manage to arrange some mutually beneficial dowry arrangements. In the meantime, he is much occupied with the affairs of his older daughter **Lucile**, who seems to be slandered when Valère and **Mascarille** reveal that a secret **marriage** has taken place. However, his anger is eclipsed by that of Lucile, who frightens everyone on the stage with her threats of reprisal. He shares a fine sequence with the wordy pedant **Métaphraste**, as his inquiries into Ascagne's strange behavior are met with a barrage of pseudo–learned drivel that drives him wild; he finally chases the tutor off stage by ringing a bell in his ears, a possible borrowing from **Gillet de la Tessonerie's** *Le Déniaisé*. Another well–developed scene is his protracted misunderstanding with Polidore, where each is seeking forgiveness from the other (Polidore for Valère's seduction of Lucile, Albert for the subterfuge of Ascagne) and is therefore all too willing to pardon his interlocutor without really knowing what the offense was.

**Albi**. City of Languedoc, northeast of **Toulouse**, where Molière performed in 1647 as part of the itinerant troupe of **Charles Dufresne**.

**Alcandre** (*Les Fâcheux*). Alcandre is apparently a viscount and impassioned **duelist**, who asks **Éraste** in Act I, scene 6 to act as his second and go deliver a challenge to a man who has wronged him. This prompts Éraste, after some deliberation, to voice his support for the **king's** ban on swordplay. Alcandre cannot muster an answer when Éraste tells him, "If you wish to disobey, find someone else."

**Alcantor** (*Le Mariage forcé*). The young lady **Dorimène** describes her father, Alcantor, as a rigid parent who brought her up in stern separation from the pleasures of society. When he appears onstage in scene 8 (Act III, scene 1, according to the different organization of the ballet), he shows himself to be a most affable fellow, at least up to the point where he begins to understand that **Sganarelle** is trying to renege on his marriage contract. At that point, he seeks out his pugnacious son, **Alcidas**, to do the necessary persuading, returning in scene 10 to make sure that Sganarelle intends to honor his commitment. According to the cast as given in the published ballet, **Louis Béjart** played the part.

**Alceste** (*Le Misanthrope*). Quite simply the greatest role in what may be the world's greatest comedy. Alceste's name comes perhaps from a character in Molière d'Essertine's novel *Polyxène*. He is a complex and deeply paradoxical character, afflicted with an archetypal sort of melancholy that has fascinated generations of theatergoers the world over. A **noble** who both exaggerates and downplays the importance of his own merit and honor, a lover despite himself who woos with insults, a silent brooder who loves to hear himself rant and rave, a man widely sought in friendship who does not believe in its very tenets, Alceste is a walking oxymoron who well befits the subtitle, "l'atrabilaire amoureux." His initial scene with **Philinte**, full of pouting, philosophizing, and rodomontades, is one of the most striking in the canon. Philinte has followed Alceste into an isolated room to find out the reason for his friend's brusque departure in the middle of a casual social encounter. Alceste turns on Philinte and berates him for making a mockery out of friendship by bestowing marks of affection on people he barely knows. There is a good deal of jealousy in this objection, just as there is a desire for attention in Alceste's ongoing threats about living alone as a hermit in some far–off retreat. But Alceste's pique is supported by an elaborate, rational theory of behavior that puts **sincerity** at the heart of human intercourse and seeks to have a **language** and a society where feelings are pronounced directly and honestly, without the indirection and inference so central to seventeenth–century French manners. He genuinely believes in his ideals, even if he cannot see very clearly the obvious contradictions between them and the exigencies of his own life. As regards his unlikely choice of **Célimène**, the consummate flirt, as object of his affections, he declares himself incapable of resisting passions that well up in him as powerfully as in any of **Racine's** tragic figures. Similarly, in mock–tragic fashion, he has decided deliberately to lose the serious lawsuit in which he is involved, rather than to engage in the scurrilous but effective rounds of bribery and influence peddling demanded by **Louis XIV's** courts. He burns to expose the dark, sinful side of human nature, and it is no wonder that René Jasinski's **Jansenist** reading of Molière focuses closely on the character of Alceste.

The second scene with the poetaster **Oronte** is just as much a tour de force as the first. Oronte, a rival for Célimène's hand, has foolishly come seeking not Alceste's advice but his unqualified approval. He hopes that his powerful political connections will cause the "proper" reaction from Alceste, but how wrong he is and how little he understands the contrary mind of his rival. Alceste is just as prepared to turn aesthetics on its head as he is to upend civility. Oronte has carefully imitated the vapid **occasional poetry** of the age, producing a masterpiece of mediocrity that deserves the empty, conventional compliments dished up by Philinte. But Alceste chooses to fight for every inch of ground, blasting each syllable of the wretched poem and the tastes that produced it. To add insult to injury he declares it inferior to an old ditty from the times of Henri IV that not only frames love in a naïve, streetwise way, but contains the extra desire to give up Paris in favor of an idyllic devotion. Even Alceste is aware of the impossibility of imparting such criticism directly, but he can only manage such a blatant disclaimer, repeatedly saying, "I didn't say that," and pretending to address a third party, so that Oronte is all the more enraged. The whole scene is nothing less than an indictment of the means and standards of poetic judgment of the age, a **satire** of literary life that is all the more disquieting because it fails to erect a positive alternative to mindless froth or brutal formalism.

One realizes by the end of the first act that nothing has happened. The spectator has witnessed two epiphenomenal, but nonetheless riveting discussions that probe to the very heart of early modern French society, but there has been minimal plot development in the **Aristotelian** sense. The beginning of Act II, with Alceste's confrontation of Célimène, risks foreshortening the entire play, since it seems to produce exactly the kind of tête-à-tête that Alceste had called for earlier and that is his sole intention in life. However, Célimène plays with Alceste like a toreador with a fresh bull, deflecting his headlong charges into a cape of illusions, denying what is most obvious and fascinating her prey with alluring nothings. Moreover, she is able to put him on the defensive at will, making him self–conscious about his **jealousy** so that he cannot focus on the reason for it. When she seizes on the arrival of company to engage in the game of social **portraits**, Alceste can only fume on the sidelines. Finally unable to contain himself, he points out to the railers that if any of their victims were to arrive in person, they would hasten to throw their arms around him and bathe him in praise. He particularly singles out Acaste and Clitandre as causes for the "vice" of demeaning gossip, accusing them of flattering Célimène's natural talent for denigration. When Philinte points out that Alceste systematically disagrees with everyone else, the misanthrope replies that he is right to do so. Shaming humanity is always in season, since people are always untimely in their praise and haughty in their criticism. Before **Éliante's** intervention can turn the conversation in a different direction, it is cut short by the arrival of the **Marshals'** guard who has come to summon Alceste to a meeting in hopes of reconciling him with Oronte. Yet another pest to interrupt Alceste's "amorous" mission!

Nor does Alceste fare much better in Act III, since before he can utter a single word to Célimène, she leaves him in the odious company of **Arsinoé**. Alceste counters each of Arsinoé's unctuous advances toward him, and one wonders how much of this is caused by his knee jerk contrariness and how much by personal distaste for the false prude. In any case, he points out that his rejection of her offers of powerful positions at **court** stem from a deeper source: he is conscious that his very nature is incompatible with the fundamental talents of the courtier. Furthermore, he is aware that his opponent in the lawsuit is a friend of Arsinoé's, a fellow member of the *dévot* faction. When Arsinoé tries to change the subject by suggesting that Célimène is betraying his friendship, he sarcastically points out that she is hardly doing him a service by revealing this. But his insistence that innuendo is worthless without empirical proof provides a pretext for her to drag him off to her home in order to show him a **letter** of Célimène's that she has intercepted.

If the third act showed Alceste at the height of his self control and in the best light of virtue, the next act reduces him to an abject fool and a puppet in the hands of deception. Just as Philinte had been about to arrange an alternative **marriage** between Alceste and the sensible Éliante, his friend bursts into the room, wild–eyed and desperate, spouting mock tragic lines and begging Éliante to avenge him with her hand, a laughable suggestion that reverses both courtship and tragedy. Despite Alceste's overblown protests that he has made an irrevocable commitment, Éliante is wise to subject his wayward passion to the proof of time, and it does not take long for Célimène to change him from a storming accuser to a groveling penitent. She allows him to give vent to all his jealous feelings, knowing that on the inside he is craving only a good excuse on her part to return to her side. But instead of offering such an excuse, she simply releases him to the torment of his own imagination by asking what if the incriminating letter were sent to a woman instead of a lover. This scene copies one in *Dom Garcie de Navarre* with one important difference: the letter in the earlier play really was to a woman and Dom Garcie's jealousy was unfounded, whereas this is not the case with Célimène. Molière has trumped and greatly improved on his earlier *prince jaloux* by focusing on the inner play of the jealous imagination rather than susceptibility to visual errors. Alceste's undignified begging for forgiveness is even more pathetic and horrible than Dom Garcie's, since there is no mercy to bless both the giver and the receiver. This time it is Alceste who benefits from the interruption of a pest, since **Du Bois's** bumbling message about news from the **law** courts distracts him from his ragged emotions.

The unfortunate verdict in the lawsuit joins with Alceste's own psychological disarray to force him to an ultimatum of his own at the beginning of Act V. He feels he has nothing left to live for except a pronouncement from Célimène. Presumably negative, it will serve as an ultimate proof of humanity's shame and a final justification for his removal to his private "desert." After a splendid jeremiad against the flaws of the human race, he is surprised to find Oronte in search of the very same pronouncement that he is seeking, and he ironically joins with his rival to corner Célimène, who is used to baffling only one man at a time. The bluntness of her suitors and the witness of Philinte and Éliante would have been enough to cause sufficient trouble for the flirt had not the arrival of **Acaste** and **Clitandre** with their damning letters driven the matter to a disclosure. Célimène is rapidly undone, pinned by her own words more effectively than any of her past victims, and every one of her visitors takes pleasure in abandoning her, as Alceste silently looks on, viewing the spectacle through misanthropic eyes. It is then that he is able to pose his question finally to Célimène, under circumstances that have fulfilled his fantasy of seeing her reduced to nothing and dependent on him for everything. Her inability to abandon **Paris** for him, as he would have abandoned it for her and with her, predictable as it might be in view of her gregarious personality, seals the fate of his retreat and gives him his excuse to stalk out into the wilderness of his own isolation.

Can Alceste ever hope to find a place where he can be free to be a man of honor, by his own definition? Can any man free himself from contingency to the point of realizing such an ideal? Having seen the flaws of both sincerity and dissimulation, can the spectator endorse or even envision such an alternative to civil life? Philinte and Éliante cannot, not without considering the universal alternative to life itself, and that is why they and the spectator would like to save Alceste and to undertake the near–impossible task of reconciling him with society. His departure and the perversity of his views cast a long shadow over subsequent plays in the canon. For instance, his words to Célimène about seeing her reduced to misery so that he could help her all by himself are echoed in *Le Malade imaginaire* by **Toinette** when she says to **Argan**, "Sir, I wish you were afflicted by every disease and abandoned by all **doctors**, hopeless and reduced to agony, in order to show you the cures and the zeal that I would put at your disposal" (III, 10). Manners have been castigated so much in Alceste's case that the possibility of their reform seems extremely questionable. It is the extremity of Alceste's position, rather like *King Lear*'s "unaccommodated man" in the midst of his lace and madrigals, that makes Alceste's character enduringly fascinating and invites actors to give the role their greatest talents, as Molière himself did.

**Alcidas** (*Le Mariage forcé*). Sent by his father to enforce **Sganarelle's** promise of **marriage** to his sister **Dorimène**, Alcidas proves a most debonair emissary. Assuring Sganarelle that there is nothing wrong with his decision, he elegantly presents a pair of swords and asks his opponent to select a **weapon**, referring to their upcoming **duel** as "a little compliment," and lightheartedly saying that they must cut each other's throat in such a situation. When Sganarelle bids him to "resheath his compliments," refusing to fight, Alcidas then matter–of–factly explains that he is forced to **beat** him with a stick, politely saying, "With your permission," before he lays on. The flogging quickly produces the desired effect. Like **Dom Juan**, Alcidas is a young aristocrat who knows how to maintain himself with perfect **politeness** while dishing out violence. Alcidas is not included in the ballet's casting, though the summary perfectly describes his role. With a slight change of clothing, the role could well have been taken by **Brécourt**, who would have worn a long robe and probably a beard to play **Pancrace** a few scenes earlier.

**Alcidor** (*Les Fâcheux*). This silent part involves an appearance with **Orphise** in Act I, scene 2. Alcidor accompanies the lady, who ignores **Éraste's** compliments because she does not want the male pest to learn of her secret relationship.

**Alcipe** (*Les Fâcheux*). Alcipe is an obsessive **gambler** who distracts **Éraste** in Act II, scene 1 with his highly detailed, though boring, account of a game of piquet that he has managed to lose, despite his deployment of card table expertise. When Éraste finally manages to dismiss him, he wanders off, muttering, "A six of hearts! Two points!"

**Alcmène** (*Amphitryon*). Of all the female leads in Molière's comedies, **Alcmène** is placed in the most morally ambiguous position. Even before the action begins, she has succumbed to **Jupiter** in the guise of her husband. This seems to have been a moment of sublime pleasure for both of them, since Jupiter enjoyed the fiery responses of a young bride still fully interested in passion and Alcmène found her divine lover far more inspired than his earthly counterpart. She confesses that he has managed to touch all the sensitive parts of her heart and she regrets sending him back to the wars and losing the perfection she has tasted. For her, it was making **love** with **Amphitryon** as she had dreamed he could be, as he never really was but should have been. Even the rather dense Amphitryon quickly realizes that he has missed the highest point of their relationship. She is uncompromised in the sense that she did not knowingly commit adultery, in fact she enjoyed the sexual encounter of her life in total innocence. After giving Amphitryon an ironically pleased account of the tryst, one that he had demanded of her, she is understandably shocked when he not only fails to share her appreciation, but denies involvement in it. No wonder she accuses him of "imposture," and the label sticks much better than it should, since his lack of belief in her faithfulness is further from "reality" than Jupiter's ability to clone Amphitryon's appearance and enjoy his wedding bed. Jupiter's casuistry about the event and his theory of loving the lover in the husband is not truly convincing to Alcmène, but she accepts it as an excuse because she is still unaware of the doubling and she deeply wanted some kind of excuse to hold onto. If there is any hope for the real Amphitryon to redeem himself with her, it is through his sense of **jealousy**, for, as she explains to Jupiter, that emotion at least has the quality of being uncontrollable and as such can be separated from intention, allowing one to believe the best about a person, no matter how badly he behaves.

**Alexander the Great**. The subject of **Racine's** tragedy, performed by the **King's Troupe** in 1665 and given by Racine to the rival players of the **Hôtel de Bourgogne**. Could Molière have played Alexander? The possibility is not out of the question, since the main roles of Porus and Taxile would probably have been taken by **La Grange** and **La Thorillière**. In *Le Sicilien*, **Adraste** recalls a story about a painter named Apelles, who executed a **portrait** of one of

Alexander's mistresses so beautifully that he fell in **love** with it and was about to commit suicide until Alexander gave him the lady as a bride. He notes that if he were to duplicate the feat of Apelles, **Dom Pèdre**, his interlocutor, might not be as generous as the Greek. Later editions of the play add a stage detail about Dom Pèdre **grimacing** at the mention of Alexander: perhaps he remembered that the conqueror was much more serious about his male companions than about any females cast his way. On the other hand, **Dom Juan** refers to Alexander in a famous passage where he wishes, like the conqueror, that there were other worlds for him to subdue, not with the sword, but with seduction.

**Algiers**. Noted center of piracy and **slavery** and supposed destination of the **Turkish** galley that "kidnaps" **Léandre** in *Les Fourberies de Scapin*.

**Almanzor** (*Les Précieuses ridicules*). Appearing only for a moment in scene 9, this lackey has but one line of response to his mistresses, as he is asked to "cart in the commodities of conversation," in other words, to bring in some chairs. He is named after one of the characters in **Gomberville's** *Polexandre*, an example of the affected girls' linguistic program.

*Amants magnifiques, Les* (*The Magnificent Lovers*). Presented five times at **Saint Germain en Laye** during February 1670, but never again performed or printed during Molière's life, this **comedy–ballet** is a model platform for the **music and dance** that filled the intervals between the five acts, as well as figuring before and after the play. Its plot is extremely thin: **Princess Ériphile** must choose a husband from among the suitors who entertain her at the **Pythian Games** in **Thessaly**. With many delays, she fends off both **Iphicrate** and **Timoclès**, as well as their stooge, the astrologer **Anaxarque**, and her mother Princess **Aristione**, for she secretly **loves** and is secretly loved by the less aristocratic general **Sostrate**. The basic dramatic structure is thus one of interruption, which had already been perfected in plays such as *Les Fâcheux* and *Le Misanthrope*. This is all the easier, since several scenes serve as transitions into or epilogues to the various musical and terpsichorean performances of the intervals. In turn, the music and dance are designed to carefully mirror the emotional themes of the heroine and her decision, even including mute **pantomime** that reflects her own unspoken thoughts.

Through the intervention of the court jester **Clitidas**, we learn the emotions of Sostrate in the very first scene of the play. He is both hopelessly in love and resigned to defeat because of his relatively low social standing and despite the martial merit he has shown in battle. His true superiority shines through in the delicacy of his sentiments, compared with the rather crude approaches of his rivals. Timocrate relies mainly on the artists he employs to woo the princess, while Iphicrate joins this baroque spectacle to an assiduous flattery of Ériphile's mother, Aristione. Both seek to enlist Sostrate on their sides, and then repeat the solicitation with Clitidas. Ériphile finally appears at the end of the act, demonstrating a great reserve and addressing some rather testy remarks to her easily impressed confidante **Cléonice**.

In the second act, Clitidas and Ériphile have a long discussion about Sostrate. Though the clown supports Sostrate's interests, and even declares that if he were a princess he would marry him, Ériphile guards her feelings and declares that she would instantly reject an offer of love from Sostrate. When the general himself arrives, Ériphile presses him to choose between her princely suitors, as though she herself were interested in them, but Sostrate parries long enough to be saved by a **messenger** who summons the princess to another show.

The third act is but a single scene, where Sostrate refuses again to judge who should be the husband, and Anaxarque substitutes his own arbitration of the matter through astrological authority. Ériphile and especially Sostrate argue against this recourse, but Aristione and the others end by accepting it.

In Act IV, Aristione probes her daughter's mind, but fares no better than the other characters in sounding her out. They fall into a carefully contrived "miracle," where **Venus** announces to them that he who saves Aristione's life shall be the lucky husband. No sooner do they rush off to sacrifice in the temple than Anaxarque explains to his son and helper how he has arranged the illusion and hopes to take advantage of it long into the future. Ériphile and Sostrate then make their long–awaited **avowals**, seemingly as the first and last expressions of doomed love.

Fortunately, during the interval, it is Sostrate who saves Aristione's life from a wild boar, instead of Iphicrate saving her from the fake **pirates** as Anaxarque had planned. Clitidas, who ran away from the beast, nevertheless takes pride in relating the rescue. After beating the astrologer nearly to death offstage, the rival princes harangue Aristione with bitter challenges to her decision, but she shakes them off by emphasizing Sostrate's manifest worthiness and by evoking the opening ceremonies for the games that are presented in the final music and dance.

Some anecdotes present the play as an allegory of the romance between La Grande Mademoiselle and her lover, Lauzun. There are historical problems with this interpretation, since the liaison was not known at **court** until a bit later in the year. In addition, Lauzun was a possible model for the foppish marquis that Molière had lambasted earlier in his career, and he seems an unlikely predecessor for the elegant, superlatively self–controlled Sostrate. **Pierre Corneille's** *Don Sanche d'Aragon* has sometimes been suggested as a plot model, but this essentially serious and political play differs tremendously in tone from Molière's. A more solid model is the artistic precedence of *La Princesse d'Élide*. *Les Amants magnifiques* represents a much purer adaptation of the comedy–ballet format, which also explains its failure to reappear on the stage of the Palais Royal Theater, since its musical and choreographic trappings were much too elaborate and expensive for that venue, and were soon rendered even more difficult by **Lully's** operatic monopolies. Its prose format, combined with the numerous developments of previous theater elements and speeches, marks this play primarily as a formalistic experiment, which, in the wake of *Tartuffe's* recent and resounding satirical success, the author thought fit to permit himself. It was also something of a pause for the ill Molière himself, whose Clitidas had major parts in only three widely spaced scenes. It was also the last new play to feature **Louis Béjart**, who probably played one of the male roles, but retired during the Lenten recess of 1670. Originally entitled simply "Divertissement royal" ("Royal Diversion"), the play was finally printed in the 1682 collected edition and was taken up some time after Molière's death by the united Hôtel Guénégaud troupe.

*See* Louis E. Auld, "Theatrical Illusion as Theme in *Les Amants magnifiques*," *Romance Notes* 16 (1974), 144–155; Jacques Guicharnaud, "Les Trois Niveaux Critiques des *Amants Magnifiques*," in MSS, 21–41; and Abby Zanger, "The Spectacular Gift: Rewriting the Royal Scenario in Molière's *Les Amants magnifiques*," *Romanic Review* 81 (1990), 173–188.

**America.** **Enrique**, the long–lost father of **Agnès** in *L'École des femmes*, is supposed to have spent the years of her childhood and adolescence in America recouping his fortunes. The source of his riches could have been Canada (the fur trade) or the Caribbean (sugar or piracy). The latter might have sprung to the mind of the audience, since **Fouquet** had been deeply involved in arming pirate expeditions and **Colbert** promoted both the corsairs and the planters, organizing the first government companies to facilitate the slave trade that would flourish in the last decades of the century. The name "Enrique" would seem more at home with the pirates of Tortuga than the *coureurs des bois* of Quebec.

**Aminte.** In *Les Précieuses ridicules*, **Cathos** chooses this novelesque name because it sounds more delicate to her ear than does her own.

**Aminte** (*L'Amour médecin*). Aminte appears only in the first scene of the play, where she advises **Sganarelle** to **marry** his daughter off promptly to the party he had negotiated with before **Lucinde's** mysterious illness appeared. He replies to this neighbor that he sees right through to the reason for her words, since she is interested in **Clitandre** herself and wishes to see Lucinde married to someone else as soon as possible.

*Amour Médecin, L'* (*Love, The Doctor*). This *comédie–ballet* in three acts was first performed at **Versailles** in September, 1665, and produced on the stage of the Palais Royal Theater only a week later. Accompanied by **Lully's music** and by elaborate dance numbers, it was a success with the public, despite the disclaimer that it is a mere trifle, composed in only five days at royal command. The basic premise of a girl who feigns dumbness in order either to forestall an unwanted suitor or to hasten **marriage** with a chosen one was probably a dramatic feature from time immortal, rather than a direct borrowing from **Charles Sorel**, as some have suggested. Some of the material may have even come from **farce** elements already existing in the troupe's **repertory** or memory. The main timely modification was the introduction of five **doctor** figures who mirrored physicians at the royal **court**. In his introduction, Molière allows it to be understood that this satirical element may have been the King's idea, like the figure of the **hunter** added to *Les Fâcheux* at the last minute. Certainly the play is unique in the number of doctors it puts on stage — no wonder it was sometimes referred to simply as "The Doctors." Molière would have of course played **Sganarelle**, with **La Grange** as **Clitandre**, **Armande** as **Lucinde**, and probably **Madeleine Béjart** as **Lisette**. The two other main actresses, **Mlle. de Brie** and **Mlle. Du Parc**, would have played the opening roles of **Aminte** and **Lucrèce**. The five doctors would have been **La Thorillière, Hubert, Du Croisy, Louis Béjart**, and **De Brie**. Since at least four of the doctors were somehow **masked,** two of them would double as Messieurs **Josse** and **Guillaume** in the first scene.

The play opens with Sganarelle, a properous **bourgeois,** in a typically self–pitying frame of mind, as he consults his neighbors and relatives about how to cheer up his despondent, mute daughter and then rejects their self–interested suggestions. Showing some tenderness mixed with irritation and impatience, he questions the girl himself, but pretends not to see when she nods at the suggestion that what she needs is a husband. The **lady's maid** Lisette then repeats the interrogation with the same results, but again Sganarelle pays no attention to her now–vocalized cries for a husband. Excusing her lack of candor to her *suivante*, Lucinde tells Lisette of her desire for Clitandre and the maid promises her help in finding a solution. Lisette twists Sganarelle around her finger by telling him a story of Lucinde's woes that leads the man to suppose first that she had defenestrated herself and then that she had died in bed. Relieved that she still lives, he sends in haste for all the doctors that can be roused, an errand performed by the dancing valet Champagne in the ballet interval.

Lisette pokes fun at Sganarelle when she learns he has sent for the medical profession and continues to needle them when they start to arrive. Distaining to examine the patient, they present diagnoses and remedies sight unseen, then fall to arguing among each other about the relative merits of bleeding and purging, which are the only cures they can think of. Forced to endure the argument, followed by painfully slow explanations from **Macroton** and painfully fast ones from **Bahys**, Sganarelle hurries off to buy a patent medicine from a charlatan, whose show furnishes the matter for the second ballet interval.

In Sganarelle's absence, Lisette manages sarcastically to rid the house of doctors, then to welcome Clitandre in a medical **disguise**. She helps the young man gain the confidence of their returning dupe through several comical rejoinders. Naturally, Lucinde and the new physician get along quite well, thanks to his gentle "mental" cures. Seeing this, Sganarelle is happy to proceed with what he believes is a deception of his daughter, promising **marriage** to the physician and providing a contract and dowry. He never suspects that the "false" elements are actually real and that he has agreed to a conventional marriage. When, after the third ballet interval and its joyous wedding dance, he learns the truth from Lisette, he can only bluster.

As one can guess from such a slight plot, much of the humor is based on verbal and physical **lazzi**, on the speech effects and repetition, on topical jokes and double entendre. Nevertheless, it is hard to miss the efficient economy of the play and the seamlessness of integration between its dramatic and nondramatic features. Here, well before *Le Bourgeois gentilhomme*, we find a perfect interpenetration of genres, waiting only for the focus to shift in that later play to **music and dance** as very elements of the thematic structure. Also present in embryonic form are several features of *Le Malade imaginaire*, from the activity of the skeptical lady's maid to the feigned death that captures the father's true sentiment. It only remains to shift the sickness from the oppressed daughter to the paterfamilias and to make it a cause rather than an effect of the oppression. Furthermore, the situation of this little play between the supposedly "high" comedies of *Dom Juan* and *Le Misanthrope* does a great deal to dismantle the theories that Molière's career underwent a radical transformation following the latter play. Here is proof that the genesis of the *comédie–ballet* was well under way during the period of the author's social struggles and that that genesis already concerned elements with a strong bearing on important philosophical as well as aesthetic values. *L'Amour médecin* shows that there was no complete changeover from advocacy to formalism after 1665.

*See* Kevin Elstob, "An Analysis of Comedia and Balletic Elements in Molière's *L'Amour médecin*," *PFSCL* 28 (1987), 131–148.

**Amour (*Psyché*).** *See* **Cupid**.

***Amours d'Alcippe, ou la Cocue imaginaire, Les* (*The Loves of Alcippe, or the Wife Who Imagined She Was Cheated*).** An extremely derivative and amateurish play by one **F. Doneau**, based on **Sganarelle** with help from notes taken by **Neufvillenaine**. The text was apparently part of **Ribou's** scheme to profit from Molière's play.

*Amphitryon.* One of the most unusual of Molière's comedies, it is an example either of a script that was quickly and masterfully finished to take advantage of topical events or of tremendous serendipity. Just prior to its January 13, 1668, premiere, **Louis XIV** had taken a new love interest and France had achieved a significant military victory in Flanders and **Franche–Comté**. Thus, although **Mlle. de la Vallière** had not even officially been displaced as royal mistress by **Madame de Montespan**, the stage was set perfectly to coincide with the plot of the play. Of course, it is almost impossible to imagine that Molière, no matter how well informed he was of **court** affairs, could have written the play specifically for this coincidence of events. The availability of **Marolles's** recent translation of **Plautus** and, perhaps, a desire for Molière to make a bid for membership in the **Academy** based on his own skills as an updater of Classical material, may have figured larger in his motivation. Whether by design or by pure accident, the three–act comedy is still a remarkable instance of art and life imitating each other.

The plot is streamlined and remarkably simple. When the play opens, **Jupiter** has already enjoyed the favors of the beautiful **Alcmène** by taking the form of her husband, who was away leading the Theban army to triumph. His henchman **Mercury** has asked **Night** to prolong her reign in favor of Jupiter's pleasures and has taken the form of the slave **Sosie** in order to help facilitate this substitution. When the real Sosie returns with a message for his mistress, the false one intercepts and beats him, persuading him eventually that he is a true double of the original. Mercury complicates matters even more by frustrating the aroused sentiments of Sosie's normally prudish wife **Cléanthis**, thus assuring an even more difficult homecoming for the slave. Understandably, Sosie has considerable difficulty reporting this state of affairs to **Amphitryon**, but the general soon finds out to his tremendous mortification that he, too, apparently has a double who has cuckolded him. Even the jewel that he has sent as a gift to his wife has disappeared from the sealed box that contained it and has already been delivered. Following this unpleasant revelation between the upper classes, it is the turn of the **servants** to quarrel, as Cléanthis bitterly complains about the lack of affection she received from the false Sosie. Even the gods get caught up in the misunderstanding, for when Jupiter, still disguised, returns to console Alcmène, she is at first quite vexed with him because of her dispute with Amphitryon. Jupiter uses all his persuasive powers and orders Sosie to summon some of "his" officers for a feast. Amphitryon soliloquizes desperately at the beginning of the third act, but when he tries to enter his home, Mercury locks him out and further exacerbates his mood. When Sosie appears with the officers **Naucrates** and **Polidas**, his master is prepared to vent his anger for the bad service until the two visitors assure him that Sosie was always in their company. A few moments later he comes face to face with his other self, which leaves him astonished and the officers so confused that they decide to go on with their banquet plans. As Amphitryon leaves seeking better witnesses, Sosie tries to assuage his hunger, but is blocked by Mercury, who refuses all attempts at reconciliation. Amphitryon returns with **Argatiphontidas** and **Posiclès**, who soon fall in with Sosie and Cléanthis, and the group is then confronted by the dei ex machina, Mercury and Jupiter explaining their true identities and the benefits to be showered upon the cuckolded couple in the future. Sosie closes the play by urging a general hushing up of the situation, for "in such circumstances, it is always best to say nothing."

With very few events or revelations, the play consists mainly of characters' psychological reactions to the double impersonation. The humans, Sosie, Alcmène, Amphitryon, and Cléanthis, all have to react to behavior that is too good or, more commonly, too bad on the part of their mates. Expectations are shattered and the limits of reconciliation are explored. In addition, Sosie and Amphitryon have to deal with the existence of the double, the uncertitude it injects into their lives, and the difficulties of making anyone believe their stories. To this brew is added some unique psychological insights on **love** itself, as Jupiter tries to convice Alcmène to think of him only as a lover, since conjugal love is to be despised as mere fulfillment of duty. To some degree, the play is something of a midsummer night's nightmare, with dreamlike reversals that prove themselves only too true in the light of reality, and unnatural acts that leave nature at a loss. After giving their thunderous speeches, the gods are whisked away to Olympus, leaving the mortals with a rather heavy fait accompli. **Language** is what lightens the moral load of the play, for from beginning to end Mercury and Sosie deploy a remarkable propensity for badinage, irreverently reducing seriousness to a laughable level. The play also incorporates an outstanding reversal of the **lovers' spite** scenes perfected in earlier Molière plays, as first masters and then servants fall out and then fail to completely make up again. Indeed, the sustained upstairs/downstairs contrast affects almost every facet of emotion, behavior, and even truth itself, providing parallel universes in which the same conflicts assume vastly different forms. It is a rare exception, one of the few comedies in the canon that ends with no prospect of **marriage**; but for Sosie's gag order, it might well end in the breaking of them.

The play was a moderate success and was published by Ribou before the end of 1668. It has since had an uneven history, alternating between periods of favor and almost complete neglect.

*See* Lionel Gossman, "Molière's *Amphitryon*," *PMLA* 78 (1963), 201–213; Jean Mesnard, "Le Dédoublement dans l'*Amphitryon* de Molière," in *Mélanges en l'honneur de Jacques Truchet* (Paris: PUF, 1992) 453–472; and L. R. Schero, "Alcmena and Amphitryon in Ancient and Modern Drama," *American Philosophical Association Transactions*, 87 (1956), 192–238.

**Amphitryon** (*Amphitryon*). One cannot actually call him a protagonist, since Sosie is a more compelling presence onstage, and in fact the Theban general is not a very likeable character. He is pompous and irritable with both his servant and his wife. His rigidity about the truth is turned inside out when the truth goes against him and he is confronted with a double of himself, a double who has enjoyed life more than the real person. From that moment on, his main characteristic is **jealousy**, rendered all the more pathetic because he is jealous of "himself." The pathos is deepened when he meets the double face to face and is unable to assert himself, even to witnesses that know him well in life. One gets the impression that he is almost as doubtful of his own existence as Sosie is in the first scene of the play. Unlike Sosie, he does not learn to live with the unpleasant doubleness or to try to achieve a reconciliation with it. Instead, he sputters and fumes like a Matamore, promising retribution that never comes. At the end of the play, he barely seems worthy of being the stepfather of Hercules and enjoying a shower of wealth and power. If there is a flaw in the play, it is the absence of a scene of understanding between Amphitryon and his spouse in the third act. However there seems to be a good reason for this omission, since the general's weak character lends serious doubt as to the future possibility of a true reconciliation. He is nearly tragic, a person who believed profoundly in the reliability of appearances and is thrown into complete disarray when he learns that reality is not always what it appears to be.

**Amsterdam**.    Site of many pirated editions of Molière's individual and collected works, the most important of which was the 1683 edition of *Dom Juan* that passed on the original acting version of the play, complete with the "pauper's scene." This text has recently been edited by Joan De Jean, *Le Festin de Pierre (Dom Juan), édition critique du texte d'Amsterdam (1683)* (Geneva: Droz, 1999).

**Anaxarque (*Les Amants magnifiques*)**.    This astrologer has been inviting bribes from all sides, but mainly from the family of **Iphicrate**, in order to influence the Princess's choice of a marriage partner. Though **Clitidas** makes fun of his pretended ability to read **dreams** in the first act, Anaxarque is mainly quiet until the third act, where he proposes that all parties let the heavens decide, through his agency, a means of choosing the husband. He deftly steps into the breach when Sostrate tries to shrug off the task of choosing and **Ériphile** admits that she is confused by the obligations the princes rush to throw upon her. Though the latter two persons express considerable incredulity about Anaxarque's abilities and the "science" of astrology in general, the proposal is readily accepted by Iphicrate, **Timoclès**, and **Aristione**. The wizard accordingly ordains, by means of a contrived apparition of the goddess **Venus**, that Ériphile should wed the man who saves Aristione's life. Anaxarque immediately admits responsibility for this miracle to his son (IV, 3) and explains that Iphicrate is making ready to fulfill the prophecy by saving the elder princess from some putative **pirates**. But after Sostrate preempts this rescue with his own, we learn from **Cléonice** (V, 3) that the jealous princes have taken out their rage on the astrologer and wounded him, a just punishment for his treachery.

**Andrée (*La Comtesse d'Escarbagnas*)**.    This young maid with a peasant name incurs her mistress's wrath by clumsily doing her hair and by calling parts of the household by their common names (armoire, attic, toilet) instead of the fancy terms imagined by the Countess. In this respect she resembles other female servants such as **Marotte** and **Martine**. The role was taken by the hireling **Mlle. Bonneau**.

**Andrès (*L'Étourdi*)**.    A rival lover of **Célie** who is at first thought to be a **Gypsy** in her entourage. Appearing only in the final act, after **Mascarille's** attempt to have him kidnapped by corrupt **police** fails, he manages to spirit her away from **Trufaldin** and lodge her in Mascarille's "boarding house," where her headache detains them. His intervention in the fight between two old hags in the final act leads to the elaborate recognition scene, where he learns that Trufaldin (Zanobio Ruberti) is his father and Célie his sister. The death of his tutor had caused him to lose touch with his Neapolitan family. Failing to find a trace of them, he went to **Venice** for several years. He explains his passion for Célie is based on "the cry of the blood." **Pandolphe** suddenly produces a daughter at the end of the play, guaranteeing a mate for Andrès.

**Angélique** (*George Dandin*).  Wife of the protagonist and dramatic descendent of the character by the same name in *La Jalousie du Barbouillé*, she is nevertheless deeper than her predecessor in many ways.  The name, of course, is ironic, since she is by her own admission no angel.  Indeed, it is her frankness about her coquettish ways and about her desire to cheat on her husband that makes this character interesting.  Like **Célimène**, she says that she is not at all displeased that men find her beautiful and that she can do nothing about it.  It is true that she lies consistently, both in public about her affair and in private discussion with **Dandin**, but it must be admitted that these untruths are "lies of convenience" that are designed to avoid conflict and counterbalance to some degree the **marriage** of convenience to which she has been subjected.  Indeed, she explains her flirtations as a natural byproduct of a marriage in which she had no say.  Thus, she flatly rejects the kind of civil death that Dandin expects of his wife and rebels against what she considers mere **slavery**.  This candor raises the question of whether good behavior can ever be logically expected of such a person in such a situation.  However, she is not exactly a passive party in the seduction.  She denies as quickly as **Clitandre** the charge of infidelity brought in the first act, and their conversation is so parallel that it suggests some preparation in advance.  It is she who invents the stratgem to fool her parents in Act 2 by pretending loudly to reject the **vicount's** advances, merely for the sake of show.  She goes so far as to **beat** her husband during the scene, pretending to aim at Clitandre.  And in the final act, when Dandin has caught her meeting outside with her sweetheart and shut the door on her, she not only contrives to reenter the home and turn the tables on him, but also accuses him of drunkenness in order to disarm his accusations.  Whatever the justifications for her behavior, one cannot help but find her to be as cold–blooded as she is clever, and in that she marks a step toward the evil **Béline** of *Le Malade imaginaire*.  The part was of course played by **Armande Béjart**.

**Angélique** (*La Jalousie du Barbouillé*).  The eponym's coquettish and clever wife.  She feigns death to regain entrance to the family abode when her husband has locked her out.  A forerunner of the character in *George Dandin*, though in *La Jalousie* her father **Gorgibus** is apparently an ordinary **bourgeois**.

**Angélique** (*Le Malade imaginaire*).  The part of **Argan's** elder daughter was played by **Armande Béjart**.  Though the name is the same as the wife in *George Dandin*, the character is completely different, for this Angélique is tender, sentimental, and completely sympathetic.  When she first appears (I, 4), she makes great show of her languishing love and begs **Toinette** to talk about her sweetheart **Cléante**.  The maid warns her that love is not always sincere, but we soon learn that Cléante has not only exchanged *paroles de futur*, or oral promises with Angélique, but has also put his intentions in print and has received a corresponding commitment from her.  Thus, she is understandably excited when her father rushes in speaking of her impending **marriage**, and deflated when she learns he is talking about a union with the junior **Diafoirus**

instead of Cléante. Toinette starts a prolonged argument with her master, partly to deflect any further disagreement with the daughter, and when she leaves at the end of the scene, her first thoughts are instead for his health, for she warns him not to put himself in distress by pursuing the saucy maid. The two women return in the last scene of the act to discuss strategy. Angélique expresses no interest in her father's potentially dangerous financial transactions, as long as he leaves her heart alone, but she urges Toinette to help her get word of developments to Cléante. In the second act (II, 3) she is so surprised to see her lover dressed as a music master that she almost gives her secret away, but cleverly covers her emotion by saying that the young man stunned her because he resembled someone who had saved her during a **dream**. The couple had hoped for a moment alone, but they are interrupted by the visit of the Diafoiruses, both father and son, and it is only after awkwardly listening to the young **doctor's** even more awkward greetings that they can exchange a few words. Because of their audience, they are obliged to do so in song. Angélique shows much genius in responding to Cléante's professions of love, not only in cadence, as he had instructed, but in rhyme as well. She assures him toward the end of their duo that she would rather die than consent to become Madame Diafoirus. When pressed to accept the proposal by Argan, Thomas, and her stepmother, she stalls for time and reminds them that marriage is primarily a matter of **love**. **Béline's** increasingly harsh attitude prompts Angélique to denounce her indirectly as a golddigger and a black widow of a wife, but she manages to say this without crossing the rules of civility or losing her own temper. We know from the testimony of Béline and **Louison** that she has a brief moment with Cléante in her bedroom after retiring from the argument, but she does not reappear until Argan's feigned death sequence (III, 13), when she erupts in tears at the news of his death and exclaims that she is all the more devastated because he expired while angry at her. When offered consolation by Cléante, she flatly tells him that there can now be no talk of marriage and that she intends to follow her father's bitter will of sending her to a **convent**. Of course, she is at first terrified when the corpse arises and starts to embrace her, but she recovers her wits quickly to express her joy and also to ask him to bless her engagement with Cléante. Instead of being upset at Argan's obstinate refusal to accept Cléante unless he becomes a doctor, she is worried that the deception planned by **Béralde** and Toinette will cause her father some real pain, and hesitates to become involved until her uncle assures her of their benign intent.

Here is a daughter without the timid weakness of a **Mariane** or the coquettishness of Madame de la Dandinière, wise almost to the point of being philosophical, and filled with empathy for those around her. Closest to **Henriette** of *Les Femmes savantes*, she is a perfect example of female "honnêteté."

**Angoulême.** City in western France between **Bordeaux** and **Poitiers**. Molière is almost certain to have visited it with **Dufresne's** troupe during their years in

Bordeaux. It is the setting of *La Comtesse d'Escarbagnas*, where it is portrayed as a remote, unsophisticated place. Perhaps this depiction is due to its proximity to **Limoges**, home town of **Monsieur de Pourceaugnac** and already a primary place of internal exile within the kingdom.

**Animals.** Molière chiefly uses the animal world as grounds for comparison with human behavior. In *Sganarelle,* the eponym compares **Lélie** to a marmoset and a starling. In *L'École des maris*, he compares men who wear fancy shoes covered with ribbons to show pigeons. When **Valère** blocks his way with unwanted civility, he calls him an ox. In contrast, the young man refers to **Sganarelle** as a dragon because of the way he rudely stands guard over **Isabelle**. Several other plays refer to prudish women as dragons of virtue, and in *Les Femmes savantes*, **Chrysale** refers to his manipulative wife as a dragon and **Armande** calls **Clitandre** a "moral monster" because he has deserted her. **Dom Juan's** father calls him a "monster in nature" for having proven unworthy of his noble status. Sganarelle, in the same play, has numerous animal epithets for his master, such as "earthworm," "ant–man," "tiger–heart," and "Epicurean pig." For a young lady with an aversion to everything that belongs to the "animal part" of existence, Armande is not averse to animal metaphors, for she also calls **children** "marmots." **Arnolphe**, in *L'École des femmes,* says that **Agnès** is like the **proverbial** serpent saved from freezing, which stings its benefactor. In *Le Misanthrope*, **Philinte** likens human nature to that of wolves, monkeys, and buzzards, who merely obey their instincts. **Dorine** compares **Tartuffe** to a monkey (*Tartuffe,* II, 3) when she asks **Mariane** if she really wants an ape for a husband; the comparison captures both Tartuffe's talents for mimicry and his physical repulsion. **Toinette** compares **Argan** to a milk cow in *Le Malade imaginaire* (I, 2) because he is such a steady source of revenue for **Purgon** and the **doctors**; we would say today that he is a cash cow.

It is hardly surprising that **Lucas** and **Jacqueline**, the **peasant** couple in *Le Médecin malgré lui,* frequently use **proverbs** about such animals as cows and goats to reinforce their thoughts. In the same play, Sganarelle, who has been dubbed "the parrot doctor" because of his green and yellow clothes, uses the example of the parrot, who purportedly learns to talk while being fed sops of bread and wine, to justify that same prescription for the mute **Lucinde**. **George Dandin**, a somewhat more lofty peasant than Lucas, uses the metaphor of flies attracted to honey to describe how his wife attracts lovers (II, 2) and later compares her repentance before the locked door to a crocodile shedding tears to fool its prey (III, 6). Another lower–class character fond of animal metaphors is **Martine** in *Les Femmes savantes*. To explain her expulsion from the household, she says, "Whoever wants an excuse to drown their dog says it has rabies" (II, 5). To justify **Chrysale's** taking a more active role in decision making than his wife, she exclaims, "The hen should never sing before the cock" (V, 3). Animals as a marriage metaphor also come to mind in *Dom Juan,* when Sganarelle tells **Gusman** that along with his mistress, the rake would also have wed "you, her dog, and her cat." When **Nicole** is speculating about

**Monsieur Jourdain's** conspiracy with **Dorante**, she comments, "There's some eel under that rock!" Though not a peasant, Jourdain's simple mind is beset with animals. When he tries to recall an air he wants the **Music Master** to sing, all he can remember is that "it has sheep in it." The same ditty has a cruel tiger for contrast. But Jourdain cannot keep his bestiary straight. After the son of the Grand Turk wishes him "the wisdom of the snake and the courage of the lion," he manages to get the animals reversed in his compliment to Dorante in Act V.

Sometimes the animal references involve practical early modern matters of sport, nourishment, or transportation. *Les Fâcheux* contains extended discussions of horses, dogs, and **hunting**. In Act II, scene 3 of *L'Amour médecin*, the doctors **Tomès** and **Des Fonandrès** discuss the relative merits of a mule and a horse, both of which have carried them around and around the city of **Paris**, presumably disseminating bad medical advice wherever they stopped. The comic effect of the mule's journey, marked by so many prominent Parisian landmarks, is not unlike that of Emma Bovary's carriage, traversing all the famous streets of Rouen while she and Léon make love inside. In the same play, **Lisette** mentions, as proof that doctors are not needed for most ills, a cat that had fallen from the height of the rooftop to the ground and recovered on its own in a few days. In *La Critique de l'École des femmes*, **Climène** brands Molière an antifeminist because Arnolphe had called women animals, until **Uranie** reminds her that the words came from a character who was deranged. Uranie herself, however, uses the term on her poor doorman, **Galopin**, when he admits Climène to the house.

Beasts play a particularly large and active part in *La Princesse d'Élide*, where **Moron** makes his entrance pursued by a vicious boar. This incident leads to his burlesque account of his hunting adventures, which he gives safely flanked by his listeners, lest the boar return. After **Aristomène** and **Théocle** dispatch the animal, thinking to protect the Princess, she upbraids them for depriving her of the kill. Later, as Moron bumbles through the forest, he manages to attract a bear that embraces him a little too heartily. Though he addresses the animal in terms reserved for princes of the blood royal and praises its fine face and body, he is only saved by some hunters who happen on the scene. Once the bear is safely dead, Moron attacks it like a wild man. He later has a *bon mot* based on the animal kingdom when he compares the spiteful Princess to the proverbial dog in the manger. In similar fashion, a wild boar attacks **Princess Aristione** between the fourth and fifth acts of *Les Amants magnigiques*. She is saved by **Sostrate**, who thus becomes the designed husband of **Ériphile**. Once again it is the clown, **Clitidas**, who delivers the account of the animal attack in a comical way. He interjects that such rude and disorderly animals should be ousted from well–managed forests and excuses himself for lack of a complete description on account of his own cowardly flight.

Pets are seldom mentioned in Molière's plays. One exception is the sparrow that **Myrtil** captures and tames in *Mélicerte*. Intended as a gift for his beloved, he composes a very gallant little piece of verse addressed to the bird.

Other animals incur man's violence for no good reason. Arnolphe swats Agnès's puppy when it barks at his hostile behavior during one of his tantrums. Another of Agnès's pets, a kitten, has died during Arnolphe's absence in the country.

*Amphitryon* contains a reference to mythological animals when **Night** says that she cannot understand how **Jupiter** can enjoy making **love** under the guise of a bull, a swan, a snake, or some other loathsome beast. Later in the play, when **Mercury** catches **Sosie** muttering under his breath about revenge and calling him a son of a bitch, Sosie denies it and says it must have been some passing parrot that said the words. In *Psyché*, everyone thinks that a mythological, snakelike monster will be sent to devour the princess at her sacrifice, but **Zephir** precludes this by carrying her off to **Cupid's** realm.

Actual onstage use of animals was rare in the seventeenth century for obvious logistical reasons, but it was not unknown to Molière's troupe. They used a live donkey for the protagonist's mount in *La Gouvernance de Sanche Pança* and trained monkeys in the ballet interval before the final act of *Le Malade imaginaire*.

**Anne of Austria** (1601–1666). Wife of Louis XIII and mother of **Louis XIV** and **Monsieur**, this lady had been rumored in earlier times to have had a relationship with **Cardinal Mazarin**. By 1658, she had mainly turned toward piety and from the time Louis assumed personal rule in 1660, she was little more than an extra fixture at the **court**. According to **La Grange** and **Vivot**, she was present with her sons at the first command performance in 1658. Molière dedicated *La Critique de l'École des femmes* to her on the pretext of congratulating her on recovering from an illness, but she was not of a temperament to have liked either that play or its prequel. She would certainly have been angry at the veiled praise of **Mlle. de la Vallière** presented in *La Princesse d'Élide*. Her death in early 1666 was the occasion for closing the theaters for two months, an event that brought an abrupt close to the bitter affair of *Alexandre le grand*.

**Anselme** (*L'Avare*). An aged suitor whom **Harpagon** has lined up for his daughter **Élise** and who is willing to take her without a **dowry** (!) as the miser keeps repeating Anselme finally arrives in Act V, just in time to hear **Valère's** attempts to exonerate himself after he has seemingly confessed (in an effusively emotional way) to the theft of Harpagon's "dear strongbox." When the young man claims to be the son of the Neapolitan noble, **Dom Thomas d'Alburcy**, Anselme is ready to call him a liar, but Valère's story of being saved from shipwreck by a **Spanish** sailor, together with various **jewelry** keepsakes and witnesses to be produced, causes a different effect. Anselme reveals himself to be no other than Dom Thomas. He further recognizes **Mariane** as his daughter. Of course, since Mariane's sick mother is still alive, there is no longer any question of marrying **Élise** (much to her relief), and Anselme proceeds generously to provide for the weddings of both his **children**, as well as various appeasements to Harpagon.

**Anselme** (*L'Étourdi*). One of three elderly men in the play, he is an old moneybags who mutters often to himself about the drawbacks of the early modern credit system. In the first act, **Mascarille** almost manages to filch his purse while cajoling him with tales of a woman who pines for him, but **Lélie's** untimely questions thwart the scheme. Only minutes afterward, the valet concocts a scheme to have Anselme buy **Célie** as a proxy for **Pandolphe**, in order to cut off Lélie's access, but this, too, fails. Later, the valet nearly manages to negotiate a loan from Anselme, ostensibly to pay for a fancy funeral for Pandolphe. Lélie makes such a show of mourning and blubbering that they even manage to escape without signing a receipt. But the reappearance of the **"ghost"** shows Anselme his error, and he is once again able to lay hands on his **money** by convincing Lélie that he needs to examine the coins to search for counterfeits. When **Léandre** almost gets control of Célie for his own lustful purposes, Anselme gives him a firm but convincing speech about the fleeting nature of passion and the more lasting benefits of a fat **dowry** on the bitter morning after. The speech has its desired effect and brings Léandre back to his engagement with Anselme's daughter, **Hippolyte**.

**Apollo.** As the god of **Delphi** and dedicatory of the **Pythian Games**, Apollo figures in *Les Amants magnifiques*. The comparison between him and **Louis XIV** is implicit in the musical finale. *See also* **Phoebus Apollo**.

**Apothecaries.** As the natural assistants and accomplices of **doctors**, pharmacists appeared frequently in Molière's plays. Like doctors, their black robes could furnish an easy **disguise**, as when the young lover **Léandre** dons an apothecary's costume and wig to woo and later run off with **Lucinde** in *Le Médecin malgré lui*. A band of flunkies masquerading as apothecaries pursues **Monsieur de Pourceaugnac** with syringes full of enema materials, splattering him thoroughly between Acts I and II. **Fleurant**, the minion of the **Diafoirus** family in *Le Malade imaginaire*, is certainly the most vocal and detestable of the profession to appear in Molière's comedies. It is the bills from Fleurant that **Argan** is reviewing and critiquing in the opening scene of that play.

**Apothecary** (*Monsieur de Pourceaugnac*). When **Éraste** speaks with this druggist about his plans to have **Pourceaugnac** treated as a lunatic, the apothecary lauds his colleague, the **doctor**, "Faith! You couldn't have consulted a brighter doctor; that man knows medicine backward and forward, as well as I know the alphabet, and when it's time for someone to die, he clings to the ancient ways like a limpet" (I, 5). He goes on to expound on what a comfort it is to die according to the rules, especially when the physician is so quick to rush to a conclusion. When the musical enema crew pursues Pourceaugnac offstage at the end of the act, the Apothecary leads the charge, armed with his "harmless little detergent."

**Apuleius**. The second century AD author of *The Golden Ass*, which served as the earliest source for the story of **Cupid** and **Psyche** taken up in Molière's *Psyché*.

**Arbate** (*La Princesse d'Élide*). **La Thorillière** played the role of this aged advisor to **Prince Euryale**. Despite the fact that he is full of "old days" and about to see his "last sunrises," Arbate urges his master to open up to **love**, only to find that the young man is already smitten. Arbate notes in particular that love is a very suitable emotion for princes, since it balances and complements their other attributes. His opinions thus rapidly become superfluous, all the more so when Euryale decides to make the fool **Moron** his main go–between with the Princess.

**Argan** (*Le Malade imaginaire*). Along with Proust's Tante Léonie, Argan is perhaps the most famous hypochondriac in all of French literature. The title character of Molière's last play, *Le Malade imaginaire*, Argan is typical of a certain category of Molière protagonists, including **Orgon** (*Tartuffe*), **Harpagon** (*L'Avare*), **Monsieur Jourdain** (*Le Bourgeois gentilhomme*), and **Philaminte** (*Les Femmes savantes*), insofar as all these characters embody a misplaced, excessive preoccupation with a single concern that comes to dominate their entire existence and threatens to interfere with the proper choice of a spouse for their marriageable daughters. Argan, a prosperous, middle–aged **bourgeois** with two daughters from a first **marriage** and a second wife who is interested only in his **money**, spends all of his time and a good deal of his wealth on **medical** treatments of various sorts. It is fairly clear that Argan is not actually in bad physical health; rather, his obsession with his health is presented as a symptom of his unbridled "imagination," a key term for Molière's comedy.
In the case of Argan, as in much of Molière's theater, to be an *imaginaire* is a complex business. It does not suggest simply that one is wont to conceptualize other possible worlds — how things might be — but rather points to a dangerous detachment from the real world — of how things actually are. At the same time, Argan's scant comprehension of himself and of those around him is one of the principal sources of comedy in the play, and as is the case for Molière's other *imaginaires*, Argan's comical excesses have an endearing quality that makes his refusal or inability to be fully enlightened at the end of the play acceptable to the audience at some level. Thus, while Argan relents in his choice of a husband for his daughter, he never gives up his obsession with the medical profession; rather, the real world is finally made to humor his imagination when he is "initiated" as a doctor by the fantastic ceremony that closes the play.
While analogies between Molière himself and several of his earlier protagonists — most notably **Sganarelle** in *L'École des maris*, **Arnolphe** in *L'École des femmes*, and **Alceste** in *Le Misanthrope* — have been pointed out,

none of them can hold a candle to the macabre association between the ailing playwright and the role of Argan, which Molière embodied up to the very moment of his own death shortly after the fourth performance of the play on February 17, 1673. Molière's preoccupations with his health were well enough known to have inspired **Le Boulanger de Chalussay's** *Élomire hypocondre*, and the extraordinary paradox of a playwright and comedian expiring while playing the role of a hypochondriac, including two key scenes in which the character of Argan plays dead (III, 12–13), was remarked upon as early as the day after Molière's death.

One of the most taxing roles Molière ever created, Argan is onstage in twenty–six of the play's thirty–one scenes. The 1674 **Amsterdam** edition of *Le Malade imaginaire* describes Argan's **costume** as including thick stockings, house–slippers, a red robe with a bit of lace, a loosely attached neckerchief, and a lacy nightcap. After Molière's death, the role was assumed by other members of his troupe, **Baron** and **La Thorillière**, and after they left the troupe the role was taken over by **Rosimond**.

*Richard E. Goodkin*

**Argante** (*Les Fourberies de Scapin*). Irascible father of **Octave**, he is tricked out of 2,000 *livres* by **Scapin** and **Silvestre**, who does a surprisingly convincing job of impersonating **Hyacinte's** swashbuckling brother. Thus cured of his infatuation with the law courts, he learns in the conclusion that **Zerbinette** is none other than his own daughter. The role was probably played by **Du Croisy** or **Hubert**.

**Argatiphontidas** (*Amphitryon*). One of the second pair of witnesses summoned by **Amphitryon** to establish his true identity (III, 7), Argatiphontidas differs from **Posiclès** in his belligerent talk. However, though he is present until the conclusion of the play, he never does anything to back up his warlike words.

**Argus**. In **Greek** mythology, a being with a thousand eyes that watches over Io. **Valère** compares **Sganarelle** to Argus twice in *L'École des maris*.

**Ariste** (*L'École des maris*). The indulgent, rather foppish older brother of **Sganarelle**. In the first scene of the play, Sganarelle criticizes Ariste's showy, **court**–inspired attire such as *canons* and tight jackets. Ariste defends himself on the grounds that one must bend to the fashions of the times. Sganarelle then attacks the freedom that Ariste gives to his ward, **Léonor**. Ariste ripostes that a woman who is virtuous only by constraint is not worth much, but that one acquainted with the ways of the world is better able to withstand temptation and inspire confidence. Having consigned his honor to his partner's good faith, he does not reappear until Act III, scene 6, where Sganarelle tries to convince him that Léonor has run off with **Valère**. Ariste professes much confusion and skepticism, but agrees to sign a wedding contract anyway. When Léonor returns home from the frivolous ball she had attended, she gives proof of the efficacy of

Ariste's method of social education. His mild–mannered reproach for her supposed relations with Valère elicits a stern denial and a willingness to marry Ariste immediately, despite his advanced age. Soon it is revealed that Léonor's sister, **Isabelle**, who had been under Sganarelle's draconian rule, was the one who has eloped. Then it is Ariste's turn to try to comfort his odious brother, which meets with little success. Instead he invites everyone to his house to celebrate, in hopes of a later reconciliation.

Critics have said that Ariste reflects some of the ideas on age and **marriage** that are expressed in **La Mothe Le Vayer's** *Prose chagrine*. He is the first, if not the most eloquent, of many *raisonneur* figures in Molière's later plays, from **Chrysalde** in *L'École des femmes* to **Béralde** in *Le Malade imaginaire*. As such, he serves not so much as spokesman for the idealized values of the author, but rather as a more rational foil to the eccentricities of Molière's loquacious Sganarelle, likewise the first of a long line of monomaniacs. It is most likely that this role was played by the aged actor **Lespy**.

**Ariste** (*Les Femmes savantes*). Tradition plausibly says that **Baron** played this part as the (presumably much younger) brother of **Chrysale**. Enlisted by **Clitandre** to back his proposal of **marriage** to **Henriette**, Ariste appears as a kind of cheerleader, encouraging Chrysale to act more forcefully. Happily, he has an extra stratagem in hand, for when Chrysale collapses yet again in the final act, Ariste delivers two forged **letters** that cause the family fortune to disappear before their eyes. Though **Trissotin** immediately heads for the doorway, unwilling to share his literary income, Clitandre rushes forward with the offer of aid, changing the mind of **Philaminte** and garnering her support. Thus, he provides the benevolent deception usually supplied by the scheming valet rather than the *raisonneur* advice one might expect from the brother–in–law.

**Aristione** (*Les Amants magnifiques*). Mother of **Ériphile**, this elder princess has allowed her daughter complete freedom in the choice of a husband. She is extremely impressed by the various entertainments that **Iphicrate** and **Timoclès** offer her daughter, but later admits to Ériphile that she is perhaps beginning to find the almost endless series of **music and dancing** to be somewhat of a burden. However, she is remarkably civil in her compliments on the various spectacles, and is also much more **polite** than necessary when enduring the personal obsequiousness of Iphicrate, who admits to wooing the daughter through the mother. She pleads in vain for her daughter to open her heart and explain her real feelings. If she has one weakness, it is her conviction that astrology is a true science that is capable of revealing the hidden future. Though she quickly falls for the trap that **Anaxarque** has set by staging an apparition of **Venus** through intricate **machinery**, her credulity does no harm in the long term. **Sostrate** saves her from the real danger of a ferocious wild boar just in time to fulfill the prophecy and marry Ériphile. The role was probably played by **Mlle. de Brie** or **Madeleine Béjart**.

**Aristomène** (*La Princesse d'Élide*).  Prince of **Mycenae**, this character was played by **Du Croisy**.  Summoned along with **Théocle** by the Prince of **Elis**, Aristomène is to participate in a series of sports and games designed to impress the Princess and lead her to choose a husband from among the contestants. Things start out badly for the pair, however, when their gallant act of killing a boar that they thought was threatening her leads only to a reprimand from the tough young lady.  Likewise, when **Euryale** tells him that he is loved by the Princess (a profession that Euryale knows to be untrue), Aristomène rushes to her side, only to be flatly rejected and told by her he is "too credulous."  In the final act, he makes an apparently successful offer on behalf of himself and Théocle for the hands of **Aglante** and **Cynthie**, though it is unclear who would marry whom.

**Aristotle**. Though still widely respected throughout Europe in the early modern intellectual community, poor Aristotle fares badly in the hands of the skeptical Molière.  The ridiculous **Doctor** in *La Jalousie du Barbouillé* offers to read the other characters a chapter of the philosopher "only sixty or eighty pages long" that will prove that the various parts of the universe are held together by the agreement that exists between them (his interlocutors understandably decline). He also refers to Aristotle's five universals.  **Gros–René**, in *Dépit amoureux*, also cites Aristotle among other learned sources in his diatribe against women. In the prefatory letter to *Les Fâcheux*, Molière mentions that he could cite precedents for his play in Aristotle if he wanted to write a self–justification, but that such a work would probably never be forthcoming.  In *La Critique de l'École des femmes*, **Monsieur Lysidas** cites Aristotle and terms from his poetics when arguing with Dorante.  In the opening scene of *Dom Juan*, **Sganarelle** refutes Aristotle's pretended stance against **tobacco** use.  **Pancrace**, in *Le Mariage forcé*, is an Aristotelian philosopher through and through, preoccupied as he is in a dispute with a colleague over whether it is more proper to say "the form of a hat" or "the figure of a hat."  As protagonist of *Le Médecin malgré lui*, Sganarelle makes frequent citations of Aristotle, both before and after he is mistaken for a doctor.  He tells his wife in the first scene that, according to the philosopher, women are worse than demons, and implies that such learning comes from his few years of schooling.  In Act II, scene 4, during his medical masquerade, he tells **Géronte** that Aristotle has "many fine things" to say about the action of the tongue and, punning on the word "grand," that he was taller than Sganarelle by half a yard.  This leads him into a discussion of peccant humors, dear to the heart of old–fasioned French doctors.  Aristotle's peripatetic philosophy is mentioned as one of the schools of interest to **Philaminte's** circle in *Les Femmes savantes*.

**Armande** (*Les Femmes savantes*).  This prudish, **jealous**, flesh–shy elder sister of **Henriette** earns the qualification of "odious" from Georges Couton.  Others may find her more pathetic than hateful.  Before the play begins, she has spurned **Clitandre's** amorous advances in an attempt to keep him as the kind of perpetual swooning suitor (*soupirant*) one finds in the novels of **Mlle. de Scudéry**. Instead he found consolation in the arms of Henriette, who finds the physical side of **marriage** quite desirable. Armande is not completely without feelings, but it is clear in the scene where her mother's salon welcomes the insipid poet **Trissotin** that she has sublimated normal desires into a poetic frenzy. She responds nearly orgasmically to Trissotin's stupid verses, just as her mother and **Bélise** do. She at first expresses a nasty, vengeful attitude toward her sister, and later gloats when she thinks Henriette will be compelled to marry the poetaster. When she lies to her mother about Clitandre's supposed insults to the family, she must suffer the personal rejection that he once again expresses, this time in front of a witness. However disagreeable she may be, she is primarily a person who lies to herself as much as her aunt does when she imagines every man in the world desires her. Despite Armande's prudishness, she aches internally for some kind of gratification; despite her concern for purity, she reacts with wretching, physical disgust when faced with anything unacceptable; despite her devotion to elevated **language**, she quickly lapses into rather vulgar expressions when she does not get her way.

The name of this character may lead one to expect that she was played by **Armande Béjart**, but a fairly reliable tradition says that **Mlle. de Brie** was cast in this role. Certainly de Brie would appear to be the elder of the two. Furthermore, de Brie would soon have a far more wicked part written for her in *Le Malade imaginaire*, where she appears as the black widow **Béline**. These late roles were a far cry from the innocent **Agnès** of 1662.

**Armenian.** **Lélie** is **disguised** as an Armenian in Act IV of *L'Étourdi* in an attempt to get closer to **Célie**. Having learned of **Trufaldin's** true identity as **Zanobio Ruberti**, the young man and **Mascarille** purport to bring him news of his long–lost son, seen by the Armenian in **Turkey** or **Barbary**. Lélie's many blunders in his testimony, his failure to remember critical details of the story, and particularly his fawning behavior at the table with his sweetheart, cause Trufaldin to suspect something.

**Armor.** Medieval armor was no longer worn in the seventeenth century, though cavalry still wore a breastplate for some occasions. Nevertheless, Sganarelle produces what appears to be a set of armor for his **duel** with **Lélie** in *Sganarelle*. When asked what his **costume** means, he explains it is a "rain outfit." **Bourgeois** men sometimes maintained military gear for times of strife, when they were called upon to defend the city. There may have been some bourgeois engagement during the 1648–1652 **Fronde** revolts, but Sganarelle's armor probably dates from the late sixteenth–century Wars of Religion. In *George Dandin*, **Monsieur de Sotenville** also appears in the frontispiece illustration to be wearing an obsolete helmet and breastplate.

**Arnolphe** (*L'École des femmes*). One of the most extensive roles in Molière's theater, Arnolphe represents the first in a long line of the dramatist's strong comic characters. Given his constant stage presence (he appears in thirty–one of thirty–two scenes, ends each act, and begins the following one with a soliloquy), his role dominates the play both scenically and verbally. An incarnation of both the *barbon* (ridiculous old man) of traditional comedy and the seventeenth–century French **bourgeois** in **love**, Arnolphe's character may best be elucidated in terms of the psychodynamics of fear: his profound insecurity is at the root of his obsessive behavior inasmuch as he suffers, on the one hand, from a deep–rooted fear of women and, on the other, from an equally pervasive fear of ridicule. Not only is he desirous of eliminating all risk from his world, but he has perfectly displaced his fears: instead of being concerned, at the outset, with **Horace** as a potential rival (I, 4) and with the consequences of **Agnès's** emotional and intellectual vulnerability, he is fearful of all other men and all other women. An impenitent misogynist, Arnolphe espouses a worldview grounded in an antithetical vision opposing cuckolded husbands and diabolical wives. His antifeminism leads him to believe that a woman's freedom is tantamount to her propensity for infidelity. The protagonist's hubris resides in his desire to escape the fate that befalls other men. By dint of pure intellect and planning, he is supremely confident of being able to preserve his honor. For him, knowledge is power, a commodity he uses to his own end. Desirous of creating an aesthetic distance between himself and ordinary men, Arnolphe believes that he alone, as self–appointed spectator of the human condition, possesses the wisdom necessary to protect himself from the vicissitudes of **married** life. If he directs his aggressive laughter against the undifferentiated mass of cuckolds that surrounds him, this is a form of self–valorization on the part of an individual who confers upon himself an aura of invulnerability; he steadfastly resists, in short, being reduced to what he considers the commonality of man's conjugal experience. To become a cuckold is, for Arnolphe, tantamount to the loss of his identity, and constitutes the ultimate de–valorization of self. Hence, his adoption of the name **Monsieur de la Souche** emanates from his desire to escape the implications of his real name, derived from the patron saint of cuckolds. Like **Alceste** in *Le Misanthrope*, Arnolphe takes great pains to set himself apart from others in order to avoid the public suffering caused by their mockery of him.

As a result of his comic folly, Arnolphe attempts to subvert and regulate Agnès's natural aptitudes. He also perverts the **educational** process by trying to mold his young ward according to his pathological needs. The reifying effect of Arnolphe's repressive pedagogy is such that he strives to "create" the perfect wife by carefully defining her rights and responsibilities. By using religion as an instrument of terror, he aims to maintain Agnès in a state of psychological, moral, and economic subservience; he thus seeks to deny her personal autonomy and access to womanhood. In addition to his role as spiritual director, he serves as a proprietary father figure and as a prospective husband for Agnès, whose innocence represents, in his eyes, a triumphant repudiation of the worldliness of the *précieuses*. His dogmatic vision of a perfect wife presupposes, in fact, her renunciation of all traditional forms of social life. The greatest irony of the play is that Arnolphe is outsmarted by the naïve Agnès, by the bumbling Horace, and by his simple–minded **servants**. He is thus defeated by those whom he wishes to keep in ignorance. In his blatant smugness and self–satisfaction, he attempts to control the spontaneous, unforeseen developments of life, in short, its very unpredictability. He fails spectacularly in his effort to outwit fate. Paradoxically, the protagonist who aims systematically to control his own destiny and that of others ends up totally out of control and dependent on the whims of Agnès. Also, it is precisely because of Agnès's ignorance that Arnolphe experiences tremendous suffering. His comic discomfiture is due to his fall from a position of moral superiority over others to an abject position of anger and vindictiveness. Ultimately, his strong discursive power is reduced to complete silence, as his final utterance of "Ouf!" marks his departure from the stage. He remains unrepentant, trapped in his monumental fear of cuckoldry. His downfall being concomitant with the revelation of his true identity (V, 7), his playing of the double role of Arnolphe and Monsieur de la Souche places him in the paradoxical situation of benefiting logistically and suffering emotionally from what the unsuspecting Horace tells him. This convergence of both the comic (the intellectual dimension of his being) and the tragic (his emotional dimension) accounts for the psychological depth and lucidity of this great *imaginaire*, and hence, the considerable number of soliloquies and asides that constitute his engaging role. Upon becoming emotionally involved with Agnès, Arnolphe is unable to keep the intellectual distance he once enjoyed. The burlesque aspect of his suffering notwithstanding, Arnolphe incarnates the remarkable weakness of Molière's men in love, in short, the pathos of the male tyrant who tries to force his young ward to love him.

*Ralph Albanese, Jr.*

**Arras**. City northeast of **Paris** on the Flanders road, site of many battles throughout the ages. In *Les Précieuses ridicules*, when **Mascarille** reminds **Jodelet** of the half–moon (a kind of bastion) that they supposedly captured at the siege of Arras, Jodelet replies ridiculously, "What do you mean a half–moon? Surely it was a full moon!" They refer probably not to the best–known seventeenth–century siege of Arras in 1640, but to a smaller, more recent action that pitted **Condé** against Turenne in 1654. The biographer **Tallemant des Réaux** attributes the original of the "full moon" remark to the Marquis de Nesle.

**Arsinoé (***Le Misanthrope***)**. This unsympathetic lady is Molière's archetypal prude and bigot, hiding her persistent lust and intrigue under the veil of holy thoughts. When she arrives at **Célimène's** house, it is clearly with the intention of embarrassing and shaming her, rather than offering her edifying advice and comfort. The spectator finds himself on the coquette's side for once as she turns Arsinoé's acid remarks against her. The prude is also interested in **Alceste's** affections and prepared to buy them through her political connections at **court**. This is Molière's most audacious swipe at the warped **religion** "cabale des dévots," whose influence already reached as far as the King's intimate circle.

Just as Arsinoé serves to show Célimène in a more favorable light, she allows Alceste the opportunity to put his virtue to good use by rejecting her offers of promotion and belittling his own achievements. Arsinoé's denunciation of Célimène through the stolen **letter** that she gives to Alceste is truly a base act, showing the depravity of her contentiousness. She fully deserves the shattering rejection she receives in the last act of the play. The first performance of this interesting part is usually attributed to **Mlle. de Brie** on the basis of 1685 casting, with the assumption that **Mlle. Du Parc** played **Éliante**. The casting of *L'Impromptu de Versailles*, where de Brie is given the role of a scheming prude, suggests this may have been true.

**Ascagne** (*Dépit amoureux*). A girl **disguised** as a man. She believes she was switched in infancy with the deceased boy Ascagne in order to conserve a great inheritance for **Albert's** family and to save the boy's mother from the wrath of her greedy husband. According to this story, the false Ascagne's mother was wet–nurse to the two children and willingly participated in the deception because of the benefits both she and her daughter hoped to receive. Twelve years have passed in the interval, making Ascagne now fifteen or sixteen years of age (early modern **children** normally stayed with the wet nurse until the age of four or five). **Frosine**, her **confidante**, must also be an honored member of Albert's family, rather than just a **servant**, because the two use the formal "vous" in addressing each other. By the beginnning of the play's action, Ascagne has fallen in love with **Valère** by a type of deflection, sympathizing with him when he was rejected by her sister **Lucile**, rather like Shakespeare's Viola. But going much further, Ascagne actually took on Lucile's identity at night, made assignations with Valère that led to the complete expression of their passion, and even secretly **married** him, without his catching on to the disguise! This accounts for Valère's nonchalant and light–hearted attitude in Act I, when Éraste tries to cast doubts on his success with Lucile; Valère thinks he has already enjoyed her favors and won her hand. In reality, Ascagne's heritage and identity are even more complicated than she thought. After commiserating with Frosine in Act IV, scene 1 over the dangers of being exposed, which are growing as Valère's claims come to a head, the two girls disappear from stage for another interval, reappearing in the final act. There we learn (unfortunately by *récit* rather than more directly) that Ascagne is actually Albert's younger daughter, born instead of the nonexistent male Ascagne, switched at birth with a neighbor's little boy, and switched again when the boy's death left open a place in the family that the mother had somehow to fill. She makes the most of her opportunities to flirt and mystify her husband in the preparations for the denouement's first **duel**, just as she had when she exchanged pleasantries with him in the opening act. Ascagne's unique situation, the unusual circumstances of her love, and her boldness in consummating the relationship "under cover" compensate to some degree for the lack of stage action associated with her role, for most of her story is told in a series of long accounts. She is far more unique and interesting than the usual heroine of intrigue comedy, as **Polidore** testifies when he greets her as his daughter–in–law, and at least comparable to her counterparts in Shakespeare. Following her final transformation into a girl, she is given the name **Dorothée**.

**Astorga.** City in Leon, Spain, where *Dom Garcie de Navarre* is set. **Dom Garcie** has rescued **Elvire** from the tyranny of the usurper **Mauregat** and taken the town of Astorga to serve as her refuge.

**Astrology.** The only play where stargazing plays an explicit role is *Les Amants magnifiques*. It is at first presented in a surprisingly multi–faceted way, with **Clitidas** mocking it openly and associating it with necromancy, while **Ériphile** and **Sostrate** express doubt. Sostrate frames his personal views in terms of skeptical **philosophy**, noting that his own "imperfect" senses can give no empirical support for belief in astrology. He then switches to turn one science against the other, drawing on astronomical observations and calculations that had only fairly recently established the tremendous distances that separated the other heavenly bodies from the earth and the remoteness of any influence they could extend. It seems that astrology may be able to furnish as objective a measure of marriage partners as anything else, for by Act III the two main lovers are desperately hiding their feelings and all other methods of choice seem to fail. Perhaps Molière was alluding to **Rabelais's** use of astrology and other methods of divination in the *Tiers Livre*, where they are seriously consulted by Pantagruel and Panurge. However, in Act IV the astrological enterprise is shown to be entirely bogus, as **Anaxarque** cynically admits to his son how he has cozened princes and princesses alike, with the intent of using his increased influence to blackmail the royal family long after the **marriage** itself has taken place. Gods, planets, and heaven are reduced to a few skillfully manipulated pulleys and cords. The victims of such schemes are simply superstitious fools. Yet the fools are not too powerless to beat the astrologer within an inch of his life, as we learn in the final act. The astrological connection between the pagan heavens and the Christian notion of heaven is implicit, leading to a tacit critique of **superstitions** in the early modern as well as the ancient contexts. It has been suggested by Couton and others that the European astrologer **Jean–Baptiste Morin**, who had died in 1656, was the model for Anaxarque and his machinations.

**Astronomy.** Recent discoveries by Galileo and others had brought astronomy to the forefront of intellectual discussion in **Paris** by the mid–seventeenth century. The science is mainly discussed in *Les Femmes savantes*, where it is the object of much derision. In the second act, **Chrysale** asks the ladies to take down the fearsome telescope they have installed in the attic, along with "a hundred other suspicious–looking doo–dads," and stop worrying about what is happening on the moon. His fears are right on the mark, for **Philaminte** later claims to have seen men walking on the moon and **Bélise**, whose eyesight was not so sharp, adds that she could only see the steeples of their churches (III, 2).

**Trissotin** later hurries in with news that the earth has barely missed collision with another heavenly body, perhaps referring to a comet (IV, 3). This attitude of wholescale dismissal seems a bit strange in a person with Molière's **philosophical** interests, but it reflects very popular anxiety about astronomy. **Rousseau** will report nearly a century later that his early experiments with telescopes were viewed with much fear by the neighbors, who suspected him of conjuring spirits and alerted the local religious authorities.

**Atis**. This "incomparable" painter is mentioned as the one who executed the locket **portraits** of **Myrtil** cherished by **Daphné** and **Éroxène** in *Mélicerte*. The handsome youth seems to have inspired a whole line of art! Molière's friend **Mignard** was also, of course, an accomplished portraitist.

**Audience**. More so than most dramatists of his time, Molière was really composing for two distinct but overlapping audiences, the **court** and the town. As a royal retainer, he obviously was required to direct his talents to pleasing **Louis XIV** and to concocting suitable entertainments for the mainly aristocratic milieu of the court whenever commanded to do so. But he also had to tend to the needs of the Palais Royal Theater and its mainly urban spectators. He was clever enough to balance the interests of both. Within the **theater**, there was a hierarchy of social types who came to the plays. Nobles tended to monopolize the rent of expensive box seats and seats placed directly on the sides of the stage. Several rows of bench seats, called the amphitheater, lined the walls of the great room, and these tended to be taken up by the upper levels of the **bourgeoisie**. The large space in the middle of the room contained no seats and was given over to groundlings who stood during the whole performance and paid the lowest ticket prices. Most of these groundlings were actually bourgeois in good standing, for the price of admission kept the lowest socioeconomic elements out of the building. The most annoying presence was often that of soldiers, who insisted on being admitted free on the basis of their service to the King, and often misbehaved when they grudgingly agreed to pay. Molière was a very wise manipulator of the groundlings, or "parterre." As an experienced "harangeur" or opening comic, he knew how to grab their attention and affection, as well as how to quell their often rowdy or rebellious moods. He was frequently criticized by opponents as catering too much to the *parterre*, but this charge obviously sprang from jealousy. It is true that he never directly insults the groundlings out beyond the stage, while often making jokes about the aristocrats lolling on the fringes of the stage or lording it up in the boxes.

*Aulularia*. A **Latin** comedy by **Plautus** on which Molière loosely based his *L'Avare*. Euclio, the protagonist, does not make his fortune as does Molière's **Harpagon**, but only finds it buried in his hearth by a previous resident of the house. His fears about losing the nest egg revolve more around typical Roman superstitions than around the capitalistic concerns that animate the French miser. Harpagon's wild soliloquy at the end of Act IV, reacting to the theft of his strongbox by the servant **La Flèche**, is based on a similar, somewhat longer, scene in Plautus. The misunderstood interrogation of **Valère** also has a parallel in the Latin text.

**Aurora.** *See* **Dawn.**

**Auteuil.** Village east of **Paris** where Molière had a country house. He often went there as a refuge from the cares of the city, and perhaps from his wife during their legendary marital troubles. A picturesque anecdote reported in **Grimarest** and later biographers claims that one evening he got drunk with **Boileau, Chapelle**, and a few other friends. The guests were so despondent about life that they resolved to throw themselves into the river and drown. However, Molière convinced them that such a brave act should only be performed by light of day. Of course, by sunrise they were so preoccupied with their hangovers that they had no more thoughts of suicide. This "evening at Auteuil" was even made into a short story in the early nineteenth century. According to the memoirs of the Chevalier d'Arvieux, a Turkish expert called in to help with the composition of *Le Bourgeois gentilhomme*, much of the work was done at Molière's cottage. The village is mentioned in *Les Femmes savantes* by **Martine**, who, when asked if she knows where the word "grammar" comes from, replies that she doesn't care if it comes from **Chaillot**, Auteuil, or **Pontoise**.

*Avare, L'* (*The Miser*). This five–act prose comedy loosely based on **Plautus's** *Aulularia* premiered September 9, 1668, at the Palais Royal Theater. It is one of Molière's most socially engaged plays in that it shows an early modern capitalist in action. Unlike Plautus's Euclio, who merely happened to find his fortune buried in the hearth, Molière's protagonist **Harpagon** is a self–made investor experienced in all facets of the business of credit and loans. Instead of just hoarding his wealth, he insists on keeping it actively invested to gain maximum interest. But unlike many a sharp businessman, he works to the detriment of his own family and household, denying them the basic necessities required by their station in life. The intrigue, which is more tightly woven than in most of the later plays, involves a triple **marriage** plot, with Harpagon and his son **Cléante** courting the same indigent girl and Harpagon's own daughter **Élise**, though promised to a rich old geezer by her father, being secretly wooed by her admirer **Valère**, who has slipped into the household in the guise of a low–cost manager. Auxiliaries to the plot include an aging matchmaker, **Frosine**, Cléante's valet, **La Flèche**, and the mansion's combination cook and coachman, **Maître Jacques**.

While Cléante has been attracted to **Mariane** by both charitable and romantic motives, neither **dowry money** nor sex seem to be driving Harpagon's suit. Instead, it seems to be a product of Frosine's panderings and the constant desire to find a bargain. Having given away all the money at his disposal, Cléante is looking for more, not only to be able to dress in fashion and to lavish more gifts on his beloved, but to run off with her far from the rigid economies of Harpagon's home. He has unwittingly made contact with his own father's agent in order to obtain an illegal loan. He makes the shocking discovery that Harpagon is deeply involved in black market finance, floating unsecured loans at usurious rates in order to obtain claims to the estates of young spendthrifts. He is a devourer of family heritage, a social parasite of the lowest order. The son, on the other hand, is a typical wastrel, having learned to live with an aristocratic burden of debt and mindless of the real sources of family income. Harpagon gives the youth a tongue–lashing, but cannot disinherit him from his mother's dowry principal, of which he has only usufructuary control. Meantime, Harpagon has been making plans with Frosine to examine the young lady she promises will bring him a fortune merely by not spending anything at all on her person. Maître Jacques presents a number of logistical obstacles to the miser's entertainment plans, since he insists on the need for supplies. But Valère plays the "yes man" to Harpagon and argues with the **servant**, eventually shoving him around the room. When Cléante learns that Mariane is coming for a visit, he conceals his interest in her and takes over plans for the entertainment, scrapping the cheap, unappetizing fare his father had ordered and substituting elegant catered dishes. He compliments the lady right under his father's nose and takes a diamond **ring** off the old man's finger to give her as a gift. Sensing something wrong, Harpagon pretends to favor his son's inclination to marry and traps the young man into admitting his feelings for Mariane. He then chases him from the house, but not before the quick–fingered La Flèche can steal a large sum of cash Harpagon had buried for safe keeping in the garden. Rejected by Mariane and bereft of his gold, Harpagon goes berserk and calls in the **law**, asking the local police **commissioner** to arrest the entire town on suspicion. Instead, the lawman interrogates the handiest witness, Maître Jacques, who decides to settle accounts with Valère by fingering him for the crime. Valère is duly summoned and assumes, because he knows nothing of the gold or its theft, that Harpagon is accusing him of stealing his daughter, which leads to a very comical misunderstanding scene. Before more harm can be done, Élise's elderly fiancé appears and recognizes Mariane and Valère as his long lost daughter and son. He eagerly grants them their desired marriage partners, and Harpagon is willing to relinquish his obstacles to Cléante's wedding if he and La Flèche return the stolen cash.

The play is filled with interesting gestural gags, such as Maître Jacques's whirlwind changes of uniform, the servants assuming grotesque poses to hide the holes in their threadbare garments, Harpagon's indecent searches of La Flèche's undergarments to prevent pilfering, the pratfalls of the clumsy footman La Merluche, and the miser's own raving over his lost strongbox. It also contains scenes of ironic confrontation, including the mutual accusations of usurer and spendthrift, the son entertaining the sweetheart on his father's date, the labor dispute between the good and bad servants, and Valère's bizarre confession to the passion he felt for Harpagon's lost treasure. Yet it was perhaps the prosaic, naturalistic quality of the play, together with the lack of any now–familiar **comedy–ballet** elements, that limited *L'Avare*'s success to a solid but mediocre level. Its unseasonably early release, at a time when many theatergoers were still on their estates supervising harvests or preparing for the fall **hunts**, helps explain the lack of a full house — perhaps it was also the fact that he was bringing the light of ridicule on some financial practices that were a little too close to the conscience of his urban **audience**. It was completely eclipsed when *Tartuffe* finally appeared, unbanned and unleashed, in 1669 and rightly or wrongly has come to be considered something of a stopgap play designed to keep the troupe solvent until the great verse masterpiece could be staged. **Boisrobert** and **Chappuzeau** may have furnished some precedents for the play, but in general Molière went to great lengths to separate this work from the existing French traditions. The text was published by **Ribou** in 1669.

See John McCann, "Harpagon: The Paradox of Miserliness," *Papers on French Seventeenth–Century Literature* 22 (1995), 555–569; and M. J. McCarthy, "The Black Economy in *L'Avare*," *Australian Journal of French Studies* 28 (1991), 235–248.

*L'Avare dupé ou l'Homme de paille* (***The Duped Miser, or the Straw Man***). A comedy by **Samuel Chappuzeau**, printed in 1662, and later retitled *La Dame d'intrigue*. Although the general theme is similar to Molière's *L'Avare*, there is little else in common. The role of **Ruffine**, instead of paralleling **Frosine**, is quite different and much more extensive. Chappuzeau's retitling of his play may have been an attempt to distance his text from the later, more popular comedy.

**Avignon.** City of the Rhone valley and ancient capital of the Comtat Venaissin. The wandering troupe of **Charles Dufresne**, which contained young Molière and his companions, passed through Avignon on their way up and down the Rhone and into Languedoc. **Madeleine Béjart** had relatives (the **L'Hermite** family) and business relationships here, and it is likely that here Molière first met the painter **Mignard**, who stayed in the same building with some mutual friends on his way back to **Paris** from the Academy in Italy in 1655.

**Avowal of Love.** Because of seventeenth–century senses of propriety, literature was less concerned with the description of **love** itself, especially its physical description, than with its psychological effects and the moment of avowal, when a person would drop his defenses and admit to being in love. This admission of feeling was tantamount to the complete physical expression of love, which was seen conventionally as a mere follow–up to the avowal. For a person to admit love placed him or her at a great weakness, since the love offered could be rejected, mocked, or broadcast to the world through gossip. In some cases, especially among the upper classes, a degree of importance was attached to the delay of the avowal, since too ready an admission would indicate that the emotion was easily come by and did not entail a high emotional price, especially in terms of sacrificing other interests or values. The classic avowal scene is often cited as the one in Madame de Lafayette's novel, *The Princess of Cleves*. This, however, is a somewhat unusual one in that it is a woman's admission to her husband (not to the lover himself) of an illicit, albeit unconsummated emotion. She never professes her love to its object, the Duke of Nemours. In Molière's works, avowals are often exchanged between characters offstage, before the beginning of the play. When they do take place, they are often of an exaggerated, ludicrous, or burlesque quality, such as the avowal **Arnolphe** offers to **Agnès** in the last act of *L'École des femmes* or the ones **Dom Juan** makes simultaneously to two peasant women. In *Le Misanthrope*, **Alceste** pursues **Célimène** throughout the play in search of an avowal on her part. She claims that he should be satisfied simply with "the happiness of knowing that you are loved" (II, 2). But when **Philinte** is actually making a proposal to **Éliante**, in John Alden fashion, Alceste bursts in and substitutes a far blunter and less respectful version to the young woman. *Les Amants magnifiques* portrays an interesting mutual avowal between **Ériphile** and **Sostrate**, neither of whom sees the possibility, or even the necessity, of fulfilling the admission (IV, 4). In *Monsieur de Pourceaugnac*, **Éraste** attempts to dictate an avowal from **Julie**, who replies, "My God, Éraste! Be content with what I am doing now and don't make future bets on the resolution of my heart" (I, 2). *Psyché* features a double avowal that is only possible because the Princes **Agénor** and **Cléomène** are perfect friends and have vowed that the one preferred shall have both their realms to offer to Psyché. The young lady uses their friendship as her pretext for rejecting them both, claiming that it is too beautiful to disrupt by favoring one over the other. In *Les Femmes savantes*, **Clitandre** is not afraid to make a very public avowal of his passion for **Henriette**, even in front of his former sweetheart **Armande** (I, 2). Molière innovatively uses the scene for plot exposition. Henriette, no less frank, mirrors this admission by openly declaring her lack of love for **Trissotin** to his face at the beginning of Act V. She includes a thinly veiled threat that she will make him a cuckold if he persists in his plans for marriage.

# B

**Babylon**. This ancient city is mentioned in a comical way by **Madame Pernelle** when she talks of the "tower of Babylon" in the first scene of *Tartuffe*. She goes on to concoct a folk etymology for the name, saying *Babylone* comes from the fact that people there would babble (*babiller*) "by the yard long" (*l'aune* in French, homonymic with *lone*).

**Bahys (*L'Amour médecin*)**. This **doctor** is one of the four originally summoned by **Sganarelle** to cure his daughter of her strange illness. Based on the court physician Esprit, Bahys speaks in a rapid mumble, while, in contrast, Macroton does so with painfully slow articulation, causing Sganarelle to remark, "One goes like a turtle, the other like a post–horse."

**Ballard, Robert**. As **music** publisher to the French crown, Ballard had a monopoly on publishing musically related scripts. The ballet of *Le Mariage forcé* (1664), which contained a summary of the play's action, and the edition of *Les Plaisirs de l'Isle enchantée* (1664), complete with the text of Molière's comedy, *La Princesse d'Élide*, fell within his purview, as did both booklets for the **Tuileries** and Palais Royal Theater productions of *Psyché*. Ballard also published the booklet for the **Grand Divertissement Royal de Versailles** in 1668, but without the text of *George Dandin*, which Molière printed separately a year later. Similarly, he printed the booklet for the musical framework for *Le Malade imaginaire*. If he did not print the booklet for *Monsieur de Pourceaugnac*, it was presumably since the spectacle was staged at **Chambord**, far from Ballard's presses; a local printer in Blois did the honors. In the case of *Le Bourgeois gentilhomme*, he must have had enough advance time to work with the text that he was able to prepare it beforehand and ship it to the Loire valley in time for the performance.

**Ballet des Ballets**. This entertainment, held in December 1671 and January 1672 in honor of **Monsieur's** second marriage with the **Princess Palatine**, combined bits of all the major **court** spectacles over the past several years with a few new elements, including *La Comtesse d'Escarbagnas*, which itself encapsulated other plays.

**Ballet des Incompatibles (Ballet of the Incompatibles)**. Presented before the **Prince de Conti** and his wife in **Montpellier** in 1655 and published locally, this entertainment contained fifteen *entrées*, each containing **music and dance**, as well as a primitive skit outlining some variant of incompatibility. Molière appears in the sixth as a poet and in the tenth as a fishwife. **Louis Béjart** also figures in the sixth as a painter and in the ninth as a drunk. There has been much speculation over whether Molière is the author of the text, for its verses have nothing in particular that resemble his mature style. They could just as easily have been penned by Conti himself or by one or more of his noble friends who took part in the dancing.

**Ballet des Muses (The Muses' Ballet)**. This **court** entertainment, presented on December 2, 1666, at the palace of **Saint-Germain-en-Laye**, was not so much a ballet in the modern sense of the term (dances grouped around a coherent theme and story line) as a revue or suite of dances, thirteen in number, later raised to fourteen. If there was a theme, it was **Louis XIV** himself, since the King featured prominently among the dancers. The festivities mobilized nearly all the cultural resources of the royal household: not only Molière's troupe, but that of the Hôtel de Bourgogne, the Italians, and a host of musicians and professional dancers, as well as court figures like **Madame, Mlle. de la Vallière, Madame de Montespan**, and others. Obviously, the mythological Muses formed an important element in the representation, but as there were more dances than Muses, some liberties of association were taken. Abundance was the watchword, rather than careful organization, and it was more important to cram in all the participants than to present a unified whole.

One of the most curious facets of this entertainment was that it was presented over and over again, with numerous changes and variations, until February 19, 1667. Thus, Molière's contributions changed in the course of time. His first contribution was the *Pastorale comique*, of which no text remains today. We do, however, have a summary of the play written by Molière himself. The play is more of a fantasy than a comedy. Along with Molière, **La Grange**, and **Mlle. de Brie**, three of the royal dancers figured as main characters. The very thin plot, based on **Lycas's** amorous misadventures, is merely a framework for **music and dance**. No fewer than fifteen numbers were attached to this flimsy base. Next, the fragmentary "pastoral heroical comedy" *Mélicerte* was inserted into the ballet, although La Grange clearly states in the 1682 collected works that it was unfinished at the time. The two versified acts were cobbled into the ensemble and served as well as anything else as a pretext for more footwork and melodies. Eventually, the small but complete prose comedy, *Le*

*Sicilien*, was tacked onto the ballet in a final fourteenth *entrée*. Though the troupe was richly rewarded for their extended stay at Saint–Germain, some of this material was wasted as far as presentation for the Parisian public. The *Pastorale comique* depended far too heavily on the involvement of dancers and other outsiders to be presented successfully at the Palais Royal Theater. *Mélicerte* might conceivably have fared better with an ending, but Molière left it as it was, unfinished and (until 1682) unpublished, perhaps out of some consideration for his royal patron's acceptance of two acts or perhaps because he did not want to show the nation what a sad morsel had satisfied the Sun King. Only *Le Sicilien* was salvaged for regular production, and it succeeded surprisingly well despite its obvious limitations.

**Ballet des Nations**. This was the musical and dancing accompaniment to the original version of *Le Bourgeois gentilhomme*. The comedy, with its interludes of **music and dance** and its **Turkish** ceremony, opened the event, with the Ballet des Nations constituting the entertainment **Dorante** had arranged for **Dorimène**. It is worth mentioning that this original version of the play was in three acts instead of five. In addition to a naturalistic crowd scene involving the distribution of the booklet to the ballet and a second number portraying three bothersome individuals who irritate the others in the crowd, there are songs by **Spanish–**, **Italian–**, and finally French–speaking vocalists, thus accounting for the name.

**Balzac**. *See* **Guez de Balzac**.

**Barbary**. Mentioned in *L'Étourdi* as a location where the "**Armenian**" (**Lélie** in **disguise**) may have seen **Zanobio Ruberti's** (**see Trufaldin**) lost son. **Mascarille** explains that the idea is not beyond possibility because the Barbary **pirates** frequently kidnap and ransom hostages.

**Barbin, Claude**. Parisian printer very active in dramatic publishing, he was involved with several of Molière's works, including *L'Étourdi*, *Dépit amoureux*, *Les Précieuses ridicules*, and *L'École des maris*. He was part of the eight–printer coalition that published *L'École des femmes* and *La Critique de l'École des femmes*. He also joined with **Thierry** and later **Trabouillet** in printing the 1674 collected edition of Molière's works. The site of his shop must have been a popular gathering place for authors, since **Vadius** challenges **Trissotin** to a **duel** there in *Les Femmes savantes* and **Boileau** makes a similar reference in *Le Lutrin*. Rumor had it that Barbin was the illegitimate son of a royal finance superintendant and the infamous Mme. Concini and that the printer himself assumed a **Chrysalde**–like tolerance of his own wife's affairs.

**Barbouillé, Le** (*La Jalousie du Barbouillé*). This part of a suspicious, drunken husband was probably played by **René Du Parc** and perhaps later by Molière. The name is descriptive, referring to the makeup that was daubed onto the actor's face. It is known that **Gros–René** usually adopted this technique, probably using flour or powder to produce a clownlike effect. One could also be daubed with wine sediment or charcoal, and it is possible that other actors used these materials when playing the role. **La Grange** lists the play as *La Jalousie de Gros–René*.

**Baron (stage name of Michel Boyron,** 1652–1729). Son of a couple of prominent thespians in the **Hôtel de Bourgogne,** Baron adopted his father's stage name. As an actor in the Troupe du Dauphin, a children's ensemble organized by Mme. Raisin, Baron received critical acclaim and gained Molière's attention. The playwright took him under his wing in 1665, and again four years later, when he was summoned back to take the place of the retired **Louis Béjart.** According to **Grimarest** (and probably Baron himself), he had been forced to leave in late 1666 or early 1667 by the antipathy of **Armande Béjart.** At the time, Baron had been playing **Myrtil** in *Mélicerte*, opposite her. It is not clear whether the intimacy between Baron and Molière or some forwardness by the boy toward the female lead was the source of a famous slap from Armande. Ironically, he played against her again as **Cupid** in *Psyché*, where she was the heroine. He probably played **Ariste** in *Les Femmes savantes* and **Béralde** in *Le Malade imaginaire.* Soon after Molière's death, at which he claimed to be present, he jumped to the rival Hôtel de Bourgogne troupe with **La Thorillière,** and later married that actor's teenage daughter, with **Racine** and **Pierre Corneille** among the witnesses. He eventually took over some of Molière's roles as an adult and distinguished himself after 1680 as one of the greatest members of the **Comédie–Française,** until his abrupt retirement in 1691. He is suspected being a source for many of the anecdotes passed on by Grimarest, but many of the stories may be fabrications of his imagination, since some present obvious anachronisms. Baron became a dramatist himself, and his best–known work, *L'Homme à bonnes fortunes* (1686), bears the influence both of Molière and of **Dancourt.**

**Basque (***Le Misanthrope***).** Célimène's footman may not have perfect command of the French **language** ("du dor"), but he seems quite accustomed to the social whirl at her house. He is even a bit blasé in the way he introduces her guests.

**Basques. Marinette** mentions in the first act of *Dépit amoureux* that she has been "trotting like a Basque" to find **Éraste.** To this day, Basques are noted for their stout constitutions and their propensity to take a little walk of twenty miles or so whenever the spirit moves them.

**Bear (***La Princesse d'Élide***).** Though unlisted among the dramatis personae, a bear (presumably played by a man in a suit) appears in the second scene of the second *intermède* to threaten **Moron.** After roughly handling the fool, the bear is attacked by a group of **hunters,** who then dance around the kill as Moron rudely vents his anger on the carcass.

**Beatings.**  A stock ingredient of seventeenth–century comedy, beatings were usually done onstage with a slapstick made from hinged pieces of wood that made a loud noise when they came together on the victim's rump or back.  Thus, any reference to wood or sticks in the play implies the threat of a beating, especially for **servants**, who were more or less open game to such punishment by their masters or even by other social superiors.   The tables are turned somewhat in *L'Étourdi*, where the valet **Mascarille** is "forced" to deliver a beating to his stupid master **Lélie** in order to avoid one himself, after one of their schemes goes awry.  *Dépit amoureux* sees **Albert** punishing the loquacious **Métaphraste** not with a stick, but with a ringing bell.  Slapping was also a form of beating.   Mascarille receives an enormous slap from **Lucile** in *Dépit amoureux* when he alleges she has secretly married **Valère**.  In *Les Précieuses ridicules,* it is he who slaps the Second **Porter** for the impudence of asking to be paid.   But when both Porters threaten him with the sticks from their **sedan chair,** he quickly relents and pays them extra for the slap.  Later, he and **Jodelet** are roughed up, though mildly, by their masters who arrive to strip off their finery and embarrass them in front of the affected girls.  In *Sganarelle*, the protagonist first speaks of beating Lélie when he sees him on his doorstep with his wife and thinks they have just had a tryst.  He says that he feels like knocking off his hat, throwing a rock at him, or tossing mud on his cloak, not exactly brave or conventional forms of fighting.  Later, in his soliloquy in scene 17, Sganarelle tries to rouse himself to revenge against the young man, but admits his cowardice and fears that he might die if he tries to beat him. Dressed in his outmoded **armor,** he tries to pump up his courage to beat the young man, but winds up giving himself a burlesque beating in the process.

At the end of Act IV of *L'École des femmes*, **Arnolphe** trains his servants to give **Horace** a proper thrashing when he tries to climb in **Agnès's** window from a ladder.  They apply their clubs so well, however, that he is worried at the beginning of the next act that the young man may be dead.   When Alain complains he was only following orders, Arnolphe says that they were ordered to strike on the back, and to wound rather than murder.  Horace later describes how he feigned death in order to avoid further blows and profited from his charade by escaping with his sweetheart.  Feigned death was commonplace in seventeenth–century theater and will be used again in *George Dandin* by **Angélique** to regain admittance to her locked home and in *Le Malade imaginaire*, when **Argan's** little daughter **Louison** avoids her father's spanking by pretending to expire and then revives out of sympathy for his genuine mourning, explaining, "I don't think I'm quite dead."

Despite the master's right to discipline his servants, such beatings are more often threatened than given in the comedies, perhaps because the desperate masters are unwilling to part with the aid or pleasure the servants can render. **Alceste** angrily says that he will bash **Dubois's** head if the valet does not stop speaking in mysterious riddles.  **Dom Juan** continually threatens Sganarelle with violence, at one point speaking of beating him with a bull whip; **Dandin** threatens to beat his sleepy, inattentive groom **Colin**, and Sganarelle. Likewise, **Sosie** is often threatened with a beating by **Amphitryon**, but the only time he is actually beaten is by himself, that is, by **Mercury** pretending to be Sosie and punishing the real servant for the temerity of demanding his identity back. When the general threatens to beat the false servant Mercury, he receives only a shower of rebuke in return.

Masters also had the right to beat their female servants for disciplinary purposes in seventeenth–century France, and **Orgon** threatens to give **Dorine** the back of his hand when she resists his **marriage** plans for **Mariane** in the second act of *Tartuffe*. However, his clumsy slap misses its target. Wives are not exempt from beatings either, as Sganarelle shows in the first scene of *Le Médecin malgré lui* when, unable to contain his exasperation at **Martine's** scolding, he takes a stick to her. Oddly enough, this husband's prerogative is defended by both spouses against the intervention of their neighbor, **Monsieur Robert**, who seeks to break up the domestic disturbance. **George Dandin** soliloquizes about beating his unfaithful wife (I, 3) and later in direct discussion overtly threatens her (II, 2), but it is he who winds up on the wrong end of the stick when he tries to eavesdrop on her tryst with **Clitandre** (II, 8). A later **Martine** in *Les Femmes savantes* agrees that she wants her husband to be a he–man who would not hesitate to "lower her tone" with a few slaps if she spoke too loudly or protested against his decisions (V, 3).

Beatings begin to take on special importance in Molière's later farcical comedies. In *Le Médecin malgré lui*, beating assumes a very unique feature as a plot element, for Martine convinces **Lucas** and **Valère** that her husband will only admit to being a **doctor** if they beat him. Having once suffered this proof, Sganarelle turns the tables on his client **Géronte** by beating him until he admits he is not a doctor. *Le Sicilien* features many threats of beatings, presumably because of the setting of the play. **Dom Pèdre** is eavesdropping when **Hali** wishes he could give the old man a thrashing: "How I would take pleasure in avenging on his back every useless step his **jealousy** has made us take!" (I, 4). As Hali and **Adraste** creep about in the dark, Dom Pèdre hails them with a "Who goes there?" accompanied by a slap, to which Hali answers, "Friend!" and returns the blow in kind. Later, in a different **disguise**, Hali and his musicians perform the number "Chiribirida ouch alla!" before Dom Pèdre, but he shows his understanding of Sabir and his disgust by intoning, "Mi ti non comprara, / Ma ti bastonara, Si ti non andara" ("I not buy you, / but I beat you, / if you not go!" scene 10). In order to effect the change of clothes that will allow **Isidore** to escape from Dom Pèdre, **Climène** slips into the house in the guise of a young wife whose husband had threatened her not just with a stick, but with a sword. The old man's generous protection in this instance is commendable and shows that he can act more humanely when his own interests are not at stake.

Molière's most famous usurpers are quick to threaten with the rod, despite their humble origins. **Monsieur de Pourceaugnac** threatens to beat not only those onstage, but also the **audience**, if they continue to laugh at him and his ridiculous **costume** (I, 3). When he consults two **lawyers**, one of whom drawls and the other babbles, he punishes them with a beating, for they tell him to his discomfort that bigamy is a hanging offense. **Monsieur Jourdain** threatens to beat his servant **Nicole** when she cannot stop laughing at his clothes. Shortly afterward, he slaps her for listening in on his conversation with **Dorante**. But he himself must bend over while the masquerading "**Turks**" beat his behind in the mamamouchi ceremony at the end of Act IV. Punning in **Sabir**, they tell him not to be ashamed, because this is "the final indignity" ("ultima affronta").

The slapstick of punishment also looms large over *Les Fourberies de Scapin*. As early as the first scene, when **Octave** moans about the approaching storm of paternal punishment he can expect for marrying **Hyacinte**, **Silvestre** replies, "Would to Heaven that I could get off so cheaply! But in my line of work I'm more likely to pay a hundred times for your follies and I see forming on the horizon a cloud of blows that will rain down upon my back." It is, however, **Scapin** who almost incurs the first beating, and with a sword at that. When **Géronte** lies to **Léandre** about the source of his information on Léandre's misbehavior, he threatens to run the cringing, kneeling valet through, unleashing Scapin's string of untimely confessions. One of these confessions concerns a beating prank on Léandre not unlike that which he will pull on Géronte. Only Octave's intervention holds Léandre back from severely hurting Scapin. Silvestre warns Scapin again at the beginning of Act III, but the bolder servant makes fun of the danger and instead sets about his plot to beat Géronte while the latter is hiding in a sack from Hyacinte's homicidal "brother" (III, 2). Scapin only avoids a beating at the end of the play by pretending to have received a more serious injury from a roofer's hammer that fell on his head.

In Molière's last play, *Le Malade imaginaire*, beatings take on a more fanciful quality, which at the same time reveals more about the psychology of the characters. In the **comedy–ballet** interval between the first two acts, the old usurer **Polichinelle** disturbs the peace by firing a gun at a group of **musicians**. When the watch comes to arrest him, they first demand a bribe of six "pistoles" or sixty **livres**, in lieu of which he can suffer thirty finger–snaps on the nose or a dozen blows with the stick. He first chooses the former, then suffers the latter as well, before coughing up the coins and going on his way. Later, when **Argan** wishes to enforce his paternal authority and to punish **Louison** for holding back testimony against her sister, he tries to spank her with switches, but her feigned death turns the penalty into a farce. The transformation of the beating from an archetypal ritual into a more deeply meaningful psychodrama marks the culmination of a long comic evolution in the author's theater.

**Beauvais**. City east of **Paris** where the **Poquelin** family originated. It was famous for textiles, hence the associations of Molière's father and relatives in the cloth trade.

**Beauval, Jean Pitel, sieur de** (d. 1709). Itinerant actor who was summoned with his wife to join Molière's troupe in 1670. They had been together for years at the **Marais** and in various touring companies. Beauval's own talents seem to have been eclipsed by his wife's. He took the role of **Bobinet** in *La Comtesse d'Escarbagnas* and is said to have played the clumsy **Thomas Diafoirus** in *Le Malade imaginaire*.

**Beauval, Mlle., née Jeanne Olivier–Bourgignon** (1647–1720). The adopted daughter of the traveling player Filandre, this young lady started her acting career in the provinces at the age of ten. In 1664 she became the second wife of Beauval. Her success in **servant** roles made her ideal for many parts in Molière's troupe, which she joined in 1670. Thus, although she and her husband joined **Baron** and **La Thorillière** in deserting the **King's Troupe** for the **Hôtel de Bourgogne** after Molière's death, they eventually were reintegrated into the newly consolidated **Comédie–Française** in 1680. Besides taking over **Madeleine Béjart's** roles, including **Dorine**, she played either **Aglaure** or **Cidippe**, probably the former, in *Psyché*, **Julie** in *La Comtesse d'Escarbagnas*, and **Toinette** in *Le Malade imaginaire*. Though tradition holds that the part of **Martine** in *Les Femmes savantes* was played by an unknown servant, that myth probably derives from one of **Grimarest's** anecdotes. The part suits Beauval perfectly and was probably played by her.

**Béjart.** The family with which Molière's theatrical career was most closely linked. Molière as a lifelong colleague of **Madeleine** and **Louis Bejart** and married **Armande Béjart**, a much younger sister of Madeleine. Other members of the family with whom he was associated include the elder Joseph, Madeleine's father, and her sister Geneviève (**Mlle. Hervé**) who appear on the contract of the **Illustre Théâtre**. The father, Joseph, died before the troupe fled to the provinces, but Geneviève accompanied her sisters and Molière throughout their travels, as did two brothers, Joseph and Louis.

**Béjart, Armande** (1641–1700). This beautiful young sister of **Louis**, Joseph, **Geneviève**, and **Madeleine** was known as Mlle. Molière after her 1662 wedding with the dramatist. She was apparently born shortly before her father's death in February 1642. She was brought up with the troupe of **Dufresne** as they traveled in southern France. Over twenty years junior to Madeleine and Molière, she may have been mistaken for the actress's child, and Molière's enemies took advantage of this confusion to accuse him of incestuously marrying the offspring of the woman they labeled as his mistress. However, in view of the fertility of their mother, Marie Hervé, who started her family young and continued to have children regularly to a fairly advanced age, there is no reason to doubt the consistent documentary evidence that Armande was actually a much younger sister, the last of the Béjart household. Armande Béjart bore three children to Molière: **Louis** (born January 19, 1664), **Esprit–Madeleine** (born toward the end of July 1665), and **Pierre Jean–Baptise Armand** (born September 15, 1672). There was most likely trouble in the **marriage** in the late 1660s. Certainly there is little intimacy between the two onstage, since in *L'Impromptu de Versailles*, Molière's most memorable words to her are: "Shut up, wife, you're an idiot." Though there is no firm documentation, many anecdotes mention Armande Béjart having one or more affairs, the perhaps most damaging stories coming from an anonymous 1687 pamphlet entitled "**La Fameuse Comédienne.**" Several anecdotes also point to a reconciliation between the two around 1670. Most of the roles she played were female leads and love interests: **Célimène**, the **Princess of Elis, Elmire, Elvire, Lucinde,** several **Angéliques, Mariane** of *L'Avare*, **Julie, Alcmène, Psyche, Ériphile, Lucette, Lucile** in *Le Bourgeois gentilhomme*, and **Henriette**. Other possible roles include **Mélicerte, Hyacinte**, the slave **Zaïde**, and **Climène**. Following Molière's death, she married the actor **Isaac–François Guérin**, who had come from the dissolved **Marais** to join the company. There are more rumors of dissolute life during their marriage. Armande Béjart was a founding member of the troupe of the Hôtel Guénégaud and entered the **Comédie–Française** in 1680 with a full share membership. She retired at the Easter break of 1694.

**Béjart, Louis** (1630–1678). Brother of **Madeleine** and a long–time member of Molière's troupe. He generally played secondary roles and often incorporated into his characters the limp he had acquired as the result of an injury in a sword fight. In the role of **La Flèche** (*L'Avare*), **Harpagon** thus refers to him as a "limping dog." It is also known that he played the role of **Dom Louis** in *Dom Juan*, since none of the previous plays on the subject had given that name to the protagonist's father. It is also likely that in repertory he had taken the forerunner role of **Géronte** in **Corneille's** *Le Menteur*, where the paternal admonishment scene involved him with the same two colleagues, Molière and **La Grange**. In similar fashion, he took the roles of **Sganarelle's** elder brother **Ariste** in *L'École des maris* and of **Arnolphe's** neighbor **Chrysalde** in *L'École des femmes*. He probably played at least one of the swordsmen in *Les Fâcheux*: either **Alcandre, Filinte**, or **La Rivière**. In *L'Impromptu de Versailles*, he played a royal **servant**, and in *Le Mariage forcé* Sganarelle's future father–in–law, **Alcantor**. He was given the role of **Theoclès**, Prince of **Pylos**, in *La Princesse d'Élide*. It is probable that he was **Damis** in *Tartuffe*. The last production he was associated in was probably *Les Amants magnifiques*. After leaving the theater with a pension in 1670, he went on to a career as a military engineer, a most surprising change unless we remember that one of the many business ventures of his father, Joseph, had been a military training academy.

**Béjart, Madeleine** (1618–1672). Associated with Molière at least from the time of the **Illustre Théâtre** until her death, Madeleine was already an experienced actress by 1641, and by all accounts, a red–haired beauty admired by all. Many anecdotes make her a mistress of the dramatist, and some of the nastiest rumors said that she was actually the mother of Molière's wife, **Armande**. Nevertheless, the latter accusation appears to bear no weight in reality, and even during the years wandering the roads of the provinces, her main beau appears to have been the courtier playboy Esprit de Rémond, Count of Modena, by whom she had a child in 1638. Likely roles included **Magdelon** in *Les Précieuses ridicules*, **Sganarelle's wife** in *Sganarelle*, the confidante **Élise** in *Dom Garcie de Navarre*, **Lisette** in *L'École des maris*, and either **Clymène** or **Orante** in *Les Fâcheux*. We know that in the prelude to the latter play, she played the Water Nymph who delivered **Pellisson's** poem to the **audience** at **Vaux–le–Vicomte**. One evil–minded observer remarked that the troupe had offered a beautiful nymph and delivered an old herring instead. Probably, she was the first to play **Georgette** in *L'École des femmes*. She played herself and a prude in the *Impromptu de Versailles*, the First **Gypsy** in *Le Mariage forcé*, the **lady's maid Philis** in *La Princesse d'Élide*, and probably **Dorine** in *Tartuffe*. She turned her talents to composition on at least one occasion, when she adapted a text called *Dom Guichot ou les enchantements de Merlin*, though it flopped on stage. Like Molière, she was quite close to **Pierre Mignard**, for whom she had modeled and whom she made executor of her estate. She seems to have continued acting almost right up to the time of her death, during the **Ballet des Ballets** festival at **St–Germain–en–Laye**.

**Béjart, Mlle.** (*L'Impromptu de Versailles*). **Madeleine** plays herself as the most assertive of the female members of the troupe, often giving Molière friendly advice about his work. She is the one who suggests to the dramatist that he should have taken a meaner and more personal approach in parrying the attacks launched by the **Hôtel de Bourgogne**. In the play–within–the–play, she is assigned the part of a prude, but has only a few lines. Her overall demeanor seems to suggest that at this stage in the troupe's development she exercised a vigorous and guiding influence, despite her advancing years.

**Béline** (*Le Malade imaginaire*). This wicked stepmother, apparently played by **Mlle. de Brie**, skillfully manipulates **Argan**, while plotting against his two daughters and apparently carrying on an affair with the crooked **notary**, **Bonnefoy**. If we are to believe **Angélique's** denunciation of her in the second act, Argan is not her first spouse, for the daughter accuses her of "running from husband to husband." She outwardly dotes on Argan, muffling him up in pillows, and reduces him to almost infantile status by continually calling him, "my son." Yet we know that she has been campaigning hard to have him send the girls off to a **convent**, thus saving all the potential **dowry** money for herself. If he has hesitated to put this plan into effect, it is only because of his selfish wish to use Angélique to get a **doctor** in the family. And if Béline has hesitated to take advantage of Argan's continual medications to slip him a dose of poison, it is only because of **Toinette's** watchful care and because she has not yet optimized cash arrangements with Bonnefoy's help. Indeed, one senses that she takes advantage of Argan's immobility to flirt with Bonnefoy (I, 7), which gives a sharp irony to the notary's predictions about a possible pregnancy for her. Her honeyed tone disappears in Act II, however, as she joins in the urging for Angélique to marry **Thomas Diafoirus**, mainly because she knows this issue will drive a wedge between father and daughter, furthering her own interests.

The more Angélique keeps her composure and refutes the **marriage** plans, the more bitter and hateful Béline becomes, casting insults as their conversation comes to an end. We can imagine her nastiness as she returns to tell Argan that she has seen a young man in the daughter's bedroom and asks him to question **Louison** about it. By the way, the business she claims as a pretext for leaving may well be a tryst with Bonnefoy, which adds irony to Argan's request to be sure to consult with him about the will. She had wanted Argan to simply give her all his property, but French common **law**, with its forced inheritance system, forbade this unless the couple was childless on both sides. Bonnefoy suggests several clever dodges to the legal code, including the direct transfer of cash and promissory notes, to which Argan readily agrees. It is this thought that preoccupies Béline when she hears of Argan's death in the third act and is taken in by the ruse. She cannot wait to get her hands on any cash or convertible securities that may be in the house and urges Toinette to keep the death a secret until she has had time to search. Since she has betrayed her motives so completely, we can imagine her surprise and distress when the husband comes back to life. We can also imagine that she may keep on running and rid the household of her presence, for her behavior can only raise questions about a past that may hold many dark secrets. Ever since *Le Misanthrope*, the controlling woman had been a theme of Molière's comedies, but Béline finally realizes all the evil potential in a witchlike figure that combines beauty and social skill with greed and malice. Molière, the unhappy husband, finally meets his demon face to face and bests her.

**Bélise** (*Les Femmes savantes*). This spinster who believes that she is the secret desire of every man in the world is clearly patterned on Hespérie in **Desmarets de Saint–Sorlin's** *Les Visionnaires*. She flirtingly gives **Clitandre** leave to court **Henriette** in Act I because she knows he cannot make an open **avowal** to her. Even when he repeats his sincere profession of **love** for Henriette, she refuses to believe it and thinks it a ruse, "a subtle false flight deserving praise" that is unparalleled in the vast store of romantic novels she has devoured (I, 4). When she announces this imaginary liaison to **Chrysale**, he tries to reason with her. But she insists she is loved not only by Clitandre, but also by Damis, Dorante, Cléonte, and Lycidas, even though the first has stopped coming to the house, the second insults her in public, and the last two are married. She simply explains that Damis is just being respectfully submissive, Dorante **jealous**, and the others could find no other way of drowning their sorrow. **Ariste** and Chrysale agree that their sister is mad (II, 4). When seen in the salon with **Armande** and **Philaminte**, Bélise seems less out of place because she subscribes to the same program of autodidacticism and **language** censorship as the others. She reinforces the leader Philaminte and swoons along with her companions as **Trissotin** reads his vapid verses. She is just as carried away by **Vadius's** command of **Greek**. It is she who voices the ridiculous request that Henriette's **dowry** be enumerated not in contemporary financial units, but in ancient minas and talents. Likewise, she announces the new form of love that will be instituted by the female **academy**, where all "extended matter" will be banished ("substance étendue" is a term belonging to Neoplatonic **philosophy**, but the pun on masculine sexuality is clear in English, as well). A tradition tracing to 1723 holds that the part was played by **Mlle. Hervé**, but Molière never trusted his wife's aunt with such an extensive part in other plays. More likely, it was given to **La Grange's** future wife, **Marie Raguenau**, who was soon to play the **Countess of Escarbagnas**.

***Belle Plaideuse, La (The Beautiful Plaintiff)***. A 1655 comedy by **Boisrobert** that furnished some precedents for the second act of Molière's *L'Avare*.

**Beltrame (stage name of Niccolo Barbieri)**. Italian actor and author of *commedie sostenute*, he penned *L'Inavvertito overo Scapino disturbato e Mezzetino travagliato*, published in 1629 and adapted by Molière (*L'Étourdi*) and **Quinault**. Molière later developed his own play around the persona of **Scapin**. Beltrame became the inherited name for a stock character of the *commedia dell'arte*, supposedly a Milanese like Barbieri himself.

**Bensserade, Isaac de** (1613–1691). This academician was also a dramatic author and penned a version of the **Cupid** and **Psyche** story in ballet form (1656) that may have influenced Molière's to some degree, perhaps more for what was avoided than for what was copied. However, he is mainly remembered as the author of rather frothy **occasional poetry**, including the famous "Sonnet of Job" that was one of the most remembered lyrical pieces of the century. He was also the official **court** librettist for the young **Louis XIV** and collaborated with Molière in many **comedy–ballets**, but Molière took over the task himself in the 1670 **Divertissement Royal** that evolved into *Les Amants magnifiques*. Louis XIV thought so much of Bensserade that he sometimes over–rewarded the industrious but mediocre author. The 10,000 *livres* accorded to Bensserade for his *Metamorphoses* was one of the century's most questionable acts of **patronage**.

**Béralde (*Le Malade imaginaire*)**. This man is **Argan's** brother–in–law, related to the family by his first wife, and he takes an avuncular interest in the well–being of his niece **Angélique**. He does not appear until the last scene of the second act, but then remains onstage continually until the conclusion, planning and organizing the burlesque medical ceremony that closes the play. This lively deception clashes with the reasonable presentations he has made up to that point and puts the lie to those who would see him only as a *raisonneur* embodying Molière's purest logic. He is most notable for his open attack on medicine. According to him, the body has the capacity to heal itself gradually and cannot be helped by the various treatments masquerading as remedies in seventeenth–century France. He tries to convince Argan that his very ability to withstand a regime of reiterated purging and bleeding, punctuated with enemas, is proof of his fundamental good health and resilience. He goes so far as to accuse **doctors**

of willful trickery and delusion of their patients, pointing out how their quasi–religious **costumes** and mumbo–jumbo protect them from public scrutiny. All this falsehood he describes as "the fiction of medicine." He astonishes his brother–in–law first by prescribing no other cure than Molière's comedies, which are guaranteed to heal the spirit, and then by dismissing and insulting **Fleurant** when the latter comes to administer an enema. Béralde tells the blubbering **apothecary** that he obviously is not used to speaking to people's faces! Béralde is an amused spectator as **Purgon** puts his curse on the wayward patient. He suggests that this is a great opportunity to be rid of the doctors forever, but when Argan shows too much separation anxiety, he can only conclude that he is extremely contrary and sees the world through weird eyes. Having observed the effects of **Toinette's** medical **disguise**, he takes advantage of Argan's momentary confusion to warn him against **Béline's** even more dangerous intrigues, and this leads directly to Argan's feigned death and the unmasking of the evil spouse. It is only after this, too, fails to shake Argan's faith in medicine that he suggests to the family that they use the ploy of the fake medical ceremony to satisfy the hypochondriac's uncontrollable need. Rather than a spur–of–the–moment idea, it is a plan he has apparently been contemplating for some time, since he has already engaged a troupe of actors to help with the arrangements. Although it is not clear from the stage directions, we can readily see Béralde assuming the disguised role of the "Praeses" of the Faculty in the ceremony and conferring the degree upon the "Bachelierus" Argan, especially if the original stage version of this ceremony was a little less elaborate than the one described in the 1682 collected edition, which seems to mirror the 1674 **court** performances after Molière's death. It is unclear who played this role originally. Perhaps the most likely candidate was **La Thorillière**, who eventually took over the role of Argan. Béralde is onstage with Argan from the end of Act II to the end of the play and La Thorillière would have already learned all the cues and dialogue for that part of the play. Had he played **Diafoirus** or **Bonnefoy**/Purgon, this would not have been the case. Another possibility is that **Baron** took the role, as he probably played a similar part in *Les Femmes savantes*.

*Berger extravagant, Le.* An immensely popular burlesque novel by **Charles Sorel** that may have suggested some of **Gorgibus's** comments in *Sganarelle* regarding devotional literature.

**Berlin.** Site of the 1699 **edition** of *Dom Juan* that Auger used to restore the original text in his 1823 complete works.

**Bernier, François** (1620–1688). Physician and amateur **philosopher**, Bernier was one of the few men who traveled widely in the East during the seventeenth century, becoming very familiar with the realms of the Ottomans and the Moguls. After returning from a thirteen–year period in the Orient in 1668, he associated both with the most libertine circles and with high society salons, such as that of Mme. de la Sablière.  He penned a notable French summary of **Gassendi's** philosophy, which had originally appeared almost entirely in **Latin** texts.  His knowledge of the Orient may have contributed to the **Turkish** elements in some of Molière's comedies, especially *Le Bourgeois gentilhomme*. It has been demonstrated that Molière displays there an excellent knowledge of **Sabir**, a Levantine form of trade **language** that he could scarcely have had a chance to encounter in the south of France.  Bernier, however, would have necessarily been proficient in it, as well as possessing knowledge of Turkish customs.

**Béziers**.  Town in Languedoc that was one of the three sites for parliamentary meetings in the province.  Molière's troupe played during sessions of the body, especially during the November 17, 1656, to June 1, 1657, session, when *Dépit amoureux* premiered.  Legal records show that the troupe had left **Bordeaux** on or around December 5, passed through **Agen**, and arrived in Béziers by December 16.  They had gone on to **Lyon** by early February.

**Bienséances**.  *See* **Proprieties**.

**Billaine, Claude**.  Parisian publisher and book dealer.  He was part of the eight–printer coalition that published *L'École des femmes* and *La Critique de l'École des femmes*.

**Bobinet, Monsieur** (*La Comtesse d'Escarbagnas*).  This silly schoolmaster appears with his pupil, the **Count**, to show off the latter's performance in **Latin**. He gives some hint of pedophilia when he promises to "inoculate the young master with the sowings of virtue."  The role was taken by **Beauval**.

**Boccaccio, Giovanni** (1313–1375).  Often cited as a possible source for *La Jalousie du Barbouillé* and *George Dandin*, to which two of the stories in the *Decameron* bear a resemblance, Boccaccio himself was beholden to the traditions of the *fabliau* and the **farce**, which may have been a more direct source for Molière.

**Bohemians**.  *See* **Gypsies**.

**Boileau, Nicolas**.  Usually known during his lifetime as Despréaux (1636–1711).  This poet and critic, though younger than Molière, seems to have been a friend and associate of the playwright beginning at least with the latter's return to **Paris**.  Many anecdotal stories are told of their common involvement with Parisian **libertine** circles, along with such freethinkers as **Chapelle** and **Bernier**. It is fairly sure that both Boileau and Chapelle frequented the **White Cross Tavern** that was something of a libertine stronghold.  The majority of these tales may have little substance, but their sheer number hints at the underlying reality of some kind of skeptical group involving these four and perhaps various other more purely philosophical men of letters, such as Naudé and Saint–Evremond. Boileau was, like Molière, a child of the Parisian **bourgeoisie** and a former **law** student, but unlike some of his numerous relatives (he had fifteen siblings, not counting cousins!) seems to have practiced very little. Just as whimsically, he took minor orders and briefly dabbled in theology so as to gain a clerical stipend. Boileau spent much time, as Molière did, in the outlying village of **Auteuil**. Reportedly impotent from a childhood injury or operation, the bachelor Boileau seems to have been at least as sardonic as Molière about much of the field of sexual relations. He was, if anything, more pugnacious in his attacks on various cliques, such as the *précieuses*, of whom he spared not even the most eminent members. It was about the time of the *Précieuses ridicules* that Boileau seems to become aware of Molière, and they had certainly met by 1663. Boileau and several of his friends, such as **Cotin** and the younger **La Mothe Le Vayer**, addressed verses to Molière or supported him during the **Quarrel of the School for Wives**. Calling *L'École des femmes* a masterpiece and comparing it to **Terence**, Boileau's "Stances" praise Molière's ability to combine wisdom and satire. They even defend Molière's appeal to popular tastes, which would be reprimanded later in Boileau's career. Several of Boileau's early *Satires* (1660–1666) testify to a strong commitment to Molière and his artistic methods, especially number 2, which begins with an homage to Molière's poetic technique, and 3, which mentions Molière's private readings of *Tartuffe* during the period when the play was banned in public. There is a reference to the *Satires* in *Les Femmes savantes* (III, 3). In late 1664 or early 1665, Molière is said to have taken part with Boileau in a mock trial weighing the merits of Bouillon's translation of Ariosto's *Joconde* against **La Fontaine's**. Molière is supposed to have served on a tribunal with **Brienne** and Langlade, with Boileau's brother Jérôme as spokesman for La Fontaine. As late as 1671, Molière is reported to have collaborated with Boileau on the *Arrêt burlesque* that lampooned the faculty of the University of Paris and its limpet–like attachment to **Aristotle**.

Boileau's older brother **Pierre de Puymorin**, a hard–drinking member of the White Cross Tavern group and former retainer of **Monsieur**, served as godfather for Molière's second son, **Pierre–Jean–Baptiste–Armand** in 1672. Others of the family were not always so supportive, such as the testy academician Gilles and the religious brother Jacques. Despréaux himself, though he was officially a tonsured member of the clergy until 1669, was considered by some as a model for **Alceste**. Others considered him the model for the would–be poet **Oronte**. But from 1667 onward, Boileau's increasing integration in the group of intellectuals surrounding the Parlementarian **Lamoignon**, a bigot and an old enemy of Molière, is perhaps reflected in the much more ambivalent tone that Boileau assumes toward the playwright's work in his *L'Art poétique* (1675). There, while rendering praise to his late friend, and even comparing him with the finest of Roman dramatic authors, Boileau nevertheless disparages the more physical and slapstick elements of his style, stating that he cannot find the sublime author of *Le Misanthrope* in the farcical bag–beating of **Scapin**. Ironically, two years later Boileau's "Epistle to **Racine**" seeks to console the badgered playwright with the example of Molière, pointing out that Molière's petty detractors no longer had any credit after his death. Boileau went on to become co–historigrapher royal with Racine and to engage heavily in the Quarrel of the Ancients and the Moderns, taking the ancient side against Charles Perrault and his cohorts.

   *See* Jules Brody, *Boileau and Longinus* (1958); Antoine Adam, *Histoire de la littérature française au XVIIe siècle, Tome III* (1962); Gordon Pocock, *Boileau and the Nature of Neo–Classicism* (1980).

**Boisrobert, François Le Metel, sieur de** (1589–1662). Playwright and man of letters of the age of **Richelieu**, he served as the Cardinal's literary ambassador in the **Académie Française** and aided in drawing up the list of writers to be subsidized by the state. His comedy of *La Belle Plaideuse* (1655) contained a scene where a father is caught arranging a usurious loan to his own son, which probably influenced the scene in Act II of *L'Avare* where **Harpagon** and **Cléante** discover that they have arranged to do the same thing. Boisrobert's scene mentioned a bill of goods involved in the transaction that contained some of the same items included in Molière's play. Another of Boisrobert's plays, *La Folle Gageure* (1653), was a mainstay of the troupe's repertory in their early years in **Paris**.

**Bonneau, Mlle**. An obscure hireling who originally took the role of the maid **Andrée** in *La Comtesse d'Escarbagnas*.

**Bonnefoy, Monsieur** (*Le Malade imaginaire*). This character is ironically named, since the last thing he represents is good faith. The running dialogue identifies him as "the **notary**," but he is clearly named in both the text and the dramatis personae. Bonnefoy has been engaged by **Argan**, presumably with **Béline's** recommendation, to draw up a new will and make other financial arrangements beneficial to the second wife. He is clearly aware of the limits of the **law**, both in **Paris** and other provinces, for he tells his client that a community property regime (*donation mutuelle entre vifs*) is impossible in his case because of the existence of **children**, even though they are not of the union in question. He also realizes that the nature of the **dowry** of Argan's first wife would reserve most of that principal for the children and that as usufructuary Argan could not legally transfer it to anyone else. However, he suggests several slippery plans for getting around the law, such as transferring **money** through false loans made to a third party and making unrecorded transfers of cash and bearer bonds. Argan expresses his interest in following this advice and urges Bonnefoy to proceed with the will, evidently with the intention of disinheriting the daughters from his own wealth and giving if all to Béline. Bonnefoy may well have been flirting with Béline during this interview, since Argan is almost cocooned in pillows and can't see most of the room. The notary's odd comments about the possibility of a pregnancy for Béline add piquancy to the conversation. Furthermore, he may be the business she is about to attend to when she leaves the house in Act II; unknowingly, Argan reminds his wife to consult Bonnefoy about the papers. Bonnefoy represents the negative pole of the legal system that was introduced on such a positive note by the faithful notary in *L'École des femmes*. It is unclear who played the role — perhaps **Du Croisy** — but it was probably doubled with **Purgon** or **Fleurant**, since both of those characters appear heavily robed and bearded in the third act, where Bonnefoy is absent.

**Bordeaux.** Capital of Guyenne, on the Garonne River. This city was the base for much of the activity of **Charles Dufresne's** acting troupe from 1645 to 1656. Its governor, the **duc d'Épernon**, was patron to the troupe. This was the refuge where Molière and the **Béjarts** fled the jurisdiction of the **Parlement** of **Paris** after the financial collapse of the **Illustre Théâtre** in 1644–45. From it, the troupe made excursions northward as far as **Nantes** and eastward through Languedoc to the Rhone valley. Bordeaux was a hotbed of activity during the **Fronde** and held out in rebellion even after the submission of Paris in 1652. Thus, while Molière was away from Paris during this troubled period, he was not unfamiliar with the causes and meanings of the uprising.

**Bossuet, Jacques–Bénigne, Bishop of Meaux** (1627–1704). Prominent Counter–Reformation churchman and man of letters, he was best known during Molière's life for his funeral orations for **Henrietta of England** in 1669 and for her daughter, the then Duchess of Orleans, shortly afterward. His sermons were also legendary and on a level with those of **Bourdaloue**. Like the latter, he had harsh words for Molière, but mainly after the playwright had died.

**Bouhors, Father Dominique** (1628–1702). This Jesuit was one of the most widely respected authorities on **language** and poetry of his time. Despite his religious affiliation and his friendship with such anti–Molière parties as **Lamoignon, Racine**, and **Mlle. de Scudéry**, he addressed to Molière a poetic epitaph that became famous, crediting him with reforming both the city and the **court**, though he was rewarded only with ingratitude.

**Boulanger de Chalussay, Le.** The little–known author of *Élomire hypocondre*, an invective play written against Molière and published in 1670. It is not entirely sure whether Boulanger is a family name or the profession of the author (baker). He is identified in the publisher's *privilége* as "le sieur de Chalussay." Georges Couton has suggested that the name may hide that of the younger **Montfleury**, Molière's known rival and enemy, as well as the author of another derogatory playlet. Boulanger's other works include a lost play, *L'Abjuration du marquisat*, and a booklet entitled *Morale galante ou l'art de bien aimer*. *Élomire*, an anagram of Molière's name, casts the dramatist as an obsessive cuckold who has married his own daughter. It also avers that he copied all his dramatic techniques from the Italian actor **Scaramouche** (this is the subject of the frontispiece) and that his troupe is a bunch of scoundrels. Surprisingly, it treats **Armande Béjart** in a rather positive way.

**Boulonnois**. A hireling, probably a child, who took the role of the little lackey **Jeannot** in the original production of *La Comtesse d'Escarbagnas*.

**Bourdaloue, Louis** (1623–1704).    Jesuit preacher and rival of **Bossuet**. Bourdaloue joins other religious figures in explicitly condemning Molière's plays as immoral. His attack on *George Dandin* in the Easter sermon of 1682 is particularly harsh, claiming that Molière holds the entire institution of **marriage** up to ridicule.

*Bourgeois gentilhomme, Le*.  Widely considered the crowning achievement of the collaboration between Molière and **Lully**, this five–act prose comedy premiered on October 13 or 14, 1670, at the château of **Chambord**. A royally commanded *divertissement* offered to the **court**, it was an immediate (or almost immediate) success, presented three times at Chambord and again three times at **Saint–Germain** before opening in **Paris** on November 23. Its success there was very great also, with nearly fifty performances during Molière's lifetime. It became a staple of the troupe's **repertory** and having been presented over 600 times at the **Comédie–Française**, has remained one of Molière's best known and beloved works. Thirty years later, Molière's biographer **Grimarest** reported that the King had withheld any praise after the work's début, but then praised it highly after its second performance, expressing worry about having been "seduced by the manner of its performance." If the (unproven) anecdote is correct, it could be taken as a sign of how novel the work really was: performance is central not just to its impact on stage, of course, but also is at the heart of the work's entire dramaturgy.

The work is the last original **comedy–ballet** produced by the "two Baptistes." Molière played the title role, Lully the role of the Mufti in the **Turkish** ceremony.  Benefiting from their experience gained in writing eight previous comedy–ballets together as well as other works with **music and dance**, the work integrates comedy, music, and dance to a degree never previously attained. The result, often called a "total artwork," infuses each art employed with elements of the others in a dazzling synthesis, the paradigm of the "new secret of pleasing" theater audiences, leading directly to the newly fashionable opera, which **Donneau de Visé** attributed to Molière in 1673.

*Le Bourgeois gentilhomme* has occasionally been called a comic opera *avant la lettre*, a designation with considerable merit. This achievement is accordingly difficult — if not impossible — to judge fairly without reference to its music and dance. The structure of the work has been identified as based on musical or balletic principles rather than on those of a more traditional comedy; plot considerations are often diffused into stylization and atmosphere. The old charge of shaky or unbalanced dramatic structure falls when the musical and choreographic components are accounted for; and in any case the work's continued popularity over centuries belies such a view.

The work evidently originated in **Louis XIV's** desire to stage a play with a Turkish theme. The French court had felt insulted during the previous year by Turkish envoy Soliman Aga's contemptuous dismissal of the elaborate reception that the court had offered him in the hope of improving diplomatic relations with the Ottoman Empire. According to the chevalier d'Arvieux, Louis XIV ordered Lully and Molière to employ d'Arvieux's expertise in matters Turkish in order to confect the work, which could capitalize on the then–current fashion for things "Oriental." Long tradition, although never proven, has it also that the work was intended to belittle the Turks in turn.

Whatever the precise truth concerning the work's beginnings (d'Arvieux is not reliable in every detail), it soon surpassed the original motivation. Molière, Lully, and d'Arvieux had several months during which to elaborate a spectacle that eventually incorporated comedic, musical, and danced elements, ranging from the most outlandishly farcical to the most elegant and courtly, these being staged in an exceptionally sumptuous and colorful manner. The costumes alone cost some 20,000 *livres*. Vigarani designed sets that not only reflected the title character's extreme wealth, but even accommodated nearly the whole cast of characters onstage as audience for the final spectacle, the *Ballet des Nations*. As in all the royal entertainments, the finest actors, musicians, singers, and dancers were employed. The work was accompanied at Chambord by elaborate fountain displays and fireworks; clearly, conspicuous and expensive display characterized all aspects of the entertainment.

*Le Bourgeois gentilhomme* concerns **Monsieur Jourdain**, a very wealthy cloth merchant completely taken by the idea of **nobility**. Instead of realizing his desire of ascending to the status of nobleman in the only realistic manner available to a **bourgeois**, that is, by buying an official *charge* and waiting to be given a minor title, he dreams of leaping directly into its upper ranks, as the title makes clear: "gentilhomme" designated a purely hereditary nobleman, the King being the "premier gentilhomme" of the land. M. Jourdain wishes to accomplish this realistically impossible social leap by the equally fanciful means of imitating noble manners, clearly intending to convert himself thus into an elegant and cultivated *honnête homme*. He pursues his dream by taking lessons in music, dance, fencing, and philosophy, by ordering expensive dress and associating with a count, **Dorante**. His outsize mania is evident to all around him, but he will brook no objection, whether from his tart–tongued wife or his **servant Nicole's** helpless **laughter** at the extravagance of his new clothes. His "teachers" (for he rejects their learning, believing that he has already mastered the particular arts and sciences that they represent) regard him as a hopelessly inept pupil but do not fail to charge him handsomely for their services. Likewise Dorante, who borrows enormous sums from the deeply flattered Jourdain, claims to be advancing his name at court and with a beautiful widow, the marquise **Dorimène**, of whom Jourdain is enamored. Jourdain orders music, a banquet, a diamond, and even the concluding ballet to court her on a princely scale.  In reality, Dorante is himself courting Dorimène with the means borrowed from Jourdain. The work makes clear that Dorante has neither the means nor the inclination to repay the "loans," being instead quite content to feed Jourdain's dream and, through it, his own plans. When Jourdain's dream is fulfilled as he believes himself elevated to the (purely imaginary) status of *mamamouchi*, the work's gradual passage from social satire anchored in depiction of recognizable contemporary society to the triumph of an exhilaratingly festive fantasy is completed.

Several models for Jourdain have been proposed, including Colbert, Louis XIV's finance minister, but none is particularly convincing. It is more probable that Molière took the generalized desire to rise into the nobility, evident in countless members of the bourgeoisie, as the basis for Jourdain's desire. Grimarest claimed that each bourgeois in the audience perceived his neighbor as being "realistically depicted" in Jourdain's pretentions.

Numerous sources for other aspects of *Le Bourgeois gentilhomme* have been proposed, among them a "Turkish" *ballet de cour* by Lully from 1660, **Poisson's** *Les Faux Moscovites*, **Rotrou's** *La Sœur*, *Don Quixote*, and Aristophanes's *Clouds*. Of perhaps more historical interest is the apparent amalgam in the *Cérémonie turque* of elements of various Muslim and Christian rites. Throughout *Le Bourgeois*, however, Molière's synthetic gifts make the borrowed elements serve their dramatic ends without palpable trace of disparate provenance.  The original form of the work specified three acts, but the printed versions (from 1671) used a five–act designation, which has become traditional. In either form, however, the action is continuous, with music or dance forming a dramatic bridge between acts rather than an interruption or contrast. There is an overall increase in concentration of **music and dance**, already important from the work's beginning, toward the two longest and most elaborate *intermèdes*, the *Cérémonie turque* and the full–scale *ballet de cour*, the Ballet des Nations. The music and dance that permeate the entire work unobtrusively form integral parts of the very dramatic texture in the guise of lessons for Jourdain or works composed as gifts for Dorimène, and furnish a wide variety of entertainments. Beginning with a full orchestral overture, a direct association with royal entertainment, the opening scene reveals a student composer finishing an *air de cour* with music emphasizing its hyper–refined, **précieux** lyrics. When the finished song is performed for Monsieur Jourdain (I, 2), he judges it to be soporific and states his preference for a ditty with "sheep in it," "Janneton," which he proceeds to sing as unartistically as possible (the burlesqued song afforded the opportunity to deliver a satirical slap at its authors, Perrin and de Sablières). He reacts similarly — "Est–ce tout?" — to a three–part sung pastoral "dialogue" (well over ten minutes of music) but reacts more positively toward a display of varied dance forms.

Immediately following, he insists on displaying his own dancing ability in the famous minuet, a dance considered a high test of noble carriage and dance mastery (II, 1). Jourdain considers the minuet "his" dance, but the Dance Master's comments reveal the grotesque buffoonery of Jourdain's movements.

The arrival of the Fencing Master continues the display of Jourdain's profound corporal awkwardness, while the sententious **Philosophy Master's** entry provokes a fight among all of Jourdain's teachers, each of whom believes his art or science supreme.

When the philosophy master returns from his drubbing by the other teachers, he inquires what M. Jourdain would wish to learn. Rejecting ethics as too confining and physics as too noisy, he settles on spelling and thus "learns" to articulate vowels and consonants, culminating in the braying of "I, O, I, O" and the growling and barking of "R, R, R, Ra." Having conquered the alphabet, he requests help forthwith in writing a **love letter** for the elegant Dorimène. Unsure whether he should use verse or prose — or even what these terms represent — Jourdain soon learns that he has been "speaking prose" for the last forty years and is nearly overwhelmed by this news. While Jourdain believes himself to have mastered difficult arts like singing and dancing without ever having studied them, the simplest, most obvious facts — vowels and consonants, verse and prose — strike him as revelations.

The arrival of the **tailor** to dress Jourdain in his new, would–be noble, finery culminates Act II (in the five–act schema). After skirmishing with the tailor over the clothing's fit and design, as well as the tailor's own appropriation of some of Jourdain's cloth, wherein the tailor easily quiets each objection by assuring that noblemen also dress in the same fashion, Jourdain is outfitted in cadence to music suggesting a pastiche of royal ceremony. The tailor's apprentices then nourish M. Jourdain's already–expanded notion of himself with words like "Monseigneur" and "Mon gentilhomme" and dance for joy at his extravagant tipping.

Throughout the first two acts, social satire is directed not only at M. Jourdain, whose pretensions are recognizable albeit extreme, but also at the masters and tailor who profit from his dream. Much of the satire is conveyed implicitly through the music and dance, which contrast the elegance, polish, and stylized artifice of the masters' productions with the naive Jourdain's vocal, sartorial, and corporal excesses — a virtuoso comic role for Molière and all subsequent actors. The masters' narrow–minded pedantry and general disdain for their client form other contrasts with Jourdain's openly naive and sincere ignorance. Yet despite his broadly drawn bumptiousness, Jourdain remains an appealing character through his infectious enthusiasm and because his manifest harmlessness disarms the barbs directed at him. The exposition of the enormous dimensions of his comic mania in any case dominates these acts and makes his forthcoming acceptance of the fantasy title of *mamamouchi* dramatically credible and pleasurably satisfying.

Various critics state that the plot begins only with Act III. Elements of a fairly conventional comic plot do indeed appear, with Jourdain shown as the dupe of Dorante (as earlier of teachers and tailor) and also as the obstacle to his daughter Lucile's desired marriage to her suitor, **Cléonte**. The latter, evidently a member of the *noblesse de robe* (the lower ranks of nobility), costs himself M. Jourdain's direct approval of his request for **Lucile's** hand by refusing to pretend to the higher status of a "gentilhomme" (others at the time falsely claimed noble status, a matter of wide legal inquiry by the crown during this period). Luckily for Cléonte, his quick–witted **servant Covielle** (a role derived from the *commedia dell'arte*) organizes a masquerade, the *Cérémonie turque*, which will fulfill Jourdain's dream by giving him a "noble" title, *mamamouchi*, and will thus allow Cléonte, disguised as "the son of the Grand Turk," to gain Lucile's hand.

The *Cérémonie turque*, a quarter–hour–long affair of pompous march music, pseudo–Turkish exotic chant and dance, and generally exhilarating nonsense, mystifies Jourdain even further. Emerging from the ceremony fully believing in his newly exalted title, he finds all around him people ready to play along with his belief, which now furthers their interests. This circumstance allows the desired marriages (Cléonte with Lucile, Covielle with Nicole, and Dorante with Dorimène) to be quickly concluded. All take seats onstage to enjoy the forty–minute–long Ballet des Nations, which recapitulates and elevates artistically the previous themes of love and incomprehension, cultural differences, social pretension, and discord. All previous disharmony is resolved in the elevated, indeed quasi–divine, pleasures of courtly art: "Quels spectacles charmants, quels plaisirs goûtons–nous! Les dieux mêmes, les dieux, n'en ont point de plus doux" ("What charming spectacles, what pleasures we savor! The gods, the gods themselves, have none that are sweeter!").

*Le Bourgeois gentilhomme*'s dramaturgy is of the subtlest. It remains the greatest product of a close and lengthy collaboration between two of the greatest theatrical creators of the century. Despite a flood of critical writings, this work remains in various respects among the most elusive in the Molière canon. It is very possible that in addition to its "multimedia" nature, its elusiveness derives primarily from its most important qualities being unexpectedly right on its surface, hidden, as it were, in plain view: a work at once obvious and recondite.

Throughout the work, easily identifiable dramatic themes such as the impact of appearances in society, especially the appearance of nobility; clashes between noble and bourgeois values; the quest for love; and the creation and enjoyment of art are turned into ingenious dramatic means within the spectacle's texture, not just through overt action, but as much through atmosphere and pattern inspired by music and dance. Thus Dorante's elegant noble manners allow him to attract Jourdain into bankrolling Dorante's own pursuit of Dorimène, notably in an elegant banquet with music and dance to match; to deflect **Mme. Jourdain's** acerbic confrontations; and ultimately to win his lady. Jourdain's quest for the same lady furnishes the immediate impulse (as well as the means) for all the music and dance on display. The artistic endeavors of all prefigure, and also whet, the audience's appetite for the great, courtly spectacle of the Ballet des Nations. In many respects, the work succeeds in turning *style* into its very *substance*.

Incorporating Jourdain's insatiable thirst for imitating nobility into a highly original, seamless design, Molière and Lully also present a new sort of comic character, one destined to be crowned on the very throne of his folly rather than returned, chastened and humiliated, to a realistic world, as were previous protagonists of Molière's works. It is arguable that the lengthy series of sketches allowing the audience the thoroughly pleasurable absorption of the fantastic depth and range of Jourdain's folly in Acts I and II is necessary to make the "ennobling" of the *Cérémonie turque* dramatically workable: no realistically drawn character of the Parisian bourgeoisie could convincingly accept such outlandish fakery. Throughout the work, realistic and unrealistic elements are in tension, chiefly through the effects of Jourdain's own mania. Beginning with the *Cérémonie turque*, then with the rapid triple–marriage dénouement, and the immediately succeeding Ballet des Nations, all realistic considerations are swept away. Satire recedes and plot considerations evaporate before a festive enjoyment of the ballet's refined pleasures.

The work's enduring popularity over three centuries — its eminent worthiness in many stagings and adaptations — makes doubtful the charges of its alleged shortcomings. Close attention to its overall original form shows a ubiquitous desire for pleasurable spectacle, especially in the service of love interests, which culminates in the Ballet des Nations and leaves behind narrower, purely comic concerns. Productions that jettison all or most of the music and dance without finding equivalents (as often happened from the eighteenth century on), therefore, lose much of the savor — but also dramatic substance — of the original.

Like many of Molière's works, *Le Bourgeois gentilhomme* was quickly translated into various languages and produced abroad. Of note also is Richard Strauss and Hugo von Hofmannsthal's adaptation of the work as a curtain raiser to their opera *Ariadne auf Naxos* (1912). Among recent productions that have sought to update the work are Jean–Louis Barrault's of 1972, which used a rock music adaptation of Lully's score; Bernard Ballet's of 1970 using music of the rock group Pink Floyd; and that of Jérôme Savary's Grand Magic Circus (1982). Both the latter and the consummately traditional production of Jean Meyer, which was in continuous use at the Comédie–Française for many years from the early 1950s, have been filmed. The filmed Meyer production in particular features a brilliant performance by Louis Seigner as Jourdain with a flawless supporting cast, elegant sets, and much of Lully's music in good, if stylistically dated, performance. More recent recordings of the music by La Petite Bande (1971) and Le Concert des Nations (1999) are attentive to historical style considerations.

*Le Bourgeois gentilhomme* constitutes a touchstone of Molière and Lully's conjoined comic art, one of the two highest achievements in the comedy–ballet genre (the other being *Le Malade imaginaire*), and an immortal comic character, Monsieur Jourdain, who is transformed from the grotesque imitator of noble airs who naively discovers vowels, consonants, and prose to his eternal amazement, into the fabulous figure whose comic mania eventually furnishes all spectators with the sublimely elegant pleasures of music and dance at the height of the seventeenth century's artistic form.

Selected Bibliography: Claude Abraham, "Farce and Ballet: Le Bourgeois Revisited," *Cahiers du Dix–septième* 2.1 (Spring 1988), 171–179; Gérard Defaux, Gérard "Rêve et réalité dans Le Bourgeois gentilhomme," *XVIIe Siècle*, no. 95 (1977); H. Gaston Hall, *Molière's Le Bourgeois gentilhomme: Context and Stagecraft* (Durham: University of Durham, 1990); Dorothy F. Jones, "Law and Grace in *Le Bourgeois gentilhomme*," *Studi Francesi* 94 (1988), 15–22; Volker Kapp, ed. *Le Bourgeois gentilhomme: problèmes de la comédie–ballet* (Tübingen: Biblio 17, 1991); Catherine Kintzler, "*Le Bourgeois gentilhomme*, trois degrés dans l'art du ballet comique," *Comédie Française* 154–155 (Dec. 1986–Jan. 1987), 10–15; Charles Mazouer and Martine Mazouer, *Le Bourgeois gentilhomme* (Paris: Ellipses, 1999); Robert McBride, "The Triumph of Ballet in *Le Bourgeois gentilhomme*," in I. D. Macfarlane et al., eds., *Form and Meaning: Æsthetic Coherence in Seventeenth–Century French Drama* (Amersham: Avebury, 1982), 127–141; Odette de Morgues, "*Le Bourgeois gentilhomme* as a Criticism of Civilization," *MSS,* 170–184; Orest Ranum, "Visions of Nobility and Gallantry: Understanding the Jourdains Historically," *ATTOP,* 104–109; David Whitton, *Molière: Le Bourgeois gentilhomme* (London: Grant and Cutler, 1992).

Discography: Jean–Baptiste Lully, *Le Bourgeois gentilhomme, complete music* (La Petite Bande, dir. Gustav Leonhardt, Deutsche Harmonia Mundi 77059–2–RG, 1971); Ibid. (La Simphonie du Maris, dir. Hugo Reyne, forthcoming in 2002 from Accord–Universal); *L'Orchestre du roi soleil* (Le concert des Nations, dir. Jordi Savall, Alia Vox AV 9807, 1999); Lully–Molière, *Comédies–ballets* (Les Musiciens du Louvre, dir. Marc Minkowski, Erato CD 2292–45286–2, 1988); Molière–Lully, *Le Bourgeois gentilhomme. Comédie, musique* (Collegium musicum de Paris, dir. Roland Douatte, Auvidis–Hachette 7914).

*Stephen H. Fleck*

**Bourgeoisie**. This is usually understood as the urban component of the "third estate," or common people, under the *ancien régime* social system. To be more precise, the status of *bourgeois* was actually conferred only upon property–owning burghers, possessing "a gable on the street." Status as a bourgeois often included important rights with regard to elective municipal offices and taxation, especially for Parisian bourgeois. Originally, there had been duties, as well, such as helping to defend the city in times of military conflict. Most of the duties and elective advantages had disappeared by the time of **Louis XIV**, or would be discontinued during his reign. Artisans, even if they possessed a fairly modest home, could claim to be bourgeois, but journeymen, laborers, apprentices, and other employees could not. Thus one can note **Sganarelle's** pride in his status, however humble, as woodcutter in *Le Médecin malgré lui* (I, 5), where he boasts of the quality of his sticks and the high prices he receives for them. Within the bourgeoisie, there was a definite hierarchy, with the poorest of the guilds and professions at the bottom, the grander guilds and merchants in the middle, and the royal officers and legal professionals at the top. The latter often enjoyed personal nobility because of their callings and eagerly sought to convert this to hereditary nobility by keeping an office in the same family for three generations. The uppermost levels of the bourgeoisie thus overlapped with the nobility, causing much controversy on both sides. Within the bourgeoisie, **money** also formed a hierarchy of **marriage** patterns, which were converted by Furetière in his *Roman bourgeois* into a chart of "partis sortables" or proper marriage partners. A parallel exists in the discussion of the "sortabilité" of **Angélique** in *Le Malade imaginaire*. The active upward mobility of the bourgeoisie that had characterized the reigns of the late Valois and early Bourbon kings had greatly decelerated by Molière's time, though some opportunities continued to exist in the military, particularly in the artillery and the engineers, and in other limited areas. The various levels of the bourgeoisie, while proud of their own prerogatives, tended to be very protective against the mobility of lower groups. Each had strong forms of identity in **language**, **education**, **costume**, and habits that defined tastes and activities, at least across a single generation. Such characters as **Chrysale** and **Madame Jourdain** appeal to these patterns of identity to safeguard family unity against change. The uppermost elements of the **peasant** groups, which owned land and means of production and lent money to other farmers, tended to form a "rural bourgeoisie." This is the stratum to which **George Dandin** belongs. With the passage of time, the designation "bourgeois" would come to be a virtual synonym of *rentier*, a person who had retired from active commerce to live off investment income. However, this change had not yet taken place during Molière's lifetime. The different nomenclature would lead to considerable gaps of misunderstanding in the interpretation of Molière's plays by later generations.

**Boursault, Edmé** (1638–1701). A dramatist associated with the **Hôtel de Bourgogne**, Boursault penned the vitriolic attack on Molière, *Le Portrait du Peintre* (1663), as part of the controversy over *L'École des femmes*. Molière scorns and belittles him as a publicity–seeking hack in *L'Impromptu de Versailles*. Six years later Boursault would collaborate with **Cotin** to attack **Boileau** in *La Satire des satires*. During Molière's career, he also wrote unsuccessful little comedies in competition with him, including *Le Mort vivant* (1662), *Les Nicandres* (1664), and a version of *Le Médecin volant* (1665) that Boursault claims he translated from the **Italian**. In his declining years he would achieve success in keeping with plays about writing, such as *Le Mercure galant*, *Les Fables d'Ésope*, and *Ésope à la cour*.

**Bowling**. In the second–act ballet of *Les Fâcheux*, **Éraste** falls in with a group of bowlers who appeal to him to judge their throws and present a dance made up of bowlers' gestures.

**Boyer, abbé Claude** (1618–1698). This tragic playwright regularly composed for the rival troupes, but when he gave Molière's troupe his *Tonnaxare* in 1662, they had a respectable run of fifteen performances and paid him handsomely.

Though elected to the **Academy** in 1666, Boyer was lambasted in famous epigrams by both **Boileau** and **Racine**.

**Brécourt (stage name of Guillaume Marcoureau,** 1638–1685). An actor in Molière's troupe who also became an author of comedies, notably the peasant-centered *Les Noces de village (Village Wedding,* 1664) and a postmortem tribute to his former patron, *L'Ombre de Molière* (1674). The latter play was so successful that it was printed with *Le Malade imaginaire* in the 1674 collected **edition** of Molière's works. He also published *La Feinte Mort de Jodelet* 1660) and *Le Jaloux invisible* (1666). Brécourt joined Molière's troupe in the spring of 1662 along with **La Thorillière**, who had been with him at the **Marais**. One of Brécourt's specialties was playing **peasant** characters with distinctively rural language mannerisms. As a member of Molière's troupe, he is thought to have taken the role of **Alain** in *L'École des femmes* and played himself and a gentleman in *L'Impromptu de Versailles*. Georges Couton maintains that Brécourt was also the original **Dorante** of *La Critique de l'École des femmes*, a role that devolved to **La Grange** after his departure. Documents indicate he played **Pancrace** in *Le Mariage forcé*, and may have doubled as **Alcidas** a few scenes later. He may also have taken the role of **Dorante** in *Les Fâcheux* (though not the original, since it premiered in the summer and autumn of 1661). This character, in recounting a deer **hunt** gone awry, mentions "un grand bênet de fils aussi sot que son père" ("a big oaf of a son as stupid as his father"). Brécourt composed a play by the same name that was performed by Molière's troupe in 1664. Since the title character was a country bumpkin, it probably gave Brécourt ample opportunity to employ his peasant dialect. He left the troupe later that year for the Hôtel de Bourgogne. After more than a decade with the Hôtel de Bourgogne, he left to make an acting tour of the Low Countries and returned in January 1682 to join the recently formed **Comédie-Française**. His half–share was raised to a full share by the Dauphine before he died.

**Brécourt** (*L'Impromptu de Versailles*). Representing himself in the frame play, Brécourt has relatively little to say. His role as the *honnête* aristocrat in the play–within–the–play mirrors the one he played in *La Critique de l'École des femmes*. It is perhaps noteworthy that, while he bears this important burden, Molière corrects him more often than **La Grange** or **Du Croisy**, sometimes demonstrating a whole speech. Perhaps Molière, while playing the foolish marquis himself, could not resist the opportunity to mouth the words of the "reasoner" in this important instance.

**Brennus**. Name of at least two Gaulish leaders. One, leading the 279 B.C. incursion into **Greece**, was beaten at Delphi and Thermopylae. *Les Amants magnifiques* credits **Sostrate** with this feat.

*Bretteur*. Obsolete term for a professional swordsman or thug of early modern times. **La Rapière**, who appears in Act V of *Dépit amoureux*, is such a hireling, offering to lend his sword against **Valère's** enemies and to add the aid of two friends, as ready as he to unsheath at any call. However, when he describes how his other sidekick, le petit Gille, died on the rack for his crimes, Valère decides to forgo their services. In *Les Fâcheux*, both **Éraste** and **Damis** appear to employ *bretteurs*, though the former turns against his own gang, led by La Rivière, in order to save the latter. **Dom Juan** employs a *bretteur* in the person of **La Ramée**, though most texts break with the original wording and call him a *spadassin*, which amounts to the same thing. **Argatiphontidas** in *Amphitryon* seems to be something of an ancient **Greek** *bretteur* because he can't wait to draw sword on the one who has been impersonating his friend. **Scapin** transforms his colleague **Silvestre** into a false *bretteur* in order to scare **Argante** and **Géronte**. Silvestre plays his Matamore role to the hilt, thrusting and slashing in all directions in an outburst of swordplay **lazzi**. Scapin's description fits the whole category of sword–wielding thugs, "He is one of those hired ruffians, those bullies who are all cut and slash, who talk only of breaking backs, and have no more conscience about killing a man as about swallowing a glass of wine" (II, 5).

**Brie, De (stage name of Edmé Villequin,** 1607–1676). He entered the troupe of Molière and **Dufresne** around 1650 and married Catherine Leclerc, who was already a member. He probably played the roles of **Villebrequin** in *La Jalousie du Barbouillé* and *Le Médecin volant*, but seems to have been relegated to minor parts soon after the troupe's return to **Paris**. He may have taken the part of **Monsieur Loyal** in *Tartuffe*. In *L'Avare*, he may have tripled as **Maître Simon**, either **La Merluche** or **Brindavoine**, and either the **Commissioner** or his **clerk**. He was a **River God** in *Psyché*. His wife, known as **Mlle. de Brie**, was one of the principal actresses of the **King's Troupe**.

**Brie, Mlle. de (stage name of Catherine Leclerc du Rozay,** 1630–1706). Already a stage veteran of many provincial seasons by the time Molière's troupe returned to **Paris**, Mlle. de Brie was **Cathos** of *Les Précieuses ridicules* and the original **Agnès** of *L'École des femmes*. She played many a daughter's role in plays that followed, including that of **Mariane** in *Tartuffe*, and Molière sometimes inserted subtle jokes about her height and slenderness, as in *L'Avare*, where she played **Élise**, who according to her shorter father had "grown like a weed." She also played **Uranie** in the *Critique de l'École des femmes*, herself in the *Impromptu de Versailles*, the Second **Gypsy** in *Le Mariage forcé*, **Cynthie** in *La Princesse d'Élide*, **Arsinoé** in *Le Misanthrope*, **Charlotte** in *Dom Juan*, **Isidore** in *Le Sicilien*, **Venus** in *Psyché* and perhaps in *Les Amants magnifiques*, **Julie** in *Monsieur de Pourceaugnac*, and **Dorimène** in *Le Bourgeois gentilhomme*. Taking on less benevolent and less innocent roles in Molière's later career, she was reportedly cast as **Armande** in *Les Femmes savantes*, and followed with the evil **Béline** in *Le Malade imaginaire*. When the Palais Royal Theater was terminated, she continued on into the troupe of the Hôtel Guénégaud and entered the **Comédie–Française** as a full–share member. She retired at the Easter break of 1685, having been pressured to do so by the Dauphine, who had been given authority over the theater.

**Brie, Mlle. de** (*L'Impromptu de Versailles*). In the frame play, this actress professes ignorance of some aspects of the **Quarrel of the School for Wives** and begs an explanation from Molière. Whether this was merely a pretext for his speeches or she really did not know much about the intrigue is unknown. The part he assigns her in the play–within–the–play is that of a woman who is flirtatious but covers it with a veneer of decency, rather like **Célimène** in some ways. However, she has little chance to display this personality in the ensuing conversation, which focuses almost entirely on Molière and the theater.

**Brindavoine** (*L'Avare*). A lackey who, along with his companion **La Merluche**, complains about their ragged livery in Act III.

**Brissart, Pierre**. One of the engravers who produced the series of illustrations for the 1682 collected **edition** of Molière's works.

**Brussels**. Site of a 1684 **edition** of *Dom Juan* that helped pass on the tradition of the original text during the time it was lost to most French readers. Brussels passed back and forth during the seventeenth century between Spanish, French, Dutch, and Austrian control. The **Queen Mother** exiled herself there for a period during the reign of **Louis XIV**.

# C

**Candles.** Everyday necessities in the seventeenth century, they were a fairly costly item for the **theaters** and also for **bourgeois** and aristocratic households, which called for wax candles (*cierges*). The common people had to content themselves with cheap, smoky tallow candles (*bougies*). The fact that the **Countess of Escarbagnas** has only the latter in her household testifies to her low economic and social status.

**Capitan.** A stock figure in French farce and comedy of the early half of the seventeenth century, the Capitan was a swaggering **Spanish** soldier whose bombastic speech scarcely concealed the heart of an inveterate coward. **Pierre Corneille's** comedies adopted the persona and gave him the more precise identity of Le Capitaine Matamore. This resurrection of the Roman *miles gloriosus* would continue on the French stage through the Classical era. The painting of great farce actors by Verio shows him wearing a colorful red and blue outfit with a conquistador–style breastplate, a large plumed hat, and, of course, a long sword. Molière mentions the Capitan, along with the Docteur and **Trivelin**, in the preface to *Les Précieuses ridicules*, saying that real **soldiers**, savants, or judges should not be insulted by such characters who ape them on the stage. When **Éraste** refuses to serve as **Alcandre's** second in Act I, scene 6 of *Les Fâcheux*, he mentions that even though he has served for fourteen years in the army, he doesn't want to play the Capitan. In **Le Misanthrope**, **Philinte** mentions a person of the Capitan type to **Alceste** when he asks him if he thinks Dorilas should be told that the **court** is tired of his accounts of his own bravery. **Argatiphontidas** in *Amphitryon* embodies some of the characteristics of the fire–breathing Capitan, but does not have a chance to prove either bravery or cowardice.

**Carcassonne**. Fortified city in Languedoc where Molière performed as part of the wandering troupe of **Charles Dufresne**. Acts show that the troupe was present in October 1647.

**Caritidès (*Les Fâcheux*)**. One of the more bizarre figures in this play, the pedant Caritidès appears in Act III, scene 2 and explains that he has shunned **Latin** names ending in "us" as too affected, but instead taken an even more affected **Greek** name ending in "des." He asks **Éraste** to use his influence at **court** and present to the King a petition asking him to create for Caritidès the position of royal corrector of signs. He claims that those existing in the capital are filled with errors of etymology and spelling that demand correction. Although the plan is preposterous and **Louis XIV** took little interest in trade signs, he did during his reign create an academy of inscriptions that followed Caritidès's plans on a loftier level! The role was played by Molière himself.

**Carle (*Les Fourberies de Scapin*)**. Though described in the dramatis personae as a *fourbe*, Carle actually engages in no tricks, but simply serves as a messenger to announce offstage events. **Beauval** or **de Brie** probably played the role.

**Carnival**. There is a carnival atmosphere in several of Molière's comedies, thanks to the presence of groups of **masked** figures or mummers. **Madame Jourdain** calls attention to these festive characters when she deplores the constant parade of "Mardi Gras characters" who are always parading through her home (III, 3). She later asks the newly installed *mamamouchi* if he is some kind of a *momon* (V, 1). A production of ***Tartuffe*** in Louisiana in the 1990s took this idea a bit further, successfully staging the play during Mardi Gras season, with all the characters in hilarious costumes and the Kingfish himself, Huey Long, emerging to give the **Exempt's** speech at the end of the play.

**Carriages**. These conveyances were undergoing rapid technological and aesthetic development in seventeenth–century France, and they had become one of the prime factors in fashion. Molière was well aware of it, since some of his relatives were in the carriage–making trade. The daily ritual parade of carriages in the **Cours la Reine** is described in the opening scene of *Les Fâcheux*, where the theatrical pest shows off his *galèche* and is greeted by a fellow fop in a superb carriage overloaded with lackeys front and back (one thinks of the well–known portrait of Chancellor Séguier surrounded by his followers). Later **Orphise** mentions that she also has a carriage, to which **Alcidor** was merely walking her when **Éraste** had seen them earlier. A measure of the social success of **Orgon's** family in *Tartuffe* is the constant line of carriages stopping at their door, which **Mme. Pernelle** detests. One of these carriages is surely that of the suitor **Valère**, who reappears in Act V and puts his rig at the disposal of Orgon so that he can flee the impending prison term that seems to hang over him. Mention of a coachman occurs in Act II, scene 2 of *L'Amour médecin*, where **Lisette** explains that she had seen the doctor **Tomès** at the home of **Sganarelle's** niece's friend, where he was "curing" the sick coachman who later died, a fact that Tomès heatedly denies, despite eyewitness testimony. **La Bruyère** poked fun at the excessive importance attributed these vehicles and the emotions they could produce when they arrived in the courtyards of the newly rich. **Célimène**, sophisticated as she is, comes running at the sound of an approaching carriage in Act III, scene 2 of *Le Misanthrope*. Had she known it was only her nemesis, **Arsinoé**, she might not have bothered to be so curious. Arsinoé later uses her carriage, whose return she must await, as an excuse to linger in Célimène's house in hopes of meeting **Alceste**. It is known from existing records that Molière himself maintained a carriage and team at considerable expense, perhaps because he did not want to offend the prevailing trends. Few people would allow their carriage and team to fall into the deplorable state one finds in *L'Avare*, where **Harpagon** is not only too miserly to pay for a full–time coachman, but has let the horses starve for want of oats. While not exactly a carriage, **Night's** chariot in *Amphitryon* causes some envy on the part of **Mercury**, who is tired of crossing the earth and heavens on foot and would like a nice ride for a change. Molière includes a poem on a carriage in *Les Femmes savantes*; the silly epigram develops around the conceit of a rig covered in gold leaf that cost so much it should not be called "amarante" (yellow), but "de ma rente" (from my income). Ironically, the usurper **Monsieur de Pourceaugnac, disguised** as a "lady of quality," gives a hilarious impersonation of a foolish aristocrat yelling for her carriage. As one of the most conspicuous elements of the new society of consumerism, the carriage receives more than its share of satirical attention in the comedies.

**Cassia.** An herbal purgative that was frequently used with rhubarb and senna in various "cleansing" formulas administered to the early modern ill. When **Toinette** jokingly compares it to **wine**, **Argan** distorts a common folk saying about the grape to reply, "Yes, good cassia is very good."

**Cathau (***La Jalousie du Barbouillé***).** The few lines given to this serving woman concern her role as an accomplice for **Angélique** in her nocturnal assignations.

**Cathos (***Les Précieuses ridicules***).** Niece of old **Gorgibus**. Judging by the diminuitive of Catherine, the role was probably taken by **Catherine de Brie**. In the play, Cathos seeks to rename herself **Aminte**, in imitation of a character from **Gomberville's** *Polexandre*. Cathos generally follows the lead of her cousin in all things. Her most famous remark is probably her question about how anyone could manage to sleep next to a man who is naked.

**Cato.** Famous statesman and orator of the Roman republic. **Orgon** shows off a bit of his **Latin** by comparing his brother–in–law **Cléante** to Cato when he undertakes to criticize **Tartuffe** and to denounce false devotion.

**Catullus.** **Latin** poet of the first century B.C., he was mainly known for his light **love** verses, which **Vadius** accuses **Trissotin** of copying.

**Célie** (*L'Étourdi*). The female lead in the play, she is described as a **slave** girl belonging to **Trufaldin**. She turns out to be Trufaldin's long–lost daughter, who has undergone a series of kidnappings before being sold by **Gypsies**. She seems to have picked up the Gypsy trade of fortune telling, since **Mascarille** consults her in Act I, presumably to inquire about a "friend," but really to convey a message of **love** from **Lélie**. It is not her fault if this interview is less than successful, for her own replies show a great deal of poise and cleverness. She is also much sought by **Léandre** and **Andrès**. After escaping with the latter in the final act, she soliloquizes about which of the lovers she should choose. Perhaps this, rather than the headache of which she complains, is the real reason for her going no farther than Mascarille's "boarding house." She has a witty exchange of compliments with **Hippolyte**, who gloats a bit at Léandre's return to her. The last act finds her full of surprise at learning her real identity, but she has little chance to express much joy for her upcoming **marriage** to Lélie. Apart from some elegant badinage, the part contains nothing very outstanding or very original, but intrigue comedy placed women in a very dependent condition and gave them little room for character development beyond the conventional traits. If the role was originally taken by **Madeleine Béjart**, it certainly devolved to another actress in the troupe after her retirement.

**Célie** (*Sganarelle*). Daughter of **Gorgibus** and sweetheart of **Lélie**. Alarmed that her father is on the point of forcing her to marry **Villebrequin's** son **Valère**, Célie opens the locket her absent lover Lélie has given her and pines away over his **portrait**, eventually falling into a faint. **Sganarelle**, happening to pass by, comes to her aid and manages to fondle her thoroughly while trying to revive her. The locket, which has fallen on the ground, is picked up by the eavesdropping Mrs. Sganarelle, giving rise to an argument between her and her husband. When Célie has recovered, she reappears onstage just in time to see Lélie departing, and is told by Sganarelle that the young man is involved in an affair with his wife. She naturally tells her father that she is now prepared to follow his orders with regard to the arranged **marriage**. Her subsequent confrontation with the apparently unfaithful suitor is interrupted first by Sganarelle's armored entrance and then by the intervention of his irate wife, who stuns everyone by accusing her of seducing Sganarelle. By the end of scene 22, everyone has explained what they actually saw and what they inferred, and everyone is reconciled except Gorgibus, who still insists on his authority. Only Villebrequin's embarrassed announcement that his son is secretly married already frees the couple to fulfill their vows with the fathers' blessings. Célie appears as a sensitive girl with highly volatile emotions. Her fainting provides only gestural proof of the depth of her feelings, for her dialogue is rather sparse and conventional.

**Célimène** (*Le Misanthrope*). Object of **Alceste's** perverse love, cousin of **Éliante**, and chatty friend to the entire world of Parisian menfolk, Célimène is unlike most other female roles in Molière's theater and has few parallels in the previous seventeenth–century plays. She will, however, be much imitated on both sides of the Channel for her combination of flawless worldliness and stinging wit. As an aristocratic widow, she enjoys great freedom of association, unencumbered by a wife's sense of decorum. Her house is open to any and all who share her appetite for gossip and **portrait** games. She explains to Alceste that she does have an ulterior motive for this hospitality in that she is using several of her suitors to further her interests in a **lawsuit**. However, it is also obvious that she is naturally gregarious and thrives on attention. Alceste's persistence amuses and flatters her, for she knows that *galant* gentlemen such as **Acaste** and **Clitandre** would desert her at the first sign of rejection, while the misanthrope only clasps himself to her more closely. She is no more inconvenienced by his sermons than by the moral quibbles of **Arsinoé**, taking neither of them very seriously. In this, she appears as a kind of feminine equivalent of **Dom Juan**, convinced of her own superiority and boldly facing down an inferior universe. This probably explains the presence of her cousin Éliante, as well. The **philosophical** woman offers a challenge to her conversational skills that helps keep boredom at bay. Ennui is her only real danger, and that is why she must refuse to follow Alceste into his rural retreat at the end of the play, despite the fact that she is quite tempted to accept his **sincere**, though rather totalitarian, offer of **marriage**. She is what Chamfort would later call "a product of the perfected civilization." Endowed with a resilience that will characterize Madeleine Renaud's famous interpretation of the role in the 1950s, she would rather face the difficulties of calumny than give up the social game she plays so well. Viewed from this perspective, her willingness to launch herself back into **Paris** society is just as heroic, in an opposite sense, from Alceste's withdrawal to his "desert." There is a strange complementary nature to this couple, even in their comic incompatibility. By giving the role to his wife Armande, Molière proved his absolute confidence in her theatrical maturity and his fearlessness of the Parisian gossip mill that had been working against him in recent years, for in many ways the couple was probably acting out a symbolic version of their own domestic struggles.

**Ceres**. The goddess of grain is mentioned by **Éroxène** in *Mélicerte* when she greets **Lycarsis** with wishes for his prosperity (I, 4).

**Chaillot**. In Molière's time and well into the following century, this village lay beyond the western edge of the city of **Paris**, though its site is now just across the river from the Eiffel Tower. It is mentioned by **Martine** in *Les Femmes savantes*.

**Chambord**. Royal residence in the Loire valley used principally during the **hunting** season by the young **Louis XIV**. It was there that *Monsieur de*

*Pourceaugnac* was first produced on October 6, 1669, and *Le Bourgeois gentilhomme* just over a year later.

**Champmeslé (stage name of Charles Chevillet**, 1642–1701). Having collaborated as early as 1666 with **Rosimond's** troupe in Rouen, this actor was brought to the **Hôtel de Bourgogne** in 1670. He continued on through the period of unification of the French **theaters** to become a member of the **Comédie–Française**, with the exception of 1679–80, when he and his wife belonged to the Hôtel Guénégaud company. He also tried his hand at writing, and in doing so displayed the strong influence of Molière on his themes and style. An example is his comedy, *Les Grisettes, ou Crispin chevalier* (1671), which owes much to *Les Précieuses ridicules*. He gave tribute to Molière in a posthumous piece, *Les Fragments de Molière* (1676), which summarized some scenes of *Dom Juan* and tacked on a happy ending. Champmeslé seems to have worked along with **La Grange** as a director of the Comédie–Française. His wife, who died in 1698, was one of their most accomplished tragedians.

See Joseph F. Pritavera, *Charles Chevillet de Champmeslé, Actor and Dramatist* (Baltimore: Johns Hopkins University Press, 1938).

**Chapelain, Jean** (1595–1674). Though his best work is mainly confined to correspondence and literary essays, this intellectual exercised an immense influence on the writing of the century through his place on the **Academy** and his role in preparing the list of annual literary stipends for **Louis XIV**. **Boileau** was not alone in lacerating Chapelain's masterpiece, the Joan of Arc epic *La Pucelle* (1655). But old Chapelain seemed to be able to shake off quarrels and keep a remarkably open mind in assessing his more talented colleagues. Thanks to his opinions, Molière joined the stipend list in 1663.

**Chapelle, aka Claude Emmanuel Luillier** (1626–1686). Legitimized natural son of a rich **bourgeois**, Chapelle is noted for having received a fine **education**, including studies with the great skeptical **philosopher, Gassendi**. The rumor that Molière and Chapelle studied together under Gassendi is traceable at least as far back as **Voltaire**. However, Gassendi only began his teaching in Paris in 1645, when Molière was already fleeing to the provinces with the remainder of the **Illustre Théâtre** troupe. Many colorful anecdotes are told of Chapelle and Molière's other friends of the "Circle of the **White Cross**," named for a tavern where **libertines** congregated. One of the best–known is the famous "evening at **Auteuil**" story where Chapelle, **Boileau**, and others, despondent over unfortunate **love** affairs and quite drunk, decided to throw themselves into the Seine. Only the cool–headed Molière refrained, persuading the others that such a glorious sacrifice should only be performed by the light of day. Of course, by daylight the tipplers were more concerned with their hangovers than with suicide. There is no way of verifying this picturesque story, and one may take it as one wishes.

**Chappuzeau, Samuel** (ca. 1625–1701). A comic author who was both a rival and an emulator of Molière. The troupe staged his comedy *Le Riche impertinent* in May 1661 with very modest results. The play was staged as early as the next year by the **Hôtel de Bourgogne**. However, Chappuzeau's subsequent work, though written for other companies, continued to bear a strong mark of Molière. This is evident in *Le Colin–Maillard* and *L'Avare dupé*, both of which premiered at the Hôtel de Bourgogne in 1662, and *Les Eaux de Pirmont* (1669).

**Charlotte** (*Dom Juan*). This **peasant** girl, played by **Catherine de Brie**, appears through the length of the second act. At the outset, she is with her fiancé **Pierrot**, who recounts to her how he saved **Dom Juan** and **Sganarelle** from the waves. His description of their courtly **costumes** stimulates Charlotte's interest, making it clear that this country lass is ill pleased with the swains in her village and yearns for a knight in shining **armor** to carry her away to a better life. She rejects Pierrot's pleas for signs of love from her, since she has little interest in the peasant jostling that constitutes village romance. Dom Juan is no sooner onstage than he seems to make her dreams come true. He showers her with inappropriate compliments, even though Sganarelle points out that she is dressed in rags and has hands as dirty as pitch. The seducer has no trouble overcoming her few qualms, convincing her that he is not only interested, but totally committed and prepared to seal the relationship with marriage. When Pierrot returns to lay claim to his beloved, she does not hesitate to indicate her change of plans, hoping to mollify her former suitor with promises of the milk and cheese trade at her new château. She shows little affection for Pierrot, as he uses her for a human shield while denigrating Dom Juan and all other nobles who spoil the quiet patterns of rural life. Soon a new challenge arrives in the form of her counterpart, Mathurine, to whom Dom Juan has already promised **love**, devotion, and marital bliss. Obviously the two women have an ongoing rivalry and this latest issue simply rekindles their existing competition. This makes it easier for Dom Juan to woo both of them simultaneously and unscrupulously, since neither is willing to listen to the other's words or to believe what the seducer is telling the rival. He manages to bring them to a kind of dumbfounded agreement by assuring both of them that they know their claims are true. The women remain trapped in this situation, while Dom Juan learns from La Ramée that his enemies are at his heels and he must flee. He assures both Charlotte and Mathurine that he will soon be in contact with them. However, it is obvious that Dom Juan is a man who is only interested in whichever women are handy, and that he will not go out of his way to fulfill the peasants' dreams once he has departed from their village. Like the other characters in the play, they will be left to pick up the pieces of their lives and resolve their disputes if they can. This role is substantial not only because it calls for a good impersonation of an ingénue, but also because it demands familiarity with rural **language** patterns and a certain amount of physical stamina. It is one of Molière's most genial inventions, since the original seaside seduction in **Tirso's** *Burlador* involved a mermaid, rather than a true human being. Molière once again shows his propensity for naturalistic depiction and his skill in creating a rather well rounded peasant character who shows emotional development and imagination far beyond the usual stereotypical limits.

**Charpentier, Marc–Antoine** (1643–1704). Charpentier is in may ways the opposite of Molière's other musical collaborator, **Jean–Baptiste Lully**. He was associated with **Italian music**, never held a post at **court**, composed more sacred than theatrical music, and published almost none of his music; indeed, many of his more than 500 compositions are yet to be published. Like his career, his reputation has been overshadowed by that of Lully, yet his work is of high quality and remarkable diversity. He worked with the major Parisian theaters for almost fifteen years, and his one opera, *Médée*, rivals those of Lully and Rameau.

Little is known about his life, especially the early years. Born in **Paris** in 1643, he probably received his early musical **education** from family members. He went to Rome around 1665, where he worked for three years with Carissimi, the best known Roman composer of the time, and made the acquaintance of Dassoucy. The latter claimed that Molière had promised to commission music from him, as **Corneille** had for *Andromède*, but when Molière broke with Lully in 1672 it was to Charpentier that he turned.

Between the performances at **court** of *La Comtesse d'Escarbagnas* in December 1671 and the Paris revival in July 1672, Lully founded his Académie Royale de Musique and tried to keep other troupes from including more than two airs and two instruments in their plays. The protests by Molière and others resulted in less draconian restrictions, but it was out of the question for Molière to use Lully's music. Charpentier composed a prologue for *La Comtesse d'Escarbagnas* and new *intermèdes* for *Le Mariage forcé*, which accompanied it. He also contributed music to the revival of *Les Fâcheux* in August, but the music is lost.

The only work that Charpentier and Molière created together was *Le Malade imaginaire*, which Charpentier had to revise often because of restrictions imposed by Lully on the number of musicians other troupes could use. It was first performed "in its splendor," but with a second prologue to replace the magnificent one intended for the court premiere that never came, then "with the restrictions" in the 1674 revival. It was finally performed at court during the fêtes of July and August 1674, then again, "revised for the third time," in 1686. **Louis XIV** was definitely in Lully's camp, although he did allow Molière's successors in 1673 and 1674 to use more musicians than the letter of Lully's ordinance allowed.

After Molière's death Charpentier continued to work with the troupe in the Hôtel Guénégaud, setting new text by an unknown author for a revival of *Le Sicilien* in June 1679. He also supplied a new overture for *Le Dépit amoureux* in July.

When the actors decided to take advantage of the popularity of **machine plays**, they turned to Charpentier for music. He wrote over 1,000 measures for

*Circé*, with a libretto by **Thomas Corneille** and **Donneau de Visé**, which was a huge success from March to October 1675. Lully again took legal action, since the performances employed more than the two singers and six instrumentalists allowed by the April 30, 1673, ordinance; a new ordinance, on March 21, 1675, specified that the two singers had to be members of the company rather than professional singers. Their next venture, *L'Inconnu*, was nonetheless a success in late 1675 and again in 1678 and 1679. Charpentier's music is lost, as is his music for his last machine play with the Guénégaud troupe, *Le Triomphe des dames*, in August 1676.

Charpentier supplied incidental music for several plays by the newly formed **Comédie–Française** from 1680 to 1685, including the December 1684 revival of *Psyché*. Several of these bear witness to the continuing rivalry with Lully, including **Poisson's** *Les Fous divertissants* (1680), which includes airs from Lully's operas *Bellérophon* and *Proserpine*, probably to mock their exaggerated popularity, and **Dancourt's** *Angélique et Médor* (1685), which was a parody of the current **Quinault**–Lully opera, *Roland*. Charpentier wrote new music for a lavish production of Corneille's machine play *Andromède*, revived in 1682 to compete with Quinault and Lully's *Persée* and successful enough to evoke yet more legal action by Lully. He also wrote music for *La Pierre philosophale* (Th. Corneille and Donneau de Visé, 1682), *Endimion* (anonymous, 1682), *La Noce de village* (**Brécourt**, 1666, revived in 1681), *Le Rendez–vous des Tuileries ou le Coquet trompé* (**Baron**, 1685), and *Les Amours de Vénus et d'Adonis* (Donneau de Visé, 1669, revived 1685).

While he was writing music for the theater he was also in the service of Mlle. de Guise (Marie de Lorraine), who offered him an apartment in her **hôtel**. He remained there until 1687 or 1688, singing and composing sacred and profane works as a member of a musical establishment of about fifteen that outshone that of many royal courts.

His profane works there include *divertissements* such as *Les Arts Florissants*, *Actéon*, *La Descente d'Orphée aux enfers*, and *Orphée descendant aux enfers*, often considered the first cantata by a French composer. He also composed a *petit opéra*, *Acis et Galathée*, for M. de Rians in 1678, and a pastoral, *Les Plaisirs de Versailles*, for the **Dauphin**, for whom he also composed many sacred works between 1679 and 1682 or 1683; Louis XIV is said to have preferred them to the works of all other composers. In 1681, the *Mercure galant* published his settings of the first three of Rodrigue's *stances* at the end of Act I of *Le Cid*.

He was a candidate for a post as *maître de musique* at the royal chapel at **Versailles** in 1683. Illness kept him from completing the competition, but he did receive a royal pension, probably as remuneration for his services to the Dauphin. He would return to the court in 1692–93 as music master for the duc de Chartres, for whom he wrote a brief treatise, *Règles de composition*, which offers a rare glimpse into compositional techniques of the time, including the "characters" of the different keys.

In addition to a wide variety of sacred pieces he wrote for Mlle. de Guise and the institutions she protected, he wrote masses, motets, psalms, Tenebrae, and more for several convents, including Port–Royal de Paris (in the 1680s, after its association with the **Jansenists**). He wrote music for state occasions, such as the death of Queen Marie–Thérèse, and the famous Te Deum (of Eurovision fame) to celebrate the recovery of Louis XIV in 1687. After the death of Mlle. de Guise in 1688 he became *maître de musique* at the Jesuit church of Saint–Louis, known for its almost operatic music, and at the Louis–le–Grand college, for which he wrote two *tragédies en musique*, *Celse martyr* and *David et Jonathas*, the acts of which were performed between acts of plays in **Latin**.

His only opera, and probably his masterpiece, *Médée* (libretto by Th. Corneille), had a successful run at the Académie Royale de Musique in 1693, in spite of criticism by admirers of Lully who found Charpentier's music too complex. It has held the stage well during several runs in the 1980s and 1990s.

In 1698 he was appointed *maître de musique* at the Sainte–Chapelle, the most important position in France for sacred music, after the chapel at Versailles. He remained in the post until his death, February 24, 1704.

Selected Bibliography: *Music for Molière's Comedies*, ed. John S. Powell (Madison, WI: A. R. Editions, 1990); *Prologues et intermèdes du Malade imaginaire de Molière*, ed. H. Wiley Hitchcock (Geneva: Minkoff, 1973); Catherine Cessac, *Marc–Antoine Charpentier* (Paris: Fayard, 1988); H. Wiley Hitchcock, *Marc–Antoine Charpentier* (New York: Oxford University Press, 1990); idem, "Marc–Antoine Charpentier and the Comédie–Française," *Journal of the American Musicological Society* 24 (1971), 225–281; John S. Powell, "Charpentier's Music for Molière's *Le Malade imaginaire* and Its Revisions," *Journal of the American Musicological Society* 39 (1986), 87–142.

Selected Discography: *Incidental Music to* Les Fous divertissants *and* Le Mariage forcé (New Chamber Opera, The Band of Instruments, dir. Gary Cooper, ASV CD GAU 167, 1997, 1 CD); *Le Malade imaginaire* (Les Arts Florissants, dir. William Christie, Harmonia Mundi HMC 901336, 1990, 1 CD); *Le Malade imaginaire* (Les Musiciens du Louvre, dir. Marc Minkowski, Erato 245002–2, 1990, 1 CD).

*Buford Norman*

**Chasteauneuf.** A salaried player or *gagiste* employed by the **King's Troupe**. He played **Lycas** in *Psyché*. It is not clear if he was an actor by the same name who had earlier collaborated with Molière's provincial troupe, or if he is the A.P.P. de Chasteauneuf who published *La Feinte Mort de Pancrace (The Feigned Death of Pancrace)* in Maastricht in 1663.

**Chauveau, François** (1613–1676). The most timely of Molière's illustrators, he created frontispieces for the published versions of several plays, including *Le Misanthrope*, as well as early collected volumes. Where possible, **Brissart** and **Sauvé** appear to have simply copied their elder for the illustrations to the 1682

**edition**, though some details of **costume** show notable updating to include the *justaucorps* jacket that had become popular in the intervening years.

**Chevalier, Jean** (fl. 1660–1670). One of the main rivals and emulators of Molière, Chevalier acted in the **Marais** troupe under the comic persona of Guillot, a bumbling, drunken sot. Encouraged perhaps by the success of *Les Précieuses ridicules*, Chevalier wrote a series of imitative works, including *Le Cartel de Guillot (Guillot's Challenge,* 1661), *Les Galants ridicules (The Ridiculous Lovers,* 1661), *L'Intrigue des carosses à cinq sous (The Five–Cent Omnibus,* 1662), *La Désolation des filoux (The Crooks' Mistake,* 1662), *La Disgrâce des domestiques (The Servants' Disgrace,* 1662), *Les Barbons amoureux (The Lusty Grey–beards,* 1662), *Les Amours de Calotin (Calotin's Conquests,* 1664), *Le Pédagogue amoureux (The Love–Smitten Pedant,* 1665), *Les Aventures de nuit (Night–time Adventures,* 1666), and *Le Soldat malgré lui (The Soldier Despite Himself,* 1668). Despite the obvious influence of Molière in the titles, in some efforts of characterization, and (in the case of *The Five–Cent Omnibus*) topical satire, Chevalier's works were hampered by their very poor versification, crude sense of humor, and ham–fisted composition.

**Children and Childhood**. In general, early modern French society treated children as incomplete, problem–ridden little adults, and they are seldom depicted in art and literature. **Armande**, the voluntarily sterile sister in *Les Femmes savantes*, refers to them with a sneer as "marmots." The **King** in *Psyché* is perhaps speaking for many Frenchmen when he explains to his daughter that he was a reluctant parent: "I received from [the gods] a present that my heart had never asked for, and at that time I found nothing appealing in you, watching without joy as my family grew" (II, 1). This began to change somewhat in the time of **Louis XIV**, who was depicted in a number of notable **court** paintings with his offspring. The prospect that the mainly homophilic Louis XIII might not produce a male heir was terrifying for the French, since it would almost certainly mean a bloody dynastic civil war. When young Louis was born, he was called "Le Dieudonné" (The Godgiven) and his childhood was closely documented by the **court** physicians charged with watching over his health. On the other side of the social scale, one sees **peasant** children appearing in the genre scenes of Louis Le Nain: wistful, resigned figures that face a life of privation. The **bourgeoisie**, which had adopted the aristocratic custom of the wet–nurse and the consequent separation of the child from the married couple, is often seen as scorning and repressing childhood. However, this is not entirely true; the same custom of employing wet–nurses resulted in an actual increase in the number of children born to bourgeois women, since the pregnancy–reducing effects of lactation were foreshortened. Molière himself belonged to a numerous family from which he was never distantly separated until the failure of the **Illustre Théâtre**.

The first consideration of childhood in Molière's works occurs in scene 1 of *Le Mariage forcé*, where **Sganarelle** considers the factors that favor his projected **marriage** with **Dorimène**: "Besides the joy I will have in possessing a beautiful wife, who will give me untold caresses and pamper me . . . I believe that in staying as I am, I am allowing the lineage of Sganarelles to perish from the earth, and that in marrying I will be able to see myself born again in other little me's, and I'll have the pleasure of seeing creatures from my own loins, little faces that will resemble mine like peas in a pod, who will always run playing about the house and call me papa when I come home from work and say the funniest, silliest little things to make me happy. Why, I can see it all already, and there are a half dozen of them about me right now!" This sentimental yearning for a lap full of toddlers might seem odd coming from crusty old Sganarelle, who has, like **Arnolphe** in *L'École des femmes*, long avoided the compromises of family life. Yet, it shows that the child–bearing urge is strong enough to penetrate even the roughest exteriors and to set aside any form of logic. **Monsieur Dimanche** is so disarmed by **Dom Juan's** solicitous questions about his children, charming little Claudine and noisy Colin, with his toy drum, that he neglects to press his debtor for payment on outstanding loans. **Henriette**, in *Les Femmes savantes*, views motherhood with anticipation and joy. She teases her prudish sister with the idea that by refraining from sexual contact she is preventing "some little scholar from coming into the world."

Even parents who are less than eager to hold a baby on their lap are not immune from sentimental attachment to their children, for parental love is just as strong when gradually acquired as when it exists from the start. Psyche's father tells that his eyes and his heart became sweetly accustomed to his child as he invested fifteen years in toils, vigils, and studies with her. He had decorated her with virtues and imbued her with wisdom until he came to see her as his life's greatest accomplishment and the treasure of his old age, a source of tenderness and joy through whom his own diminished senses could live again vicariously. Molière himself wrote parts for several of the troupe's children into some of his plays and court entertainments. He often served as godfather or baptismal witness for the children of his friends.

Characters who have children are not always as sentimental about them. When **Martine** rhetorically asks Sganarelle in *Le Médecin malgré lui* what she is to do with the four hungry children she has on her hands, her husband tells her callously to put them on the ground and whip them if they whine. When three alleged offspring rush into **Monsieur de Pourceaugnac's** lap, he calls them "little sons of bitches" and recoils in horror. In *Les Fourberies de Scapin*, **Géronte** and **Argante** have obviously raised sons who do little to respect the wishes of their absent fathers, but the fathers accuse each other of giving their boys a faulty **education** (II, 1). On a more serious note, **Dom Louis** lectures his son Dom Juan on the many disappointments he has caused the family through his scandalous and thoughtless behavior. This does not prevent him, however, from reverting to maudlin joy when he believes his penitent son has undergone a **religious** conversion in the final act. The **Countess of Escarbagnas** has confided the care of her son to a tutor, in noble fashion, but the boy seems to have reached a fairly advanced age without going beyond rote recitation of the first rules of **Latin** grammar. He seems to be a "big oaf of a son as stupid as his mother," to borrow a description from another play. In *Mélicerte*, **Lycarsis** tries at first to enforce his authority over **Myrtil** in order to make him give up his feelings for the poor eponym and marry instead one of the rich "nymphes" who have asked for his hand. However, once Myrtil shares his sufferings with the old man, he is touched to the point of tears and agrees to grant his son his wishes. Like Myrtil, **Cupid** in *Psyché* finds himself at the poignant moment when childhood ends. Speaking of his love for the young mortal, he tells Zephyr, "It is time to leave this long childhood / That tries my patience. / It is time now that I grow up." To this the henchman replies, "Very well, you cannot do better, / You are now embarking on a mystery / Where a child is out of place" (II, 1).

The play with the most to say about children is *Le Malade imaginaire*, where **Argan's** relationships with his daughters are portrayed in some detail. When Argan threatens to throw the girls into a **convent**, **Toinette** mocks his bluster, "You will be overwhelmed by paternal tenderness . . . a little tear or two, arms thrown around your neck, a 'dear, darling daddy' sweetly spoken will be enough to touch your heart." Indeed, **Béline** uses the **language** of childhood to entrap Argan when she continually coddles him with the term, "my little boy." **Monsieur Diafoirus** speaks in detail of his son's backwardness as a child, and how it has led to his stupidity as an adult (II, 5). **Louison's** appearance (II, 8) gives a rare glimpse into the behavior of a parent and a truly young child, for she was played by a six year old and comports herself accordingly. We know immediately that Argan is on somewhat formal terms with his children, since he addresses the youngster with "vous" and she replies in kind. Knowing that her father expects a token of good behavior and intelligence, she wishes to recite a fable or a fairy tale for him. When he inquires into the more intimate details of what she has seen in **Angélique's** bedroom, Louison at first denies knowing anything in a typically childish way, then, threatened with a spanking from the switches her father has grasped, she begs forgiveness and offers to tell all. When he requires that she first submit to her punishment for lying, she resorts to passive subterfuge, crying out, "Oh, father, you have wounded me! Just a minute: I am dead." This performance has an immediate result, as Argan breaks down into regretful tears, which his daughter does not hesitate to kiss away. Pardoned, but still under possible cross–examination from the omniscient little finger that Argan playfully puts to his ear, she gives a young child's simplified and rather disapproving account of the sweet talk that took place and says the finger is a liar if it denies her words. As she leaves, her father wistfully says, "Ah, there are no more children!"

Argan's line is significant on many levels. On the one hand, it is an expression of the eternal nostalgia that age feels toward youth and the certainty that the young people of "today" are never quite equal to those of the past. However, on another level, it can be seen as a sad statement by a man who knew what it was to lose siblings and offspring to childhood diseases. Besides dead brothers and sisters, Molière could remember his own two sons, buried long before they had emerged from the cradle. One recalls also his poem to **La Mothe Le Vayer** on the death of that **philosopher's** son, urging the old man to give way to his tears, rather than stifling them in common stoical form. This language is echoed in *Psyché*, where the King refuses to accept stoical curbs on mourning. He rejects the consolation of his two elder daughters, saying that the two who remain do nothing to replace the one who is about to be taken away. He even goes so far as to promise life–long anger toward the gods for demanding a child's death. It is no wonder that **Béralde**, mindful of such matters and of the frightful infant and childhood death rates that barely allowed for replacement of the population, discounts the importance of planning a *dowry* for young Louison. She is, to some degree, "laissée pour compte."

**Chorèbe (*Les Amants magnifiques*).** This **Greek**–style retainer of the **court** of Princess **Ériphile** has the sole function of summoning her to meet her mother in the grove of **Diana** (II, 4). Since **Sostrate** addresses him as "little boy," one may surmise that the role was played by one of the **children** of the troupe's families.

**Chrysalde (*L'École des femmes*).** Although it is difficult to see how he could put up with such a devious, self–centered blowhard, Chrysalde is clearly shown from the beginning of the play to be **Arnolphe's** best friend. The two are similar in age, but not in temperament, for Chrysalde has listened to the call of **nature** and married, while Arnolphe, fearful of becoming a cuckold, rejected all offers. Thus Chrysalde has become a butt for his neighbor's outright mockery, for Arnolphe does nothing to spare him from the jibes he hurls at the whole community of cuckolds. The debate that ensues, with Chrysalde upholding the virtues of tolerance against Arnolphe's insistence on absolute control, much resembles the one between **Sganarelle** and **Ariste** in *L'École des maris*, so much so in fact that Chrysalde himself remarks on the similarity. This amounts to an inside joke for the players, since the same men, Molière and **Louis Béjart**, played both pairs of characters and would soon become brothers–in–law. In order to prove his point that a stupid, pliable wife is best, Arnolphe invites Chrysalde to witness **Agnès's** compliance for himself, and he relates her amusing question about whether babies could be conceived by the ear. Chrysalde is one of the few people who are privy to the secret of Arnolphe's double identity, and the latter enjoins him to stop using his old name and call him only Monsieur de la Souche, so that the public will come to think of him as a landed noble.

Despite the tongue lashing Chrysalde takes from his friend at the outset, he returns in Act IV to invite Arnolphe to dine. The debate over cuckoldry then resumes, with Arnolphe still sarcastic, but much more subdued since his personal reverses. Chrysalde, on the contrary, seems to have the upper hand as he frames the response to cuckoldry in terms of fate and personal success, rather than simple neglect. Taking a page from **Pascal**, he describes the issue of marital fidelity as a roll of the dice, where bad outcomes are unavoidable and can only be salvaged by "clever gamesmanship and a humble stance / That may by good behavior give the lie to chance." His warning to his friend about "dragons of virtue and she–devils of civility" seems to point to such future figures as **Arsinoé** and **Célimène**. Seeking to console his friend, he points out that thousands who surpass him in good looks, courage, wealth, and pedigree have already led the way down that road, allowing the audience to self–identify with the issue under discussion. Having assumed the role of *raisonneur* or voice of reason, at least for a while, Chrysalde reappears in the final act with the long–absent **Enrique** to facilitate the resolution of the plot. He learns that he is actually Agnès's uncle. Like many well–intentioned neighbors or relatives in Molière's comedies, Chrysalde is capable of rising above his own foibles to represent a convincing brand of common sense as an alternative to the rigid, but often fragile, logic of one–sided thinkers who are blinded by their pursuit of a single, often illusory, objective.

**Chrysale (*Les Femmes savantes*).** In this play, Molière cast himself as an impotent old fool, who rants and raves about paternal authority but breaks down at the slightest sign of opposition from his wife. It brings the pusillanimity of the **Sganarelle** persona into a **bourgeois** framework. Chrysale's heart is in the right place, and he shows from his opening scenes in the second act that he wants to do the right thing. He quickly seconds **Ariste's** suggestion that **Clitandre** would make a good son–in–law, tries to reason with the delusionary **Bélise**, and sets out to confront **Philaminte**, encountering along the way poor **Martine**, who has been run out of the house for misuse of **language**. He makes the mistake of taking up the **servant** issue first, running afoul of Philaminte's fixed ideas about the reform of speech and exacerbating her sense of feminine superiority. In the face of Philaminte's idealism, he can only sputter a materialistic quibble, "These strips of flesh are dear to me." She finally lets him wear himself out with a long tirade that pecks away at her preferences, then lacerates him with a single line, "Oh, gods, what vulgarity of language and soul!" After shamefully backing down on his support for Martine, he gets nowhere with the **marriage** plans and must report abashedly back to Ariste that Philaminte plans for **Henriette** to marry **Trissotin**. Re–energized by the end of Act III, he takes a bold move in his wife's absence and preempts her project by getting Henriette and Clitandre to exchange *paroles de futur* before witnesses, thus sealing their engagement. He disappears, wistfully reminiscing about the good old days, and does not come on stage again until it is almost too late, Philaminte already having sent for a **notary** to draw up the contract to suit her wishes. With the help of Ariste, Henriette, and Clitandre, Chrysale puffs himself up into a courageous stance, indeed, a parody of true courage, since he has become a "fanfaron" of masculinity. He manages to hold firm through part of the notary confrontation, matching his wife almost word for word, but finally fizzles in his usual fashion, leaving the lovers hopeless for a minute, until Ariste is able to effect a ruse involving two forged **letters**. Molière was always brave enough to take up a coward's role, from Sganarelle all the way to **Monsieur de**

**Pourceaugnac**. However, Chrysale is, like other figures in this comedy, strangely pathetic, and one is glad the author survived to step into **Argan's** shoes, at least for four triumphal performances.

**Cicero**. This Roman political leader of the first century B.C. was also revered as a great writer and stylist. Known to every early modern schoolboy, he is cited in Act II, scene 6 of *Dépit amoureux* as one of the **Latin** authorities dear to the tutor **Métaphraste**. In *Le Médecin malgré lui*, **Sganarelle** attributes to Cicero the common **proverb**, "One shouldn't put one's finger between the bark and the tree," but manages to disfigure it in a ridiculous manner. **Bobinet** claims that the **Count of Escarbagnas**, his pupil, is capable of dealing with Cicero's epistles, but modifies this by admitting that the boy is only writing a theme that he himself has dictated! The stupid young count, who has not gotten past rudimentary grammar, is taking too much time even with a simple dictation.

**Cicognini**, **Giacinto Andrea** (1606–1660). Author of an Italian version of the **Dom Juan** story, *Il Convitato di Pietra*, that Molière almost certainly used in constructing his *Dom Juan*. Less well known are Molière's debts to *Le Gelosie fortunate del principe Rodrigo*, which suggested several passages in *Dom Garcie de Navarre*. Cicognini was known as the major bridge between Italian literature and the **Spanish** theater of the *siglo de oro*.

**Cidippe (***Psyché***)**. The less glib of the heroine's jealous sisters, this role was perhaps taken by **Mlle**. **Marotte**, the future bride of **La Grange**, who was not as experienced an actress as her partner, **Mlle**. **Beauval**. Like her sister, Cidippe laments Psyche's greater popularity and denies the younger sibling any advantage in beauty. She is just as ineffective as her sister in modifying her behavior to imitate Psyche's openness and **politeness**. When they accost **Agénor** and **Cléomène** in the second scene, they show that they are both guileless and inconsiderate. They are downright rude when Psyche tries to provide them with husbands "on the rebound." Cidippe is as pleased as **Aglaure** when they learn of Psyche's impending sacrifice, and the two seem to gloat morbidly at the execution place until Psyche can get rid of them. When summoned to **Cupid's** magical home by their lonesome sister, Cidippe is instantly filled with envy. She is clearly undeserving of Psyche's kindness, a disgusting and ill–mannered pest.

**Claudine (***George Dandin***)**. This **lady's maid** is an accomplice of her mistress in flirtation and in ways an even more effective flirt herself. She deals very effectively with the awkward advances of **Lubin**, refusing him kisses and escaping his groping hands. But she does not rebuff him completely, perhaps in case he can be of some further use. Any objective observer would see that he has no chance with her, but his own mania is as strong as that of an **Alceste**, and their conversations are a kind of distorted mirror image of the scenes between the misanthrope and his beloved, quite opposed to the ones involving Dandin and **Angélique**. Unlike Lubin, Claudine is no country bumpkin. She speaks as well as her mistress and shows it, especially in the compliment she pays to **Clitandre** when he thanks her for her assistance. Dandin is right to call her a "dessalée," a completely self–possessed and disabused personality. Moreover, it is clear from her banter with Clitandre that she has set her own sights on an aristocratic lover and would not shy away from serving as a "pis aller" once he has tired of Angélique. She plays along cleverly with the denials of guilt in Act I and warns her mistress of the husband's approach in Act II. In the final act, she prudently counsels breaking off the amorous chatter and getting inside before the tryst is discovered. Since **Mlle**. **Beauval** did not join the **King's Troupe** until 1670, the original Claudine was in all probability **Mlle**. **de Brie**.

**Cléante** (*L'Avare*). The son of **Harpagon** complains often about his father's excessive thrift and its affect on his wardrobe, but he longs to provide **money** to **Mariane** and her indigent and ailing mother. Thus, he arranges with his valet **La Flèche** and the dishonest agent **Maître Simon** to contact a lender who will extend him an illegal loan, only to find out that the creditor would be his own father. The scenes in Act II where he goes over the outrageous contract and then engages in mutual denunciation with Harpagon are some of the finest in the play. Cléante did not hesitate to confide in his sister **Élise** that he planned to run off with Mariane as soon as he accumulated enough cash, but his intentions to her are couched in charitable **language** and his sweetheart later tells **Frosine** that his visits have been most respectful. During the "feast" his father hosts in honor of his own intentions for Mariane in Act III, Cléante upstages the old man, passionately kissing the hand of his "future stepmother" and presenting her with a diamond **ring** snatched from Harpagon's own hand. He also succeeds in replacing his father's disgusting dishes with fashionable catered items he has ordered. He is not a party to La Flèche's theft of the strongbox, but after his father tricks him into admitting his feelings for Mariane in the fourth act, he no doubt feels justified when he learns of the robbery. In the final scene of the play, he comes to bargain with his father, offering the money in return for the hand of Mariane — a deal that the miser readily accepts.

**Cléante** (*Le Malade imaginaire*). Suitor to **Angélique**, this young man intervened to save his sweetheart from a bully's insults before the play began — a confrontation that is recounted in the third person before they begin their duet in Act II. Cléante has managed to sneak into the house **disguised** as a substitute music master, a disguise so effective that it originally surprises **Toinette**, who knows him. We learn that Cléante and Angélique have exchanged **letters** of mutual intent to marry before the action opens. When they meet on stage (II, 3), she is so startled that she almost gives away the secret, but she cleverly covers her amazement by saying that the teacher resembles a man who saved her in a **dream**. Through Cléante's ingenuity, they manage to communicate in song under the guise of singing an opera duet. He pledges his devotion and receives the desired assurance from her that she would rather die than comply with her father's wishes. When **Argan** almost uncovers their ruse by discovering that there are no words on the pages before them, Cléante fools him with the news that a new method of musical notation has been invented that combines the words and the notes. Dismissed by the exasperated father, he waits until Angélique is free and speaks to her in her room for a minute before **Béline** espies them. We learn the content of their discussion from little **Louison**, who was present but apparently less than enthralled with the amorous goings–on. She reports to her father that Cléante said, "I don't know how many things . . . this and that. He said he liked her and that she was the prettiest girl in the world." Then he knelt before her and kissed her hands before heeding Angélique's urging to withdraw. He does not return until the last scene, where he sadly learns of Argan's death and tries to console his sweetheart. We do not get a chance to hear his reaction to her grim vow of chastity, for her father reanimates at that instant. He quickly joins her in asking Argan's blessing, throwing himself on his knees to plead with the hypochondriac. When the stubborn Argan makes the ridiculous request that he become a **doctor**, Cléante takes him at his word and promises to become a physician "and even a pharmacist" if it will garner the old man's support. He willingly joins in **Béralde's** more convenient scheme to persuade Argan that he can be a doctor himself, and we can imagine that he dons a disguise to appear as one of the Doctors who examines the Bachelierus during the ceremony. According to the usual casting pattern, this role should go to **La Grange**, who generally played the young lovers. He had already been in analogous situations in *Le Sicilien*, disguised as a painter, and in *Le Médecin malgré lui*, as an apothecary. This role is mainly demanding not for its dialogue, but for its singing. However, Cléante gives an elaborate disclaimer that he does not really have a singer's voice and is only performing in order to allow Angélique to sing her parts. This would allow for less than perfect vocal execution.

**Cléante** (*Tartuffe*). Brother–in–law of **Orgon**, Cléante is a dignified and persuasive character who wears the cloak of *raisonneur* in the play, although reason is not a very effective weapon against the likes of **Tartuffe**. His sister **Elmire** proves the more practical of the two, with her subtle understanding and manipulation of emotions and her excellent self–control. After joining the rest of the family in teasing the obstreperous **Mme. Pernelle** in the first scene, Cléante buttonholes Orgon as soon as the latter enters the house, anxious to press the young people's plans for **marriage**. He is drawn into a discussion of **religious** devotion by Orgon's foolish "Poor man!" exchange with **Dorine**, and expounds at length on the differences between real, humble piety and the ostentatious spectacle adopted by the "falsely devout." Even eloquent words can seldom convince a true believer, and the only upshot of the argument is to make Orgon unwilling to discuss the **children's** fate. Cléante apparently allows Orgon to evade him while he springs the bad news on **Mariane**, forgives Tartuffe's near–seduction of Elmire, and banishes **Damis**. It is only at the beginning of the fourth act that Cléante reappears to confront Tartuffe, who is by then so strongly entrenched in control of the family wealth and secrets that he is able to parry Cléante's good sense with clever Jesuitical phrases that constantly play off intent against effect and private versus general interests. Cléante soon surrenders the initiative to his sister. His main function in the final act is to restrain Orgon's emotions, lest he commit some further folly that would plunge him deeper into trouble. His last speech is a truly Christian appeal for mercy and reconciliation on the part of all. It seems probable that this role was taken by the distinguished actor **La Thorillière**, who was sent along with La Grange to plead the play's case before the King after its second banning.

**Cléanthis (*Amphitryon*).** **Sosie's** wife must have been played by one of the senior actresses of the troupe, either **Madeleine Béjart** or **Catherine de Brie**. She is described by **Mercury** as a prude and has been married to the **slave** for fifteen years. Yet she becomes very aroused while observing the tryst between **Jupiter** and **Alcmène** and obviously seeks something analogous when she approaches the man she believes to be her war–weary husband. However, it is actually Mercury, who, unlike his chief, has no desire to use his human **disguise** to sample mortal **love**. In fact, if he has a weakness, it is his malice in irritating humans to the point of exasperation. He actually reproaches her for her former good behavior, implying he wouldn't mind if she were unfaithful, for "I prefer convenient vice to tiresome virtue" (I, 4). When she confronts Sosie in the second act, he is concerned primarily with ascertaining her virtue, however, for he has just witnessed the horrible scene between his master and mistress and fears a parallel cuckoldry for himself. Thus, when Cléanthis recounts how she was rebuffed by Mercury, he leaps up joyfully shouting, "Vivat Sosie!" (II, 3). Confused by Sosie's line of questioning and not entirely satisfied with his pretext of drunken amnesia, she reminds him of his taunt about unfaithfulness, but he quickly shunts her onto a different topic. When he proposes a reconciliation along the model of what Jupiter manages, she threatens instead to punch him in the nose. Yet one senses that her reaction to seeing the two Amphitryons simultaneously in the final act ("You're up there, and I see you right here!") will pave the way for reacceptance of her seemingly wayward husband. If not, as he says, "too bad for you!"

*Clélie.* A multi–volume, 13,000–page adventure novel by **Madeleine de Scudéry**, published between 1654 and 1660. Supposedly set at the time of the overthrow of the Tarquins in **Rome**, it contains almost entirely imaginary events that often relate to contemporary Parisian **love** affairs in *roman à clef* fashion. The first volume contains the famous Map of Tenderness recalled by **Cathos** and **Magdelon** in *Les Précieuses ridicules*, where they specifically mention such "towns" as Billets–Doux (love letters), Petits–Soins (caring thoughts), Billets–Galants (playful notes), and Jolis–Vers (pretty poems). The rather sterile romance between the title character and her admirer, Aronce, is also cited by Magdelon. In *Sganarelle*, old **Gorgibus** laments that his daughter **Célie** speaks more often of *Clélie* than of God.

**Cléomène** (*Psyché*).  The slightly more talkative of two friendly princes, Cléomène was probably played by **La Grange**.  The pair comes courting in the first act.  Avoiding the unwanted attention of **Aglaure** and **Cidippe** as politely as they can, they explain to **Psyche** that they have both fallen in **love** with her and are such perfect friends that they have made a pact.  They shall propose simultaneously and the one preferred will get both principalities to offer to the bride.  This extraordinary proposal is treated with respect by Psyche, who tells them that their worthiness is too equal to allow a choice.  She considers her own merits to be too few to break up a beautiful friendship, and instead offers the men her sisters as a *pis aller*.  When they protest, she goes further and virtually orders them to marry Aglaure and Cidippe, but they deny that she can dispose of their love in any way other than to accept or reject it.  In any case, the sisters answer in such a rude manner that there can be no question of an engagement.  The princes return in the second act with an offer to defend Psyche from the monster that **Venus** will send to devour her, but she dismisses them with her thanks.  Unable to recover from their heartbreak and grief, the pair dies.  Psyche meets them when Venus brings her to the underworld in Act IV.

**Cléon** (*Les Amants magnifiques*).  Son to the **astrologer Anaxarque**, this character is little more than a foil for his father's description of how he has arranged the false miracle of **Venus's** appearance.  He appears only in Act IV, scene 3 and has only two lines.  He may have been played by a hireling.

**Cléonice** (*Les Amants magnifiques*).  Though she is described as **Ériphile's confidante**, this is not entirely accurate, since the circumspect Princess shares no emotions with her.  Instead, she is a lady of the **court** whom Ériphile criticizes for having a bit too tolerant a taste for artistic endeavors, since her house serves as a refuge for all the importunate entertainers of the realm.  Cléonice takes this comment graciously and later tells the others of the harsh punishment that has befallen the disgraced **Anaxarque**.  The part was probably played by **Madeleine Béjart** or **Catherine de Brie**.

**Cléonte** (*Le Bourgeois gentilhomme*).  A modest, elegant role perfectly fitted to **La Grange**, who would play opposite **Armande Béjart** as **Lucile**.  The young lovers do not get on stage until late in the play (Act III), but they debut with an impressive **lovers' spite** sequence that is the longest such passage in the canon, extending over scenes 8 to 10.  In this version the master and his man **Covielle** first refuse to speak to the women, Lucile and **Nicole**, despite much coaxing and caressing.  Their unexplained silence drives the women to distraction and they turn their backs on the men, forcing a reversed profusion of tender words and entreaties.  Finally it is determined by the **servants**, always the franker of the classes, that the dispute arises from a misunderstood gesture that was designed to do nothing but keep the lovers' secrets intact.  Cléonte has gained the unqualified support of his future mother–in–law because she believes that he is not so haughty that he will cut off relations with his lower–born relatives.  In his speech to **Jourdain**, Cléonte explains that his parents were above the Jourdains in standing, royal officers of some distinction, perhaps for several generations. Cléonte himself has had a military career (perhaps in the artillery or engineers, that attracted many well educated *nobles de robe* and were positions that would have been denied to a commoner). He denies having the status of "gentleman," which required hereditary **nobility** on all sides of the family stretching back over several generations. But his family is clearly upwardly mobile and most distinguished — an excellent match for the likes of Lucile. That Cléonte avoids asserting this superiority speaks for his modesty, dignity, and general *honnêteté*. He is not too proud, however, to play his role as heir to the Ottoman Empire to the hilt, with many mysterious words and gestures that fool Jourdain. Ingenuous, meritorious, and well spoken, Cléonte stands out against the sophisticated but unprincipled **Dorante**, tipping the balance of virtue easily to the side of the gilded **bourgeoisie**.

**Clerk** (*L'Avare*). A nonspeaking role, the clerk accompanies the **police Commissioner** and takes notes on his investigation.

**Clermont, College of**. This great Renaissance institution of learning, located in the heart of the **Latin** Quarter was, according to **La Grange** and **Vivot**, the site of Molière's pre–university schooling. Among his classmates was the **Prince of Conti**, who would later become the patron of the itinerant troupe. Much has been suggested about Molière having studied at the college with the skeptical philosopher **Gassendi**, but in fact Gassendi did not come to the school until after Molière, a very quick and able student, would have finished. Assuming that La Grange is correct in saying that Molière managed to study **law** before becoming involved with the **Illustre Théâtre** and that he did, as evidence indicates, work at least for a short time as *tapissier du roi*, he could not have attended Gassendi's classes except as a curious spectator. He might, of course, have encountered Gassendi *ex cathedra*, perhaps in the household of another likely classmate, young **La Mothe Le Vayer**. Certainly the latter would have been a help in transmitting Gassendi's ideas, which for the most part were recorded in a turgid, almost impenetrable Latin — quite a challenge even for a good humanist like Molière.

**Climène** (*La Critique de l'École des femmes*). A lady with rather vulgar and exaggerated manners, this enemy of Molière's **theater** was played by **Mlle. Du Parc**, who also played a similar role in *L'Impromptu de Versailles*.

**Climène** (*Le Sicilien*). She is described in the dramatis personae as the sister of **Adraste**, but in scene 9, when he describes to **Hali** his stratagem for eloping with **Isidore**, he says he will use a young **slave** girl for his purpose. The role seems to have undergone a change at some point, for the guide booklet to the **Ballet des Muses** lists it as a slave girl named **Zaïde**, played by **Armande Béjart**. In any case, she appears with very little preparation in scene 14, pretending to be a battered wife who seeks **Dom Pèdre's** protection against her husband's **jealous** rages. This is just a pretext for getting her into the house, where she changes clothes with Isidore, allowing the latter to leave with her "reconciled spouse," in reality Adraste. Once the couple is in the clear, Climène emerges, lifts her veil, and rails against Dom Pèdre and all others jealous enough to try to confine women. Interesting that Molière should give such a triumphantly adulterous speech to his wife, who was already suspected of extramarital flirtations at the very least!

**Clitandre** (*L'Amour médecin*). **La Grange** almost surely played this young lover, who does not appear until the third act of the play, though he is mentioned in the first as having already proposed **marriage** and impressed the silent **Lucinde** in the process. Once he does appear, he wittily explains to **Sganarelle** that he cures not by purging and bleeding, but by "words, sounds, letters, charms, and jeweled **rings**." Taking Sganarelle's pulse instead of the girl's, he fools the old man by saying that he can tell her pulse through family resemblance. After pleasing Lucinde with his words of love, he tells her father that he has practiced a mental cure already, and that she had only suffered from an "unhinged imagination" because of her "depraved desire" to marry. He pretends that he will complete the cure by agreeing to marry her himself, despite his profound disgust for the practice. Since this is just the kind of talk Sganarelle had wanted to hear, he complies completely, even allowing the gift of an engagement ring (as a medical charm) and the signing of a contract before a **notary** (supposedly Clitandre's apothecary). Then the couple hurries off to complete the "other, later remedies that will cure her completely of this fantasy." It is a light, charming role well suited to La Grange's acting strengths and to his personality, still lying within the technical domain of trickery, but brought off with such gentleness and consideration as to qualify for something better.

**Clitandre** (*Les Femmes savantes*). Like others of his ilk, this character was played by **La Grange**. His hallmark in this play is self-professed **sincerity**. In Act I, scene 2, he makes a clear profession of love to **Henriette** in front of the woman he had previously wooed, **Armande**, explaining how her refusal to grant his wish led him to find consolation with her more agreeable sister. He explains to Henriette that he is skeptical about gaining **Philaminte's** approval as long as she is in the grip of the detestable **Trissotin**. He relates that he had read the poetaster's works and formed a mental picture of him that turned out to be entirely accurate when they actually met. On his way to recruit help for his proposal, he is waylaid by Henriette's aunt **Bélise**, who assumes that he is one of her imaginary lovers and tests his patience. At the end of Act III, he has gained Chrysale's consent and hopes to realize his hopes, but in the next act he runs afoul of Armande again as she is maligning him to her mother. Their rather bitter conversation, which expands on their discordant ideas of **love** and **marriage**, does nothing to help his case with Philaminte, nor does his subsequent argument with Trissotin over the nature of wit and the good taste of the **court** in literary manners. Clitandre implicitly defends royal policy, including the trimming of the pension lists for writers. He is full of hope again at the end of the fourth act and accompanies **Chrysale** to present his demands in the fifth. Unfortunately, it looks as if his cause is doomed when the father predictably wilts under pressure from his wife. But **Ariste's** ruse of the forged bankruptcy **letters** allows him to show his generosity, and he wins the consent of Philaminte, only to be stopped surprisingly by Henriette herself, who refuses to go through with a wedding that will ruin him financially. This last minute objection gives the young man grounds to be both sad and happy, for Ariste's revelations assure him that he will not only have a wife, but an economical one at that. This Clitandre is most remarkable for both his political orthodoxy and his ability to put a positive spin on **Alceste's** doctrines of frankness.

**Clitandre** (*George Dandin*). **Lubin** tells us that this courtier is a viscount and that he has already deployed the standard means of seduction before the plot opens: bribing **servants**, conniving messengers, and extending secret approaches to the lady desired. Given this seductive acumen, he seems to be experienced in the area. It is surprising when we find him denying outright the accusations brought against him by **Dandin** in Act I that he has not actually met with the lady up to that point. If this is true, their remarkable interplay in fending off the charges is an example of a natural fit of personalities, a natural complement too strong to impede. Clitandre speaks the **language** of hollow **politeness**, mastering the forms of avoiding both conflict and obligation of any kind. He quickly sums up Dandin as a poltroon and forces his advantage further by threatening to run him through the guts with his sword if he is lying. Then he conveniently avoids doing so by nonchalantly accepting the excuses forced by **Monsieur de Sotenville** and attributing to him the sparing of Dandin's life. Alone with **Angélique**, Clitandre finds she is more difficult to control than her husband, as she alternates between come–hither invitations and gentle rebuffs. In their parting scene in the third act, he fully assumes the language and manner of a "soupirant," begging her for more time together and expressing **jealousy** toward her husband. As an accomplished adulterer, he surpasses his fellow aristocrat **Dorante** of *Le Bourgeois gentilhomme*, since the latter is merely courting an unengaged widow. Like Angélique, he is in some ways closer to the amoral courtiers of British Restoration comedy than to many of Molière's young lovers. It certainly marked a new direction for the talents of **La Grange**.

**Clitandre** (*Le Misanthrope*). Differing from several other characters by this name in other plays, this Clitandre is neither a leading man nor a handsome suitor/seducer, but a foolish and foppish **court** nobleman who is sidekick, and even alter ego, to **Acaste**. The pair are virtually interchangeable, and have been played as such. Clitandre is a little less glib than his fellow marquis, but seems no less vain or frivolous. His approach to courting Célimène is exactly the same: not so much a matter of passion or even of pleasure as an opportunity to "take coup" in the constant game against the opposite sex. Of course, Clitandre and Acaste compare **letters**, as they probably compare everything else in their existence. Indeed, one seems incapable of standing without the other. Obviously, this role was an exception to the Clitandres of **La Grange**, and it is unclear which of the other actors in the troupe might have taken it.

**Clitidas** (*Les Amants magnifiques*). Clitidas is a self–proclaimed clown or **court** jester who has through his humor gained the right to express himself freely in the entourage of **Princess Aristione**. He is on very friendly terms with **Sostrate**, so much so that the normally reticent general shares his secret feelings for **Ériphile** with him. In turn, the jester greatly admires Sostrate, to the point that he tells the princess he would marry him himself if he were in her place. Clitidas is also held in some esteem by the rival princes **Iphicrate** and **Timoclès**, who have already consulted him, and perhaps bribed him to represent their opposed interests. Ériphile, for her part, also places great trust in him, since she questions him closely on the intimate matter of Sostrate's opinions. He is bold enough to probe the princess's heart by lying to her and telling her that the general is in **love** with one of her ladies in waiting, just to see how she will react. But Clitidas proves to be less than the controlling figure he promises to be at the outset. He does not succeed in moving Sostrate's case forward or in eliciting any sign of recognition from Ériphile. His big moment comes in Act V, when he delivers the account of how Sostrate saved Aristione from a rampaging boar, thus assuring his **marriage** with her daughter. It is a tale in the burlesque mode, with saucy interjections on the part of the teller and a nonchalant attitude toward excuses and instances of personal cowardice on his part. The speech typifies Clitidas as a purely verbal virtuoso, capable of hobnobbing with his betters and turning an elegant sentence, but far from the energetic, manipulative servant of the **Mascarille** era. The part allowed the ailing Molière to take somewhat of a rest, for it concentrated his lines in a few scenes and spared him any strenuous physical activity.

**Clymène** (*Les Fâcheux*). A poetic and intellectual pest, she arrives in Act II, scene 4, along with her foil **Orante**, to ask **Éraste** to mediate a typical salon dispute on whether a **jealous** lover is better than a lover without jealousy. Clymène takes the side of jealousy, claiming that only a lukewarm admirer would fail to show signs of it. After letting them rail on for some time, Éraste cleverly slips out of the trap by decreeing, "The jealous man loves more, but the other loves much better."

**Clymène** (*La Princesse d'Élide*). This unlisted character appears only in the fifth *intermède*, where she and **Philis** sing a supposedly consoling song to the Princess. The role was undoubtedly played by Mlle. de La Barre or Mlle. Hillaire, the two female singers listed as participating in the song that closes the play.

**Colbert, Jean–Baptiste** (1619–1683). **Louis XIV's** most trusted and able minister from 1661, when he aided in deposing **Fouquet**, to around 1671, when he began to fall out of favor, to be replaced eventually by Louvois. Like Molière, Colbert came from a family with roots in the cloth trade in north central France. He first rose to prominence as an accomplice of Mazarin. Colbert fostered a protectionist policy toward French idustry, which had been badly reduced by Dutch and other foreign competition, and strongly promoted the nation's colonial expansion in **America**, India, and Africa, where he invested heavily in the slave trade. It has been pointed out that Colbert opposed Molière in artistic issues, where he favored Le Brun over the playwright's friend **Mignard**. However, Colbert was also a patron of the theater and oversaw the artists' pension lists in which Molière and his actors figured prominently. He may have come in for some *persiflage* in *Les Femmes savantes*, where ridicule is cast on one of his pet projects, astronomical observation. The completion of the Royal Observatory coincided with the production of the play. Colbert's decline was due to his reluctance to endorse the growing expenditures lavished on the royal family, including the construction of **Versailles**.

**Colin** (*George Dandin*). This sleepy, blockheaded swain appears only in one scene (III, 4), where he is involved in an extended **lazzi** sequence as **servant** and master search for each other onstage, only to collide eventually. He is then so afraid of being **beaten** that he almost flees before **Dandin** can mollify him and send him on an errand to fetch the **Sotenvilles** for another ambush on their daughter and her lover. Colin fails to respond when **Angélique** calls to him to open the door in Act III, scene 6. The part may have been taken by a wage–actor, since it would be difficult to double and the play already calls for four males and a cross–dressed **Hubert** as Madame de Sotenville.

**College**. In Molière's time, the "collège" was an institution of secondary learning administered by one of several branches of the Church. Molière attended the prestigious **Collège de Clermont**. After a liberal arts education in college, students specialized in one of the traditional disciplines of the university, such as **law, medicine**, theology, or **philosophy**. When **Monsieur Jourdain** speaks wistfully of the wonders of **education**, his wife jokingly asks him if he's going to college at his age "in order to get a good whipping." "Why not?" he replies, "Would to God I could be there now and get my hide tanned in front of everybody, if only I could know what they learn in college!"

**Comédie–ballet**. It may truly be said that this transitional art form was an innovation of Molière's. It involved the interweaving of a play, usually a one– or three–act comedy, with a series of **musical and dance** numbers. From *Les Fâcheux* onward through *Le Mariage forcé, La Princesse d'Élide, L'Amour médecin, Pastorale comique, Mélicerte, Le Sicilien, George Dandin, Monsieur de Pourceaugnac, Les Amants magnifiques, Le Bourgeois gentilhomme*, and *Le Malade imaginaire*, the genre continues to develop, eventually reaching five–act form.  Sometimes the themes of the musical interludes would very closely relate to the play material, while at other times, they would remain more distant or symbolic.  The comedy–ballet is a forerunner of both the French opera, which would rise under **Lully**, and the popular *vaudeville* genre that would flourish in the following two centuries.  Though some of Molière's contemporaries, such as **Quinault**, would develop noted careers as opera librettists, none would equal, and few would even challenge, his preeminence in the comedy–ballet.

See Marie–Françoise Christout, *Le Ballet de Cour de Louis XIV (1643–1672)* (Paris: Picard, 1967).

**Comédie–Française**.  The national French acting troupe, also known in its early days as the Théâtre–Français, was formed by the merger of the company of the Hôtel Guénégaud and the **Hôtel de Bourgogne** in August 1680.  Combining elements of Molière's company with other actors from the **Marais** and provincial troupes, the Hôtel Guénégaud troupe, named for the financier's residence where their theater was located, bridged the gap between the death of Molière and the ultimate fusion of the major French companies by royal decree.  When the Guénégaud actors joined with the remnants of a depleted Hôtel de Bourgogne company, they became the one official, subsidized French–language **theater in Paris**.  Its only nearby rivals were the Théâtres de la Foire that rose to importance on the periphery of the city around the turn of the century, and the **Italians**, who were eventually banned from the capital through the latter end of **Louis XIV's** reign.  The company continued to use the theater of the Hôtel Guénégaud until building a new one in the Saint–Germain–des–Prés neighborhood in 1687.

**Commander's Statue (*Dom Juan*)**.  The title of Commander was generally associated with a nobleman in one of the military orders of the clergy, such as the Knights of Calatrava in Spain or the Knights of Malta in France.  In some cases, membership in such an order required the gentleman to take minor holy orders and to be tonsured.  Molière's Commander is descended in theatrical tradition from the Spanish nobleman of Tirso's *Burlador* whom Don Juan killed in order to elope with Dona Ana.  However, in Molière's play, there is no indication that he is a relative of **Elvire**, whose brothers make their own quest for vengeance against the abductor.  Instead, he becomes a symbol of **Dom Juan's** transgressions against holiness, for by murdering a member of the clergy, the eponym has placed himself within the purview of canon law.  Sganarelle mentions this as evidence of his master's impiety early in the play, to which Dom Juan playfully responds, "What, didn't I kill him very properly?"  There remains a distant link between the Commander and Elvire, however, for in her case, too, there was infringement of a sacred barrier, the convent walls.  Also, Dom Juan and Sganarelle stumble upon the Commander's sepulchre in Act III shortly after their highly ironic encounter with **Dom Carlos** and **Dom Alonse**, where the brothers have to renounce their revenge because the rake has just saved the life of one of them. The aesthetic admiration of the pair for the fine workmanship of the tomb soon gives way to a typical contest between Sganarelle's superstition and Dom Juan's atheistic swagger. The nobleman forces his quivering servant to invite the statue to dinner, eliciting an unexpected and terrifying nod from the stony guest. As bidden, the statue arrives in time for Dom Juan's feast in Act IV, following on the heels of **Dom Louis**, **Monsieur Dimanche**, and Elvire. Rejecting the politeness of seating and illumination that Dom Juan had used to disarm his previous visitors, he comes not to share the rake's bounty, but only to deliver a counter–invitation that must be taken seriously. In the concluding act, when Dom Juan has effectively used his **disguise** of **religious** conversion to dispose of his family, his in–laws, and society in general, it remains for the statue to enforce the broken laws and to accompany the sinner, hand in hand, into hell. Nevertheless, it is clear from the Commander's speech that he represents a sacred rather than an infernal force, for he emphasizes, "Those whose way is lit by Heaven have no need of earthly light!" Molière employs the Commander as a means of raising the stakes in the play from a matter of personal misbehavior and family revenge to a more universal and **philosophical** plane.

**Commedia dell'arte.** A very ancient tradition on the Italian stage tracing back, some believe, directly to Imperial Roman theater companies. By the early seventeenth century, when Italian players of the commedia tradition installed themselves in Paris, their style had a number of unique characteristics. For one thing, the company in Paris did not work from elaborate scripts, but rather from loose scenarios. They were free to ad lib both actions and words. The latter were all the more free, since much of the French audience did not understand all the dialogue. Only under the later regency of the Duke of Orléans did the commedia actors begin to speak French on stage. Gestures were extremely important and stylized. They were emphasized also by the fact that most of the actors wore **masks** that permitted little or no facial expression. An exception to this trend was the great **Scaramouche**, who anticipated Molière by acting with a bare face and studiously perfecting the whole range of smiles and **grimaces**. Besides their masks, the characters of the commedia wore distinctive stylized clothing that constituted a kind of uniform, instantly recognizable to the public. Everyone could distinguish **Trivelin** or Arlequin by their clothes, which never changed from play to play. All of the roles were taken by stock characters, whose circumstances could vary, but who never altered their identities. The typical plot of a scenario revolved around love interests and included ancillary rivalries based on money or power between the various comic actors, or *zanni*. Lacking a verbal dimension for much of their comedy, the *zanni* perfected the art of sight gags or *lazzi*. These could be built around almost any kind of situation, but usually contained some fighting and the use of the slapstick, a hinged stick or bat that delivered a terrific smack while producing minimal impact on the actor. A great deal of the stage business in Molière's productions, at least as far as reported in the texts, owes a debt to the tradition of the commedia, especially in plays such as *Dom Juan*, where Molière actually used existing scenarios in fashioning his version of the story. Other debts include some to characters of the commedia, such as the Dottore or **Doctor** Balourdo, originally a product of the great medical faculty at Bologna, whom Molière transformed into personalities from the Flying Doctor through the four physicians of *L'Amour Médecin* to the odious **Diafoirus** clan and their minion **Purgon** in *Le Malade imaginaire*. The *miles gloriosus* was another element of the commedia, usually in the form of a boastful Spanish *capitan*. This inspired not only would–be bravados such as **Sganarelle** in *Le Cocu imaginaire*, but also bullies like **Arnolphe**, as well as many a shady *bretteur* who lurked in from the wings. Finally, the commedia scenarios often involved festive music, parades, and dances, which anticipated Molière's development of the French *comédie–ballet*.

**Commissioner** (*L'Avare*). This **police** investigator, who wishes he had a piece of gold for every thief he's hanged, appears with his clerk in Act V to look for **Harpagon's** stolen strongbox. No doubt frustrated by the vagueness of **Maître Jacques's** testimony about a largish–smallish, reddish–greyish box, he eventually lets Harpagon do most of the talking and sticks to taking notes. Only in the final scene does he speak up, asking who is going to pay for the cost of his inquiry (and probably bribe him to keep quiet about the rest of the proceedings).

**Commissioner** (*L'École des maris*). The *commissaire* was a **police** official roughly equivalent to a constable. In this play, **Sganarelle** seeks out the officer on his own initiative when he decides to meddle publicly in the elopement he thinks has taken place involving **Léonor** and **Valère**. The police would be interested parties, of course, because elopement was a crime. But Sganarelle plans to arrange the French equivalent of a shotgun wedding by compelling the young couple to accept matrimony in lieu of their illegal union. The commissioner goes along with this, reminding the other characters that no undue force should be exerted on the runaways. He is right to do so, since any **marriage** by compulsion would be invalid; the youngsters have to agree to wed of their own free will. This commissioner denies Sganarelle's allegations about rampant police corruption so vehemently that we suspect he might be suggesting that a discrete gratification would not be out of place.

**Company of the Holy Sacrament**. A secret organization within the Roman Catholic church, this company spanned a wide variety of social levels and maintained a large and sophisticated intelligence apparatus. Though the group had vague pietistic goals, its main preoccupation seems to have been to find and persecute its own enemies. **Louis XIV's** lieutenant of police had the company infiltrated and the King ordered it dissolved, fearing that it might have a pernicious political influence. Although it was officially nonexistent during the **Quarrel of the School for Wives** and the *Tartuffe* affair, it seems to have continued to exercise some influence, perhaps from surviving local cells. **Dom**

**Juan** refers to such dark powers during his explanation of his mock conversion in Act V. **Arsinoé's** hints at a secret Devout Party power structure in *Le Misanthrope*, with "machines" that can effect even the royal **court**, confirm the persistence of some kind of secret intelligence organization in the Church. **Harlay de Péréfixe**, the archbishop who raised the ecclesiastical ban against *Tartuffe*, is suspected of being an important member of the original Company of the Holy Sacrament, as is the **parliamentary** president **Lamoignon**, who raised a similar outcry. So was the **Prince de Conti**, who was accepted for membership after he made public penance for some of his most blatant scandals. Luckily for Molière, **Louis XIV** did not fall under the influence of the *dévots* until well after the dramatist's death.

*Comtesse d'Escarbagnas, La.* This one–act prose comedy first performed at the **Ballet des Ballets** in December 1671 is unique in that it contains no roles for Molière, **Armande Béjart**, or **Mlle. de Brie**. All of them were needed elsewhere in the production, since the play was only a small part of the festivities. The ballet contained bits of all other recent **court** ballets as a tribute to **Monsieur's** new second wife, the **Princess Palatine**. Molière's play has sometimes been characterized as little more than a platform for songs and dances. Originally, in the seven court performances given at **Saint–Germain**, it encapsulated a now–lost pastoral. In later **Paris** performances, from July 1672 onward, the pastoral was replaced for economical reasons by another short play. At first the companion piece was a refurbished version of *Le Mariage forcé* with new music by **Charpentier**, then *L'Amour médecin*, *Le Fin Lourdaud*, and *Les Fâcheux*, respectively. Performances in October and November fell at a time when Molière was still in mourning for his son, born in mid–September and buried on October 12. It was still in performance in February 1673, just before the premiere of *Le Malade imaginaire* and Molière's death, so it was not published during his lifetime and first appeared as part of the 1682 collected **edition**.

There really is no plot, just a series of conversations strung together, in which **Julie**, her secret lover the **Viscount**, and the **Countess** talk with each other, as well as with the latter's **servants** and members of her household, then finally with her amorous visitor **Thibaudier** and the indignant **Harpin**. If Thibaudier is a small–scale version of **Trissotin**, then Harpin is a kind of bush–league **Alceste**, ranting at the Countess for her duplicitous policy of keeping numerous suitors waiting for her profession of favor. The play closes abruptly with the announcement of a reconciliation between his family and Julie's that will allow the Viscount to cease his feigned courtship of the Countess and openly propose to his beloved.

Despite the minimal nature of the play, it still involved a certain amount of experimentation and development on the author's part. Simply doing without his own comic talents was something new. So was the creation of a short but memorable satirical role for **Marie Raguenau** and a sweetheart role for **Mlle. Beauval**. The fact that the show involved several young hirelings in the roles of the Count, **Criquet**, **Jeannot**, and **Andrée** was another innovation. The Viscount's attempt to woo Julie with verses that are obviously not his own and not addressed to her is an interesting development, as are the love gifts that Thibaudier bestows on the Countess. The mention of so many specific Parisian locales, albeit from the distance of **Angoulême**, leads one to wonder whether the mature Molière was planning a return to very topical satire on the model of *Les Précieuses ridicules*.

**Condé, Louis II de Bourbon, prince de** (1621–1686). This towering figure, who had defeated the last major **Spanish** incursion into France at Rocroi in 1643 and later become involved in the intricate conspiracies of the Fronde revolt, had reconciled with the crown by 1658. As a "prince of the blood royal," he occupied a central place in the social and artistic life of **Paris**, and he became an important **patron** to Molière and his troupe. His support was especially important during the evolution of the *Tartuffe* affair. As a person inclined to free thinking, Condé would have naturally been attracted to Molière's attack on blind faith and manipulative hypocrisy, but his courage and generosity in sustaining a mere "comédien" went above and beyond the call of **philosophical** *noblesse oblige*. Condé is credited by the reliable **Madame de Sévigné** as the source of a famous quote about *Tartuffe* and *Dom Juan*: the reason that the devout faction was so scandalized by the plays is that they strike a blow against hypocrisy, while other authors only attack religion, and are therefore ignored by the bigots. The **Princess Palatine**, second wife of **Monsieur**, must have shared Condé's interest in Molière, since she co–sponsored some of his command performances. In the last campaign of the War of Devolution in 1667–68, Condé led a veritable blitzkrieg attack on **Franche–Comté** and thoroughly conquered the province. Though it was given back to the Holy Roman Empire in the Peace of Aachen, it was an important bargaining chip for the vital acquisition of Flanders, and Condé destroyed its defenses to such a degree that it was an easy conquest in the next war. It was to celebrate these victories that **Louis XIV** organized the **Grand Divertissement Royal de Versailles** that included *George Dandin*. Molière also hastened to dedicate *Amphitryon* to Condé, breaking his usual silence in matters of dedicatory epistles.

**Confidante**. This was one of the stock roles in intrigue comedy, and indeed in most French seventeenth–century theater. In exposition scenes, a female lead could discuss the plot situation with her confidante. They were also useful for delivering messages or passing on bits of gossip. One occasionally encounters a male confidant with similar functions. However, Molière tended to replace conventional confidantes with servants or family members, whose interests could be more easily developed as part of the plot structure.

**Conti, Armand de Bourbon, prince de** (1629–1666). This younger brother of the great **Condé** embraced Molière's troupe and lent his **patronage** to them in 1653–54 when they were in the region of **Montpellier** and visited his estate. He was then a notorious rake, suspected even of incest with his sister, who became Madame de Longueville. As governor of Guyenne and royal emissary to the **parlement** of Languedoc, he and his minions Sarasin, Cosnac, and Guilleragues took great pleasure in Molière's acting and sponsored the players during their stay in the South. But by 1657 he had reformed and, turning to the opposite extreme, become a **religious** bigot and an enemy of the **theater**. He forbade the players to use his name thenceforth and went on to write vehemently against Molière and perhaps to take part in conspiracies by members of the **Company of the Holy Sacrament** against the playwright. His *Traité de la comédie* (published posthumously in 1666), though aimed primarily at other writers, blasts *L'École des femmes* and *Dom Juan* in the preface. Nevertheless, in the 1682 biographical preface to the collected works, **La Grange** and **Vivot** mention Conti in a kindly fashion and imply that he never reneged on his support for the playwright. This fib, which was easier to pass off because the subject was dead, may have been a gesture to Conti's family, and especially his great brother, who was still probably a staunch proponent of Molière's former colleagues.

**Convents**. Though his own sister and an aunt were cloistered nuns, Molière did not seem to think highly of convents or the sheltered life they fostered. **Arnolphe** threatens to drop **Agnès** into a "stinking convent" if she does not accede to his wishes, and **Argan** later tries to frighten his girls in the same way. **Dom Juan** has abducted **Elvire** from the cloistered sanctity of a convent before forcing his affections on her. **Henriette** is not the only woman who nearly takes to a convent herself in order to avoid a disastrous **marriage** with **Trissotin**, for **Julie** makes the same threat in *Monsieur de Pourceaugnac*, though perhaps with less seriousness. A great believer in doing what comes naturally, Molière probably saw convent life as a waste of biological resources and a needless interference with the human drive toward happiness. Nevertheless, his death documents mention that he often extended charity to nuns making collections at Eastertide.

**Coqueteau la Clairière**. A Rouen author whose tragedy *Pylade et Oreste* was performed by Molière's troupe in November 1659 with very poor results.

**Coridon (*Pastorale comique*)**. **La Grange** personified this helpful sidekick, who seems to have interceded, like **Philinte** in *Le Misanthrope*, to try to smooth out **Lycas's** battles and straighten out his **love** life. Unfortunately, none of Coridon's lines are recorded in the booklet to the entertainment.

**Corinne (*Mélicerte*)**. Corinne is Mélicerte's **confidante** and appears (II, 1) only to inform her that **Daphné** and **Éroxène** have both fallen in love with **Myrtil** and asked for his hand in **marriage**. The part would probably have fallen to **Mlle. Hervé**.

**Corneille, Pierre** (1606–1684). Though this great dramatist had a long–standing affinity for the Troupe du **Marais**, Molière began performing his plays in **repertory**, perhaps at a young age, soon after the collapse of the **Illustre Théâtre** which was to have been a rival for the Marais. Among the plays listed in **La Grange's** register as having been performed after Molière's return to **Paris** are *Nicomède, Le Cid, Horace, Cinna, Le Menteur, Rodogune, Héraclius*, and *Sertorius*. In fact, Molière's command performance before the King in 1658 consisted of Corneille's political tragedy *Nicomède*, played with indifferent success, followed by a jolly farce that the monarch found more pleasing. Molière's troupe gave two of Corneille's works their premieres. The 1667 opening run of *Attila* had only middling success, with eleven performances, but ten subsequent performances in reprises were enough to qualify the tragedy for an honorable showing. The 1670 production of *Tite et Bérénice* took place in the context of a famous battle of the playwrights against **Racine's** *Bérénice*. Though most authorities gave the nod to Racine as the winner, Corneille's play held the stage of Molière's troupe for twenty–one performances, plus three more in a reprise with *Le Bourgeois gentilhomme*. This testifies to the fact that even after the loss of Racine and of **Mlle. Du Parc**, Molière's troupe was able to achieve good results even in straight tragedy, provided they had a decent text in front of them. The closest cooperation between the young comic genius and his aged peer seems to have been in the composition of *Psyché*. Having finished the versification of one complete act and a couple of scenes, Molière turned his notes over to Corneille and had him finish the play. Molière refers to this collaboration in a rather cavalier manner, but there is no evidence of bitterness on Corneille's part. It is interesting that Molière chose to sit for his best **portrait**, by his friend the artist **Mignard**, not in one of his comic costumes, but in that of Julius Caesar in Corneille's *La Mort de Pompée*, reportedly his favorite tragic role. Nevertheless, **Le Boulanger de Chalussay** mentions Molière as having failed badly in productions of *Cinna, Heraclius. Rodogune*, and *Le Cid*, before obtaining success with *L'Étourdi*.

Corneille's comedies were also admired by Molière, especially *Le Menteur (The Liar)*, which influenced several aspects of **Dom Juan**. Molière was not above quoting from Corneille's plays in highly ridiculous or comical contexts. In *Le Médecin volant*, **Sganarelle** mentions a famous line from *Le Cid* ("Rodrigue, as–tu du coeur?" ["Rodrigue, do you have courage?"]) as part of a medical hodgepodge. Sganarelle closely paraphrases a couplet from *Nicomède* as he is congratulating himself for chasing away **Valère** in *L'École des maris*. *L'École des femmes* places a line from *Sertorius* ("Je suis maître, je parle, allez, obéissez!" ["I am master, I speak, go and obey!"]) in the mouth of **Arnolphe** with equally funny results. Sganarelle, in the play by the same name, puns on Corneille's own name with the cuckold–like term Corneillius. In *Les Fâcheux*, the idiotic **theater** pest mentioned in the opening scene claims to **Éraste**, "I know the rules that make for literary perfection / And Corneille comes to read me all that he composes." He proceeds to give a plot summary of the entire action unfolding before them on the stage and even to speak the lines out loud before the actors do.

**Corneille, Thomas** (1625–1709). **Pierre's** younger brother, also a dramatist. The literary hostilities between Thomas and Molière's troupe may have been opened by the former when he wrote to the abbé de Pure that their acting had ruined a tragedy, *Oreste et Pylade*, written by his friend **Coqueteau de la Clairière**. The troupe's success with *Les Précieuses ridicules* proved, acccording to him, that "they are only fit to dabble in such trifles and that the very best play would suffer in their hands." Thomas seems to have been the butt of Molière's joke in the first act of *L'École des femmes* about a social climber who usurped the status of **gentleman** by digging a ditch around an old lot and calling himself Monsieur de l'Isle. It is known that the younger Corneille vainly did the same thing. Some critics feel he was also the model for the self–promoting dramatist **Monsieur Lysidas** in the *Critique*. Whatever Molière thought of him as an individual, he respected the man as a playwright well enough to adopt his *Dom Bertrand de Cigarral* into the troupe's **repertory**, where it remained one of their most successful pieces. On the other hand, the younger Corneille was not above pillaging Molière's material, as he showed in the rare comedies written for the  Hôtel de Bourgogne with which he tried to challenge the master: *Le Baron d'Albikrac* (1668) and *La Comtesse d'Orgeuil* (1671). Ironically, Thomas Corneille would be called on to versify and bowdlerize Molière's originally provocative text of *Dom Juan*, and this version of *Le Festin de Pierre* was the only one generally known from February 1677 until the true text was rediscovered in 1819 by Auger. Corneille's version was not replaced on stage until November 1841, at the Odéon, and not until even later by the **Comédie–Française**. It has recently been edited by Alain Niderst (Geneva: Slatkine, 2000). Corneille split the 2,000 *livres* adaptation fee paid by the troupe of the Hôtel Guénégaud with **Armande Béjart**.

**Cosmetics**. The affected girls in *Les Précieuses ridicules* are very interested in cosmetics. They concoct them at home, using lard, mutton fat, egg whites, and other ingredients to make lipstick. The frontispiece of the 1682 **edition** also shows them wearing a profusion of *mouches*, or velvet beauty spots. These were favored by **Mademoiselle de Scudéry**, whose terrible complexion was due to illness. The adepts of *préciosité* developed a complicated taxonomy of *mouches*, depending on the location on the face or body. **Sganarelle** denounces them in *L'École des maris*. The Maxims of Marriage in *L'École des femmes* also condemn "those elixirs, ointments and pommades / And a thousand ingredients that make the complexion glow" as "deadly drugs." **Philinte** asks **Alceste** in *Le Misanthrope* whether he thinks **sincerity** obliges him to tell old Émilie that she should act her age and give up excessive powder for her face. One of the things that **Dorine** reproaches in **Tartuffe** and his **servant Laurent** is that they scold the women of **Orgon's** house for their use of cosmetics and "throw away our ribbons, our rouge, and our *mouches*."

**Costume, Men's**. Costume depended on and indicated social standing in early modern France, especially in Molière's plays, where age–old costume conventions were gradually abandoned for a much more naturalistic look. In *Les Précieuses ridicules*, male costume is at issue because of the affected girls' emphasis on fashion. Regarding the unsuccessful suitors **La Grange** and **Du Croisy**, they specifically criticize the "indigence" of plumes and ribbons on their clothes, the narrowness of their breeches, and the cheapness of their gloves. In contrast, **Mascarille** is dressed in a veritable cascade of plumes, ribbons, and lace, including his *grands canons*. His breeches are described as being of the baggy *rhingrave* style that was promoted by fops of the royal entourage. He claims that his gloves are "pure Perdigeon," presumably a well–known maker. A frontispiece illustration exists that depicts in beautiful detail Mascarille's outfit. **Clitandre**, one of the foppish marquis in *Le Misanthrope*, is lacerated by **Alceste** for similar clothing and the mannerisms that accompany it: a long claw of a nail on the fifth finger (for politely scratching on the royal doors), shocking blonde wigs, huge *canons*, piles of ribbons, a vast *rhingrave*, and a silly falsetto giggle (II, 1). The descriptions of **Dom Juan's** flame–colored costume, given by the peasant **Pierrot** in his rural dialect, confirm the extravagance of foppish clothes. Pierrot refers to shirts so big that he and **Charlotte** could climb into them together, breeches "as wide as from here to Easter," lace collars at the ends of the sleeves, and so many ribbons that "it is really a pity!" No wonder this natty dresser criticizes his wife for approaching him in her **hunting** clothes when she finally catches up with him.

In *L'École des maris*, Act I, scene 1, **Sganarelle** delivers a scathing satire of the current **courtly** fashions favored by his older brother **Ariste**. In particular, he mentions small hats, vast blonde wigs that obscure eyesight, small jackets, *jabot* collars that cascade down the chest, long sleeves bedecked with lace that are cumbersome at the table, bloomer–like breeches, shoes so covered with ribbons that they make a man look like a show pigeon, and stiff *canons* that make the wearer walk as though he were saddle sore. In opposition, he favors commodious hats, short hair, small collars, long jackets that button tightly up over the belly, thigh–hugging breeches, and roomy hose and footwear. The outmoded, more middle–class nature of his attire is highlighted by an old–fashioned purse he wears at his waist.

We know that **Éraste** of *Les Fâcheux* was clad in a fashionable marquis costume, since **La Montagne** makes a nuisance of himself by fussing with the collar, brushing the jacket, straightening the *canons*, curling the wig, and eventually dropping the hat. Even **peasants** wore hats, and **Alain** engages in some elaborate hat **lazzi** in the first act of *L'École des femmes*, where **Arnolphe** keeps removing the hat from his **servant's** head, trying to teach him respect, and Alain keeps putting it back.

Like most **bourgeois** characters, Arnolphe wore a simple suit consisting of a jacket–like doublet over a shirt, with knee breeches and high stockings, buckle shoes, cloak, and brimmed hat. In keeping with Molière's preference for odd or bright colors, this suit is mustard yellow or tawny, while the average middle–

class man wore black. In bourgeois attire, lace was fairly restrained, usually consisting of a single ring at the end of the sleeves and a single ring at the collar, and embroidery was simple and limited to seams and areas around the buttonholes. Though simple, bourgeois collars were supposed to be kept firm; old **Chrysale** in *Les Femmes savantes* presses his between the pages of a fat volume of **Plutarch**, the only book he needs in the house. He wants his women to be able to tell the difference between shirt and breeches and to know how to handle needle and thread to keep them fit. In Chrysale's bourgeois costume, the recently invented frock coat or "justaucorps" had replaced the doublet. His was black velvet with gold lining, embroidery, buttons, and matching breeches with garters. A light purple vest was worn underneath, over the shirt. It was one of the least expensive, and probably least stylized, of all Molière's costumes.

Usurpers' costumes tended to reflect both their wealth (they are of fine material) and the owners' lack of taste (they are all wrong in color and style). **George Dandin** is a veritable walking rainbow of hues, with color layered upon wildly contrasting color. **Pourceaugnac's** clashing primary colors also speak of his lack of sophistication, especially in view of the fact that he says he designed the suit to match "the court's country attire," exactly what the fashionable **Chambord** audience was wearing. **Monsieur Jourdain's** garish red–and–green "exercise suit," his silly "Indian" dressing gown, and his absurd suit of flowery brocade, with the flowers upside down, give a visual metaphor for his alienation.

Lower–class men wore whatever they could afford, unless they were servants in livery. Those better off could approximate bourgeois attire, while the penniless were reduced to hand–me–downs or nothing at all. In *Tartuffe*, **Dorine** is quick to point out that when the imposter first set foot in **Orgon's** house, he was not even wearing shoes, and was dressed like a beggar whose whole outfit was "not worth six pennies." The source of such garb was the second hand store, where many outmoded or outworn pieces of clothing found their way. A number of the items that **Harpagon** tries to foist off on his son in the bill of goods are such items from the *fripier's*, as are the old rags stored in a trunk that **Géronte** proposes for the ransom of his son in *Les Fourberies de Scapin.*

Of course, at night men of all classes wore a nightshirt and nightcap, items that **Agnès** mentions knitting for Arnolphe. Such a nightcap was worn by **Argan** during *Le Malade imaginaire* and it is one of the few Molière props, along with the armchair from that play, that has been conserved by the **Comédie–Française**. According to the stage directions of the 1674 edition, Argan wore a dressing gown over his nightshirt for warmth, as would have been common even for those who did not consider themselves seriously ill. When taking over the part from Molière after the playwright's death, **La Thorillière** had a somewhat more natty costume designed for himself, with a kind of waistcoat lined with squirrel fur. When going outdoors, men wore capes or mantles to cover their more expensive suits; such a cape allows Arnolphe to **disguise** himself from Agnès when **Horace** hands her over to him.

The exotic extremes of seventeenth–century costuming appear in the clothes of foreigners. These include **Sbrigani's** Neapolitain outfit, **Hali's** bizarre robes and pointed hat, and the outlandish turbans and gowns of the *mamamouchi* ceremony in *Le Bourgeois gentilhomme*. As for the numerous **"Greeks"** in Molière's plays, they were never clad in togas or realistic ancient attire, but in fantasy suits of current taste decorated with some exotic–looking trim or accessories. At most, **Sosie** was given something resembling a tunic for servant's garb. The definitive work on this area is Steven Dock's.

**Costume, Women's**. In general, seventeenth–century French women always wore dresses as an outer garment, and it was the fabric, cut, and design of these dresses that signaled differences in social standing. Aristocratic dresses were lower cut, made of expensive materials such as satin, silk, and taffeta (often mixing these types of cloth), complex in design, and heavily trimmed with lace, embroidery, and even jewels, in the case of the highest **nobility**. Women of the uppermost **bourgeois** levels might tend to imitate noble fashions, especially if their families were associated with the law courts and the *noblesse de robe*. This is the basis of **Mme. Pernelle's** complaint against **Elmire** in the first act of *Tartuffe*, where she says, "You are a spendthrift, and it hurts me that you go around dolled up like a princess." Later, Tartuffe pretends to examine the soft and supple cloth of Elmire's dress as a pretext for stroking her skin (III, 3).

More modest women, such as Mme. Pernelle and **Mme. Jourdain**, would have worn dresses of the finest black wool. In *L'École des maris*, **Sganarelle** crusades against makeup and ribbons for female attire and says that women should wear fashionable black only for solemn occasions and stick to "good, honest serge" the rest of the time. One imagines that **Agnès** in *L'École des femmes* must have worn such a simple robe of *grisette*, as suggested by the illustration in the 1682 **edition**. The socially ambitious fiancée in *Le Mariage forcé*, young **Dorimène**, makes her entrance in a gown with a train, an accessory forbidden to all but the higher levels of the nobility. To add to this sartorial usurpation, she employs a boy to hold it for her. Even this dress is not good enough for her, however, for she explains as she makes her exit that she is on her way to buy fancier gowns to replace "these old rags."

Serving women would normally be clad in some type of *grisette*, often with an apron and a bonnet, but **ladies' maids** would be dressed in a lesser version of their mistresses' attire, opulent enough to show off the family wealth, but not so much as to compete with the lady herself. This leads to a comic scene in *Tartuffe* (III, 2), where the bigot urges **Dorine** to cover her well–exposed breasts with a handkerchief out of modesty, and she makes fun of such sensitivity, replying that she would not become excited even if she saw Tartuffe buck naked.

Accessories were certainly important to all levels of feminine attire, with ribbon assuming particular importance. Vendors of such items were, however, sometimes suspected of delivering messages from male admirers and otherwise fomenting infidelity. Arnolphe seeks to banish from his house "ribbon peddlers, wigmakers, hairdressers, handkerchief hawkers, glovers, second–hand merchants, and all people whose daily work furthers the triumph of love."

**Cotin, abbé Charles** (1604–1682). In the early years of Molière's **Paris** career, this academician had supported him, perhaps because of the influence of **Boileau**, who with his brother Gilles and Furetière belonged to the same literary circle. By 1664, however, Boileau had broken with both Gilles and Cotin, perhaps in part over jealousy at Cotin's inclusion on the royal pension list. He disparages the old poet and man of letters in the fourth *Satire*, addressed to **abbé La Mothe**. Cotin gave a riposte in the "Satire des satires," where he writes: "Without blaming the poet, I have read bad verses. / I've read **Molière's** and never booed his plays," which seems to allude to his earlier approval. Thus, Molière was ready to fire a salvo back, especially in 1672, when Cotin and some other old–fashioned scholars had been dropped from the pension list. Cotin became the model in *Les Femmes savantes* for **Trissotin**, who seems originally to have been named Tricotin. Molière demolishes two of Cotin's poems that are repeated word for word in the comedy. He also recreates Cotin's feud with **Gilles Ménage**, whom the former had torn apart in his "Ménagerie." Molière might have had reason for revenge against both of them, for a rumor said that they had stirred up the **Rambouillet** clique against *Le Misanthrope* on the grounds that the **Duke of Montauzier**, one of its members, was the original for **Alceste**. Molière certainly achieved his tactical objectives in lambasting Cotin, but if he had strategic plans to enter the **Academy**, the opposition of the old poet would not help him.

**Count** (*La Comtesse d'Escarbagnas*). This child who has inherited his deceased father's title, for what it is worth, appears in scene 7 with his tutor **Bobinet** and recites a bit of **Latin** that is nothing but the beginning of **Despautère's** declension rules. He is obviously still at the rudiments, despite his advanced age, which says nothing for his intelligence or that of Bobinet. His mother, however, is scandalized by the lesson, since she doesn't understand any Latin and hears only the oft–repeated syllable "vi," which she associates with the French term for the male organ ("vit") pronounced the same way. She tells her schoolmaster to teach the pupil a less dirty form of Latin. **Gaudon**, an obscure young hireling, played the part.

**Countess** (*La Comtesse d'Escarbagnas*). Played by **Mlle. Marotte**, this silly provincial aristocrat obviously belongs to the class of impoverished *hobereaux*, since she cannot even afford wax **candles** and stays in the lowest sorts of **hotels** on her visits to **Paris**. She makes a great fuss over her **servants**, assigning them functions they barely understand and asking them to speak in the jargon of the **court**. Her son is being tutored at home by the pedant **Bobinet**. She also inflates her own family status, like the **Sotenvilles**, boasting that her husband's **nobility** was better than any robe nobility and referring to her parents with a royal form of honorific. A widow, she has apparently assembled a string of

**bourgeois** suitors including the court official Thibaudier and the tax collector Harpin. Both of these affairs seem to involve financial self–interest on her part.

**Cours la Reine**. A fashionable stretch of parkland, near the western borders of the city of **Paris** in the seventeenth century, where fashionable folk paraded about on foot and especially in their finest **carriages** to see and be seen. The theatrical pest described in the first scene of *Les Fâcheux* insists on bringing Éraste there to show off his new *galèche*.

**Court**. Molière was exposed at least indirectly to the royal court early in life as a result of his father's office as *tapissier du roi*. This position obliged him to care for the furniture and other goods of the royal household for three months out of the year and to accompany the court as it moved from one palace to another. Having taken over the office, Molière may have made a journey with the court himself before becoming involved with the **Illustre Théâtre**. Even during his wandering years in the provinces, Molière stayed in contact with several influential members of the court, including the **Duke d'Épernon** and the **Prince de Conti**. Having taken part in the **Ballet des Incompatibles** staged at Conti's provincial court in **Montpellier**, Molière had additional opportunities to observe courtly fashions before returning to **Paris** in 1658. Once re–established there, he had access to court circles through his status as a "servant" to **Monsieur, patron** of the junior troupe. Critical of the sartorial fashions of some courtiers in early plays, such as *Les Précieuses ridicules* and *L'École des maris*, Molière's attitude begins to change in *Le Misanthrope* toward a more ambiguous view.

Almost everyone in the most aristocratic of Molière's plays brags about his influence at court. **Oronte** is the first to offer **Alceste** the power of his political connections (I, 2). **Célimène** uses **Acaste's** presence in the court as an excuse to Alceste for receiving him in her home, though she implies that he is nothing more than an *arriviste* (II, 4). True to form, the marquis later makes sure that his companions know he has been to the ceremony of the royal rising and intends to be present when His Majesty turns in for the night, as well. Later, in the "**portrait** scene," she makes fun of a certain Adraste, who is never content with the decisions of the court and thinks he is entitled to every honor that is handed out. This is an interesting allusion, considering that Molière's friend **Boileau** had only recently leveled outspoken blame on the court for the partisanship of the royal pension lists. Alceste seems to distance himself from those he styles "my good friends of the court" when he tells the hypocritical group of gossipers that none of them would have the courage to confront their targets directly, but instead would submerge them in a flood of flattery and kisses. In the third act, it is **Arsinoé's** turn to mention the extent of her influence at court, offering to incite her friends in favor of Alceste's lawsuit, and even to obtain for him a court appointment of his own (III, 5). But the misanthrope replies, "Madame, in that circle, what could I possibly do? / My sacred honor makes me hate it through and through." Yet, despite Alceste's recalcitrance, and perhaps because of it, the "laughers" of the court circle are not entirely disgraced in this play.

By the time of *Dom Juan*, Molière's ambiguity deepens. The eponym's father **Dom Louis** criticizes his son's behavior in the name of courtly behavioral standards and warns him that he has exhausted all his own credit at court in defending **Dom Juan's** transgressions. Those who criticize the taste of the court become increasingly sociopathic and marginalized individuals, from the salon members in the *Critique de l'École des femmes* to **Trissotin** in *Les Femmes savantes* and **Monsieur Diafoirus** in *Le Malade imaginaire*. Bumpkins like **George Dandin, Monsieur de Pourceaugnac,** and the **Countess of Escarbagnas** are implicitly and explicitly denounced from the point of view of court values. Rare are the idiots, like **Monsieur Jourdain**, who can idolize the court and those who frequent it (**Dorante**), while remaining impervious to its codes of behavior. As his career develops, Molière tends more and more to endorse the taste of the court as an arbiter of all that is good, beautiful, and true. The spokesman for this attitude is **Clitandre** in *Les Femmes savantes*. He defends the tastes of the court, and implicitly their choices for the royal pension list for writers, from the attacks of Trissotin, whose original, the **abbé Cotin**, had recently been dropped from them. Clitandre tells his rival that the royal circle is "not as stupid as some of you writers seem to think" and that "worldly wisdom is worth more there than the obscure learning of you pedants." During Molière's lifetime, the royal circle had not yet become dominated by the shadowy **religious** figures that would come to influence **Louis XIV** from the 1680s onward, nor was the court physically and geographically withdrawn from Parisian life, as it would become during the residency at the palace of **Versailles**.

**Covielle** (*Le Bourgeois gentilhomme*). This valet to **Cléonte** is a variation on the theme of the *fourbe* or trickster tradition that goes back, within Molière's comedy, to **Mascarille**. Yet he blends to Mascarille's cleverness the lower–class romantic interests of the **Gros–René** character, for he is in **love** with the maid **Nicole** just as his master is in love with **Lucile**. Together, the foursome have one of the notable **lovers' spite** sequences in the canon (III, 8–10). He mirrors Cléonte's ill humor, and later his begging for forgiveness, in a lower social register. But when Cléonte mishandles his interview with **Monsieur Jourdain**, refusing through modesty to claim the title of **"gentleman,"** Covielle points out how wrong he was and sets in motion the stratagem of the **Turkish** masquerade. He disguises himself as the "world traveler" who offers to serve as translator and matchmaker in order to marry Jourdain's daughter to the son of the Grand Turk. The **disguise** is good enough to fool not only Jourdain, but **Dorante, Madame Jourdain**, and Lucile. He spouts gibberish with ease, completely befuddling the would–be aristocrat, and winning himself the hand of Nicole at the end of the play. The role could have been taken by **Baron** in the original version, if not by **Beauval**, who thus would have been playing opposite his wife.

**Credit**. In the financial sense, credit is always an ambiguous or pejorative element in Molière's **theater**, perhaps because the cash–poor nature of the French economy depended inordinately on credit and was always fearful of a collapse of mutual obligations. Thus, in ***Dépit amoureux***, **Gros–René** says that he is not the type of man to "make himself miserable on credit," that is, to be jealous before the appearance of a genuine reason. In ***Le Misanthrope***, **Acaste** expresses reluctance to "make love on credit and pay all the costs," or to make all the concessions expected of a suitor while receiving no promise of love in return. Those who lend at excessively high rates of interest, like **Harpagon**, deserve the label of usurers, while those who extend their credit without guarantee or profit, like **Jourdain**, are merely fools.

***Cri du sang, Le*** (**The Cry of the Blood**). A literary convention, inherited from Classical times, that family members who have been separated and are unaware of their relationship will nevertheless be mysteriously drawn to each other by an innate emotional force. This is frequently used to explain what would otherwise be incestuous yearnings in literary and theatrical plots, such as those of **Andrès** in ***L'Étourdi*** and **Dom Sylve** in ***Dom Garcie de Navarre***.

**Criquet** (***La Comtesse d'Escarbagnas***). The little lackey whose tendency to drop the formulas preferred by his mistress and address people by their proper names makes the lady infuriated. He was played by the young hireling **Finet**.

**Criticism of Molière**. *See* **Seventeenth–Century Criticism** (1660–1715); **Eighteenth–Century Criticism** (1715–1798); **Early Nineteenth–Century Criticism** (1798–1850); **Late Nineteenth–Century Criticism** (1850–1914); **Early Twentieth–Century Criticism** (1914–1960); **Late Twentieth–Century Criticism** (1960–2000).

***Critique de l'École des femmes, La***. This one–act comedy was presented for the first time at the Palais Royal Theater on June 1, 1663, though it had been announced in some sense months before, in the preface published with ***L'École des femmes***, where Molière excused himself from making a full–scale apology for his play by saying that he envisioned the possibility of a dramatic defense that would soon appear. One reason for the delay is that, as further criticisms emerged, Molière no doubt wanted to incorporate answers to them in his response, and also to enliven a revival of the original play.

The play consists of a very naturalistic representation of a fashionable salon where a mainly noble assembly will debate the merits of Molière's hit play. Before the arrival of the guests, the hostess **Uranie** and her cousin **Élise** discuss the openness of the gathering. Élise disapproves of some improper elements being admitted, especially a **Marquis** whose **language** leaves something to be desired in terms of decency. Uranie defends her taste for a varied crowd, though we later learn from her lackey's protestations that she herself had forbade entrance to the same man. However, the first to arrive is the prude **Climène**, whom Élise describes as "the silliest beast ever to try to reason." Before Climène manages to enter, Élise describes a ridiculous supper she gave, where the man she had mistakenly invited as a great wit and conversationalist sat mute and taciturn all night long. Climène issues a whole-scale condemnation of Molière's masterpiece, accusing it of filthy language. Yet, in the absence of any sound examples for her opinion, her overly explicit reactions to the play constitute the true vulgarity. While Uranie delivers a little lecture on the true nature of female decency, Élise delights in egging on Climène with satirical comments and a defense of the article "le" that the prude found so offensive. (In *L'École*, **Arnolphe** was worried that the oft-repeated "le," linked with something **Agnès** had lost to a young man, would be followed by *pucelage* [her virginity], but it merely designated a ribbon.)

Next to arrive is the Marquis, who literally fights his way past the lackey **Galopin**, clearly not caring whether he is welcome or not. **Dorante**, a much better mannered guest, soon joins him. The best justification the Marquis can give at first for denouncing *L'École* is that the groundlings in the **audience** adored it. Dorante parries this reverse aesthetic with a defense of the common man's taste and common sense in things dramatic. The Marquis then cites various authoritative figures who disapproved of the play, but Uranie and Dorante dismiss them as being too self-centered or affected to render a clear judgment.

The coming of the poet **Lysidas**, who has been reading his latest play around the town, allows for a more penetrating discussion, especially since Élise, in order to tease her suitor Dorante, pretends to change sides and argues sarcastically for the enemies of Molière. Finally getting closer to the text itself, Climène argues that Molière is antifeminist because Arnolphe calls women **animals**, but Uranie reminds her the words came from a deranged character. Then the Marquis keeps repeating "tarte à la crème" without being able to explain why the words are so offensive (the cream pastry was mentioned innocently by Agnès in the course of a word game where some more explicitly sexual double entendre might be expected). When Climène objects that their age is ignoring nobler genres to concentrate on low humor, Dorante launches a spirited defense of Molière's brand of naturalistic comedy, which he dubs more difficult to perfect than tragedy. Lysidas attacks the **court** for approving of the play, which incites Dorante to defend the aristocrats' sense of taste as strongly as he had that of the groundlings. The poet's claim that the comedy violates Classical rules causes Dorante to respond that it, like the rules themselves, are merely based on common sense. At last, Lysidas levels five specific objections at the text (it lacks action; people object to certain expressions; Arnolphe waits too long at the door in Act I; he gives money too readily to Horace; and his loving gestures in Act V are exaggerated). The nobleman quickly gives reasonable explanations for all of these things, leaving the Marquis with nothing further to do but sing an idiotic tune in lieu of conversation. The party finally agrees that their exchange should be set onstage and they charge Dorante with getting Molière to do it.

Set in polyphonic dialogue, this aesthetic discussion is much more convincing and entertaining than it would have been as a mere essay. The very enactment of the dispute makes many of Molière's points, without even needing the support of words. While avoiding prescriptive poetics, Molière manages to make all his central points about reason and human nature, leaving the whole question of style quite open to whatever works best. The play was a timely success as long as the **Quarrel of the School for Wives** raged on. Accompanied by a rather flippant dedication to (of all people) the prudish **Queen Mother**, it was published right away in 1663 by a coalition of no fewer than eight printers, indicating a phenomenal literary success for so slight a text. Two works that give most penetrating analyses of this play and relate it superbly to the rest of Molière's theater are Ron Tobin's *Tarte à la Crème: Comedy and Gastronomy in Molière's Theater* (Columbus: Ohio State University Press, 1990) and Larry Norman's *The Public Mirror: Molière and the Social Commerce of Depiction* (Chicago: University of Chicago Press, 1999).

**Cupid (*Psyché*).** **Baron** played the Love God in this extravaganza. In the prologue, he appears alongside his enraged mother, who bids him to arrange for the sacrifice of her rival in beauty, Psyche. Having fallen in **love** with her instead, he sends **Zephyr** to bring her to his palace in Act II. He converses with the windy spirit at the beginning of Act III, asking him about the lady's beauty, to which Molière, as Zephyr, replies with elegant badinage. In the parts of the play finished by **Pierre Corneille**, Cupid appears before Psyche incognito and confesses his love, allows her to visit with her sisters, continues to conceal his identity until she forces him to do so, then disappears in disgust, leaving his beloved to throw herself into the river. Following Psyche's rescue by the **River God** and her journey through the underworld with **Venus**, Cupid reappears and gets into a violent argument with his resentful mother, until **Jupiter** comes on the scene and grants his wish to **marry** the mortal. The part certainly drew on Baron's still youthful looks.

**Cupids (*Psyché*).** Besides the major character of the god of Love, there were two minor cupids, his attendants or *putti*, played by young Thorillon and Barillonet.

**Cynthie (*La Princesse d'Élide*).** Played by **Mlle. de Brie**, this cousin of the Princess does little but join with **Aglante** in defending **love** near the beginning of the play. She is part of the **marriage** arrangement proposed by **Aristomène** in the final act, but it is unclear if she is to wed him or **Théocle**, and she is given no lines for a reaction.

**Cyrano de Bergerac, Savinien de** (1619–1655). Legendary swordsman, freethinker, and author, Cyrano is now known primarily for his imaginative **philosophical** tales, *L'Autre Monde* and *Les États et Empires du Soleil*, which stand among the precursors to science fiction. However, these works were only published after his death, when the author was out of range of any backlash from censors and **religious** authorities who objected to their irreverence. Cyrano had already attracted the attention of such authorities with his successful tragedy, *La Mort d'Agrippine* (1653). His pen was also very active during the political troubles of the Fronde (1648–1652), writing on both sides in the controversy over Cardinal Mazarin. However, the most influential work known during his lifetime was probably his comedy, *Le Pédant joué*, published in 1654 but written and produced nine years earlier. Here a father signs what he thinks is a false **marriage** contract in hopes of fooling his daughter, only to find out that it is real and that he has actually consented, against his intention, to her marriage. This ending would be much emulated, especially by Molière in the conclusion of *L'Amour médecin*. Molière also uses parts of *Le Pédant joué* in *Les Fourberies de Scapin*, where he includes an odd internal reference to his borrowing in the form of Scapin's feigned wound at the end of the play. Cyrano was killed by a roofing tile that fell on his head, allegedly thrown by assassins too cowardly to challenge his legendary sword. Scapin pretends that he has been hit by a roofer's hammer in order to obtain pardons from his employers, then miraculously recovers. Some accounts had Cyrano sitting with **Brienne** and Molière on the jury that judged between Bouillon's version of "La Joconde" and **La Fontaine's**, but of course Cyrano was long dead by that time.

# D

**Dame Claude** (*L'Avare*). This "cleaning lady," who has no lines and appears in Act III with her broom at "present arms," may perhaps have been played by a man, given the unisex possibilities of the name in French. She is put in charge of the bottles at **Harpagon's** feast but warned that anything missing will be deducted from her presumably minimal salary.

**Damis** (*Les Fâcheux*). Damis is a blocking character, the guardian of **Orphise**, with whom **Éraste** is in love. We know that he plans a speedy **marriage** for his ward, but there is no indication that he is in **love** with her himself, like the guardians in *L'École des maris*. Though much talked about, he only appears in the final scenes of the play, where he plots with his servant **L'Espine** to attack and kill Éraste, only to be saved by that very man when **La Riviére** and his companions turn the tables and fall upon Damis. In view of this life–debt, he naturally gives his sanction to the marriage of the young lovers.

**Damis** (*Tartuffe*). As son of a man of apparent parliamentary status, young Damis may well be a third generation noble, at which point the honor switches from personal to hereditary. He certainly acts the part, denouncing **Tartuffe** as a flat–footed commoner (lacking the high heels of aristocratic boots) and threatening to punish him physically. The sword he carries is also a noble prerogative, and other documents, such as **Sorel's** novel *Francion*, are full of stories of young *nobles de robe* who make a point of this practice. Damis loves the noble lifestyle and is quick to defend it at all times. His brashness makes him spy on **Elmire** and Tartuffe in the third act, despite **Dorine's** negative advice, for she knows how hotheaded he can be. True to form, he ruins Elmire's subtle scheme by bursting out as soon as he feels he has heard enough, threatening vengeance against the hypocrite for his personal slights. We learn that this "just anger" is based on Tartuffe's machinations against Damis's **love** interests. But Damis would have been better served by more courtroom skill, for he underestimates the power of his enemy's self–incriminating histrionics, which from the beginning captivate **Orgon,** the judge. The inept prosecutor finds himself in contempt of court, beaten, banished, and cursed by his father. But his noble spirit is not all bad. It leads him to return generously in Act V, though he still has sword in hand and speaks of cutting off the bigot's ears. Furthermore, he threatens to flog **Monsieur Loyal** when the officer preparess to seize Orgon's house. Like father, like son: Orgon longs to punch his former colleague in the nose and Damis itches to teach him a lesson with his blade. His violence is ineffectual at the end of the play, and one wonders whether the removal of his nemesis will really change his character. The swaggering role fit Molière's brother–in–law **Louis Béjart** quite well, and he was probably the first Damis.

**Dance.** *See* **Music and Dance.**

**Dancers.** In all of Molière's **comedy–ballets**, dancers performed their art according to the latest fashion of the day. These dancers were usually members of a royal troupe headed by Beauchamp. However, the professionals were sometimes joined by talented members of the **court**, including the King himself. Perhaps the greatest number of dancers was employed in the super–spectacular **Tuileries** production of *Psyché*, where no fewer than seventy appeared in the finale. Among the troupe that regularly performed were the brothers Saint–André, Favier, Pesan, Du Gard, Lestang, and Vaignard; the father and son teams of Dolivet and Foignard; and the individual dancers Joly, Doyat, de Launoy, de Lorge, Bonnard, La Pierre, Le Prestre, Jouan, Joubert, Paysan La Vallée, Charpentier, Chauveau, Favre, Isaac, Girard, Hidieu, Noblet, Chicanneau, Magny, Le Chantre, Mayeu, Desbrosses, Desgranges, La Montagne, and Arnald.
    *See also* **Music and Dance.**

**Dancing Master** (*Le Bourgeois gentilhomme*). In conversation with the **Music Master** during the first act, the Dancing Master is the more idealistic of the two, deploring **Monsieur Jourdain's** lack of appreciation for his art, while his companion points out practically that their client "has discrimination in his purse." Later the two men get into a small argument over which of their disciplines is the most crucial, the Music Master pointing out that his must be the key to civilization, since any kind of mistake in domains of war or state is referred to as a *faux pas.* Both masters give admirable demonstrations of their abilities, but the battle heats up when the **Fencing Master** insists his "art" is more important than theirs. It blazes fully when the **Philosophy Teacher** enters the fray. This character must have been played by a very competent performer from the royal dance troupe, and one wonders whether the great Beauchamp himself did not fill the role.

**Dancourt, stage name of Florent Carton** (1661–1725). Perhaps the most successful of the generation of comic dramatists that followed Molière. Although he pillaged the works of Molière's contemporaries for titles, characters, scenes, and even nearly whole plots, Dancourt refrained from raiding the great dramatist too openly, since his works were still being staged very regularly. Instead he took pains to imitate Molière's style in many ways. His debts to Molière have nevertheless been somewhat exaggerated by those unfamiliar with the works of such other playwrights as **Poisson, Hauteroche**, and **Donneau de Visé**. Dancourt did follow the master in that he wrote almost exclusively, and always most successfully, in prose. While promising much through their titles in the way of topical satire or **comedy of manners**, Dancourt's plays actually are direct forerunners of Marivaux and often unfold in a neutralized social setting, such as a country retreat or a fair. His best–known works, *Le Chevalier à la mode*, *Les Bourgeoises à la mode*, and *La Famille à la mode*, feature amoral but clever characters closely related to British Restoration comedy. Dancourt eloped with Thérèse, **La Thorillière's** daughter and Molière's godchild, in 1680, forcing the family to allow them to marry. Both joined the **Comédie–Française** after Easter 1685. Their original half–shares were augmented to full shares in the coming years, as other actors retired.

**Daphné (*Mélicerte*).** One of two women, variously described as **shepherdesses** or "nymphes," who are in love with **Myrtil**. She seems to belong to a higher class than the latter, judging from the text, but we are not told why. In the first scene, the two ladies reveal their secrets to each other: they both wear lockets with Myrtil's miniature **portrait** inside. They go together to **Lycarsis** to ask him to give Myrtil's hand to one of them, and he decides to leave the matter to his son. Myrtil pays compliments to both of them, but rejects both offers, managing not to offend his admirers. The role was probably taken either by **Catherine de Brie** or **Madeleine Béjart**.

**D'Aquin, Louis–Henry.** One of the court physicians and Molière's landlord from 1661 to 1665. A noted proponent of bloodletting, D'Aquin was probably the model for Tomès in *L'Amour médecin*. Some of the invective writing against Molière said that there was a real estate quarrel between the dramatist and the doctor, but this is unlikely. Historic documents show that Molière sublet his property in D'Aquin's house from another person and that he left when his party moved away from the property, not because of any direct problem with the landlord.

**Dauphin.** Title given to the eldest child of the French king and heir to the throne. **Louis XIV's** oldest son was born November 1, 1661, and is referred to in *L'École des maris*, Act I, scene 3, and again implicitly in the first "day" of the *Plaisirs de l'Île enchantée*. This child, named Louis after his father, showed little improvement despite the elaborate education given him at **court**, and predeceased the Sun King in 1711.

**Dawn** (*La Princesse d'Élide*). Singing a couple of stanzas at the opening of the first *intermède*, Dawn, represented by Mistress Hilaire of the royal singers, makes way for Molière's **Lyciscas** and his gestural comedy.

*Dépit amoureux (Lovers' Spite)*. Five–act comedy in verse that was first produced at **Béziers** in 1656–57 and published in 1663. The dedication by the printer, **Gabriel Quinet**, to a justice official named Hourlier. It was adapted from the *commedia sostenuta L'Interesse* (1585) by **Nicolo Secchi**, with some elements borrowed from **D'Ouville's** *Aimer sans savoir qui* (1646). Though adapted from another Italian comedy, this play is very different from *L'Étourdi*. Instead of astounding the spectators with a dizzying succession of ingenious plots, the action is actually rather restrained and focuses attention on the psychological reactions of characters to the revelations that come forth as the comedy progresses. In a complicated series of infant swappings that only becomes clear at the end of the play, **Ascagne–Dorothée** has come to represent a lost brother in order to secure a large inheritance that otherwise would go to **Valère's** family. Valère had contested **Éraste's** successful courtship of Lucile, only to be rejected, but Ascagne, **disguised** as the older sister, gave him nocturnal trysts and made him marry her secretly. All this is recounted in lengthy *récits*, so that the main elements emerge as Éraste's pathological **jealousy** over Lucile, the guilt of old Albert and young Ascagne over the impersonation, and the growing confusion of Valère over a **marriage** he had thought to be happily consummated. The first of these leads to the scene from which the play got its name, which takes place in Act IV and involves a double lovers' quarrel, with the Éraste–Lucile dispute mirrored in a different social register by **Gros–René** and **Marinette**. The second moves toward a beautiful misunderstanding sequence where **Polidore** and **Albert** forgive each other for offenses that they do not clearly understand, as well as further efforts by Ascagne and Frosine to clear up the mysteries of the family. The third element leads to increasingly hostile encounters with Albert and Lucile, and almost to a duel with Ascagne, whose final revelations involve a sex–changing recognition scene and a blessing on all three **marriages** (Éraste–Lucile, Valère–Dorothée, and Gros–René–Marinette). But the importance of this play for Molière's career lies not on the level of the larger plot, but in his experimentation with the way **language** generates itself on the scenic level. The power of words to interact, whether in conflict or in harmony, is clearly the focus of this innovation, as the playwright devises an incredible array of new scenic forms involving misunderstandings, flirtations, love's capacity to provoke spite (and its inability to let go), the reciprocal quality of blame, the replication of negation or affirmation, and the impenetrability of self–justifying pedantry.

*See* Molière, *Dépit amoureux*, ed. Noel Peacock (Durham: University of Durham Press, 1989).

*Déniaisé, Le* (*The Disabused*). A comedy by **Gillet de la Tessonnerie** that contributed some elements to *Dépit amoureux*.

**Descartes, René** (1596–1650). During Molière's lifetime, the great expatriot philosopher was still considered quite marginal in the French intellectual world. But it is almost impossible that Molière would not have heard of his many works, which were causing a stir in all realms of **philosophy**. The most direct allusion to Descartes comes in *Les Femmes savantes*, where **Philaminte** and her circle mention his ideas on physics, especially the theory of vortices. The learned ladies are quite caught up in this dizzy concept, though the playwright distances himself from what he considered pseudo–science, just like the idea of men and cities on the moon. Indeed, despite the support of Malebranche, Descartes's views on the physical sciences would continue to be blasted for over a century, until discoveries about the nature of the atom would rehabilitate to some degree his vortex theory. Perhaps more important and pervasive in Molière's work, if less explicit, is the Cartesian concept of **reason**. Most of Molière's monomaniacs, from **Arnolphe** and **Alceste** through **Dom Juan**, **Monsieur Jourdain**, and **Argan**, act as though they have misread Descartes's *Discourse on Method*. Though the opening sections of the *Discourse* clearly advocate that reason should never be stretched beyond the boundaries of common sense and social custom, Molière's protagonists consistently do just that. They fasten upon a single concept and use reason to build around that obsession an entire universe that is very logical, but also very wrong, regardless of supplied evidence or established manners. Was Molière truly anti–Cartesian? It might be argued that his plays satirize "false Cartesianism," just as he continually cited as his targets false piety, false tastes, false **medicine**, or even false cuckoldry. The difficulty lies in determining where the true ends and the false begins. But considering Molière's reiterated warnings about the inability of humans to escape from the innate preoccupations and emotional foibles, one can scarcely doubt that he would find Descartes's mission of reasoning himself all the way to God to be a little presumptive.

*See* Hiram Caton, *The Origin of Subjectivity: An Essay on Descartes* (New Haven: Yale Univ. Press, 1973).

**Desert**. When **Alceste** speaks of retiring to his desert in *Le Misanthrope*, he does not mean the Sahara or the Mojave. The term could refer in seventeenth–century France to any retreat away from the city or court society. Sometimes this could be a luxurious country estate, such as the Grande Mademoiselle's retreat at Saint–Fargeau. More commonly, it could designate a religious establishment of some kind, though seldom one of total ascetic isolation. It was used particularly by the Huguenots to indicate places of exile away from French Catholic persecution. Though this does not seem to be the case for Alceste, the mere association tends to link him with the idea of dissidence, all the more so since the embattled Jansenists also employed such terminology. If one is not tempted to adopt Jasinski's reading of the play as something of a Jansenist allegory, one can always assume that "desert" simply designates a retreat to Alceste's rural properties.

**Des Fonandrès** (*L'Amour médecin*). One of the four **doctors** summoned by **Sganarelle** to cure his aphasic daughter, Des Fonandrès is based on the **court** physician Des Fougerais. He disagrees with the rabid bloodletter **D'Aquin**, favoring purges in all cases.

**Desjardins, Marie Catherine** (ca.1640–1683). A talented female author who penned prose descriptions of some of Molière's works. Best known for her novels, such as *Les Désordres de l'amour* and perhaps *Les Mémoires de la vie de Henriette–Sylvie de Molière*, she also dabbled in the **theater**. When Molière had the goodness to perform one of her plays, *Le Favori*, she was miffed by his use of the **bourgeois** "mademoiselle" on his posters and heatedly remarked, "I should be Madame to the likes of him." Other plays, such as the tragedies *Manlius* (1662) and *Nitétis* (1663) appeared at the rival **Hôtel de Bourgogne**. Also known under her alternative identity as Mme. Villedieu, she led an adventurous and sometimes scandalous private life.

**Desmarets de Saint–Sorlin, Jean** (1596–1676). A Jesuit and one–time member of **Richelieu's** stable of authors, Desmarets is chiefly known for his comedy, *Les Visionnaires* (1637). This work belongs to the Renaissance tradition of the fools' play, where a succession of people suffering from various mental disorders is paraded before both onstage and offstage **audiences**. It is particularly well written and was a major element in the **repertory** of Molière's troupe for several years after their return to **Paris**. It had a wide–ranging influence over many of his plays, especially *Les Fâcheux* and *Les Femmes savantes*. The Jesuit also penned one of the many devotional texts that may have served as models for the Maxims of **Marriage** in *L'École des femmes*. Desmarets was a member of the **Academy** during Molière's productive period and had long since given up the theater. He praised Molière soon after the dramatist's death.

See James Dryhurst, "Des Marests, le Tartuffe et l'ombre de Molière," *Revue d'Histoire Littéraire de la France* 7 (1974), 20–28.

**Despautère, Jean**. Grammarian whose standard **Latin** manual is cited in *La Comtesse d'Escarbagnas*.

**Deus ex machina**. The literal appearance of a god or goddess descending or ascending in a **machine** was not unknown in Molière's theater. In his own comedies, we find such an event at the conclusion of *Amphitryon*, where both **Mercury** and **Jupiter** rise on mechanical clouds.

**Devils**. *See* **Satan**.

**Diafoirus, Monsieur** (*Le Malade imaginaire*). This **doctor** is the brother–in–law of **Argan's** physician, **Monsieur Purgon**, and father of the awkward **Thomas**. His opening exchange of words with Argan is a form of verbal **lazzi**, where both men speak at the same time, each eager to say his piece but uninterested in listening to the other. He seems to be only slightly brighter than his son, explaining at length that Thomas showed signs of remarkable stupidity from an early age, but affirming that this defect was merely a sign of the great powers of judgment that would serve him as a doctor. He confirms each one of Thomas's ridiculous diagnoses and never tires of prompting his son with lines from his rehearsed, but not mastered, greetings. He brags mightily of Thomas's virility. When Argan suggests, however, that such a great pair of doctors should serve the **court**, the elder Diafoirus replies that his ilk seldom succeeds with the aristocracy because they have the audacity to demand a cure for their illnesses, instead of being ready to die in good order, like the **bourgeoisie**. His parting advice to Argan's question about how many grains of salt he should put on an egg is that it should always be an even number, but that doses of medicine should always be odd numbers. The family name translates, roughly, as "through the liver." The role may have been played originally by **Hubert** or **Du Croisy**.

**Diafoirus, Thomas** (*Le Malade imaginaire*). The classic "big oaf of a youth," this role is traditionally ascribed to **Beauval**. It recalls the play written for the troupe much earlier by **Brécourt**. Thomas is a total idiot. He cannot even remember with whom to begin his rehearsed compliments, but he actually manages to finish his speech to **Argan**. **Toinette's** sarcastic comment on his learning leads us to think it was filled with numerous verbal glitches and accompanied by grotesque facial contortions. Reassured by his father, he asks crudely if he should kiss Argan, using the verb "baiser" rather than the more formal "embrasser." Then he mistakes **Angélique** for her mother–in–law, but finally proceeds with his speech, comparing her to the statue of **Memnon** and himself to a sunflower. As a gift, he presents her with his thesis against the theory of the circulation of blood (complete with illustrations, with which Toinette claims she can paper her room) and invites her to the dissection of a female cadaver. After this gallantry, it is not surprising that he insists on marrying her even against her will, since all that matters for him is the father's permission. This opinion recalls that of **George Dandin**. When **Béline** appears, he again cannot finish the speech meant for her, because she interrupts him with thanks and he is unable to get restarted. At last, when he tests Argan's pulse before leaving, he delivers a nonsensical analysis and concludes, against even Purgon's conclusion, that the patient has a bad spleen. This part of a clumsy, vulgar fellow, a dolt from start to finish, recalls to some degree the fat **servant** roles of preceding decades, but lacks even the meager sympathetic characteristics of a **Gros–René**.

**Diana**. This Greco–Roman goddess is mentioned several times in Molière's comedies, often by comparison with her traits of chastity and **hunting**. She has a sacred grove in **Tempe** in *Les Amants magnifiques*.

**Diderot, Denis** (1713–1784). As with many other subjects, this subtle *philosophe* was often ambiguous in regard to Molière. He acknowledged him as a great writer and in his essay on dramatic poetry, he even claimed a considerable personal debt to Molière via **Goldoni**. However, in *Le Neveu de Rameau,* he claimed that even Molière's perceptive social analysis could be put to misuse: the Nephew uses *Tartuffe* to study how he can perfect hypocrisy rather than avoid it. Diderot's later dramatic writings tend to view Molière through the lens of his own experiments with **bourgeois** drama. Thus he tended to paint a picture of Molière as an obsolete moralist who had catered to the whims of the courtiers rather than trying to effect societal reforms. He added that by making his characters universal, combining all the idealized traits of the types depicted, he had missed the chance to create a true comedy of manners. This latter goal could only be achieved, he opined, through the focus on "conditions" in works such as his own dramas, *Le Fils naturel* and *Le Père de famille,* as well as the odd successful comedy, such as Sedaine's *Le Philosophe sans le savoir.* Diderot drew heavily in his discussion of dramatic character and audience sensibilities on the British actor, David Garrick, and on the ideas he had developed in his own analysis of Richardson's writings. His contention that Molière had failed to achieve any meaningful moral criticism was taken up by **Rousseau**.

**Dijon.** Capital of the province of Burgundy. Molière's troupe gave performances there before leaving the Rhone valley area for **Paris**, notably in June 1655, and during the summer of 1657.

**Dimanche, Monsieur (*Dom Juan*).** The principal **creditor** of the notorious *roué* is entirely hamstrung by his debtor's recourse to false civility, which turns the tables on financial obligation. Monsieur Dimanche becomes the one who is owing to **Dom Juan** for his professions of unending friendship and his obsequious interest in the Dimanche family, right down to the yapping family dog. Dom Juan uses **politeness** to stay one step ahead of the businessman, smothering him so profusely in compliments that Dimanche literally cannot get a word about payment into the conversation. In the following scene, **Sganarelle**, who also is indebted to Monsieur Dimanche, uses a slightly different strategy to silence his demands, pushing him physically off the stage, while simply denying any talk of repayment with "Fie, fie!" The character serves to show just how hard it is to impose earthly obligations on a man who will do absolutely anything in order to avoid acknowledging them. The original casting is unknown, but one can easily imagine **Du Croisy** in the role.

**Director of Conscience.** The term *directeur de conscience* originally seems to have referred to a member of the clergy who, like a confessor, was designated to watch over the spiritual interests of a given person or group, such as nuns in a **convent**. By Molière's time, the laity had become heavily involved in such activities, often in an unofficial way that was frowned on by the Church. In Molière's works, the term first comes up in *L'École des maris,* where **Sganarelle** uses it sarcastically to refer to his brother's lax moral teachings. *L'École des femmes,* however, finds **Arnolphe** consciously aspiring to play the role of director to his "ward" **Agnès**. One of the most controversial aspects of the play was that he used actual devotional texts as a close model for the "Maxims of **Marriage**" that he has Agnès study. He also adopts the language of spiritual direction in painting for the young lady the kind of spiritual torment that supposedly punishes disobedient girls. In the second scene of *Tartuffe* **Dorine** sarcastically refers to him as a "prudent director," making his function in the household dangerously explicit. **Orgon** acknowledges this role, and marvels at how the man has undertaken to govern the behavior of the entire family, but especially the women. Several real–life bogus directors of conscience, including a certain Charpy de Sainte–Croix, have been mentioned as prototypes for the character of **Tartuffe**. Like him, they crossed the line between conventional direction of conscience and crime by getting directly involved in the sexual and financial affairs of those they claimed to advise.

**Disguises.** The use of disguise is so widespread in Molière's comedies that it is almost impossible to avoid. There are characters who disguise their sex (**Ascagne**), their class (**Arnolphe**), their past (**Henrique**), and their beliefs (**Tartuffe**). Gods take on the guise of men (*Amphitryon*) and men of gods (*Les Amants magnifiques*). Characters switch identities (**Dom Juan** and **Sganarelle**, **Isidore** and **Climène**) or appear as shadowy strangers (**Arnolphe, Du Bois**). To gain entrance to their sweethearts' houses, lovers take on the **costumes** of apothecaries (*Le Médecin malgré lui*), painters *(Le Sicilien)*, music masters (*Le Malade imaginaire*), or even **servants** (*L'Avare*). Few of those who disguise themselves are willing, however, to go to the lengths of cross–dressing, as **Monsieur de Pourceaugnac** does in an effort to flee **Paris** and its many troubles. At first he has some fun aping the manners of aristocratic ladies, but the disguise only attracts the unwanted amorous attention of a couple of **Swiss** guards, who play a game of tug–of–war with the "pretty little thing." The theme of disguise not only furthers the mechanics of intrigue comedy but also contributes to the great baroque concern of appearance and reality, illusion and impression, which underlies so much of the art of the period.

*Docteur amoureux, Le* (*The Amorous Pedant*). This **farce** was given along with **Corneille's** *Nicomède* at the first command performance by Molière's troupe before the royal family in 1658. It is credited with amusing the King so much that he accepted his brother's sponsorship of them and launched Molière's **Paris** career. The text is lost. What is known of the action does not resemble any of Molière's longer plays; perhaps it remained in that stock of farce material that **La Grange** and **Vivot** refer to as a reservoir for future development, which contained such texts as *Gorgibus dans le sac* (the model for *Les Fourberies de Scapin)*.

**Doctors** (*Monsieur de Pourceaugnac*). In order to thwart Pourceaugnac's **marriage** plans, **Éraste** arranges for him to stay at a doctor's house and tells the doctor that the visitor is a mad relative. Éraste observes the doctor and his colleague in action when they are consulted by two **peasants** about a woman who suffers from migraines. The doctors respond that the trouble is not in the head, but in the spleen. They comment that the patient's six months of diarrhea are a good sign, because it shows "his insides are becoming unblocked." When they learn that the patient has been bled fifteen times without result, they conclude the problem is not in the blood (if he has any left), and order fifteen purgatives instead, failing which, the prescription is the baths. After checking Pourceaugnac's pulse and peppering him with questions about his **dreams** and his bowels, the two launch into medical tirades that consist of a great deal of disconnected nonsense sprinkled with **Latin**. As their patient shows signs of rebellion, they assure him that they know more about his health than he does, before sending a legion of enema–toting **apothecaries** to chase him with their vile cures.

**Doctors and Medicine.** The figure of the doctor had been a standard element in the **Italian** *commedia dell'arte*, where he was often represented as a Bolognese from the medical school at that great old university. In the generation before Molière began to write, the doctor had moved into French **farce**, as can be seen in *Le Médecin volant*, which is probably based on an older original. The association between medicine and comedy was all the more intimate in the Parisian mind, since street comics like **Tabarin** and hawkers selling all sorts of medical remedies performed on the Pont–Neuf as part of the daily spectacle of street life. In practical terms, the doctor's long black robe was a wonderful theatrical **disguise**, easily recognizable and apt for involvement in all sorts of plots. However, Molière was to bring medical satire to a whole new level by exploiting the subject matter of medicine itself and its relationship to the fear of death that lies so close both to the comic spirit and to the **philosophy** of **Lucretius** that Molière favored. The **language** of doctors, larded with **Greek** and **Latin** terms that seemed bizarre to ordinary Frenchmen, lent itself very well to this enterprise. It ensured that they would appear otherworldly and divorced from logical reality. Their reliance on ancient authorities like **Galen** and **Hippocrates**, and on authority itself rather than rational analysis, made them ready butts for irreverent jokes. Moreover, their pretentious claim to understand and even control the forces of nature must have rankled a skeptic like Molière, who was steeped in the Lucretian precept that **nature** surpasses man's efforts to organize and dominate it. Thus, the doctor appears in this light as another form of charlatan, a seller of indulgences, a professional trickster who could live well by manipulating the **superstitions** of others and giving them nothing in return for their payments.

In *Dom Juan* we literally see this development take place on stage, since **Sganarelle** puts on medical clothing in order to disguise himself from his master's enemies, but then begins to fleece his fellow countrymen of their meager possessions in exchange for blithering diagnoses and false advice. Astonished that his master is "impious in medicine" as in all other areas, he proposes "emetic wine," a contemporary favorite, as a cure–all, explaining that if it fails to restore health, it will at least hasten death. Sganarelle had already discussed the pseudo–medical benefits of **tobacco** in the opening scene, so it is no surprise that he takes so readily to the role of a doctor. Having hidden in the bushes while his master was fighting with **Dom Carlos** against a gang of **robbers,** he crawls out of the scenery, remarking that the **costume** seems to have had a purgative effect on him. **Dom Juan** joins his servant in playing doctor when the occasion calls for it. Sganarelle's first tale of the **Commander's** moving statue is attributed to "a case of the vapors that has troubled your sight." When he catches Sganarelle stealing morsels from the table and hiding them in his cheeks, Dom Juan pretends that the servant has a boil on his cheek and pokes him with a knife, offering to lance it for him.

*L'Amour médecin* raised the stakes even further, for Doctors **Tomès, Macroton, Des Fonandrès, Bahys,** and **Filerin** are almost universally acknowledged to represent prominent **court** physicians: **D'Aquin,** Guénaut, Des Fougerais, Esprit, and Yvelin. Since the playwright imitated the prominent speech traits of each man and even constructed names that gave clues to their identities, it is obvious that the real doctors knew that they were being laughed at in the theater. Moreover, D'Aquin was at one time Molière's own landlord! It seems impossible that the men's personal vanity could have blinded them to their personification in the comedy. Yet, there is no indication that they fomented a feud or even took the humor badly. Were they capable of taking part in the collective joy of comedy and laughing at themselves? On the other hand, was Molière totally against medicine and unbelieving in its powers? By 1665, Molière was beginning to have health problems, perhaps from an ulcer, and may have consulted these very men. Though he jokes about the ineffectiveness of remedies, there are a number of reports that he followed a careful diet to try to treat his own illness. All this suggests that, if satire is at work, it is far more complex and self–mocking than is usually understood. There can be no doubt that Molière lashes out at the contemporary remedies of purging and bleeding that seemed to many doctors fit for any disease. Nor can there be any uncertainty that Molière uses Filerin's tirade in Act III, scene 1 to condemn the complicity of the entire medical community in obfuscating truth from the public and in crassly exploiting ignorance to fill their own pockets. He goes so far as to compare doctors to flatterers, alchemists, and fortune–tellers. But the exposure of medical abuse in all its falsehood does not prevent Sganarelle from running to an even more blatant scoundrel, the snake–oil salesman or *opérateur* who peddles "orviétan," an elixir that was supposed to cure all ills. In his song, the hustler enumerates them: mange, hives, scurvy, fever, plague, gout, pox, dropsy, and measles. Furthermore, medicine does have its uses, since it allows **Clitandre** a pretext to visit his beloved and to plot with her to obtain permission for their **marriage**.

In *Le Mariage forcé*, Sganarelle complains of a headache after he realizes his fiancée intends to be unfaithful every chance she gets, and she attributes his distress to a case of the vapors. **Monsieur de Pourceaugnac** relates that his cousin has died of smallpox, but Éraste spreads rumors that the provincial visitor is not only insane, but suffering from a venereal disease as well. Pourceaugnac barely escapes from the posse of apothecaries armed with enema syringes that chases him around **Paris**. The doctors in the play, who specialize in snap diagnoses, confirm the presence of mental disease after only a brief examination and a very long speech. **Arnolphe** in *L'École des femmes* shows that he is familiar with an alternative to enemas and bloodletting, for when **Horace** recounts his first visit to **Agnès**, the old man mutters, "Oh, the frightful pill!" He later complains of heart palpitations when he rants and raves at his servants. In *Tartuffe*, we learn that **Elmire** has been subject to a malady that caused severe headaches and lack of appetite, as well as causing her to be attended all night long. Though a bloodletting immediately cured the supposed disease, it is clear that the real pain was having to spend the evening alone in the house with **Tartuffe**; the symptoms were an excellent deterrent to his unwanted attentions. In *Amphitryon*, it is the **servant Sosie** who demonstrates some medical knowledge, for he recommends "six hellebore seeds" as a remedy for **Alcmène's** apparent madness (II, 2). In the next scene, he tries to use doctor's advice as an excuse for not satisfying **Cléanthis's** desires, claiming that drunkards who indulge in sex risk conceiving unhealthy **children**. For her part, the wife rejects all medical advice, especially that offered on the subject of intercourse and female physiology, such as prohibition of sex during the summer heat.

Sganarelle boasts in the opening scene of *Le Médecin malgré lui* that he has served a doctor for six years. Nevertheless, his knowledge of medicine consists strictly of a few overheard and misunderstood phrases and a great deal of made–up nonsense. Having admitted under the coercion of a beating to being a doctor, he marvels at the miracle cures that **Martine** has attributed to him (they amount to two instances of raising people from the dead) and wonders how he can have received his degree without remembering it. He takes advantage of the ignorance of his interlocutors by spouting a great deal of macaronic **Latin** and **Greek** containing schoolboy exercises, adages, and bits of prayers. He tries to persuade them, for instance, that "armyam" is Latin for lungs, "nasmus" is Greek for the brain, and "cubile" **Hebrew** for the vena cava. Furthermore, he pretends to diagnose **Lucinde's** muteness from her pulse and later declares that **Léandre** is sick on the same evidence. When **Géronte** catches him in an obvious mistake about the heart being on the right side of the body and the liver on the left, he tells the old man that modern medicine has changed all that and reversed the positions. In the process of concocting his nonsense, he mentions many actual medical terms and beliefs, such as peccant humors, laudable feces, ventricular theory, and sympathetic ailments. He and his fellows also mention such remedies as potable gold, purgative herbs (including **cassia**, senna, and rhubarb), enemas, bloodletting, the "universal cure," poultices, and juleps (according to Sganarelle, his **wine** bottle is full of them). As a cure for hydropisia (symptoms of which resemble gout, diabetic coma, and dropsy), he foists off on the peasants **Thibaut** and **Perrin** an old hunk of cheese that is supposed to be chock full of precious remedies such as gold, pearls, and gems. Sganarelle concludes in the third act that medicine is the finest trade, since no one criticizes how one butchers the human raw material and the dead make no complaints.

Medicine plays a pervasive role in *Le Malade imaginaire* because **Argan** is actually convinced that he is seriously ill and has organized his entire life and that of his household around this conviction.  We see in the first couple of scenes that medicines and bedpans dominate the rhythm of his existence.  As a kind of professional patient, he has come to know as much about the subject as the doctors and apothecaries themselves.  He wishes to trade his daughter, like a **slave**, in order to get a doctor in the house, and he believes **Purgon** has a nearly supernatural control over his very life–force.  The visit of **Diafoirus** and son gives the **audience** a chance to see him interacting with the practitioners themselves, typical, backward–thinking University of **Paris** products who refuse to believe in modern experimental discoveries such as the circulation of blood.  They found their nonsensical diagnoses on the authority of misunderstood ancients, tossing about much Greek and Latin vocabulary to impress their patients.  Yet their own understanding of anatomy and physiology is nil.  When Thomas Diafoirus determines from Argan's pulse that his problem is in the spleen, contradicting Purgon's analysis that it is the liver that is at fault, the senior Diafoirus  traces an impossible journey through real and imaginary organs to show that the two are really connected, one and the same.  Medicine is shown as a source of false authority that challenges both Church and state, as when Purgon accuses Argan of treason against the medical faculty.   As laughable as one may find the ceremony at the end of the play, it mimics the training of real doctors, whose answer to every disease is the same rote–learned regimen of enemas, bloodletting, and emetic drugs.  Clearly Molière is focusing on the automatic, Bergsonian quality of early modern medicine as a prime source of comedy.  But the degree conferred on the Bachelierus at the end of the rite has an ominously realistic ring, as it authorizes him to purge, bleed, slash, and kill to his heart's content, as long as the public is willing to follow the godlike words of the doctor.  Thus, the play carries a double–edged blade that cuts to the illusions of what **Béralde** terms "the fiction of medicine," while also satirically underlining the true dangers that stem from it.

**Dom Alonse (*Dom Juan*).**  The violent and one–dimensional brother of **Elvire** and **Dom Carlos** is focused entirely on killing his offensive in–law and thus wiping the family honor clean again.  He does not really share or appreciate his brother's noble ideals, only hesitating to slit **Dom Juan's** throat because his brother puts himself in his way.  He sums up his attitude in the observation, "O what a strange lack of strength and a frightful blindness, to set the interests of one's honor at risk merely for the sake of ridiculous thoughts and illusory obligations!" (III, 4).  He appears in only one scene and was played by an unknown actor.

**Dom Alphonse (*Dom Garcie de Navarre*).**  Brother to **Elvire**, he goes through most of the action of the play under the name **Dom Sylve**, unaware of his own identity as he courts his own sister.  His passion is explained, of course, as an instance of *le cri du sang*.  He is the heir to the throne of Leon and has been hidden in Castille for several years to protect him from the conspiracies of

**Mauregat**. Oddly, there is little satisfactory explanation given of why he was originally unaware of his own identity.

*See also* **Dom Sylve**.

**Dom Alvar** (*Dom Garcie de Navarre*). He is an aide to Dom Garcie and the successful suitor to **Élise**, who has preferred him to the evil **Dom Lope**. His role is largely limited to that of a messenger. His excuses for his master's behavior are much less interesting and convincing than his sweetheart's.

**Dom Carlos** (*Dom Juan*). **Elvire's** more civil brother appears first in the third act, where immediately after the **pauper** scene **Dom Juan** sees him offstage, set upon by three men. Declaring somewhat cryptically that the mathematics of the battle is all wrong, Dom Juan comes to the aid of the underdog and has no trouble dispersing the attackers, who were **robbers**. It is somewhat unclear whether Dom Juan realizes he is doing a good deed, though the censored, seventeenth–century version of the text contributes to that impression. When Dom Carlos reveals his reason for being in the forest, namely, that he has been pursuing Dom Juan, the so far unnamed benefactor maintains his anonymity, but says that Dom Juan is a friend. Dom Carlos cordially refuses to speak further ill of the rake in his new friend's presence. Just at that moment, Elvire's other brother, **Dom Alonse**, who is a hot–blooded and vengeful man, happens on the scene and recognizes Dom Juan instantly. Dom Carlos has all he can do to separate his brother from the enemy, almost finding it necessary to let his brother stab him instead. Dom Juan looks on with amusement as Dom Carlos explains how the **laws** of honor and civility forbid him from instant revenge against a man who has saved his life. Inviting Dom Juan to change his ways, he finally succeeds in getting his brother to vouchsafe a few days of truce, after which they will be free to pursue their vendetta.

Dom Carlos appears in the fifth act to remind Dom Juan that his period of grace has expired. In the meantime, **Elvire** has spoken once more with her husband and informed him of her desire to retire from the world, presumably into **religious** life, but perhaps into suicide. In the absence of Dom Juan's recognition of his **marriage** vows, Dom Carlos is thus once again obliged to set out on the trail of revenge. Dom Juan is only too ready to play along, for while he gives only sardonic and casuistic answers to Dom Carlos, he sets a time and place in a nearby lane for a **duel** to the death. The fact that Dom Carlos delivers this ultimatum alone is determined by his promise to his brother that he would assume personal responsibility for the failure to kill Dom Juan when he was at the brothers' mercy in the forest. He is prepared for the almost certain death that awaits him in single combat with the master swordsman. Fortunately, Heaven intervenes before Dom Juan can add another victim to his list of homicides. Dom Carlos is an ambiguous and troubling figure, admirable in his insistence on noble values, but undermined by his inability to bring the villain to bay or to effect a practical end to the troubles he causes. Through him, the **audience** is forced to confront the results of their own moral qualms and absolute values. It is unknown who played the part in the original play.

***Dom Garcie de Navarre, ou le Prince jaloux (The Jealous Prince)***.  Begun as
early as 1660, first performed at the Palais Royal Theater on February 1, 1661,
and not published until 1682, this play is often referred to as Molière's one
signal failure.  The facts merit some qualification of that statement.  Its original
run, in the height of Mardi Gras season, was only two weeks long and receipts
dropped noticeably at the end.  That was very unusual for one of Molière's
plays, even that early in his career, but not at all a rare phenomenon in the
theater as a whole.  The play was revived for only five performances in 1662 and
1663.  One of these was before the **Prince de Condé**, always a faithful fan and
supporter, but two were royal command performances, and the remaining two
ordinary theater **repertory**.   There were many plays that never got the
distinction of appearing twice before the King and **court**.  Although he had
obtained a printing privilege as early as 1660, Molière's failure to publish the
play during his lifetime is seen as a mark of disgrace.  However, he was still
using it onstage through 1663, and it was considered unwise to publish a play
that was still of some financial use, since its appearance on the bookstalls put it
in the public domain and authorized anyone to stage it.  Even more importantly,
Molière was conserving parts of *Dom Garcie de Navarre* for his own
"recycling" purposes.  Many of the better lines, including two virtually complete
scenes, would be lifted from the earlier play and included in *Le Misanthrope*.
Another sequence is modified into part of Act II, scene 6 of *Amphitryon*, where
**Jupiter** tries to regain **Alcmène's** good graces after his look–alike Amphitryon
has insulted her.  The playwright did not want to release this text before he had
incorporated it in a more important work, nor did he want to call attention to his
own re–use of it by publishing the original source.  The same reluctance to call
attention to the recycling would affect dramatic performances after *Le
Misanthrope*'s premiere.  Viewed in this light, *Dom Garcie* was not so much
swept under the rug as dressed up in different clothes and sent out into the world
with a new name.  It is true that anecdotal criticism of *Dom Garcie* tends to
characterize it as less than a success and to use this to emphasize the
shortcomings of both Molière and his troupe in the area of serious drama.
Certainly, Molière conceived of the play as an experiment in genre, a *comédie
héroïque*.  Exactly what he meant by this designation is somewhat unclear.
Some critics feel it was simply supposed to be a Hispanic–flavored tragicomedy
in the tradition of *Dom Sanche d'Aragon* and *Dom Bertrand de Cigarral*.  But
the extreme contrast between Dom Garcie's civic virtues and his irrational
jealousy was incorporated later into **Alceste**.  This suggests that Molière was
working on a more innovative level, trying to realize his important goal of
showing an otherwise admirable and noble character afflicted with a single
immobilizing flaw — one so laughable that could lead others to avoid such a
dilemma.  It is certain that by 1661 Molière was already beginning to formulate
his various stylistic innovations into a more or less comprehensive theory of
comedy.  This implicit theory, of which we catch only snatches in his ***placets***
over the ***Tartuffe*** affair and in the polemical works surrounding *L'École des
femmes*, involved much more than the established principal of *castigat ridendo
mores*.  Fundamentally, it had to do with the relationship between **nature** and

the individual human character and the extent to which comic conscience allowed man to improve on what nature gives him.

Though contemporaries such as **Donneau de Visé** criticized the plot as being "more overloaded with incidents than *L'Étourdi*," it is in fact rather compact. A great deal of the political background is revealed through accounts in the first and second acts: **Mauregat's** usurpation of the throne of **Leon** and his imprisonment of **Ignès**, Dom Garcie's rescue of **Elvire** and her establishment in the fortress of **Astorga**, the campaigns of Dom Garcie and Dom Sylve against the tyrant, Dom Sylve's unfaithfulness to Ignès in pursuing Elvire, and the anticipated return of Elvire's long–hidden brother, Dom Alphonse, heir to the thrown of Leon. The primary psychological elements of the play are likewise revealed in the development phase: Elvire has preferred the love of Dom Garcie to that of Dom Sylve, despite the enormous esteem she feels toward the latter and her exasperation with the former's **jealousy**; Élise has preferred Dom Alvar to Dom Lope; Ignès has complained to Elvire of Dom Sylve's betrayal and has obtained her sympathy. The action revolves mainly around Dom Garcie's mistaken outbursts of jealousy. In Acts I and II the misunderstandings involve **letters**. The first is a simple political communication that Elvire forces Dom Garcie to read aloud before chastizing him and making him swear to control his emotions. The second is half of a torn letter whose contents do sound suspicious until they are united with the missing half, and it is revealed that the letter was destined for Dom Garcie himself. The next two misunderstandings involve meetings. In Act III Dom Garcie barges in on a discussion between Elvire and Dom Sylve. Instead of exchanging **love** vows with the rival, the princess was actually lecturing him on his duties toward Ignès. Later, Dom Garcie thinks he sees Elvire in the compromising position of embracing a man, only to find that the male in question was the **disguised** Ignès, who was celebrating her escape from the tyrant with the princess.

The inner drama of Dom Garcie's jealousy is almost completely detached from the outer politics of the play, so that one always has a bit of trouble remembering that the jealous man is also a prince. Dom Garcie's one chance to perform a princely act during the play falls flat, as he fails to assassinate Mauregat between Acts IV and V because the mob beats him to the event. The denouement is one of Molière's weakest, leaving a great deal unsaid about the political side of things and much dissatisfaction about the emotional dimension. Dom Garcie is morose and dejected, the proud Elvire suddenly reverts to sympathy for the man she had thrown into disgrace, and the complex Dom Sylve resolves his divided feelings too quickly when given a political expedient. Nothing is made of **Dom Lope's** betrayal, nor of the romance between Dom Alvar and Élise. The main elements that Molière would salvage from *Dom Garcie* to incorporate in *Le Misanthrope* involve the eponym's conversations in the final three acts with Elvire. The jealous male at his most angry and most abject points, especially when he begins to impute his problems to fate or some evil star, is the essence that will be transferred to Alceste.

See W. D. Howarth, *"Dom Garcie de Navarre, ou le prince jaloux?" French Studies* 5 (1951), 140–148.

**Dom Garcie** (*Dom Garcie de Navarre*).  Prince of **Navarre**, Dom Garcie has enlisted his country's aid in the cause of the throne of **Leon**.  He has freed **Elvire** from the power of the usurper **Mauregat** and conquered the town of **Astorga** to employ as her secure base of operations.  He has also so impressed the princess with his bravery and good qualities that she has preferred him to his Castilian rival, **Dom Sylve**.  The only thing that stands between Dom Garcie and happiness is his pathological **jealousy**, all the more so since **Dom Lope** is exploiting that weakness in his own quest for political power.  However, Dom Garcie proves as early as the first act that his real enemy lies within himself. After professing his willingness to control his jealous impulses, he fails to do so when Elvire receives a simple political missive.  In abject fashion, he is forced to read the text aloud, to admit his wrong, and to promise effusively to do better in the future.  Yet when he comes across a torn **letter** in the next act, he becomes even more irate, only to be forced once again to swallow his words, since the other half of the incriminating letter reveals it was addressed to him. By this time, he has become more realistic about the extent of his problem, but no more effective in controlling it.  In fact, his charges against Elvire become more outrageous and insulting in Act III, when he finds her engaged in conversation with Dom Sylve and accuses them both of dishonesty and collusion, while Elvire had actually rejected Dom Sylve's vows and reminded him firmly of his previous commitment to **Ignès**.  An element of bathos enters into Dom Garcie's obsession in the next act, where he mistakenly thinks Elvire is embracing a man, only to find that the stranger is the escaped Ignès.  He is now in the position of fearing to be cuckolded by a woman.

     Dom Garcie's **love** does have a noble side to it, for he dismisses any interest at all in ruling Leon, making a point that his emotions are totally divorced from usual self–interest.  Like **Alceste** in *Le Misanthrope*, he wants Elvire to take everything from his all–providing hands: "Yes, with all my heart I yearn to prove to everyone / That in you I seek nothing more than yourself."  There is a subtle change in character in Act IV, where Dom Garcie begins to impute his bad behavior and the rest of the world's troubles to destiny, bad luck, the heavens, and other unavoidable causal forces, rather than to the individualism that has so far been associated with him.  When he realizes that he has doomed himself by hastily requiring an explanation from Elvire, he resolves on suicide and decides to take Mauregat with him by assassinating the tyrant.  Dom Sylve appears to preempt this desire (actually, though, Mauregat was killed by a mob), leaving the protagonist depressed and impotent throughout the final act.  The "jealous prince" has by this time ceased to be either princely or jealous.  Though he clearly expresses his feelings of guilt and self–loathing, he never achieves any compensatory act that would have mitigated the stain of his jealousy. Instead, Elmire absolves him of his wrongs because she feels sympathy for the underdog and the political situation changes dramatically in her favor.

**Dom Gilles d'Avalos.**  This is the name of a **disguise Hali** uses in *Le Sicilien* (scene 12) to distract **Dom Pèdre** while the false artist **Adraste** converses with

**Isidore**. He pretends to discuss a point of honor, for he says he has been slapped and wants to know how to respond.

***Dom Juan, ou le Festin de Pierre (The Feast of Stone).*** This five–act prose comedy, patterned on tragicomic models, is one of Molière's most interesting and puzzling plays. Perhaps most importantly, it presents a figure who, much more than any miser or misanthrope, embodies tendencies and awakens desires and anxieties typical of modernity and, to a degree, of all of us. It is a play about which spectators and critics have always been ambivalent. Is it really a comedy? Is the main character a hero of resistance to oppressive tradition or an unpardonable sociopath? Is his mathematical rationalism an admirable corrosive of superstition or merely a new superstition? Is he a hypocritical seducer or the most ruthlessly sincere of all literary figures? The play confronts us with all of those questions and more.

The Don Juan "myth" is one of modernity's central literary and **philosophical** preoccupations. From **Tirso de Molina's** *Burlador de Sevilla*, to the Donjuanesque, Faustian, and Promethean heroes of recent literature and cinema, by way of **Cicognini**, Mozart, Pushkin, Lenau, and Nietzsche, avatars of Dom Juan abound in early modern and modern works. Many critics and commentators have pointed out that modern man's conception of himself is Promethean and Faustian. Early modern thinkers, such as Pico, Ficino, and Manetti celebrated the Protean restlessness of modern man and identified freedom with his ability to transform the material and social worlds to man's own specifications. The Don Juan figure is, especially in Molière's version, the archetype of this early modern, self–fashioning individualist. He is arrogant, seems spectacularly free, is unconstrained by traditions and relationships, and eloquently expounds his mathematical rationalism. He is what every would–be individualist envies and fears. We are fascinated by Don Juan because we are ambivalent about him and what he represents.

Dom Juan is thus both the ideal and the nightmare of modernity. We might say that he is the repressed double of adventurous, entrepreneurial, emancipated, innovative modern man. He is an uncompromising individualist who rejects all "archaic" authorities and claims the right to invent himself. He shares with Galileo and **Descartes** the belief that mathematics is the **language** of truth, and he awakens in others the desire for social mobility that provides much of modernity's dynamism. In some ways, Molière's play can be read as anticipating **Jean–Jacques Rousseau's** denunciation of the painful ambition and the hateful envy at the heart of modern man's motivations. At the same time, Dom Juan ruthlessly exploits the advantages conferred on him by the same social system whose values and constraints he flouts and undermines. The difficulty of finding Molière's play entirely comic or completely serious reflects our ambivalence about Dom Juan. The play enacts the consequences of the emerging modern society's high valuation of individualism, **money**, free circulation, and novelty. Dom Juan represents the regime of universalization, repeatability, transferability, and number; he systematically devalues the past and its "folkloric" beliefs and practices; more, perhaps, than any other Molière character, he insists on inhabiting a world of words, a world that is his own artifact or hallucination. He is the twin of Faust, the dark side of the Cartesian transcendental Subject.

Composed quickly to fill the void created by the banning of *Tartuffe*, *Dom Juan* exploits what was already a popular legend. In addition to Tirso's play, which Molière may not have known, several versions of the story preceded Molière's. Two French playwrights, **Villiers** and **Dorimond**, produced versions in **Paris**, in 1659 and 1661, respectively. These were no doubt inspired by the **Italians**, Cicognini and **Giliberto**, whose works were based on Tirso's *Burlador*. One of Molière's principal innovations within this familiar framework is his emphasis on the theme of **religious** hypocrisy. Dom Juan's adoption of this new **disguise**, in Act V, permits Molière to stage a condensed version of the banned *Tartuffe*. His enemies immediately recognized this and successfully lobbied to have the new play suppressed.

So, Molière's play makes use of the Don Juan phenomenon to place us squarely on debatable ground, to locate us in a boundary zone of unstable borders and ambiguous meanings. Molière, who created *Dom Juan* in the context of an enforced silence imposed by the banning of *Tartuffe*, uses the final act of this play to put a religious impostor on stage, thus gaining a partial victory over those who, like Dom Juan himself, try to silence inconvenient speech and suffocate critical thought. In the character of the **nobleman**, however, Molière combines the motives of pompous moralism with those of modern rationalist epistemology, in effect denying that the latter deserves unambiguous status as an improvement over the former. By showing the ease with which a Dom Juan becomes a **Tartuffe**, Molière suggests that his society provides huge opportunities for hypocrites, pretenders, and seducers. Language or rhetoric is a major issue in both plays, since both Dom Juan and Tartuffe speak like books. Identification of authority with bookish rhetoric, another tendency of early modernity, is thus thematically central to both plays.

The episodic structure of *Dom Juan* and its synthesis of farcical and somber materials make it the best example in Molière's *oeuvre* of the differences between neoclassical theory and early modern theatrical practice. The **unity** of place is not observed, and the unity of time is certainly stretched beyond the critics' approved twenty–four hours. There is a kind of unity of action, or psychological unity: Dom Juan himself is central to all of the play's episodes, either physically present or being talked about. The character's inconsistencies, along with the structural and thematic idiosyncrasies of the play, confront emerging modernity with some of its own fundamental contradictions. A number of students of early modernity have emphasized that reality in that period, like the world of Molière's play, was a zone of instability, inconsistency, and unmanageable metamorphoses.

Why, specifically, should early modern writers be preoccupied with Promethean figures? Perhaps it is the rapid widening of systems of exchange and the consequent erasure of borders and limits that engenders this anxiety about man's growing ambition. Is the consolidation of enormous political and technological power a major factor? Molière's Dom Juan certainly resembles the absolute monarch in many ways, sharing **Louis XIV's** social and sexual exhibitionism and his propensity to finance his pretensions by borrowing from wealthy **bourgeois**. To admire man as Protean is to place a high value on mutability and, by implication, to devalue stability and tradition. Modern man's power to accomplish large social, political, and environmental metamorphoses relativizes things and people, making the world appear as a vast system of theoretically unlimited exchanges, as a "language." Reality thus becomes rhetoric, and Donjuanism becomes a great temptation, even a kind of virtue. Emerging capitalism establishes egotistical calculation in place of old, patriarchal, idyllic relations and resolves personal worth into exchange value.

Molière's play seems in many ways to echo those, like **Pascal**, Nicole, La Rochefoucauld, and **La Bruyère**, who denounced the corrupting effects of luxury, spectacle, and increasingly pervasive social ambition. By seducing duchesses and **peasant** women, Dom Juan mimics the social leveling that is fundamental to the logic of modernity and that was implicit in Louis XIV's systematic elevation of serviceable bourgeois. Dom Juan promises the kind of social transformations that have become the basis of the modern state's legitimacy and the essential feature of our consumer economy. It is as if Hermes, the god of transitions and transgressions and the seductive master of hypocritical manipulation, were the modern deity, and Dom Juan his earthly embodiment. In replacing *Tartuffe* on his play–bill, Molière seems concerned to show that Tartufferie is not just an explicitly religious phenomenon.

In a larger sense, however, religion or the sacred is the central issue: the desacralization of the world associated with modernity is a source of tension and anxiety in the early modern period. Bruno Latour says that modernity was born from the marginalizing of God and the radical separation of the self from the world, a separation underlying modern science. Freed from "bondage" to tradition and religion, "emancipated" from old, local, and limited corporate entities and exchanges, early moderns could denounce the supposed obscurantism of traditional authorities. Dom Juan is a very militant practitioner of desacralization. The play's ending, in which the rationalist Dom Juan is consumed by the fires of hell, certainly authorizes us to make the issue of modern rationalism's contempt for the sacred part of our interpretation.

Closely related to eliminating the sacred is the idea of a Great Divide separating the supposedly ridiculous constraints of the past from modern "progress." For moderns, time erases the past in its wake, supposedly leaving no accumulated debt to the past or the future. Another of modernism's critical innovations is the conversion of exchange into competition, combined with the assertion that competition is actually a superior form of exchange. In Molière's play, Dom Juan's contempt for his father and for the latter's conception of nobility as a debt to the past rather than an advantage to be exploited in the competitive present links the son to this progressive logic of modernity. Dom Louis represents the past, with its network of corporate obligations and exchanges, from which his son is determined to be emancipated. Dom Juan shares the modern rationalist tendency to regard limitations on the self as mere relics of obsolete traditions. He exists in an open market that reflects the early modern divorce of economics from ethics. He is the rival and the enemy of all that constrains individualism. It is no surprise, then, that he eventually comes into conflict with all that is represented by the supernatural.

The sudden emphasis on money and credit during and after the Renaissance created an economy so pervasive that even salvation could be bought. This had a corrosive effect on communities, substituting competitive transactions for traditional exchanges in which benefits were supposed to be mutual and equal. The impact of this development on social relationships and on the sense of sacredness is admirably dramatized in Act II, scene 2 of *Dom Juan*, the famous pauper scene. From the sixteenth century on, in France, corporate groups and localized communities loosened, widened, and subdivided under the pressures of commercial enterprise and political centralization. Old networks were regarded as barriers to the expansion of the new political and economic systems and as constraints on individual enterprise. Economic rationalization redefined exchange as competition taking place in an open market unbounded by local realities. Dom Juan's offer to give money to a poor hermit if the latter will commit blasphemy condenses into a single gesture the divorce of ethics from economics and the convertibility of all other values into money.

Tirso's play inaugurates the tradition in which the Don Juan figure enacts an ironical commentary upon, as well as a direct challenge to, the prevailing values of his society. The rebellious **Spanish** nobleman embodies a revealing caricature of his culture's conception of honor, which was first codified in the *Poem of the Cid*. The world of the Cid is the background of the conquistadors' world, to whose excesses much of early modern Spanish literature is a reaction. Rodrigo de Vivar, El Cid, inhabits a world wherein women serve as exchangeable symbols of male honor and of alliances between males. They are also sometimes the objects of violent mistreatment whose purpose is to dishonor the male whose status they represent. So, Don Juan's "conquests" mimic the invasive, exploitative behavior of the colonialist conquistadors and the patriarchal use of women as transferable signs of male prestige. In Molière's play, too, Dom Juan uses women in what is really a competition with other men. Dom Juan obviously regards women as interchangeable acquisitions serving as signs of his autonomy.

Molière's play goes far beyond Tirso's dramatic meditation on conquest to create a figure incarnating modernity itself. Dom Juan exemplifies all the desires and delusions associated with competitive individualism, fear of and fascination with women, rejection of ethical constraint, and dominance through the deployment of rationalism and bookish language. As an object of others' desires and fears, Molière's Dom Juan inspires social ambition, patriarchal possessiveness and rage, narcissistic gullibility, and a spectacular divine punishment. The latter can be read as simply the negation of individualistic autonomy in favor of ethics and obligation. The play can also be read as a meditation on absolutism. Like Louis XIV, Dom Juan arrogates unlimited sexual privilege to himself, and he attempts to be an irresistible display of social, discursive, and erotic power. Moreover, as Louis Marin makes clear, the absolute monarch himself is created by representations. He thus has much in common with Dom Juan, whose ability to manipulate others depends on his dexterity with signs and on his being a living signifier of authority and status. Here, Molière is essentially in agreement with those among his contemporaries, most notably Pascal and Nicole, who made the overwhelming prestige of the King a leading example of social delusions based on taking wealth and power as signs of personal quality. The absolute monarch also resembles Dom Juan in his increasing recourse to borrowing to finance his pretensions. In Act IV, scene 3, Dom Juan flatters **Monsieur Dimanche**, his bourgeois creditor, by lavishing on him words and gestures implying great respect and honor. He actually pays the bourgeois nothing. This scene parodies both the normally hardheaded bourgeois who are mesmerized by dreams of high social status, and the King, who borrows their money and sells them titles of nobility.

Growing monarchical power and the frenetic pursuit of wealth and social mobility are keys to a thorough understanding of what the writers we refer to as the seventeenth–century moralists perceived about their times. Molière certainly qualifies as a moralist. Paradoxically, at least on the surface, rapidly increasing and centralizing state power was the Siamese twin of growing individualism and personal autonomy. *Amour–propre* was both a character flaw and the engine of progress, as the emerging capitalist economy understood that concept. Widening and intensifying exchange demanded the production of abstract information which, in order to be reproducible and highly portable, had to be separated from context and "ground." One effect of early modern secular humanistic pragmatism was to provide the ruling classes with an ideology more consonant with their worldly aims, less inconvenient to power and acquisitiveness, than either Christianity or feudalism. All of these social and cultural phenomena are thematized in *Dom Juan*.

The play is interestingly related to **Jean–Baptiste Colbert's** economic policy of encouraging specialization in the production and commercial marketing of refined, luxurious goods. Colbert saw much profit for the French economy, and therefore for the monarchy's treasury, in producing and marketing an aristocratic veneer, or what we would call an upscale lifestyle. To this day, France is regarded as a principal source of the accoutrements that serve as signs of good taste and refined living. Of course, in order to profit from such products, the French had to market them to wealthy non–nobles who aspired to imitate aristocrats, or perhaps even to pass for aristocrats. *Le Bourgeois gentilhomme* is another play that, by very clear implication, puts this exploitation of social ambition and envy on the stage. It is interesting and entertaining to think of Dom Juan as complementing, perhaps even authorizing, the ambitions of the many socially ambitious or pretentious Molière characters. In this connection, too, Dom Juan can be seen as implementing systematically, perhaps even sincerely, some of the social practices of his time.

It is possible to see in Colbert's policy a foundational stage of the modern consumer economy, in which the acquisition and display of commodities that have been defined as signs of important personal qualities are taken to be vehicles of social mobility. In effect, Dom Juan markets himself as signifying and bestowing transformed social status. His seductive words and gestures function in much the same way as does advertising. In Act II, scene 1, a peasant woman, **Charlotte**, is seduced by a description of Dom Juan's clothes. His seductiveness clearly depends on his veneer. Dom Juan's abuse of his power, his seductive exploitation of his sophistication as a symbol–manipulator, is made acceptable to Charlotte by his promise to transform her social status. By consenting to marry him, Charlotte believes, she will be consummating an exchange in which she will obtain status like his. This is only possible, of course, if nobility is already conceived as a transferable commodity. A further interesting commentary on the relationship among public economic policy, political and cultural power, and private profit is implied in the fact that Colbert was the scion of a prosperous family of Reims cloth–merchants. Again, we inevitably think of **Monsieur Jourdain**. Dom Juan foreshadows the persistence of aristocratic power and consumption as a model for the modern, bourgeois conception of progress and happiness. When it loses its concrete social functions, the aristocracy acquires a less substantial and more pervasive existence, as the image of modernity's promise to generalize the level of status and material consumption once enjoyed only by the greatest nobles permeates society.

In our context of reception, at the beginning of the twenty–first century, the play is perhaps even more powerful than it was 300 years ago. We can see Dom Juan, parading the verbal and sartorial signs of privilege among the bourgeois and the peasantry, as a forerunner of the commercial dream–merchants who sell us costumes and other commodities associated with individualist emancipation and enhanced status. We live in a culture of mirrors, in which every reflection is a model for insatiable desire. That same desire is intensified by rage against its origin in envy and imitation of an arrogant, impossibly free model. The irrational, impossible promise of an essentially aristocratic level of material consumption and of unlimited social mobility for an ever–increasing number of individuals is what the legitimacy of our institutions seems to depend on. Unfettered mobility is what Dom Juan represents — and pretends actually to offer — to the common women who cannot resist the prospect of marrying him. For men, there is the idea of being like Dom Juan and the simultaneous fear of being one of his defeated rivals. However, a relationship with Dom Juan is really only a seduction permitted by perceiving the world as mere display or spectacle. Being a Dom Juan would be synonymous with alienation. Thus, again, the character is both a dream and a nightmare. In fact, it is only this delusive conversion of the material world into an abstract, represented one that permits the excessive desire that characterizes Dom Juan and modernity. It is this conversion that allows the grandiosity of the modern Subject. Dom Juan's promiscuous distribution of empty flattery and promises allows everyone to dream the modern dream of power, status, and endless metamorphoses. His is the subjectivity whose mobility is the object of an increasingly generalized envy, whose superiority is purely semiotic, and whose rationality ignores its complete dependence on the same physical world that it purports to manipulate or transcend.

The play confronts us aggressively with lessons in the interpretation of comedy. We are intimately connected with, even implicated in, what we are challenged to interpret and evaluate. Moreover, in this powerful play, it is to a degree what we take to be our virtues, rather than what we are willing to acknowledge as our foibles, that confronts us. For each trait or act of Dom Juan that offends us, there is one that enacts some of our own wishes, fantasies, or convictions. In fact, they are sometimes the same traits and acts. *Dom Juan* denounces the fetishization of mobility, the emancipation of individual behavior from its ethical context, the epistemology of quantification, and the myth of the Sovereign Subject. In the process, it subjects to critique some of what we have come to take for granted, and even to celebrate as liberating, about modernity. In Dom Juan's character, there is a deep convergence or continuity of religious hypocrisy with the rhetoric of rationalism; of individualist aspiration with irresponsible waste; and of impassioned appreciation for female beauty with narcissism, abstractionism, empty literary rhetoric, and an incapacity for real pleasure and relationships.

*Dom Juan* illuminates an early phase in the advent of a comprehensively competitive society wherein minimally differentiated individuals battle for the exchangeable wealth that defines status. Often, this wealth is entirely abstract, consisting of mere signs signifying status. Max Vernet, in his excellent study of Molière, emphasizes the importance of this competition for the signs of more and more marginal distinction in seventeenth–century France and in Molière's plays. Vernet argues that the comedian sees the modern culture emerging in his time as tending to substitute a system of two–dimensional abstractions for the given world of concrete relationships. Molière's types always make the mistake of inventing an abstract nature in order to be able to control it. They try to live in a world defined by knowledge or power that they can regard as their property and that will permit them to control others. In other words, they want to function as what Descartes called "masters and proprietors" of the world.

Dom Juan ruthlessly and self–destructively follows the contradictory modern logic defining progress as the ever–freer circulation of commodities and signs of status that lose their power to confer real distinction even as they intensify the desire for that distinction. Like Dom Juan, modernity relativizes social status without eliminating it, and, in the process, releases a huge appetite for the now–transferable signs of status. The aristocracy becomes both obstacle and ideal in this process. Dom Juan, as a noble, is playing the game that will destroy him and his class. The very advantages that he trades on are constituted by superstitious awe; *qualité*, itself, is defined by a kind of folklore or **superstition**. Thus, Dom Juan's systematically corrosive treatment of belief and traditional exchange steadily undermines the basis of his power and influence. Aristocracy itself will be a victim of rationalism's corrosive critique of conventions.

*Dom Juan* exhibits the implications of conceiving exchange as purely economic, as empty of ethical implications. Removing from exchange the ethical element denies the origin in social exchanges of the very individualist identity whose interests are supposedly advanced by the bracketing of ethics.

This, precisely, is Dom Louis's point in his reproach to his son. In fact, it can be argued that the very concepts of the autonomous self and of self–interest are historical products of early modernity. One of modernity's errors is locating substance in the individual Subject, rather than in relationships.

It would be absurd, of course, to argue that excessive, alienated desire is an exclusively modern problem. Systems of wisdom as old as Taoism and **Greek** tragedy counsel the avoidance of excessive desire for reasons much like those implied in Molière's play. What is particular about modernity is that envious desire has ceased to be regarded as a temptation to be avoided; it has become, instead, the engine of collective progress and the motive of individual improvement. Dom Juan quite literally embodies the operations of individualistic desire as they are idealized by modern ideology and exploited by advertising.

Suggested Bibliography: Camille Dumoulié, *Don Juan, ou l'héroîsme du désir* (Paris: Presses Universitaires de France, 1993); Pierre Force, *Molière ou le prix des choses: morale, économie et comédie* (Paris: Editions Nathan, 1994); James F. Gaines, *Social Structures in Molière's Theater* (Columbus: Ohio State University Press, 1984); Michael S. Koppisch, "Dom Juan's Equal Opportunity Rivalry," *Papers on French Seventeenth–Century Literature* 27. 53 (2000), 385–392; Bruno Latour, *We Have Never Been Modern*, trans. Catherine Porter (Cambridge, MA: Harvard University Press, 1993); Larry W. Riggs, "Dom Juan and Harpagon: Molière's Symbiotic Twin Archetypes of Modernity," *Papers on French Seventeenth–Century Literature* 26.51 (1999), 405–423; idem "Dom Juan: The Subject of Modernity," *L'Esprit Créateur* 36.1 (Spring 1996) 7–20; Max Vernet, *Molière: côté jardin, côté cour* (Paris: Nizet, 1991).

*Larry W. Riggs*

**Dom Juan Tenorio (*Dom Juan*).** This role marked a departure from the young romantic leads **La Grange** had previously played in Molière's comedies. Whereas earlier figures had demonstrated little more than sporadic youthful lust for a single well–chosen woman, here was a character with a worldwide agenda of seduction, deliberately casting his net wide and far to bring in women of every type and social category. Instead of wooing them with naïve **sincerity**, he lies continually and with cynical light–heartedness whenever he feels it will advance his cause. Indeed, his attitude is beyond that of the facile *galanterie* described by **Acaste** in *Le Misanthrope*. He seeks only a minimum investment in **love**, actually no investment at all, though he is always willing to pervert marriage into a mere trap for his sweethearts. It will not guarantee them against the most summary abandonment as soon as he grows bored or feels temptation from another source. His success with women is based on his ability to tell them — literally — anything they want to hear, no matter how outrageous or patently false. He does not merely exaggerate words or twist them, as **Éliante** claims lovers do in *Le Misanthrope*, but drains them altogether of any significance. They mean no more than the imaginary **money** he promises to his creditor **Monsieur Dimanche** or the empty courtesy that he offers his overwrought father.

This Dom Juan is not as barbaric and violent as his predecessors in the string of plays that already stretched through the **Spanish, Italian**, and French traditions. He does not kill fathers or rape daughters onstage, for he has no need to. Discreet murders can always be performed offstage. But he was certainly capable of bullying his inept valet **Sganarelle** or unarmed **peasants** like **Pierrot**, as well as hatching plots for armed abductions, such as he forms at the end of the first act. We find further on in the play that he is an accomplished swordsman. Not only has he killed the **Commander**, and "killed him well," but he can also put to flight the gang of robbers attacking **Dom Carlos** as well as cold–bloodedly set up a **duel** with the same man whose life he had earlier saved. Dom Juan's violence is well mannered and carefully restrained.

Disdaining any organized **philosophy**, Dom Juan contents himself with a superficial materialism that gives him liberty to blaspheme. Yet he derives the greatest pleasure from coyly engaging Sganarelle in mock–philosophical debate and from tempting the most pious people to blaspheme for him.

Brave enough to confront an unsheathed sword or to take the hand of a walking statue, Dom Juan is afraid only of committing himself. At the end of the play, he finds bogus bigotry to be a most convenient refuge from any kind of pursuit. His own playfulness is his most potent adversary, for it robs him of any type of lasting contentment, forcing him ever further on a universal quest for gratification. Love becomes so easy that real passion can come to him only under the most perverse circumstances, when a woman is reduced to tears by her useless self–sacrifice or prepared to abandon life itself. The "great lord, miserable man" is a walking paradox, a lewd **Quixote** accompanied by his *demi–habile* Sancho, Sganarelle. His odd tale leaves us with the Calderonesque impression that life itself may be nothing more than a strange dream.

**Dom Lope (*Dom Garcie de Navarre*).** This character is the personification of the old–fashioned evil parasite of morality plays. Bitter because **Élise** has given preference to the bland **Dom Alvar**, Dom Lope admits to her that he is misguiding Dom Garcie in order to work toward political power. He is passing on bits of false or distorted information that he knows will exacerbate Dom Garcie's hyper–**jealous** nature and destroy his chances of courting **Elvire**. He suddenly disappears after Act III, having been blamed for provoking Dom Garcie's interruption of the conversation between Elvire and **Dom Sylve**. It is dramatically disappointing that the evil parasite is banished in such a summary manner, without even having a chance to say another word, much less to atone or pay for his crimes.

**Dom Louis (*Dom Juan*).** The protagonist's father appears in only two scenes, but both are highly significant to the moral context of the play. The first is Act IV, scene 4, where the aging courtier delivers a stern reprimand to his son, admonishing him for failing to live up to the standards of behavior set by his ancestors and accusing him of derogating from his status as an aristocrat through his shameful behavior. It is interesting that the old man assumes a share of the guilt himself, acknowledging that he had prayed so hard for a son to carry on his name that he had spoiled the one granted to him by heaven. He also admits to a lack of empathy with Dom Juan, observing, "To tell the truth, we seem to embarrass each other strangely." Reviewing the whole theory of early modern **nobility** in the course of his speech, Dom Louis concludes, "Know that I would make more of the son of a stevedore who was a decent man than the scion of a king if he acted like you." His concern about derogation is quite real, since some of Dom Juan's crimes could well entail loss of nobility as well as other punishments, and that opprobrium would fall on the entire family rather than on the individual, since his heirs would also lose their status. Instead of contradicting his father's arguments, Dom Juan merely continues the display of false politeness he had carried on with **Monsieur Dimanche**, saying, "Sir, if you were seated, you would be much more comfortable for your speeches." Dom Louis warns him as he stalks out that his paternal tenderness has been pushed to the breaking point and that Dom Juan faces imminent disaster as a result of his actions. The scene reproduces to some extent one in **Pierre Corneille's** *Le Menteur* where Géronte reproaches his son Dorante for his habitual lying. The same two actors, **Louis Béjart** and Molière, were involved, and Molière made an inside joke by calling the father Dom Louis, a name never before used in the other versions of the play. However, he also took care to make Dom Juan's behavior quite different from his predecessors, for the earlier impersonations of the character brutally struck the father, a violation of the **proprieties** as well as a shocking sin against family respect. Molière's "great lord, bad man" is thus far more subtle than the prototypes in his response and in his moral makeup.

The second scene involving Dom Louis is Act V, scene 1, where Dom Juan fools his father with a fake conversion to Christian living. In this totally original scene, Dom Louis is taken in not only by Dom Juan's change of clothing, to the simple shirt of a penitent, and by his mastery of the **language** of penance, but even more so by his own fatherly propensity to wish for his son's return to the right path. Like the father of the biblical prodigal, Dom Louis is willing to forget all and to rejoice that the lost one has returned. One must presume that this performance is good enough to deceive not only Dom Louis and Sganarelle, but the audience as well, for like the valet in the next scene, they must feel a certain revulsion and also a degree of disappointment in themselves when they realize that the sinner has not repented at all, but only learned to ape the actions of the righteous. Unlike Dom Louis, the **audience** does not have a ready excuse for its failure to exercise caution in accepting the rake's alleged change of heart.

**Dom Pèdre** (*Dom Garcie de Navarre*). He appears only briefly to deliver a **letter** silently in the first act and in a transition scene in Act IV, where he leads **Ignès** into **Elvire's** castle, having helped her escape from **Mauregat**.

**Dom Pèdre** (*Le Sicilien*). It is known from the **costume** in Molière's postmortem inventory that he played the role of this crotchety bully, who has bought the **Greek slave** girl **Isidore** and emancipated her, only to imprison her again as his wife. Dom Pèdre seems more bellicose than the average pantaloon. He sleeps with a sword by his side and summons his **servants** to bring an arsenal of **weapons** when he feels threatened by interlopers. The quick slap that he gives **Hali** is met with an equally quick one in reply. He also seems quite natural as a consultant on affairs of honor, as Hali impersonates **Dom Gilles d'Avalos** to lure him away from his fiancée in scene 12. Yet his answer is hardly that of an honorable Frenchman, for he advises Dom Gilles that assassination is the best way to deal with the problem. When he faces the fact of Isidore's elopement with **Adraste**, he flies immediately to the courts for satisfaction instead of seeking it himself on the field of honor. He frankly admits his **jealousy** to Isidore, comparing it to that of a tiger or a devil. To his credit, Dom Pèdre offers shelter to **Climène** in scene 14 when she pretends to be pursued by a murderous, furious husband. He even puts himself in the role of peacemaker, asking Adraste, who impersonates the jealous husband, to forgive her on the basis of the smallness of the offense, her lack of bad intentions, and even his own personal credit as a mediator. Though often on stage, Dom Pèdre has few strenuous gestural scenes, an obvious concession to Molière's ill health, which delayed the **Paris** opening of the play. It is unknown if he conjured up a **Spanish** accent for this role, since the printed version contains no dialectal misspellings or other clues.

**Dom Sylve** (*Dom Garcie de Navarre*).    Thought by everyone, including himself, to be a Castilian prince, Dom Sylve is actually Dom Alphonse, **Elvire's** brother and prince of **Leon**, who has been hidden from the treachery of the usurper **Mauregat**. Dom Sylve has bravely come to the aid of Elvire in her efforts to expel the tyrant and regain the throne for the rightful heir, her brother. Having earlier given his vow of **love** to **Ignès**, he becomes enamored of Elvire and forsakes his former sweetheart. When Elvire meets with him in Act III and reproaches him for his lack of faith, he gives an interesting explanation of his feelings, revealing that his mysterious attraction for Elvire has not erased his love for Ignès. He confesses to being torn between the two women, while experiencing grief and shame over both relationships. The interview is cut short by **Dom Garcie's** heated intervention.    Despite aspersions cast against his honor, Dom Sylve shows admirable restraint and consideration for Elvire's presence, but makes it clear he is willing to settle things later with Dom Garcie if he persists in his accusations. There is little indication that he is setting off to kill Mauregat before Dom Garcie can get to him, as everyone believes he has done through the first half of Act V. His heroic status is somewhat deflated by his honest admission that it was the mob, and not he, who killed the tyrant. His transition to Dom Alphonse, in mid–speech, is abrupt and poorly managed, with no proper explanation given over his mysterious ignorance of his own identity. In the same manner, his revelation that his feelings for Elvire simply vanished when he knew he was her brother, to be replaced by the submerged passion he had never stopped feeling for Ignès, is too coincidental to be really satisfying.

**Doneau, F.**  Little–known author of a worthless imitation of **Sganarelle** called *Les Amours d'Alcippe ou la Cocue imaginaire*. The name probably belongs to a hack author working for **Ribou** or hides that of a better–known man of letters who did not want to take credit for the text.

**Donneau de Visé, Jean** (1638–1710).  This Parisian playwright and man of letters began writing as Molière's enemy, writing the scurrilous *Zélinde, ou la véritable critique de l'École des femmes* in 1663.  Later, for reasons that remain a mystery, he seems to have become an ally.  He hastened to write an approving but rather uninteresting *Letter on Le Misanthrope* that was often included in early editions of the play.  *La Mére coquette* (1665), arguably his best play, bears testimony to a strong emulation of the great dramatist.  It was Molière's troupe that premiered the play, with some success (fourteen performances in the first run, with a four–performance reprise a bit later).  In staging this text, the **Palais–Royal** company was confronting a play of **Paul Quinault** by the same name staged at the **Hôtel de Bourgogne**.  Two years later, the troupe presented *La Veuve à la mode* with only moderate receipts.  *Les Maux sans remède* (1669) and *Les Maris infidèles* were outright flops, with *L'Embarras de Godard* (1667) only slightly less so.  Still imitating Molière, Donneau turned to the **Marais Theater**, desperate for comic material, with *Le Gentilhomme guespin, Les Intrigues de la loterie* (both 1670), and *Le Mariage de Bacchus et d'Ariane* (1672).

Shortly before Molière's death in 1672, Donneau founded the first real French periodical, the *Mercure galant*.  At first an irregularly appearing mixture of all sorts of literary and social drivel (**La Bruyère** is scathing in his criticism, qualifying it as "immediately below null"), it eventually became a real newsletter of sorts.  With a few changes of name, it outlived the Old Régime, the Revolution, and even Napoleon.  The fact that Donneau collaborated on the *Mercure* and on some dramatic projects with **Thomas Corneille** may give a hint at his changing point of view on Molière.

In his *Nouvelles Nouvelles*, Donneau said that had *L'École des maris* only been in five acts, it would have rivaled **Corneille's** *Le Menteur* and **Desmarets de Saint–Sorlin's** *Les Visionnaires* as one of the greatest comedies of the age (the playwright obviously took this to heart and showed how right it was in creating *L'École des femmes*).  However, the same collection contained much criticism of Molière.  Donneau enlarged upon these attacks in *Zélinde*, which in turn takes *L'École des femmes* to task on the grounds that it is derivative and filled with compositional errors.  Donneau refrained from the most invective smears of Molière, concentrating mainly on aesthetic matters and lavishing his observations on other authors, as well.  His last shot against the playwright seems to have been *La Vengeance des marquis*, where he responded to Molière's send–up of the pompous Hôtel de Bourgogne style of declamation by lampooning the comic's own weaknesses, particularly in his attempts at tragic acting.

**Dorante (*Le Bourgeois gentilhomme*).**  Dorante represents the ultimate evolution of the ridiculous marquis in Molière's canon.  In the earlier plays, it was the stodgy **bourgeois** who found the weak point of the flighty aristocrat by criticizing his outlandish attire and affected ways. Now the courtier has become totally fashionable, completely elegant, and utterly in control. It is the bourgeois who is wearing the shamefully discordant clothes and who is being gulled as well. Dorante seems to be quite a cold–blooded parasite, a cynical, worldly version of **Tartuffe**. Unlike in that play, we are given no description of how **Monsieur Jourdain** fell in with this nobleman. We do not know which of the two was the active party in deception. Suffice it to say that they found each other. Jourdain's self–interest is served by Dorante's willingness to bring the marquise closer to him, while Dorante's pockets are filled with Jourdain's gold so that he can arrange costly entertainment and buy gifts. We must remember, however, that the diamond Dorante presented to **Dorimène** actually was obtained at Jourdain's own expense; it was not part of the loan discussed by the two men in private. That accounting scene serves only to paint Dorante with a darker brush, for it recalls the way **Dom Juan** dealt with his creditor, **Monsieur Dimanche**. Both Dom Juan and Dorante disable their lenders with excessive courtesy and avoid reimbursing a penny of their debt. Dorante actually does better than the blasphemer, since he obtains an additional loan on top of what he already owes, just to "round out the figures." No wonder that, despite much cajoling on the part of Dorante, **Madame Jourdain's** social defense sensors are immediately placed on alert whenever the wily courtier approaches. It is as though she can measure the depth of his cynicism, compared to the candor of her darling **Cléonte**, a **noble** who knows not how to swindle or lie. Yet in objective terms Dorante is hardly the family disrupter that one finds in either Tartuffe or Dom Juan. He has no designs on **Lucile** and he is only too happy to aid Cléonte in the **Turkish** masquerade, for it costs him little and will add to his amusement. The sums that he obtains from Monsieur Jourdain are not a significant portion of the family fortune, only "fun **money**" that the fellow can afford to throw into speculations without his wife knowing about it. One hardly gets the impression that Dorante ever intends to reimburse Jourdain, but perhaps he classes himself in with the various masters in the first act as someone who is simply selling himself for needed revenue, as much a courtesan as a courtier, selling refinement to someone willing to buy. One can certainly say that Dorante is a precursor of many figures on the stage of the English Restoration theater, a man who can stand as spokesman for culture and civility and still have larceny in his heart. **La Thorillière** is most generally given credit for playing the original role.

**Dorante** (*La Critique de l'École des femmes*). This fashionable and eloquent *chevalier*, who defends the common man, the **court**, and common sense against the attacks of Molière's enemies, is also a lover who flirts with **Élise** during the discussion on drama. The role was originally played by **Brécourt**, who took analogous ones in *Les Fâcheux* and *L'Impromptu de Versailles*.

**Dorante** (*Les Fâcheux*). The last of the pests presented in Act II, Dorante is a **hunting** maniac. He gives an extremely detailed account of a deer hunt that was spoiled by the intrusion of a country bumpkin, badly mounted on a mare still nursing its foal, and accompanied by a "big oaf of a son as stupid as his father." In the course of various events, in which Dorante purports to show off his skill at the chase, the bumpkin and his pack of mongrels actually manage to corner the stag, which is finished off crudely with a cavalry pistol. Dorante makes much of his own horse, a beautiful animal with Arabian bloodlines. Molière announces in the dedication that the King himself contributed the idea for the best of the pests in the play, and the *Ménagiana* explains that this was none other than the Dorante incident. According to the anecdote, **Louis XIV** remarked to Molière that de Soyecourt, the future leader of the royal hunt, was a "real character" who deserved to be included in the play. Molière proceeded to obey the King's implied command by composing the scene, though there is little reason to assume, as have some editors, that he obtained the hunting terminology from Soyecourt himself. As for the "big oaf" and his father, it is known that **Brécourt**, who specialized in countrified characters, composed a play called *Le Grand Benêt de fils aussi sot que son père* that Molière's troupe would stage in 1664. The text to this play is now lost. However, its association with Dorante may suggest that Brécourt played the part of this pest after the original 1661 production.

**Dorimène** (*Le Bourgeois gentilhomme*). **Mlle. de Brie** is usually credited with playing this part for the first production, and it is not at all out of keeping with her general aura of seriousness and straightforwardness. As a widow, she is a woman enjoying unusual freedom of association and equally particular financial circumstances, in that her wealth has become personal, no longer tied to the legal constraints of dower and **dowry**. Thus, she is a great prize for someone seeking wealth, and one must consider that **Dorante's** interest in her is partly financial. Since he seems to possess nothing but debts, it would be a great advantage for him to find a woman who might be willing to enter into a community property agreement, such as this rich widow. Aside from this financial consideration, there is another troubling side of her relationship with Dorante, since she seems to be attached to him mainly out of what contemporaries would call "reconnaissance." He professes unqualified **love** to her in a one–sided **avowal**, but she gives no evidence of tender feelings for him other than sensible concern and gratitude. He is clearly trying and succeeding in pushing her toward commitment by dint of extravagant spending. Dorimène has qualms about going to **Monsieur Jourdain's** house for entertainment, and would have many more if she knew what kind of loans were being made to facilitate the feast.

Like her admirer, Dorimène is a model of civility and wit. She serves in Act IV as a sounding board of surprise at the extent of Jourdain's crudeness and his wife's rudeness. But she maintains her dignity by adhering to **polite** formulas in even the most trying circumstances. She manages to reply with a very clever *bon mot* when the new *mamamouchi* presents excuses for the couple's previous behavior: "It's nothing at all, and I pardon her [Madame Jourdain] for such an overflow of emotion; your heart must be dear to her, and it doesn't surprise me that living with a man like you could cause no small alarm"

(V, 3). Dorimène's charm and intelligence are striking, and she seems to lack the malice of such aristocratic ladies as **Célimène** and **Arsinoé**. She seems to deserve a better man than Dorante.

**Dorimène** (*Le Mariage forcé*). This bride–to–be of **Sganarelle** appears in scene 2, where she complains of the rigidity in which she was brought up and exults in the freedom and luxury she intends to enjoy as a wife. Her ambitions are made very clear by her entry, where she is accompanied by a little page whom she instructs to hold up the train on her gown. Although she cajoles her fiancé with reassuring words, her intent to lead a life of coquetry is only too clear to him, as well as to the **audience**. She tells him that she doesn't intend to be an unsociable "werewolf" like some of the **bourgeoisie**, but instead says, "I like games, visiting my friends, parties, banquets, and **carriage** rides, in a word, all things pertaining to pleasure, and you should be overjoyed to have a wife like me." She explains that she wants complete freedom of action and association and is willing to grant Sganarelle the same "mutual tolerance, " adding, "In fact, though married, we'll live as two people who know the ways of the world." Rushing off to buy new clothes to replace "these rags," she leaves her future husband with a furious headache that she promises to cure once they are wed. Later, in scene 7, she reiterates to her lover **Lycaste** that she only intends to marry for **money**. This role conforms very much to that of the *marquise façonnière* that Molière had assigned to **Mlle. Du Parc** in *L'Impromptu de Versailles*, so much so that one wonders whether he was not simply type–casting it again in this play.

**Dorimond (stage name of Nicolas Drouin** ca. 1628–1693). Itinerant actor and contemporary of Molière. His *Le Festin de Pierre ou le fils criminel* (*The Feast of Stone or the Criminal Son*), performed in **Lyon** in 1658, was one of the sources for *Dom Juan*. In addition, it is possible that another comedy, *La Femme industrieuse* (*The Scheming Lady*), published in the spring of 1661, may have given Molière the idea of **Sganarelle's** serving as an unwitting go–between for **Isabelle** and **Valère** in *L'École des maris*. The **Doctor** in Dorimond's play performs a similar service for the young lovers, Isabelle and Léandre, although he is not the young lady's guardian. A third comedy, *L'École des cocus ou la Précaution inutile* (1661) may have given rise to the vogue of plays by Molière and others with "school" in the title.

See Alice Pianfetti, *The Theater of Nicolas Drouin, dit Dorimon, a Contemporary of Molière* (New York: Philosophical Library, 1970).

**Dorine** (*Tartuffe*). Dorine is one of Molière's most outspoken and active female characters, a **lady's maid** who clearly sees herself as the mainstay of **Orgon's** household. She joins her superiors in laughing at the departing **Mme. Pernelle**, delivering two long tirades in which she lambastes the nosy neighbors and excoriates women who turn from flirts into prudes when they can no longer attract men. It is she who also provides much of the description of **Tartuffe** and his hold over Orgon, including some slightly off–color remarks on belching that are explained in the text as being "**servant's language**." She continues in the same vein in Act II, sniping at Orgon while he tries to convince **Mariane** to accept **marriage** with "an **animal**," upbraiding her mistress for failing to respond forcefully, and then overcoming the **lovers' spite** that develops between her and **Valère**. At the beginning of the third act, she vainly tries to reason with the hot–headed **Damis**. Then she has one of her funniest exchanges with Tartuffe, who urges her to cover her breasts with a handkerchief, only to draw the response, "As for myself, I'm not so quickly aroused, / And I could see you naked from bottom to top / Without being tempted in the least!" Orgon finally manages to cow her into silence in Act IV, and her comments in Act V are limited to a few pert, sarcastic rejoinders, especially in regard to **Monsieur Loyal**. While she falls short of being a true *meneur du jeu* in the way that **Toinette** of *Le Malade imaginaire* will be, she nevertheless marks a lively step in the evolution of feminine theater roles. **Madeleine Béjart** most probably figured as the original Dorine, distilling into her much of her rich theatrical experience, since it was in most respects her last great part.

**Dorothée**. The real name of **Ascagne** in *Dépit amoureux*, not revealed until the final scene.

**D'Ouville, Antoine Le Metel, sieur** (ca. 1600–ca. 1657). Author of numerous comedies and tragicomedies in the decades before Molière's plays began to appear. His *Aimer sans savoir qui* (1646) may have suggested several items in *Dépit amoureux*. D'Ouville was the brother of the influential **Boisrobert**.
    *See* Roger Guichemerre, *La Comédie avant Molière 1640–1660* (Paris: Colin, 1972).

**Dowry**. *See* **Marriage**.

**Dramatic Poetry**. Molière is seldom given all the credit he deserves for developing dramatic poetry to its ultimate form in Classical France. Before him, comedy existed in two distinct and incompatible modes. One was the farcical remnant of the Middle Ages that continued to be composed in clumsy octosyllables, a rhyme scheme much better suited to the morphology of Old and Middle French. Its characters were hobbled by their speech, expressing themselves in a sort of doggerel suited only for wenches, drunks, and rakes. One need only disinter some of the plays of Molière's contemporary, **Jean Chevalier** of the **Marais Theater**, to see the obvious limitations of this style. The second, higher form was mostly imitated from the **Spaniards** and gave rise to the comedies of **Pierre Corneille** and **Rotrou**. Its alexandrine verses were well suited to lofty sentiments and delicate expression. But this very quality kept it distant from the true essence of laughter. It remained too often sterile and contrived, depending more on the intricacies of unlikely intrigue to generate laughter, rather than on the development of character and the juxtaposition of ludicrous forms of manners. Even its funny men were confined to verbal comedy in the style of the Spanish *gracioso*, who was so often merely a sarcastic spectator to the action instead of a participant and ingredient.

In creating the grand comedy, Molière first had to master the alexandrine and adapt it to comic form as no one had before. This involved the extreme inventiveness in rhyme for which **Boileau** (and almost Boileau alone) gives him credit in the second *Satire*. But more than just end–rhymes were needed, and Molière infused the alexandrine with all the salty vocabulary of the street and the marketplace as no one before him had ever dared. Then, having brought formal verse to a new threshold, he boldly leaped across and showed that prose deserved a place in dramatic discourse. This was a daring move that is still not appreciated by everyone. The prejudice for verse was long entrenched and would remain so. It was easy for detractors to say that he simply lacked the time or dedication to versify, an impression to which he lent some credence by subcontracting the verses of most of *Psyché* to **Pierre Corneille**. However, as he teaches **Monsieur Jourdain**, prose is just the reverse side of verse; the sign on the coin is different but does not lessen its value. From *Les Précieuses ridicules* through *L'Avare* and on to *Le Malade imaginaire*, Molière's prose plays represent a chain of experiments in dramatic language seeking an ever freer and more supple means of expressing human thoughts and emotions.

Finally, one must appreciate that Molière sought to shorten the distance between dramatic **language** and the language of **music**. Experimenting at first with free verse songs and passages inserted into the early **comedy–ballets**, he went on to explore in *Amphitryon* and *Psyché* the effects of free verse in entire works, approaching the operatic in the latter work. This free verse was metered and rhymed, but non–isometric, similar to the kind used by **La Fontaine** in the *Fables*. It provided for stress and silence, for emotional percussion and punctuation, much better than the closely ordered alexandrine couplet. French literature would have been much the richer if it had followed these experiments further instead of merely picking up the tried and true forms of prose or couplets as it moved ahead into and beyond the Classical period. Those who find Dryden's style a bit stilted would add the same for English literature of the Augustan age.

*See also* **Alexandrines**; **Proprieties**; **Unities**; **Verisimilitude**.

**Dreams.** A common comic element. On the eve of what promises to be a violent day, the cowardly **Mascarille** of *Dépit amoureux* says that he has dreamt ominously of broken eggs and unstrung pearls and pleads to be excused from his master's upcoming **duel** with **Albert's** family. **Clitidas** mockingly mentions that he has also dreamed of broken eggs and dead fish, which **Anaxarque** interprets as evil omens. In *Le Mariage forcé*, **Sganarelle** blames his new–found scruples about **marriage** on a dream, where he found himself in a ship on a raging sea (scene 3). **Dorine**, the quick–witted **lady's maid** in *Tartuffe*, advises **Mariane** to forestall marriage with the dreaded hypocrite by citing bad omens, such as crossing the path of a corpse, breaking a mirror, or dreaming of muddy water.

Dreams may also reflect the preoccupations of daily life rather than the intrusions of the supernatural. In *Psyché*, **Aglaure** tells how her **jealousy** of her younger sister causes insomnia, but when she does fall asleep, her dreams bring her back to the same subject, making it impossible to escape the cause of envy in daytime or at night. In *Monsieur de Pourceaugnac*, the **doctors** who are studying the protagonist's mental condition ask him if he has had dreams lately, showing that Freud was not the first to delve into such matters. However the patient is not much help to the budding psychologists, for when asked what the dreams were like, he simply replies, "Like dreams" (I, 8).

The convenient tendency to describe any uncanny vision or event as an unreal, unsubstantial dream is both highlighted and criticized by Molière. **Amphitryon** at first tries to dismiss **Sosie's** nonsensical (but true) story of encountering a double as a dream. Later when he hears from **Alcmène** that another Amphitryon has visited her during the night, he again tries to explain it as a dream, but finds himself in the reverse position of being mocked for lack of verisimilitude. In *Le Malade imaginaire*, the practical **Angélique** uses a dream as a pretext for explaining her astonishment at seeing **Cléante** in their house dressed as a music teacher; saying she had dreamt that such a man had saved her from danger. The latter example shows that the notion of dreams as insubstantial trifles may be exploited by those clever enough to seize the advantage.

**Du Bois (*Le Misanthrope*). Alceste's** valet makes a sudden and apparently hilarious interruption into the play in the last scene of Act IV. Bursting in unannounced, he causes **Célimène** to remark, "But here comes Mister Du Bois, in a most laughable fashion." Alceste then asks him, "What means this outfit and this frightened appearance; what's wrong?" We may infer from this that he was wearing something different from the normal servant's attire, perhaps a long cloak and hat to conceal himself. He goes on to explain, all too slowly for Alceste's taste, why he has come in this unusual costume and what has happened at Alceste's lodgings. The "man of dark clothes and countenance" who left an indecipherable paper in the kitchen with Du Bois was certainly, as the man assumes, an officer of the court involved with Alceste's lawsuit. An hour later, one of Alceste's friends came to warn him that things were going badly and that he risked arrest if he stayed in the jurisdiction. Though he meant to bring along the note that the thoughtful friend had written to explain things more fully, Du Bois searches his pockets and can produce neither the legal writ nor the note. This was probably the occasion for search **lazzi** in the original production, and many modern performances also deploy considerable sight gags as Du Bois goes through his clothes looking for the papers. An interesting aspect of Du Bois is that he is, like his master, highly superstitious, not only ascribing all the mysterious events to a gloomy fate, but frequently mentioning devils and demons in his speech. Not only does this illustrate the old proverb, "Like master, like servant," but it reinforces a whole side of Alceste's character that is often obscured by his bumptious intelligence. The role may originally have been taken by **Louis Béjart**, among others.

**Du Croisy (stage name of Philibert Gassot,** ca. 1630–1695). This rubicund actor came from a theatrical family and had already led his own troupe, albeit unsteadily, when he joined Molière's in 1659, having perhaps met the playwright in **Rouen** the preceding year. His technical expertise served the troupe well during their move from the **Petit–Bourbon** to the refurbished Palais Royal Theater. His wife Marie Claveau was also a player, but was so untalented that she eventually gave up her share in the troupe and slipped into the background. Du Croisy played numerous roles throughout the Parisian years, including his homonym in *Les Précieuses ridicules*, the poet **Lysidas** in *La Critique de l'École des femmes*, himself and Lysidas in *L'Impromptu de Versailles*, the **philosopher Marphurius** in *Le Mariage forcé*, **Aristomène** in *La Princesse d'Élide*, the **senator** in *Le Sicilien*, **Jupiter** in *Psyché* and perhaps in *Amphitryon* as well, **Sbrigani** in *Monsieur de Pourceaugnac*, and **Harpin** in *La Comtesse d'Escarbagnas*. He was probably **Tyrène** in *Mélicerte*, **Monsieur de Sotenville** in *George Dandin*, the **Philosophy Teacher** in *Le Bourgeois gentilhomme*, and **Vadius** in *Les Femmes savantes*. He could have been cast as the **Notary, Diafoirus, Purgon,** or **Fleurant** in *Le Malade imaginaire*. His greatest part is undoubtedly **Tartuffe**. His sister was married to the prominent tragedian Bellerose and his daughter, Marie–Angélique, to the actor Paul Poisson, sibling of the more famous Raymond. After Molière's death, he continued into the company of the Hôtel Guénégaud and in 1680 joined the **Comédie–Française,** along with his daughter, as half–share members. He retired at the Lenten break of 1689.

**Du Croisy** (*L'Impromptu de Versailles*). There is little conversation between Du Croisy and his counterparts in the frame play where he represents himself, though he complains less than the other players about having to learn his lines, perhaps reflecting his dependable nature in real life. Molière assigns him the part of the poet **Lysidas,** just as he had played him in *La Critique de l'École des femmes,* and advises him to sound out his phrases pedantically, indicating that the pedant may have been a stock role for Du Croisy. He discharges his role very well, continuing in the vein of the earlier play.

**Du Croisy** (*Les Précieuses ridicules*). Playing under his own stage name, Du Croisy is mainly an accomplice to his fellow **bourgeois La Grange** in a few scenes at the beginning and end of the play. Conventional suitors, they react to the bad reception they have had from the would–be *précieuses* and later "punish" their valets, **Jodelet** and **Mascarille,** for having impersonated them, although it was the masters themselves who devised the scheme.

**Du Croisy, Mlle.** (*L'Impromptu de Versailles*). In what must have been one of Marie Claveau's last appearances on stage, she notes that, like **Mlle. Hervé,** she has very few lines, but still can't promise to get them all correct, perhaps a reference to her faltering talents, which would eventually drive her from the boards. Molière assigns her the role of a lady who cannot stand to say anything good about anyone, but she does not take a large part in the discussion that follows.

**Duels**. Frequently mentioned and often threatened in comic theater, duels had been officially banned since the time of **Cardinal Richelieu**, and were further forbidden on stage by the conventions of the *bienséances*. **Louis XIV** renewed and reinforced this prohibition during Molière's lifetime.

In *Dépit amoureux*, two duels threaten to break out in the final act, the first between **Ascagne** and **Valère** over **Lucile's** honor and the slander that she appears to have received from Valère, and the second (nothing more than a joke) between **Mascarille** and **Gros–René** over the hand of **Marinette**. Neither comes to blows, since Ascagne eventually reveals her true identity as a woman and Valère's very secret wife, while Mascarille shows himself to be a total poltroon in avoiding a clash with his fellow valet.

Similarly, in *Sganarelle, ou le Cocu imaginaire*, the title character arrives in an ancient suit of **armor**, intending to provoke **Lélie** into a duel, but after a few shoves, it becomes clear that his opponent is stronger and more fearless, and the **bourgeois** in his "rain gear" quickly gives in.

*Les Fâcheux* introduces a pair of dueling fanatics. The first is **Alcandre**, who explains that he has just been challenged (I, 6) and wants **Éraste** to serve as his second and deliver his reply. After some reflection, Éraste answers that his fourteen years of military service are proof enough of his bravery, but that he refuses to disobey the King's edicts against such combat. Later on (III, 4), **Filinte** arrives to announce that Éraste has been challenged and that he intends to guard him everywhere he goes. Though Éraste tries to explain that he is awaiting his mistress and wants no company at all, Filinte persists until the lover threatens to draw and fight himself if the pest will not leave him. At this point, all that Filinte strikes is a hasty retreat. Like Alcandre and Filinte, **Monsieur Jourdain** seems to have a serious interest in swordsmanship, so much so that he has hired a **fencing master**. He quickly reveals, however, that he is interested in fighting only if he can be sure of winning, asking for assurance that in fencing "without possessing courage, one can kill a man and avoid being killed oneself."

All proper duels began with a formal challenge, or "cartel." One is delivered in *Pastorale comique* to **Lycas** from his rival **Filène**, but we must wonder what **weapons** were involved, for swords do not seem appropriate to the **shepherds** of that play. Perhaps this was part of the gestural comedy involved in their two "combat" scenes. *Le Sicilien* provides a more seasoned duelist in the form of **Dom Pèdre**. This **Spaniard** is armed to the teeth with both blade and bullet and carries a sword with him to bed, if we are to judge by scene 4. **Hali** uses a **disguise** and the pretext of an upcoming duel to beguile his attention while **Adraste** makes love to **Isidore**. Ironically, the dueling expert advises his questioner to simply ambush and murder his opponent, but one must remember that the speaker is not a Frenchman. Another who has received a more realistic challenge is **Monsieur de Pourceaugnac**. He recalls to **Éraste** how he was slapped by a gentleman from Périgord back in **Limoges**, but responded only with a shower of bad **language**. Oddly enough, when he learns that the **doctor** has diagnosed him as afflicted with a venereal disease, Pourceaugnac shouts that he wants to meet the liar sword in hand.

**Amphitryon** finds himself in the unusual position of trying to provoke a duel with a god. He wants to punish **Jupiter** for assuming his identity, but is unaware of that of his opponent. Jupiter, for his part, enrages the Theban even more by treating the challenge as a joke and dismissing the enemy as unworthy. Even Amphitryon's friend **Naucrates** is unwilling to let a man duel against himself. The most serious duel in Molière's theater almost occurs in the final act of *Dom Juan*, where the protagonist responds to **Dom Carlos's** challenge by fixing a time and place for single combat, already assured that he is a far superior swordsman and can easily dispatch his victim, resorting to foul play if necessary, since the spot chosen is an unfrequented lane leading to a remote **convent**.

**Dufresne, Charles.** Leader of a troupe of traveling players attached at first to the Governor of **Guyenne** and later to the **Prince de Conti**. The remnants of the **Illustre Théâtre** took refuge with Dufresne beginning in 1645, after the failure of their enterprises in **Paris**. Little is known of the man, but he gives the impression of an active and careful leader who saw his troupe through many difficult times. Based in **Bordeaux** where they regularly played before the **parlement** of Guyenne, the troupe eventually performed in a great crescent route stretching from **Nantes** in the west, southward through **Poitiers** and **Bordeaux**, up the Garonne valley through **Agen**, **Albi**, and **Toulouse**, through the Languedocian cities of **Carcassonne**, **Narbonne**, **Béziers**, **Pézenas**, and **Montpellier**, and up the Rhone valley via **Avignon**, **Vienne**, **Grenoble**, and **Lyon** to **Dijon**. Dufresne trusted Molière to take up the demanding roll of *harangueur*, which involved a stand–up opening act designed to capture the goodwill and attention of rowdy provincial **audiences**. Later, after Dufresne's retirement in 1656, Molière himself became head of the troupe.

**Du Parc (stage name of the actor René Berthelot, also known as Gros–René**, d. 1664). Noted for his rotundity, Du Parc was obliged to ride an elephant at one royal entertainment because he was too hefty for any other type of mount. Nevertheless, he was married to one of the most beautiful women in **Paris**, the actress Marquise–Thérèse de Gorla, who, after René's death, had an affair with **Racine**, defected from Molière's troupe to the **Hôtel de Bourgogne** and went on to become one of the great interpreters of Racine's tragedies. Du Parc was already a member of **Dufresne's** troupe when Molière joined. He probably had the original role of **Le Barbouillé** and played slow–witted **servants** in *Le Médecin volant, L'Étourdi, Dépit amoureux*, and *Sganarelle*. He worked with Molière from 1647 to 1664, except for a year with the **Marais** in 1659–60.

**Du Parc, Mlle. (stage name of Marquise–Thérèse de Gorle or de Gorla,** ca. 1635–1668). More talented as a tragic actress than as a comedienne, Mlle. du Parc was somewhat ill–matched with Molière's troupe. To judge from her part in *L'Impromptu de Versailles*, she was often bickering with **Mlle. de Brie** and

**Armande Béjart** over theatrical privileges. Similar to her part of the *marquise façonnière* in the play–within–the–play of that work was her role as **Dorimène** in *Le Mariage forcé*. After the death of her husband René in 1664, the troupe continued to pay her his share of the earnings through the end of the yearly contract. Whether this was due to their fondness for the old *farceur* or to respect for Marquise's tragic talents is open to debate. Racine's plays seemed to offer her a new lease on professional life. When the young poet, blaming Molière's troupe for the tepid reception of *La Thébaïde*, underhandedly withdrew his script of *Alexandre le grand* and gave it to the rival **Hôtel de Bourgogne**, she eventually followed him, but not until the year's contract ran out on Ash Wednesday 1666. Racine is widely rumored to have become her lover. The incidents surrounding her mysterious death in 1668, at the height of her career, still give rise to speculation about murder. Among the roles attributed to her are those of **Célie** (*Sganarelle*), **Done Elvire** (*Dom Garcie de Navarre*), **Orante** (*Les Fâcheux*), **Climène** (*La Critique de l'École des femmes*), **Éliante** (*Le Misanthrope*), **Dorimène** (*Le Mariage forcé*), and **Aglante** (*La Princesse d'Élide*), as well as **Night** in **Gilbert's** *Endymion*. However, in the absence of documentary or vestimentary proof, some of these have to qualify as speculative.

**Du Parc, Mlle.** (*L'Impromptu de Versailles*).     This is one of the most interesting roles in the small play.   Molière clearly pokes fun at the actress for her affected, apparently vampish way of presenting herself and makes her one of the loudest protestors against the difficulty of learning lines in the frame play. In the play–within–the–play, she has a sequence where **Armande Béjart** teases her about her looks, perhaps revealing a type of real rivalry between the troupe's two beauties, one of them barely out of adolescence and the other in the prime of her adulthood.   Her role continues the character of **Climène** in *La Critique de l'École des femmes*, and she joins in the silly criticisms leveled against Molière and his theater.

**Du Ryer, Pierre** (ca. 1600–1658).   Parisian playwright and translator.   A contemporary and rival of **Pierre Corneille**, Du Ryer wrote two Classical tragedies that were performed by Molière's troupe, both in the provinces and after the return to **Paris**. A legal act mentions that the **Illustre Théâtre** had purchased the text of *Scévole* (1643) from the author.   Taken from the life of Caius Mucius Scaevola, it concerns Roman heroism in the face of Tuscan oppression.     Apprehended before he can assassinate Lars Porsenna, the protagonist burns off his own hand in a brazier, which convinces the Etruscan king to leave Rome in peace. It was still being performed in 1659–60, according to **La Grange's** Register.   The troupe also gave at least one performance of *Alcionée*, another work dealing with the limits of legitimate royal authority.

   *See* James F. Gaines, *Pierre Du Ryer and His Tragedies: From Envy to Liberation* (Geneva: Droz, 1987); **Repertory**.

**Dutch Renditions of Molière.** Along with Britain, Holland was very much affected by Molière's comedies. There were innumerable editions pirated in French, but some translations can be noted. *Scapyn* appeared in a collection published in 1696 by Gusbert de Groot of **Amsterdam**. *George Dandin* was rendered in 1686 as *Lubbert Lubbertze, of, de Geadelde Boer*, published by Albert Magnus of Amsterdam. The same printer issued *'t Gedwongene Hunwelyk (Le Mariage forcé)* in a 1682 collection. A 1711 volume printed by J. Lescaille, also in Amsterdam, contains the foregoing play along with *Fielebout of de Doktor tegens Dank* (a combination of *Le Médecin malgré lui* and *L'Amour médecin*), *De Schilder door Liefde (Le Sicilien)*, and *De Listige Vryster (L'École des maris)*. It is clear from this list, and perhaps from the absence of authorial claims, that the Dutch appreciated the **farcical** elements most highly.

# E

**Early Nineteenth–Century Criticism** (1798–1850). During the Napoleonic period (1798–1815), Molière's work was often scorned or ignored by the public in general, from barely literate elements through the intellectual classes. The main exception to this tendency came from neoclassical intellectuals such as Cailhava, La Harpe, and Geoffroy. The first two of this trio wrote mainly pedagogical and aesthetic works, but the latter was something of a cultural journalist, associated with the *Journal des Débats*. The neoclassicists defended Molière against low–brow modernists and newly minted Romantics alike, upholding the dramatist as a great model of style, if not of moral perfection. It was easiest to defend Molière when he was placed in contrast with the views of Schlegel, who openly touted the imaginative superiority of Anglo–Germanic literature. For some early Romantics, such as Stendhal, Molière was admirable for the same brusqueness of manners and freedom of expression that modernists flouted, but in other ways he represented a tradition that was obsolete. Along with Chateaubriand and Madame de Staël, who also saw herself as a bridge between French and "Northern" literatures, Stendhal was responsible for creating the image of a sad, brooding Molière that would dominate during the following years. The Restoration of the Bourbon monarchy in 1815 marked a departure in attitudes toward Molière. The imposition of reactionary political and religious controls in France caused a resurgence of interest in Molière and especially in *Tartuffe*, idolized as a supremely effective protest play by the dissidents of the age. The new generation of rising Romantics tended to embrace Molière while rejecting **Racine's** tragedy in favor of Shakespeare's. Nodier, Hugo, Musset, and Sainte–Beuve all saw in Molière a profound poetic genius as well as a stylistic innovator who heralded their own priorities. At the same time, they assimilated Molière's characters, and even his historic person, to the image of the melancholy Romantic hero, suffering from *mal de siècle* and world–weariness generated by his deep, visionary understandings. Molière seemed perfectly suited to the goals of humanitarian romanticism, which took seriously the motto of *castigat ridendo mores*, correcting human behavior through ridicule. This tendency reached its peak with the historian Jules Michelet, an ardent Republican who saw Molière as an avatar of liberty, equality, and fraternity, struggling subversively against the oppression of his age. Others, such as the critic Jules Janin and the writers Alfred de Vigny, Musset, and Emile Deschamps, more enthusiastic about the austere humor of *Le Misanthrope* than the energetic, heterogeneous drama of *Dom Juan*, followed Théophile Gautier's inclinations toward the doctrine of *l'art pour l'art*. Musset's poem, "Une soirée perdue," presents Molière's genius hovering far above the petty values of social improvement that preoccupied the Hugo wing of Romanticism. Anti–bourgeois thinkers such as Théodore de Banville, Gustave Flaubert, Proper Mérimée, Baudelaire, and Leconte de Lisle were quick to rally to the altar of this aesthetic Molière. Sainte–Beuve's *portrait littéraire* of Molière, written as the heyday of Romanticism was passing, sums up these divergent trends very well. The half–century that had opened with the exhumation of Molière's remains from the cemetery (they turned out to be the wrong bones) culminated with the dedication of a memorial to him at the Fontaine de Molière, near his last home in the rue de Richelieu. The unsuccessful efforts of the Revolution to assimilate Molière had given way to increasing popularity, as social reformers and antisocial stylists alike found plenty of inspiration to claim Molière as a forerunner for their schools.

*See* Otis Fellows, *French Opinion of Molière (1800–1850)* (Providence: Brown University Press, 1937).

**Early Twentieth–Century Criticism** (1914–1960). Following the intense biographical detective work and the arguments about Molière's morality that had characterized the end of the previous century, scholars from World War I on tended to work on integrating new–found knowledge and opening new fields of critical perspective. One result was a spate of "new" Molière biographies, all of which are now quite dated with the exception of Gustave Michaut's monumental biographical triology, published between 1922 and 1925, that traces the dramatist from his youth, through his first trials, and into his period of great struggle. Unfortunately, a final volume was never finished, though notes in the form of an article were later published. Michaut's understanding of the relationship between the events of Molière's life and his development as an artist and writer still pertains to modern studies.

Another important area of progress even before the 1914 dividing line was in source studies, with E. Martinenche providing a major review of Moliere's debt to the **Spanish** theater in 1906 and Pietro Toldo doing the same for **Italian** sources in 1910. Toldo's volume would receive an important updating from Gustave Attinger in 1950. Further contributing to this growing context for understanding Molière was the monumental *History of French Dramatic Literature in the Seventeenth Century* in nine volumes completed by Henry

Carrington Lancaster between 1929 and 1942. The outbreak of World War I coincided with the first great study of Molière's *comédies–ballets* as a unique art form by Maurice Pellisson.

Exciting new outlooks on comic theory in Molière came from a variety of directions. The Spaniard Ramon Fernandez published a book in 1929 that strives to understand Molière as the inventor of a new and more universal type of comedy; it has reappeared since in various titles and languages, without losing any of its original verve. The Dane Valdemar Vedel contributed an important study in 1935 that is also able to detach Molière's artistic contributions from the cultural attitudes that have become second nature to French observers. From within the French hexagon, Daniel Mornet's 1943 aesthetic biography of the author enhanced on Michaut's vision of Molière's career and the inter–relationships between the separate plays. Will G. Moore's 1949 study, *Molière, A New Criticism*, successfully applied Chicago School methods to the analysis of his works, while at the same time laying the groundwork for later studies concentrating on the strictly theatrical elements of the canon. These would be provided by Jacques Audiberti in 1951 with *Molière dramaturge* and by René Bray in 1954 with *Molière, homme de théâtre*, both of which argue that Molière can best be appreciated from the point of view of the stage itself and its needs and conventions.

At the same time, the abiding interest in Molière's **philosophical** and intellectual connections was not being abandoned. A. L. Sells in 1933 published articles in *Modern Language Review* that amount to a substantial little monograph on Molière's relationship with the skeptical philosopher **La Mothe Le Vayer**. René Jaskinski's 1951 study, *Molière et le Misanthrope*, views the dramatist's work through the lens of **Jansenist** Christian ideas, highlighting the unlikely echoes of this sect in the comedies. Antoine Adam's third volume of the *Histoire littéraire de la France au XVIIe siècle,* published in 1954, is devoted to Molière and **Boileau** and emphasizes their contributions to the whole constellation of French Classical literary values arranged around rational philosophy, though often achieved through means of irony and subversion. The Marxist–inspired criticism of John Cairncross goes further; he delivered a strident image of Molière as a **bourgeois** and libertine forerunner of revolution against all forms of neo–feudal tyranny. On the other hand, Paul Bénichou's 1948 study, *Morales du Grand Siècle*, returns to the old moral framework through the new methodology of mentalities, demonstrating persuasively the many links between Molière and an emergent nobility built around **Louis XIV's** powerful nation state and its political and aesthetic pretensions.

The new era was not without its anti–Molière cranks. Just as the seventeenth century had its **Boulanger de Chalussay**, the eighteenth its **Fabre d'Eglantine,** and the nineteenth its Veuillot, the early twentieth produced Henri Poulaille, who in 1951 tried to convince the world that Molière's masterpieces could only have been written by — Corneille!

*See* Laurence Romero, *Molière: Traditions in Criticism (1900–1970)* (Chapel Hill: University of North Carolina Press, 1974).

*École des femmes, L'* (*The School for Wives*).  Premiering at the Palais Royal Theater on December 26, 1662, this was the first of Molière's five–act plays in verse to emerge from the **Italian** model of the *commedia sostenuta*.  *L'École des femmes* is considered a *grande comédie*, which, by virtue of its psychological depth and subtlety, represents perhaps the greatest triumph of his career.  The exposition scene highlights a debate in which **Arnolphe** and **Chrysalde** present opposing views on women and **marriage**.  Having delayed his marriage until the rather advanced age of forty–two, Arnolphe, the comic, and at times farcical, *barbon*, has elaborated a fail–safe theory of a perfect marriage predicated upon the social, moral, and intellectual subordination of his wife.  He acquired his bride–to–be, **Agnès**, at the age of four and has succeeded in keeping her, for the past thirteen years, in total seclusion from the world in order to cultivate systematically her innocence; he has thus maintained her, both intellectually and emotionally, in a state of infantile dependency.  In his steadfast attempt to reason with his friend and to convince him of the limitations of this strategy, Chrysalde contends that a wife needs to possess the essential ingredients of *honnêteté* (sensitivity and judgment) to be able to distinguish between right and wrong.  He also holds that the fate of any husband is ultimately beyond his control.  Imperturbably self–assured, Arnolphe takes particular delight in mocking the conjugal misfortunes of husbands in his town, which he documents scientifically by means of his memoirs or *tablettes*.  Moreover, he has selected simple–minded servants, **Alain** and **Georgette**, in order to ensure the success of his plan.  The dramatic irony of Arnolphe's first encounter with **Horace**, his youthful rival, stems from the fact that the **money** that Arnolphe has generously loaned him will be used to advance the latter's amorous plans with Agnès (I, 4).  As the result of a double quid pro quo concerning the protagonist's identity (Horace does not know that Arnolphe is also his unseen rival, Monsieur de la Souche) and the fact that he owns two homes, the *jeune blondin* (golden–haired boy) will continually inform his "friend" Arnolphe of the various schemes he designs to develop his relationship with Agnès.

After flying into a rage against his **servants**, whom he accuses of betrayal, Arnolphe proceeds to interrogate comically the disingenuous Agnès, since he is anxious to be apprised of all details surrounding her encounter with Horace.  Upon discovering that Agnès has only yielded a ribbon to her suitor and that her virtue is thus still intact, Arnolphe warns her of the mortal dangers to which she has exposed herself in the presence of her young male visitor.  He also orders her to discourage Horace when he next visits by slamming the door in his face and throwing a stone at him (II, 5).  Believing he has regained control of the situation, he decides to advance the time of his proposed marriage, brings a **religious** tract for Agnès's edification, and has her recite the Maxims of **Marriage**, which constitute a thorough presentation of the austere wifely duties he assigns to marriage (III, 2).  In a movement of self–congratulation, Arnolphe exults in his ward's apparent docility, envisioning her as a piece of wax he can mold to his liking (III, 3).  Horace then informs the protagonist, in an unexpected revelation, that Agnès attached a poignant **love letter** to the stone she hurled at him (III, 4).  In this meeting with Horace, as well as in others,

Arnolphe is forced to view himself in terms of the negative alter ego that Horace presents in descriptions of Monsieur de la Souche (cf. I, 4; IV, 6). To the extent that the young rival assumes the role of Agnès's "teacher," her eventual liberation from Arnolphe's tyranny will occur in the miraculous "school" of love. Then, in one of the more profound ironies of the play, Arnolphe becomes cognizant of his love for Agnès (III, 5).

Feeling once again betrayed, Arnolphe is more and more intent upon not losing his prized possession and vows to prevent Horace and Agnès from sharing their love (IV, 1). After a scene of comic relief with the **notary** who was to arrange his wedding contract (IV, 2), he seeks to enlist the support of his servants by having them rehearse a scene in which Horace tries to bribe them (IV, 4). Chrysalde, Arnolphe's comic foil, advises him to adopt a posture of stoic acceptance of the inevitability of cuckoldry, but the protagonist vehemently rejects his proposal (IV, 8). In a desperate attempt to preserve his honor, Arnolphe endeavors to rally his servants to his cause and arranges for them to ambush his young rival, by **beating** Horace as he seeks to gain access to Agnès's room (IV, 9).

Responding to the servants' mistaken belief that they have inadvertently killed Horace by pushing him off a ladder, Arnolphe criticizes them for seriously mishandling the affair (V, 1). Thereupon, Horace appears and informs Arnolphe that he and his servants were duped by the rival's pretending to be dead (V, 2). In preparation of his flight with Agnès, Horace asks the protagonist to safeguard her in his home (V, 3). After removing his **disguise**, Arnolphe chastises Agnès for her ingratitude (V, 4). He then threatens, orders, and cajoles her to display affection for him. Recognizing his vulnerability to her charms, Arnolphe capitulates unconditionally in front of his young ward and grants her the freedom to behave as she pleases. However, enraged by Agnès's categorical rejection of his offer and by her clear choice of the appealing Horace over him, Arnolphe recants and threatens to re–imprison her in a "cul de couvent." Instead of helping the disconsolate Horace, whose father **Oronte** had previously made plans for him to marry **Enrique's** daughter, the protagonist betrays him, advising his father to exert parental authority by carrying out his son's arranged marriage (V, 7). Much to his chagrin, Horace is then made aware of Arnolphe's second identity of Monsieur de la Souche. In a poetic denouement highlighting the ultimate triumph of the young lovers, Oronte reveals the final turning point of the play: the daughter of Enrique is no other than Agnès (V, 9). Utterly despondent, Arnolphe leaves the stage after Chrysalde tries to console him by telling him that remaining single will be the only way for him to avoid cuckoldry.

Though based on the already hackneyed theme of useless precautions, the play's timely elements ensured its overwhelming financial success. Playing for an exceptionally long time at the premiere rate of double the usual admission price, it was also much in demand for private performances. The triumph was to prove durable, as Arnolphe became as famous a role for Molière the actor as the earlier figures of **Mascarille** and **Sganarelle**. It was in Arnolphe's mustard–colored outfit that Molière was depicted in Verio's portrait of the prominent

French and Italian comic actors of the century. Such success did not come without its detractors, however, and within months Molière's enemies had launched the **Quarrel of the School for Wives** that was to occupy the literary and artistic imagination of France for over a year. So confident was Molière of the inability of his rivals to create a character as fine as Arnolphe, that he published the play soon after production. Its first print run was finished only five days after the theaters had closed for Easter in 1663. It was so much in vogue that the main printer, **Guillaume de Luynes**, had to share his privilege with seven other colleagues in order to keep up with the demand.

Bibliography: David Clarke, "*L'École des femmes*: Plotting and Significance in a 'Machine à rire,'" *Seventeenth–Century French Studies* 11 (1989), 117–135; Judd Hubert, "*L'École des femmes*, tragédie burlesque," *Revue des Sciences Humaines* 97 (1960), 41–52; Denis Porter, "Comic Rhythm in *L'École des femmes*," *Forum for Modern Language Studies* 1 (1969), 205–217.

*Ralph Albanese, Jr.*

*École des maris, L'* (*The School for Husbands*). First performed in June 1661 at the **Palais Royal Theater**, this play was far more successful and far more experimental than is often recognized. First of all, it was fairly unconventional to launch a new comedy during the slow summer season. True, Molière had done it at least once before with *Sganarelle*, but in that case the one–act play served as an accompaniment to a series of **repertory** tragedies, rather than as a full–fledged three–act comedy. Here, one senses that comedy is about to break free of its daily ties to tragedy, freeing the troupe from an onerous two–performance requirement and granting far greater poetic freedom to the author. The fact that the play ran until October proves that Molière's gamble was right: the public could be called upon to attend such types of plays, even in the off–season, provided they contained enough originality and verve. Together with the earlier play, *L'École des maris* solidified both the position of **Sganarelle** as the major new comic persona of the French stage and the form of the twelve–syllable alexandrine couplet as the prime vehicle for the genre, replacing the clumsy octosyllable comic couplets that had reigned since the Middle Ages. In the use of the word "school" in the title and in the opposition of two contrasting brothers, Molière was probably influenced to some degree by the dramatist **Dorimond**, and perhaps by **Samuel Chappuzeau**, though the latter was more likely an emulator of Molière. Other possible sources have been identified as **La Mothe Le Vayer** and **Hurtado de Mendoza**. Since Molière hinted in his contract negotiations for the 1661–62 season that he was planning to marry before the next Lenten season, we know that the theme of **marriage** and the precautions taken for it were even more than usually on his mind. He had stipulated that the troupe give him an extra share as author and an extra share for his wife, if he should marry during the season — a very extraordinary measure for the times. He also strove to take the artistic high ground by dedicating the play to **Monsieur** and by taking a publishing privilege himself rather early in the play's run, counting on its success almost from the first performance.

The first act opens with a strong dose of the timeliness that had fueled *Les Précieuses ridicules*. The subject is male fashion in this case, with brothers **Ariste** and Sganarelle engaging in a lengthy and detailed debate, the latter assailing all elements of the current **clothing** trends and the former defending some concessions to prevailing tastes. The addition of the young wards, **Isabelle** and **Léonor**, accompanied by the **lady's maid Lisette**, leads to a much faster–paced second scene, stichomythic in character, as the debate extends to the issue of how much freedom to tolerate in young women's social lives. Once again Sganarelle berates his more progressive brother with his repressive theories, but the voices of tolerance rise in the form of a lively speech by Lisette and a lengthy peroration by Ariste. Then the scene again becomes punctuated by short, balanced replies as the argument heats up until Sganarelle dismisses those "laughers" who mock him as impertinent fools and finishes the encounter with a near soliloquy that prefigures the speeches of **Arnolphe** in *L'École des femmes*. In fact, Sganarelle attempts to continue his pompous tirade into the next scene, while **Valére** and his valet **Ergaste** try to interrupt with much display of bowing and hat tipping. He eventually is forced to recognize their presence, whereupon Sganarelle brusquely evades the young man's attempts at polite conversation with curt fragments of sentences. Left alone in scene 4, Valère and the **servant** become more explicit about their attempts to approach Isabelle, who is so tightly guarded by Sganarelle that Valère has not been able even to determine if she reciprocates his emotions. They end the act by retiring in puzzlement, but it is clear that someone else in the meantime has been busy plotting a way around those cloistered conditions.

Act II opens with Sganarelle setting out to chastise Valère for bothering Isabelle with his attentions, a stratagem she has imagined in order to communicate, albeit paradoxically, with her intended lover. In no time, the curmudgeon has accosted the young man and cut straight through his attempts at **politeness** with a rather churlish request to turn his attentions elsewhere. As he rants on, the youth realizes that he must have captured the lady's eye after all, and that she would only have responded in such a way if she wanted him to know it and to respond in due fashion. Sganarelle immediately congratulates himself on the young man's visible change of countenance, thinking it must signal embarrassment and defeat. Yet he no sooner returns to Isabelle in scene 3 than she recounts another imaginary visit in which an emissary of Valère has delivered a **love letter** in a golden box. She pretends to return this missive, still sealed, as proof of her honor. Actually, she is sending out Sganarelle with yet another unwitting message, which promptly finds its way first to Ergaste and then on to Valère. When they open the letter, they find nothing less than a bold–faced declaration of intent by Isabelle to give herself to Valère if he will save her from the disgusting future she faces as the bride of Sganarelle. It is, as Ergaste points out, a particularly frank and unrestrained document. Scene 6 opens with another near–soliloquy by Sganarelle, this time on the positive effects of **sumptuary laws** in suppressing coquettry. He scoffs at Valère's lack of fortune in choosing a target as unattainable as Isabelle, but the lover turns the tables on him and uses him in the same fashion as Isabelle had. He makes

Sganarelle promise to unveil to her all the details of Valère's passion, as well as his continued interest and his implicit acceptance of the bargain set forth in her letter. By this time, Sganarelle has been transformed into an ironic self–persecutor, delightedly repeating to himself, point by point, the details of his downfall. Isabelle profits one more time by his gullibility in complaining that Valère is planning an elopement, thus communicating to her partner the very means of their happiness. Predictably, Sganarelle rushes back to Valère with this new accusation, which he accepts so skillfully that Sganarelle outdoes his own evil fate by urging him to come talk with Isabelle in person, in order to show without a shadow of a doubt whom of the two she prefers. The **jealous** guardian's supposedly superior logic not only fails to see through his adversaries' tactics, but actually works against itself by making their plans easier. Scene 9 is thus the first of several in the course of Molière's works in which the two young lovers are able to communicate their sentiments to each other through a kind of coded **language** while in the very presence of their oppressor. Just as Isabelle is enjoying her success, Sganarelle threatens to destabilize it by declaring, after Valère has left, that he is so pleased with the developments that he has decided to marry her tomorrow, instead of waiting a week. Thus, he ups the ante in this game of deception and calls upon Isabelle's wiles to invent yet another trick; she will not fail to do so.

As in the previous act, Isabelle bluntly puts forward her plan in the first scene of Act III. In a reversal that is quite transparent to the audience, she accuses her sister of planning to run off with Valère, now that she has so flatly refused him. This ploy might have been unlikely to work with anyone more reasonable than Sganarelle. But she has chosen her dupe wisely, for he wishes for nothing more than to prove his superiority to Ariste, even at the expense of his brother's honor and domestic happiness. Consequently, he readily agrees to let Léonor leave the house, hoping to turn the affair into a glaring scandal. Of course, Isabelle herself takes advantage of the open door that Sganarelle unlocks. To add to the irony, he follows her to Valère's door, and denies, in an aside, that it is Isabelle who arrives, thinking that the young man has been fooled by a **disguise**. He then seeks out, in scene 4, a **police Commissioner** and a **notary**, who will not only witness the scandal, but document it in legal fashion. He then summons his brother, telling him that Léonor has eloped instead of going to the ball and offering concrete proof to the confused old fop. Naturally, he himself has already, without realizing it, experienced the firsthand recognition of shame that he promises to Ariste. When they arrive at Valère's abode, they hear him telling the policeman and notary that he wishes them to draw up formal marriage papers as proof of his good intentions, and Sganarelle takes advantage of this perceived opportunity by insisting that they should both set their names to the paper. When Léonor returns from the ball, bored with the jaded young playboys she has encountered there, the men accuse her, drawing an angry defense of her virtue and an offer to prove her loyalty to Ariste by marrying him on the spot. Imagine Sganarelle's discomfiture when he learns that the signature he thought to give as witness has actually provided formal approval for Isabelle and Valère to marry. Instead of being the butt of scandal, old Ariste enjoys a flattering direct and public declaration of love from his young ward. Sganarelle concludes that this intrigue can only be the work of the devil and he ends the play by consigning Isabelle and the entire female race to hell.

The structure of the play is quite simple and more appropriate to its format than to a full five–act comedy. The first act is an exposition with timely satirical elements added as a lure to the spectators' interest and to compensate for the uncomplicated nature of the characters' personalities. The second is a series of tricks or *fourberies* resembling those in the middle acts of an **Italian** *commedia sostenuta*, and grouped around the role of Sganarelle as ironic messenger. The last act is fittingly limited to a single deception that unknots the plot, while enhancing Sganarelle's aspect as a self–tormentor, whose insistence on bringing a moral issue into the legal realm actually formalizes and eternalizes his shame. The overall scheme sets Sganarelle as a would–be master of reason who first fails to detect the tricks around him and then actually outdoes his opponents by working against his own interests, eventually completing his doom by appeal to the forces of law and order. Molière would exploit this form time and again with infinite variation and inventiveness in the plays to come. *L'École des maris* would remain one of the most dependable and best known of Molière's early comedies, and one to which later plays such as *L'École des femmes* and *Le Misanthrope* would refer.

**Editions of Molière's Works.** The earliest French editions of individual works have been indicated under their respective headings. Most have since been reedited innumerable times. Apart from *La Jalousie du Barbouillé*, *Le Médecin volant*, *Dom Juan*, and *Le Malade imaginaire*, they present few variants or editorial problems. The first collective edition done during the author's lifetime was issued in two volumes in 1666. Published by a consortium of **Guillaume de Luynes, M. de Sercy, Claude Barbin**, Thomas Joly, **Louis Billaine**, and others, it was embellished by a pair of fine frontispiece engravings, the one showing Molière in the costumes of a marquis and **Sganarelle**, the other depicting **Arnolphe** and **Agnès** receiving laurel crowns from a muse. It contains *Les Précieuses ridicules, Sganarelle, L'Étourdi, Dépit amoureux, Les Fâcheux, L'École des maris, L'École des femmes, La Critique de l'École des femmes*, and *La Princesse d'Élide*, as well as the various prefatory material to those works, and is dedicated to **Monsieur**. In 1674, a posthumous six– volume collective edition was issued by Barbin and **Thierry**, featuring as frontispiece an engraved version of **Mignard's** famous **portrait** of Molière in tragic costume. It was issued under a *privilège* granted to Molière in 1671 and valid for nine years. The first two volumes emulate the 1666 edition. The next four volumes contain Molière's major plays, except for *Dom Juan* and **Dom Garcie de Navarre**. The two provincial **farces** are also missing, along with *L'Impromptu de Versailles, Mélicerte, Les Amants magnifiques*, and *La Comtesse d'Escarbagnas*. A seventh volume was added the following year containing *Le Malade imaginaire* and **Brécourt's** *L'Ombre de Molière*. Numerous Dutch pirated editions followed in the years to come.

Sixteen eighty–two saw the publication of the great eight–volume collection of works edited by **La Grange** and **Vivot** and published by Thierry, Barbin, and **Trabouillet**. It rearranged the plays in chronological order, starting with *L'Étourdi*, added the series of engravings of each play by **Brissart** and **Sauvé**, and contained the invaluable life of Molière offered by the editors. It contained almost all the texts, with the exception of the two farces. However, *Dom Juan*, though finally available in prose instead of in **Thomas Corneille's** versified and edulcorated version, was severely censored, with almost all copies containing paper strips glued over the offensive sections. The 1682 version of *Le Malade imaginaire* differs somewhat from the earlier one and boasts of corrections from the author's own copy. This monumental edition, almost complete, was quickly pirated in **Holland**, Belgium, and **Germany** and remained the standard, with only two important variations, until the nineteenth century.

Only a few of the many subsequent editions are noteworthy. The 1734 Paris edition by La Serre restored the farces that had been rediscovered by **Jean–Baptiste Rousseau**. From 1739 onward (the edition printed by Prault), most also carried the life of Molière prepared by La Serre's rival, **Voltaire**. The 1819 edition by Auger was the first to contain the true text of *Dom Juan*, which had been restored from a German pirated edition (Berlin, 1699) and replaced Thomas Corneille's weak verses and the censored 1682 version. The 1844 works published by J.–J. Dubochet were edited by **Sainte–Beuve** and contained his excellent portrait of Molière. Garnier published the 1863 edition by Moland in seven volumes, which was redone in 1885 in a twelve–volume format, containing a valuable critical study updating knowledge about the author and an extensive lexicon of his **language**.

The great Hachette edition of 1873–1900, in thirteen volumes, reset the bar for all subsequent Molière studies, for besides superlative annotation of the plays by E. Despois and P. Mesnard, it contained an extensive bibliography and lexicon. Reissued from 1886 to 1924, it remained the standard until the late twentieth century. Many subsequent efforts, including the 1947 Gallimard edition by Maurice Rat and the 1965 Garnier Classiques edition by Jouanny, pale in comparison. The 1949 Michaut edition published by the Imprimerie Nationale is noteworthy for its inclusion of the notes to Michaut's unfinished fourth volume on the life of Molière and a new study of the **language** of Molière by G. Matoré.

The contemporary standard is George Couton's two–volume edition of 1971, which replaced Rat's in the Bibliothèque de la Pléiade collection. It represents the best available versions of the texts, together with very extensive and accurate annotation. Its one weakness is a lack of visual imagery on the plays, for not even the Brissart and Sauvé illustrations are included. However, visual images are readily available in the many individual editions of the plays printed for scholastic use by Bordas, Hachette, and Larousse. Unfortunately, there is no standard edition of Molière's collected or complete works available in English. Richard Wilbur has translated most of the great verse comedies individually in witty, sparkling couplets. Just a few months ago, he published his long–awaited translation of *Dom Juan*, which promises to open new perspectives for that play in the English–speaking world.  Some of the prose comedies have also been rendered adequately in acting versions, such as *Les Fourberies de Scapin*.  However, many others are available only in very outdated or Anglicized versions.  Whatever the level of the translations themselves, most of these renditions are almost totally lacking in any kind of critical apparatus or bibliography.  The great *Complete Works of Molière* in English has yet to happen.

**Egyptian.** *See* **Gypsy.**

**Eighteenth–Century Criticism** (1715–1798).  First read before the **Académie Française** in 1714 and disseminated the following year, Fénelon's *Lettre à l'Académie* did much to set the tone for Molière criticism throughout the Enlightenment period.  On the one hand, it not only acknowledged him as a great playwright for France, but also as an international genius and as the inventor of an entirely new and superior type of comedy that carried earlier influences from farce or foreign comic traditions to a lofty and yet-to-be-appreciated pinnacle.  At the same time, it sought to "correct" Molière in terms of language, audience, and moral message, opening a line of inquiry that will be pursued by the trio of great *philosophes*, each for his own purposes.  **Voltaire**, primarily interested in his own career as a tragic playwright, wished to claim Molière as a forerunner of Enlightenment, but at the same time was eager to show that, by catering too closely to the tastes of the **court**, he had avoided an opportunity to engage fully the cause of the common man.  **Denis Diderot** also had a personal dramatic agenda, that of the *drame bourgeois*.  Though he originally spoke of his links to Molière, he later sought to cut them due to the increasing importance of originality as a literary value and as a disclaimer to the troubles his own plays had encountered with critics.  Consequently, he, too, tended to fault Molière for remaining too much a creature of his times, mired in archaic vocabulary and customs.  **Jean–Jacques Rousseau** harbored an animus against civilization throughout his literary career.  However, he showed little interest in Molière as an individual until the affair of the *Encyclopédie* article on Geneva induced him to focus on the playwright.  Rousseau reasoned that he could best ingratiate himself to his intended hosts in Calvinist Geneva by excoriating the entire sinful block of French theater, and at its summit the genius Molière.  So he attacked *Le Misanthrope* as the aesthetically best, and at the same time morally worst, play of all times, seeking to frame its author as the ideological dupe of Parisian decadence.

    In a separate vein from Voltaire, Diderot and Rousseau, another influential voice was that of the former star of the *comédie italienne*, Luigi Riccoboni.  In a rather partisan crusade for his own company against the Théâtre Français, Riccoboni's earlier works exaggerate Molière's borrowings from **Italian** sources, both in number and scope.  According to Riccoboni, the dramatist was little more than a translator and adapter, as derivative from Italian models as **Boisrobert** or **d'Ouville** were from **Spanish** ones.  Though his 1736 *Observations sur la comédie et sur le génie de Molière* seek to retract some of his earlier pronouncements, he remains subtly critical of his French predecessor. After undergoing a religious conversion, Riccoboni amplified his complaints again, concentrating this time on the old bigot theme of the plays' indecency, and demanding large–scale bowdlerizing of the canon.

In contrast to the great *philosophes'* ambiguous approach to Molière, a more stable and positive response came from rank–and–file members of the movement, such as Marmontel and Chamfort, who generally lauded both the dramatist's stylistic talents and his moral message of reform. The latter, mainly remembered for his collections of aphorisms about the "perfect civilization," wrote a stirring if somewhat repetitious *Éloge de Molière*. Additional praise came from the unlikely quarter of the anti–philosophical writer Palissot, one of the few authorities in the century to focus on the actual comedy and gaiety of Molière's works and to stress their value apart from the controversies of the day. Palissot is joined in this vein by J.–F. d'Estandoux de Cailhava. Cailhava, one of the first Frenchmen who can be classified mainly as a literary scholar, also insisted on the intrinsic qualities of the plays, in a version of Chicago New Criticism *avant la lettre*. As a rare survivor of the guillotine, he carried his message into the next century and influenced the first generations of Napoleonic and Romantic writers.

**Éliante (*Le Misanthrope*).** The character of **Célimène**'s cousin, played according to Georges Couton by **Mlle. Du Parc**, is one of the few genuinely sympathetic parts in the play. It is natural that she eventually promises herself to **Philinte**, who is equally likeable. However, early in the play, Philinte himself is trying to promote a match between Éliante and his friend **Alceste**, on the grounds that she would be far more tolerant and compatible than the coquettish Célimène. He tries to steer Alceste toward this idea in the first act, but is told by the misanthrope, who is very willing to require rigorous self–mastery of others, that he simply cannot control his amorous impulses. Éliante is present during much of the second act, for it is she who accompanies the two ridiculous marquis up to the salon from the ground floor. Though she is involved in the entire sequence of the "**portrait** scene," as Célimène and her guests mock their absent acquaintances, she has very little to say. The one exception comes in the form of a correction she makes to Alceste, who has just loudly averred that lovers should not hide the faults of their beloved, but should speak openly of them. Nearly quoting word for word a passage from **Lucretius**, Éliante says that true lovers are not even conscious of such faults, which the nature of **love** causes them to overlook or distort into virtues. Thus, the qualities that the public would consider negative become advantages in the eyes of the lover. It is significant that she should choose to make herself heard on this particular point, for it shows that she is closely considering the issue of love with Alceste and cares deeply about his attitudes toward it. The passage also qualifies her as one of the relatively few female characters in the canon who can be termed *raisonneurs*, or spokespersons for the rational mean so close to the dramatist's heart. Yet for all her Classical learning, Éliante is not meant to be either a spokesperson, or a character solely devoted to reason, or a mate for Alceste. At the beginning of the fourth act, when she talks with Philinte about Alceste's ludicrous behavior at the court of the **Maréchaussée**, she makes it clear that she admires the man's outspoken sincerity.  She would even accept him on the rebound if her cousin were to reject him, though she would prefer for him to wed Célimène.  But this does not blind her to other possibilities.  As Philinte, who had intended merely to be a go–between, begins to unfold his own passionate feelings for her, she seems more and more ready to respond to him.  This tête–à–tête is broken up when the misanthrope stalks into the room, moved beyond reason by Arsinoé's accusations against the coquette, and intent on vengeance.  When he makes it clear that this vengeance would entail marrying Éliante to spite Célimène, the former wisely suggests that he should not make such a decision in a heated state, but wait until calm restores his ability to weigh all circumstances carefully.  Éliante may have been able to accept marriage on the rebound, but marriage strictly out of spite is too bitter a dish for any reasonable woman to choose.  She correctly guesses and states to Alceste that his true emotions are still linked to the woman who seems to have wronged him, and that he is not capable of replacing her in his heart with another.  Though she retires after this remark, leaving the misanthrope to excoriate Célimène and then abjectly grovel before her for forgiveness, one senses that Éliante not only knows what will happen during that intimate confrontation, but that she has made up her mind on the basis of Alceste's most shameful demonstration of **jealousy**.  Therefore, the audience is not surprised when, in the final act, she sets aside Alceste's last respectful but untimely compliments by telling him that she intends to marry Philinte.   The attraction of similarities overpowers the attraction of opposites, uniting the two most *honnête* persons in the play — not so much on the basis of implacable reason as on that of mutual pleasure.  Lucretian in ends as well as in means, Éliante is a most unusual feminine role, far ahead of her time in all aspects.

**Élise** (*L'Avare*).  **Harpagon's** daughter appears mainly as a confidante for her suitor, **Valère**, and her brother, **Cléante**.  Before the action of the play begins, Valère has saved her life, and he takes on the identity of an overseer in Harpagon's household to be near the object of his affection.   Selected as a dowerless bride for the aged Anselme, she confronts her father more courageously than the daughters in *Tartuffe* or *Le Bourgeois gentilhomme*, but is somewhat nonplused when her **disguised** sweetheart appears to agree with the plans.  She is skeptical about Valère's idea that she can feign illness (although it works for many other daughters in Molière's comedies), and if she has any more confidence in **Frosine's** conspiracy to distract Harpagon with other prospects, she does not show it.  In the final act, she makes an impassioned plea for mercy on behalf of the accused Valère, but to no avail.  Based on the reference in Act III to Élise's height (Harpagon says she is as tall as a weed), the role was probably given originally to **Mlle. de Brie**.

**Élise** (*La Critique de l'École des femmes*).  Like **Éliante** in *Le Misanthrope*, this cousin of the *salonnière* **Uranie** is distinguished by her brains.  However, her tendency toward mordant satire and her playfulness make her more akin to **Célimène**. Thus, the role was taken by **Armande Béjart**, who plays a similar one in *L'Impromptu de Versailles*.

**Élise** (*Dom Garcie de Navarre*). She is mainly remarkable for her apology of **jealousy** as a laudable shortcoming that gives proof of the liveliness of passion and the seriousness of a lover's commitment. She manages to extract a confession of envy and evil intentions from her former suitor **Dom Lope**, but is unable to warn **Dom Garcie** about the dangers of listening to this advisor. She gives proof of her prudence in trying to prevent Dom Garcie from interrupting **Elvire's** discussion with **Dom Sylve** in Act III, and of her mercy by trying to help him regain Elvire's good graces after that debacle. Unfortunately, her presence fades in the denouement, and nothing is ever made of her relationship with **Dom Alvar**.

**Elmire** (*Tartuffe*). Along with **Célimène**, this was one of **Armande Béjart's** greatest triumphs. As the witty, beautiful second wife of **Orgon**, Elmire assumes a place in the family that is more of a friend than an authority figure. She joins in the merriment in the first scene as everyone jokes at **Mme. Pernelle's** expense, but tries to temper the effect of the jibes on the old woman's sensitive character, and even goes to the door with her to bid her to stay. Having shown herself an apt mistress of the worldly salon, she also must be a mistress of the boudoir, for she retires there to await her husband, and probably to lay a clever love–trap, while her brother accosts him downstairs. Her bedroom ways are a mystery, but when she next appears, it is to entice **Tartuffe** into an intimate conversation where he may make a declaration of affection, one that she intends to use to blackmail him into silence while she arranges the children's weddings. She very nearly succeeds, skillfully leading the wary hypocrite into her ambush until **Damis's** rude and untimely interruption spoils her plans. She knows better than to be drawn into his downfall and beats a quick retreat, the better to fight again. Thus she is ready in Act IV, when her brother's reason has been worn to a frazzle and **Dorine's** guerrilla activity has been subdued, to assume family leadership and attempt her boldest venture yet by getting Tartuffe to reveal his true intentions while her husband hides under the table. Even she underestimates her husband's capacity for absorbing punishment, however, when he ignores her repeated coughing signals and she almost finds herself forced to let Tartuffe have his way with her. Elmire represents a pinnacle of the principle of female *honnêteté* or civility. A brilliant psychologist and conversationalist, she loves pleasure but seeks that of others before her own. She uses her beauty as a powerful lure for men, but stops short of selling herself, requiring instead that the men in question accept her fully and on her own terms if they, in turn, wish to be accepted.

***Élomire hypocondre, ou les Médecins vengés*** (***Élomire the Hypochondriac, or the Doctors' Vengeance***, 1670). This nasty little verse invective in four acts, accompanied by a separate text called "Le Divorce comique," inserted between the fourth and fifth acts, is the work of someone called **Le Boulanger de Chalussay**. The author was apparently a literary hack associated with the **Hôtel de Bourgogne**, but perhaps the name masks one of the Hôtel de Bourgogne actors or regular authors. After discussing his declining health with his wife, Isabelle, who refuses to believe he is ailing, Èlomire consults first with the famous charlatans Bary and l'Orviétan, then with some doctors in a **Turkish** masquerade, then with Sennelay, the great reader of urine samples. The latter is really a man named Oronte, who plays a trick on Élomire in the final act, with the connivance of some **police** officers. The play has numerous references to the actors and plays of Molière's theater and the Hôtel de Bourgogne. The entire text of the inserted "Divorce comique" concerns a revolt by Molière's players against the leader of the troupe, who is depicted as an unreasonable martinet. In the course of the latter, an actress named Angélique, patterned on **Madeleine Béjart**, claims that Élomire only turned to the theater after failing at the legal profession and as a of snake–oil salesman. The play also accuses **Armande Béjart** of being Madeleine's daughter rather than her sister, and shows Élomire to be almost as frightened of cuckoldry as of disease. It is the source of several anecdotes about Molière's legal studies and career, and contains much misinformation about the entire **Béjart family** as well. It went to at least four editions, the latter ones accompanied by a letter stating that Molière had tried to suppress the first through collusion with the printer. Le Boulanger claims a court victory freed him from this problem. He threatens to unleash upon Molière more plays that will be a thousand times more damaging than *Élomire*, but there is no record of further dramatic publication by the author, despite his having obtained permission to print one more book. In many ways, this play can be seen as a late reverberation of the **Quarrel of the School for Wives**, for it chiefly mentions that play, along with *L'Amour médecin* and the second version of *Tartuffe*. This suggests it was actually composed closer to 1666 at the latest. It is astonishing that in view of the play's many biases and errors, it could nonetheless be taken quite seriously by many critics in the course of history.

**Elopement.** *See* **Marriage**.

**Elvire (*Dom Garcie de Navarre*).** This part is perhaps the most crucial of the play, even more so than that of **Dom Garcie** himself. As the potential reasoning figure in the plot, Elvire could have precluded a great deal of the trouble that the **jealous** prince gets himself into. But she is also afflicted with a personality disorder, in the form of overweening pride. It is this imperious spirit that accounts for her unwillingness to deliver a clear vow of **love** in the first act, when Dom Garcie wanted it most. Indeed, her efforts to avoid an open explanation make her **language** quite turgid in places. She doggedly insists that Dom Garcie must be able to read her true feelings strictly from the tone of her voice, the look on her face, and other aspects of body language, without the actual articulation of her feelings. **Reason** gives way to anger and sarcasm as Dom Garcie's acts become more and more threatening to her sense of decorum.

In conversation with Élise, she expresses a preference for avoidance of direct contact and a concern for her own vulnerability that are reminiscent of *préciosité*. Elvire is at her best in her conversation with **Dom Sylve**, where she is much less restrained in her emotional language, more willing to listen to the man's problems, and more forthright in her advocacy of **Ignès**. When Dom Garcie thinks he has caught her embracing a man in Act IV, she makes him choose between winning her hand, provided he accepts her innocence at face value and asks no questions, and losing her forever, if he requires an explanation of the apparent intimacy. By choosing the latter, for the contrary purpose of proving that no good explanation could be found, Dom Garcie seems to doom his pursuit of Elvire. Elvire's self–control and her handling of the outraged lover during this sequence constitute the high point of her role and contribute much toward the characterization of **Célimène** in *Le Misanthrope*, even though Célimène's approach to **Alceste** will differ fundamentally in its deceit. Elvire's sudden change of sentiment in the final act, when sympathy for Dom Garcie's downfall melts her pride even before the politically expedient **recognition scene** is unveiled, is far less convincing. However, her plea to the still **disguised** Dom Sylve to return to Ignès and allow her to retreat to a nunnery carries a note of pathos and elevation that does suit her character. In fact, the spectator can imagine her more easily in the seclusion of a **convent** than as a happy partner in Dom Garcie's bed, and there lies not the smallest problem of the contrived ending.

**Elvire (*Dom Juan*).** We learn from her coachman **Gusman** that **Dom Juan's** wife Elvire, or perhaps one should say, one of his wives, has been pursuing him across the face of **Sicily** in hopes of getting him to recognize the **marriage** vows he privately made. Only in this way can he make an honest woman of her, for he has abducted her from a cloister and forced her to succumb to his sexual advances. If she can get to him before her vengeance–crazed brothers, perhaps she still has a chance to live a decent, civil existence. Thus, still clad in her travel **clothes**, she catches up with him at last, but her first few seconds with her husband convince her that she has made the trip in vain, for he shows no hint of tenderness or consideration. In the speech that follows, she admits her own responsibility for her willingness to accept the seducer's lies. "I have been good enough or, I admit, foolish enough to want to deceive myself and to disagree with the evidence of my eyes and my reason" (I, 3). She desperately wishes even now that he would lie and lie well, and she feeds him possible excuses he could use to cover up his treachery. These remarkable speeches constitute a kind of "**avowal** after the fact" that has few parallels except in the nascent genre of fiction, where works like *La Princesse de Clèves* and *Les Lettres portugaises* will probe the feminine soul to new depths. Finally revolted by Dom Juan's fake **sincerity**, she observes, "It is cowardly to sit by while my shame is laid out before me," and leaves him with the anger of a woman scorned.

Elvire visits Dom Juan a second time in the fourth act, this time coming onstage with a veil that at first **disguises** her identity. She explains that she has found spiritual serenity and plans to withdraw from the world, though the spectator is unsure whether she is speaking of re–entering the **convent** or facing death.  Her heart–wrenching words cause **Sganarelle** to weep, but have a much different effect on Dom Juan, for he finds her tearful presence strangely erotic instead of edifying.  If anything, the tenor of her speech about repentance will give him something to imitate in the final act when he feigns religious conversion.  After all, he sees how powerful an influence the admonishment has on his valet and reasons that he can use it to fool others easily.  One can hardly doubt Elvire's sincerity or question her predictions of her own imminent demise, so it is natural to link her to the specter that appears in the fifth act, just before Dom Juan's immolation.

Elvire differs significantly from the figure in the earlier versions on whom she is based.  **Tirso de Molina's** noblewoman is the victim of rape rather than seduction.   Dom Juan kills her father when he tries to rescue her, thus prefiguring the **Commander** in Molière's play.  Molière is not responsible for all the changes, since the **Italian** versions of the story had already made profound alterations.  But he is the one who brought the character to her well–rounded potential.  She does not simply succumb physically to the rake, but first of all emotionally.  Through her, the public judges the effectiveness of Dom Juan's persuasiveness, as well as the weakness of their own defenses.  More than just a virtuous doll, Elvire is a complete woman who must bear the weight of her own surrender.  The **spectre** that appears in Act V is often interpreted as the ghost of Elvire, a thoroughly logical extension of her speeches in Act IV.  This would have been an extremely unusual part for **Armande Béjart**, and one more easily imagines **Mlle. Du Parc** in this serious, tragic role.

**Elzevier, Daniel.**   The crown prince of the **Dutch** pirate printing industry, Elzevier's presses churned out many a copy of Molière's plays.  However, it is doubtful that he was directly implicated in the 1673 Dutch pirated edition of *Le Malade imaginaire*, since it was of such low textual quality and contained a suspiciously variant spelling of the family name.

**Engagement.**  This act had an official status in the Old Regime civil justice system and thus was not to be approached lightly.   The mere exchange of promises (*paroles de futur*) was legally binding, especially if backed up by physical proofs (**letters**, exchanged tokens, etc.).  The specifics of engagement differed greatly with social rank.  In *Dépit amoureux*, the **servants Gros–René** and **Marinette** seal their engagement simply by touching hands, peasant–style: "Touch right there, nothing more is needed."   **Chrysale** tries to preempt his wife's plans to marry **Henriette** to **Trissotin** in *Les Femmes savantes* by arranging an exchange of vows before witnesses between **Henriette** and **Clitandre**, sealed by a similar handshake.  In the **bourgeois** realm, however, engagement traditionally involved elaborate negotiations leading to the signing of the formal **marriage** contract, which laid out the details of the all–important dower and dowry.  These formalities make their appearance in *L'École des maris* and again in *Les Femmes savantes*.  There is much confusion in the latter play, for the father and mother of the bride are insisting on different husbands, and the **notary** insists that they sort the matter out before he can finish his papers. In *L'École des femmes*, **Horace** explains to his father that he and **Agnès** are engaged by mutual promises or *paroles*.

*See* **Marriage**.

**England.** In *Le Mariage forcé*, **Géronimo** recalls that his friend **Sganarelle** has spent seven years in England, presumably engaged in commerce of some type. Relations with England had been stormy during the time of Cromwell, but **Louis XIV** took personal credit for restoring the Stuarts to the throne and referred to England almost as a protectorate. **Henrietta of England,** carrying the title of Madame as wife of Louis's brother Philippe, was the most prominent British person in Paris, although she was in most ways a cultured Frenchwoman. One of the imports made by Stuart followers returning to England after 1660 was the theater of Molière, which formed the basis for Restoration comedy. Davenant, Etheredge, Dryden, Shadwell, Wycherly, Colley Cibber, Richard Flecknoe, Suzanna Centlivre, Aphra Behn, and a host of other writers hastened to adapt Molière's successful plays to the English idiom soon after they were presented in **Paris**. For his part, Molière seems to have little interest in or knowledge of the British Isles, and he probably shared the popular view that this formerly barbarous land of regicides had become happier and more civilized as a result of its inclusion in Greater France.

**English Renditions of Molière's Plays.** As stated above, Molière's influence on the Restoration stage is so deep and pervasive that it cannot be briefly summarized. Well into the 1700s, most of the plays produced in **England** carried some echo of his style, his characters, or his plots. In particular, figures of the French fop, including Etheredge's Sir Fopling Flutter, became enduringly popular offshoots of the ridiculous marquis tradition. Imitations of **Alceste**, **Philinte**, **Cathos** and **Magdelon**, **Bélise**, and **Elmire** also abound. The influence of **Mascarille**, **Sganarelle**, and **Scapin** was more muted, since the English had a very different approach to the representation of **servants** on stage, nor were they quite as concerned with cuckolds and doctors as the French genius. A reasonably complete list of plays which imitate Molière in their entirely must include: Richard Flecknoe, *The Damoiselles à la Mode*, 1667; Thomas Shadwell, *The Sullen Lovers* (*Les Fâcheux*), 1668, *The Miser*, 1672, *Psyche*, 1675; Charles Sedley, *The Mulberry Garden* (*L'École des maris*), 1668; M. Medbourne, *Tartuffe, or the French Puritan*, 1670; John Dryden, *An Evening's Love* (*Dépit amoureux*), 1671, *Sir Martin Mar–all* (*L'Étourdi*), 1697; J. Caryll, *Sir Salomon* (*L'École des femmes*), 1671; Edward Ravenscroft, *The Citizen Turned Gentleman*, 1672; J. Lacy, *The Dumb Lady* (*Le Médecin malgré lui* and *L'Amour médecin*), 1672; William Wycherly, *The Country Wife* (*L'École des femmes*), 1675; Thomas Otway, *The Cheats of Scapin*, 1677, *The Soldier's Fortune* (*L'École des maris*), 1681; Thomas Rawlings, *Tom Essence* (*Sganarelle*), 1677; Thomas Wright, *The Female Virtuosos* (*Les Femmes savantes*), 1693; Thomas Crowne, *The Countrey Wit* (*Le Sicilien*), 1693; Susanna Centlivre, *Love's Contrivance* (*Le Médecin malgré lui* and *Le Mariage* *forcé*), 1703; John Vanbrugh, *Squire Trelooby* (*Monsieur de Pourceaugnac*), 1704, *The Mistake* (*Dépit amoureux*), 1706; Charles Molloy, *The Perplexed Couple* (*Sganarelle*), 1715; and Colley Cibber, *The Non-juror* (*Tartuffe*), 1718.

See Dudley H. Miles, *The Influence of Molière on Restoration Comedy* (1910; reprint, New York: Octagon, 1971).

**Enrique** (*L'École des femmes*). This aged character is said to have been "in **America**" since the time that he left his daughter with a wet–nurse in the vicinity of **Arnolphe's** home town. He is onstage only during the concluding scenes of the last act, and has few lines. At first supposed to be the father of the "other woman" whom **Oronte** proposes as a bride for his son, he is revealed in the denouement to be the father of **Agnès** herself. It is unexplained if the wealth he has amassed during his absence is due to the fur trade, sugar plantations, or piracy, the three lucrative forms of American activity for a Frenchman of the 1660s. Enrique mentions to **Chrysalde** that he had married the latter's sister and that the two are brothers–in–law.

**Épernon, Bernard de Nogaret de la Vallette, duc d'** (1592–1661). Courtier and governor of Guyenne who sponsored the troupe of **Charles Dufresne** in the 1640s. This patronage undoubtedly meant a great deal to the players in terms of commissions to play before parliamentarians and other eminent citizens of **Bordeaux**. His mistress, Ninon de Lartigue, lived in **Agen**, which may help explain the presence of Molière's troupe in that town, as well. Since d'Épernon added the governorship of Burgundy to his portfolio in 1654, Molière's visits there may have included homage to his former patron. Bernard de Nogaret's children had lives no less colorful than his own: his daughter Anne Louise Christine became a Carmelite nun in 1648 after her beloved Chevalier de Fiesque was killed in battle, a notable example of romantic devotion at the time; and his son, Louis Charles Gaston, was the noted **court** figure Candale, a fop who may have served as model for some of Molière's marquis.

**Epicurus.** When **Sganarelle** mentions the great third–century B.C. **philosopher**, he commits the common sin of misinterpretation, assuming that by making the pleasure principle the center of his system, he was advocating a totally sybaritic code of life. In fact, Epicurus's notion of sensual pleasure was rooted in the golden mean and in a strict doctrine of morality and responsibility. Epicurus's thought was taken up by **Lucretius**, Molière's favorite philosopher. Thus, Sganarelle's epithet of "Epicurean pig," hurled at his master, takes on ambiguous meaning. Despite the fact that **Dom Juan** did not live by true Epicurean standards, the ignorant people around him were happy to paint him with that brush. But then Sganarelle, who misquotes almost every philosophical or religious authority he invokes, is hardly a reliable guide to the truth.

**Erasmus, Desiderius** (1469–1536). Early humanist of Rotterdam and author of the famous volume *In Praise of Folly*. **Gros–René** briefly refers to it when he gives his diatribe against women in *Dépit amoureux*. Given Molière's interest in **Lucretius** and skeptical authors, one is not surprised to find him frequenting this secular rationalist.

**Éraste** (*Dépit amoureux*). One of the principal characters of the play, Éraste is afflicted at the beginning of the action with a terrible case of **jealousy,** as he confides in his valet **Gros–René.** Not only does he distrust his beloved **Lucile** and her other suitor **Valère,** but he even doubts the loyalty of the fat **servant,** despite his explanation that people like him treat their employers "quite roundly in all ways." He worries because Valère does not seem anxious or jealous enough to be truly smitten, nor bitter enough to be rejected. Gros–René mentions his master's surpassing jealousy to his own mistress **Marinette** when she comes to deliver a **letter** from Lucile. Éraste, worried about appearances as well, begs Marinette not to reveal his "passing fears" to Lucile. She is only too happy to comply if he will reward her with the pretty **ring** she has been promised. Just when things appear to be going Éraste's way, Valère arrives on the scene and stokes his suspicions by gloating over his own preferment (I, 3). Seeking to learn the truth, Éraste tricks **Mascarille** into revealing that Valère has already been admitted to a tryst with his beloved. What neither Éraste, nor Valère, nor Mascarille knows is that the woman in bed with Valère was not Lucile, but the disguised **Ascagne–Dorothée.** Éraste gives warning of the impending **lovers' spite** confrontation as early as Act I, scene 5, but does not give vent to his full transport of jealousy until he meets with Lucile in Act IV, scenes 2 and 3. After having heaped abuse on the young lady, he realizes he cannot live without her and wheedles himself back into her affections, finally accepting her pleas of innocence. Éraste seems almost cured of his mania when he returns in Act V, where he abdicates all interest in quarreling with Valère, leaving Ascagne–Dorothée to straighten out matters with his rival. If so, he is one of the few Molière characters who manages effectively to rein in the demon of jealousy and achieve a degree of true emotional control.

**Éraste** (*Les Fâcheux*). A handsome and dashing young marquis, Éraste is in **love** with **Orphise,** but is prevented from seeing her by the interference of the various pests who appear in the course of the action, by the opposition of her guardian **Damis,** and even by Orphise herself, who sometimes engages in subterfuge to hide their relationship and other times seems **jealous.** For someone so beset with unwanted attention, Éraste seldom loses his temper, except perhaps with his bumbling valet **La Montagne.** He not only shows considerable patience, but displays wit in his efforts to rid himself of his troublesome company. His longest speech is his opening tirade against the pest at the **theater,** who insisted on interrupting the play with his antics and then would not leave Éraste alone, pulling him along to see his coach and to parade on the **Cours la Reine.** This speech certainly voices a great deal of Molière's own frustration at thoughtless **noblemen** who, having bought seats onstage, distracted the audience and actors instead of showing discretion. Perhaps one of the greatest insults was that they commonly departed before the conclusion of the play. Éraste shows considerable bravery in confronting Damis's attackers, although it is not clear whether or not he recognizes that they are his own retainers. The incident prefigures **Dom Juan's** defense of **Dom Carlos**, all the more so since **La Grange** played both roles. But he was not the only one! An interesting note in the register tells that when La Grange fell sick with a terrible fever in the midst of the play's run, **Du Croisy** took over his part for two months.

**Éraste** (*Monsieur de Pourceaugnac*). This young **lover** is less well defined than most others in Molière's works and has a great many of the aspects of the trickster about him. He has laid a number of traps for **Pourceaugnac** before the latter can even arrive in **Paris**, with the help of his accomplices **Sbrigani** and **Nérine**. He accosts the provincial in a most notable manner, claiming to know him from past visits to **Limoges**, and allowing Pourceaugnac to fill in all the details he needs to know, simply by supplying a few vague hints about his family and acquaintances that might apply to almost anyone almost anywhere. This was a fairly well established type of comic scene, tracing back at least to the medieval *Roman de Renart*, where the fox manages to trick Chantecleer the rooster into thinking they are kin, because he is able to extract so many details about the family. Having placed Pourceaugnac, on the basis of false confidence, into the hands of the doctors, Éraste retires until the third act, where he pretends to bring the love–crazed **Julie** back to her father. **Oronte**, who has been scandalized by the behavior of his daughter and her country suitor, is only too happy to give her hand to Éraste before any more harm can come to him. Éraste makes a point of mentioning how Oronte had broken off the engagement between him and Julie over a trifling matter of some 4,000 or 5,000 *écus* (about 12,000 to 15,000 *livres*, a considerable sum). Since Julie feigns resistance at the idea of marrying Éraste, the old man throws another 30,000 *livres* into her dowry to sweeten the pot. Perhaps all is fair in love and war, but Éraste certainly falls back on some unscrupulous methods in winning his bride. Only the fact that Pourceaugnac is utterly unsympathetic prevents him from standing out as even more cynical and manipulative. If **La Grange** played the usual part of the young lover, this must have been one of his more ambiguous roles, along with **Dom Juan**.

**Ergaste** (*L'École des maris*). Valet to **Valère**, Ergaste appears in the last two scenes of Act I, as well as briefly in Act II and in the concluding scene of Act III. He is a more or less conventional **servant**, functioning mainly as confidant and messenger for his master. He has the occasional witty commentary line in the tradition of the **Spanish** *gracioso*, as when he describes **Sganarelle's** manners as a "werewolf's welcome." His longest speech urges Valère to undertake **Isabelle's** seduction for, he affirms, a woman closely guarded is already half won.

**Ergaste** (*L'Étourdi*). A servant who appears twice to warn **Lélie** and **Mascarille** of potential problems looming on the horizon. The first of these is **Léandre's** project to abduct **Célie** during a **mascarade** and the second is the involvement of the "**Gypsy**" **Andrès** in the ever–more–complicated suitor situation. He also consoles Mascarille on the failure of his **police** operation in the final act.

**Ériphile** (*Les Amants magnifiques*). This princess is being wooed openly by the princes **Iphicrate** and **Timoclès**, while **Sostrate**, whom she **loves**, keeps his passion a secret. Timoclès courts her with splendid spectacles of song and **dance**, while Iphicrate reinforces this approach by profusely complimenting her mother **Aristione** and conspiring with the **astrologer Anaxarque**. Aristione has given her daughter complete freedom of choice and even authorized her to choose a husband from any rank, showing uncommon credit for the meritorious acts of men below her station. However, Ériphile is tighter than a clam when it comes to expressing her emotions. Unlike the Princess of Cleves, she owes this wary attitude not to her mother's protection, but to her own sense of pride. She refuses to confide either in **Cléonice** or in Aristione. Having almost revealed herself in her interview with **Clitidas**, who tested her by falsely reporting that Sostrate loved a member of her retinue, Ériphile refuses to give the general a hint of her inclinations during their first conversation. Only in the fourth act does a mutual **avowal** take place, and only then because both lovers sense their passion is doomed by the astrologer's prediction that Ériphile must marry the man who saves her mother. It is a somewhat remarkable scene because the woman takes it upon herself to speak first. She reveals to Sostrate that she has been consciously delaying the **marriage** choice, for although she has surrendered her heart to him, she wishes to maintain the honor and reputation that prevent her from accepting a husband lower than herself. She tells him, "There are conditions where it is not socially acceptable to desire to do all that one is able to do; there is shame in placing oneself above all restraint, and vicious rumors can make one pay dearly for yielding to one's inclination" (IV, 4). She goes on to tell him that she looks forward to married life with disgust and that if she were truly free to choose, she would have chosen him or no one. Having performed this duty of disclosure, she is reluctant even to grant Sostrate's plea that she will remember him. But she eagerly listens to Clitidas's good news in the following act and readily accedes to the wishes of her mother and "the gods" when they decree that she must become Sostrate's wife. Ériphile is an embodiment of Molière's idea that dictatorial authority produces far less efficient constraint than internal self–controls derived from one's sense of honor. This makes her something of an ice princess, a role well suited to **Armande**, but different from her usual coquettish stand and closer to her role in *Les Femmes savantes* than to the character of **Célimène**.

**Éroxène** (*Mélicerte*). Like her virtual double, **Daphné**, she is a **shepherdess** of high stature who rebuffs a suitor of her own age and condition, **Tyrène**, to pursue the young **Myrtil**. In the second scene, each lady shows the other the locket **portrait** of the youth she carries. Éroxène accompanies Daphné to visit **Lycarsis** in hopes of arranging an **engagement** with the boy, but both are disappointed when Myrtil, in galant and diplomatic fashion, reveals his passion for **Mélicerte**.

***Esprits, Les (The Ghosts).*** A prose comedy by Pierre Larivey, published in 1579, perhaps the funniest and best constructed of the French Renaissance. The character of Séverin probably influenced that of **Harpagon** in *L'Avare*, especially the monologue where Molière's miser complains of the theft of his strongbox (IV, vii).

***Étourdi, L', ou le Contretemps (The Blockhead, or the Blunder).*** Five–act comedy in verse, first performed in **Lyon** in 1655 and published in **Paris** in 1662, adapted from **Beltrame's** *L'Inavvertito*. Dedicated by the publisher **Barbin** to the royal attorney Armand Jean Des Riants. It is in this French version of an **Italian** *commedia sostenuta* that Molière first appears in the role of the tricky valet **Mascarille**. The plot is really nothing but a series of consecutive schemes devised by Mascarille to get the beautiful **Célie** out of the clutches of **Trufaldin**, who has bought her from **Gypsies**, and into those of his master, **Lélie**. Two rivals, **Léandre** and **Andrès**, must be overcome, as well, perhaps with the help of Lélie's cantankerous father **Pandolphe** and the wealthy neighbor **Anselme**. There is no real connection or transition between one scheme and another, and they alternate between stealth and violence, robbery and abduction, false identity and faked death. The female characters are overwhelmingly passive, with Célie receiving surprisingly little stage time and few lines, and **Hippolyte** only engaged in two major scenes, both of which are peripheral to the main developments. Even though they have much more presence, the male characters fare scarcely better, since the majority of their dialogue is oriented around the details of intrigue, rather than on their inner thoughts or feelings. There is nothing at all timely about the play; it might unfold almost anywhere and involve almost anyone. Indeed, the identities of the characters and the basic elements of intrigue are almost entirely analogous to Greco–Roman comedy. The **recognition scene** in the denouement, though contrived, does at least have some grounding in the text, since Trufaldin's true identity has already been revealed in Act IV, but the picturesque fight between a couple of old hags that unclenches the disclosure is unfortunately conveyed in a secondhand account. Lélie hugs Mascarille much more fervently than his sweetheart and the future brides of Andrès and Mascarille are not even introduced. Nevertheless, the play continued to be performed with much acclaim throughout Molière's career and probably owes its considerable seventeenth–century popularity to the sheer verve of invention displayed by Mascarille, who generates no fewer than ten stratagems in five acts, and to his witty, sarcastic commentary on his master's blunders. It is certainly equal to all but the very best comedies by **Corneille** and **Rotrou**, already identifying Molière as a budding genius far above the likes of **Jean Chevalier** or **Villiers**.

See Carlo François, "*L'Étourdi* de Molière, ou l'illusion héoïque," *Revue d'Histoire Littéraire de la France* 59 (1959), 87–91; Quentin M. Hope, "Molière's Coup d'Essai," *Kentucky Romance Quarterly* 69 (1970), 163–178;

David Maskell, "Molière's *Étourdi*: Signs of Things to Come," *French Studies* (1992), 12–25; Edith Potter, "Molière's Comic Artistry in *L'Étourdi*," *Kentucky Romance Quarterly* 72 (1973), 89–97.

**Euryale** (*La Princesse d'Élide*). Originally played, as were most other young lover roles in the Molière canon, by **La Grange**, this young prince of **Ithaca** describes in the first scene how he suddenly became enamored of the **Princess of Elis** when he learned that she spurned all lovers. Before, she had seemed to him merely a "beautiful statue," but her pride, exciting his, made him long to succeed where others had failed. This perverse attraction, which overcame his previous disdain for **love**, caused him to develop a distant and as yet unrevealed passion. He explains to his counselor **Arbate** that he has hesitated to disclose his feelings partly because he has seen the way **Aristomène** and **Théocle**, despite their earnestness, have been rebuffed. Arbate spurs him on, but questions the Prince's decision to put his suit in the hands of the clown **Moron**, which seems to be an unwise move. Indeed, Euryale takes over negotiations himself by the end of Act I. He shows a considerable degree of surprise and adaptability usually missing in pining young suitors. His icy reaction upon winning the chariot race shocks the audience as well as the Princess, for he had not given any hint of the secret plan he was developing between the first and second acts. When she questions him about it in Act III, he explains that he not only refuses to love, but avoids being loved, since it would seem to impose a reciprocal obligation. These unsympathetic attitudes produce the desired result, as the Princess becomes more and more determined to make Euryale love her, if only to deflate him with rejection once he does. But when she tries the same ploy by claiming to have chosen Aristomène, Euryale once again astounds her by congratulating them and saying that he has chosen **Aglante**. Fresh from the success of this double–reversal, Euryale consults with the Princess's father and wins his support. Thus when she makes a last–ditch effort in the fifth act to block Euryale's **marriage** and then to preserve herself, she is completely isolated and doomed to failure. The production of an entire plot, thin as it may be, through psychological manipulation rather than the usual array of contrived obstacles, is a triumph both for Euryale and for Molière.

**Exempt** (*Monsieur de Pourceaugnac*). Unlike the honest **policeman** in *Tartuffe*, this one has clearly been corrupted by **Éraste** and **Sbrigani** to play along with their many–layered ruse on the provincial bumpkin. When **Pourceaugnac**, dressed as a woman and amorously pursued by a couple of randy **Swiss** guards, screams for help, the Exempt arrives with a couple of *archers*. After scaring off the bullies, however, he instantly recognizes Pourceaugnac as a wanted man and threatens him with jail. He extorts an enormous bribe from the Limousin, and claiming that he, too, must now go into hiding, personally escorts him from the stage. Given the number of roles in this play, the Exempt must have been played by an actor who doubled the part, perhaps with one of the doctors from Act I, or else was played by a hireling.

**Exempt** (*Tartuffe*).  The **police** official who appears in the fifth act of the play stays quietly in the background through much of the conclusion, apparently ready to execute **Tartuffe's** order to arrest **Orgon** and his family and take them to prison.  In a stunning reversal, when the moment arrives, he instead taps his wand of authority on the hypocrite's shoulder, signaling his demise.  He then goes on to deliver the astonishing panegyric of **Louis XIV** as the ultimate lord of justice, a monarch with a God–like ability to see into the very souls of his subjects and to winnow out the good from the bad.  The Exempt would not have appeared in the earliest performances of the play, which did not get beyond the third act.  Who played the role is something of a mystery, since all the share–holding male members of the troupe already seem accounted for onstage, except for **De Brie**, whose comic powers would presumably have been needed for **Monsieur Loyal**.  Could De Brie have done a quick costume change in the space of fifty lines that separate Loyal's exit from the Exempt's entry?  It seems unlikely, especially since **Dorine's** remarks call attention to Loyal's face, which the public would have easily seen.  Would Molière have entrusted such an important, albeit small, part to a mere hireling?  In the absence of more evidence, one can only conjecture that perhaps he gave it to a theatrical professional who would not need much comic presence, such as one of the royal singers or dancers.  In recent times, as a result of retrospective thinking, the part has often been portrayed as representing the Secret Police, linked to the burgeoning apparatus of absolute monarchy as a forerunner to the totalitarian state.  But such interpretations undercut the mythic power of release that the role represents and the prospect for a successful reintegration that Molière so strongly underlines in his text.

**Eyeglasses.**  Spectacles were often used as props for old pantaloons, such as the various **Géronte** and **Gorgibus** characters in Molière's comedies, and also were commonly featured on misers.  Thus, it is not surprising that **Harpagon**, who is both elderly and a miser, is described as wearing them in *L'Avare*.  **Frosine** brings the protagonist's attention to the possibility of **marriage** with **Mariane** partly by saying that she considers no man handsome unless he is wearing eyeglasses.  It is possible that **Hubert** also used them for some of his old lady roles.  One thinks particularly of **Dorante's** admonition to **Madame Jourdain** that she should "get better glasses" when she is ranting against **Dorimène**.  This might simply be a figure of speech, but one can easily imagine Jourdain's wife, as well as **Madame Pernelle, Madame de Sotenville**, and perhaps even **Philaminte**, in glasses.  Among its Molière mementos, the **Comédie–Française** conserves a pair of spectacles thought to have been worn by Molière himself when playing Harpagon or **Argan**.

# F

**Fabre d'Eglantine, Philippe** (1750–1794). This revolutionary follower of Danton is remembered not only for inventing the months of the Republican calendar, but also for popular songs ("Il pleut, il pleut, bergère") and for the drama *Le Philinte de Molière*. Resetting the play in **Paris** of the 1790s, Fabre tries to put into effect **Rousseau's** moral judgments on the original play by making Jérome Alceste the drama's hero in his opposition to **Philinte's** scurrilous and false civility. Fabre eventually ended his life on the scaffold like his political idol.

*See* Ronald Tobin, "Civilité et convivialité dans *Le Misanthrope* et ses suites," *Le Nouveau Moliériste* 4–5 (1998–1999), 145–168.

*Fâcheux, Les* (*The Pests*). It is astounding that a play constructed on such a simple premise could have played such a great part in the history of drama as this one. If we are to believe Molière himself, it was hastily written in a span of two weeks for the great feast at **Vaux–le–Vicomte** where the superintendent of finance, **Fouquet**, would try to impress young **Louis XIV**. However, this disclaimer was used so frequently by the dramatist that one comes to take it with a pinch of salt. Certainly he had already experimented with pest–like characters, most recently in *L'École des maris*, where **Valère** pesters **Sganarelle** with his polite attentions in Act I. It was, however, a major step to move from the use of a single character in the context of a full–blown comedy to the idea of an entire play based on the intervention of pests that beset a man waiting for a rendezvous with his sweetheart. This is the entire plot of *Les Fâcheux*: the waiting lover **Éraste** is distracted by a succession of boors, including people infatuated with **music** and **poetry (Lysandre)**, swordplay (**Alcandre** and **Filinte**), intellectual trivialities (**Orante** and **Clymène**), political intrigue (**Caritidès** and **Ormin**), **hunting (Dorante)**, and **gambling (Alcipe)**. The concept of such a review of weird types may have come from **Desmarets de Saint–Sorlin's** *Les Visionnaires*, where a series of deranged and deluded individuals present their warped versions of reality, one after the other. This play was a major part of the troupe's **repertory** and afforded a ready model for the actors. The succession of intruders is more of an obstacle to Éraste than either **Orphise's** guardian **Damis** or the somewhat quixotic young lady herself. Each one of Éraste's pests insists on having his or her say, until the young man finally manages to free himself with a witty remark or a timely retreat. Sometimes he is too late, as when Orante and Clymène force him to arbitrate their quarrel over jealous lovers, and Orphise, espying him with the women, becomes **jealous** herself. It is chance alone that ends the deferral of Éraste's pleasure. In the third act, just after rejecting Filinte's rather frivolous proposal for swordplay, Éraste happens upon an actual ambush upon him being organized by Damis. It seems that Éraste is not the only eavesdropper, for a tough character named **La Rivière** and two of his friends, who are apparently retainers of Éraste, also overhear the plot and decide to launch an attack on Damis. Éraste can then jump from his hiding place and save Damis, who is so grateful that he gladly consents to the previously unappealing **marriage** of Orphise and the new hero.

It would be a mistake to try to understand the importance of *Les Fâcheux* on dramatic values alone, for it was the first of Molière's *comédie–ballets*, a new mixed genre that combined traditional acting with **music and dance**. The characters move almost seamlessly between the art forms. The nymph who delivers **Paul Pellisson's** verse prologue magically makes part of the cast appear, then leads off certain actors, saying, "Pests, now depart! Or if His Majesty must see you / May it only be to increase his pleasure." She leaves the others to perform the opening dance number to the sound of the oboes and violins. At the end of Act I, Éraste is pushed aside by a group of players engaged in a *jeu de mail*, a primitive form of croquet, and then enveloped in a crowd of gawkers who dance around him in their curiosity. Éraste returns to center stage at the beginning of Act II with the remark, "Have all my pests at last deserted me?" At the end of that act, Éraste has no sooner separated himself from the hunting maniac Dorante, perhaps using a band of lawn bowlers as cover, than the bowlers seize him to judge a disputed point in their game. These bowling dancers are run off by a band of urchins with slingshots, only to be pursued themselves by their shoemaker parents, and these by a gardener, whose solo leaves the stage open again for Éraste's return. The happy conciliation scene at the end of the play is suitably invaded by masked mummers who come to join the fun. This causes Éraste, in search of peace and quiet, to call for reinforcements, "What, still nothing but pests? Ho! Some **Swiss** guards here! / Kindly show these wretches to the door!" The guards, whirling their halberds in cadence, chase away the mummers, leaving an entry of **shepherds** to finish the entertainment with a dance that is more harmonious, if less realistic, than those that preceded it. The onset of the *comédie–ballet* raised the stakes for comedy, both by making it a more expensive and challenging undertaking, but also by requiring a sense of integration with the other lively arts that had hitherto been unheard of. More than just a transitional form in the development of musical opera, the *comédie–ballet* marked the legitimacy of collaboration between music and theater, which has since found expression in more modern times as the Broadway musical, among others.

Of course, one of the most remarkable aspects of *Les Fâcheux* was that it also accompanied a political event of tremendous scope. Conceived as a crowning ceremony for Fouquet's new country house and a seal to his important relationship with the young monarch, the feast of Vaux would lead Louis XIV to imprison Fouquet and his family, exile many of his followers, and use their shame to reinforce his status as an autocrat who would not share power with anyone. The importance of this angry response could not have been lost on Molière, for shortly afterward he was called upon to present the play twice before the King himself. Thus placed under the King's umbrella of **patronage**, like the trio who had designed Vaux, the playwright hastened to separate himself from Fouquet by composing an unprecedented double introduction to the play. The first part was a dedicatory letter directly to the King, emphasizing that the finished text contained a sketch commanded by the crown itself, involving the hunting fanatic Dorante. Molière claims in this letter that the comedy owes its success entirely to the King. The second, more general introduction dispenses with such sycophantic language and places the *comédie–ballet* under the aegis of public approval, flippantly saying that he could explain it in terms of **Aristotle** and **Horace** if needed, but that that day would probably never come. Having justified the play in terms of ancient and modern standards, the author suggests that it will not be the last of such experiments. These introductions set the pattern for the defense of his work that Molière will henceforth deliver in all times of controversy: he calls simultaneously upon the judgment of the most general public and the most specific and lofty of patrons to justify his writing. Éraste's little endorsement of Bourbon anti–dueling policy in his scene with Alcandre textually manifests Molière's high–profile alignment with the throne, a call that will be echoed again and again, even as the content of his comedies comes perilously close at times to upsetting the public order the King represents.

Not surprisingly, *Les Fâcheux* was a huge success, both in the short run (with many private and command performances and a healthy public run) and in the longer term, as it remained a staple repertory element throughout Molière's lifetime. It was his third most popular play, performed 106 times prior to his death.

The term *fâcheux* would go on to be used after this play for any character who makes a pest of himself. In *Le Misanthrope*, **Acaste**, who is considered a pest by **Alceste**, recounts how the impertinent windbag Damon kept him out in the sun for more than an hour while he ranted on about unimportant topics (II, 4). The **Viscount** in *La Comtesse d'Escarbagnas* tells **Julie** how another loquacious busybody tied him up with discussions of politics while he was on his way to see her (I, 1). This type of scene would be passed on into Restoration comedy and from there into the theatrical tradition.

**Fagotier, Le (*The Stick Collector*).** The title of this farce is mentioned by **La Grange's** register as early as 1661. It indicates **Sganarelle's** profession, someone who collected sticks in the forests and sold them as firewood in the streets. Obviously a very low–level livelihood, it was made possible because windfall lumber was not subject to the same laws as that which was cut down. This was clearly an early version of *Le Médecin malgré lui*. In fact, La Grange reverted to that title several years after the production of the latter play.

**Fainting**. A fairly common comic technique that Molière uses sparingly. In *Sganarelle*, **Célie** faints after contemplating **Lélie's portrait** and thinking that she might have to wed **Villebrequin's** son, while Lélie faints after **Sganarelle** tells him that the lady from whom he got the portrait is his wife.

**Faked death**. This was a commonplace element in seventeenth–century comedy, and entire plays were even built around it. Molière was among those who used it most skillfully, from **Horace's** supposed demise in *L'École des femmes* and the feigned deaths in *Les Fourberies de Scapin*, including **Scapin's** own "assassination," to the fabrication of both **Louison's** and **Argan's** deaths in *Le Malade imaginaire* (II, 8 and III, 11). Frequently part of a scheme involving the extortion of **money**, and sometimes linked with the appearance of a "**ghost**," the faked death could be employed to sound out the true intentions of characters and sort out their grimaces from their true expressions of emotion.

*Fameuse Comédienne, La* (*The Famous Actress*). An anonymous pamphlet published as early as 1687 and often thereafter, sometimes under the title *Les Intrigues de Molière et celles de sa femme*, that accuses **Armande Béjart** and her two husbands of various immoral acts. It appears to have little value other than as invective, but it does confirm the impression of a falling out between Molière and his spouse in the late 1660s.

**Farce**. A type of short, ribald comedy originally developed in the liturgical theater of the Middle Ages. As Passion plays and mysteries grew longer and more elaborate and were divided up between urban guilds to handle the multitudes of biblical characters, some episodes were turned by their performers into comic skits. These were designed to showcase the talents of comedy–minded burghers, to relieve the solemn atmosphere of the more serious spiritual drama, and to retain the attention of audiences obliged to stand for hours in the squares where the liturgical dramas unfolded. Since they were "stuffed" into the fabric of the larger works, these skits were called *farces* (stuffing) and eventually took on a distinct form and identity of their own. Full–blown farces of the late fourteenth and fifteenth centuries abandoned the original religious context and focused on everyday squabbles in the lives of medieval citizens. Typical of these were the famous *Farce of the Vatmaker*, constructed around the problems of contracts, and the *Farce of Master Pierre Pathelin*, which involves a shyster lawyer. **Law** was an apt subject for the farces as more and more law students in medieval universities became involved in drama and formed societies to put on the *sotie* plays that were given during carnival season. The Renaissance looked with a jaundiced eye on such vulgar entertainments and sought to replace them among the learned classes with translations of Greco–Roman comedy, or plays based on **Terentian** models, such as Pierre Larivey's *Les Esprits*. While this campaign worked well for the upper levels of the public, there was a constant audience among the lower **bourgeois** elements for more slapstick and pratfalls. Thus, farce survived, often in the form of medieval octosyllables, well into the seventeenth century. In the early decades of the century, such figures of the **Hôtel de Bourgogne** as Gautier–Garguille, Gros–Guillaume, and Turlupin kept the genre alive on stage, while street players like Tabarin made their living among the crowds of the Pont–Neuf. **Jodelet** and Capitaine Matamore were considered by many admirers to be representative of the farce tradition, as was Molière's fat colleague **Gros–René**. The latter was almost certainly the original protagonist of the play now called *La Jalousie du Barbouillé*, as **La Grange's** register indicates. This play, as well as *Le Médecin volant* were farces, as were several other short plays in the Palais Royal Theater **repertory**, such as *Le Docteur amoureux* and *Gorgibus dans le sac*. Although the latter texts are lost, at least in their original form, parts of them were preserved in later comedy productions. While dropping the face masks and some of the more stereotypical elements of early seventeenth–century farce, Molière deliberately preserved its emphasis on physical and gestural humor, its free range of **language** and topics, and its often irreverent approach to established values. Even late in his career, *Les Fourberies de Scapin* shows that Molière remained interested in all the comic potential of the farce, which he refused to abandon in favor of an exclusively refined brand of humor. This decision cost him some support in the decades following his death, as critics like **Boileau** called for an increasingly lofty form of drama. However, in general history has applauded Molière's choices, which greatly enhanced the heritage of all comedy that followed him.

See Bernadette Rey–Flaud, *Molière et la farce* (Geneva: Droz, 1996); Barbara Bowen, "Some Elements of French Farce in Molière," *L'Esprit créateur* (Fall 1966), 167–175; Bernard Faivre, *Répertoire des farces françaises des origines à Tabarin* (Paris: Imprimerie Nationale, 1993).

**Fates.** When mocking **Argan's** superstitious belief in **Purgon's** powers, **Béralde** implicitly compares him with the mythological Fates: "It seems, to hear you, that Mister Purgon holds in his hands the thread of your life and that, by supreme authority, he stretches it or shortens it at his pleasure" (*Le Malade imaginaire*, III, 6).

***Femmes savantes, Les* (*The Learned Ladies*).** This five–act verse play is arguably Molière's most carefully crafted work. In 1668 he announced that he was writing a comedy, "tout à fait achevée." Four years later, after reading his "complete" comedy in worldly gatherings, he presented *Les Femmes Savantes* on March 11, 1672, at the Palais Royal Theater and published it on December 16. For this comedy of manners he rejected the more natural prose of *L'Avare* that had drawn criticism and adopted the more highly valued alexandrine form. Molière's painstaking composition of *Les Femmes Savantes* reveals his desire to be seen as a serious, accomplished playwright. Although popular, his "model" comedy was not the huge success he might have expected it would be.

For this serious professional statement, Molière returned to a theme that had inspired him throughout his career: women's roles and place in society. This was the first time Molière did not write himself the principal role, opting instead to have all the attention focused on the "learned ladies." In a second departure from his previous compositions, Molière created two individualized **portraits**. Contemporaries immediately identified the ridiculous poets **Trissotin** and **Vadius** as **Cotin**, a celebrated Hellenist and Academician, and the equally learned **Ménage**, both of whom were also renowned in the salons as poets. According to an anecdote, the realism was heightened when Molière donned an old outfit of Cotin's to play him. *Les Femmes Savantes* is thus designed to satirize the seventeenth–century salon milieu as well as address the more general theme of "learned ladies."

Molière had already treated these questions in his first Parisian success, *Les Précieuses Ridicules*, and to a lesser degree in *L'Ecole des Femmes*. In *Les Femmes Savantes*, Molière depicts a Parisian, bourgeois household under the maniacal grip of its matriarch, **Philaminte**, a woman infatuated with knowledge. Her daughter **Armande** and sister–in–law **Belise** follow her lead and live only for the mind. In contrast, another daughter, **Henriette**, is totally lacking in culture and often serves as the spectator to the other women's follies. Only Henriette is not humiliated at the end and is rewarded when she is betrothed to her choice, **Clitandre**. As in *Les Précieuses*, the principal scenes depict a salon where the "learned ladies" entertain poets and reveal their stupidity and lack of taste when they judge mediocre works as masterpieces. Once again women's desire to control **language** and their capacities as arbiters of literary taste, two traits of *préciosité*, come under attack. Molière again denounces the literature of the salons, as Belise takes her cue from these literary models. But in *Les Femmes Savantes*, Molière's satire goes beyond the phenomenon of *préciosité*. The *précieuse* is replaced by a more generalized female pedant imbued with the philosophy of **Descartes** and fascinated by **astronomy** and physics, an exaggerated version of the Parisian salon woman. Molière designed his comedy to show that like their *précieuses* forebears, the "learned ladies" are proof that women who go beyond the limits of their sex as dictated by society create chaos in their households and become humiliated social outcasts. The more than 1,600 presentations of *Les Femmes Savantes* at La **Comédie–Française**, as well as the thousands of performances of the play throughout the world, confirm Molière's sense that putting learned ladies in their place would always find an appreciative audience.

See *Les Femmes savantes*, ed. H. Gaston Hall (Oxford: Clarendon, 1974).

*Faith E. Beasley*

**Fencing Master (*Le Bourgeois gentilhomme*).** Of the three worldly teachers who cater to **Monsieur Jourdain** in the first act and dispute the relative importance of their disciplines, the Fencing Master is the most laconic, speaking mostly in monosyllabic orders and curt phrases. He enters the house already clad in his fencing **costume**, including a *plastron* or chest protector and, if we can believe **Nicole**, stomps about the place, shaking the china and muddying the floors. The Music Master calls him a "clumsy draft horse" and his superior arms do not prove decisive against the combined forces of two fine arts teachers. His pupil fares no better, for despite his training and his course in the "demonstrative reason" of combat, he is quickly beaten into retreat by a mere maid. The Fencing Master thus joins the ranks of false bravery along with the **Capitan** and the *miles gloriosus* of Roman comedy. It is unknown who played the part originally, for Molière's sword–toting brother–in–law, **Louis Béjart**, had already retired when the play premiered.

**Filène (*Pastorale comique*).** This "rich" **shepherd** takes umbrage when he hears **Lycas** making up amorous verses for **Iris**, whom he loves as well. He threatens Lycas with dire consequences if he does not give up his pretensions, but the latter dismisses the threats as a trifle. So Filène has another shepherd deliver a formal challenge and the pair eventually tries to settle the matter on the field of battle. After they are parted by others of their kind, they put the matter before the lady, who coyly refuses to pick a favorite, driving both men nearly to the brink of self–slaughter. Fortunately Filène, like Lycas, heeds the voice of a younger shepherd who denounces the folly of their fight, and he joins his rival in the fun at the end of the play. Destival, a court singer who often performed with Molière in official spectacles, played the part.

**Filerin (*L'Amour médecin*).** The last of the five doctors to arrive on stage, Filerin tries to quell the disagreement between his colleagues in order to preserve **medical** orderliness and to better fool the general public. His strategy of confusing and manipulating the common folk is very explicit, as he compares his profession to such illustrious practices as flattery, alchemy, and fortune telling. He probably represented the prominent physician Yvelin.

**Filinte (*Les Fâcheux*).** The last of the pests presented in this play, Filinte is a fellow marquis to **Éraste**, but he is preoccupied with swordplay. He announces to Éraste that he has been challenged by someone and insists on lending his unwanted services to the young lover. The affaire that he discusses does not match the details of Damis's planned ambush, and the spectator may assume, with Éraste, that it is imaginary. When Filinte refuses to leave, Éraste threatens to fight against him, which causes Filinte to beat a hasty retreat, indicating perhaps that he would have been of little assistance in a real brawl. Although his name is homonymic with the famous friend of **Alceste** in *Le Misanthrope*, this pest has a sleazy air, and the spelling of the beginning of his name may be meant to recall "filou," a criminal.

**Fin Lourdaud, Le (*The Subtle Idiot*).** A play, probably in one act, that was first shown on November 20, 1668, and represented thirty more times until 1672, and probably thereafter until at least 1678. It accompanied *L'Avare* on the bill of the latter's first reprise. **Hubert's** register refers to the same play as *Le*

*Procureur dupé*, a possible subtitle that hints at a judicial theme, since it involved duping a prosecutor. One imagines a legal equivalent of *Le Malade imaginaire*'s **Thomas Diafoirus**. That this relatively successful piece remained anonymous suggests that the author may not have been Molière. The text has been lost.

**Finet.** An obscure young hireling who played **Criquet** in *La Comtesse d'Escarbagnas*.

**Flamme.** The French word for "flame" was standard theatrical vocabulary for "love" in the seventeenth century. It was necessary not so much as a euphemism as because the sheer frequency of "amour" made it useful to have other rhyming synonyms.

**Flemish.** This **language**, or rather an ethnic representation of it, makes an appearance in *Monsieur de Pourceaugnac*, when **Sbrigani** fakes a Flemish accent to impersonate a merchant to whom the protagonist supposedly owes much **money**. It is really a parody of the way a Fleming would pronounce French, rather than an attempt to recreate the Dutch language.

*Fleur des Saints, La* (*The Flower of the Saints*). A collection of **religious** devotional writings, possibly one of several translated from the **Spanish**, where *flor* was used even more often than in French as a term for anthologies. Such books, extremely common in **bourgeois** libraries, were typically hefty tomes, and **Dorine** mentions in *Tartuffe* that she was innocently using one to press her handkerchief when the bigot Laurent ripped it away and said it was a sin to pollute holy words with such vile objects.

**Fleurant, Monsieur** (*Le Malade imaginaire*). This **apothecary**, whose name roughly means "sniffer," since he gains his living sniffing chamber pots, appears only in Act III, scene 4, where **Béralde** prevents him from giving a scheduled enema to **Argan**. After Béralde insults him by saying that he is not used to speaking to people's faces (usually being occupied directly with the posterior of the body), he threatens reprisals, and in fact sends **Purgon** to punish the unbelievers. However, Fleurant is much spoken of in the play as early as the first act, where Argan counts up and discounts his bills and **Toinette** puns on his name. The part may have been played by **Hubert**, **Du Croisy**, or **de Brie**, and may have been doubled with **Monsieur Bonnefoy**.

**Flipote** (*Tartuffe*). **Mme. Pernelle's** maid is a mute part and her only function is to receive a slap from her mistress when she is not quick enough to follow orders. Mme. Pernelle calls her a slut and says she's only good for gaping at the sky. No wonder she appears only in the first scene of the play. The original Flipote may well have been **Marie Raguenau**, but in at least one modern production, the part was played by a Great Dane!

**Flora.** This fertility goddess sings in the original prologue to *Le Malade imaginaire*, where she calls the **shepherds and shepherdesses** to leave off their toil and celebrate the return of the victorious **King Louis**.

**Fontainebleau.** Royal palace located in an extensive forest about fifty kilometers southeast of **Paris**. Often used as a summer retreat by the **court**, it was the site of Molière's second production of *Les Fâcheux* on August 25 and 27, 1661, a little over two months before being shown in Paris and less than a fortnight after the controversial feast of **Vaux–le–Vicomte**. Donneau de Visé's *Lettre sur le Misanthrope* was written under the pretext that he was making a report on the play to a friend who was with the court at Fontainebleau during the August 1666 opening.

**Fontenay–le–Comte.** City in the Vendée region. **Charles Dufresne** took his wandering players, including young Molière, to this city to perform in the summer of 1648.

**Food.** The main feasts in Molière's plays are: the meal **Dom Juan** shares with **Sganarelle** and the **Commander's statue**; **Monsieur Jourdain's** *collation* for **Dorimène**; and **Harpagon's** dinner in honor of **Mariane**. The latter two occasions offer contrasts of elegant cuisine and polite conviviality with crude behavior and unfashionable food.

For a complete discussion of the very important food and drink metaphors that pop up almost everywhere in Molière's theater, *see* Ronald Tobin, *Tarte à la crème: Comedy and Gastonomy in Molière's Theater* (Columbus: Ohio State University Press, 1990).

**Fouquet or Foucquet, Nicolas** (1615–1680). As superintendent of finance, this clever social climber became one of the most powerful men in France after the death of **Mazarin**. It was he who assembled the talented trio of the architect Le Vau, the landscape architect Le Nôtre, and the painter Le Brun to create his spectacular château at **Vaux–le–Vicomte**, some twenty miles southeast of **Paris**. Even before the famous and ill–fated feast that was to take place there, Fouquet demonstrated his taste for Molière's work by ordering a command performance in Paris during the October–November 1660 period when the **Petit–Bourbon** theater had been demolished and the Palais Royal Theater's refurbishing was not yet completed. Several such "visits" allowed the troupe to remain comfortably solvent during this difficult transition. For the great celebration at Vaux, Fouquet again spared no expense in assembling the greatest artists of his age: singers, dancers, stage designers, and of course, actors. They were probably all under the general direction of his secretary **Paul Pellisson**, himself a noted poet and author of the lines spoken by **Madeleine Béjart**, the charming water nymph who opens *Les Fâcheux*. The story of **Louis XIV's jealousy** over Fouquet's power and his beautiful estate, which led to a trumped–up trial and lifelong imprisonment, is well known. Unlike such adherents as Pellisson and **Jean de la Fontaine**, Molière did not suffer exile or other punishment for his role in the feast, partly because he took pains to distance himself from the superintendent and to inflate Louis XIV's own contribution to his play.

***Fourberies de Scapin, Les (The Tricks of Scapin)****.* The title of this three–act prose comedy is one of the most difficult of Molière's to translate. "Tricks" is a somewhat weak rendering of "fourberies," which are not just gratuitous pranks, but elaborate and self–interested deceptions. "Swindles" conveys the degree of planning involved, except that *fourberies* are not always financially motivated. Indeed, in this play, **money** is just a means to the end of marrying the two desired women, and the major trick is strictly for revenge. Moreover, *fourberies* can only be properly carried out by a *fourbe*, someone who makes something of a profession of these ruses, a kind of mercenary "fixer" who solves other people's problems. A recent English version of the play calls itself *That Scoundrel Scapin*, which comes close, but does not quite convey the professionalism of *fourberies*.

The play was first performed on May 24, 1671, at the Palais Royal Theater and soon after published by Le Monnier. It is somewhat unusual among the later plays in that, although less than five acts, it lacks a comedy–ballet dimension. Was this intentional, or a result of Molière's betrayal by **Lully**? In any case, it is fairly obvious that the major events of the third act were developed from an earlier **farce** Molière presented in **Paris**, *Gorgibus dans le sac*. This little play was never listed among his own works and may have been borrowed from the store of traditional farces tracing back to medieval times. Tabarin has bag tricks in some of his comic sketches, as did one of Straparola's tales. Other elements suggest **Terence's** Latin comedies, particularly *Phormio*, where two young men develop relationships with forbidden women while their fathers are away on business and enlist the help of a slave to cover their misdeeds. This is the play, in fact, that **Boileau** had in mind in his *Art poétique* when he accuses Molière of catering too much to the common people and "joining Terence to Tabarin." There are also scenic borrowings from **Rotrou**. However, the great originality in this comedy derives not from its farcical antecedents, but from its experiments with dramatic **language**, for Molière succeeds here in muting the gestural, plot–based elements of the farce form, while adapting its characters to an entirely new type of speech–based text.

Consider the exposition. It begins with a sequence in which the **servant Silvestre** and his master **Octave** review the latter's problems. What is important is not the "content" of the father's return to impose a **marriage**, but the means of its conveyance: Octave has to review the information within his questions, while Silvestre simply repeats the last few words of each of his master's lines. This type of leading interrogation alternating with reluctant repetition is a novel idea for exposing intrigue, and it dovetails nicely with the next scene. Just when Octave is lamenting, "What shall I do?" up pops **Scapin**, as if to say, "You rang?" Having obtained a promise of help, Octave launches into an account of the preliminary events that is complete, but prolix and sentimental. Scapin pushes the tale along with comments, then Silvestre cuts in and finishes it off logically, ironically supplying the last details from the least likely source. The real theme of the first two scenes is the management of words, and it segues into scene 3, where Octave and his sweetheart **Hyacinte** share a nice **lovers'** duo, until Scapin sends the girl away and makes Octave rehearse for the scolding he expects on his father's return. He first works on posture, positioning his subject as well as he can, then imitates the father so convincingly that it makes the young man cower in fright. Here the comic rehearsal, used to such good effect in the first act of *Amphitryon*, gains a new dimension by being too close to real life. Of course, the approach of the father makes the terrified son take to his heels, leaving the servants to deal with his ire. Scene 4 first offers the kind of disconnected conversation that Molière first developed in the notary scene in *L'École des femmes*. Old **Argante** is so emotionally preoccupied with his son's misbehavior that he does not answer Scapin's solicitous advances. Then, when Argante spots Silvestre and seeks to vent his spleen on the guardian who was supposed to have prevented trouble, Scapin must distract the father by literally stealing the conversation and directing it to his own version of the rehearsal just finished, where he claims Argante's friendship by showing how he had scolded the boy. In the ensuing dialogue, he always stays one step ahead of the old man, leading him through one possible scenario after another. When Argante threatens to disinherit the disobedient youth, Scapin leads him through a denial sequence that recalls **Dorine's** conversation with **Orgon** and prefigures **Toinette's** with **Argan**. All three involve the same pre–emptive appeal to paternal affection, which the interlocutor does his best fretfully to deny. Despite the fact that Scapin cannot quite shake Argante from his fixed ideas about the inheritance, he closes the act by rehearsing again, this time with Silvestre, who is to portray a brawling *bretteur* in the next phase of trickery.

The second act, like the first, opens without the trickster. Argante and his fellow geezer **Géronte** play a verbal game of "tag," each blaming the other for failing to educate his son properly. Then Géronte's son, Léandre, arrives to greet his father warmly and generates a **lazzi** sequence as the irritated old man resists his embraces. This is linked to another gestural tableau in the third scene, where Léandre, wrongly blaming Scapin for disclosing his secret affair with **Zerbinette**, demands a confession at swordpoint from the penitent **servant**. In a scene that recalls and amplifies **Valère's** misunderstood confession to **Harpagon**, he admits first to consuming a keg of Spanish wine with his friends, then to stealing the watch Léandre had sent to his loved one, and finally to **disguising** himself as an evil spirit in order to beat up his master in the dark. Unfortunately, none of these is the confession Léandre was looking for, and the interrogation might have gone on forever had not the messenger **Carle** arrived with news of Zerbinette's impending departure. In scene 4, it is the tormentor's turn to become the beggar, as Léandre implores Scapin to aid him and the scoundrel pouts as long as he can before agreeing to procure the necessary cash for both young men to buy the freedom of their girlfriends. He sets to the task immediately with Argante. In an exchange that recalls **Frosine's** review of an imaginary dowry with **Harpagon**, Scapin lists all the legal expenses that Argante will save if, instead of suing to break off his son's marriage, he simply pays off the young lady's bully brother. When Argante resists, the brother, in reality Silvestre, appears to exact payment or revenge. Like a **Capitan**, he swaggers and swears and thrusts his sword in every direction, dispatching a whole company of imaginary defenders and scaring the wits out of Argante. The old man pays up, and Scapin falls on Géronte as his next victim in scene 7. Here, recalling a passage in **Rotrou's *La Soeur***, he claims Octave has been stolen by **Turks** in a galley in the harbor and that if ransom fails they will take him to the slave market in **Algiers**. This verbal sequence again plays on automatic responses (the old man keeps repeating, "What the devil was he doing in that galley?") with insufficient solutions (first Géronte offers only some old **clothes** as ransom, then he literally will not let go of the money until Scapin tears it away). The act ends with Scapin doling out the gold to the two eager youths.

The third act finally permits us a look at the pair of liberated young ladies, who have so far failed to appear. Scapin sends them off under guard of the pusillanimous Silvestre and begins his revenge on Géronte, who had told Léandre that he learned of the misbehavior from Scapin instead of Argante. Warning Géronte of a death threat from the "brother" and his gang of thugs, Scapin induces the old man to hide in a bag, then impersonates a variety of different voices in order to beat his victim. After quite an impressive performance in **Gascon** and **Swiss** dialect, Scapin flees when Géronte catches on to the trick. But it was not enough for Géronte to suffer the actual blows. He must relive the experience in shameful silence as Zerbinette recounts the whole story to her own great amusement. The idea of a man as the painful audience to his own punishment recalls Arnolphe's listenting to Horace in *L'École des femmes*. Though Zerbinette slips away after divulging too much of the truth, Géronte manages to nab Silvestre and he commiserates with Argante before the denouement begins to unfold in an ironically self-conscious double recognition, with both old men commenting on how unlikely the coincidences are of their daughters reappearing as the young women courted by their sons. Octave almost ruins the chance to fulfill his dreams by resisting the marriage, until he realizes that he is now on the same wavelength as his father; this passage recalls and reverses yet another at the end of *Le Bourgeois gentilhomme*, when **Madame Jourdain** almost destroys her daughter's chances. Finally, Scapin uses the tried and true technique of **feigned death** to extort a pardon from his masters, appearing as though mortally wounded by a roofer's fallen hammer. But no sooner are the words of forgiveness spoken than he hops off his pallet and proclaims that he is suddenly feeling better, foreshadowing **Louison's** remarkable recovery in *Le Malade imaginaire*.

Boileau is entitled to his supercilious opinion, but it was clear to the audience that this play was no relapse on Molière's part. It was nothing less than a review of comic technique and a remarkable encapsulation of all the types of scenes he had perfected in his career. He did not wait for his emulators to amass this type of retrospective after his death (**Brécourt, Champmeslé**, and others would hasten to do so), but achieved it himself while still alive. Scapin's miracle recovery at the end of the play is a kind of personal statement to the audience that he did not feel "quite dead yet" and was still able to give them what they loved. *Les Fourberies de Scapin* is a living grammar of theatrical dialogue that is still without parallel.

See *Les Fourberies de Scapin*, ed. John T. Stoker (London: University of London Press, 1971); Dorothy F. Jones, "Insiders and Outsiders in *Les Fourberies de Scapin*," *Studi francesi* 106 (1992), 67–72.

**Franche–Comté**. A province of the Holy Roman Empire, sometimes under **Spanish** control, located between Burgundy and Switzerland. **Condé** conquered the area in a lightning attack in the winter of 1667–68. Although it was traded back to the Empire in the Peace of Aachen in exchange for territory in Flanders, Condé had so reduced its defenses that it was easily regained.   It was permanently added to France by the Treaty of Nimeguen in 1678. The original campaign was the subject of **occasional poetry** by Molière and others and for **court** celebrations that involved several of the plays.

**Francisque (*Dom Juan*)**. *See* **Pauper**.

**Fronde, La**. A series of desultory revolts which took place between 1648 and 1652 in various parts of France, involving different elements of the population. The uprisings took their name from the slingshot, which was their symbol.  On the one hand, the *Fronde des princes* sprung from challenges by powerful members of the nobility, notably the great **Condé** and **Mlle. de Montpensier**, who sought to manifest their independence from royal decisions and decided to make a last stand for feudalism.  Condé was eventually captured and when liberated changed allegiances and fought for a while under the Spanish flag that he had helped defeat earlier at Rocroi and Lens. Mlle. de Montpensier, in her capacity as governess of the Bastille, at one point ordered the cannons of the fortress to open fire on the royalist troops that were maneuvering outside the walls of Paris.  This was perhaps less a matter of military strategy than a stubborn reflex by the daughter of the ever–conspiring Gaston d'Orléans.  She was later made to pay bitterly for her action through internal exile and condemnation to life as a spinster.  Young La Rochefoucauld took the side of Condé and the princes, but was wounded and had to retire from court as a result of his rebellion.

Another feature of the hostilities was the *Fronde parlementaire*. Certain of the sovereign courts, inspired perhaps in part by the Revolution led by English parliamentarians, sought to extend or at least manifest their rights within the political structure. In **Bordeaux**, a particularly active branch of the Fronde was called the Ormée, after the great elm which served as rallying place and liberty tree. One of the sticking points of the dispute was taxes, and in some rural areas the opposition to these was fierce enough to assume the dimensions of a *jacquerie*.  Popular outrage largely bypassed the official tax administration to focus on tax farmers, privileged royal minions, and especially the odious Cardinal **Mazarin**, who was blamed for bleeding the country dry.  A series of pamphlets called the *mazarinades* lambasted him for everything from large–

scale embezzlement to sleeping with the Queen Mother. **Retz** was especially dogged in his campaign against Mazarin, but deserted the principles of the revolt in exchange for appointment as a cardinal.

Through all this, very little hatred was focussed on the person of the young king, as all parties mouthed the battle cry of "Vive le roi sans gabelle," targeting the despised salt tax. Nevertheless, the royal family was not immune from disturbance by the Fronde. At one particularly confusing moment Louis XIV and his family were startled to find municipal guards from the city of Paris intruding into their palace and placing them briefly under a form of house arrest, supposedly for their own protection. The monarch never forgot this affront. As soon as he had assumed personal power, he began a long and vigorous campaign to stamp out all vestiges of independent elective power and to place the country under a centralized, autocratic chain of command. There is a rather clear allusion to the Fronde in *Tartuffe*, where Orgon is described as having played a laudable role in supporting the king during the country's late troubles. Orgon's friend, Argan, who has left a case full of incriminating papers in the judge's keeping, undoubtedly represents a less lucky magistrate who took the opposite side during the *Fronde parlementaire*.

**Frosine** (*L'Avare*). The best–known of Molière's *entremetteuse* figures, she is remembered chiefly for the "negative dowry" that she concocts for **Mariane**, consisting of the sums of expenditures she would never make, and for gulling **Harpagon** with the prospect of a young woman in love with bespectacled old pinchpennies.

**Frosine** (*Dépit amoureux*). Listed in the dramatis personae simply as **Ascagne's** *confidante*, this Frosine is far different from the elderly go–between of the same name in *L'Avare*. She is obviously a young lady and a member of **Albert's** prominent family, since she and Ascagne employ the honorific "vous" in speaking with each other. She refers to Albert's household as "our home." Of course, she is quite aware of the real nature of Ascagne's identity and sex (or thinks she is), the only one besides Ascagne's two mothers who appears to know all the details, although she correctly suspects that Albert has unearthed at least part of the secret. Until Act II, however, she does not know that Ascagne has managed to usurp **Lucile's** identity by night and to seduce and marry **Valère**. When at the beginning of Act IV events seems to be pushing Ascagne's identity toward disclosure, she half–forms a sentence about wanting to consult the woman she believes to be Ascagne's birth mother. That visit having taken place between acts, she reveals in Act V that Ascagne is actually Albert's own daughter, twice switched with a neighbor's male infant (once with his knowledge, once without), and the "the shopkeeper Ignès," whom Ascagne had believed to be her parent, is in fact no relation. Following the second switch, Ascagne and Frosine were brought up together and were for a while *soeurs de lait* (that is, Frosine's mother was Ascagne's wet–nurse).

# G

*Galanterie*. This important notion in early modern France had little to do with military bravery. It was a code of flirtation that existed to some degree at most levels of society, but was especially important among the **court** aristocracy and the fashionable elements of **Paris**. The best authority on the many gradations of *galanterie* is Jean–Michel Pelous, who points out that, in its truest forms, it differed from abstract *préciosité* in embracing the physical aspects of joy, **love**, and beauty. Nevertheless, the proponents of *préciosité* mention it frequently and develop their own watered–down version of it. *Galanterie* differed from true amorous passion in that it was deemed to be light, witty, and eminently controllable. It called for just the right measure of interest and compliment, without the imposition of any absolute conditions. Thus, it differed from debauchery or hedonism, since the enjoyment of physical happiness was itself subject to restraint and highly contingent on local conditions. *Galanterie* was especially prized in the occasional verse of the age of **Louis XIV**, such as one finds in **Mascarille's** impromptu in *Les Précieuses ridicules* or **Oronte's** sonnet in *Le Misanthrope*. Its highly conventional nature, facile hyperbole, lack of elevated themes or metaphors, and verbal playfulness tended to drain lyric poetry of much of its force during the period.

**Galen**. Ancient **Greek doctor** considered as one of the fathers of medicine. He is cited by **Sganarelle** in *Le Médecin volant* and by the First Doctor in *Monsieur de Pourceaugnac*.

**Galleys**. Lest one consider the frequent reference to galleys in French comedy as an anachronism, it is important to remember that they were still a primary base of naval power in the Mediterranean in the seventeenth century. The French navy's galleys, based in Toulon and rowed by convicts almost in the fashion of *Ben Hur*, were the joke of the seas. The **Spanish** called their commander "el amiral de la comedia." In *Les Précieuses ridicules*, **Jodelet** boasts that **Mascarille** has served in the galleys of **Malta**, which were actually quite well known, but since they were operated by the Knights of Malta, he makes the mistake of saying his friend commanded a regiment of cavalry. The idea of a hundred horses clambering about on those thin, exiguous vessels must have provoked a great laugh among any military men in the audience. Almost any mention of the galleys, especially applied to **servants** or lower–class characters, is tantamount to calling them "jail–bait." Such references are made to **Sbrigani** in *Monsieur de Pourceaugnac* and to **Scapin**. A **Turkish** galley is supposed to have abducted **Géronte's** son in *Les Fourberies de Scapin*, recalling a similar incident in **Rotrou's** *La Sœur*, where the exotic kidnappers struck the ferry plying between the **Louvre** and the Tour de Nesle on the Seine.

**Galopin** (*La Critique de l'École des femmes*). This young **lackey**, obviously still a child or a youth, has the tough job of doorman in **Uranie's** household. When he announces **Climène's** arrival, he is told he should have told her the mistress was away. When he tries to prevent the **Marquis** from entering, he is told he should not have stood in his way, even though Uranie had previously told him she did not wish to see the man. No wonder he fetches the chair for the Marquis in a most surly manner.

**Gambling**. The character of **Alcipe** in *Les Fâcheux* introduces the gambling obsession that swept through France during Molière's time. The particular card game described in his tirades is *piquet*. It was an immensely popular but terribly complicated game, somewhat resembling whist, that was played between two players and involved a system of points for the types of hands and conditions under which they were taken. Card counting was essential for success in this game, but Alcipe has counted his hearts badly and winds up being narrowly beaten on the last hand by Saint–Bouvain with a six, when he has just sloughed the ace. No wonder he walks off muttering like a zombie, "A six of hearts! Two points!" In the inner play of *L'Impromptu de Versailles*, the two silly marquis played by **La Grange** and Molière set a wager on which one of them is the model for the figure in *La Critique de l'École des femmes*. Their bet reflects not only the mania for such wagering among the vapid **nobility**, but also their weak financial standing, for of the 1,000 *livres* at stake, they can only come up with 100 in cash. Among the ruses used by loose women to cover their infidelity that **Arnolphe** reels off in the first scene of *L'École des femmes* is the practice of saying that the **money** received from lovers was won at the gaming tables. *Monsieur de Pourceaugnac* alludes to a far more dishonest practice, for **Sbrigani** accuses **Nérine** of luring a young nobleman to her house and swindling him out of 12,000 *écus* (36,000 *livres)*. Not surprisingly, **Arnolphe's** favorite reading matter, the Maxims of Marriage, also forbids women to gamble, lest she "gamble with her honor." Other religious bigots, such as **Tartuffe** and **Orgon**, are equally opposed to gambling, and Orgon uses **Valère's** fondness of the practice as a pretext for breaking off his **engagement** to **Mariane**, in order to **marry** her off to his minion.

**Games and Pastimes.** The ballet interludes in *Les Fâcheux* show several popular games of the seventeenth century. The first–act ballet opens with a band of dancers involved in the *jeu de mail,* an ancestral form of croquet. The second–act ballet features an *entrée* of bowlers, whose game was probably closer to *bocci* or *pétanque* than to British or Dutch pin bowling. This group is chased off by a band of child dancers playing with their slingshots, who are in turn pursued by their parents, shoemakers and their wives, who constituted the lowest rung of the **bourgeoisie.** In *Le Mariage forcé,* **Dorimène** mentions among the favorite pastimes of the young upper classes **gambling**, visiting friends, parties, feasts, and **carriage** rides. The ancient sport of chariot racing makes its appearance in *La Princesse d'Élide,* where **Euryale** engages in a contest with his rivals for the hand of the **Princess.**

**Gascon.** The dialect of southwestern France is extensively parodied by **Scapin** in his famous bag scene (III, 2). He switches "b" and "v" and replaces mute "e" with a hard version of the vowel, adding a few patois terms like "cadédis" and "adusias." **Lucette** also gives extensive speeches in Gascon in *Monsieur de Pourceaugnac,* where she pretends to be a wife who has been seduced and abandoned by the alleged bigamist (II, 7). Her speech includes consistent use of Hispanic verb endings as well as the features noted above. The Gascons who sing in the crowd scenes of the **Ballet des Nations** use only the pronunciation variants that Scapin employs.

**Gassendi, Pierre** (1592–1655). Skeptical philosopher from Digne in southern France, often associated with the thought of Molière. By the time Molière was in the **Collège de Clermont,** Gassendi had already accrued a formidable reputation by attacking the neo–Aristotelian thought that dominated French academic circles in a series of *Exercitationes* written in rather turgid **Latin.** Indeed, his ideas were not readily available to most of the French public until **Bernier** published a compendium of his work in the vernacular. Later he strongly objected to the rationalism promulgated by Descartes. Gassendi's own line of thought descended from Epicurus through Sextus Empiricus. Though usually branded as completely negative Pyrrhonism, Gassendi's ideas in fact embraced a type of optimistic skepticism based on the concept of probability of doubt as a counterpoint to absolute truth. Besides Bernier, Molière's close friend **Chapelle** was linked with the philosopher and may well have taken classes with him. However, Gassendi did not arrive in the capital to join the Clermont faculty until after Molière finished his courses. The anecdote that he and Chapelle were personally tutored by Gassendi was propagated by **Grimarest** and most likely has little grounding in truth. It is not beyond possibility that Molière may have eavesdropped on some of his lectures, but by that time he was devoting most of his time to the adventure of the **Illustre Théâtre** and had enough practical worries to distract him from philosophy.

Gassendi was also closely linked to another intimate of Molière, **La Mothe Le Vayer**, who shared many of his inclinations in a more veiled and cautious way.

**Gaudon**. An otherwise unknown young actor, probably a hireling, who played the **Count** in *La Comtesse d'Escarbagnas*.

**Gauls**. In *Les Amants magnifiques*, the general **Sostrate** is given credit for defeating the 279 B.C. incursion into **Greece** under the leadership of **Brennus**. After early victories, the actual invasion was beaten back before Delphi in Phocia and shattered at Thermopylae in **Thessaly**.

**Gautier–Garguille**. One of the favorite farcical characters of the generation before Molière, Gautier–Garguille was easily recognized by his stylized **mask** and **costume**, depicted in the Verio painting of great seventeenth–century comic actors. He played at the **Hôtel de Bourgogne** and was famous for his "comeback" lines, or *rencontres*. The author of the *Observations sur le Festin de Pierre* reproaches Molière for lacking this talent.

**Gazette**. The earliest forerunner of the French newspaper was a semi–official summary of important weekly events at **court** and in **Paris**. Composed in octosyllabic verse, it was founded in 1631 by Théophraste Renaudot, who also introduced employment agencies and pawn shops into France. It was continued after Renaudot's death in 1653 by Loret, and then Robinet, both of whom regularly mention Molière's comedies. The periodical lasted well into the next century, and contains much important information and corroborative evidence on Molière. It was eventually joined by the *Mercure de France* and other news sources. Like **La Bruyère**, who had little respect for the *Mercure*, Molière's **Alceste** considers the "honor" of being cited in the *Gazette* to be minimal: "It's scarcely an honor to be praised these days, / One's loved and lauded to the point of regret, / And the man who cleans my socks is in the Gazette" (III, 5). Alternative views were provided by the **Gazette de Hollande**, an illegal but widely read publication that is mentioned in *La Comtesse d'Escarbagnas* as the favorite reading matter of a provincial busybody.

**Gentleman**. The terms *gentillesse* and *gentilhomme* were not just mild honorifics, like their English counterparts, gentility and gentleman, but very particular marks of noble standing. To qualify as a gentleman in France, a person had to be able to trace hereditary **nobility** back at least three generations on all sides of the family tree. Officially this was measured by heraldry experts in terms of so many "quarters of nobility," but the rule of thumb of three untainted generations seems to have been used frequently in society. Keep in mind that personal nobility also required three generations to transform into hereditary nobility, but did not require antecedents on all sides of the family tree, merely from father to son. Thus, a *noble de robe* could conceivably qualify as a gentleman, but only if his own line had held nobility for six generations and had intermarried with people of equal or higher noble standing along the way.

This rigid definition sheds some light on the absurdity of **Monsieur Jourdain's** pretensions, as well as those of **Monsieur de Pourceaugnac**, "gentleman lawyer," to the true status of gentleman and on **Cléonte's** admission that he is not entitled to call himself one.

**George Dandin** (*George Dandin*). What we know of Dandin's **costume**, both from Molière's death inventory and from the **Brissart** and **Sauvé** engraving, solidly establishes his social position.   He is quite richly, but very inappropriately clad, with fine materials, but bright, clashing colors that bespeak his usurpation of rank.   In fact, he is an enriched **peasant**, probably from the class of "laboureurs" who were actually rural entrepreneurs.  They rented their livestock and equipment to tenant farmers, sharecroppers, and even the gentry. In addition, they often sold seed and bought up crops, monopolizing farm production at both ends of the growing cycle.   Such people could amass considerable fortunes, when compared with the relative misery of much of the rural nobility, who were often heavily over–mortgaged and lacked the initiative and know–how to manage their own lands.  Their very status prevented them from taking up any other economic activity and doomed them to gradual decadence.   Such a family was the **Sotenvilles** with whom Dandin had allied himself, relying on their influence to establish a noble identity for himself.  This was a big mistake in **Louis XIV's** France, when the "recherches de noblesse" were busily removing many a Sotenville type from the tax–exempt rolls of the aristocracy and demoting them to commoners.   Dandin is therefore both a bumpkin and a usurper, for his claim to nobility seems to rest, at best, on fief ownership, which by itself was not grounds for noble status.

Dandin is onstage for almost the entire play, with the exception of a few short scenes of intimate discussion between **Angélique** and **Clitandre** and between **Lubin** and **Claudine**.  His presence is accentuated by monologues and by his spying on the lovers at times when they believe themselves to be alone. In this sense he is closer to **Arnolphe** than other protagonists in the canon.  Like Arnolphe, he is unable to control his servants, **Colin** and **Claudine**, with any degree of success.   The only person inferior in intelligence to him is the bumbling Lubin, and that advantage is gained only because Lubin is even quicker than Dandin to open his mouth at inopportune times.  Indeed, Dandin's logorrhea contrasts with the very measured speech of Angélique and Clitandre to show that the management of words is one of the themes of the play, as is so often true with Molière.   Inability to control speech is matched by inability to control action, especially one's own, as we see repeatedly in the plot and particularly in the denouement, where Dandin's momentary fears of actually killing his wife let her get the better of him.

There is an interesting progression in the three proofs by which he tries to establish his wife's infidelity.   In the first act, he presents an accusation based only on his own testimony and hearsay from an absent party (Lubin). This, of course, is easily denied by personal testimony from the parties implicated, and Dandin suffers a verbal chastening.  In the second act, he tries to present active, firsthand, visual evidence by having the Sotenvilles eavesdrop on their daughter's tryst. However, Angélique, warned of the trick, turns the scene into a staged rejection of Clitandre, thus garnering compliments for herself and a physical humiliation (blows from a brickbat) for her husband. In the third act, Dandin hopes to geographically prevent such distortion by locking his wife outside the house and showing her shame to her parents. By **feigning death**, she reverses the scheme and instead convinces the Sotenvilles that Dandin has been out on a drunken escapade and that she has locked him out. This results in humiliation that is both verbal and physical (he must kneel to her in submission).

*George Dandin, ou le Mari confondu (The Thwarted Husband).* A combination of **farce** and court ballet, *George Dandin* premiered in July 1668, the same year as *Amphitryon,* as part of the **Grand Divertissement Royal de Versailles.** The text of the three–act play, written in prose, was first published in 1669, in **Paris,** by **Jean Ribou.** The action centers on the woes of the eponymous character, a wealthy **peasant** who has entered into a misalliance by marrying **Angélique,** the daughter of a pair of caricatural provincial **nobles, Monsieur** and **Madame de Sotenville.** In spite of his three attempts to show his in–laws proof of the infidelities of their daughter, who carries on relations with the aristocrat **Clitandre** but always manages to foil her husband's plans to prove it, **George Dandin** must repeatedly endure the humiliation of recognizing the social superiority of the Sotenvilles and of apologizing to the wife who is cuckolding him all the while. George Dandin, the object of farcical ridicule, including a *bastonnade,* also takes the stage in a number of monologues with tragic undertones, including the final scene, in which he finds that the only solution to his failed **marriage** is suicide.

Angélique is also the name of the unfaithful wife in *La Jalousie du Barbouillé,* where this character uses a similar ruse to foil her husband's accusations, locking her husband out of their house and then calling to him from the window to accuse him of drunkenness. There are several possible sources for the farcical elements that Molière put to use. The twelfth–century *Disciplina clericalis* by Petrus Alfonsi includes a scene of a husband locking his wife out, telling her from window that he will prove her infidelity once and for all. The wife pretends to commit suicide by throwing a rock into a well, the husband goes out to look, and the wife slips inside and locks the door, thus turning the tables on him (in *George Dandin,* Angélique, mimicking the heroines of the *tragédies sanglantes* of preceding years, claims she will kill herself with a knife). The anonymous "De celui qui enferma sa femme en une tor," a thirteenth–century fabliau that was an adaptation of the *Disciplina clericalis,* was a widely read text in the Middle Ages and the Renaissance. The *Dolopathos sive de Rege et septem sapientibus* (ca. 1184–85) by Jehan de Haute–Seille includes a similar ruse. This text was translated ca. 1223 by Herbers as *Li Romans de Dolopathos. L'Ystoire des sept sages,* a French version of the fifteenth–century Latin work, appeared in 1577. In **Boccaccio's** *Decameron* (VII, 4), the hapless husband Tofano falls prey to the same tactic and ends up resigned to being humiliated in front of his in–laws and neighbors. Boccaccio's tale had been adapted for the German stage by Hans Achs in the mid–sixteenth century, entitled *Das Weib im Brunnen*. During the same time, another adaptation of Boccaccio, a comedy by Andrea Calmo entitled *La Rhodania*, included the same scene of trickery. The situation is a borrowing from the **Italian** farce tradition. The anonymous "Il villano geloso," a scenario of the *commedia dell'arte*, which may have been in circulation in Molière's time, also contains the principle elements of the anticlimactic scene of George Dandin's ultimate failure to gain the upper hand on his wife (III, 6).

The name *George Dandin* has a number of semantic and literary connotations. Furetière defines the term "dandin" as a "grand sot qui n'a point de contenance ferme." In Old French, the term "dandin" refers to a bell worn by sheep. In **Rabelais's** *Quart Livre*, Panurge buys a sheep from a merchant named Dindenault. A judge named Perrin Dendin and his son Tenot Dendin appear in the *Tiers Livre*. In **Racine's** *Les Plaideurs* (1668), the character of the judge is named Dandin.

The cuckolding tale of Molière's *George Dandin* was performed, during the play's premiere, as part of a pastoral ballet, for which the music was composed by **Jean–Baptiste Lully** (1632–1687). The **comédie–ballet** was part of the Grand Divertissement Royal de Versailles of July 1668, a fête that celebrated **Louis XIV's** conquest of the **Franche–Comté** and the signing of the Treaty of Aix–la–Chapelle earlier that year. According to the *Gazette*, 3,000 people were in attendance, including the king and queen, the nuncio of the Pope, the **cardinal de Retz**, and such literary figures as **Mlle. de Scudéry**, Mme. de Lafayette, and **Mme. de Sévigné**. Félibien gives July 18 as the date of the premiere of *George Dandin* at the fête, whereas Robinet, in the *Gazette en vers*, gives July 16, and the Paris *Gazette* July 19. The program of the performance was published by **Robert Ballard** in 1668. It is likely that Molière had a hand in authoring the parts of the program that introduced the libretto of Lully's portion of the **comédie–ballet**. Robinet attests that the verses sung during the pastoral portion of the comédie–ballet were by Molière. Lully would base the third act of his first opera, *les Fêtes de l'Amour et de Bacchus* (1672), on the final act of the pastoral he composed for *George Dandin*. The performance ended with over 100 singers, dancers, and instrumentalists on the stage, performing the work's final cadence.

Molière himself most likely played the role of George Dandin, with **Armande Béjart** in the role of Angélique. **La Grange** described the **costume** that portrayed the ambitions of the wealthy peasant: "Musk–colored breeches and mantel with similar collar; the whole outfit decorated with silver lace and buttons, with matching belt; tight jacket of crimson satin with a second jerkin worn over it and made of multi–colored brocade with silver lace; old–fashioned 'strawberry' collar and shoes."

Events of the fête were recorded by André Félibien (1619–1695), *Historiographe des bâtiments du Roi*, in the "Relation de la fête de **Versailles**." Félibien describes in detail the processions, entertainments, feasts, fountains, and fireworks that made up the Grand Divertissement. Another account was written by the poet and academician the abbé de Montigny, who provided a list of noteworthy ladies who attended the event.

According to **Grimarest**, the play was well received at the **court** in July and also during its first public performance in **Paris** — henceforth without the trappings of the comédie–ballet — on November 9 of the same year. During Molière's lifetime there were four performances of *George Dandin* at the court: the premiere at Versailles in July of 1668 and three performances at **Saint–Germain–en–Laye** in early November 1668; there were also thirty–nine performances of the play in Paris, at the Palais Royal Theater, starting on November 9, 1668 — according to La Grange, ten during the last two months of 1668, thirteen in 1669, ten in 1670, three in 1671, and three in 1672. From 1673 to August 25, 1680, the date of the founding of the **Comédie–Française**, thirty performances were given at the Hôtel Guénégaud. The play would be performed twenty–one times at court during the years 1682 to 1789. On February 17, 1681, *George Dandin* entered the repertoire of the Comédie–Française, where, as of 1999 (when the play was directed by Catherine Hiegel) the play has been performed 1,262 times — 135 times during the years 1680 to 1700, 519 during 1701 to 1800, 273 during 1801 to 1900, and 335 during 1901 to 1999.

*George Dandin*, with its cynical characters and repeated scenes of humiliation, has been considered by some to be one of Molière's darkest comedies, dramatizing the isolation and alienation resulting from social stratification. Other approaches center on comical and farcical elements in the actions of the main characters. The play's perceived crassness and bitterness aroused the critical indignation of **Bourdaloue**, Riccoboni, **Voltaire**, and **Rousseau**. Situated in the historical context of its premiere at Versailles and of its reception in the years following its premiere, the play has in more recent years aroused the interest of scholars, such as Chartier, who have provided sociohistorical readings of the play situated in the context of its premiere at Versailles.

Selected Bibliography: Ralph Albanèse, "Solipsisme et parole dans George Dandin," *Kentucky Romance Quarterly* 27 (1980), 421–434; Claude Bourqui, *Les Sources de Molière. Répertoire critique des sources littéraires et dramatiques* (Paris: SEDES, 1999); Roger Chartier, "George Dandin, ou le social en représentation," *Annales HSS* 49.2 (March–April 1994), 277–309; *Dandin*, dir. Roger Planchon, perf. Claude Brasseur, Zabou, Daniel Gélin, Nelly Bourgeaud, Jean–Claude Adelin, Evelyne Buyle (Alliance Vivafilm Video, 1990); James F. Gaines, "Dandin on the Big Screen of History," *PFSCL* 26.51 (1999), 309–317; Jean–Léonor le Gallois, sieur de Grimarest, *La Vie de Molière* (Paris: Michel Brient, 1955); Charles Varlet, sieur de La Grange, *Le Registre de La Grange (1659–1685)*, ed. Bert Edward Young and Grace Philputt Young, 2 vols. (Geneva: Droz, 1947); Charles Mazouer, "*George Dandin* dans le Grand Divertissement Royal de Versailles (1668)," in Frank Rutger Hausmann, Christoph Miething, and Margarete Zimmermann, eds., "*Diversité, c'est ma devise,*" *Festschrift für Jürgen Grimm*, (Tübingen: PFSCL, 1994), 315–329; Molière, *Œuvres complètes*, ed. Georges Couton, vol. 2 (Paris: Gallimard, 1971) and idem, *Œuvres de Molière*, ed. Eugène Despois and Paul Mesnard, vol. 6 (Paris: Hachette, 1881); Noel Peacock, "The Comic Ending of *George Dandin*," *French Studies* 36.2 (1982), 144–53.

*Roland Racevskis*

**Georgette** (*L'École des femmes*). This serving woman is specifically described in the list of characters as a **peasant** and her speech reflects her background. Like her male counterpart, **Alain**, she has been hired to watch over **Agnès** in **Arnolphe's** secret second house. Also like him, she is a stumblebum. In Act I, scene 2, one first hears her voice, as she and Alain argue about who should open the door for the master. When Arnolphe threatens to withhold four days rations from those who fail to obey, she and Alain collide with each other in their rush to admit him. This "beautiful ceremony," as Arnolphe calls it, has sometimes been staged as if the two **servants** were surprised *in flagrante delicto* rather than simply being lazy. The latter interpretation underlines all the more the fact that Arnolphe has recruited badly for positions of such importance, for the two are supposed to be guardians, rather than servants, of his ward. Stupid as she is, Georgette understands her master's vanity and verbal manipulation, for when he asks a second time with menacing mien if Agnès hasn't been sad since his departure, Georgette changes her tune to "yes, indeed" and explains, "Whenever a thing in the street would pass, / She took it for you, whether horse, mule, or ass." Of course, she mentions nothing about **Horace's** appearance. Later, in Act II, scene 2, when Arnolphe attempts to interrogate the two peasants, Georgette is so frightened that she screams, "Please, sir, I conjure you not to eat me!" She remarks to Alain that she has never seen a more hideous Christian in her life. It is Georgette's professed naivete about **jealousy** that provokes Alain's ridiculous description of woman as "man's stew."

In Act III, she promises to listen no longer to Horace's fine words. She appears to prove her words in the following act while rehearsing with her master, calling the "seducer" a clod and an impudent fool. However, when a bribe is offered, her hand is very ready and she forgets all the rules. She runs to warn Arnolphe in the final act that Agnès is desperate enough to throw herself from the window in order to escape, which justifies her mute witness to the denouement. Unless usually silent **Mademoiselle Hervé** was able to master peasant dialect, it is quite probable that the original part was played by the aging **Madeleine Béjart**, later passing to **Mlle. Beauval**.

**German.** Not one of Molière's languages, he uses it as an example of the most incomprehensible of tongues. In *Dépit amoureux*, old **Albert** explains that the only **Latin** he knows is his prayers and that despite fifty years of saying them, he understands them no better than "High German."

**German Renditions of Molière.** Molière seems to have been nearly as popular across the Rhine as he was in **Holland** and **England**. Not only were numerous pirated editions done in such cities as Cologne and **Berlin**, but **Nanteuil's** acting company imported his works into the interior of Hanover and Brunswick. A 1670 collection published in Frankfurt by J.–G. Schiele contains translations of

*L'Avare* (*Der Heissige*) and *George Dandin* (*Der verwirrete Ehemann*), along with versions of French plays by **Du Ryer** and others.

**Géronimo** (*Le Mariage forcé*).  Géronimo is a fellow merchant allied with **Sganarelle**.  They had met in **Rome** about thirty–two years ago.  Asked to give his advice about Sganarelle's idea to marry, Géronimo first asks to calculate his age and then strongly tries to dissuade his colleague from taking a wife at the age of fifty–two.  When he learns that Sganarelle has not only already been courting, but has also made a promise to wed **Dorimène**, he skeptically withdraws his advice and bids Sganarelle the best of luck.  He returns in scene 3 with a proposition about a wedding **ring** from a jeweler he knows, but leaves when his friend begins to describe his ominous **dream**, advising him to seek advice from the two **philosophers**, **Pancrace** and **Marphurius**.  One wonders if, unable to take advantage of Sganarelle's rashness by getting a commission on the ring, Géronimo is not making fun of him by sending him to two thinkers who are bound to disagree with each other, at best.  The role was played by **La Thorillière**.

**Géronte** (*Les Fourberies de Scapin*).  Father of **Léandre** and (unbeknownst to him) of **Hyacinte**, he pays dearly for wrongly telling his son that **Scapin** betrayed his trust.  Not only is he bilked out of 1,500 *livres* by the trickster's tale of the **Turkish galley**, but he is also the victim of the famous **beating** in the bag.  The role was most likely played by **Du Croisy** or **Hubert**.

**Géronte** (*Le Médecin malgré lui*).  **Lucinde's** aged father is a typical pantaloon, who serves mainly as a straight man for **Sganarelle's** ridiculous gags.  Before the appearance of the latter in Act II, Géronte explains that he has no faith in **Léandre's** promise of an inheritance: "Death doesn't always open his ears to the sighs and prayers of Milord the Heir.  One can grow long in the tooth waiting while one's fancies depend on the death of another."  He prefers the ready fortune of a young man named Horace, who never appears in the play, in order to marry off his daughter.  He is awestruck by Sganarelle 's seeming medical powers and cowed by his daughter's defiant stand against his **marriage** plans.  Ironically, he expresses his confidence in his precautions even as his daughter is eloping with her sweetheart, and turns angrily on Sganarelle , calling for the help of the **police**, when he learns she has belied him.  However, he is just as quick to forgive and forget when the couple returns to beg his forgiveness and receive his blessing.

**Ghosts**.  The spirit of dead **Pandolphe** seems to appear to **Anselme** in Act II of *L'Étourdi*, but it is really a very lively (and angry) old man returning from a useless trip to the country.  Anselme's attempts to send the spirit away are very amusing.  They belong to an old tradition of "walking dead" scenes that trace back to Renaissance plays, such as **Larivey's** *Les Esprits*, and ultimately back to Greco–Roman theater.  A similar affect is achieved in *Le Malade imaginaire*, where **Argan** "comes back from the dead" to frighten his evil wife **Béline**, having learned how to **feign death** from his little daughter. When **Sosie** tries to reconcile with his double **Mercury** in *Amphitryon* he asks if he might not become his own ghost or shadow, in order to follow the original through the world and take part in some simulacrum of life. To no avail he promises to be "such a well–behaved little shade that you will be proud of me." Even the ghost is an important element of the individual identity, which the usurping Mercury claims in its entirety. Not exactly a ghost, but more of a spooky monster, the *loup garou* had ceased to be a true werewolf for seventeenth–century Frenchmen. **Scapin** admits to pretending to be one in order to administer a prankish beating on his master **Léandre** (II, 3). Although he pretends to fear no ghosts or enemies, **Dom Juan** must deal with that of the **Commander**, which has apparently chosen to haunt his memorial statue, as well as with the ghostly apparition in the fifth act that announces his doom, before changing into a figure of Father Time with his scythe.

**Gifts**. Frequently a means of seduction or conspiracy, gifts appear often in Molière's works. In *Dépit amoureux*, **Éraste** gives **Marinette** a **ring** in exchange for her help in courting **Lucile**. On a more modest social level, she and **Gros–René** have exchanged **love** tokens: a box of cheap pins and scissors with a tin chain for her; a little knife, a lace hat decoration, and a piece of cheese for him. Éraste and Lucile have exchanged richer, more conventional gifts: a **portrait** locket, a bracelet of woven hair, a diamond, and a cameo locket. Two of these, apparently the bracelet and the cameo, have poetic inscriptions. Both **Harpagon** and **Monsieur Jourdain** give costly diamonds to the women of their dreams, but in each case the gift is problematic. Harpagon's ring is literally ripped off his hand by his son, who offers it to young **Mariane**, while **Dorante** takes all the credit for the gifts he offers **Dorimène**, leaving Jourdain to believe that he is considered the donor.

**Gilbert, Gabriel** (1610–1680). Mainly in hopes of finding a reliable source of tragic material, Molière's troupe tried out a series of authors before they found **Jean Racine**. However, most of them (Coqueteau, Magnon, Prade, and Boyer) contributed just a single play. Only Gilbert had three, beginning with *La Vraie et la Fausse Prétieuses* (May 1660). Premiering in August, *Huon de Bordeaux* at first fared badly (only three performances), but redeemed itself with a respectable showing in reprises. Though given a much more auspicious slot in the carnival season of 1661, *Le Tyran d'Égypte* achieved only mediocre results. Gilbert later turned to the **Hôtel de Bourgogne** to stage his five–act verse comedy, *Les Intrigues amoureuses*, perhaps as early as 1663. The play's scheming valet, Marot, has clearly gone to school with **Mascarille**. Molière's company also revived Gilbert's **machine play** *Endymion*, which had premiered at the Hôtel de Bourgogne. This play had been composed at **Rome** while Gilbert was in the service of Queen Christina of Sweden. Previously, he had served as secretary to the Duchess of Rohan.

**Giliberto.** Author of an **Italian** version of the **Dom Juan** drama, dated 1652, which Molière may have consulted while working on his comedy. Giliberto's text is now lost.

**Gillet de la Tessonnerie** (fl. 1640–1650). Author of several plays that influenced Molière's works. *Le Déniaisé*, Act I, Scene 4 may have given Molière the idea for the conclusion of **Albert's** conversation with **Métaphraste** in *Dépit amoureux*, where the old man chases away the bombastic tutor by ringing a bell in his ears. The same play contains a scene prefiguring the **philosophical** conversation of *Le Mariage forcé*, where **Jodelet** asks a windy pedant named Pancrace if he should marry. *Le Campagnard*, a comedy that lambastes bumpkins, was an element of the troupe's **Paris repertory**, though it had debuted at the **Hôtel de Bourgogne** in 1655. The play had some influence on such Molière bumpkins as **George Dandin**, **Monsieur de Pourceaugnac**, and the **Comtesse d'Escarbagnas**.

**Girard, Théodore.** Parisian printer involved in the publication of *L'Amour médecin*.

*Gloire du Val de Grâce, La.* Encomiastic poem to **Pierre Mignard**. The "gloire" in the title is most literally the interior dome painting of the Val de Grâce chapel, but also puns on the painter's artistic glory. About 1661, Pierre Mignard was commissioned to paint a fresco for the cupola of the magnificent Val de Grâce church. Constructed in **Paris** between 1645 and 1665, Val de Grâce fulfilled **Anne of Austria's** vow to honor the Virgin Mary for granting her a son, the future **Louis XIV**. Presented to the Queen Mother on August 11, 1663, the immense painting shows her surrounded in a radiance (or glory) by more than 200 figures of saints, as she offers the new church to God.

The fresco appears to have been controversial, though the extant evidence is scant and inconclusive: (1) an implicitly anti–Mignard tract, *La Peinture, poème* (1668), by Charles Perrault, future architect of the Louvre colonnade, **Jean–Baptiste Colbert's** deputy for buildings, and thus a partisan of Mignard's rival, Charles Lebrun, Colbert's hand–picked director of the Académie de peinture; and (2) Molière's *La Gloire du Val de Grâce* subtitled *Poème sur la peinture de Molière. Mignart* (1669), which not only defends Mignard and chides Lebrun, but may be read as a discreet attack on the authoritarianism that had invaded the intellectual world under Colbert.

The text of Molière's verse essay derives from and embroiders on a foundational work of French art criticism, *L'Art de peinture* (1668), Roger de Piles's French translation of, and commentary on, *De arte graphica liber* (also 1668) by Charles–Alfonse du Fresnoy, Mignard's collaborator on the Val de Grâce fresco. Among the many themes touched upon are: the consanguinity of poetry and painting; the triple exigency of unity, concision, and clarity; the importance of fidelity to the subject; and the compositional use of color.

The interpretation of Molière's poem began with his contemporary, **Boileau**, who assured its place for posterity. According to Boileau's table talk, the key to *La Gloire du Val de Grâce* is a distinction between oil and fresco painting, the former permitting leisurely elaboration and *retouches* or revisions, the latter requiring quick, even spontaneous, and absolutely sure brushwork. Reading *La Gloire du Val de Grâce* poem reflexively, Boileau asserted that it was the work of Molière the "oil painter," whereas his comedies were "frescos."

*La Gloire du Val de Grâce* appears to be the first attempt by a major French literary figure to write technical art criticism. Among those to follow the same line were **Diderot**, Baudelaire, Zola, and Malraux.

Selected Bibliography: Molière, *Oeuvres complètes*, ed. Georges Couton, Bibliothèque de la Pléiade, (Paris: Librairie Gallimard, 1971) II, 1186–1195 (text) 1524–1531 (notice and notes); also François Bluche, ed., *Dictionnaire du Grand Siècle* (Paris: Fayard, 1990), entries on Boileau, Colbert, Le Brun, Mignard, Perrault, Val de Grâce.

*David Lee Rubin*

**Gomberville, Marin Le Roy de** (1600–1674). Author of extremely lengthy novels such as *Polexandre*, Gomberville is associated with the movement of *préciosité* in *Les Précieuses ridicules*, by virtue of the fact that **Cathos** and **Magdelon** have named their little valet **Almanzor**, after one of the novelist's characters.

**Gorgibus, Cardin**. The actual name of a transport barge operator, skipper of the *Belle Image*, who moved the goods of Molière's troupe from Rouen to Paris in 1658. He seems to have exercised his trade on the quays of Paris from 1658 onward. There is no indication that he showed any resentment at Molière's use of his name for a series of crotchety old men in the plays.

**Gorgibus (*La Jalousie du Barbouillé*)**. An irascible father–in–law, Gorgibus and his friend **Villebrequin** seem most interested in reestablishing harmony in the household of his son–in–law **Le Barbouillé**, by preaching the virtues of domestic life at the beginning and end of the play.

**Gorgibus (*Le Médecin volant*)**. Father to **Lucile** and master to **Gros–René**, Gorgibus sees his **marriage** plans for his daughter thwarted by the other characters. He is distracted from family affairs by the "**doctor**" who is supposed to cure his daughter of her mysterious ailments. Trying to patch up the family quarrel between the physician and his "brother" **Sganarelle**, Gorgibus does not notice when **Valère** makes off with Lucile. However, he willingly pardons them when they return to beg his forgiveness in the final scenes.

**Gorgibus (*Les Précieuses ridicules*)**. This grouchy bourgeois patriarch, father to **Magdelon** and uncle to **Cathos**, is one of the most fully drawn of Molière's farcical pantaloons. Though critical of the girls' infatuation with affected literature that he does not pretend to understand, he is angrier at their excessive spending on cosmetics. He claims that their lipstick recipes have cost him, besides various arcane ingredients, the lard of a dozen pigs and so many legs of lamb that four **servants** could have lived all year on it, all this to allow the girls to "grease their snouts." He is even less pleased to learn of their high–falutin' refusal of the proper middle–class husbands he has found for them. He threatens to send them to a **convent** if they persist. His **language** is liberally laced with nearly profane insults such as "pendardes" (bodies fit for hanging, or jail–bait) or "coquines" (scoundrels). However, Gorgibus also complains that he is tired of supporting a couple of full–grown women in his household and that such dependents are too much for a man of his age. At the end of the play, he unleashes his fury on the embarrassed girls, the would–be **noblemen Mascarille** and **Jodelet**, and finally the poor violinists who simply ask for their wages. Admitting that the family will now be the laughing stock of the whole neighborhood, he ends the play by consigning all novels, poetry, songs, and "sonnets et sonnettes" to the devil. Originally this role was probably played by the aged **Lespy**.

**Gorgibus** (*Sganarelle*). Described in the dramatis personae as a "bourgeois de Paris," he is the old father of **Célie** and neighbor of **Sganarelle**. In this play, Gorgibus is a rank authoritarian who rants about obedience through most of his scenes onstage. He has arranged a **marriage** for Célie with **Valère**, the son of **Villebrequin**, and intends for her to follow through with his promises. To justify his choice, he notes that Valère has a fortune of 20,000 ducats, while **Lélie** is relatively poor. Confident of the appeal of **money**, he avers that **love** is often the fruit, rather than the cause, of marriage. He blasts his daughter for her worldliness, saying that she speaks much more often about *Clélie* than about God. According to him, such devotional reading as **Pibrac**, Matthieu, or Louis of Grenada would be more appropriate. In scene 18, when Célie seems to relent, he exclaims that the filial kiss she gives him makes him feel ten years younger. He is not amused when she backslides after reconciling with Lélie, but Villebrequin's news of Valère's secret marriage obviates the paterfamilias's plans, and he readily accepts Lélie as son–in–law under the circumstances. Typically irascible and materialistic, this Gorgibus offers little depth of character. In early productions, the role was taken by **Lespy**, one of the senior actors of the troupe.

**Gorgibus dans le sac.** A short play, presumably by Molière but never published, that served as the basis for part of *Les Fourberies de Scapin*, notably the famous scene of the **beating** in the sack. However, the character who is beaten in the latter is named **Géronte**, not Gorgibus.

**Graces**. The mythological trio of Aglae, Thalia, and Euphrosyne was thought to represent the ultimate in feminine beauty. **Vadius** refers to them in *Les Femmes savantes* and the daughters of **Du Croisy** and **La Thorillière** silently represent two of them in *Psyché*, though Molière alters the names to Aegiale and Phaène.

**Gracioso.** The **servant** character typical of the **Spanish** *comedia* of the *siglo de oro*, the *gracioso* was less devious and less physically active than his French and **Italian** counterparts. His place was to provide an ongoing ironic commentary on the more serious action pursued by the **nobles** in the main plot of the play. This sort of "comic relief" was not needed in Molière's works, where the humorous elements emerged from the plot itself. **Gros–René** occasionally approaches the character of the *gracioso*, as does **Sganarelle** in ***Dom Juan***, where he recalls the related persona of Sancho Panza. **Raymond Poisson's** Crispin character dressed and spoke much like the Spanish *gracioso* and preserved the tradition that was handed on to Marivaux in the 1700s.

**Gramont or Grammont, Antoine, Duke de** (1604–1678). Colorful and well respected **court** nobleman and dean of the **Marshals of France**, Gramont was a patron of Molière's theater. The indirect reference to him in *Le Misanthrope*, where he arbitrates the dispute between **Alceste** and **Oronte**, is a deft nod to a powerful figure. Gramont had by no means ceased his activities by that time, and took part in the military campaign in Flanders the following year.

***Grand Cyrus, Le.*** The better–known subtitle of **Mademoiselle de Scudéry's** multivolume adventure novel, *Artamène*. It purports to feature the **love** lives of eminent Frenchmen such as **Condé** under the guise of ancient Persians. It was one of the primary vehicles of ***préciosité*** and is mentioned prominently in ***Les Précieuses ridicules***. In that play, **Magdelon** answers her father's insistent calls for **marriage** by saying, "What a fine thing if Cyrus wedded Mandane right away, or if Aronce up and married **Clélie**!" Proclaiming her inability to adjust to the affected girls' stilted vocabulary, the maid **Marotte** complains, "Mother o' God, I don't understand **Latin**, and I didn't study philophy [*sic*] in *The Great Stud* (a pun on Cyrus/Cyre) as you did."

**Grand Divertissement Royal de Versailles, Le (The Great Royal Entertainment at Versailles).** This type of royal spectacle, which became the personal specialty of **Louis XIV**, was a baroque extravaganza designed to appeal to all the senses and overwhelm them with the King's magnificence. As such, it featured both vocal and instrumental **music, dances**, processions, banquets, and other activities. Both real and artificial architecture and greenery was used in an impressive display, and as always Louis insisted on a variety of waterworks, canals, and fountains to astound the imagination. Both courtiers and some of the general public were admitted to the events, with the latter serving as part of the entertainment for the former. The comedy of ***George Dandin*** fits particularly well in this context of social raillery. It was itself inserted in a "pastoral" suite of songs and dances that likewise filled the intervals between the acts. For the most part, the pastoral provided a sense of refined counterpoint to the play, just as the courtiers did to the commoners present. A sense of closure is provided at the end of the play, when the thwarted **Dandin** is led away to join in a Bacchic dance performed by inebriated **shepherds**. Held to celebrate the victories of the royal army under **Condé** in the

**Franche–Comté** and the acquisition of Flanders in the treaty of Aachen signed on May 2, the festival unfolded on July 15, 1668. Since the palace was still in the early phases of construction, it was an outdoor event, making use of the new gardens still being laid out by Le Nôtre. Molière wrote the poetic passages used in the event and reprinted in the guide booklet, while **Lully** was responsible for the music.

**Gravelines.** A town near the Belgian border that was the site of numerous early modern military confrontations between the French and the Spanish or Dutch. When **Mascarille** and **Jodelet** start to show the girls in *Les Précieuses ridicules* their supposed war wounds, Jodelet shows one that he claims to have received at the attack on Gravelines. A minor engagement that took place there in 1658 makes this claim slightly less unbelievable.

**Greece and Greeks.** Ancient Greece is the setting for *Mélicerte, La Princesse d'Élide, Pastorale comique,* and *Les Amants magnifiques.* **Isidore**, a female **slave** in *Le Sicilien*, is also supposed to be Greek. Numerous references are also made to ancient Greek warriors, **philosophers**, and **doctors**. Other than these literary references, knowledge of ancient or modern Greece in **Louis XIV's court** was very dim. Their **costumes**, for example, were extravagant mixtures of current seventeenth–century dress and bits of Roman **armor**. For Molière, Greece usually functioned as an idealized pastoral setting for **love**.

**Greek Language.** Frequently cited in macaronic fashion by the pedants, physicians, and other swelled head of Molière's comedies. **Métaphraste** blurts out a few syllables in *Dépit amoureux*. In *Le Médecin malgré lui*, Sganarelle tells his clients that "nasmus" is Greek for the brain. In *Les Fâcheux*, the character **Caritidès**, a sort of would–be professional etymologist, explains that he has added the Greek ending "des" to his name because he considers the **Latin** ending "us," used by many intellectuals in Holland and Germany, to be too pompous. In Act II, scene 5 of *L'Amour médecin*, **Doctor Macroton** mentions the Greek word "atmos" as a synonym for "vapor" in his pompous explanation that Sganarelle's daughter is, in his opinion, constipated. A different kind of pedant, **Monsieur Lysidas** in *La Critique de l'École des femmes*, tries to impress his salon audience by using the **Aristotelian** terms "protasis," "epitasis," and "peripeteia." However, **Dorante** urges him to "humanize his speech" by using the more common equivalents: exposition, plot, and denouement. In *L'École des femmes*, **Arnolphe** cites one of **Plutarch's** apothegms saying that it is best to calm oneself by saying the alphabet when one is enraged. **Chrysale** finds that most respected biographer useful for pressing his collars between the pages of his monumental tome. **Argan** and **Béralde** maintain that Greek is as desirable as Latin for doctors, so that they can name all the maladies in a foreign tongue. The glory that was Greek stumbles into **Philaminte's** salon in the form of **Vadius**, modeled on the writer **Gilles Ménage**, who was one of the few people in France, along with the adepts of Port–Royal, who were really proficient in the language. Though he pronounces only the words "ithos" and "pathos" to describe Philaminte's circle, the ladies swarm over him to kiss him for the sake of his ancient learning, except for **Henriette**, who excuses herself by remarking, "Sorry, sir, I don't know Greek." Vadius claims Greek authority for refusing to read his verses aloud, but that does not prevent him from circulating copies to all interested parties. **Martine** later deforms the word "Greek" when discussing Henriette's **marriage**: "She needs a husband, not a schoolmaster, / And since she don't need Grease nor Latin, / She won't be wanting Mister Trissotin" (V, 3).

**Grenoble.** Capital of the province of Dauphiné. **Dufresne's** itinerant players were present in this alpine city for a christening in August 1652 and probably performed there before returning to **Lyon**. **La Grange** and **Vivot** imply in their 1682 biography of Molière that he stopped there immediately before going to **Rouen** on his return to **Paris**, but this remains unsubstantiated.

**Grimaces and Facial Expression.** Mentioned as early as *Dépit amoureux*, Molière's grimaces were legendary. He is often said to have learned the art of facial expression from **Scaramouche**, and it is true that the playwright's "parenthesis moustaches" and other similarities date from the period of their contact. It is clear that Molière is the first major French comic actor to rely entirely on a "natural" face rather than a **mask**. Facial contortion certainly lent a great deal to the portrayal of characters like **Arnolphe** and **Sganarelle**, who are often filled with inchoate anger and frustration, and **Alceste**, who is always scowling at his fellow man. Gradually, in the evolution of Molière's career, the notion of the grimace comes to have a more symbolic meaning associated with the ever–present possibility of human deception in a society so conscious of appearances.

The turning point in this process comes in *Le Misanthrope*, which is full of references to grimaces as means of dissimulation. When Alceste talks about his low–born and unscrupulous opponent in a lawsuit, he says, on the one hand, that "one can see the traitor right through his mask," but, on the other hand, that "his grimaces seem welcome everywhere." Later in the play, in the "**portrait** scene" (II, 4), **Célimène** criticizes a neighbor named Timante, who uses grimaces and "wild looks" to gain attention, conveying in a whisper mysterious secrets that turn out to be nothing. She applies this same quality of deception, with more ulterior motives, to her prudish visitor **Arsinoé**. Speaking with **Acaste**, she dismisses Arsinoé's zeal as pure simulacrum, "franche grimace," used to hide the worldliness of her soul. Alceste usually associates the baseness of deception with his legal opponent, however, and he returns to the theme in the final act when he acknowledges that the man has managed to outmaneuver him in court, "The power of his grimaces, masterpieces of falsehood, overcome my legal rights and turn justice upside down" (V, 1).

It is the deceptive, malevolent side of grimaces that prevails in later plays. **Toinette** cautions **Angélique** against "the grimaces of **love**" in *Le Malade imaginaire* (I, 4). When **Thomas Diafoirus** cites the authority of the ancient **Greeks** to maintain the necessity of compulsion in marriage, supposedly to preserve feminine honor, **Angélique** counters, "The ancients, sir, were ancient, and we are the people of today. Grimaces are no longer needed in our century, and when a **marriage** pleases us, we are quite capable of rushing into it without being dragged" (II, 6). **Dom Juan**, on the other hand, upholds the efficiency of deceptive behavior: "By the power of the grimace, one can forge unbreakable links to all the members of the [Devout] party. Anybody who rubs one of them the wrong way soon finds that all the others descend on him; and even those who are known to act in true faith and to be truly inspired by Heaven all inevitably become dupes of the hypocrites. They walk right into the web of the grimace masters and unwittingly support those who ape their devotions" (V, 2). Using the benevolent grimace of comic acting to alert his audience against those who put grimaces to more wicked purposes, Molière walks a thin line on the edge of satire.

**Grimarest, Jean–Léonor Le Gallois, sieur de** (1659–1713 ). Minor Parisian man of letters and author of the *Vie de Monsieur de Molière*, the first book–length biography of Molière. Grimarest draws heavily on the biography that appeared with the 1682 collected works of Molière, presumably the work of **La Grange** and **Vivot**, though mysteriously attributed by some eighteenth–century sources to an otherwise unknown actor named Marcel. He lards his text with innumerable anecdotes, many of which are credited to the actor **Baron**. Yet Baron was only a child when he worked with Molière on a couple of plays and his stories usually seem to be little more than self–promoting name–dropping. Numerous factual errors appear throughout the text of this biography. The date of Grimarest's book, 1705, more or less precludes any firsthand evidence by people who actually knew the author, but this did not prevent it from being translated into **Dutch** and **German**. Attached to the duc de Noailles, Grimarest was also known as a teacher and translator. He also penned a history of Charles XII of Sweden, as well as treatises on **language**, eloquence, and military science. His life of Molière has been well edited by Georges Mongrédien.

**Gros–René (acting name of Guillaume Du Parc)**. Usually a slow–witted valet used as a foil to Molière's sharp–witted **servants, Mascarille** and **Sganarelle**. As depicted in the painting by Verio, Gros–René is clad in a baggy outfit with a tiny hat and his face is painted with a white makeup, perhaps flour or powder. The stock character was undoubtedly based on Gros–Guillaume, a farce actor of the previous generation who had enjoyed great popularity

**Gros–René (*Dépit amoureux*)**. The role given to **Du Parc** in this play is far more nuanced and developed than he was used to in farcical situations. True, Gros–René is once again cast in the role of the slower–witted **servant** and a foil to Molière's ingenious trickster. However, Gros–René is aware of this polarity and even makes fun of it in the first act, when he says to his master **Éraste** that people of his build are generally honest, more likely to be the dupe than the duper. Composing a pun on the term "round," which in French can figuratively mean frank and reliable, he says he is "a very round fellow in all the senses of the word." Furthermore, he is endowed with a very interesting arsenal of linguistic traits that include all sorts of literary pretentions, as when he poetically calls **Marinette** "the rainbow of my soul," but later, when he thinks she has deceived him, accuses her of "being worse than a satrap or even a Lestrygonian." His function in this play is to act in concord with Éraste, as a sort of mirror–image in the master–servant relationship, as well as in opposition to **Mascarille**. His courting of Marinette is a double of his master's pursuit of **Lucile**, minus the element of suspicious **jealousy** that is unsuited to his nature. Thus, in reflection of the famous "**lovers' spite**" scene between Éraste and Lucile, Gros–René and Marinette also have to quarrel in Act IV, scene 4. Their spat is a *reductio in absurdum* of the other conversation, complete with the giving back of **gifts**: a box of Paris pins and a cheap pair of scissors that Marinette has received, and a "noble blade" or jackknife, a lace hat decoration, and a hunk of cheese that she has given him. Without the elaborate psychological steps that the master and mistress require in their rapprochement, only a few syllables and a handful of giggles are enough to reconcile the servants. Gros–René gets the better of Mascarille twice in the final acts of the play, once by keeping him waiting at the door with a bit of clever repartee and then by enforcing his husband's privileges against marauders who would flirt with Marinette. In vain, Mascarille fires a parting shot at this picture of a "husband–confidant." Prior to the lovers' quarrel, Gros–René has a most interesting speech (IV, 3), a wandering diatribe against "that flighty sex" that refers to **Aristotle**, **Erasmus**, and **Pichou** and tries to develop metaphors of women as waves, winds, and shifting dunes before they become completely unraveled. It is a perfect example of the kind of false reasoning that **Sganarelle** will use in *Dom Juan*.

**Gros–René** (*Le Médecin volant*). This **servant** happens to see **Sganarelle's** trick of changing identity by jumping out the window and putting on different **clothes**, but when he tries to reveal the deception to **Gorgibus**, he is outdone by his fellow valet, who appears to be two people at once by embracing his own hat and collar, propped on his elbow.

**Gros–René** (*Sganarelle*). Valet to Lélie. Limited to a single scene, this very slight role restricts Gros–René to complaints about the hard riding he and Lélie have done to respond to **Célie's** plea for help and to conventional professions of gluttony.

**Groundlings**. As in Shakespeare's theater, the biggest part of most seventeenth–century French audiences stood on the ground, before and below the stage in buildings that were usually converted tennis courts. These were the cheapest places, at least half as expensive as the bleacher–like seats in the "amphitheater" that extended along the walls. There is sometimes a tendency to assume that this *parterre* was filled with the lowest elements of Parisian society, but research has shown that to be false, since even these places were too pricey for many commoners. Also, few genuinely poor people had the leisure to spend four or five hours of the afternoon dallying with the players. The average groundlings were prosperous tradespeople and merchants who could afford to leave their shops in the hands of their workers and take the evening off for some culture and recreation. Some valets were probably brought in by noble masters, who naturally sat in the more expensive loges or on the stage itself. The most troublesome members of the *parterre* were troops such as musketeers, who often barged in drunk and claimed that, as members of the royal household, they were entitled to free admission. There are several records of Molière taking legal action against these intrusions, which sometimes led to scuffles and even injuries. But Molière was no enemy of the *parterre*. As the official announcer for his wandering provincial troupe in the pre–Parisian years, he had developed techniques like those of today's stand–up comics to catch the crowd's attention, gain its sympathy, and placate any troublemakers. Many of his techniques play directly to the audience in this way, including **Arnolphe's** many soliloquies, **George Dandin's** moments of reflection, and **Harpagon's** enraged search for his stolen gold. One of the most persistent, if unverifiable, anecdotes in **Grimarest's** biography says that Molière always read his scenes to his charwoman to test them out. Whenever Molière writes about the audience, he constantly reaffirms the importance of the groundlings as judges of good taste and success. Characters such as **Mascarille** in *Les Précieuses ridicules*, who considers his fellow commoners to be "brutes" and opposes the opinion of the groundlings, are always shown in a negative light. In *La Critique de l'École des femmes*, the repulsive **Marquis** cites the applause of the groundlings to show Molière's play was bad, but **Dorante** delivers a stern rejoinder defending their common sense and good taste in humorous matters. No doubt Molière's rivals must have been **jealous** of his magnetic appeal to the **bourgeois** who crowded at the edge of the stage.

**Guard** (*Le Misanthrope*). *See* **Marshals' Guard**.

**Guérin, Eustache–François, sieur d'Estriché** (1636–1728). Second husband of **Armande Béjart**, who became his colleague when the **Marais** company was merged with the Palais Royal Theater in 1673 to form the Hôtel Guénégaud troupe. Reputed to have better conduct than his wife, Guérin went on to become a founding member of the **Comédie–Française**.

**Guez de Balzac, Jean–Louis** (1594–1654). This retired statesman became one of the great models of epistolary style in French literature. From his country estate near Angoulême, he wrote letters to his Parisian friends that were praised as paragons of proper grammar, orderly composition, and clear, precise wording. Along with **Malherbe**, he is considered one of the great "regularizers" of the language, and the two are cited together in *Les Femmes savantes* by the ranting **Chrysale**, who bellows, "Balzac and Malherbe give us fine words, no doubt, / But here in my kitchen, they'd be nothing but louts" (II, 7). Balzac's elegant but sometimes wordy and formal style was replaced eventually by the more sprightly and more emotional epistolary manner of **Madame de Sévigné**.

*Guide des Pécheurs, Le* (*Guide for Sinners*).  A devotional book by Brother Louis of Grenada that **Gorgibus** recommends to his daughter in *Sganarelle*.

**Guignard, Jacques.**  One of the Parisian printers who collaborated in publishing such works of Molière as *L'École des maris* and *Les Fâcheux*.  He was part of the eight–printer coalition that published *L'École des femmes* and *La Critique de l'École des femmes*.

**Guillaume, Monsieur** (*L'Amour médecin*).  Guillaume is, like Molière's own father, an upholsterer or furniture merchant.  Appearing only in the first scene of the play, he advises **Sganarelle** to cure **Lucinde's** mysterious illness by buying her a fine tapestry, either a landscape or one with human figures, to brighten up her room.  Sganarelle dismisses this mercenary suggestion.

**Guillot–Gorju.**  One of the team of farcical comedians at the **Hôtel de Bourgogne** who were popular in the 1630s.  He was a **masked** actor with a stylized **costume**, which one can see in the Verio painting of great French comedians of the seventeenth century.  According to a disparaging rumor, Molière bought Guillot–Gorju's memoirs from his widow and pillaged them in order to write his plays.  Judging from the nature of the comic works of **Tabarin**, another of the early **farce** actors, such material would be far too thin and repetitious to generate the kind of comedy developed by Molière.

**Gusman** (*Dom Juan*).  **Elvire's** coachman chats with **Sganarelle** at the beginning of the play.  He seems little interested in Sganarelle's thoughts about **tobacco**, but is appalled by the valet's revelations about his master's character, which he passes on to his mistress.

**Gypsies.**  This ethnic group functions in an entirely conventional way in the seventeenth–century French theater.  Molière uses them principally in two ways: as dancing characters to introduce or expand exotic elements, and as vehicles for hidden identity.  In *L'Étourdi*, Andrès is thought to be a Gypsy until he learns that he is related to **Trudaldin** and **Célie**, who are of **Italian** origin.

In *Le Mariage forcé*, Gypsies are described both by the usual term "Egyptians" and by the less common name of "Bohemians."  The ballet edition explains that after Act II, scene 3 (scene 5 of the later version of the play), **Sganarelle** encounters six "Egyptians," two male (played by the King and the Marquis of Villeroy) and four female (played by the Marquis of Rassan and the professional dancers Raynal, Noblet, and La Pierre).  Following this third of the ballet entry numbers, he meets two "Bohemians," whom he asks to tell his fortune.  These women, played by **Madeleine Béjart** and **Mlle. de Brie**, mock him and send him on his way.  In the printed version of the play, which was based on the text adapted to Parisian staging, the six initial dancers never appear and the two women, who are called "Egyptians," offer to tell his fortune if he will cross their palms with silver.  They forestall his questions about cuckoldry and tease him by predicting that his wife will be "gentle ... cherished ... loved by everyone." They add that she will "bring [him] lots of new friends ... fill the house with abundance ... give [him] a great reputation." When he asks them point–blank if he will be a cuckold they merely sing and dance.

Gypsies "dressed as Moors" are featured in the **comedy–ballet** interval between the second and third acts of *Le Malade imaginaire*. A mixed company of dancers performs several types of steps, while a quartet of female vocalists sings very un–Gypsy–like airs of **love**. In the exotic **Italian** setting of *Les Fourberies de Scapin*, Gypsies seem to abound. They have brought their slave **Zerbinette** to town with the intention of selling her, and with **Scapin's** help **Léandre** manages to buy her with his father's own **money**. A bracelet reveals that she is **Argante's** long–lost daughter. Like the pirates in **Greek** romances, Gypsies fulfill the dramaturgically useful task of carrying off **children** who will later be reunited with their parents in recognition scenes.

# H

**Hali** (*Le Sicilien*). A most unusual role, in that it was one of the few clever **servants** not played by Molière himself, who takes **Dom Pèdre** in this play. Instead, it was **La Thorillière** who played this **Turkish slave**, proud of his trickery and masterful at costume changes. In the first two scenes, he displays a certain verbal virtuosity, reminiscent of **Mascarille**, with witty comparison of the black night to the **costume** of **Scaramouche** and elaborate wordplay on musical terms such as B–sharp and B–flat in the serenade to be presented. After the number, he shows some signs of traditional poltroonery, first ranting about how Dom Pèdre deserves to be thrashed and then hiding when the Sicilian calls out his household guards. Once they are safely out of sight, he threatens to **beat** them if they should return. He refers to the challenge of tricking Dom Pèdre as an affair of honor for him. Approaching the old man with exaggerated bowing, he tries to introduce himself into the household as a **musician** and forms a band with four other slaves to sing the melody, "Chiribirida ouch alla!" The music does not please Dom Pèdre, who chases the group away in their own **Sabir** tongue. Hali had apparently donned some sort of **disguise** for this scene, since Dom Pèdre exclaims at the end when he recognizes him, and Hali admits to his ruse, promising that they will have the girl in the end. Instructed in **Adraste's** painterly plot, Hali runs off to arrange another **disguise**, for when he reappears it will be in **Spanish** garb under the name **Dom Gilles d'Avalos**. This "Spaniard" pretends to consult with Dom Pèdre about the details of a challenge, thus distracting him while Adraste and his model discuss their plans for the future. When he leaves the stage at the end of this discussion, he does not reappear.

**Halles, Les.** The market neighborhood where Molière was born and raised. The **Poquelin** family's second house was located under the pillars of one corner. It was considered as filthy by the upper classes of their day as it was in the nineteenth century, when Zola dubbed it "the Guts of Paris." In *Les Femmes savantes*, **Philaminte** justifies her dismissal of **Martine** on the basis of the crudeness of her **language**, including "**proverbs** dredged up from the gutters of Les Halles."

**Harlay de Champvallon, François de** (1625–1695). Successor to **Hardouin de Péréfixe** as archbishop of **Paris**, Harlay was very harsh to **Armande Béjart** when she requested a church funeral and Christian burial for Molière. Under intense royal pressure, he relented only so far as to permit a limited night time funeral, without Mass. He was hardly a model of piety himself, figuring in some of the more scabrous entries of Tallemant's *Historiettes*.

**Harpagon** (*L'Avare*). Molière's miser occupies the same archetypal niche in French culture as Dickens's Scrooge in ours, but he is just as often misinterpreted or misestimated. Like **Argan**, Harpagon is an ultimate form of the pantaloon of **farce**, but both are much more socially engaged than their comic ancestors. The miser is actively wooing a young lady, albeit for economically perverse reasons. He is just as energetically transacting business with everything he gets his hands on, including his own **children**. Like Scrooge, who begrudges each chunk of coal his clerk puts on the fire, Harpagon is a classic withholder, refusing to buy new clothes for his **servants** or even oats for his horse. But he continues to squeeze each penny out of everything in his power. He is an active capitalist who literally capitalizes each thing, living or inanimate, that falls within his reach. If he has his way, he will rid himself of human contingencies, exchanging each human relationship for its capital value. Then he will undoubtedly sell off the leftover objects at many times their value, as he proposes to do in the loan he unwittingly arranges for his son. This loan, which he tries to disguise under legitimate financial procedures, actually involves usurious hidden interests rates and a bill of goods inflated to many times its imaginable worth. The former he ascribes to the necessity of negotiating secondary loans that are mere shams; the latter was an old financial trick denounced by **Pascal** in the *Lettres provinciales* under the name of the Mohatra Contract. Harpagon is on the cutting edge of fraud and his victims are the most vulnerable in **bourgeois** society — the heirs who stand to inherit family fortunes that will disappear before their eyes as the bills roll in. Thus, Molière's miser is no social militant using his acumen to undermine the feudal powers of times past, but a dangerous parasite preying on his own class. It is essential to understand him as a great danger to, and not a representative of, the French bourgeoisie.

On the psychological level, Harpagon's quasi–sexual relationship with his strongbox full of gold is most intriguing, approaching that of Old Grandet in Balzac's famous novel. He does not like to keep his **money** immobilized, but prefers to have it safely invested and under contract, so the presence of the strongbox in his household is unusual and problematical. But he is just as **jealous** over it as a superannuated lover over his sweetheart: he is constantly slinking off to make sure no one is ogling or fondling it. He calls it "dear" and goes into a panic when it disappears, just like the pantaloons in earlier Molière plays when their fiancées elope with young chevaliers. Clearly, Harpagon fears the status of becoming a "financial cuckold." But he is far more effective than **Dom Pèdre** in *Le Sicilien* when it comes to mobilizing the institutional forces of law and order on his side. His **policemen** first interrogate **Maître Jacques** and are all ready to arrest **Valère** for the robbery. Valère's bizarre misunderstanding, which conflates the strongbox with **Élise's** virtue, completes the comic equation of money with sexuality in such a way that Harpagon ironically questions the values he himself stands for. It is he, and not young Valère, who yearned for money and wanted to revel in its physical caress.

Molière created this part for himself very deliberately, and it would be a great mistake to dismiss Harpagon as a kind of mental incompetent, as some actors and critics have also done with **Monsieur Jourdain**. Like Jourdain, Harpagon has his own implacable logic, though it seems ludicrous to others; his own sharp senses, though they do not delight in the sensations most find pleasant; his own vulnerability, though others question his sensitivity. Above all, he constitutes his own threat to civilization, which threatens the stability of his own family and all others, gnawing individualistically at the foundations of society and business in a land where everything was interdependent and mutually obligated. As precocious as Harpagon's *laissez faire* attitude seems in retrospect, it was too strong a drug for the early modern economy of Molière's time. In the name of **nature** and pleasure, Molière seeks to defend that social fabric against the self–justifying predator and the intrinsic imperatives of capitalism. With its notion of a social plan for business, France still does the same today.

**Harpin** (*La Comtesse d'Escarbagnas*). This tax official, played by **Du Croisy**, makes a pun on his own function ("receiver of taxes") when he says that he has presented so many **gifts** to the **Countess** that he should be called "Mister Giver" instead of "Mister Receiver." Recalling **Alceste** in a lower and more ludicrous mode, he irately demands that the Countess cease her policy of encouraging any suitor who can contribute to her financial well–being.

**Hauteroche** (**stage name of Noël Breton**, 1617–1707). Associated with the **Marais** troupe as early as 1655, Hauteroche moved to the **Hôtel de Bourgogne** in 1659 at about the same time that Floridor recruited **Raymond Poisson**. Both actors were intended to shore up the troupe against the competition of Molière. He is one of the targets of Molière's clever parody of tragic styles in *L'Impromptu de Versailles*, where his role as Pompey in **Corneille's** *Sertorius* is lampooned. When Floridor died in 1671, Hauteroche succeeded to the leadership of the Grands Comédiens. As an author, Hauteroche emulated Molière's comedy in such plays as *L'Amant qui ne flatte point* (1668), *Le Souper mal apprête* (1669), *Crispin médecin* (1670), *Le Deuil* (1671), and *Les Apparences trompeuses* (1673).

**Heavens.** As part of the **proprieties** of seventeenth–century **theater**, nothing sacred was supposed to be shown on stage. This ranged from God himself, through representatives such as priests, to sacramental ceremonies, such as **marriage.** Earlier in the century, exceptions had been made for biblical stories and plays based on saints and martyrs, but these were becoming less conventional and less common by 1650. Pagan divinities, of course, were an exception, since they were deemed imaginary. In order to represent the powers of **fate,** the supernatural, or even the notion of a Judeo–Christian God, playwrights sometimes had recourse to the term, "the heavens," as a neutral indicator. Molière often used this device when discussing anything touching on God or his powers, as throughout *Dom Juan* and in **philosophical** passages of such plays as *Les Amants magnifiques.* But even there, it was dangerous to try to represent such things and one's attitude to them on stage. A self–labeled blasphemer like **Dom Juan** may barely get away with it, but for most other characters it was safer to maintain an attitude of awe and mystery toward heavenly powers. In general, Molière tried to explicitly associate charlatans such as **Tartuffe** with earthly appetites and deceptions. Yet the problem becomes more complex with a character such as **Orgon,** who sincerely believes that Tartuffe's pretenses are really connected to God. If this level of imitation is successful, that is, if a man can successfully imitate God, how can any belief defend itself against abuse? Molière's implicit answer, that one must adopt a skeptical stance in all matters of faith that intersect with the real world, would not have satisfied the majority of churchmen in his day, nor perhaps in ours. Incredulity is a hard thing to measure.

**Henrietta of England, (known at court as Madame,** 1644–1670). Daughter of Charles I of England and Princess Henrietta of France. She was married to **Monsieur,** that is, Philippe d'Orléans, younger brother of **Louis XIV,** and lived with him at the French court, where she was considered one of the most brilliant ladies, as well as a most astute **patron** of the arts. Molière dedicated his *L'École des femmes* to her. Two years later, in February 1664, she served as godmother for Molière's first son, **Louis,** through the proxy of her first chambermaid. She is remembered in one of **Bossuet's** most famous *Oraisons funèbres* and in a biography by Madame de Lafayette.

**Henriette (*Les Femmes savantes*).** The younger daughter of **Chrysale** and **Philaminte** is completely different from both her parents and much more similar to her fiancé **Clitandre** in her frank, down–to–earth approach to life. In her opening dialogue with her sister **Armande,** she represents one vast part of womanhood, rooted in the pleasures of the physical world, partnership, and motherhood, while her sister soars in the giddy heights of intellectual abstraction. The pair represents a very original variation by Molière on the old medieval division of women into saints or whores: his modern dichotomy is the family woman and the bluestocking. Henriette defends her **love** with Clitandre on the grounds that she simply offered kindness to someone that her sister had thrown away. She does not understand Armande's desire to surround herself with male zombies whom she will forever hold in thralldom with her charm, while refusing them any reciprocal favors or devotion. Henriette avoids arguing openly with her mother, perhaps because she realizes it does little good. Yet she mirrors Clitandre's first–act **avowal** to her by candidly explaining to **Trissotin** why she does not love him, and even goes so far as to threaten him with the punishment of cuckoldry if he should persist in his plans. She tells Clitandre that she would rather take refuge in a nunnery than submit to her mother's **marriage** scheme. Though she and Clitandre exchange promises in front of witnesses, this act of **engagement** could be superceded by a marriage contract of the kind **Philaminte** wishes drawn up. We never see exactly how far she would go in opposing Philaminte (she could have simply refused to sign the contract) because **Ariste's** ruse of the forged **letters** stops the process before they arrive at that point. The letters announcing the family's financial ruin allow Clitandre to ingratiate himself to Philaminte and gain her approval, but they have an unexpected effect on Henriette. Showing her sensible side, she is unwilling to accept a marriage that would entail misery for her husband and uses her bankruptcy as an excuse to refuse him. This sort of test in the extreme will also be put to **Angélique**, under very different circumstances, in *Le Malade imaginaire*. Clearly the dramatist wished to rise above the idea of the female lead as a lovestruck maiden with heaving breasts and little brain. He wanted her to be a fully dimensional moral person, capable of facing and evaluating challenges and, if necessary, of demonstrating the same sacrificial courage that men displayed in the **Cornelian** theater of heroism. Those who would rush to condemn Molière for antifeminism because of the caricatures of the *salonnières* would do well to consider first this portrait of Henriette in the denouement.

**Hercules.** The birth of this demi–god is foretold in the final scene of *Amphitryon*, which concerns the events immediately following his conception.

**Heresy.** Molière's enemies did not stop short of accusing him of heresy, a capital crime (and more importantly, a canon one, outside the authority of secular courts) in early modern France. Molière self–consciously includes the epithet *Hérétique* along with those of "Devil," "**Turk**," "Epicurean pig," and "Sardanapalus," all leveled by **Sganarelle** at his master **Dom Juan**. While Molière had already been called a devil during the **Quarrel of the School for Wives**, he had not yet played any Turks, nor does the equivalence with Sardanapalus seem justified. Molière indirectly uses the character of Sganarelle (portrayed, of course, by himself) to contaminate the real charges against him with overblown, patently ridiculous accusations.

**Hervé, Mlle.** (*L'Impromptu de Versailles*). In one of her very rare opportunities to emerge from the shadows of the theater, Geneviève **Béjart** notes that she has very few lines. Indeed, her part in the frame play is minimal compared to the other women in the troupe. Though Molière assigns her the role of a *soubrette* or maid in the play–within–the–play, her tiny part merely echoes the others.

**Hippocrates**. Great medical authority of ancient **Greece** and developer of the Hippocratic oath. He is mentioned along with **Galen** by **Sganarelle** in *Le Médecin volant*. Naturally, he is frequently quoted by the group of **doctors** in *L'Amour médecin*. **Tomès** cites him as authority for the fact that the coachman mentioned by **Lisette** cannot have died, since Hippocrates said that such a disease could not produce death in a mere six days. To this the maid wittily responds that Hippocrates could say whatever he wants, but the man is dead. **Doctor Macroton** later mentions Hippocrates as justification for his failure to act in a given case, since consequences may be very dangerous. The Doctors in *Monsieur de Pourceaugnac* invoke his name to give authority to their ridiculous diagnoses (I, 8). Even Sganarelle, the false doctor in *Le Médecin malgré lui*, invokes Hippocrates (in his chapter on "hats") to order that the men should always keep their hats on.

**Hippolyte (*L'Étourdi*)**. Daughter to **Anselme** and engaged to **Léandre**, who is about to abandon her for **Célie**. Hippolyte uses some of her father's considerable fortune to engage **Mascarille's** services in winning back her fiancé and reminds him of his obligations in the second act. However, Mascarille does little to deserve this retainer, other than to work against Léandre's schemes in the service of **Lélie**. Predictably, those efforts go astray through the latter's blockheadedness. Hippolyte emerges again in the final act to confront Célie with many clever compliments, but also with the assurance that her financial clout will force Léandre back into her arms.

**Hobereau**. A provincial noble with limited resources who is unable to maintain an expensive lifestyle suitable for the **court**. The **Sotenvilles** and the **Comtesse d'Escarbagnas** are examples of this type. **Nicole** in *Le Bourgeois gentilhomme* refers to "the son of our village squire, the clumsiest oaf and the silliest ninny I have ever seen" (III, 12).
   *See also* **Nobility**.

**Holland**. **Géronimo** recalls that **Sganarelle** has spent five years in Holland as part of his commercial career in *Le Mariage forcé*. The Dutch were at war with France during some of Molière's creative period, but this did not prevent an active commerce from continuing between the countries. Anticipating the age of Bayle, Leclerc, and other French intellectuals operating in Holland, figures such as **Descartes** and Huyghens already opened channels of literate communication. As part of this process, the Dutch regularly pirated all popular French books, including those of Molière. Though **Louis XIV** fulminated against the Protestant republic and encouraged hack writers to devote their pens to anti–Dutch propaganda, the French state itself was in many ways dependent on its industrious neighbor. For example, the only truly fit fighting ships in the French navy were imported from Holland, including the King's flagship.
   *See also* **Gazette**.

**Horace**. First–century Roman writer and critic whose satires and *Ars poetica* would be imitated by Molière's friend **Boileau**. In the prefatory letter to *Les Fâcheux*, Molière says tongue–in–cheek that he could cite Horace and **Aristotle** if he wanted to justify his new work, but that he would probably never complete such a project. **Monsieur Lysidas**, the pedantic poet of *La Critique de l'École des femmes*, alleges that Molière has broken the laws laid down by Horace and Aristotle for literature, but **Dorante** counters that those ancients based their judgments on nothing but common sense, exactly like the playwright. **Vadius**, of *Les Femmes savantes*, praises **Trissotin** for his well–made odes "that leave Horace far behind." He retracts this later in his letter to **Philaminte**, where he accuses his rival of plagiarizing the Latin author.

**Horace (*L'École des femmes*).** This is certainly one of the most interesting parts that Molière created for his young colleague **La Grange**, showing far more depth and range than the average young lover role that had prevailed up to that moment. Horace begins typically enough in Act I, scene 4, as a youth who has quickly developed designs for **Agnès** as soon as he arrives in **Arnolphe's** town. He is both libidinous and naïve, struck by the girl's beauty, but interested at first in little more than a physical, exploitative relationship. He seems ready to live up to Arnolphe's prediction that he is "cut out to make cuckolds." However, it is also clear from the beginning that he possesses not only a high degree of innate charm, but a mastery of politeness that particularly impressed Agnès when the couple exchanged bows and curtsies all day long from balcony to street. Furthermore, Horace's account of their initial meeting demonstrates a considerable amount of verbal skill that will be required throughout the play, as he is constantly obliged to balance Arnolphe's soliloquies and asides with extensive descriptions of his meetings with Agnès that take place offstage. During these speeches, he must be vulnerable enough to cause Arnolphe to gloat whenever he thinks he has the upper hand, as when he thinks Horace has been stoned or shut out from the house. He must also have enough verve to drive the bully to despair when he adds that all has turned out well for him, whether through messages sent on a rock or secret visits to Agnès's chamber. Horace also becomes somewhat of a *raisonneur*, or voice of reason, in the play. It is he who is witness to Agnès's transformation from a beautiful ignoramus into a young woman able to manage and communicate her increasingly complex emotions. Duly touched by this metamorphosis, he changes himself, becoming a mature lover instead of a mere playboy, a man of understanding who strives in Cornelian fashion to be worthy of his chosen soul–mate. Fittingly, he delivers the lines that sum up Molière's thoughts about **love** and **nature**: "One must admit what a great teacher is this Love, / Whatever our faults, he makes us rise above, / And in a single lesson moves our heart / To transcend all the defects of its start, / Removing all our inner nature's obstacles, / To liberate our feelings like a miracle." Horace himself becomes an example of sublime feeling in Act V, as he relates how Agnès's daring escape filled him with "an ecstasy impossible to translate" and made it unthinkable for him to dishonor her in any way. The effect of this emotional transformation adds to the verisimilitude of an ending where he literally put his beloved into the hands of her tormentor, an act that could only be judged as idiotic under any other circumstances. His subsequent distress at learning of his father's approach further underlines Arnolphe's apparent triumph, which seems due more to ill fate than to his success in outwitting Horace or seducing Agnès. Thus, the otherwise unbelievable climax, with its unlikely recognition scene and unanticipated reversal of fortune for everyone, becomes far more acceptable. Horace's own rapid restoration of his wits, which allows him to cajole his previously irate father, is a suitable finale for a youth who has truly become a man of the world as a result of his adventures with Agnès. Horace's character marks as well a higher step for Molière the writer. His previous young leads had existed very much on the surface of the world, amounting to little more than the sum of their good looks and fine clothes. To the misguided Arnolphe, Horace seems to incarnate these same airy qualities; he continually underestimates his opponent as nothing more than a walking pile of lace and feathers. By developing a more profound, more perceptive personality beneath the exterior of a marquis's finery, the playwright took a giant step toward the perfection of the comedy of character.

**Hôtel.** In the seventeenth century, this term could be applied to almost any large and important building, regardless of whether it offered accommodations. Thus, the **Hôtel de Bourgogne** was actually a **theater**. Private mansions were called "hôtels particuliers"; the Hôtel de Rambouillet was that duke's private residence. It is true that such noble mansions often had rooms for people who were considered attached to the great person's entourage. **La Fontaine** was one of many writers who made use of such largesse. Rich **bourgeois** built "hôtels" as well, and often sought to defray some of the phenomenal costs by renting space to distinguished members of the public. The institution of the traveler's hotel was also beginning to appear at the time, and a guide was actually issued in 1692. The Hôtels de Mouhy, de Lyon, and de Hollande mentioned by the **Countess of Escarbagnas** were either in the lowest class of such accommodations or did not appear at all on the list. One must consider that they were little more than ordinary inns.

**Hôtel de Bourgogne.** The building from which Molière's principal rivals drew their name was situated in the rue Mauconseil and belonged to a lay religious association called the Brotherhood of the Passion. The Brotherhood (*confrérie*) had intended to produce Passion plays in the structure, but the public performance of such plays was discontinued soon after they procured the building. They leased it to the senior company of royal players, who had occupied the premises for nearly a century by the time Molière came back to **Paris** in 1658. As a boy, he had undoubtedly attended performances there by great tragedians of past generations. The main members of the troupe in the Great Comedians in 1658 were all veteran actors: Floridor (Josias de Soulas), Villliers/Philipin (Claude Deschamps), Montfleury (Antoine Jacob), and Beauchasteau (François Chastelet), along with their respective wives

(Marguerite Baloré, Marguerite Béguin, Jeanne de la Chappe, and Madeleine de Pouget). The widows of the great Bellerose and the senior Baron were also still with the troupe. All were present at Molière's first command performance in the **Louvre**, and though he addressed words of respect to them, they soon realized the seriousness of his challenge to their dominance. Indeed, they enjoyed a virtual monopoly of the French stage in the capital, since the **Marais** troupe had seen only minimal activity between 1653 and 1658. They quickly added new associates in the persons of **Hauteroche** (Noël Breton) and Crispin/Bellerose (**Raymond Poisson**). The former was eventually to lead the troupe and the latter was to prove its most gifted comic actor, surviving until the time when the French troupes would all be blended into the **Comédie–Française** decades later.

Relations between the Hôtel de Bourgogne and Molière's troupe soured fairly quickly, for **La Grange** notes in his register that the Great Comedians were soon petitioning the King to help them because of the rude competition put up by the junior players. Some critics, such as Deierkauf–Holsboer, feel the senior group was also offended by certain lines in *Les Précieuses ridicules,* which they took as an insult. Their first attack (or counterattack, depending on one's view) took the form of two derisive little plays from the pen of **Antoine Baudeau de Somaize**, *Les Véritables Prétieuses* and *Les Prétieuses . . . mises en vers* (published almost simultaneously in 1660) that, most ironically, accused Molière of plagiarism, although they are almost entirely derived from his work. Molière's subsequent staging of **Gabriel Gilbert's** comedy, *La Vraie et la Fausse Précieuse*, may have been a reply to Somaize, though none was needed to such feeble barbs.

Lancaster is among critics who believe that the next shot from the Hôtel de Bourgogne was equally weak; **F. Doneau's** play, *Les Amours d'Alcippe et de Céphise, ou la Cocue imaginaire*, was as derivative as Somaize's texts, simply copying and sexually reversing the plot of *Sganarelle*, to very little critical or popular effect. Deierkauf–Holsboer feels that the Great Comedians also intended satire in Raymond Poisson's popular little sketch, *Le Baron de la Crasse* (1661), where traveling actors appear who parallel those of Molière's provincial years. However, they are not really a source of humor in the play, whose strong satire is directed against a ridiculous provincial noble who embarrassed himself at **court** and slunk back into the hinterlands; if anything, this rural version of a ridiculous marquis is yet another tribute to Molière's models.

The **Quarrel of the School for Wives** opened the floodgates of invective against Molière and the Hôtel de Bourgogne surely took advantage of every scurrilous text that came their way to blacken the reputation of their rival on stage. **Donneau de Visé's** *Zélinde*, presented in June of 1663, was a whole–scale but mainly literary attack against Molière's hit comedy, listing all the various textual complaints that had been raised in print or voice. **Edmé Boursault's** *Portrait du peintre* was a far more vicious, ad hominem item, attacking Molière's moral character and raising unpleasant insinuations of incest in the dramatist's recent marriage with **Armande Béjart**. Molière more than compensated for Donneau's formal objections in *La Critique de l'École des* *femmes*, but he did not reply in kind to the disrespectable Boursault. Instead, he launched a very effective parody of the acting styles of the principal members of the Hôtel de Bourgogne in *L'Impromptu de Versailles*, where he apes the pompous declamation of Beauchasteau and his wife (in their roles as Rodrigue in *Le Cid* and Camille in *Horace*), **Montfleury**, **Villiers**, and **Hauteroche** with devastating results. It is uncertain whether Montfleury was more insulted about this criticism of his delivery or over comments in the *Impromptu* about his elephantine size, but he was so enraged that he wrote a placet to the King personally libeling Molière for incest and adultery.

These exchanges were not enough, however, to dissuade the Hôtel de Bourgogne from answering Molière's withering salvos with stray potshots. They again went to Donneau de Visé to commission *La Vengeance des marquis*, where their actors turn the tables on Molière, mocking his performance as Caesar in *La Mort de Pompée* (as a tragic actor, Molière admittedly made an easy target). Montfleury's son Antoine composed another puny satire, *L'Impromptu de l'Hôtel de Condé*, and Boursault, again accusing Molière of plagiarism while openly practicing it himself, published an altered version of the farce, *Le Médecin volant*, which had been in the junior troupe's repertoire for years. The obscurity of these texts and the fact that Molière chose not to dignify them with the slightest response testify to their ineffectiveness.

More pithy and professional competition came in the form of a series of play–to–play contests between the two troupes. The first of these came in the fall of 1665, when both companies staged plays called *La Mère coquette*, Molière using a text by the turncoat Donneau de Visé and the Hôtel countering with one by **Quinault**. Neither was an overwhelming success, though Donneau's may qualify as his best comedy. A more serious clash came in December, when **Racine's** *Alexandre le grand et Porus*, staged at the Palais Royal Theater, was challenged by a revival of Boyer's *Porus, ou la générosité d'Alexandre* by the Great Comedians. Though Racine's text was in every way superior to **Boyer's** and the receipts were favorable, the shortcomings of some Palais Royal Theater actors must have shaken Racine's confidence enough to make him overlook **Mlle**. **Du Parc's** splendid performance as Axiane and give the text in an unprecedented fit of theatrical treason to the rival company. The last of the company battles took place five years later, as the Palais Royal Theater pitted **Corneille's** *Tite et Bérénice* against Racine's *Bérénice* at the Hôtel de Bourgogne. Both plays were actually quite successful, with Racine's obtaining slightly stronger recognition, for its text as well as for its performance.

By the end of 1671, the membership of the Great Comedians had changed markedly. Floridor, Montfleury, and Beauchasteau had all died, and Villiers had retired. Gone also were Mlles. Montfleury, Villiers, Bellerose, and Baron. They had been replaced by Molière's former associate **Brécourt** and his wife (Étiennette Des Urlis), **Champmeslé** and his spouse (Charles Chevillet and Marie Desmares), La Fleur (François Juvenon), Poisson's wife (Victorine Guérin), and the excellent tragic actress Mlle. Dennebault (Françoise Jacob, daughter of Montfleury). Mlle. Du Parc, lured to the Hôtel de Bourgogne by her lover and writer Racine, had had a short but glorious interval with the troupe before her mysterious death. Mlle. des Oeillets, another outstanding tragic actress, had enjoyed a stellar career with the Great Comedians between 1662 and her death in 1670. The new generation at the Hôtel had little reason to quarrel with Molière personally. Some of them had contacts with him and others were eager to try to imitate his new comic style, especially the actor/authors Brécourt, Poisson, Hauteroche, and Champmeslé.

It had been a challenging decade and a half of competition, with the Hôtel de Bourgogne generally prevailing in tragedy, thanks to its experience and talents in that genre. Nevertheless, their advantage was not steady, since apart from Racine, their authors were notoriously inconsistent, with such writers as **Thomas Corneille** alternating between great successes and dismal failures. Even in tragedy, the Palais Royal Theater had its occasional momentary advantages. In comedy, the situation was roughly reversed, with the Great Comedians striving to both emulate and outdo the master and mounting many a flop in the process. It was mainly after Molière's death that some of their writers were able to achieve a degree of independent success. Some of the comedies by Poisson, Hauteroche, Brécourt, and Champmeslé only stayed in the Comédie–Française repertory as long as they did because their authors occupied important posts once the troupes were united.

See S. Wilma Deierkauf–Holsboer, *Le Théâtre de l'Hôtel de Bourgogne: Le Théâtre de la Troupe Royale, 1548–1680*, 2 vols. (Paris: Nizet, 1968–1970).

**Hôtel Guénégaud.** *See* **Comédie–Française.**

**Hotot, Jean.** Printer in the Loire valley city of Blois who produced the booklet for the comedy–ballet of *Monsieur de Pourceaugnac* in 1669. Presumably the arrangements were so rushed that the job could not be done by a Parisian printer before the departure of the **court** for the royal **hunting** holiday at **Chambord**.

**Hubert, André**. This versatile actor was already married and a veteran of the **theater** when he joined Molière's troupe in Eastertide of 1664. Like **Brécourt**, whom he replaced, he had been a member of the **Marais** troupe immediately before joining Molière, but his ties to that theater went deeper than most, since his mother was one of the co–owners of the building. He was part of the company when the Marais reopened in 1659, and had probably acted in touring troupes before that. Hubert seems to have been unpretentious and truly professional. Besides taking over Brécourt's roles, he excelled in all sorts of different supporting parts. In line with the personality of **Alain** in *L'École des femmes*, he probably played the **peasant** parts of **Lucas** in *Le Médecin malgré lui* and **Pierrot** in *Dom Juan*. Able to cross–dress with ease, he was the original **Madame Pernelle** in *Tartuffe* and is usually credited with playing **Madame de Sotenville** in *George Dandin*, **Madame Jourdain** in *Le Bourgeois gentilhomme* and **Philaminte** in *Les Femmes savantes*. He was **Iphitas** in *La Princesse d'Élide*, the **First Doctor** in *Monsieur de Pourceaugnac* and **Thibaudet** in *La Comtesse d'Escarbagnas*. In *Psyché*, he was either **Cléomène** or **Agénor**, most likely the latter. Probably he was cast as one of the medical men in *Le Malade imaginaire*. He helped administer the troupe as Molière grew older and left a register of their activities in 1672–73 that is an important supplement to **La Grange's**. Following Molière's death, he remained with his colleagues through the various fusions that ensued, retiring from the **Comédie-Française** at the Easter break of 1685.

**Humors.** An ancient medical theory held that the human body and mind were governed by the relative influences of four fluids or humors: blood, phlegm, bile, and black bile. A predominance of one over the others produced mirth and courage, impassivity, anger, or melancholy, respectively. The most obvious reference to this theory in Molière's works is in *Le Misanthrope*, which was subtitled "L'Atrabilaire amoureux," or the melancholy lover. It must be remembered that this constitutes something of an oxymoron, for an "atrabilaire" by his very nature should not be capable of falling in love. Molière is certainly citing this paradigm tongue–in–cheek, since he pays little respect to the prevailing medical knowledge in his **doctor** plays.

**Hunters** (*La Princesse d'Élide*). After killing the bear that threatened **Moron** in Act II, the mute company of hunters dances around their trophy while the fool rains blows upon it. They were played by the royal dancers Manceau, Chicanneau, Balthazard, Noblet, Bonard, Magny, and La Pierre, who also appeared in other ballet numbers in the production.

**Hunting.** A **pastime** almost entirely restricted to the **nobility** by seventeenth–century law, hunting was a favorite **court** occupation during **Louis XIV's** youth. **Mascarille** boasts about being invited to hunt deer with a duke in *Les Précieuses ridicules*. In *Les Fâcheux* (II, 6), **Dorante** gives an impassioned, if long–winded, account of a deer hunt in which he mentions the hunters' typical lunch (hard–boiled eggs), the different cries and horn calls that were used, the succession of dog packs, the work of the beaters, and innumerable points of lore and etiquette. He drops a great deal of hunting vocabulary, undoubtedly for comic effect. His own skill is contrasted to that of a rude bumpkin who joins the party with his awkward son, disrupting the order of the chase and finally finishing off the prey in lubberly fashion with a cavalry pistol. It is said that this character sketch was the idea of Louis XIV himself and was based on Monsieur de Soyecourt, who would later become the head of the royal hunt.

Hunting plays an important part in *La Princesse d'Élide*, where a boar hunt at the beginning of the play involves two characters played by Molière, the dog–handler **Lyciscas** who is aroused in the first *intermède* and the fool **Moron** who flees from the beast in the second scene of Act I. Moron's comical description of his hunting feats is a gem of burlesque rhetoric. For the princely suitors **Aristomène** and **Théocle**, however, the hunt is a disaster: their kill gains them only a tongue lashing from the proud **Princess**. Later, some hunters save Moron from an overly friendly bear. Hunting is also mentioned as one of the forms of aristocratic entertainment in *Les Amants magnifiques*. While **Aristione** was not hunting when she met the savage boar that threatens her life, **Sostrate** employs his skills in killing the beast, thus winning her daughter's hand in **marriage**.

While the foregoing examples show the noblest forms of hunting, the poor country squire or *hobereau*, usually with a rank no higher than baron, could not afford the wooded expanses necessary for such sport. He was often reduced to lesser game that could be found in the fields. Thus **Monsieur de Sotenville** in *George Dandin* offers his fellow aristocrat **Clitandre** the pleasure of "chasing the hare" with him, a laughable prospect for any courtier of rank. The impoverished **Countess of Escarbagnas** mentions that her husband kept "a pack of running hounds" as one of the proofs of his nobility.

**Hurtado de Mendoza, Diego** (1503–1575). Spanish statesman, historian, poet, and playwright whose *El Marido hace mujer* (1643) may have given Molière the idea of a pair of brothers marrying a pair of sisters, with the older and less oppressive brother winning the love of his partner, while his doctrinaire sibling fails, a scenario that appears in *L'École des maris*.

**Hyacinte (*Les Fourberies de Scapin*).** The unfortunate young woman whom **Octave** meets when she is crying over the body of her dead mother. The pathetic scene is described in rather too much detail by the youth, whose attaction to her at that moment, with her clothes and hair in disarray and tears streaming down her face, recalls, on the one hand, Pyrrhus's fatal encounter with the grief–stricken Andromaque in **Racine's** tragedy and, on the other, **Alceste's** desire to see **Célimène** reduced to nothing so that she may owe everything to his aid. **Cléante's** meeting with **Mariane** in *L'Avare* also presents similarities. Despite this important introduction, Hyacinte has rather little to say for the short time she is onstage. The role was probably taken by **Armande Béjart**, who had also played **Mariane**.

# I

"**I didn't say that!**" This phrase rises to the status of a set piece in Molière's comedy, where he employs it often with varying types of effect. The most notable instance is probably in *Le Misanthrope*, where **Alceste**, forced to give his opinion of **Oronte's** fluffy little sonnet and incapable of gilding the pill, relates advice he would give to "someone else." Each time the insulted Oronte asks him if he is saying that his writing is not good, Alceste uses the disclaimer, "I didn't say that," and proceeds to give an even more damning assessment of the verses.

**Ignès**. The name given in *Dépit amoureux* to the woman who is thought to be **Ascagne's** mother during much of the play. She is described as a shopkeeper. Actually, she had switched her son with **Albert's** younger daughter **Dorothée** and then switched back after the boy died, both times in hopes of gain from Albert's family.

**Ignès** (*Dom Garcie de Navarre*). Much discussed in Acts I through III because she is **Dom Sylve's** jilted love, she appears in Act IV dressed as a man, which causes **Dom Garcie** to make his most fatal mistake in accusing **Elvire** of infidelity and falsehood. Actually she had escaped from her captor, the tyrant **Mauregat**, by pretending to be dead and then donning the masculine garb. She has made her way to **Astorga** with the help of **Dom Pèdre**. In Act V she professes great esteem for her friend Elvire, saying she is not unhappy to lose Dom Sylve to one so beautiful and virtuous. After Dom Sylve reveals his true identity as **Dom Alphonse**, prince of Leon, she forgives him immediately and expresses no qualms about being a bride seized on the rebound. Similarly, she shows considerable sympathy toward Dom Garcie. It is she, rather than Elvire, who explains to him that he is now free to realize his happiness with the princess. The catalytic effect of her goodwill is nonetheless not enough to save an unraveled and disappointing denouement.

**Illustre Théâtre.** An ill–fated acting company founded by Molière and a group of others, including several members of the **Béjart** family, in 1643. This was a time of change in the **Poquelin** family, as some of his younger siblings moved with their father to a new house and **Jean–Baptiste** himself ceded the office of royal upholsterer, which he had held for only several months, to his younger brother. The would–be thespian was only twenty–two, and several of his associates were even younger. Most lacked professional acting experience. Nevertheless, they contracted to turn a tennis court, the Jeu de Paume des Métayers, into a proper theater and acquired new plays from such well–known authors as **Pierre Du Ryer, Tristan L'Hermite,** and perhaps André Mareschal. They engaged musicians and even lured a dancer away from a rival group (it was on the dancer's contract that Jean–Baptiste Poquelin first signed with the stage name of Molière). Unhappily, their location was remote from the traditional entertainment district, rather far down river on the left bank of the Seine, and the ensuing winters brought some of the worst weather of the century to **Paris,** causing patrons to stay home by the fire.

Having already experienced financial problems in the preceding months, the troupe took the extraordinary step of relocating in the middle of December 1644 to a new location at the Jeu de Paume de la Croix Noire, closer to the center of town, but still in a questionable location for performances. By April of 1645, with their new playhouse barely furnished, lawsuits based on their loans began to proliferate. By summer they had accumulated to the point that Molière faced prison for unpayable debts. He seems to have quit the capital in October, perhaps only a few steps ahead of the police. The remnants of the Illustre Théâtre joined the troupe of **Charles Dufresne** in **Nantes.** This wild and sometimes dangerous adventure, a kind of *saison en enfer* for a young man of his background, had the effect of forcing Molière to choose forever between his past life as a somewhat comfortable *moyen bourgeois* and the romantic, but ephemeral life of an actor. After breaking his ties to the past, he was free to throw himself with abandon into his new profession.

*See* Madeleine Jurgens, "L'Aventure de l'Illustre Théâtre," *Revue d'Histoire Littéraire de la France* 72 (1972), 976–1006.

**Impromptu.** A minor genre of *vers libre* poem popular in mid–seventeenth–century salons. **Mascarille** recites one in *Les Précieuses ridicules* and then sets it to **music** with comical results. The term was also used for spontaneous dramas.

***Impromptu de Versailles, L'.*** This unusual one–act comedy, written and performed in 1663 and published in the collected works of 1682, was instigated by **Louis XIV** himself, who ordered Molière to reply to the attacks made against him by his enemies in the **Quarrel of the School for Wives.** While the dramatist does mention the latest and most vicious of these, **Boursault's** *Portrait du peintre*, he explicitly refuses to answer in kind with ad hominem slanders.  Instead, he discusses the issues on several levels, including a gentle but comically effective critique of the **Hôtel de Bourgogne's** acting styles.

The play opens with most of the members of the Palais Royal Theater company playing themselves, waiting for Molière to begin the rehearsal of a new comedy.  Unfortunately, they all tell him immediately that they have not learned their lines and are incapable of going on stage.  These whining pleas for more time and less stress appear to be very realistic and may reflect the real preoccupations of the actors in the face of Molière's demands for shorter and shorter deadlines in royal command entertainments.  The men of the troupe are fairly diffident and quiet, while the women, in a definite pecking order dominated by **Madeleine Béjart**, with **Mlles. Du Parc** and **de Brie** in second position, have a lot more to say, both to Molière and each other.  None seems completely happy with her part.  Instead of launching into the rehearsal, they begin to discuss the attacks recently made on Molière and the ways he can respond to them.  Mlle. de Brie pleads with him to tell her more about some ideas for parody that he had discussed with Madeleine, and he obligingly lampoons five of the leading stars of the  Hôtel de Bourgogne (**Montfleury**, Mlle. Beauchasteau, Beauchasteau, **Hauteroche**, and **Villiers**).

Next, they get back to rehearsing, with Molière giving preliminary instructions to some of the players, while saying very little to others.  Before they can actually begin, an impertinent **marquis** played by **La Thorillière** interrupts them with his questions.  Once rid of him, Molière and **La Grange**, as ridiculous marquis, engage in a silly dispute over who is the model for the marquis in the *Critique*.  Calling on **Brécourt**, as a polite **nobleman**, to mediate their argument, he disagrees with both of them and says that Molière can never exhaust the ridiculous models their counterparts provide.  At this point, Molière gets so caught up that he intervenes and performs a whole speech to demonstrate to Brécourt the way it should be delivered.   The entry of **Armande Béjart** and **Mlle. Du Parc**, as the salon butterflies **Élise** and **Climène**, allows for a series of **lazzi** over **politeness** and a teasing exchange between the vain women.  The arrival of the rest of the cast brings the discussion around to the matter of Boursault's *Portrait du peintre*.

At this point, Madeleine stops the rehearsal to ask why Molière has not answered the hack more harshly, but the dramatist explains his reluctance to allow such people to exploit his private life in order to gain scandalous publicity.  Having been so reasonable about this troubling slander, Molière is reduced to a dithering wreck when a series of messengers demands the beginning of the performance.  He is greatly relieved when the last of them, played by **Louis Béjart**, dispenses the company from its obligation in exchange for an easier **repertory** piece.

The little comedy is a compendium of aesthetic and professional ideas, conveying Molière's comic sense much more effectively than any "objective" essay could.  While it failed to completely silence the writers affiliated with the Hôtel de Bourgogne, it permanently claimed the moral high ground for Molière and put an effective end to the Quarrel of the School for Wives.

*See* Abby Zanger, "Acting as Counteracting in Molière's *The Impromptu of Versailles*," *Theatre Journal* 38 (1986), 180–195.

*Interesse, L'*. An **Italian** *commedia sostenuta* by the Venetian author **Secchi** that was adapted in *Dépit amoureux*.

**Iphicrate (*Les Amants magnifiques*)**. This prince vies with **Timoclès** to obtain the hand of **Princess Ériphile** in **marriage**. He presents a somewhat ridiculous and unworthy face as a suitor, since he stoops to smothering Ériphile's mother with untimely compliments in hopes of swaying her judgment. This obsequiousness is matched by his fervor in trying to capture the good will of others, such as **Sostrate** and **Clitidas**, to support his cause. **Anaxarque** later admits to having accepted numerous bribes from Iphicrate and his relatives in exchange for astrologically recommending him as a husband. In fact, Iphicrate underwrote the cost of the **Venus** illusion that fools **Aristione** at the beginning of Act IV, and he has agreed to the scheme to pretend to save her from fake **pirates** in order to prove the astrologer's prediction true. Having laid out so much money in advance, he is understandably outraged when the plot fails to come off, and he joins Timoclès in thrashing Anaxarque between Acts IV and V. However, he finishes the play on a ludicrous note by coming with his rival to complain about Aristione's choice in the final scene. Though both men had agreed wholeheartedly to the fortune teller's proposal, neither accepts it once the prediction comes to pass, for they claim that Sostrate is unworthy of Ériphile and such a choice wounds their honor. Their behavior seems to bear out the princess's earlier remark about vicious rumors and unspoken threats, and one wonders whether the play's closing spectacle can put such feelings of pique to rest.

**Iphitas (*La Princesse d'Élide*)**. The part of the **Prince of Elis**, father to the eponym, was played by **Hubert**. While drawing on his expertise with elderly roles, this one does not offer the actor much opportunity to speak. Before he can even address his daughter in Act II, scene 4, she preempts his arguments by simultaneously pledging to do her filial duty and expounding on the repugnance of **marriage**. He accordingly tempers his exhortation and comforts her by saying he will not force her to do anything against her will. When he appears again at the beginning of Act V, he is overjoyed to learn that **Euryale** has overcome his daughter's resistance and he proceeds to aid the young man and to dismiss his daughter's denials. He puts her in a very delicate position by insisting that if she blocks Euryale's marriage with **Aglante**, she must be prepared to marry him herself; he takes her hesitations as a sign of consent.

**Iris (*Pastorale comique*)**. This **shepherdess** is loved by both **Lycas** and **Filène**. We know none of the details from her interview with Lycas in scene 4 or from her talk with **Coridon** in scene 11, but the guidebook does report her parting words to the rivals at the end of scene 12: "Expect me not here to sing my own praises: / For the choice that you face, you must look to yourselves. / You have eyes and I love you — / That tells you enough." She seems to have faced a situation like **Célimène** in *Le Misanthrope* and to have handled it in much the same way, by refusing to endorse either suitor in public and telling them both to follow their hearts. Unlike **Alceste**, Lycas and Filène appear to interpret this nonchalant reply correctly, to mean that neither is really preferred. This despair almost leads them to mutual suicide. The part was played, according to the guidebook, by **Mlle. de Brie**.

**Isabelle** (*L'École des maris*). Sister of **Léonor** and ward to **Sganarelle**. Although subject to a harsh regime of lock and key on the part of her **jealous** guardian, she says little to directly confront his tirades in Act I, preferring to let her sister do the talking. Undoubtedly she has already learned her role as a passive–aggressive woman very well and knows that Sganarelle is more likely to be taken in by feigned agreement than by overt opposition. Thus, in Act II, she devises the stratagem of communicating with **Valère** by means of Sganarelle himself. This is achieved by telling the sociopathic burgher that Valère has been bothering her with his continued attentions, whereas the reality is quite the opposite. When accused, Valère sees the significance of the message immediately and replies in kind. We also learn that she has contrived to send him a **love letter** by way of a gilded box that he has supposedly sent to her. She even keeps Sganarelle from snooping (and garners his confidence) by making a point that she has not even broken the seal on the letter and is returning it intact to the sender. Though the missive lacks the poignancy and candor of **Agnès's** letter to **Horace** in *L'École des femmes*, it nevertheless gives proof of her initiative and strength of character. As the valet **Ergaste** remarks, "It's not bad stuff, for a young lady!" She manages to accuse Valère so effectively that she even obtains a tête-à-tête with him right under Sganarelle's nose, where she can give and receive a "coded" profession of love without the old man's suspecting a thing. It only remains for her to take things one step further in Act III by concocting the tale of Léonor's elopement in order to facilitate her own. The excuse she offers Sganarelle for her flight is extremely witty, though not very contrite: she says that knowing herself to be unworthy of such a man, she preferred to see herself in the hands of another rather than to feel guilty for her shortcomings! Those lines distance her from the likes of Agnès and place her closer to the satirical spirit of **Célimène**.

**Isidore** (*Le Sicilien*). Played by **Mlle. de Brie**, according to the guidebook to the **Ballet des Muses**, this **Greek slave** girl is rather forward and frank toward her former owner and would–be husband, **Dom Pèdre**. She tells him outright that she resents his attempts to sequester her and that any woman so treated would be justified in fleeing him. She admits that she has enjoyed the serenade **Adraste** arranged and that she also enjoys the attention men have managed to give her, presumably referring to Adraste's longing looks. Thus, given the chance to speak with him directly by the ruse of having her **portrait** painted, she wastes no time in engaging in amorous banter and in exploring the depths of his passion. She seems quite satisfied with what she discovers, telling Dom Pèdre, "This gentleman seems to me to be the most polite man on earth, and one must agree that the French have some kind of native civility that lacks in other nationalities" (scene 13). When Dom Pèdre frets about this flirtatious quality, she does not lie directly, but answers him obliquely, "What they do is only a game." A game she quickly masters herself, changing clothes with **Climène** and fleeing her household prison as fast as her legs will carry her. Isidore is one eloping female who never looks back.

**Italian Influences.** It is unclear where Molière learned his Italian, but by the time his career reached its height, he clearly commanded the **language** in both oral and written form. There does not seem to be any direct Italian presence in the **Poquelin**–Cressé family, in the **Illustre Théâtre**, or in **Dufresne's** provincial troupe. Had Molière not obtained some instruction in the language in school, he may have met wandering Italians in the south of France during the nearly two decades he and his colleagues crisscrossed the region. Even the scurrilous *Observations sur le Festin de Pierre* credits Molière with the ability to translate Italian passably well. By 1656 he was familiar enough with the language and literature of Italy to transpose **Beltrame's** *L'Inavvertito* into *L'Étourdi* and, shortly after, **Secchi's** *L'Interesse* into *Dépit amoureux*. Both of these late Renaissance plays derive from the learned genre of the *commedia sostenuta*, but there was no clear line of distinction in Italy between the higher form and the more farcical *commedia dell'arte*. In fact, Beltrame himself was a noted practitioner of the latter. Both of Molière's surviving short farces, *La Jalousie du Barbouillé* and *Le Médecin volant*, may owe a debt to models in the *commedia dell'arte*. Such influences are difficult to prove in many cases because the Italian players tended to work from scenarios that were not always committed to paper and always contained a great deal of patterned improvisation. A more obvious inspiration was **Cicognini's** *Le Gelosie fortunate del principe Rodrigo*, which was the basis for several passages in *Dom Garcie de Navarre*. It has been conclusively shown, however, that Molière knew of two Italian scenarios of the Don Juan story, a lost 1652 text by **Giliberto** and **Cicognini's** *Il Convitato di Piedra*, which contains many elements adopted in his own *Dom Juan*. This is scarcely astonishing when one considers that by 1665 he had shared two stages with the Italian players resident in **Paris** for a number of years. He had met and, many say, imitated the great comic **Scaramouche**, one of the first of his kind to work without a **mask**. Molière's theater face was quite like that of Scaramouche. If the persona of **Mascarille** was originally masked, as the name suggests, he soon lost the artificial cover, since no illustrations exist showing him with one. From **Sganarelle** onwards, it is clear that Molière's characters were designed to be played with a "natural" face enhanced by cosmetics but essentially uncovered. Rather vague Italian antecedents have been suggested for a number of Molière's characters, especially **Tartuffe**. Despite the seeming likelihood of some of these connections, they still await, for the most part, documentary proof. Late in his career, Molière returned to an Italianate mood for his *Fourberies de Scapin*. Scapino had been a stock character of the Italian theater at least as far back as **Barbieri's** career. Italian singers, along with dancers dressed in the stylized costumes of Scaramouche and **Trivelin**, form part of the **Ballet des Nations** that accompanies *Le Bourgeois gentilhomme*. Soon after Molière's death, it was time to reverse the influence, as the Venetian Carlo Goldoni fell strongly under the spell of Molière, and developed an Italian theatrical tradition based on the comedy of manners.

See Gustave Attinger, *L'Esprit de la commedia dell'arte dans le théâtre français* (1950); Philip Wadsworth, *Molière and the Italian Theatrical Tradition* (Birmingham, AL: Summa, 1987).

# J

**Jacqueline** (*Le Médecin malgré lui*). Although she is often on scene as a confidante or messenger, this buxom country wet–nurse, the wife of **Lucas**, takes part significantly in Act II, scenes 1 through 4, and in Act III, scene 3. Her speech is just as hilarious as that of her husband, deforming vowels and consonants alike. She begins by trying to persuade **Géronte** to let his daughter marry her beloved **Léandre**, noting that "a husband is a poultice that cures all the girls," and citing the example of a neighbor who, when married against her fancy, "grew yellow as a quince and never prospered ever again since that very day." Admiring her breasts, **Sganarelle** employs many tricks and *lazzi* to fondle them in the presence of her husband, despite his efforts to pull the **doctor** away. He claims, "It's the official duty of any doctor to inspect the titties of a wet–nurse." She admires his apparent medical skill and his macaronic **Latin**. But when he offers to administer some personal treatments to her, she retorts, "Fie, fie, none of that! I'll not turn my body into an **apothecary's** shop!" Later, when the doctor tries to seduce her, she professes loyalty to Lucas: "What do you want, sir? It's penance for my sins, and wherever the goat is tied, there must it graze." However, she agrees that Lucas deserves all the names Sganarelle calls him: an outright **animal**, a brute, an idiot, and a fool. Before the seduction can progress further, Lucas surprises the pair, and no further conversations between them take place. It is likely that the original Jacqueline was **Madeleine Béjart**, who was apparently better endowed physically and more adept at **peasant** roles than **Mlle. De Brie**.

*Jalousie du Barbouillé, La* (**The Dauber's Jealousy**). One–act farcical comedy written by Molière during his touring period and not published until 1819. The title refers both to the name and to the appearance of the title character, whose face was daubed with white flour–based makeup. The text is based on manuscripts found by the eighteenth–century lyric poet, **Jean–Baptiste Rousseau,** and eventually edited by the antiquarian Viollet–le–Duc. **La Grange's** register refers to seven performances, notably from 1660 to 1664. It is quite likely that Molière's corpulent colleague, **René Du Parc,** played the title role for some time, since the troupe is listed as having performed a comedy called *La Jalousie de Gros–René.* Molière may also have played the lead role of Le Barbouillé at some point, with **Madeleine Béjart** taking that of his wife, **Angélique.** The intrigue mainly consists of an extended argument between the drunken protagonist and his spouse, who criticizes him for his coarseness and debauchery. Le Barbouillé suspects his wife of infidelity — perhaps rightly, since she flirts with a gentleman named **Valère.** Angélique's father **Gorgibus** and his companion **Villebrequin** are drawn into the fray, as is a ridiculous and pseudo–pedantic **Doctor** who happens to be in the neighborhood. Catching Angélique as she returns from one of her visits, Le Barbouillé tries to lock her out of the house, but she turns the tables on him by pretending to die and locks him outside instead, exposing him to the criticism of his father–in–law. The latter sequence would eventually be employed again by Molière in *George Dandin.* Though rather crude in places, especially in le Barbouillé's dialogue, the **language** of the play contains the germs of the type of quick repartee that Molière would develop in his maturity. The Doctor, who attempts to demonstrate rhetorically that he is a doctor ten times over, seems to be based rather directly on the *commedia dell'arte* figure of Doctor Balourde. The thirteen scenes are cobbled together with little thought for transition or character development. A possible source, though distant, is **Boccaccio's** tale of Tofano in the fourth story of the seventh day of the *Decameron.*

**Janissaries.** These special forces in the armies of the Ottoman Empire are evoked indirectly in *Le Bourgeois gentilhomme* when **Covielle** and **Monsieur Jourdain** discuss Paladins. The Paladins of legend were, of course, Christians. To add to the confusion, **Madame Jourdain** confuses "paladins" with "baladins," or song–and–dance men. The Janissaries were much in the minds of seventeenth–century France, since they took part in the Ottoman drive through the Balkans toward Vienna and the expansion into the Venetian islands of the eastern Mediterranean. Both of these theaters of combat involved French expeditionary troops, either under royal orders or organized privately by **noblemen** like the **Marquis de la Feuillade.**

**Jealousy.** One of the great themes of seventeenth–century theater, and of Molière's works in particular. It appears, of course, in the **farce** of *La Jalousie du Barbouillé,* but only in a rather crude form. For one thing, Le Barbouillé's feelings appear to be well justified, since his wife is flirting with **Valère,** making assignations, and running around town at night. Thus, there is little imaginative element in this play's portrayal of jealousy. Furthermore, Le Barbouillé's reaction is straightforward. Without any self–doubt or *états d'âme,* he takes direct action and seeks to simply lock out the offending party. It is only when he thinks she might have killed herself from shame, throwing blame back on him, that he relents and allows her to turn the tables on him.

A far more profound and complex treatment of the emotion is found in *Dépit amoureux*. For one thing, the conversation between **Éraste** and **Gros–René** at the beginning of the play establishes that jealousy is linked to one's fundamental character. Frank and phlegmatic Gros–René is not going to fret about **Marinette's** faithfulness, even though he claims she has flirted with **Jodelet** in the past. Éraste, however, recognizes that he is drawn to suspicion and worry by his very temperament. He further admits that small and illogical fears are at the base of this syndrome, even though major shocks are bound to unleash its full fury. Though aware of the fact that investigation tends to deepen rather than assuage jealousy, he cannot help himself from trying to gain reassurance by questioning **Valère** and **Mascarille**. He immediately takes silence to be a very bad sign. Despite the fact that he has a **letter** professing **love** from **Lucile**, a very explicit and dangerous gage for a seventeenth–century woman to give, he doubts its contents from the beginning and finds its very existence somewhat suspect.

An interesting debate takes place in *Les Fâcheux*, when the ladies **Orante** and **Clymène** accost **Éraste** and insist that he decide for them whether a jealous lover is better than a tolerant one. Orante maintains that a jealous man is simply too disagreeable and insulting, whereas Clymène claims that failure to be jealous is a sign of tepid emotion at best. Éraste cleverly solves this issue by saying that the jealous lover loves more, but the indulgent one far better. Prefiguring the situation that will develop in *Le Misanthrope*, Molière thus appears to take the side of *honnêteté* in agreeing that excessive emotions, though **sincere**, often are pernicious in **polite** society.

One of the most jealous of Molière's protagonists is **Alceste** in *Le Misanthrope*. After he derides her for receiving too many men in her home, **Célimène** accuses him of being jealous of "the whole universe," a point that is not far from the truth. Of course, he is not the only one in the play to be bitten by that bug. Célimène notes that **Arsinoé** offers an eminent example of female jealousy, since she envies those with numerous lovers, all the more so because she is no longer capable of attracting such attention with her "sad merits." **Acaste**, **Clitandre**, and **Oronte** also show clear signs of jealousy, for despite their swagger they are just as unsure as Alceste about which man is preferred. The misanthrope, however, is unable to hide the transports of his emotions, such as when he erupts in anger over the love letter he thinks he has found, addressed from Célimène to Oronte (IV, 2). Though he hysterically begs **Éliante** to avenge this wrong by accepting his offers, she wisely points out that such jealous rages are often of short duration because they are based on little more than illusion. True to form, when he has fulminated sufficiently against Célimène, she silences him by answering, "Your jealous rage, so foolish through and through, / Does not deserve the love I have for you." She goes on to scold him until he feels that he, and not she, is on trial, and must prove his devotion by groveling abjectly as he asks for forgiveness. The irony lies in the fact that in this instance where he was absolutely right in doubting her faithfulness, it is he who backs down. Having humiliated himself in this way, Alceste seems to reach the limits of his flexibility. When Oronte approaches Célimène with an ultimatum to choose among her suitors, Alceste chimes in that "jealous or not jealous," he no longer wishes to share any part of her affections with other men. He goes on to explain his desire for absolute domination of his loved one: she must be reduced to nothing and receive no help from anyone in the world but him, so as to owe everything to her man. This concept of jealousy borders, of course, on sadism. It shows how incompatible love and jealousy can become, since the latter tends to stifle all sympathy and compassion for the well being of others.

Jealousy plays a preponderant role in **Amphitryon**, where both the Theban general and the god **Jupiter** are jealous of each other in different ways. Jupiter feels hemmed in by the prison of his own grandeur and wants to experience some of the freshness of human existence, particularly the fiery **love** of a newly married bride, who has not yet grown tired of sex. Having enjoyed the complete cooperation of **Alcmène** in his amorous play, he is worried that she may have given him so much in part out of conjugal duty. He wants to have her favors given as a lover to a lover, without any of the social compulsion that, to him, constitutes a poison to pleasure. It is not enough for him to know that he has pleased her more than her mortal husband ever did or could, for to some degree he is competing against the limits of his own imagination, rather than against a physical rival. Amphitryon, on the other hand, is chagrined to learn that he has lost not only the sweet homecoming that he was planning on, but perhaps the greatest sexual opportunity of his life. His wife has experienced the peak of pleasure in the arms of another. Not only does this make him reject his still affectionate wife, but it also ruins all aspects of his military triumph, and he tells the audience in soliloquy that he can no longer stand the "killing friendship" of his countrymen. Alcmène, on the other hand, would welcome a simple case of jealousy in exchange for the incomprehensible reactions of her cloned husband, since she could at least dismiss jealousy as an uncontrollable urge, rather like a sickness instead of a product of the human will. As Jupiter leaves, he not only states that sharing one's wife with a god is no grounds for jealousy, but if there should be a jealous party, it is he, since Alcmène remains "completely yours ... since the only way of pleasing her is to appear to be her husband." No wonder this statement elicits from the sarcastic **Sosie** the remark, "Master Jupiter certainly knows how to sweeten the medicine!"

Jealousy always seems to be either deficient, as in the case of **Orgon**, or exaggerated, as in that of **Dom Pèdre**. When **Isidore** asks him whether he is jealous merely of the glances she gets from admiring men, he responds, "Yes, jealous of those things like a tiger or, if you will, like a demon. My love wants you entirely for myself. It is sensitive to a smile, takes offense at a look that they can steal from you. And I spare no effort to cut off all approach by your admirers and to assure myself of possessing your heart and not allowing one bit of it to be stolen from me" (scene 6). Isidore warns him in vain that a heart is impossible to guarantee, especially if one tries to do so by force. Even **Dom Juan**, the legendary seducer who has enjoyed legions of women, is susceptible

to jealousy.  He admits to **Sganarelle** that he became interested in the young
bride he plans to abduct because he was jealous of the joy she shared with her
young husband.  This "dog in the manger" attitude does much to explain why
the rake can never be satisfied with the extent of his achievements.  He cannot
feel satiated as long as someone else is capable of feeling joy.  Thus, his
purported pursuit of pleasure is actually a sadistic crusade to inflict pain and
separation on others.  A spiritual variant of this jealousy causes him to try to
corrupt the pauper's ascetic serenity with gold.

    *Les Femmes savantes* shows us further examples of jealousy out of place.
**Armande** envies her sister's attachment to **Clitandre**, even though she herself
had rejected his suit.  She can only justify her emotions with the *précieuse*
doctrine that women are allowed to have a stable of male admirers that they can
keep forever in limbo, enjoying their attentions and giving no love in return.
The unreasonable nature of this jealousy is set in context by her aunt's dotty
logic.  When **Ariste** points out to **Bélise** that **Dorante** cannot be in love with her
because he is always insulting her, she retorts that it is merely the product of his
uncontrollable jealousy.

**Jeannot** (*La Comtesse d'Escarbagnas*).  This little lackey arrives to deliver a
message from **Thibaudier**.  He was played by the hireling Boulonnois.

**Jewelry**.  The ultimate **love** token in early modern intrigue comedy, jewelry is
also sometimes given as a reward for help, as in *Dépit amoureux*, where **Éraste**
rewards **Marinette** with a **ring** in exchange for her help in courting **Lucile**.  The
gift apparently came from the young man's own finger, although Marinette
hinted at it by mentioning a jeweler's shop nearby, perhaps just offstage or
visible in the painted scenery.  Lockets were also highly important, and the one
with a miniature **portrait** that **Sganarelle's wife** finds on the ground in *Le Cocu
imaginaire* leads to the protracted misunderstanding that fuels the plot.  She
praises the fine enamel work, the engraving, and even the scent of this "bijou,"
as well as the painting itself.  **Daphné** and **Éroxène** have lockets that are
suspiciously similar in *Mélicerte*.  In fact, they contain the **portrait** of the same
sweetheart, **Myrtil**.  Products of the workshop of the renowned **Atis**, they were
not gifts from the partner, since Myrtil rejects both women in favor of Mélicerte.
In the same play, **Lycarsis** refers to the fancy cage containing a sparrow Myrtil
gives to Mélicerte as a "jewel."  Jewelry is suggested as a remedy for illness in
*L'Amour médecin*, but it is a somewhat self–interested cure, for it came from a
goldsmith.  **Amphitryon** had hoped to spice up his homecoming after triumph
in battle by giving his wife a precious jewel containing five great diamonds that
had belonged to the vanquished Ptérélas.  However, **Jupiter** has magically
stolen it from a sealed box and already presented it to **Alcmène** before he slept
with her.  The pocket watch that **Léandre** sends to his beloved **Zerbinette** also
fails to reach its destination, but in this case it is stolen by the greedy **Scapin**.
However, Léandre's interest in jewelry is not in vain: a bracelet discovered late

in the play leads to the revelation that Zerbinette is really **Argante's** daughter, and therefore a suitable **marriage** partner.

    *See also* **Rings**.


**Jodelet (stage name of Julien Bedeau**, 1620?–1660). Comic actor attached for most of his life to the theater of the **Marais**, where he was famous for his white pancake makeup and his good–natured, clownish style. In some ways, Jodelet may be considered the last of the French *farceurs*, for his humor was forged in the company of **masked farce** specialists such as Turlupin and Gaultier–Garguille and harked back to medieval roots. He left the Marais only for a short time in the 1640s, under royal order. But by 1657, the Marais company had all but dissolved, so he and his brother sought a home in Molière's company soon after they came to **Paris**. Molière jumped at the chance to team up with the dominant comedian of the previous generation. As the **Marquis de Mascarille** and the Viscount de Jodelet, the two made a smashing impression in *Les Précieuses ridicules*. Molière also added a number of Jodelet's standard comedies to the **repertory**, including **Scarron's** *Jodelet maître et valet* and *Jodelet prince*. Though Jodelet died during the Lenten break of 1660, the plays were not removed from the repertory; it is interesting to speculate whether Molière himself took over the part of his elder predecessor.

    **Gros–René** refers to Jodelet in *Dépit amoureux* as a former suitor to **Marinette**. This is an interesting reference, since the play was written before Jodelet joined Molière's troupe. Was it an original element of the play when Molière first staged it in **Béziers**, referring off–handedly to a comic known all over France? Could it be a theatrical in–joke, referring to a previous liaison between him and the actress playing Marinette? Or was the line added after Jodelet had joined, but before the 1663 publication, perhaps in memory of the fallen colleague?


**Jodelet (*Les Précieuses ridicules*).** Jodelet is **Du Croisy's** valet and has been dressed up, like **Mascarille**, to pass for an aristocrat in order to play a trick on the affected young ladies, **Magdelon** and **Cathos**. His entrance must have been a treat for the public, uniting a great veteran with a very different new generation of actor in the person of Molière. During the scenes they share on stage (11 through 15), they act as perfect foils to one another. Very little divides them, except for Jodelet's inability to keep pace with Mascarille's break–neck dancing, due to the very real malady that was sapping his strength and would claim him during the Lenten interval before next year's theater season. Otherwise, the two strive to outdo each other in discussing fictional military glories, in showing off their war wounds, in speaking of fashionable outings and **pastimes**, and eventually in dodging blows from their masters as their clothes are torn off to reveal the unaccommodated men beneath. To the very end they parallel each other, for when the **musicians** demand **money** from Mascarille, he tells them, "Ask the Viscount," and when they turn to Jodelet, he responds, "Ask the Marquis!" Following Jodelet's death, this role, along with those in *Jodelet maître et valet* and *Jodelet prince*, probably devolved to veteran funny man

**René Du Parc**, who rejoined the troupe after Easter 1659. When Gros–René in turn passed on, the easiest reassignment might have been to shift them to the versatile actor **Hubert**, but in the absence of further discoveries, casting after 1664 remains speculative.

**Joly, Claude.** Parisian bookseller. He was part of the eight–printer coalition that published *L'École des femmes* and *La Critique de l'École des femmes*.

**Josse** (*L'Amour médecin*). Addressed as Monsieur Josse, this character is a **bourgeois** like **Sganarelle**, and a goldsmith by profession. He appears only in the first scene, where he advises Sganarelle to cure his daughter's mysterious illness by buying her a fine arrangement of diamonds, rubies, or emeralds to cheer her up. Sganarelle dismisses this advice as clearly self–interested. There was also a Josse in the entourage of the bigoted **Prince de Conti**.

**Jourdain, Madame** (*Le Bourgeois gentilhomme*). The frank and blustering character of Jourdain's wife was originally played by **André Hubert**. Her purpose in the play is twofold: to denounce the Mardi Gras madness of her husband's schemes and to support the suit of **Cléonte** for her daughter's hand. Both of these are tied to her fundamental **bourgeois** feelings. She wants a son–in–law who will not separate her from her daughter (and eventually, her grandchildren), who will not look down on the old neighborhood and its mercantile inhabitants, who will not try to impose shame on her as the **Sotenvilles** do on **George Dandin**. Her husband's outlandish behavior has already got the neighbors whispering, and she wants no such notoriety. As a member of the bourgeoisie, she is extremely skeptical, and a bit afraid, of the motives of the hereditary **nobility**. Their spendthrift habits go against generations of inherited frugality in her own family tree. She is more at home with homely wisdom and time–tested proverbs than with the wispy, abstract expressions used by courtiers. Like **Chrysale** in *Les Femmes savantes*, she is happily rooted in the material world and lacks curiosity about the immaterial issues of higher culture. When she thinks that her family honor has been threatened by the visits of **Dorante** and **Dorimène**, she is not reluctant to give vent to her feelings, despite the possibilities of reprisals by "her betters." In like manner, when she thinks that her daughter is about to be sent off to the edge of the earth in exchange for some noble trinkets and a lot of mumbo–jumbo, she clamps to her opinion like a mussel to its rock and refuses to allow the **marriage**. She even insults her daughter for going along with such a hare–brained plan and seems prepared to hold out forever, insisting that a mother's authority is as great as a father's, until she finally realizes the nature of the ruse and plays along. This lady is a far more likeable battle–axe than Hubert's other harridans, such as **Madame Pernelle**, **Philaminte**, and **Madame de Sotenville**.

**Jourdain, Monsieur** (*Le Bourgeois gentilhomme*). Certainly one of the most famous roles in Molière's theater and in his personal career, the would–be gentleman is also a deceptively difficult role, like that of **Harpagon**. Jourdain seems so utterly stupid in most situations that it is all too easy to play him as Jean Meyer did, as a gigantic baby. Yet Jourdain's intellect, for all its flaws, is not that of an ordinary child. It has its moments of acuity and insight. Despite his apparent propensity to wear any silly cut of cloth the **tailor** slaps together for him, he has such a sharp eye that he realizes the man has purloined some of his own material to make himself a coat. Moreover, Jourdain's brain is eminently corruptible. His mind is one that has been warped by its own logical distortions. As with **Arnolphe**, the drive for superiority is important, and the desire to forget or condeal his ancestors and their work is significant. While underemphasizing the strategic importance of Jourdain's usurpation, Jules Brody is right to correct Meyer's image of an infantile character, for he does clearly seek in his own way to be "one of the beautiful people." The whole problem is that, even with the help of able teachers, Jourdain is incapable of discerning beauty. Some people have a "tin ear," but it may be said that all of Jourdain's senses are of tin. His judgment is, as the **Music Teacher** notes, in his purse, but one should add "only in his purse." It is true that he has come to patronize the elegant arts, but only because he got it into his head that these things were necessary for him to be what he wanted to be. He places no value on beauty or love for its own sake or for any measurable physical good that it can procure for him. Jourdain cannot exchange money for beauty, as he wishes to do in all his transactions, but only be a donor, albeit unwillingly.

Along with his distorted logic, Jourdain resembles Molière's other maniacs in numerous ways. He is unable to discipline or control his **servants**, which in this case is a happy circumstance. His erotic impulses are channeled toward an unattainable ideal, in mockery of the very real opportunities and responsibilities that he tries to evade. He is incapable of true communication, speaking mainly to himself or to the hired folk he uses as sounding boards. Indeed, he is never more comfortable than when babbling away in an exotic tongue he neither speaks nor understands. He is a poltroon who rails away at his tailor, sending him in effigy to the sickbed, to the grave, to the devil in hell, and then wilting away with a pitiful, "Ah, there you are! I was just about to get angry at you" (II, 5). He is conspiratorial and suspicious, tending to reject common wisdom simply because it is common. His fantasies come to constitute a kind of parallel world where he lives alone; for other people become merely the shadows he projects onto them. Other humans, even his own flesh and blood, are reduced to the status of pawns in his battle to achieve an ultimate form of transformation. If he is willing to employ Dorante as a pimp to obtain a *marquise* for him, if he is willing to trade his daughter to a dimwit or an animal to make her a *marquise*, it is because his ease has focused his desire on a single object. "I have money enough for my daughter," he explains (more lucidly than one may wish to admit), adding, "The only thing I need is honor, and I want to make her a *marquise*" (III, 12). Dimly aware of this isolation, he is obsessed with the fragility of his world of desire and will go to almost any expense to defend it. In a way, he already is a *mamamouchi*, a chimerical creature only his imagination can form, and by acceding to the title, he is only acquiring what he already has, just as he speaks prose without realizing it.

Is Jourdain the ultimate portrait of a rising middle class that seeks total domination and non–contingency as its goal? One cannot completely dismiss this troubling vision conjured by the richly associative brush strokes of the dramatist. But if he represents an incipient tycoon, an early modern Daddy Warbucks, a baroque General Bullmoose, it is in the manner of a photographic negative, for Jourdain is empty of the very traits required for bourgeois hegemony. He has failed as a husband, father, businessman, singer, dancer, fencer, writer, seducer, and manipulator. Moreover, unlike **Dom Juan** or **Tartuffe**, he cannot even convince anyone that he is capable of success. He is a monster of **Nature**, of the kind that Nature herself produces from time to time for unknown reasons. Yet even as the spectator laughs at this product of weird evolution, so freakish and impotent that he seems destined to oblivion, he cannot fail to reflect that perhaps one century's *avorton* is the next century's successful mutation, provided the environment welcomes it.

**Judges**. In general, Molière is content to represent the judicial world through the lesser figures of **notaries** and **policemen**, but in *Le Sicilien*, he creates a magistrate or "senator" whom **Dom Pèdre** consults in his search for justice in the elopement of **Isidore**. However, the legislator can speak of nothing but the masquerade he has organized. As in the medieval masterpiece *La Farce de Maistre Pierre Pathelin* or in **Racine's** *Les Plaideurs*, the judge and the plaintiffs cannot manage to stay on the same topic.

**Julie** (*La Comtesse d'Escarbagnas*). This role, played by **Mlle. Beauval**, is more witty than sentimental, and her lines to her lover, the **Viscount**, and to her hostess, the **Countess**, are likely to contain a clever satirical edge in either case. In the absence of a comical **servant**, it is she who assumes the place of sardonic commentator on the dialogue.

**Julie** (*Monsieur de Pourceaugnac*). Ample evidence exists to show that **Mlle. de Brie** was cast as **Éraste's** sweetheart in this three–act **comedy–ballet**. She has relatively little to say in the opening scenes, refusing to oblige her lover with a full–blown **avowal**, and promising to enter a **convent** rather than follow her father's instructions to marry **Pourceaugnac**. Her part only becomes interesting in the second act, where she literally throws herself at the visitor in a feigned fit of lust. She smothers him with tender compliments and kisses and insists on holding his hand, much to the consternation of her father, who has just had an icy meeting with Pourceaugnac and believes him to be infected with syphilis. Neither the characters onstage nor the audience are prepared for this amorous onslaught, which must have been doubly hilarious coming from the normally reserved Mlle. de Brie. Éraste brings her back to her father in the third act, for she has supposedly run away to be with her dear Limousin. She continues to act infatuated as her father arranges a match with Éraste, whom she tells that she is marrying with the greatest reluctance. This travesty succeeds so well that she not only gets the husband she wishes, but a much bigger dowry, to boot.

**Julien** (*Les Femmes savantes*). **Vadius's** valet bursts in to deliver his master's incriminating **letter** in the fourth act. When **Philaminte** reproaches him for entering directly, instead of having himself announced through one of her **servants**, he sarcastically replies, "I'll remember to note that in my book." It is not only a witty rejoinder, but a suggestion by Molière that even the domestics of self–styled intellectuals cannot wait to get into print. The role may have been taken by **Beauval** or a hireling.

**Jupiter** (*Amphitryon*). In an attempt to escape from the "prison of grandeur" and to taste the untainted and spicy fruits of first **love**, the king of the gods has taken the form of the Theban general **Amphitryon** and slept with his bride **Alcmène**. Their delicious tryst is just coming to an end as the play opens, with **Night** lengthening her stay so as to give the lovers extra time and cover Jupiter's retreat. For someone who has taken such liberties, Jupiter has strange scruples, and he wishes to owe Alcmène's enthusiasm strictly to his own powers and not in the slightest to her sense of wifely duty. She has no trouble at all uniting the two concepts, since she is unconscious of any wrongdoing. But he preaches on at length about how duty destroys the sincerity of love, revealing himself to be something of a divine **Alceste** in his hunger for total domination. She makes fun of this blasphemous thinking and enjoys him as if he were her lawful mate. He has failed to take into account that he must also inherit the spite she will feel for Amphitryon when he returns home. He is on the defensive in their second conversation, where she calls him a monster, little knowing how accurate she really is. Once again, Jupiter spews casuistry, blaming all the bad things on the husband in Amphitryon and all the good things on the lover he has chosen to be. When she condemns this "frivolous subtlety," he goes into an even more hypocritical act, pronouncing **Tartuffe**–like self–abasement. This behavior would be entirely shameful, if it were not for the fact that Jupiter is likely to derive less good from it than his poor double Amphitryon. By preserving the unsullied pleasure of his love, he ironically takes away some of the shame he has left for the mortal, if only the general is able to pick up where he left off. Both males are ultimately lucky that Alcmène's inherent kindness and lack of resolve contribute more to Jupiter's pardon than any real sentiment of forgiveness for the offenses received. Jupiter's nonchalant appearance in Act III, where he coolly shakes off Amphitryon's hot–headed threats, recalls **Dom Juan's** chilly civility in its imperviousness to human blame or responsibility. The only person who can respond sensibly to his thundering promises of a heroic heir in the person of **Hercules** and riches galore for the foster father is the sarcastic **Sosie**, who saw from the very beginning of the play that gods were subject to all human foibles. He is only the person without any "éclat" who can ultimately cut to the truth of the matter, shaking off the stupefaction caused by the gods' baroque machinery and optical trickery. If one reads the play as an allegory of **Louis XIV's** conquest of **Madame de Montespan**, the King emerges as an ambiguous figure at the very least. But considering the reality of the royal seduction, where la Montespan was probably much more adept at laying traps for the monarch than he for her, one can see that disclaimers could come quite easily that would dismiss the play as merely a flight of fantasy, despite the famous line to the effect that sharing with a king entails no shame. In view of the role in *Psyché*, it is possible that **Du Croisy** played Jove in this play as well.

**Jupiter** (*Psyché*). The king of the gods, played by **Du Croisy**, appears only in the final scene of the play, where he stills **Venus** and gives the heroine to **Cupid** as a bride.

**Juvenal.** The great Roman satirist of the first and second centuries is mentioned by the **Philosophy Teacher** in *Le Bourgeois gentilhomme*, who will copy his works, responding in print to the punishment the other teachers have inflicted on his person.

# K

**King's Troupe** (*Troupe du Roi*). This was one of the titles originally claimed by the troupe of the Hôtel de Bourgogne, and even after the official royal sponsorship of Molière's troupe in 1665, the senior company much resented its use (or, in their point of view, usurpation) by the newcomers. Molière's group did distinguish themselves from the Bourguignons by using the formula: Troupe du Roi au Palais–Royal.

# L

**La Bruyère, Jean de** (1645–1696). Jean de La Bruyère was the first child of a solidly **bourgeois** Parisian family. Little is known with certainty about his early years. He received a law degree from the University of Orléans in 1665 and eight years later, probably with the help of an inheritance from his uncle, purchased the post of Trésorier Général de France for Caen, which provided him with both an annual income and a title. His installation in this office was the occasion of La Bruyère's only visit to Caen.

On the recommendation of **Bossuet**, he was named tutor to the Duc de Bourbon, the grandson of the **Prince de Condé**. The Condé household, into which La Bruyère now moved, was one of the grandest in France and must also have been among the most disagreeable. Saint–Simon described the young duke's father as a "fils dénaturé, cruel père, mari terrible, maître détestable, sans amitié, sans amis." To judge from La Bruyère's letters to his charge's grandfather, the young duke was a less than dedicated student. After the marriage in 1685 of the Duc de Bourbon and Mademoiselle de Nantes, daughter of **Louis XIV** and **Madame de Montespan,** and the death of the Prince de Condé in 1686, La Bruyère's duties as tutor came to an end, but he was to remain attached to the Condé family as a *gentilhomme ordinaire* at Chantilly, where he lived and attended to the chateau's library. He had resigned his post in Caen just before Condé's death. With the support of the party of the Ancients, **Boileau–Despréaux, Bossuet,** and **Racine** among them, La Bruyère was elected to the **Académie Française** in 1693. On the evening of May 10, 1696, he was stricken by an attack of apoplexy and died at the Condé residence in **Versailles**.

La Bruyère is recognized today for one major work, *Les caractères ou les moeurs de ce siècle,* which he appended to his translation from the **Greek** of the *Characters* of Theophrastus. Between 1688 and 1694, he published eight editions of his book. A posthumous ninth edition, which the author himself undoubtedly reviewed and modified before his death, appeared in 1696. The first edition of the *Caractères* included 420 remarks. By the eighth edition of 1694, this number had grown to 1,120. The fragmentary, discontinuous form of the *Caractères* lent itself to changes and accretions, and the nature of those has been the source of much scholarly debate. La Bruyère's book is divided into sixteen chapters treating a wide array of subjects, such as personal merit, the city, the **court**, the King, men, fashion, and free thinkers. It is composed of aphoristic statements not unlike the maxims of La Rochefoucauld, somewhat longer reflections on aspects of the human condition, and individual **portraits** that may or may not be based on real people. Despite the author's insistence that he intended to "peindre les hommes en général," keys identifying various of La Bruyère's characters circulated freely among the work's readers.

La Bruyère knew and admired Molière's theater. In the first chapter of the *Caractères*, "Des ouvrages de l'esprit," he compares Molière to **Terence**. If the great French playwright's style was less pure and elegant than that of his Roman predecessor, Molière's jokes, his portrayal of manners, and his sharp eye for the ridiculous were without peer. What a brilliant author one could create, La Bruyère opines, by combining the two. Like other writers in the French *moraliste* tradition, including Molière, La Bruyère is a keen observer of humankind. He claims to do nothing more in his work than return to the public what it has loaned him by way of subject matter. La Bruyère and Molière have a similar goal for their writing: that it will lead readers and audiences to see their own faults and, as the moralist says in the preface to his *Caractères*, "s'en corriger."

Not by inclination a reformer, La Bruyère accepted and benefited from the social and political order of his day. The chapter "Du souverain ou de la république" shows its author to be a convinced monarchist who respects Louis XIV and even defends his revocation of the Edict of Nantes. Class distinctions and social hierarchies do not in themselves trouble La Bruyère. However, as incisive an observer as he cannot but see that much is amiss. Without explicitly contesting the principles underlying seventeenth–century French society, the *Caractères* offer a penetrating, often harsh critique of social and political realities. The royal court, for example, makes slaves of its inhabitants by filling their lives with superficial pleasures and spectacles, but the "applaudissements aux théâtres de Molière et d'Arlequin" only cover up the courtiers' profound unhappiness ("De la cour" 63). If he had to choose between the empty showiness of the life of society's great men and women and the solidity of the people, La Bruyère would not hesitate: "Je veux être peuple," he declares ("Des grands" 25). One of the longest passages in the *Caractères* depicts war as a human perversity ("Des jugements" 119), and La Bruyère, in a famous remark, movingly portrays **peasants** reduced to the state of wild **animals** ("De l'homme" 128). Why, he asks, ought they not have bread from the grain that they themselves have sowed?

La Bruyère's vivid, theatrical portraits of individuals distinguish him from moralist writers like La Rochefoucauld and Nicole. La Bruyère tries to delve beyond the surface of human **masks** and find the essence of a character. This would permit him to define the individual. What he discovers, though, is that human beings have no fixed, determined character that makes sense of all they are and do ("De l'homme" 147). So he draws his characters as he observes them: empty, changing, never at rest, always in motion. At times, they become automatons, playing out their roles mindlessly, mechanically. Day after day, Narcisse gets up in the morning, spends hours dressing, attends Mass, meets his friends, plays games, reads, goes to bed, wakes up to start all over again. Then in a final meaningless gesture no different from all the others, he dies ("De la ville" 12). Cimon and Clitandre chase about trying to impress everyone with their importance to the state. They are always on the run, but to slow them down would be destructive, for it would break the rhythm of the mechanism that keeps them on the move: "vous démonteriez leur machine" ("De la cour" 19). The animation of many of La Bruyère's characters places them in the line of descent from some of Molière's great creations.

Editors have called attention to many references in the *Caractères* to Molière. Timon, La Bruyère's **misanthrope**, is a direct response to **Alceste** but in some ways resembles **Philinte** more closely. Although he has no use for other people, Timon is careful always to be **polite** and formal in his relations with them ("De l'homme" 155). His misanthropy is less blatant, more refined than Alceste's. A casual observer might well not detect that Timon is a misanthrope. Among the most subtle **portraits** in the *Caractères* is that of Onuphre, who is explicitly a version of **Tartuffe** ("De la mode" 24). That Onuphre would never talk about his hair–shirt and his scourge, as Tartuffe does in his entrance line, signals La Bruyère's intention to refashion and improve upon one of Molière's greatest comic figures. So clever is Onuphre in his imitation of piety — La Bruyère calls it a perfect imitation — that it is hard to distinguish Onuphre's brand of *fausse dévotion* from real devoutness.

La Bruyère concludes the *Caractères* with the declaration that he will be surprised if readers do not appreciate his little book — and just as surprised if they do.

*Michael S. Koppisch*

**Lackeys (*Le Sicilien*).** These two **servants** have no lines and appear only in scene 2 to hold torches for the serenade offered by **Adraste** to **Isidore**. They were probably played by hirelings or employees of the theater.

**Lady's Maid or *Suivante*.** The lady's maid in seventeenth–century France could also be called a lady's companion, since she occupied a unique echelon in the system of household **servants**. She was considered to be above other women who worked in the house and to be uniquely attached to the woman she served. Her dress was supposed to be nearly equal to that of her lady, and she would often eat and associate closely with her, which ordinary servants were forbidden from doing. Thus, the *suivante* was a kind of **bourgeois** equivalent of the aristocratic lady–in–waiting. She was not considered to be a strict chaperone, like the Spanish duenna, but rather someone to share in the pleasures of social life. Because of this, the institution of the lady's maid was harshly criticized by those opposed to independence for young women.

In Molière's works, the lady's maid first appears as an unnamed character in *Sganarelle*, where she is attached to **Célie**. This is a very conventional and arid *confidante* role, except for an interesting tirade on the physical joys of **marriage**. The maid is a widow, whose late husband Martin kept the conjugal bed so warm that she needed no fire in winter. Combining pathos with bathos, the maid declares that there are innumerable comforts provided by a husband in the house, if nothing more than to say "God bless you!" when his wife sneezes. Quoting a pedant, she says that women are like ivy and collapse as soon as their men (trees) are taken away.

In *L'École des maris*, **Lisette** is described as a lady's maid to **Léonor**. **Sganarelle** detests this practice, preferring to have his ward, **Isabelle**, sleep with an old *duenna* called Lucrèce, who does not appear in the play, but whose name evokes rigid chastity. Lisette is capable of giving just the type of uppity, worldly advice that Sganarelle wishes to stifle.

**La Feuillade, François, vicomte d'Aubusson, later marquis and duc de** (ca. 1625–1691). This ostentatious courtier became a military hero thanks to his actions in the battle of St. Gothard in 1664. He personally formed an expeditionary corps to assist the Venetians at Candia in Crete in 1668–1672, but the mission failed to prevent **Turkish** takeover of the island. As a reward for his valor, his fief was erected into a duchy upon his return. He ascended further to the rank of **Marshal of France** in 1675. **Grimarest** relates in an anecdote that this fashion–conscious courtier was so mad at Molière because of the naughty jokes in *L'École des femmes* that he mutilated the playwright's face in an ambush. This seems unlikely, however, since the real viscount was one of Molière's patrons, having ordered a private performance listed in **La Grange's** register. Another late report, by the poet **Jean–Baptiste Rousseau**, that Molière made references to La Feuillade in speeches by **Monsieur de Sotenville**, must be considered very dubious, given that Sotenville is clothed in a nearly medieval outfit, while the marquis was one of the court's showiest and most modern dressers. Jean–Baptiste Rousseau was not even born when the play premiered.

**La Flèche** (*L'Avare*). Valet to **Harpagon's** son, **Cléante**, La Flèche is not as direct as **Maître Jacques** in criticizing his superior, for when he is caught muttering, "A plague on misers!" he deftly explains that he was only speaking to his hat. Other clever lines include the observation that it doesn't matter to the **servants** whether Harpagon has **money** or not, since they never see it. After the hilarious search scene in Act I, when Harpagon pays rather too much attention to the contents of the valet's pants, La Flèche helps Cléante try to arrange a loan, but runs away soon after the lender turns out to be Harpagon. He reappears toward the end of Act IV to announce to Cléante that he has just stolen the strongbox full of gold, which the son eventually returns to his father in exchange for permission to marry **Mariane**. La Flèche's pre–emptive justification for the crime resembles the Jesuitical defense of Jean of Alba discussed in **Pascal's**

sixth *Provincial Letter.* Harpagon's reference to La Flèche as a "limping dog" probably means the role was taken by Molière's brother–in–law, **Louis Béjart**.

**La Fontaine, Jean de** (1621–1695). Closely associated with the disgraced **Fouquet** and considered something of a freethinker in his own right, the composer of the *Fables* was probably known to Molière by the time of *Les Fâcheux*. Anecdotes generated mainly during the eighteenth and nineteenth centuries often insist that they were close associates in **libertine** gatherings at the **White Cross Tavern** or at Molière's cottage in **Auteuil**. In reality, there is a remarkable lack of evidence of such association on either side. La Fontaine did include an account of the **Grand Divertissement Royal de Versailles** in one of his later *Contes* (*Tales*), and both authors shared an obvious fascination with **animal** metaphors often drawn from **peasant** life and language. According to Brienne, Molière took part in a mock trial that weighed the merits of La Fontaine's tale of "La Joconde" against Bouillon's, finding in favor of the former. Molière and La Fontaine shared an ambiguous attitude to **Louis XIV**, looking to the monarch as a source of greatness and a focus for an often chaotic society, while at the same time harboring a fundamental distrust of authority and its misuses. Molière includes an implicit reference to the popularity of the *Fables* in *Le Malade imaginaire*, where he has little **Louison** offer to recite "The Crow and the Fox" to her father. Perhaps Molière enjoyed similar recitations from his own daughter. The playwright almost certainly consulted La Fontaine's popular novel, *Les Amours de Psyché et de Cupidon*, as he worked on his version of the myth. At the time of the Revolution, the government ordered the exhumation of the bones of both authors, who were thought to be buried in the Cimetière Saint–Joseph. However, the bones obtained were in neither case a complete set, nor were they of the correct age and sex to belong to the writers. Nevertheless, the false remains were later entombed in the Père–Lachaise Cemetery, where many today mistake them to be genuine.

**La Grange, Charles Varlet de** (ca. 1635–1692). The young actor who from Easter of 1659 on played most of the lover roles in Molière's comedies. He married **Marie Raguenau**, an actress specializing in **servant** roles. It was he who kept the invaluable register of receipts that gives us an intimate glance into the finances, **repertory**, and other affairs of the troupe. Short of stature, but endowed with liveliness, grace, and a strong voice, he was by all accounts a paragon of **politeness** and charm. This surely influenced the most well known part that Molière created for him, that of **Dom Juan**. La Grange's aptitude for such a major role was probably suggested by his success in repertory with that of Dorante in **Pierre Corneille's** *Le Menteur* (*The Liar*). Other roles included the many **Valères** and **Clitandres** of Molière's various plays, **Horace** in *L'École des femmes*, **Lycaste** in *Le Mariage forcé*, **Euryale** in *La Princesse d'Élide*, **Cléonte** in *Le Bourgeois gentilhomme*, **Philinte** in *Le Misanthrope*, **Coridon** in *Pastorale comique*, **Acante** in *Mélicerte*, **Adraste** in *Le Sicilien*, either **Agénor** or **Cléomène** (probably the latter) in *Psyché*, and the **Viscount** in

*La Comtesse d'Escarbagnas*. He was the original **Éraste** of *Les Fâcheux*, but was replaced for two months in that role by his colleague **Du Croisy** when he became sick with a raging fever. He was cast in that role again in *Monsieur de Pourceaugnac*. He played under his own name in *Les Précieuses ridicules* and *L'Impromptu de Versailles*. Following Molière's death, he assumed the leadership of the troupe, even though the comedian Rosimond was hired to take many of Molière's roles. He continued to guide his colleagues as they were fused into the company of the Hôtel Guénégaud and later the **Comédie–Française**. Along with the mysterious **Vivot**, he prepared the 1682 collected edition of the playwright's works and wrote the brief biographical introduction that serves as the most authoritative summary of Molière's career by a contemporary.

**La Grange** (*Les Précieuses ridicules*). La Grange is the more active of the spurned **bourgeois** suitors in the play. He takes the rejection more to heart, delivering a scathing analysis of the girls' warped values of *préciosité*. It is he who devises the **disguises** for the two valets. He also seems to take the lead in stripping them and humiliating them and the girls in the denouement. The title of "seigneur" by which **Du Croisy** addresses him, perhaps ironically, at the beginning of the play, indicates that he is a property owner, though this is obviously not enough to deserve the girls' respect.

**La Grange** (*L'Impromptu de Versailles*). La Grange's role in both the frame play and the play–within–the–play is remarkably restrained. He is one of the quieter members of the cast. Assigned the role of an auxiliary ridiculous marquis, Molière gives him almost no instructions and pays much more attention to **Brécourt's** far more important role.

**La Meilleraye, Charles de la Porte, duc de** (1602–1664). Courtier before whom the **Dufresne**–Molière troupe performed at **Nantes** in 1648. Perhaps coincidentally, one of the duke's lackeys was apprenticed to Molière's father in the furniture trade. This may have been done not so much to provide a new career for the lackey as to train him to care for the duke's household property. Several noblemen seem to have sent apprentices to **Jean Poquelin** for this purpose. It testifies to his stature as royal upholsterer, an expert in the acquisition, care, and moving of fine furnishings. La Meilleraye was something of a self–made man. Made Grand Master of the Artillery in 1635, he became General of the Army of Poitou during the **Fronde** revolts and took **Bordeaux** for the royal party. This, again, may have been of some aid to the troupe. Ugly and disagreeable in his person, he was nevertheless a major figure at **court**. He achieved the rare rank of duke and peer of the realm by royal letter in 1663 and his son became Duke of Mazarin as a result of his **marriage** with Hortense Mancini.

**La Merluche** (*L'Avare*). This lackey appears in the preparations for the feast in Act III and, with **Brindavoine**, complains about the sorry state of his clothes, only to be told to make sure that the holes are facing the wall, so that the guests will not notice.

**Lamoignon, Guillaume de** (1617–1677). First President of the **Parlement** of Paris and member of the **Company of the Holy Sacrament**, this jurist presided over the trial of **Fouquet**, irritating the monarch by returning a sentence of life imprisonment instead of death. He also played a role in the *Tartuffe* affair, signing a legal ban on the public performance of *L'Imposteur* in his jurisdiction (August 6, 1667). This would be over–ridden by royal decree. After 1666, **Boileau** became increasingly involved in Lamoignon's intellectual circle.

**La Montagne** (*Les Fâcheux*). This valet is a complacent commentator on the play's sometimes feverish action. He becomes a pest himself when he fusses over his master **Éraste**, straightening his tie, touching up his hair, and dusting his jacket at inopportune times. The role was almost certainly conceived for **Du Parc**, himself a mountain of a man.

**La Mothe Le Vayer, François de** (1588–1672). Trained as a jurist, this Parisian intellectual served as tutor to the young **Louis XIV** from 1652 to 1660. During this time of association with the **court**, he dampened his skeptical views that had stood out more prominently earlier in his career, when he was associated with Richelieu. He did not cease to take controversial stands, however, and in particular took up an anti–**Jansenist** position in theological matters. His son seems to have been a particular friend and perhaps a schoolmate of Molière. The young abbé La Mothe was also a friend of **Boileau**, who in 1664 adressed his fourth satire ("On Folly") to him. When this son died, Molière addressed to the father a poignant sonnet that, in marked contrast to the fashionable type of Stoical lament made popular by Malherbe, justifies the tears of the bereaved, both on human and philosophical grounds. The elder La Mothe's *Prose chagrine* may have lent elements to *raisonneurs* such as **Ariste** in *L'École des maris*. One also finds many common elements among his rather disparate **philosophical** writings. It may well have been more through La Mothe than through personal contact that Molière knew of the ideas of Gassendi. Even in early life, La Mothe wrote under other identities, and it is extremely possible that he is responsible for some of the anonymous pro–Molière literature associated with the plays, as Robert McBride has recently argued, most convincingly, in regard to the *Lettre sur l'Imposteur*.

**Languages**. Molière's comedy is truly a multilingual realm. Besides **Latin**, which was a stock necessity for pedants and **doctors**, and **Italian**, which was still the predominant musical idiom in the seventeenth century, the playwright shows an awareness of many other tongues. His own Latin and Italian were good enough to allow him to translate from the original, as well as to add to parts in his plays and *comédies–ballets*. Though no Hellenist like **Racine**, he injects some **Greek** into the medical and **philosophical** language of his scholars. He mentions **German** and **English** and has some characters converse in Dutch and **Swiss** dialects or accents. His borrowings from Alarcon, Tirso de Molina, and Moreto suggest at least some knowledge of **Spanish**, and characters also speak in the **Gascon** patois of the southwest borders. Even farther afield, a song in *Le Sicilien* and the **Turkish** ceremony in *Le Bourgeois gentilhomme* demonstrate a familiarity with the **Sabir** trade language of the Levant. Molière of course never traveled that far east, but his friend **Bernier** certainly did, and may have advised him in writing those scenes. We know that the chevalier d'Arvieux, another Turkish expert, was consulted for the play. However, the "Turkish" (as opposed to Sabir) words in the text seem to be imitated from **Rotrou** or simply fabricated. When **Monsieur Jourdain** points out that the translation does not seem to match the gibberish very well in length, **Covielle**, **disguised** as an interpreter, replies, "Yes, the Turkish language is like that; it says much in few words" (IV, 4). In a scene reminiscent of Panurge in **Rabelais's** *Pantagruel*, **Pancrace** of *Le Mariage forcé* mentions eleven different languages in trying to find a common idiom to discuss **Sganarelle's** complaint. Among them are Hebrew, Arabic, Syriac (presumably Aramaic), and Turkish.

There is much discussion of language in the plays dealing with *préciosité*, whose affectations verged on the creation of a separate language for "**polite**" society. **Cathos** and **Magdelon** thus create much confusion by referring to simple objects like mirrors by indirect wording. **Philaminte** and her circle make their pretensions quite explicit, claiming that by controlling words, they will control society. They run into the same communication problems with the cook **Martine**, whose attitude to language is comically expressed when she says, "Let words clash or let them get along together ... what does it matter as long as one is understood?" At the same time, the members of her circle seek to bring language to a new level of abstraction, cutting away "all those nasty syllables that make the finest words seem scandalous." Once again the issue of proper language comes up between the **Countess of Escarbagnas** and her **servants**, who are astonished when she appears to tell them to throw a piece of clothing in the toilet. Molière implicitly favors the great French Classical goal of clarity, which allows that language can be elegant, but demands that it be transparent to speaker and listener.

Of course, as a great gestural comedian, Molière was also quite familiar with various forms of "body language," and in *Le Sicilien* **Adraste** gives a moving description of how he and **Isidore** have communicated for months without being able to speak to each other, leading **Hali** to comment, "But in **love** there are many ways of speaking, and it seems to me that your eyes and hers having been saying much to each other for nearly two months now" (scene 2).

**La Ramée** (*Dom Juan*). Described in different versions as a *bretteur* or a *spadassin*, this hired thug alerts **Dom Juan** to the approach of his pursuers at the end of Act II.

**La Rapière** (*Dépit amoureux*). Described as a *bretteur* or thug, he arrives to warn **Valère** of the **duel** that awaits him at **Albert's** house and offers his services. Valère wisely declines when he learns of La Rapière's criminal connections.

**La Reynie, Nicolas–Gabriel de** (1625–1709). As **Louis XIV's** lieutenant of **police**, this **Limousin** nobleman exercised considerable powers over the population from 1667 onward, including perhaps censorship. He owned one of the few copies of the 1682 *Dom Juan* text that was not defaced by paper strips over the bolder passages.

**Larissa**. The chief town of the rural Vale of **Tempe** in ancient **Greece**, setting for *Mélicerte*.

**Larivey, Pierre [Giunto] de** (1540–1619). This great Renaissance humanist and translator influenced Molière not only through his own well–known comedy, *Les Esprits* (*The Ghosts*), but through versions of **Italian** works, such as Luigi Pasqualigo's *Fedele*.

**La Rivière** (*Les Fâcheux*). In Act III, scene 5, La Rivière, who is attached to **Éraste**, overhears **Damis** plotting to ambush his master and falls upon him with several companions, only to be routed by Éraste himself, who seizes the chance to come to the aid of the only man separating him from **Orphise**.

**La Rochefoucauld, François duc de** (1619–1680). This aristocrat had immersed himself in the swashbuckling intrigues of the Fronde revolts between 1648 and 1652, only to be wounded and disgraced as a result of having chosen the wrong side. His exile from the **court** did not prevent him from becoming a regular fixture at several **Paris** salons, especially that of Mme. de Sablé, where he cultivated a long–term literary and personal friendship with Mme. de La Fayette, whose novels bear his influence. The *Mémoires* he wrote to clarify his role in the Fronde elicited less interest than his popular *Maximes*, which went through numerous editions. These pithy and cynical aphorisms may seem at face value to have little to do with Molière, but on closer examination one finds that the spirit of the *Maximes* constantly dovetails with that of the great comedies in intriguing ways. Both stem from an irresistible urge to correct society, while at the same time recognizing the virtual impossibility of changing human nature on an individual or collective level. In this fundamental contradiction and its vast ramifications in various human situations lie the similarity of the two authors, each of whom was far too proud to borrow more directly from the other.

**Late Nineteenth–Century Criticism** (1850–1914). One of the trends to emerge from the second half of the nineteenth century was an extended critical debate over the moral message in Molière's theater. That such a message should even be sought was largely a product of the philosophy of positivism that flourished following Auguste Comte's philosophy teachings a decade earlier (1830–1842). Comte encouraged a wave of thinking that refocused attention on societies, as opposed to individuals and historical movements, and this in turn invited re–evaluation of Classical writers in terms of their relationship to the society as a whole. Thus, C.–J. Jeannel in 1867 published his *La Morale de Molière*, establishing the playwright as the spokesman for a broad–based message of bourgeois common sense that would be attached to the collective rise of the middle class, rather than the political goal of a revolution. This line of thinking was seconded by Émile Faguet and received great impetus from the launching of the Third Republic in 1872. While refuting the kind of revolutionary spirit that had animated the Paris Commune during the Franco–Prussian War, the new republic actively sought Classical authors associated with the rise of the middle class and with a solidly laic worldview. Molière, along with such colleagues as **Boileau** and **La Fontaine**, seemed to fit this need perfectly; Ralph Albanese has recently shown how their works became canonical in the new national school system organized by the Third Republic.

However, the other major movement that resulted from the war, the Catholic Revival, had diametically opposed views concerning the country's literary heritage and Molière in particular. The effort to discredit Molière as a moral voice for his class was led by Louis Veuillot, a rabid ultra–Catholic, whose *Molière and Bourdaloue*, appearing in 1877, sought to repaint the dramatist with the dark stain of immorality. Veuillot was seconded by the more influential Ferdinand Brunetière, who from 1879 on became a leading intellectual of the Revival. Rather than engaging Molière directly on the field of good and evil, Brunetière chose the easier and less controversial approach of searching for anticlericalism in the plays and extending any evidence over his writing career in general. But in doing so, Brunetière invited a powerful counterattack and it came from Raoul Allier and A. Rebelliau, who shortly after the turn of the century made in–depth studies of the "cabale des dévots" and the more active and insidious steps taken by religious extremists of the seventeenth century to destroy Molière and his ilk.

Much of this discussion of Molière's morality and moral message had distracted attention from the plays as artworks. By 1900, corrective measures were under way in the critical community. Gustave Larroumet's study of *La Comédie de Molière* in 1903 promised to put the canon in better perspective, but failed due to its neo–Romantic viewpoint and excessive reliance on dubious anecdotes. Abel Lefranc's 1904 series of lectures succeeded much better by promoting a standpoint of subjectivism that heralded North American New Criticism by detaching literature from the social framework and emphasizing the coherence of individual texts. Gustave Lanson became the great synthesizer of the Belle Époque period and set the tone for French Classical studies well into the twentieth century. Although originally a student of Brunetière with interests rooted in religious discourse, he developed a method of artistic analysis applicable to nearly all writers. As his own inclinations shifted toward the democratic, laic stance, he came to advocate the study of literary history as a discipline, subject to both the old–fashioned academic rigor of philology and Comtean scientific inquiry. His official consecration of Molière into French literary history, along a line of compromise owing to the traditions of **Boileau**,

**Voltaire, Sainte–Beuve,** and the positivists, made an authoritative statement in the years just prior to World War I.

As this interpretive debate raged during the late nineteenth century, a parallel movement was taking place on a different footing. Research into the actual facts of Molière's life and theater had been greatly accelerated by the work of Louis Beffara, a police official whose *Dissertation sur J.–B. Poquelin–Molière*, breaking new ground in 1821, had launched a vogue of biographical and archival studies. Anaïs Bazin followed this with an important revision in 1851, leading to Eudore Soulié's even more revealing *Recherches sur Molière et sur sa famille* in 1863. This new intellectual hobby found a collective outlet with the founding of the periodical *Le Moliériste* by Georges Monval in 1879. For a decade, its pages would be full of discoveries, ranging from the most pertinent to the most trivial, and biographically based, arguments about every facet of the author's existence. This intense interest coincided with the greatest edition of the author's works since the mid–eighteenth century, and one on which modern scholarship today still largely rests. Begun by Soulié and completed by Eugène Despois and Paul Mesnard between 1873 and 1889, this was the monumental Grands Écrivains edition of the complete works of Molière, capped by an entire volume on philological and linguistic matters and an immense bibliography. But for a few small items that have arisen since then relative to editorial matters, it still stands as the equivalent of a Varioriem Molière. It incorporated all that was important out of the *Moliériste* activity and provided text that resituated all the plays within the ken of the average Frenchman to the extent then permitted by print. Even before Lanson's critical blessing, it turned Molière into an enduring cultural institution.

**Late Twentieth–Century Criticism** (1960–2000). The boundary between the largely structuralist criticism of the cold war era and the post–modern era is fluid and hard to fix, with 1968 springing forward as an obvious, but not always reliable, dividing line. In reality, many new critical trends had begun to manifest themselves in the early 1960s, though it is difficult to see a direct relationship between *Tartuffe* and Sputnik, for example. One thing that is certain is that much of the new scholarship was generated by Americans, Britons and Frenchmen working abroad. One example is the book by Yale professor Jacques Guicharnaud, *Molière, une aventure théâtrale*. Limiting himself to the major five–act plays that Michaut had highlighted in *Les Luttes de Molière*, Guicharnaud re–reads the texts closely in New Criticism style, but from the point of view of dramatic values that had been emphasized by Will G. Moore, Jacques Audiberti, and René Bray. The result is a much more complete understanding of the artistic processes of the playwright than had been achieved before. It can safely be said that after Guicharnaud, Molière could never again be read as a nondramatic text.

At the same time, several works of predominantly philosophical approach were investigating the crucial bond between Molière and the notion of reason that developed during his time. Most notable in this regard are Judd Hubert's *Molière and the Comedy of Intellect* and Robert McBride's *The Skeptical Vision of Molière*. Hubert's concise book, arguably the best treatment in one volume of the entire canon, traces Molière's portrayal of reason from his earliest works through his perfection of grand comic form and into his maturity, devoting a separate chapter to each phase in his development. Hubert shows Molière's sense of reason to be more penetrating than the *bon sens bourgeois* accorded him by the Third Republic or the tool of anticlerical libertinage identified by observers from the extreme right or the extreme left. Rather, it is inseparable from his sense of art itself, much as the playwright cunningly implies in *L'Impromptu de Versailles* or "La Gloire du Val de Grâce." McBride sets the record straight on Molière's skeptical antecedents, sweeping away much of the accreted crust of anecdotes and philosophical *idées reçues* to show a clearer profile of systematic doubt at work in several of the major plays. In this regard, it would be appropriate to mention Francis Lawrence's *Molière and the Comedy of Unreason*, a brief but piquant monograph presenting a more Erasmian perspective on several texts and on the way characters short–circuit rationality because of their own obsessions and appetites.

Among the many books of recent decades delving into the relationship of Molière to comic theory in general, it is appropriate to cite W. D. Howarth's *Molière, a Playwright and his Audience*, Marcel Gutwirth's *Molière ou l'invention comique*, Peter Nurse's *Molière and the Comic Spirit*, and Andrew Calder's *Molière: The Theory and Practice of Comedy*.

Following in the wake of Lionel Gossman's *Men and Masks: A Study of Molière*, an impressive group of studies has sought to understand the playwright from a socio–critical viewpoint, taking into consideration the advances in history of mentalities pioneered by the *Annales* school of French historians. Ralph Albanese's *Le Dynamisme de la peur chez Molière* examines several of the major plays as power struggles involving the imposition of authority and the resistance of freedom. James Gaines's *Social Structures in Molière's Theater* sets forth a scale of values applicable to the entire canon and concludes that Molière's outlook was more conservative than revolutionary, though subversion often backed him into ambiguity. Larry Riggs's *Molière and Plurality: The Decomposition of the Classical Self* applies post–structuralist thinking to the plays' analysis in surprising new ways. Ronald Tobin's *Tarte a la crème: Comedy and Gastronomy in Molière*, while appearing to be a strictly thematic study, investigates the issue of conviviality and its social ramifications throughout the works. Stephen V. Dock's *Costume and Fashion in the Plays of Jean–Baptiste Poquelin Molière* provides an exhaustive repertory of the clothes worn by characters and their often overlooked significance for interpersonal relations. Max Vernet's *Molière, côté cour côté jardin* re–evaluates the social thematics of the plays mainly from philosophical standpoints in subtle and revealing ways. Jurgen Grimm's *Molière en son temps*, originally written in German, proposes a historico–social reading of the theater from a fresh perspective unfettered by Marxist notions.

A giant step in biographical study came in the form of Madeleine Jurgens and Elizabeth Maxfield–Miller's *Cent Ans de recherches sur Molière, sur sa famille et sur les comédiens de sa troupe*, which updated and improved upon all documentary evidence available since the publication of the Despois–Mesnard edition of the complete works. Molière emerges as a man much more engaged with his class and his family. Virginia Scott's very recent *Molière: A Theatrical Life* offers a rich view of his life based on evidence rather than on the fictionalization that has run rampant in Molière biography throughout much of history.

Among other successful perspectives to the canon, one can note Alvin Eustis's *Molière as Ironic Contemplator,* which studies the linguistic elements of the plays, and Harold Knutson's *Molière: An Archetypal Approach.* A flurry of studies has shed light on the long–neglected stock of **court** entertainments, including Claude Abraham's *On the Structure of Molière's Comédies–ballets,* Stephen Fleck's *Music Dance, and Laughter: Comic Creation in Molière's Comedy–ballets,* and Charles Mazouer's *Molière et ses comedies–ballets.*

In France, efforts have been concentrated on perfecting the traditional literary–historical and thematic models, with important contributions from Roger Garapon's *Le Dernier Molière* (an important study of the last plays in the canon); Jacques Truchet's collection of essays in *Thématique de Molière*; Gabriel Conesa's thorough linguistic study, *Le Dialogue moliéresque*; Georges Forestier's compendium, *Molière en toutes lettres,* which follows his broader earlier studies on **disguise** in seventeenth–century drama; and Patrick Dandrey's *Molière ou l'esthétique du ridicule,* a thoughtful re–measuring of the doses of *le bon, le beau, et le vrai* in Molière's comedy.

With few exceptions, Molière studies have been relatively unmarred by the wilder flights of deconstruction and post–modernist fancy that have characterized much of world literature. A distinct interest in mentalities, social formations, and reappraisal of the *grand siècle,* informed by French historical research, has often been present, but inquiries have largely avoided descending into the morass of political correctness that has marked the emergence of New Historicism in English studies. Instead, a general attitude of eclecticism has prevailed, favoring measured development in all traditional areas, with an increasing focus on the entire canon in order to account for Molière's career as a work in progress, a ground for constant experimentation and innovation in dramatic art, where early modern concepts were continually being born and nurtured.

**La Thorillière, François Lenoir, sieur de** (1626–1680). Son of Charles Lenoir, who had founded the **Marais** theater in 1634, La Thorillière had a distinguished military career before marrying Marie Petitjean, daughter of the head of the Marais in 1658. He was thus already experienced when he passed into Molière's troupe in 1662, along with **Brécourt,** just at the moment when the Marais had re–established itself by succeeding with a series of spectacular **machine plays.** He played **Géronimo** in *Le Mariage forcé,* the impertient **marquis** in *L'Impromptu de Versailles,* **Arbate** in *La Princesse d'Élide,* **Hali** in *Le Sicilien,* and the **King** in *Psyché.* Such parts as **Cléante** (*Tartuffe*), **Lubin** *(George Dandin),* **Dorante** (*Le Bourgeois gentilhomme*), **Silvestre** (*Les Fourberies de Scapin*), and **Trissotin** *(Les Femmes savantes)* have been attributed to him. However, he probably played the tragic leads in **repertory** and in **Racine's** first two plays. His own tragedy of *Cléopâtre* achieved a modest success with eleven performances by the troupe in Advent of 1667. The inventory of his **costumes** made after his death testifies to this astounding range of parts, with everything from **peasant** garb to a Roman emperor's outfit. The two partial registers he kept of the company's plays and receipts serve as an important supplement and confirmation to **La Grange's**. Along with La Grange, he made the trip to the front lines of the siege of Lille to appeal to the King after *Tartuffe* was banned for the second time. After Molière's death, he briefly took the role of **Argan**, but soon left the troupe for the **Hôtel de Bourgogne**. It was his death, among other factors, that caused the ultimate fusion of all French companies in Paris into the ancestor of the **Comédie–Française**. His oldest son, Pierre, played as a child in *Psyché*, as did a daughter, presumably Charlotte, who later married **Baron**. His younger daughter, Thérèse, Molière's god child, eloped with **Dancourt** in 1680, forcing the family to allow them to marry. Pierre and Charlotte later became members of the Comédie–Française.

**La Thorillière** (*L'Impromptu de Versailles*). One of the few players who does not represent himself in the frame play, La Thorillière has the "real" role of an impertinent **marquis** who interrupts the rehearsal with his questions. Through this "comic relief," Molière takes the focus off the **Quarrel of the School for Wives** for a moment and adds an extra layer of metatextuality to the play, further blurring the distinction between performance and actual life. The perfect way La Thorillière acquits himself of this role suggests he is probably enlarging on a character he played in *Les Fâcheux*.

**Latin**. In their biographical introduction to the 1682 collected works, **La Grange** and **Vivot** credit Molière with great skills in Latin during his schooling at the **Collège de Clermont**. **Terence** was, they say, his favorite author. He also kept in close enough touch with the language to undertake a translation of **Lucretius's** *De rerum natura* into French, perhaps in an effort to establish his eligibility for membership in the **Academy**. *Amphitryon* and *L'Avare* are based on Latin models, and there is good evidence that Molière went beyond existing translations to consult and draw on the original **language** of **Plautus**. Nevertheless, in Molière's plays, Latin is generally a sign of pedantry, and false pedantry at that.

In scene 6 of *La Jalousie du Barbouillé*, the **Doctor's** speech is larded with mostly inappropriate Latin phrases gleaned from all sorts of sources. In *Dépit amoureux*, the exhausted **Marinette** complains that she has run so much that she has lost her Latin (a humorous saying in the mouth of a female **servant**), but she later manages to throw a few words of Church Latin into her conversation. **Albert**, speaking with the wordy tutor **Métaphraste**, repeatedly asks him to leave off Latin, since he himself only managed to commit his prayers to memory and even after so many years understands them no better than "High **German**." Indeed, Latin was a language often heard but seldom understood in **Louis XIV's**

France. In *Les Précieuses ridicules*, the illiterate servant **Marotte** assumes that her mistresses' *précieux* jargon is Latin and complains that she knows none of it. **Caritidès**, the professional etymologist in *Les Fâcheux*, derides the use of Latin in surnames and explains he has transformed his own name with a Greek ending to be less pretentious.

Medical Latin is an indispensable ingredient of Molière's verbal humor. The unlettered **Sganarelle** who poses as a physician in *Le Médecin volant*, knows better than to insist on Latin, but when accosted by the **Lawyer**, he manages to throw together a few syllabes of Latin–sounding words that actually fool his interlocutor. In *L'Amour médecin*, **Doctor Macroton** deploys his knowledge of Latin by using the phrase "experimentum periculosum." He also slings around Latinate words that the audience would have trouble identifying without a good dictionary: "fuliginous," "mordicant," "conglutinous," and so forth. In all, the doctors in this play fulfill **Lisette's** prediction that all the edification Sganarelle can expect from them is that they will tell him his daughter is sick in Latin. In *Le Médecin malgré lui*, it is the masquerading **doctor** Sganarelle who spews bits of nonsensical Latin phrases to justify his charlatan's tricks. Early in the play, he explains that he had picked this up during his "extensive" schooling (all the way to the sixth form, or less than two years), when he learned his rudiments, and during six years of service to a physician. The two physicians who diagnose **Monsieur de Pourceaugnac's** mental illness also have their turn, but are more interested in coining bizarre words with Greek and Latin roots ("cacochymie," "melanogogue") than in speaking the ancient language itself. The greatest spouters of Latin in the canon are the doctors in *Le Malade imaginaire*. **Thomas Diafoirus** and his father bandy about common schoolroom terms such as "optime," "nego," "distinguo," "concedo," and "quid dicis." Yet neither seems able to finish a single sentence in the language, and their anatomical references are often scrambled. **Toinette** makes fun of them when, during her own medical **disguise** scene, she rejects **Purgon's** prescriptions with the mock declension "ignorantus, ignoranta, ignorantum!" **Argan**, for his part, placed great importance on Latin as an element of the medical profession, lauding it in Thomas Diafoirus and requiring it of **Cléante** before he can marry his daughter. The fractured Latin, sprinkled with French, that appears in the concluding medical ceremony is apparently just what he had in mind, since he answers in similarly macaronic fashion to each question: "Clysterium donare, / Postea seignare, / Ensuitta purgare." His reception speech is riddled with French words welded to Latin endings and others like "rhubarbe" and "voilà" that don't even both to pretend to Latin morphology.

Pedantic Latin, almost inseparable from its medical cousin, lards the discourse of **Pancrace**, the **Aristotelian philosopher** consulted by Sganarelle in *Le Mariage forcé*. Besides Aristotle's *Categories* and precepts from his physics, Pancrace runs together quotes from Macrobius and Terence, as well as Latinized versions of country **proverbs**. **Lubin**, in *George Dandin*, claims that he knows Latin because he has recognized the meaning of the word "collegium" printed on a sign. **Monsieur Jourdain's** philosophy teacher threatens to use his command of Latin to punish the colleagues who have beaten him, lacerating them with a satire in the manner of **Juvenal**. He translates a Latin phrase in praise of learning for his pupil, but soon finds that Jourdain has not even the rudiments of Classical learning, so he must begin with French.

The **Count of Escarbagnas**, despite his having a tutor, has not gone much beyond this point. Although **Bobinet** claims he is reading **Cicero**, he can really only take dictation about Cicero, and mighty slowly at that. Despite his advanced age, he is still on the rudimentary rules of **Despautère's** grammar. It must run in the family: his mother is so ignorant, she takes all the syllables that contain "vi" for dirty words, demanding that the pedant teach her son a cleaner language. A few minutes earlier, she had mistaken **Martial** the Latin epigram writer for Martial the Parisian glove–maker, to which her equally ignorant suitor **Thibaudier** replied, "No, he's talking about a writer who's been dead for thirty or forty years." Thibaudier has obviously confused the Roman poet with the comic playwright André Maréchal, who had written at the time of the **Illustre Théâtre**. Neither **Chrysale** nor his maid Martine have any respect for the "Latin folks" Philaminte has attracted to their home in *Les Femmes savantes*. The names of **Horace, Vergil, Terence**, Catullus, and Theocritus are bandied about by the salon figures, but at least Philaminte's group does not explicitly massacre the language as so many of Molière's pretentious characters do.

**Laughter.** Molière shows the range of every sort of laughter in his works, from the most refined intellectual titter to the irresistible belly laugh resulting from Bergsonian situations. His literary critics have often reprimanded him for the latter, declaring **farcical** laughter of the impulse–response variety to be unworthy of high comedy. This simply coincides with the aristocratic bias of Molière's contemporary detractors, who felt he catered too much to the **groundlings** in the theater at the expense of his better paying customers. Molière not only persisted in arousing the happy spirits of the multitude, but he implies in many places that such unsophisticated laughter is more natural and more healthy than snide snickers against those who fail to come up to social muster. Of all the people who laugh at **Monsieur Jourdain**, it is the maid **Nicole**, who can only react with uncontrollable guffaws, who is the most benign toward the warped protagonist. Her motives are less mercenary than all the teachers and leeches that Jourdain's fortune attracts, and in her simplicity, she never swerves from loyalty to the family. There is no way of proving the anecdote that Molière always tried out his scenes on his cleaning lady before hazarding them at the theater, but one cannot deny that such a practice would be in character.

**La Vallière, Louise de La Baume Le Blanc, duchess of** (1644–1710). The first of **Louis XIV's** "official" mistresses, who was in favor in the early 1660s. She was known for her equestrian and athletic abilities and undoubtedly served as a model for the figure of the **Princess** in *La Princesse d'Élide*. She had long been supplanted by **Mme. de Montespan** when she entered the Carmelite order in 1674.

**La Violette (*Dom Juan*).** This lackey plays a role in the **lazzi** of the feast scenes in the fourth act of the play.

**Law.** The law that is mentioned in Molière's plays is the pre–Revolutionary common law of the area governed by the Parlement of **Paris**, which included much of France beyond the immediate capital area. If he seems well acquainted with many legal areas, from inheritance and property to criminal law, it is because he is reputed to have had legal training on the authority of his good friend and *protégé*, **La Grange**. Though some of his **notaries** and **lawyers** cross the line of legality a little too freely, Molière in general shows great respect for the *coutume de Paris* as a source of wisdom and justice. The **Notary** in *Les Femmes savantes* puns on this body of common law when, faced with two husbands cited on the same **marriage** document, he slyly remarks, "That's too much for the 'custom.'" He fends off **Philaminte's** demands to omit legal terms from the marriage contract, saying, "My style is perfectly good and it would be absurd, / To change so much, Madame, as just a single word." He points out to **Bélise** that if he honored her request of calculating the dowry in ancient monetary units, he would become the laughingstock of his colleagues.

Indeed, common law almost proves impervious to any tinkering, even to the schemes of a crook like **Monsieur Bonnefoy** in *Le Malade imaginaire*. When **Argan** mentions that he might consult a lawyer, the notary cautions against it because "they imagine it is a great crime to act fraudulently against the law" and "they cause difficulties because they do not know how to make a detour of the conscience" (I, 7). The surprisingly accurate discussion of inheritance law found in this play, in *L'École des femmes,* and especially in *Les Fourberies de Scapin*, may well derive from legal training that Molière received. In trying to dissuade **Argante** from filing a lawsuit to dissolve **Octave's marriage** (a likely recourse, since the boy did not have parental consent), **Scapin** reels off dozens of legal terms. He runs through the entire personnel of the courts and outlines all the things that could go wrong with a suit on its way to judgment, including all the people who could sabotage it if they were not bribed. He further lists all the legitimate costs and fees involved in such suits, referring not, of course, to the written law of Hispanic Naples, but to the common law of Paris.

**Monsieur de Pourceaugnac** alternates between pride in his legal studies and efforts to cover them up whenever his **nobility** is questioned. After he has been accused of bigamy by the pretended wives from **Gascony** and **Picardy**, he quickly reels off a series of terms quite accurately summing up the appeals process under common law in the *ancien régime*. **Sbrigani**, who is no stranger to the courtroom because of his criminal record, recognizes the legalese terms employed by the **Limousin**, but Pourceaugnac claims, "Those words come to me without my knowing it" (II, 11). Taking him at his word, Sbirgani arranges for him to consult two musical lawyers, who both assure him that his case is clearly a hanging offense, not only in the Paris jurisdiction, but in **England**, **Holland**, Denmark, Sweden, Poland, Portugal, Spain, Flanders, Italy, and Germany, as well. This assessment is quite true, by the way, since bigamy was considered a capital offense even if the parties in question brought no complaints, and the punishment entailed not only death, but loss of nobility as well, since hanging was an "infamous" punishment reserved for commoners. They cite as authorities the entire contents of the law library: Justinian, Papinian, Ulpian, Tribonian, Fernand, Rebuffe, Jean Imole, Paul, Castre, Julian, Bartholo, Jason, Alciat, and finally the venerable Cujas. Molière must have had fun enumerating all the great names from the lectures and readings of his youth.

The only strong indictment of the early modern French law comes from **Alceste**. The misanthrope refuses from the outset to take part in the process of lobbying judges and bribing them to ensure the victory of one's suits. He implies he would rather lose his case a hundred times over than pass up the opportunity to demonstrate the corruption of the system, with the courts becoming a metaphor for all collective human endeavors. **Du Bois's** appearance in Act IV underlines the suspicion and even superstition that surrounds their concept of the justice system, associated with darkness, magic, and diabolical processes. No wonder Alceste unleashes his fury at the beginning of the concluding act against a perverted, upside–down form of justice that places greater emphasis on the successful appearance of what is obviously artificial than in the more permanent, if less discernible, notion of rights. It is only **Philinte's** confidence that the decision against Alceste could be easily appealed and overturned, given the proper counsel, that prevents a wholesale condemnation of the law. No matter how much Alceste has tried to lose his suit, the eventual verdict may well shift to his favor if the slow–grinding gears are allowed to move forward.

It is not surprising that an early modern playwright would come from the law schools, since the same rhetoric applied to both domains, and law students had been deeply involved in the Parisian theater since the days of the medieval *soties* they staged during Carnival.

*See also* **Judges**.

**Lawyer** (*Le Médecin volant*). Unconnected to the central plot, the lawyer is a sort of pest who appears to try out his **Latin** on a fellow intellectual, the doctor portrayed by **Sganarelle**. His own learning is so flimsy that he accepts Sganarelle's nonsense as learned wisdom.

**Lawyers** (*Monsieur de Pourceaugnac*). The two lawyers appear in the interval between the second and third acts of the play and are strictly singing roles, though **Sbrigani** introduces them in the prose text. They confirm that **Pourceaugnac** is guilty of bigamy according to all the legal systems of Europe and all the learned scholars in the law library.

**Lazzi**. The Italian term for gestural comedy on the stage. Molière was an expert in this area, thanks in part to his association with the **Italian** players, but also to his familiarity with French farce traditions. The numerous situations giving rise to lazzi are, for the most part, not marked in the text, but must be inferred, as when the valet **La Montagne** fusses with his master's clothes and then knocks off his hat in the first act of *Les Fâcheux* or when **Dubois** searches unsuccessfully in his clothes for the note he wishes to give **Alceste** in *Le Misanthrope*. Stage directions for lazzi are indicated in *George Dandin* (III, 4), where Dandin and **Colin** cross each other unknowingly several times while searching for each other before they collide in the middle of the stage. **Pierrot** initiates a different form of lazzi in *Dom Juan* when he argues with the nobleman while maneuvering around **Charlotte** to avoid any blows. Molière's most elaborate eating lazzi also occur in that play when Sganarelle attempts to grab a quick dinner from an even quicker serving crew that lifts away his plates before he can touch them. There are also hat lazzi in *Le Médecin malgré lui*, where they accompany other visual gags based on bottles, enemas, and breast fondling. *Les Fourberies de Scapin* has equally amusing stage business involving a purse that tight–fingered old **Géronte** involuntarily hangs onto (II, 7). Greeting lazzi consisting of elaborate bows are noted in *Le Sicilien*, scene 7, where **Hali** also interjects "with your ladyship's permission" into every few words he utters, and also occur in Act II, scene 3 of *Les Fourberies de Scapin*, where Géronte avoids his son's fervent embraces. Another more gestural form of greeting lazzi occurs in Act III, scene 16 of *Le Bourgeois gentilhomme*, where the tactless **Jourdain** asks **Dorimène** to back up so that he will have room to execute the silly four–step bow that his dancing master has taught him to perform. Other lazzi in the latter play involve Scapin's kneeling confessions to **Léandre**, **Silvestre's** swashbuckling impersonation of a *bretteur*, and the famous bag **beating** that Géronte endures in the final act. Lazzi could become sexually suggestive, as when **Mascarille** and **Jodelet** offer to show the girls their "wounds" in *Les Précieuses ridicules*, or when **Harpagon** searches **La Flèche's** "third hand" and his pants in *L'Avare*.

**Léandre** (*L'Étourdi*). Described as a "fils de famille," Léandre is one of **Lélie's** potential rivals in the play's complex **love** interests. He has already been engaged to **Anselme's** daughter, **Hippolyte**, but is so attracted to the **slave** girl **Célie** that he is willing to neglect his obligations. Toward the end of Act II, **Mascarille** pretends to leave the service of Lélie and work for Léandre. He convinces his new master to give him **money** to buy Célie, intending to hand her over to Lélie instead. However the ruse fails when Lélie breaks up the sale with a fake **letter** from Spain, pretending to offer a father's ransom for the girl. The blockhead did not realize he was the intended beneficiary of Mascarille's purchase. In Act III, Léandre almost abandons the pursuit of Célie when Mascarille says she is really a woman of loose morals. Léandre's qualms are somewhat hypocritical, but they foreshadow his eventual return to Hippolyte later in the play. For the time being, he quickly drops his worries when Lélie contradicts everything Mascarille has said. His attempt to abduct Célie during a masquerade ends when **Trufaldin** dumps a chamber pot on his head. A sermon from **Anselme** about the relative merits of short–lived lust versus long–term dowry profits has a profound effect on Léandre and by Act V he has resolved to return to his fiancée. Léandre is a rival figure quite typical of intrigue comedy, lacking any salient personality traits except what are necessary for the plot.

**Léandre** (*Les Fourberies de Scapin*). One of the young lovers, he has a remarkable greeting scene with his father **Géronte** that is full of **politeness lazzi**, since the old man rebuffs his advances and scolds him for his misdeeds. Smitten with the **Gypsy slave Zerbinette**, he manages to buy her freedom with the **money** extorted from Géronte by **Scapin's** tale of abduction in a **Turkish galley**. His announcement at the end of the play that the Gypsies have admitted to kidnapping the girl and given him an identifying bracelet allows **Argante** to recognize his missing daughter. The part was probably played by **La Grange** or **Baron**.

**Léandre** (*Le Médecin malgré lui*). This young suitor, probably played by **La Grange**, is mentioned several times before he appears at the end of the second act. He has been rejected by **Lucinde's** father in favor of a rival who has his inheritance already in hand. He deploys his **money** immediately to make an impression on **Sganarelle** and does not miss his mark. Sganarelle promises his help most readily and has Léandre don the **disguise** of an **apothecary** so that he can approach the object of his **love**. Not even bothering with a fake identity, Léandre is introduced to **Géronte** with a series of comic gestures that undoubtedly mime to injections of enemas for which apothecaries were famous. It is to Léandre that Lucinde addresses her first words upon breaking out of her feigned dumbness. Sent into the garden to walk with the patient, Léandre takes Sganarelle's advice and rushes off to administer a quick dose of "matimonium" to her. However, he returns with the girl, claiming to have adopted a more honest method of dealing with his father–in–law, thus acquiring the old man's admiration and consent. Since the audience hears nothing of Léandre's loving discussion with Lucinde, this must qualify as one of the least interesting suitor roles in the canon.

**Le Brun, Charles** (1619–1690). Baroque painter, who became chief artist to the King in 1662 and director of the Gobelins tapestry works and of the Academy of Painting in 1663. Along with the landscape architect André Le Nostre and the architect Louis Le Vau, Le Brun had designed **Vaux–le–Vicomte** for **Fouquet**. The same trio was immediately set to work on **Versailles** following Fouquet's arrest. Le Brun became a kind of unofficial minister of culture for **Louis XIV**, with central power over all works commissioned for the huge enterprise at Versailles. As such, he must have worked with Molière on several of the **court** entertainments held there, such as the **Grand Divertissement Royal de Versailles** and the *Plaisirs de l'Îsle enchantée*. However, Molière's friendship with Le Brun's rival, **Pierre Mignard**, and the playwright's advocacy of Mignard's style in "**La Gloire du Val de Grâce**" must have created some distance between the two men.

**Lélie** (*L'Étourdi*). The blockhead referred to in the play's title, Lélie naively manages to bungle each of the schemes **Mascarille** devises to try to further his love affair with **Célie**. In Act I, he bungles three plots: he appears at just the wrong time in Mascarille's pretended fortune–telling session with Célie; he blurts out, "Whose purse?" when the valet has just succeeded in robbing **Anselme**; and he breaks up the plan whereby Anselme would purchase Célie on behalf of **Pandolphe**. Act II features his one moderately clever moment, as his sobbing helps persuade Anselme that Pandolphe has died. But once he has Anselme's **money** in hand for a short time, he readily relinquishing the purse when Anselme pretends to search for counterfeit coins. When Mascarille nearly succeeds in purchasing Célie from **Trufaldin**, using Léandre's cash, Lélie lets his creativity get the best of him and interrupts the sale with a forged **letter** from a **Spanish** nobleman who is supposedly the girl's father. In the following act, he errs twice, first by contradicting Mascarille's warnings to Léandre about Célie's bad character, and then by warning Trufaldin of the masquerade abduction and unmasking the valet, who had been trying to pre–empt the rival. Lélie's own **disguise** as an **Armenian** who knows Trufaldin's lost son miscarries very badly in Act IV, as he makes numerous geographic mistakes and fails to remember key details that Mascarille had tried to drill into him. He undoes the last two stratagems in the final act by vouching to the corrupt **police** for the man they are about to arrest and by revealing to **Andrès** that Mascarille's rooming house is a fake. The role is more psychologically interesting than many in the realm of intrigue comedy, since Lélie's emotions vary between self–sufficiency and desperation, self–recrimination and blame of others, confidence and fear, good–natured courage and stupefied confusion. His naivete makes a good foil for Mascarille's sarcasm. His efforts at good manners and sound morality make him all the more ridiculous, a trait that undoubtedly contributed to the lasting popularity of the play during Molière's lifetime and to its influence on British Restoration comedy. **La Grange's** register tells us that in 1659 the role was played by **Joseph Béjart**, who got sick during one performance and died shortly afterward. It is unclear whether La Grange himself, who had recently joined the troupe and would have been an excellent understudy, took over this role that seems suited to him in some ways. Joseph Béjart had suffered from a stammering problem well into adulthood and may well have exploited this a bit in playing Lélie. With this in mind, it is possible that the role may have been given to another actor, such as **Du Croisy**.

**Lélie** (*Sganarelle*). Suitor to **Célie** and master of **Gros–René**. Lélie is debonnaire and a bit vapid, for as soon as he learns that his beloved Célie is supposedly married to **Sganarelle**, he faints. He responds to Sganarelle's armed challenge and to Célie's angry accusations of faithlessness more with confusion than with sternness. The revelations of the denouement, which finally place paternal blessing on his engagement to the young lady, are greeted only with conventional expressions of contentment. Lélie has given his sweetheart a fine locket as a token of their **love**, and the **portrait** inside it gives rise to much of the misunderstanding that fuels the plot.

**Le Monnier**, **Pierre**. A member of the Parisian printing guild who took part in the publication of the text of *Psyché*, *Le Bourgeois gentilhomme*, and *Les Fourberies de Scapin* in 1671.

**Léonor** (*L'École des maris*).  Sister of **Isabelle** and ward of **Ariste**.  **Sganarelle** concedes in the second scene of the play that she has a quick wit, and she does not hesitate to confront him over the silliness of his plan of denying young women contact with the social world.  She then disappears until Act III, scene 8, where she returns bored and exasperated with the flirtations she has had to endure at a fashionable ball she attended.  She reacts strongly to Ariste's suggestion that she has misused his policy of leniency and offers to marry him on the spot if that is the proof he requires.  Her words to Sganarelle, who actually accuses her of elopement, are somewhat harsher, as one may expect.  Though her lines are limited and her opinions succinct, she is the predecessor of such strong feminine figures as **Éliante** in *Le Misanthrope* and **Henriette** in *Les Femmes savantes*.

**L'Épine** (*Les Femmes savantes*).  This lackey stumbles as he carries in a stack of chairs, causing **Philaminte** and **Bélise** to ask if he knows anything about gravity, instead of giving him better instructions.

**L'Espine** (*Les Fâcheux*).   This character is apparently a **servant** who accompanies **Damis** in Act III, scene 5, when the latter hopes to arrange an ambush to catch **Éraste**.  Damis sends L'Espine to fetch some thugs who are supposed to murder the suitor.  His only lines announce the arrival of a pack of mummers at the end of the play, ushering in the third–act ballet.

**Lespy** or **L'Espy** (**stage name of François Bedeau**).  Brother of the famous clown **Jodelet**, Lespy was a veteran of the **Hôtel de Bourgogne** and **Marais** troupes when he joined Molière's Paris troupe on April 1, 1659.  Already aged, Lespy probably took the role of **Gorgibus** in early productions of *Les Précieuses ridicules* and *Sganarelle*.  He also played **Ariste** in *L'École des maris,* and perhaps **L'Espine** in *Les Fâcheux*.  After Easter, 1663 he retired to a village in Anjou, where he died six months later.

**Letters**.   Although they are supposed to be a means of communication and sometimes a proof of loyalty, letters more often seem to function in comedy as a grounds for misunderstanding and suspicion.  Thus, in *Dépit amoureux*, **Éraste** is unnecessarily skeptical about **Lucile's love** letter, just as he is indiscreet in showing it to **Valère**.  From a woman to a man, a love letter was a very overt and dangerous expression of emotion, all the more so if she had not already received something at least as explicit already.  In *Dom Garcie de Navarre*, a letter intercepted by the eponym is enough to send him into a fit of **jealous** rage, until **Elvire** demonstrates it was not even written by a man, but rather by her imprisoned friend **Ignès**.  Later, **Dom Garcie** finds half a torn letter that seems incriminating enough for him to blame Elvire even more outrageously, but when she combines the halves and has him read it aloud, he finds to his chagrin that it was actually addressed to him.  In *Le Misanthrope*, the letter from **Célimène** (alleged to **Oronte**) that **Arsinoé** shows **Alceste** has a similar effect, though Célimène uses the mere suggestion of a feminine author to reduce her suitor to an even lower level of abjection. Like Éraste, **Acaste** and **Clitandre** cannot resist showing each other the written "proof" they have received of Célimène's affections. But their personal triumphs of a written **avowal** lose all value when it emerges that she has sent such letters to more than one man. Instead of keeping their shame secret, they flaunt it in public, showing the pertinence of La Rochefoucauld's observations that one's faults often contribute more to popularity than one's virtues. The scene where they read from their respective missives (V, 4) is remarkable because it shows the danger of **portraits** once they cross over from the oral to the written realm. The insults dished out by Célimène then become as damaging to her as they are to the targets, if not more so. In much the same way as Acaste and Clitandre, **Harpin** vows to disclose to the citizenry of Angoulême the **Countess of Escarbagnas's** letters of commitment to him.

**Isabelle**, in *L'École des maris*, manages to deceive Sganarelle by complaining that **Valère** has written annoying love letters to her. Yet it is she who sends him a letter, still sealed in a golden box, through the unwitting agency of her persecutor. While not as admirable as Agnès's famous letter to Horace, this one nevertheless prefigures it as a means of female liberation. *L'École des femmes* gives evidence that a love letter can be not only sincere, but even somewhat heroic. **Agnès's** missive, tied to a rock she obediently hurled at **Horace**, convinces him that she not only reciprocates his passion, but also deserves a better treatment than he had been prepared to give her. It is surprisingly elegant and eloquent in its frankness and gives proof that much has been going on underneath the calm exterior of the young lady. It is not the only letter in the play, since **Arnolphe** in Act I peruses a letter of credit that Oronte has sent along with his son Horace. While full of compliments that Arnolphe shrugs off, such a letter would have had legal standing and was indispensable in the cash–poor economy of seventeenth–century France. A formal letter of presentation is read by **Dom Pèdre** in *Le Sicilien*, indicating **Adraste** will substitute for the painter scheduled to do **Isidore's** portrait. Perhaps Molière thought this unusually trite step was necessary, since this is the only instance, among many substitution tricks, where the original "expert" is not present to endorse his replacement. Without the letter, the scene might have been thought to lack **verisimilitude**. In *Le Malade imaginaire*, the letters exchanged by **Angélique** and **Cléante** are not only love letters, but mutual promises of **marriage** as well, a documentary form of "paroles de futur" almost as binding as the marriage contract itself.

If Agnès's love letter is a positive example of style, then the one sent by **Thibaudier** to the **Countess of Escarbagnas** with a gift of pears must be the opposite. His conceit consists of punning on the word "pears" and on the variety "Bon–chrétien" in a very awkward way. Comparing a lady's **love** to an unripe fruit, for example, is not very likely to please her unless she is as ignorant as the Countess. His allusion to having to swallow "poires d'angoisse" as a result of her reluctance is also less than a happy image, since those words designate a medieval torture device used to reduce the skull to a bloody mess.

Molière's letters go far beyond the status of simple plot devices to become interesting standards of epistolary style and communicative efficiency.

*See also* **Messages**.

***Lettre sur la comédie de l'Imposteur*** (*Letter on the Comedy of "The Impostor"*). Dated August 20, 1667, fourteen days after **Lamoignon's** ban and nine days after the Archbishop's, this document on the second version of *Tartuffe* reveals important details about Molière's intentions. In fact, it reveals so much that Molière has often been suspected of being the author, a hypothesis that is not entirely out of the question. Be that as it may, one finds that the character of **Tartuffe** has been totally recast on the outside since the first version four years earlier. Instead of being dressed in quasi–clerical **costume**, this Tartuffe is a fop named **Panulphe**, clad in the latest fashions of the **court** marquis. This interpretation would have us believe that bigotry was not just a fashion, but also in fashion. It also makes much of certain amendments to the language of the text, designed to deflect criticism of impiety or even blasphemy in the work. We also find that the 1667 version was truly a complete five–act play, very similar in its plot to the final 1669 product. The letter is full of praise for Molière, especially for his cleverness in character construction. A long parenthesis is opened in the account of the third act in order to examine the various attacks leveled at Molière on account of his hypocrite's realism and his outrageous language. The author of the letter hides behind the rampart of hearsay, and after presenting a synopsis entirely favorable to Molière, calls on the reader to make up his or her own mind on the matter. Assuming a bolder pose after finishing the account of the play, the author of the letter discusses at length the objection to the play on the basis of the **proprieties** and their condemnation of religious matters on stage. Declaring "it is certain that religion is nothing if not the purification of Reason, at least as concerns morality," he goes on to justify discussion of divine matters from the point of view of practical behavior. The correspondent's second major point in summation is that the representation of the hypocrite as a worldly *galant* strikes a useful blow for domestic fidelity and against the dangers of seduction. Various authors have been suggested for this letter, including, apart from the dramatist himself, **Donneau de Visé**. However, Robert McBride has recently made a compelling case that the author is none other than **La Mothe Le Vayer**. This hypothesis is supported not only on the basis of prose style, but also by some interesting internal evidence, such as stray remarks about the paradoxes that La Mothe Le Vayer and his skeptical cronies were so fond of using.

***Lettre sur la comédie du "Misanthrope"*** (*Letter on the Comedy of "The Misanthrope"*). A text, published in pamphlet form by **Donneau de Visé** almost immediately after the premiere of the play in August 1666. Purporting to relay information on the performance to a friend at the **court** of **Fontainebleau**, this letter marks a distinct change in the attitudes of the author toward Molière, which had heretofore been mainly hostile. While summarizing the action of the play in some detail, Donneau does not hide his admiration for the playwright, the main character, and the overall construction of the comedy. Stressing the social utility of such satire, Donneau explains, "I find it all the more admirable since the hero is funny without being ludicrous and that he makes polite folks laugh without recourse to the witless or vulgar jokes that one is accustomed to hear in comedies." Otherwise, the letter is not remarkable for any insightful analyses. It was often reprinted with the play.

*Lettre sur les Observations d'une Comédie du sieur Molière intitulée le Festin de Pierre* (*Letter on the Observations on a Comedy by Mister Molière entitled The Feast of Stone*). An anonymous pro–Molière pamphlet published in 1665 by **Gabriel Quinet**. Its author attacks the writer of the *Observations* as being too envious and spiteful for rational analysis. He further declares that his counterpart misuses **religion** in the course of his argument and misunderstands aesthetics. If the writer of the *Observations* had known more about higher comedy and less about **farce**, he would have realized it is impossible to mock a really devout person.

*Lettres portugaises, Les* (*The Portuguese Letters*). An anonymous epistolary novel in the form of letters purportedly from a Portuguese nun named Sister Mariana to her unfaithful French lover. Immensely popular because of their sentimentality as well as their style, these letters were considered by the public to be genuine when they were published in 1669 and for a long time thereafter. Most scholars now attribute them to Gabriel–Joseph de Lavergne, vicomte de Guilleragues, though at least one attempt has been made to link them with Molière. Guilleragues left **Paris** in 1669 to become ambassador to the Ottoman Empire.

**L'Hermite**. This family had members related to both Molière and the **Béjarts**. The playwright was related to the **Paris** branch through his mother's family, and **Madeleine Béjart** was related to a branch in **Avignon**. The most famous literary member of the clan was the playwright Tristan L'Hermite, a contemporary of **Pierre Corneille**. The **Illustre Théâtre** is known to have purchased the right to act his tragedy, *La Mort de Chrispe*, but unfortunately this work did not have the success of his well–known *Mariane*. Both of these plays were performed in **repertory** by Molière's troupe after their return to Paris.

**Libertines and Libertinage**. Though the word is usually taken today in the sense of licentious living, libertinage in the seventeenth century referred more frequently to the learned pursuit of freethinking. The libertine tended to be skeptical, if not downright contrary, to orthodox **religious** doctrines. Among the more prominent Parisian personalities associated with this position were Guy Patin, a noted physician, and Gabriel Naudé, the librarian at the Arsenal. Despite the religious motivation of **Descartes's** *Discourse on Method*, he was commonly held to be a libertine, since his approach shook the foundations of orthodox authority. Moreover, his writings on physics challenged the theories sanctioned by Rome. Molière was accused of placing a libertine on stage in the form of **Dom Juan**. Indeed, he seems to have anticipated the accusation, given the way he has **Sganarelle** define his master as a man who believes only in mathematical proofs and who fears neither God, the Devil, or spooks. Dom Juan's famous quote about believing only that two plus two equals four comes from an anecdote about the earlier libertine, Maurice of Nassau. The most sensitive part of the play was the pauper scene where Dom Juan bribes a poor hermit to blaspheme, seconded by Sganarelle, who urges the man to swear "just a little." The fact that the **pauper** does not verbally accept, even when offered the coin "for the love of humanity," leaves Molière technically innocent of inciting to blasphemy, no matter how much the tenor of the conversation may have injured the Devout Party. For an orthodox fundamentalist, of course, any mention of such matters constituted guilt *ipso facto*. It is interesting that Molière's enemies, in their various blasts against him, do not mention association with the known libertine circle of the **White Cross Tavern**, a source of many posthumous anecdotes about the dramatist. It is certainly true that his friend **Chapelle** was an acknowledged libertine, and others of his entourage such as **Bernier** and Brienne were often cited as such. Even the young **Boileau**, prior to his whitewashing by the **Lamoignon** clan, was often spoken of as a libertine. Molière's favorite Classical philosopher, **Lucretius**, was a fixture on libertine reading lists. He was thus guilty of libertinage at least by association, and it is no wonder that his infringement of the **proprieties** against religious matters on stage brought him an accusation of not just one, but four different kinds of impiety from the author of the ***Observations on the Feast of Stone***.

**Limoges**. City in west–central France, capital of the Limousin province. It was already being used in the seventeenth–century as a place of internal exile for disgraced political figures and army officers, hence the phrase *être limogé* meaning "to be assigned to an obscure post." Several of the associates of the disgraced **Fouquet** were sent there, including **La Fontaine**. As the Podunk of France, Limoges is also home to **Monsieur de Pourceaugnac** and his nest of petty bureaucratic relatives. Pourceaugnac mentions specific places in Limoges during his conversation with **Éraste**, including Petit–Jean's restaurant and the cimetière des Arènes, the most fashionable promenade in Molière's time. It is unclear why Limoges was considered in such low regard. When Pourceaugnac asks **Sbrigani** what Limousins had ever done to hurt Parisians, the trickster answers, "They are brutal folk, enemies of the nobility and merit of other cities" (III, 2).

**Lisette** (*L'Amour médecin*). **Lady's maid** to **Sganarelle's** daughter, **Lucinde**, this Lisette is more active than the previous model, since she actively works with her mistress to try to arrange a **marriage** with **Clitandre**. At first, in scene 3, she questions Lucinde about her desires and repeatedly shouts to Sganarelle that what the girl wants is a husband. She might have done more had not the discreet Lucinde hidden her inclinations from everyone up to that point. When Lucinde grows despondent, Lisette upholds female choice with bold words: "Go on! You mustn't let yourself be led around like a stupid goose! As long as you don't compromise your honor, you can liberate yourself from a father's tyranny. What do you think is going to happen? Aren't you old enough to be married? Does he think your heart is made of stone?" Lisette's comical account of Lucinde's fainting, which leads the man first to think she has jumped from her window or died in bed, has the desired effect of panicking the old man. Later, in Act III, she encourages Clitandre in his **disguise** and sympathizes with him. She then makes Sganarelle dance for joy, literally, before she tells him the news of the fantastic new **doctor** who has arrived to cure Lucinde. When Sganarelle objects that the man seems to lack the beard of a doctor, she defends him by saying, "Science is not measured by the beard, and he doesn't have his brains in his chin." When the young lovers need a moment's privacy, she makes Sganarelle withdraw by warning him, "Are you kidding? You must go away. A doctor asks so many questions that a decent man should not overhear!" As the contract is signed and the ruse concluded, Lisette keeps her peace until the lovers have sneaked away, then revealing to Sganarelle that he has been tricked.

However, it is Lisette's jokes about the medical profession that are her most precocious point. Before the doctors arrive, she tells Sganarelle that Lucinde could certainly manage to die without their help, that it is better to say a man has died from four doctors and two pharmacists than from an illness, and that a cat that fell from the roof managed to live and recover because no doctors were around. She then tells **Tomès** that the coachman he had treated at a friend's house has died. When the doctor objects that it is too early, according to medical theory, for this to have happened, she retorts, "**Hippocrates** can say what he wants, but the coachman is dead." As the doctors are leaving, she tells them that someone has done their profession a great wrong by usurping their role, causing a man to die by piercing him with a sword. Tomès warns her, "Listen, laughing girl, one day you'll fall into our hands." But she answers, "The day I need your help, you have my permission to kill me." Active and witty, this Lisette certainly heralds the coming of **Toinette** in *Le Malade imaginaire*. **Madeleine Béjart**, still listed as the top actress in the troupe in 1665, might well have played the original role.

**Lisette** (*L'École des maris*). **Lady's maid** to **Léonor**. She is an unremarkable companion, except for her one substantial speech in Act I, scene 2, where she stands up for the resiliency of women's honor, attacks the barbarism of sequestration, and warns of the adverse reactions that excessive **jealousy** can produce. In doing so, she gives a glimmer of later uppity **servants**, such as **Dorine** in *Tartuffe* and **Toinette** in *Le Malade imaginaire*.

**Loret, Jean** (d. 1665). Man of letters who took over the *Gazette* from **Théophraste Renaudot** and furnished the octosyllabic verses for the publication during Molière's early career. At first the verses were composed solely for Madame de Longueville and were circulated in manuscript form, but Loret arranged for their printing from September 1652 onward under the title *La Muse historique* and obtained a royal *privilège* in 1665 to protect them from piracy.

**Louis XIV** (1638–1715). The image of the Sun King that prevails through most of Molière's theater is the one given in the "**Remerciement au Roi**" and in *L'Impromptu de Versailles*: he is an energetic monarch, constantly on the run between one great matter and another, but magnanimous, all–knowing, full of charm for everyone, and possessing an uncanny ability to deal with individuals even far below his lofty level. Molière does not hesitate to give him an active role in the gestation of his plays. He cleverly separates *Les Fâcheux* from **Fouquet's** patronship by suggesting in the introduction that it was Louis himself who suggested "the best episode," with the future head of the royal **hunt**, Monsieur de Soyecourt, serving as a model for the obsessive hunter in the play. The strategy coincides marvelously with Louis's personal assumption of absolute rule in 1661. Molière also indicates that the King ordered him to compose *L'Impromptu de Versailles* as a riposte to the enemies who had unfairly attacked and impugned him in the **Quarrel of the School for Wives**. The King, of course, was the troupe's main **patron**, even while it carried the name of his younger brother. It must have seemed the most natural thing in the world for them to become "The **King's Troupe** at the **Palais Royal**" after the crown adopted and pensioned them in 1665.

Little credence can be given to anecdotes about the King's displeasure with individual plays, such as the story that he had the first presentation of *Tartuffe* interrupted after the third act (this notion is clearly contradicted by **La Grange's** register). Molière takes pains in his first *placet* on *Tartuffe* to recall that Louis personally approved of the play; he implies in the second *placet* that the King may have suggested the specific changes of costume and wording he mentions. La Grange and **La Thorillière**, sent as ambassadors to deliver the second petition to the King near the battle lines at the siege of Lille, were apparently well received. They brought back the promise that the monarch would attend to their complaints when he came back to his peaceful concerns in the capital. Perhaps Louis was afraid that Molière would stick to his promise that he would cease creating comedies if the persecution continued. The third petition, which coincides with the successful staging of the final version of the play, is nothing less than a thank–you card to Louis for his help.

Rather than being resentful, he seems to have been mightily pleased with almost everything the dramatist produced, from the **farce** of *Le Docteur amoureux* that was part of the very first command performance in 1658, through the later works. There may be some truth to the story that *Dom Juan* was discretely rejected as too freethinking, but it was not enough to prevent the all–important royal adoption of the troupe from taking place, including the awarding of a healthy annual subvention of 6,000 *livres*. If it was the victim of censorship, it was censorship of the most gentle and dignified kind.

Louis's interest in the troupe had a great deal to do with his increasingly elaborate **court** feasts and ceremonies. The *Plaisirs de l'Île enchantée* (1664), the **Ballet des Muses** (1666), and the **Grand Divertissement Royal de Versailles** (1668) all involved Molière's players and resulted in outstanding profits for them. It is clear that the command for a **Turkish** satire that gave birth to *Le Bourgeois gentilhomme* coincided with the King's diplomatic and political interests. Louis XIV is said to have initiated the work on *Psyché* because he wanted to find a use for the **Tuileries** Theater and the underworld scenery left over there from the opera *Ercole amante*. Just how the King envisioned their contribution is another matter. He was constantly focused not on the quality of the work of art being presented, but on its effect on the audience. Though royal patronage was vital for them, he may have thought of the troupe merely as minor court **servants**, an almost insignificant part of the massive expense of bedazzling his fellow aristocrats. Details of the latter festival, for instance, show little concern about the play *George Dandin*. Instead, there is much about the elaborate banquet of pastry set pieces that was constructed each day, only to be "demolished" by a mob of lackeys and servants, who thrashed about in the remains of marzipan castles and sugar meringue mountains to the delight of their superiors.

**Louison** (*Le Malade imaginaire*). The part of **Argan's** younger daughter was originally played by Louise, the six–year–old child of the **Beauvals**. She must have been a precocious child to do this, even with Molière coaching and coaxing much of her dialogue. We know early in the play that **Béline** wants to put Louison in a **convent**, and she seems in much greater danger of going than her elder sister, on the one hand, because she would get only left–overs for her dowry, and, on the other hand, because she is somewhat of a nuisance for an aged and supposedly infirm father. However, we soon learn that there is a close and tender relationship between the two and that Argan's threats are really so much bluster. Louison is summoned in Act II because she has witnessed a conversation in **Angélique's** bedroom between her sister and her lover, **Cléante**. At first she offers to recite a fable or fairy tale for her father, for she has just learned "The Crow and the Fox" and "The Ass's Skin." When her father asks if she has heard anything unusual, she at first denies doing so, which prompts Argan to grab some switches and start to spank her. Louison is apparently used to this sort of reaction, for she instinctively **feigns death** at the first blow. Argan is so sentimental and gullible that he believes it when she says, "I'm dead!" and he begins to mourn and to regret his violence, tossing aside the damned switches and collapsing into tears. Before this can go much further, Louison realizes that she had better revive, and she announces that she thinks she is not quite dead after all. She then gives a **childish** description of the wooing that went on while she was in the room. Argan plays a little game with her, pretending that his omniscient little finger will whisper in his ear if she does not tell the truth. When he suggests she has been leaving something out, she labels the little finger a liar and is permitted to leave. Later, when Béralde is discussing the girls' future, he expressly discounts Louison, telling Argan he has one daughter to provide for. This is undoubtedly because she is still so young and liable to catch oneo of the childhood diseases that prevented so many children from reaching adulthood, including several of Molière's siblings and both of his sons. It is a somewhat grim afterthought on the charming world of childhood that holds considerable nostalgia for both the playwright and Argan, for the latter exclaims as his daughter leaves, "Ah, there are no more children!"

**Louvre**. Still a royal residence in Molière's time, especially in winter months, it is mentioned in *Les Précieuses ridicules* when **Mascarille** claims to be invited to the King's *petit coucher*, or bedding down ceremony. In *Le Misanthrope*, **Acaste** ostentatiously mentions his presence at the *lever* or rising ceremony at the Louvre, where a certain **Cléonte** made a fool of himself. Molière knew the building well, since the theater where **Louis XIV** initially permitted him to perform, the Petit–Bourbon, was right against the side of the Louvre and had to be abandoned when work began on the present colonnade of the east face, designed by Claude Perrault. In the "Remerciement au Roi," Molière gives a witty picture of courtier life in the Louvre, with its jostling marquis pressing to get close to the King.

**Love**. This topic was so minutely dissected, measured, and plotted by Molière's contemporaries that any attempt to sum up the ideas of the age would require a book of its own. However, there are some very salient points in Molière's concept of love that deserve mention. Without delving into the Neoplatonic niceties that intrigued the Renaissance, Molière portrays love as a product of natural mutual attraction. It may be triggered by a look or gaze, by an exchange of civilities (as in *L'École des femmes*), or by an act deserving recognition (as in *L'Avare* or *Le Malade imaginaire*). But **Ériphile** explains that love cannot be forced through obligation, no matter how extravagant the price.

The worst kind of love is simply a nonspecific longing for power, procreation, or pleasure — the kind found in **Arnolphe**, **Dom Juan**, **George Dandin**, or **Béline**. This reduces the love partner to a mere object necessary to carry out the mission assigned by his or her manipulative owner. **Sostrate** places the idea of "making oneself be loved" alongside that of transforming lead to gold, in the realm of imaginary delusions. Even when some reciprocity takes place, it may be unbalanced, or the product of illusion, as in **Dom Juan's** seduction of the **peasant** girls or **Clitandre's** seduction of **Angélique** in *George Dandin*. Dom Juan's love apology for noncontingent love (I, 2) deserves attention. Couching love in terms of a benefit he bestows on others, he specifically rejects **marriage** as a pre– or post–condition of love, on the grounds that it imposes artificial limits on the largesse of the universal lover. As for himself, he declares that he is incapable of resisting attraction or restricting his inclinations in any way. The attractiveness of love is its gamelike challenge to overcome the "innocente pudeur" of the ladies whose favor is sought. Such conquests are only good as long as they are unfulfilled, for the consummation of love brings on undesirable torpor and degradation. His ideas mix elements of the aristocratic warrior ethic with the virtues of *générosité* and activity, skillfully neglecting any aspects that could foul his neatly built system. As his seduction of **Charlotte** shows, his system collapses the second one questions a single element of it, and it is his ability to attach no truth at all to what he says that allows him to succeed. In an inverse application of **Pascal's** wager of faith, Dom Juan dares the woman seduced to disbelieve in what he promises. The weakest link is, of course, that he never really experiences love at all, but only the desire and satiation cycle that metonymy has given the name of love. It is

**Elvire's** poignant complaints, rather than **Sganarelle's** cock–and–bull diatribes, that furnish a positive context in which to judge Dom Juan's ways.

In Molière's universe, **Nature** not only unleashes true love, but goes far to ensure its completion, transforming the crude figures of **Horace** and **Agnès**, for instance, into highly sophisticated lovers. Love cannot be easily resisted, or even kept secret, for very long. **Éliante** in *Le Misanthrope* almost quotes **Lucretius** word for word when she says that love fundamentally alters the perception of the lover. Portly ladies become majestic, beanpoles towers of virtue, dwarfs condensed gems of beauty, and so forth. **Cléonte** gives a working demonstration of this theory in *Le Bourgeois gentilhomme* when he counters **Covielle's** reproaches of **Lucile's** small eyes, short stature, lax bearing, limited intellect, poor conversation, lack of humor, and flightiness. Substituting the desired image for the real one, he describes each defect as an advantage (III, 9). The eyes, which in Neoplatonic theory became the aggressive arms or passive targets of love, are in Molière's works more like lamps that show the existence of love within and even send **messages**. **Bélise** in *Les Femmes savantes* is a great believer in platonic love, which she characterizes as "pure as the daystar," going on to explain that it will encourage only mental intercourse, while all physical contact will be banned. However, Neoplatonism is strongly rejected in this play as early as the first scene, where **Armande's** desires to sublimate physical love into a warped intellectual game contrast sharply with **Henriette's** healthy desire for intimate companionship and a family. **Clitandre** later tries to explain to his former sweetheart that love is innocently rooted in the satisfaction of physical desires, but she is too enshrouded in her mother's theories to listen.

*Le Misanthrope* shows that, if Molière disapproves of love that is too *tendre* (divorced from the physical), he can be equally critical of the kind that is too *galant*, or superficially playful. Acaste's conceited diatribe at the beginning of Act III earns him the spectators' antipathy, as he outlines his theory that any love that is too "costly" is not worth the effort. He esteems his own "price" to be high enough that the lady must "pay in advance" with her favors if she expects to receive much recognition from him. Not for Acaste is the long–suffering submission of a *soupirant* who is prepared to sigh forever at the feet of a stern mistress. He considers himself to be handsome and convivial enough to deserve the attentions of any woman he desires. While Molière often ridicules the *précieuses'* demand for a lover who will be constantly faithful regardless of the prospect of reward, he also shows the fatuousness of those who expect to make love a commodity of easy exchange, devoid of profound commitment.

While love cannot be denied, a very strong act of the will can defer its enjoyment, provided some powerful resolve is involved; this is how **Ériphile** manages to hold out so long against naming a husband, how **Angélique** in *Le Malade imaginaire* is able to refuse marriage in honor of her dead father's will, and how Henriette can refuse to marry Clitandre if it entails his financial ruin. Fortunately, as the latter examples show, such repression is not usually needed forever, for in the comic world crises tend to work themselves out happily. One may worry, as **Hyacinte** does in *Les Fourberies de Scapin*, whether love will be enduring (I, 3), but generally once external obstacles are removed, love flourishes. Thus, once aroused, love sustains itself not with logical likelihood, but with a kind of folly. Éliante's speech about the transforming power of love, almost straight from Lucretius, touches close to Molière's central concern with the limitations of reason in the search for happiness. His theater abounds in both positive and negative examples of how to realize that search.

**Lovers' Spite.** This stock scene involves a dispute and near–breakup of a couple over trivial misunderstandings and prideful resentment that make them jump to conclusions rather than eliciting explanation. Besides *Dépit amoureux*, where this type of scene is enacted between both the upper–class and the **peasant** lovers, there are several other examples in Molière's comedies. One of the most famous is Act II, scene 4 of *Tartuffe*, where **Valère** and **Mariane** pout over apparent rejection, requiring all of **Dorine's** wiles to reconcile them. Another is spread over three scenes in the third act of *Le Bourgeois gentilhomme*, where **Cléonte** and **Covielle** at first turn their backs on their sweethearts, **Lucile** and **Nicole**, because they feel slighted over an event that happened earlier that day, when the girls pretended not to see them. They continue in their rudeness, no matter how the young ladies coax and cajole them. Finally they turn the tables, refusing to speak on their part until the young men kneel and plead forgiveness before them.

**Loyal, Monsieur (*Tartuffe*).** Appearing in Act V on behalf of **Tartuffe** to oversee the seizure of **Orgon's** house and to place the family under *garde à vue*, this officer of the courts is a precursor of Dickens's Uriah Heep. Under professions of humility and age–old friendship, he harbors a ruthless and predatory spirit that cannot wait to start picking like a vulture at the remains of the judge's wealth. He is clearly a cool operator, who does not cringe in the least at the threats of father or son, knowing he can unleash his numerous subordinates on the helpless foe. The actor who played the original role is somewhat of a mystery. It is certain that Molière played **Orgon**, **La Grange Valère**, **Du Croisy** Tartuffe, and **Hubert Mme Pernelle**; probable that **Louis Béjart** took **Damis** and **La Thorillière Cléante**. Thus, the first Monsieur Loyal was most likely the obscure **De Brie**, whose wife played **Mariane**.

**Loyson, Étienne.** Parisian printer and bookseller. He was part of the eight–printer coalition that published *L'École des femmes* and *La Critique de l'École des femmes*. He also published a rare 1674 imprint of *Le Malade imaginaire*.

**Lubin (*George Dandin*).** Lubin is a country swain, much like **Lucas** or **Alain**. He has been hired at many times his usual wages by **Clitandre** in order to deliver **messages** to **Angélique**. However, he does a poor job, since he blurts out to **Dandin** exactly what he has been doing. He is equally ineffective as a suitor to the clever Claudine, who keeps him at arm's length, despite his attempts at petting. The confusion in the dark that matches him briefly with Angélique in the final act shows how random the whole enterprise of furtive romance can be. Though he boasts to his master about his learning (which is confined to reading block printing), he is the only character stupider than Dandin himself. Strangely enough, the part was played by the normally dignified **La Thorillière**.

**Lucas** (*Le Médecin malgré lui*). This "Mr. Nursemaid," the husband of the buxom **Jacqueline**, incorporates the verbal humor of **peasant** speech with the situational humor of the valet or underling. Appearing first in Act I, scene 4, where he and **Valère** are searching for a **doctor** to cure the mistress's mysterious ailment, his **language** is peppered with picturesque curses, malapropisms, and rural expressions. Thus, he has many a laugh line — for instance, when he calls Sganarelle the "parrot doctor" because of his **costume** of green and yellow. Lucas joins in the lusty **beating** administered to the woodcutter, and later pounds **Géronte** on the chest as he lectures his wife on her duties. In scenes 2 and 3 of the second act, he engages in a prolonged **lazzi** sequence with Sganarelle and Jacqueline, as the former tries to fondle the nursemaid's breasts, to her apparent pleasure and the annoyance of her husband. The scene involves several amusing visual effects, such as pirouettes that the characters make each other execute. Later, in the third act (scenes 3 and 4), he eavesdrops on Sganarelle's attempts to seduce Jacqueline, but does not show himself. He takes his revenge in scene 8, where he denounces Lucinde's elopement with Léandre, and the doctor's part in it. He has no lines in the final scenes, so we must assume he and Jacqueline conveyed their feelings about the denouement strictly through facial expression. Both the character's speech and his minor conflict with the protagonist foreshadow the role of **Lubin** in *George Dandin*. The part was likely taken by **Hubert**, who assumed the roles originally played by **Brécourt**, himself a specialist at peasant caricature.

**Lucette** (*Monsieur de Pourceaugnac*). One of **Armande Béjart's** shorter roles, Lucette is a woman who pretends to be the **Gascon** wife of the protagonist. Her version of Gascon dialect goes far beyond the simple phonological changes found in other Gascon speeches, incorporating much Hispanic vocabulary and morphology. It must have been accompanied by a good deal of body **language**, for the average Parisian would certainly have trouble comprehending Lucette's tale of seduction and abandonment. There is little preparation or explanation for her intervention, which has apparently been planned by **Nérine**, who arrives directly afterward with a **Picard** version of the same tale.

**Lucile** (*Le Bourgeois gentilhomme*). **Monsieur Jourdain's** daughter has a small but concentrated role. She first appears in the **lovers' spite** sequence in the third act, where after sweetly attempting to reconcile with **Cléonte** to no avail, she adopts his hard–hearted attitude and makes him beg on bended knee for her pardon. She offers no direct opposition to her father when Cléonte mismanages his proposal and is rejected for failure to claim the status of **gentleman**. Later, however, she protests vociferously against marrying the son of the Grand Turk until, suddenly recognizing Cléonte beneath the bearded **disguise**, she rapidly accedes to her father's wishes. In both cases, she reveals herself to be a young lady of strong and loyal emotions, but prone to misunderstanding. **Armande Béjart** played the role during her lifetime.

**Lucile** (*Dépit amoureux*). Daughter to **Albert** and sweetheart of **Éraste**, Lucile appears to be more conventional than some of her fellow characters. She has been discreet about her relationship with her suitor, although she has gone so far as to write him a note that some seventeenth–century people might consider daring. She seems to have been rather straightforward in rejecting **Valère**, even though her "brother" **Ascagne** has donned women's clothes, for a change, and adopted Lucile's identity to marry secretly with the rejected party. Her rage in the second act is understandable, considering the vulnerable position in which she placed herself by declaring her **love** for Éraste more or less unilaterally and by doing so on paper. Such a bold move would normally call for extra concessions and consideration from a lover, and rejection at that point would be a very bitter blow. Given those considerations, her ability to relent, however reluctantly, after the **"lovers' spite"** sequence in Act IV, is proof of her genuine affections for the perhaps unworthy young man. But her ire is soon re–ignited by Valère's claim that the two have already consummated a secret **marriage**. Valère, who does not realize his wife is really Ascagne–**Dorothée**, is totally abashed by Lucile's righteous anger, and even the glib **Mascarille** is shouted into submission. We readily believe Lucile's threat that if she were a man, she would silence them at sword's point. As it is, the scene ends with her giving Mascarille a tremendous slap on the face that sends him reeling. Yet when she learns what has actually happened she laughs off the whole affair with grace and dignity.

**Lucile** (*Le Médecin volant*). **Gorgibus's** daughter, she prefers to elope with **Valère** rather than marry **Villebrequin**, as her father has arranged. We get to see little of the character. Even when she and Valère return in the last scene, it is **Sganarelle** who asks forgiveness for them all.

**Lucinde** (*L'Amour médecin*). **Sganarelle's** daughter is sticken with aphasia at the beginning of the play, forcing her father to seek advice from neighbors and relations. As this proves useless, he interrogates her himself, but once he hits on the right cause for her speechlessness, that she wants to be married, he does not seem to see her nod her head enthusiastically, since in the next scene he tells **Lisette** that he cannot tell the cause. Lisette then questions her and gets the correct answer, but Sganarelle will not listen, though the **lady's maid** repeats it no less than eight times. She goes on to explain, after her father's departure, that she wishes to marry **Clitandre** despite the fact that she has not been able to speak with him, since she has been impressed by his looks, his behavior, and the manner of his proposal. It is because Lisette tells Sganarelle that Lucinde is so upset that she is pining away that the man sends for a flock of **doctors**. Of the five doctors who answer Sganarelle's summons, none actually examines the patient, for all are ready to give a diagnosis based only on a description of the symptoms. Clitandre, however, is only too ready to don his medical robes and examine her in detail, speaking words of **love** to her and obtaining proof of her inclination toward him. She is perfectly aware of the **disguise** and of Clitandre's ruse, so she pretends to persist in her **marriage** mania, accepting Clitandre's **ring** and holding the marriage contract in her own two hands so that her father cannot change it. The young couple escapes during the **dance** interval before Sganarelle learns the truth about what has taken place. This ingenue role was almost certainly performed by **AB**, since she had been a member of the troupe already for several months when the play was produced.

**Lucinde (*Le Médecin malgré lui*).** This girl has feigned dumbness in order to delay the threatened **marriage** with Horace and to find a way to get her father to allow her to marry the man she prefers, **Léandre.** To believe **Jacqueline**, this relationship has been going on for some time and is no secret to the household. It is only **Géronte's** materialism and greed that makes him choose Horace over Léandre, forcing Lucinde into a speechless strike. She communicates her plight immediately to **Sganarelle** through a series of grotesque gestures near the beginning of the second act and cooperates with him as he apes a **doctor's** diagnosis of her malady. She then apparently retires (II, 4). She then reappears in Act III, scene 6, enjoying a moment's secret conversation with the **disguised** young man before she publicly breaks her silence. She then assails her father with a barrage of forceful statements about her marriage plans, just the kind of strong affirmation that **Dorine** had tried to coax out of **Mariane** in *Tartuffe*. It concludes as she screams in deafening tones that she will never consent to her father's wishes. However, this does little good in swaying the old man, who gloats over his control of her, even while she slips away to elope with Léandre. When the two return in the final scene to procure Géronte's blessing, she lets her mate do all the talking. The role would have been taken by **Armande Béjart**, who regularly played such female leads.

**Lucrèce (*L'Amour médecin*).** This niece of **Sganarelle** appears only in the first scene of the play, where she advises her uncle that **Lucinde** is too feeble and delicate to be a wife and face the rigors of child–birth, and should instead enter a **convent**. Sganarelle dismisses this advice by pointing out that Lucrèce hopes to profit from her advice by inheriting **money** that otherwise would go to Lucinde's dowry.

**Lully, Jean–Baptiste, né Giovanni–Battista Lulli** (1632–1687). The two Jean–Baptistes, one a musician–dancer, the other a writer–actor, and both theater directors, maintained from 1661 to 1671 one of the most fruitful collaborations in the history of the theater. Eleven of Molière's plays — when they are performed complete — contain music by Lully, and *La Comtesse d'Escarbagnas* was part of his **Ballet des Ballets**. Although Lully is known primarily as the creator of French opera, he was also a key player in the development of the **comedy–ballet**, a form in which Molière created some of his greatest works.

Giovanni Battista Lulli was baptized November 28, 1632, in Florence. He came to France in 1646 to be a *garçon de chambre* (later *valet de chambre*) in the service of **Mlle. de Montpensier** (la Grande Mademoiselle), who wanted to practice her Italian. He remained in her service until her exile in 1652 (she had been on the side of the *frondeurs*), and during this time he was exposed to the best **music and dance** being performed at the French **court**. Mademoiselle had music at the **Tuileries** every day, employing musicians such as Michel Lambert, the major composer of airs and Lully's future collaborator and father–in–law.

In February 1653 Lully danced beside **Louis XIV** in the *Ballet de la Nuit*. The following month he was appointed *compositeur de la musique instrumentale du roi*, a post that involved primarily composing dance music for court ballets. He contributed music to seven ballets from 1654 to 1656, and although in many cases it is hard to know exactly what Lully's contribution was, he was responsible for most of the *Ballet de la Galanterie du Temps* in 1656 and for all of the *Ballet d'Alcidiane* in 1658, except for two *récits* by J.-B. Boesset. In all he wrote all or most of the vocal and instrumental music for twenty ballets, mostly in collaboration with **Benserade**; he also danced at least one role in almost all of them. He increased the role of music in the court ballet while at the same time improving the integration of dance with a simple plot. In 1657, four years before the beginning of his collaboration with Molière, his *Ballet de l'Amour malade* was described as "un ambigu de ballet, de comédie et de farce."

He began to play an increasingly large role in the musical life at court, gaining more and more control for himself while contributing to Louis XIV's efforts at centralization and at increasing the role of professionals, thus diminishing that of the **nobility**. He created a new string orchestra, the Petite Bande, in 1656 and gave it a large role in his ballets. When Louis began his personal reign in March 1661, Lully was involved in the creation of the Académie Royale de Danse the same month, became *Surintendant de la musique et compositeur de la chambre* in May, and was naturalized in December. He became *Maître de la musique de la famille royale* on July 16, 1662, and when he married Madeleine Lambert on July 24, 1662, he was well enough established for the signers of the **marriage** contract to include the King, Queen, Queen Mother (**Anne d'Autriche**), **Colbert,** and his wife.

Although Lully had contributed a courante to *Les Fâcheux* in 1661, his real collaboration with Molière began in 1664 with *Le Mariage forcé*, which we call a comedy–ballet but which their contemporaries referred to as a "ballet meslé de comédie." They worked together on ten more plays (*see* Music and Dance), concluding with *La Comtesse d'Escarbagnas*, which was part of the Ballet des Ballets in December 1671. Lully had much more experience than Molière in creating spectacles that included comedy as well as music and dance, and it is likely that, at least during the first years of their collaboration, he was the leader in working out ways to integrate the three arts. In addition to helping devise the overall plan and the choreography, Lully contributed the instrumental and vocal music that was usually performed during the *entr'actes*, plus a final ballet, and, sometimes, a prologue. He also performed dancing and singing roles, such as an

**Egyptian** guitarist in *La Pastorale comique*, a *matassin* in **Monsieur de Pourceaugnac**, and most memorably, the Mufti in *Le Bourgeois gentilhomme*.

Lully did not limit his activities to his collaboration with Molière. In the realm of sacred music, he wrote his first of at least twenty–five motets in 1664, an activity he would continue until just before his death. He continued to write and coordinate court ballets until 1671, and he probably composed some *intermèdes* for the **Italian** comedians, including *Le Collier de perles* in 1672. He worked briefly with the other two major dramatists of the period, supplying ballet *entrées* for the *entr'actes* of a revival of **Corneille's** *Œdipe* in 1664 and music for **Racine's** *Idylle sur la Paix* in 1685.

He was also following closely the success of Pierre Perrin's Académie d'Opéra, which opened with *Pomone* on March 3, 1671, and began to discuss with Colbert and members of the Petite Académie the possibility of a more heroic form of court entertainment. (According to Sénecé, he had also made plans with Molière to create operas, but betrayed Molière by taking these plans to the King alone.) Perrin had difficulties with his collaborators and ended up in debtor's prison, and in March 1672 Lully bought his *privilège* for opera performances and filed *lettres patentes* creating the Académie Royale de Musique and forbidding anyone else to perform any play "entière en musique." He immediately began trying to limit his competition in Paris, mainly from Molière's troupe, which had just devoted considerable expense to renovating the Palais Royal Theater for the performance of productions such as *Psyché* that included elaborate **machinery**.

Indeed, Molière's use of Lully's music in the successful run of *Psyché* at the Palais Royal Theater from July 1671 until March 1672, for which Lully received no compensation, probably contributed as much to the breakup of their collaboration as did Lully's efforts to secure a monopoly on theatrical performances involving music and dance. He tried to limit rival productions to two airs and two instruments, but objections by Molière and others forced him to set the limitation at six singers and twelve instrumentalists (ordinance of August 12, 1672, five days after last performance of *La Comtesse d'Escarbagnas* with new music by **Charpentier**). This was further reduced on April 30, 1673, to two singers and six instrumentalists, which forced Charpentier to revise his music for *Le Malade imaginaire*. Two days earlier Lully had received permission to take over Molière's theater in the Palais Royal, which would be the home of the Académie Royale de Musique until it burned in 1763.

Another blow to Molière was the September 20, 1672, *privilège* giving Lully exclusive rights to print not only his music but also the texts to which the music was set. Molière thus lost rights to works such as *Le Bourgeois gentilhomme*, *Les Amants magnifiques*, *George Dandin*, and *La pastorale comique*, parts of which Lully and **Quinault** included in their first work at the new opera, *Les Fêtes de l'Amour et de Bacchus*, in November 1672. By this time the break with Lully was complete, and Molière had already engaged Marc–Antoine Charpentier to supply new music for *Le Mariage forcé* and *La Comtesse d'Escarbagnas*, which were revived on July 8, 1672.

Lully and Quinault created their first *tragédie en musique, Cadmus et Hermione*, in 1673. From then until his death on March 22, 1687, Lully would compose and produce an opera each year: *Cadmus et Hermione* (1673), *Alceste\** (1674), *Thésée\** (1675), *Atys\** (1676), *Isis\** (1677), *Psyché* (1678), *Bellérophon* (1679), *Proserpine* (1680), *Persée\** (1682), *Phaéton\** (1683), *Amadis\** (1684), *Roland\** (1685), *Armide\** (1686), *Acis et Galatée* (1686), and the unfinished *Achille et Polixène.* (Works marked with an asterisk have been performed, staged or set in concert versions, since the ground–breaking revival of *Atys* in 1687. The production for 1681, the year Lully became *Secrétaire du roi*, was his last, and most impressive, court ballet, *Le Triomphe de l'Amour.*) All of these had libretti by Quinault except the last two, which were after his retirement, and *Psyché* and *Bellérophon*, which were during his temporary disgrace. Lully had to move quickly to have a production ready in 1678, and he asked **Thomas Corneille** to revise the text of Molière and Pierre Corneille, leaving Quinault's *intermèdes* (and his own Italian lament) intact.

These operas, somewhat like comedy–ballets, also included dance in a *divertissement* during or at the end of each act, but they were sung from beginning to end. The key was the recitative developed by Lully, which could be described as a heightened form of theatrical declamation, more melodic than Italian *recitativo secco* but distinct from airs and ensembles. One can already see it coming of age in *Les Amants magnifiques.*

Lully's rise to fame and wealth (at his death, his fortune was estimated at 800,000 *livres*) was extraordinary, as was his control over the musical establishment. In 1686 the Italian valet Lulli could give his title on the printed score of *Armide* as "Monsieur de Lully, escuyer, conseiller, Secrétaire du Roi, Maison, Couronne de France & de ses Finances & Sur–Intendant de la Musique de Sa majesté."

Selected Bibliography: *Oeuvres complètes*, ed. Henri Prunières, 11 vols. (1933–1939; reprint, New York: Broude Brothers, 1966); *Oeuvres complètes*, ed. Jérôme de La Gorce and Herbert Schneider, Musica Gallica, 39 vols. (Hildesheim: Olms, 2000–); James R. Anthony, "Jean–Baptiste Lully," 1980, in *The New Grove French Baroque Masters* (New York: Norton, 1986), 1–70; Philippe Beaussant, *Lully, ou le musicien du soleil* (Paris: Gallimard/Théâtre des Champs–Élysées, 1992); Manuel Couvreur, *Jean–Baptiste Lully: musique et dramaturgie au service du prince* (Brussels: Vokar, 1992); Jérôme de La Gorce, *Lully* (Paris: Fayard, 2001).

Selected Discography: *Le Bourgeois gentilhomme* (L'Europe Galante, La Petite Bande, dir. Gustav Leonhardt, 1973; EMI /Deutsche Harmonia Mundi CMS 7–69282–2, 1988, 2 CD); *Le Bourgeois gentilhomme, Alceste, L'Amour médecin* (Le Concert des Nations, dir. Jordi Savall, Alia Vox 9807, 1999); *Le Bourgeois gentilhomme, Les Nopces de village, Cadmus et Hermione* (André Danican Philidor, Le Mariage de la Grosse Cathos, Marie–Ange Petit, percussion, London Oboe Band, dir. Paul Goodwin, Harmonia Mundi 907122, 1994, 1 CD); *Comédies–ballets* (Les Musiciens du Louvre, dir. Marc Minkowski, 1987, Erato 2292–45286–2, 1988, 1 CD [Also available with Lully's *Phaéton* by the same ensemble]); *Divertissements* (Guillemette Laurens,

Capriccio Stravagante, dir. Skip Sempé, Deutsche Harmonia Mundi 77218–2–RC, 1990, 1 CD).

*See also*: **Charpentier; Corneille, Pierre; Corneille, Thomas; Music and Dance; Quinault, Philippe.**

*Buford Norman*

**Luynes, Guillaume de.** A prominent Parisian publisher who was involved in editing several of Molière's plays, notably *Les Précieuses ridicules*, which **Ribou** had attempted to pirate. Molière undertook legal action and made sure that Ribou's privilege for the play was cancelled and replaced by one granting the publication to de Luynes. As was common practice, Luynes eventually shared the privilege with other booksellers, including **Barbin**. He was also involved in publishing *L'École des maris* and the "**Remerciement au Roi.**" Later, he was part of the eight–printer coalition that published *L'École des femmes* and *La Critique de l'École des femmes*. He does not seem to be associated with the powerful Provençal noble lineage of the same name. His own name may reflect, instead, an origin in the village of Luynes near Tours.

**Lycarsis** (*Mélicerte*). One of the few sure casting facts about this play is that Molière played the role of this **shepherd**, father to the eponym. He is foolish, vain, and quick–tempered, but also sentimental. When he appears in the first act (I, 3), he is making **Mopse** and **Nicandre** beg him for information about an important political development. When he goes so far as to ask for bribes, they pretend to lose interest. The pouting Lycarsis then tells them all they don't know, namely that the King has arrived in the valley for a visit. It is clear at the end of the conversation that Lycarsis still is not aware he has divulged his secret. Saluted by **Daphné** and **Éroxène**, who come to seek his son's hand in **marriage**, Lycarsis greets the two ladies politely and eagerly, but defers judgment to his son, suggesting that the less fortunate party can fall back on him for a husband. However, he warns them that **Myrtil** is still little more than a **child**, more interested in toys than in women. Thus, he is quite surprised when Myrtil shows great maturity in rejecting the suit of the two women and in naming **Mélicerte** as his sweetheart: "I find this love shocking and absolutely unnecessary!" Father and son enter into a one–sided argument, as Lycarsis attempts to enforce his authority and Myrtil answers with the power of nature. Lycarsis resents this **philosophy** that his son has picked up from a wandering Athenian sophist. Lycarsis fumes at his son's departure, still promising the ladies to answer "body for body" for his son's rejection. When he catches up to Myrtil (II, 4) and surprises him conversing with Mélicerte, he again blames the behavior on his son's new philosophy, adding that Mélicerte is guilty as well, for having beguiled his son. Defending her honor, she withdraws to allow father and son to talk the matter out. Myrtil shares his innermost desires with Lycarsis, eliciting sympathy from the old man and eventually causing his anger to break down completely: "I can't hold back any longer; he's driving me to tears / And his tender sincerity's won me over." Knowing perhaps that his father's moods are fleeting, Myrtil makes Lycarsis promise that he will forgive the son's disobedience if he changes his mind. Lycarsis leaves the stage on his way to arrange the marriage with Mopse, Mélicerte's uncle. Since, according to the dramatis personae, Lycarsis is not really Myrtil's father after all, this display of sentimentality is all the more interesting. The role mainly resembles several of the **Sganarelles**, but also foreshadows **Argan** in the relationship between parent and apparent child.

**Lycas (*Pastorale comique*).** Molière played the part of this "rich" **shepherd**, perhaps a forerunner to **George Dandin** in his bumpkin ways, and only a slightly better judge of women, for the one he picks to woo, **Iris**, quickly rejects both him and his rival **Filène**, rather than leading them on into cuckoldry. The worst that can be said of her is that she is certainly a coquette. Lycas apparently engages some magicians in order to use magic to aid his suit. He seems to confront his rival's rodomontades bravely enough, dismissing his threats as a "bagatelle," and later confronting sad death with cries of firmness and courage, but some gestural poltroonery would be more in keeping with Molière's traditional characters.

**Lycas (*Psyché*).** Captain of the King's guard in this play, Lycas arrives to announce the bad news of the oracle, reciting to **Psyche's** sisters the precise words that condemn her to be fed to a monster. The part was played by the salaried actor Chasteauneuf.

**Lycaste (*Le Mariage forcé*).** This is certainly one of **La Grange's** slimmest roles. As the lover of **Dorimène**, he is present for only one scene, where he scolds her for wanting to take a husband. As she goes on at length about the financial advantages of the union and the fact that she expects her husband to die promptly and conveniently, Lycaste spies **Sganarelle** watching them and alerts the young lady. They cleverly make the best of the situation, as she politely introduces her fiancé and he politely but ironically compliments him and offers the couple "his services."

**Lyciscas (*La Princesse d'Élide*).** Molière appears as the sleepy dog handler **Lyciscas** in the second scene of the first *intermède* that opens the play. He ignores the calls of his fellow hounds keepers and of the musicians that accompany them. After some cursing, he finally arises and calls to his counterparts, unleashing a fanfare of horns that signals the opening of Act I. He has only one scene to change into the costume of **Moron**, which he plays for the rest of the spectacle.

**Lyon.** Site of numerous Molière presentations during the 1650s, the city became troupe headquarters for a few years before the return to **Paris**. The troupe's theater was a tennis court in the Saint–Paul neighborhood. **Dufresne's** troupe spent most of the 1652–53 winter season in the city. They were back by March 1654 and may have spent most of the following year there, except for an ill–fated outing to **Vienne** in September. The same is true for the 1657–58 period, but for a few months in **Dijon**. It was from Lyon that preparations were made for the return to the north of France and **Rouen** the following summer. A major banking center for centuries, Lyon is mentioned in *Les Femmes savantes* as the place where **Chrysale's** family has placed its investments; Argante and Damon are undoubtedly bankers.

**Lyric and Occasional Poetry**. Nondramatic poetry appears in Molière's plays (for example, the sonnet of **Oronte** in *Le Misanthrope*, **Myrtil's** lines to a sparrow in *Mélicerte*, and **Trissotin's** creation in *Les Femmes savantes*). But subordinate to a plot structure and serving to portray the characters who wrote, read, or heard them, these are not, strictly speaking, lyrical pieces. On the other hand, Molière did write a small number of short, undistinguished poems commemorating special occasions: "Couplet d'une Chanson pour Christine de France" (1655); "Vers sur un air de Ballet de Monsieur Beauchamp" (published 1668); "À Monsieur La Mothe le Vayer sur la Mort de son Fils" (1664 or after; published 1678); "La Confrèrie de l'Esclavage de Notre–Dame de Charité" (1665–66); "Au Roi sur la Conquête de la Franche Comté" (published 1668); and "Bouts–rimés commandés sur le bel air" (probably 1667; published 1682). A happy exception is his "**Remerciement au Roi**" (1662/63), in which the playwright wittily and elegantly expressed gratitude for financial support that he had received from **Colbert** at the behest of **Jean Chapelain**.

See Molière, *Oeuvres complètes*, ed. Georges Couton, Bibliothèque de la Pléiade (Paris: Librairie Gallimard, 1971), vol 1, 629–633 (notice and text of "Remerciement au Roi"), 1282–1283 (notes); vol. 2, 1188–1186, 1195–1196 (text of short circumstantial poems); 1520–1524, 1532–1533 (notes).

*David Lee Rubin*

**Lysandre (*Les Fâcheux*)**. Lysandre is a musical pest, obsessed with **singing**, **dancing**, and composing. His rendition of a popular *courante* tune, preceeded by "La la, hem hem, listen carefully, I pray," must have been hilarious, as was his repeating the ending five or six times. Likewise, his dancing would have been grotesque, especially when he grabs **Éraste** and has him do the steps of the female partner. He appears in Act I, scene 2 and was almost certainly played by Molière himself, to judge by the numerous opportunities for **lazzi** that the part contains.

**Lysidas (*La Critique de L'École des femmes*)**. Addressed in the **bourgeois** manner as Monsieur Lysidas, this poet has been wandering the salons of **Paris** promoting his most recent play and even doing "commercials" for it by urging people to rent a loge in the **theater**. Drawn into the conversation over Molière's hit play, he shows himself to be both more circumspect and more learned than the ridiculous **Marquis**. His criticisms are not based just on the reception, but on the construction of the play itself. Lysidas cites **Aristotle** and **Horace** rather haughtily as authorities for his views, until **Dorante** brings him down to earth. The five specific charges he cites near the conclusion of the play were all items of controversy during the **Quarrel of the School for Wives**, but each is rather easily disarmed by Dorante. It is quite likely that **Thomas Corneille** was the "original" for Lysidas, all the more so since Molière had already made him a target in *L'École*; however, other names such as that of the abbé d'Aubignac have been suggested. *L'Impromptu de Versailles* shows that the role was taken by Du Croisy.

# M

**Machine Plays.**    During the course of the sixteenth century **Italian** architects devised a number of complicated machines and techniques that allowed for a variety of breathtaking theatrical effects.    These included, most notably, instantaneous scene changes, having characters fly across the stage, sudden appearances or disappearances of people or objects, simulation of disasters (earthquakes, volcanic eruptions, destruction of buildings, etc.), and metamorphoses (sudden changes of people into radically different forms). When these special effects were first presented to Parisian audiences at **court** performances in the 1640s, they proved so popular that for the next quarter of a century all of the major theatrical companies experimented with them and commissioned new plays specially designed to include them.  Not surprisingly, most of those plays featured plots derived from Classical mythology or medieval romance, allowing for the appearance of numerous **gods**, enchanters, demons, **ghosts**, or other supernatural beings.  In addition to the visual excitement created by special effects, they satisfied the Baroque fascination with illusion, swirling movement, and metamorphosis.  During Molière's lifetime the plays most likely to feature stage machinery were spoken tragedies and tragicomedies.  In those works the machines were the primary attraction; vocal music was used in small amounts; and **ballet** episodes were only occasionally included.  However, during the final quarter of the seventeenth century these "machine plays" lost out in popularity to the new school of French opera, which from the outset made the special effects a central component, alongside singing and dancing.

Molière, who for much of his career was director of an acting company and who would become one of **Louis XIV's** principal purveyors of entertainments, could hardly remain indifferent to the popular taste of his day.  If he long resisted utilizing stage machinery in his own plays, it is largely because at first he seemed unsure of how he could integrate such special effects into his comparatively realistic brand of comedy, where the supernatural rarely plays a role.

One can divide the role of stage machinery in Molière's career into four categories: (1) the performance of other dramatists' machine plays by his troupe; (2) the use of machines in **court** festivities that involved Molière's troupe and also featured plays by him; (3) plays by Molière using machines but without **music or dance**; and (4) plays by him using all these components.

(1) It is known that Molière's troupe performed **Pierre Corneille's** *Andromède*, the first machine play to win widespread acclaim, in the provinces probably in 1651–52. Molière himself played the male lead. Given the fact that the work had just premiered in 1650, the troupe was quick to recognize and capitalize on the popularity of the new type of play. Unfortunately, it is not known precisely where they performed it and how much machinery they had at their disposal. In 1660, while based at the **Petit–Bourbon** in **Paris**, a royal **theater** equipped with extensive machinery (and where *Andromède* had its initial staging a decade earlier), Molière's company staged two additional plays involving machine effects: **Gabriel Gilbert's** tragedy *Les Amours de Diane et d'Endimion* (first performed in 1657) and Jacques Pousset de Montauban's pastoral *Les Charmes de Félicie* (1653). These achieved only modest success, receiving eleven and six performances respectively, and would not be revived until after Molière's death.

(2) In 1661 the finance minister **Foucquet** commissioned Molière to write a comedy to be integrated into an elaborate festival that he arranged in honor of the King and **court**. Although the play itself, *Les Fâcheux*, has a realistic setting and plot, the original prologue was a mythological tribute to the king. After Molière, in street clothes, made a mock apology at not having enough time or performers to entertain the King properly, a huge shell opened to reveal a naiad, who declared that Louis's power was so great that at his command statues would walk and trees would speak, whereupon those objects opened to reveal a group of actors and dancers dressed as dryads, fauns, and satyrs. At the nymph's command the actors left to change **costumes** for the comedy and the dancers executed the first ballet of the evening. While Molière participated in this prologue, it seems clear that he did not plan it; the nymph's speech was written by **Paul Pellisson**, the minister's secretary, and Foucquet himself, who engaged the services of the Italian machine specialist Giacomo Torelli, was probably the one to decide when and how they should be used. Nevertheless, the experience must have greatly impressed Molière, who came to recognize the usefulness of mythological characters and pastoral decor: they were an elegant method of flattering the King, suggesting that he and his court were the continuation of the glories of Classical antiquity; they allowed for splendid costumes and sets, as well as for elaborate episodes of vocal music and ballet; they made a striking contrast with the prosaic and foolish characters of the comedy that they accompanied; they could add to the general mood of celebration typically required at the end of a comedy by presenting an idealized world where people have nothing else to do but sing and dance.

In 1664 Molière and his troupe were called upon to participate in *Les Plaisirs de l'île enchantée*, a three–day extravaganza intended to mark the unveiling of Louis's new palace at **Versailles**. The main entertainment of the first evening was a pageant and ballet, presided over by the deities **Pan** (played by Molière) and **Diana**, who made their entrance atop a mountain that was carried through the air. The main spectacle of the second evening was a comedy–ballet written by Molière, *La Princesse d'Elide*, which featured a machine effect only in the concluding ballet. As so often happened at the conclusion of court productions with happy endings, the celebration involved singing and dancing **shepherds** and fauns. On this occasion, although the shepherds and herdsmen entered normally, the sixteen fauns emerged from underneath the stage upon a huge tree, each playing a musical instrument (flute or violin). The use of a machine, not strictly necessary to the play, was probably mandated by the festival organizers, who wanted a spectacular finish to the day's festivities. The third and final day was largely devoted to a battle over the palace of the sorceress Alcina (a character from Ariosto's *Orlando furioso*), specially built on an island on the lake in the Versailles gardens. Special effects abounded: two additional islands suddenly appeared on the lake, each covered with instrumentalists; then Alcina emerged from behind a rock carried by a huge sea monster, accompanied by two of her nymphs seated on whales; then the palace suddenly acquired a group of tall towers; and finally a brilliant fireworks display destroyed the palace, quickly reducing it to ashes.

The *Ballet des Muses*, held in December 1665 and January 1666 at another of the king's palaces, **Saint–Germain–en–Laye**, consisted of thirteen different entertainments in different genres. The third of these was a pastoral play by Molière (*Mélicerte*, later replaced by the lost *Pastorale comique*); late in the run a fourteenth entertainment was added: Molière's comedy–ballet, *Le Sicilien*. Machines do not seem to have been featured except in the thirteenth segment, where the nine daughters of Pierus, refusing to accept the judgment by a panel of nymphs that the nine Muses surpass them in artistic excellence, are finally punished by **Jupiter,** who changes them into birds (a sudden metamorphosis effect). It is possible, though the original libretto does not specify, that Jupiter entered in a flying machine.

(3) In 1665 Molière, probably responding to the enormous popularity of the Don Juan legend, which inspired dramatic treatments at both of the rival theatrical companies, composed his own version. *Dom Juan* is the only one of his comedies to feature a separate stage set in every act. The fact that the troupe brought in two decorators experienced in stage machinery (the contract survives) indicates the unusual importance accorded to the set. Molière must have wanted instantaneous scene changes, but scholars disagree as to whether the Palais Royal Theater in 1665 possessed the technical wherewithal for them. (Given that the public theaters needed time during the intermissions to trim the wicks of the **candles**, there would have been time to change the sets manually.) Since by the middle of the seventeenth century, dramatists and audiences had accepted a highly restrictive interpretation of the unity of place that banned virtually all scene changes within a play, with machine plays constituting the one recognized

exception, Molière's intent was to write a kind of machine play. The multiple sets also possess symbolic value: the hero is a man in constant motion who refuses to be tied down, either spatially or amorously; and at the same time, wherever he goes, he finds himself unable to escape constant pursuit by forces of society and **religion** that call for his repentance. In addition, the play has two sets of special effects that directly affect the plot: there is an extra scene change within an act (III, 5) to show the tomb of the **Commander** whom Dom Juan previously slew and whom he will invite to dinner. Scholars who hold that all the scene changes were instantaneous claim that the mausoleum occupied the full stage; the alternative view is that a flat at the rear of the stage opened to reveal the mausoleum. Near the end of Act V a ghost appears in the form of a veiled woman to deliver a final warning to Dom Juan (it is not clear whether the ghost enters from a trap door or from the wings; the part was probably given to the actress playing **Done Elvire**). This is followed by two special effects: the ghost changes into Father Time with sickle in hand, then it flies up into the air and disappears. A moment later the statue reenters and hurls Dom Juan into hell. According to a stage direction in the 1682 edition, the hero is struck by lightning bolts to the accompaniment of thunder; the earth opens and swallows him; a great fire emerges from the place into which he falls. This obviously required a trap door and some kind of fireworks. The fact that the *Registre* of **La Grange**, a daily record of performances and box office receipts for the company, notes payments to the Capucin friars (who also served as firemen), for the majority of performances of this play, suggests that special precautions needed to be taken for its spectacular finale. (Prior to 1665 La Grange recorded only very sporadic payments for this service.)

In 1668 Molière staged his only other machine play without ballet, *Amphitryon*. Once again the supernatural was an essential ingredient in a well–known plot, which in this case was taken from Classical mythology. The subject had already been treated as a machine play: in 1650 the **Hôtel de Bourgogne** troupe revived **Jean Rotrou's** comedy, *Les Sosies*, renamed it, and added machine effects. Molière, who presumably wished to emphasize the comic aspect of the story more than the miraculous, used special effects with sobriety. There are no scene changes, and the machine effects, confined to aerial flight, occur only at the opening and close of the play. The prologue consists of a dialogue between **Mercury** and the personification of **Night**; the former appears on a cloud, while the latter enters in a chariot drawn by two horses. They remain in the air throughout the scene, after which Mercury descends to earth (and the cloud flies away, though this is not specified in the text) and Night moves across the stage and disappears. This episode, not found in earlier versions of the story, serves as a witty exposition and makes it visually clear that Mercury, who will impersonate a human character, Sosie, for most of the play, is really a god. When, at the play's conclusion, the deception is revealed to the characters, Molière provides both an ascent and a descent: Mercury, after giving his explanation from the balcony of the house, flies off into the air, and a moment later Jupiter arrives in a cloud to reassure the humans and foretell the birth of the hero **Hercules**. A stage direction in the 1682 edition gives further details about Jupiter's appearance: he is seated upon his eagle, armed with his thunderbolt, and his entry is accompanied with lightning and the sound of thunder (this latter, by the way, would cover up the noise made by the machines). The flying machines, besides their value as spectacle, serve to clarify a confusing plot, demonstrate the gods' physical (though not moral or amorous) superiority, and make concrete the thematic oppositions between high and low, heaven and earth.

(4) During the last dozen years of his life Molière would devote a sizable percentage of his dramatic production to a hybrid spectacle known as **comedy–ballet**. For these works, all of them intended for performance before the **court** and in most cases actually commissioned by the King, machines were not considered an essential ingredient and were rarely featured. However, *Les Amants magnifiques* (1670), an unusually elaborate court production, used machines to create a complex series of illusions, plays–within–a–play and metatheatrical reflection. Most of the main play takes place in an unspecified area of the palace, but four of the six *intermèdes* occur elsewhere, requiring simultaneous set changes. The first and third of these are intercalated spectacles offered by the two lavish princes of the title to the princess **Eriphile**, whom they are courting. The first, an aquatic festival with singing and dancing to honor the god Neptune, involves several special effects: Eole, god of the winds, enters in a small cloud; an island emerges from below the sea, bearing eight dancing fishermen, and (though this is not specified) Neptune probably arrives from below the stage, as well. The third *intermède*, consisting of a completely sung pastoral opera, is set in a forest; Eriphile is present as an onstage spectator. Although the stage directions are not fully clear, it seems that for the final celebratory section some caves at the back of the inner stage opened up to reveal a secondary stage that allowed the comic characters (little dryads and fauns) to parody the serious dancing of their elders. The fourth *intermède*, arranged by the astrologer Anaxarque, takes place in a grotto where eight statues bearing torches come to life and dance. There is no scene change at the end of this *intermède*, since the fourth act of the play proper continues in the grotto. However, when the last characters leave the grotto at the end of scene 3, the action seems to resume in the garden path outside it; presumably, there was a partial set change here. Act IV also contains a machine effect directly connected to the plot: the goddess **Venus** descends, probably in some kind of chariot, accompanied by four *putti*, to announce an oracle: the gods have ordained that Eriphile will marry the hero who saves her mother's life. Once the two ladies have left, the **astrologer** explains to his son that the goddess was really an actress hired by him and explains some of the technical details about how the machinery worked to produce such a striking illusion (IV, 3). This demystification of stage machinery and discussion of how it can be manipulated for political purposes is one of the play's most striking moments for the modern reader. The sixth and final *intermède* takes place in a temple in the form of an amphitheater. The **Pythian** games are performed in honor of the god Apollo, who enters in a ceremonial procession at their conclusion; apart from the set change this episode used no machines. The play was so incredibly lavish that

Molière did not even attempt to present a scaled–down version in his Paris theater.

The following year, however, Molière succeeded in outdoing all his previous court productions in the areas of spectacle, music, and choreography. *Psyché* combined elements from comedy–ballet and machine tragedy in a remarkable synthesis that came very close to full–fledged opera. Every act, including the prologue (which is necessary to the plot), has a separate set, though in the case of the first, second, and fourth *intermèdes* the scene change occurs prior to the dance sequence rather than after. The final *intermède* involved yet another set change to show the heavens with the residences of the gods. Molière incorporated an unprecedented number of aerial flights. In the prologue Venus, l'Amour, six *putti*, and one of the **Graces** descend in a huge machine, accompanied by two smaller machines, each bearing another of the Graces (in the Paris production only the one large machine was featured, the *putti* were eliminated, and the Graces were reduced to two). At the end of the prologue l'Amour flies away. Presumably, Venus and her companions exited in their machine, though this is not specified. In Act II the chief **zephyr** carries off the heroine on a heap of clouds with a whirlwind, according to the original libretto (the printed text has her carried off by two zephyrs). L'Amour appears in the air to sentence Psyche's mortal suitors to death. In Act III the zephyr flies off to fetch Psyche's sisters. In Act IV he takes them back in a cloud that descends for them and flies away. Later in that act there is a dramatic scene change: to punish Psyche for violating her trust, l'Amour causes the magic palace to vanish, and she finds herself in a vast and frightening countryside. The spectacular set for the fourth *intermède* and Act V showed Hades with a sea of fire, its waves in perpetual agitation (another machine effect). When Psyche faints and seems dead, l'Amour flies down to her side; soon after Venus descends in her chariot (according to the libretto); then Jupiter appears in the air seated on his eagle, to the accompaniment of thunder and lightning. When he invites Psyche to join the ranks of the immortals, two large machines descend to allow the characters to rise into the heavens (Venus and her companions enter one machine, while Psyche and l'Amour get into the other). This time Molière was determined to give his Parisian audience a taste of courtly spectacle. His troupe spent a huge sum to renovate the Palais Royal Theater and equip it with all the required stage machinery. Although he had to reduce the number of singers and dancers for the Paris production (and apparently the number and complexity of the special effects, as well), *Psyché* was a huge success.

Molière's last play, **Le Malade imaginaire** (1673) used machinery only for set changes. Since the main play has a single set, those changes occurred at the end of the prologue (in the original version this was a huge operatic scene set in a mythological pastoral landscape; the later, scaled–down version is set in a simple forest locale), and before and after the first *intermède* (set in a city street and featuring characters from the **commedia dell'arte**). On the surface, those episodes have nothing to do with the main plot. There are no further set changes, since the dancers and singers of the second *intermède* are brought into the hypochondriac's home by his brother, while in the third *intermède* that home is filled with new carpets and furniture, as well as singers and dancers, to accommodate a mock ceremony that will make him a **doctor**. The use of different sets for the first two dance episodes and the lack of them for the last two mark a symbolic progression in which two radically opposing worlds, one pastoral and ideal, the other prosaic and foolish, move progressively closer, and the play ends as fantasy invades and conquers reality.

*Perry Gethner*

**Macroton** (*L'Amour médecin*).    **Doctor** Macroton speaks very slowly, enunciating each separate syllable, in contrast to his colleague **Bahys**, who rapidly mumbles.    **Sganarelle** compares the pair to a turtle and a post–horse. Neither adds anything special to the formula of bleeding and purging proposed by the other doctors, but both believe it is better to die according to medical authority than to live in contravention to it.    Macroton represented the court physician Guénaut.

**Madame.** *See* **Henrietta of England**.

**Madness.**  Despite the many private manias of Molière's characters, wholescale madness was far less common in his works than in earlier plays, such as André Mareschal's *Hôpital des fous* or **Desmarets de Saint–Sorlin's** *Visionnaires*. Perhaps the most completely mad character is **Bélise** in *Les Femmes savantes*. On the one hand, she is recognized as such by members of her own family.  On the other, she allows her delusions of being a universal **love** object to intrude to a significant degree into her private life and welfare.    The fact that she can function "normally" in **Philaminte's** circle is perhaps proof that there is a good deal of collective insanity in their enterprise.  **Sosie** reaches the edge of madness in *Amphitryon*, for he is confronted with every paranoid's worst nightmare, the verifiable existence of a *döppelganger*.  He sounds mad as he tries to explain "the two me's" to his master, but as he cautions, the tale is quite true.  The fact that Sosie never loses his grasp on the latter fact and is able to reconcile himself with the disturbing duality that has been created speaks much for his fundamental sanity.  **Monsieur de Pourceaugnac** is diagnosed as insane by his two **doctors** after **Éraste** planted the idea in their heads.  Other than a little palliative **music**, treatment for mental disorders differed little from physical disease; enemas were in order.  **Madame Jourdain** accuses her husband more than once of being completely mad, especially when he runs around the house dressed in even more bizarre clothing than usual and chanting bits of **Turkish** nonsense, but the other characters are not willing to make this charge publicly as long as they can manipulate him for their own ends.

**Magdelon** (*Les Précieuses ridicules*).  Though the daughter of **Gorgibus**, she must have been raised in the provinces, if one is to judge by the fact that **La Grange** refers to both Magdelon and her cousin as "pecques provinciales."  She later tells her father that she wishes to get to know **Paris** better, since she and

**Cathos** have just arrived there. She gives an abridged version, in scene 4, of the proper **Scudéry** formula for gradually falling in **love**. In affected fashion, she has chosen for herself the new name of **Polyxène** from a novel by **Molière d'Essertines**. Consequently, she uses such obscure terms as "un necessaire" for a lackey, "le conseiller des graces" for a mirror, "les commodités de la conversation" for chairs, and "donner les âmes des pieds" for dancing. She is enchanted by **Mascarille's** visit, especially when he promises to introduce them to all the chief wits and gossip-mongers of Paris. Together with Cathos, she applauds Mascarille's vapid little poetic "**impromptu**," his theatrical acumen, and his taste in clothes. Yet she is faithful to prudish *préciosité* when Mascarille begins to unbutton his pants to show the girls "a whopping scar" and says they will take his word for it. She is "just splitting with rage" when La Grange and **Du Croisy** reveal their trick and strip the pretentious valets in front of the girls. The character's name probably indicates that the part was originally taken by **Madeleine Béjart**.

**Magician** (*Le Mariage forcé*). The magician was present only in the original **ballet** version of the play, where **Sganarelle** consults him right after talking with the **Gypsies**. Performed by the professional singer Monsieur D'Estival, the magician conjures four demons who execute a dance number while Sganarelle cowers in the corner of the stage. In the later Parisian version, Sganarelle mentions going off to consult the magician, but then sees **Dorimène** talking with **Lycaste** and eavesdrops on their tête-à-tête. It is not surprising that this is virtually the only mention of magic in Molière's plays, other than a couple of passing references when characters wonder whether they are under spells. Molière deliberately reduced the status of magic in comedy from the rather prominent level that had prevailed in the works of **Pierre Corneille** and his contemporaries. This was in keeping with his fundamental desire to found the theater on what is natural and reasonable, and to discredit superstition as a pernicious product of the deceptive imagination.

**Maître Jacques** (*L'Avare*). Alternately (and not, he insists, simultaneously) cook and coachman for the miser's household, Maître Jacques tries to take his dual professions seriously and chafes under the oppression of **Harpagon** and his overseer, **Valère**. It is Jacques who points out that the miser's team is unshod and starving, that his coach is in disrepair, and that the pantry is ill-stocked. He continually clashes with his superiors, making many snide remarks in the third act as Harpagon plans his "feast." He is mortified when the miser rejects his thoroughly fashionable menu for a collection of cheap cuts and stews containing little meat. It is Jacques who rails against Harpagon's avarice and directly insults him, earning a **beating** from his master and then another from Valère, when he tries to put the upstart in his place. Later, he has his revenge on the superintendent by accusing him before the **police** as the thief of Harpagon's strongbox. When Jacques's lie is discovered, Harpagon is ready to hand him over to the **Commissioner** for punishment, causing Jacques to observe that he is beaten for telling the truth and hanged for lying. However, the intervention of

**Anselme** saves Jacques from this grim end. The role is well developed and quite interesting, with numerous opportunities in both the verbal and gestural registers. For example, Jacques presides over an extended sequence in Act IV, where he thinks he succeeds in reconciling Harpagon and **Cléante** (who is on the verge of disinheritance) by agreeing completely with what each man says about the other, then happily departs before they realize that neither has obtained any concessions. Jacques figures in the 1682 frontispiece illustration, along with Harpagon and Valère. He was probably played in the original cast by **Hubert**.

**Maître Simon** (*L'Avare*). A crooked agent who helps **La Flèche** and **Cléante** arrange their illegal loan.

*Malade imaginaire, Le (The Imaginary Invalid).* **Argan**, a well–to–do, middle–aged **bourgeois**, is obsessed by his health. He spends much of his time and **money** on medical treatments of various sorts and is encouraged in his self–imposed invalidism by his second wife, **Béline**, who is interested only in taking control of his estate. In order to have a **doctor** in the family, Argan hits upon the idea of marrying off his elder daughter, **Angélique**, to a young doctor, **Thomas Diafoirus**, in spite of Angélique's love for another suitor, **Cléante**. Attempts by Argan's practical–minded brother, **Béralde**, to reason with the hypochondriac and get him to change his ways are fruitless. Finally, a plot hatched by Argan's **servant**, **Toinette**, reveals the hypocrisy of Béline and the true devotion of Angélique in spite of her father's tyrannical intentions: Toinette convinces Argan to play dead so that he can hear for himself how his family really feels about him. Argan is finally convinced to allow Angélique to marry Cléante, a non–doctor, when Béralde suggests that he, Argan, become a doctor himself by going through an initiation ritual that Béralde will organize. The play concludes with the swearing–in ceremony of Argan as a doctor.

The scenes of **music and dancing** include the original prologue, a revised prologue that was substituted for the original one after Molière's death, and three *intermèdes*, one after each of the play's three acts. In the original prologue, a group of **shepherds and shepherdesses** delight in **Louis XIV's** recent victories and his return from the war. In the much shorter revised prologue, a shepherdess laments the fact that doctors cannot cure pain of love like her own, and expresses the opinion that only a *malade imaginaire* would take doctors seriously. In the first *intermède*, **Polichinelle** serenades his mistress in **Italian** and is then interrupted by violinists and dancers whom he does his best to get rid of and whom he ends up paying off. The second *intermède* is organized by Béralde, who brings in **Gypsy** singers and dancers to entertain his brother. The third *intermède*, led by Béralde, is Argan's initiation as a doctor; the words of the ceremony are mostly in a comical, Frenchified version of **Latin**.

*Le Malade imaginaire: Comédie mêlée de musique et de danse*, Molière's last play and the one in which he died playing the title role, was conceived as a comédie–ballet, a **court** entertainment intended to celebrate Louis XIV's victories in the Low Countries in 1672. But between the time of the play's conception in 1672 and its production in February 1673, Molière's ongoing struggle with the composer **Jean–Baptiste Lully** came to a head, and the playwright was unable to perform his final comedy for a courtly audience. In 1672, the King granted Lully a virtual monopoly on all court entertainment that included singing, as well as sole publication rights to all works to which Lully contributed. A decree issued in the same year forbade all theatrical troupes in **Paris** not associated with Lully from using more than six singers and twelve instrumentalists in their productions. As a result of Lully's stunning coup, *Le Malade imaginaire* was first produced under quite different circumstances than had been originally imagined. Molière, faced with the reality that collaboration with Lully would give the musician exclusive publication rights for editions of the text itself as well as the music composed for it, asked **Marc–Antoine Charpentier** to write the music for *Le Malade imaginaire*. Moreover, because of Lully's monopoly on courtly entertainment and Molière's refusal to work with him, the play could not be staged at court. Thus Molière's last play was the only one of his comédies–ballets to open before a public audience rather than a courtly one. The play premiered successfully on February 10, 1673, at the Palais Royal Theater in **Paris**, taking in 1,872 *livres* on opening night, among the highest receipts of Molière's career (surpassed only by *Tartuffe* in 1669).

As a satire not only of the medical profession in particular but also of pedantry and orthodoxy in general, *Le Malade imaginaire* is informed by a number of events and controversies of the day. In 1671, certain leading members of the Paris Faculty of Theology, including Morel and Guyart, took steps to shore up what they felt to be their increasingly precarious authority. In response to challenges upon **Aristotelian** scholasticism, mounted mainly by various disciples of **Descartes** and **Gassendi**, the Sorbonne moved to revive a 1624 decree of the Parlement that forbade anyone, on pain of death, from professing principles that were not officially sanctioned by the Faculty. In late 1671, **Boileau** and the physician **François Bernier** joined forces to publish *Arrêt burlesque*, which mocked the Sorbonne's attempt at imposing orthodoxy at the expense of free thought; Boileau's contribution included an attack on traditional medicine and its refusal to recognize Harvey's thesis about the circulation of blood, ironically described in the *Arrêt* as "wandering and circulating through the veins and arteries without punishment, and with no right or entitlement to carry out this annoying action other than Experience." Louis XIV and **Madame de Montespan** were not supportive of critics of Harvey's thesis like Gui Patin, and Molière apparently came up with the idea of composing a comedy based on the goings–on at the Sorbonne, or at least such is the claim of Bernier in his preface to the *Arrêt*. Molière then changed his mind for some reason and only later came back to the idea in the form of a more specific critique of doctors, encouraged by the enthusiastic responses from Parisian and courtly audiences that his earlier satires of the medical profession had received. Even the narrower focus of the play's final conception was undoubtedly partially inspired by the Sorbonne controversy.

The final *intermède*, the satire of a swearing–in ceremony for a newly minted physician, was perhaps closer to contemporary practices than one might think. While the ceremony is, indeed, wildly exaggerated, seventeenth–century initiation ceremonies for medical doctors were often quite elaborate, and it was not unheard of for them to have a musical component. Molière is reported to have gathered information about such ceremonies from his own doctor, Mauvillain.

Published posthumously, *Le Malade imaginaire* is one of the hardest of Molière's plays to classify. Although in form it resembles other *comédies–ballets* like *Le Bourgeois gentilhomme*, it is also one of the few comedies in prose often considered among the playwright's greatest works, in the same lofty realm as *L'Ecole des femmes*, *Tartuffe*, and *Le Misanthrope*. And indeed, several peculiarities place *Le Malade imaginaire* in a category of its own.

The play's precise genre is difficult to determine. As a *comédie–ballet* it comes out of a long Renaissance tradition of courtly entertainments combining **music and dance** with some sort of rudimentary situation or tale, and while some critics and literary historians see the character of Argan and the plot of the comedy as hardly more developed than the simple, barely integrated stories of the *ballets de cour*, others emphasize the play's complexity: according to André Gide, *Le Malade imaginaire* reaches "a degree of greatness never surpassed in the theater." The play relies more heavily on **farce** than Moliere's other most highly regarded works, most notably in its incorporation of elements of physical comedy, especially in — but not limited to — the character of the servant Toinette, the play's most important character aside from Argan. Elements of farce include Argan's offstage forays to relieve himself; Toinette's back–and–forth scrambling to introduce the arrival of a traveling doctor and then to **disguise** herself and appear before Argan in that role; and Argan's sudden rising from the "dead" to the utter shock of first his wife, and then his daughter. This liberal admixture of farce is all the more striking in that Molière's next–to–last play, *Les Femmes savantes*, produced the previous year, is among his most refined and sophisticated works.

On a more psychological level, the play has also been read as a *comédie de caractère*, with the obsessive Argan — whose will to be ill is actually a thinly veiled means of controlling and regulating his mortality — seen as an incarnation of Molière's fear of what he must have sensed was his own impending death. Although Molière's final play is far from being the first one in which he attacks the medical establishment, his downwardly spiraling ill health almost certainly gave a particular resonance to this work, which stands apart from the playwright's earlier medical comedies in that here the satire is focused more on the patient himself than on his doctors. Molière's well–known preoccupation with his own health had been the target of **Le Boulanger de Chalussay's** *Elomire hypocondre* — "Elomire" being an anagram of "Molière" — and Molière's seventeenth–century biographer **Grimarest** was perhaps the first — but was certainly not the last — to speculate that Molière himself was the "original" of Argan.

Another peculiarity of *Le Malade imaginaire* is that it is the only one of Molière's plays to present a **child** onstage, a highly unusual practice in Classical theater. Argan's younger daughter, **Louison**, played by the young Louise Beauval, the daughter of two members of Molière's troupe, is cross–examined by her father about the carryings–on of her older sister, Angélique (II, 8), in one of Classical theater's most naturalistic scenes. Molière portrays a touching array of recognizable emotions in the little girl, including playfulness, evasiveness, fear of punishment, and the agitated excitement of tattling about an older sibling. Goethe had particular praise for this scene.

In addition to the elements of farce and of *comédie de caractère*, *Le Malade imaginaire* is also clearly a *comédie de moeurs*, a social satire critiquing not only the excesses and conservatism of the medical profession, but also the laughable, vulgar consumerism of an expanding class of prosperous bourgeois with time and money on their hands. To this extent Argan in his desire to purchase good health is as outlandish as **Arnolphe** in his attempt to buy a four–year–old girl as a future faithful wife in *L'Ecole des femmes* and as **Monsieur Jourdain** in his efforts to buy the manners of an aristocrat in *Le Bourgeois gentilhomme*.

Few contemporary sources for *Le Malade imaginaire* have been discovered. Molière seems to have been somewhat influenced by **Brécourt's** farce, *Un grand benêt de fils aussi sot que son père*, and also perhaps by Le Boulanger de Chalussay's *Elomire hypocondre*. A handful of other plays, mostly contemporary comedies, have been suggested as possible sources, but any contributions or influences of these works would appear to have been fairly minimal.

On the other hand, many affinities exist between Molière's final comedy and his earlier works. The satire of the medical profession crisscrosses Molière's entire Parisian period, including *Le Médecin volant*, *L'Amour médecin*, *Le Médecin malgré lui*, and *Monsieur de Pourceaugnac*. The basic structure of *Le Malade imaginaire*, which features an obsessive, selfish parent attempting to impose his mania on his daughter by marrying her off to a man who in one way or another satisfies his own obsession, is also operative in *Tartuffe*, *L'Avare*, *Le Bourgeois gentilhomme*, and *Les Femmes savantes*, with the obsessions involved in those earlier works being, respectively, Christian devotion, money, nobility, and aesthetic refinement. In addition to these broader affinities, Molière borrows various more specific elements from his earlier plays. Argan's initiation as a doctor is certainly reminiscent of Monsieur Jourdain's instatement as a *mamamouchi* at the conclusion of *Le Bourgeois gentilhomme*. Toinette is a younger, somewhat more boisterous, version of Orgon's servant **Dorine** in *Tartuffe*, each woman playing the role of guardian of her deluded master's family in general, and of his vulnerable marriageable daughter in particular. The revelation of the self–interested hypocrisy of Argan's wife, Béline, has been seen as an echo of the denouement of the play immediately preceding *Le Malade imaginaire*, *Les Femmes savantes*, which concludes with the unmasking of the money–hungry **Trissotin** by means of a comparable ruse. The scene in which Cléante pretends to give Angélique a music lesson (II, 5) may well borrow from a somewhat similar ploy used in *Le Sicilien, ou l'Amour peintre*. Critics have also pointed out borrowings of lines and situations from *Les Fourberies de Scapin*, *Le Médecin malgré lui*, and *Monsieur de Pourceaugnac*.

*Le Malade imaginaire* had a short performance history in its original form, with Molière playing the role of Argan. On February 17, 1673, a week after the play opened and one year to the day after the death of Molière's long–time friend and former leading lady, **Madeleine Béjart**, Molière died shortly after the play's fourth performance. Molière, who had been in failing health for quite some time, was begged by his wife **Armande Béjart** and by **Baron**, a young member of his troupe, to skip the performance in question, but he is reported to have said that he refused to let down the other members of the troupe and the employees of the theater; moreover, the **Prince de Condé** was to attend the performance, as were several foreign dignitaries. Molière's insistence on performing in spite of the alarming state of his health seems to have led to a stroke or a seizure of some kind during the final *intermède*, probably as Molière–Argan pronounced the Latin term *juro*, "I swear," during the initiation ceremony. He was taken home to the rue de Richelieu after the performance and died the same evening while awaiting the arrival of a priest.

Molière's death interrupted the play's run for only about a week. *Le Malade imaginaire* had taken in hefty receipts in its first four performances before Molière's death, averaging close to 2,000 *livres*, and although the play continued to draw well when it reopened, the loss of the author, director, and lead actor was not the only problem to beset future productions. Starting in late February of 1673 Baron and **La Thorillière** both tried their hands at playing the part of Argan, and after they left the troupe the role was taken over by **Rosimond**. Lully's increasing stronghold on the theatrical and musical life of Paris and of the court — on April 30, 1673, a decree was issued preventing comedians not associated with the Florentine composer from using more than two singers and six instrumentalists — forced the troupe to scale back the production, now being staged at the Hôtel Guénégaud, the quarters to which the troupe had been relegated after their director's death so as to allow Lully to use the Palais Royal Theater. In particular, the prologue, originally conceived and presented as a grand production number praising the recent victories over Holland, had to be rewritten to conform to the new, more stringent musical limitations imposed on the troupe, and Charpentier also had to adapt the score. The revised version of *Le Malade imaginaire* opened on May 4, 1674, at the Hôtel Guénégaud. The play's Versailles premiere, probably on July 18, 1674 — nearly eighteen months after the original Paris opening — was a triumph.

The play has received about 1,500 performances by the **Comédie–Française**. In a notable recent production directed by Gildas Bourdet in 1992, Argan's brother, Béralde, who is the main spokesperson in the play for the critique of the medical establishment as well as the principal critic of Argan's hypochondria, coughs throughout the production and falls dead in the final scene, thus underscoring the imaginary, chimerical nature of Argan's own illness and the radical dissociation of Molière's final protagonist from the realities of the world around him.

The original libretto was published as early as 1673, but the first known editions of the text of the play itself — published outside of France in highly spurious versions — date from the following year. On January 7, 1674, barely a year after Molière's death, his troupe blocked performance of *Le Malade imaginaire* by other troupes, including provincial players in **Lyon**, **Rouen**, and Orléans, until the comedy was printed. In the same year, a counterfeit edition, probably reconstituted from performances, was published in **Amsterdam** by **Daniel Elzevier**, and later in 1674 a highly corrupt pirated edition appeared in **Cologne**. In 1675 the play was printed in Paris by **Thierry** and **Barbin**, with a *privilège du Roi*, in an edition that also included Brécourt's prose comedy, *L'Ombre de Molière*. In the 1682 edition of Molière's works edited by La Grange and **Vivot** and published by Thierry, Barbin, and **Trabouillet**, the play appears in volume 8, the second volume of the *Oeuvres posthumes*, with the claim that "all false additions, etc., from previous editions" have been expurgated. This edition is generally held to be the most reliable of the early published versions of the play and has been used as the basis for most more recent editions.

Bibliography: *Le Malade imaginaire de* Molière, ed. Jacques Arnavon (Paris: Plon, 1938); *Le Malade imaginaire*, ed. Daniel Mornet (Paris: Fayard, 1947); *Le Malade imaginaire*, ed. Peter Nurse (Oxford: Clarendon, 1967); Roger Garapon, *Le Dernier Molière* (Paris: SEDES, 1977); Patrick Dandrey, *La Médecine et la maladie dans le théâtre de Molière*, vol. 2, *Molière et la maladie imaginaire* (Paris: Klincksieck, 1998); Nicholas Cronk, "Molière–Charpentier's *Le Malade imaginaire*: The First *Opéra–comique*?" *Forum for Modern Language Studies* 29 (1993), 216–231; Roxanne Lalande, "*Le Malade imaginaire*: The Symbolic and the Mimetic," *Cahiers du dix–septième* 3 (1989), 83–104.

*Richard E. Goodkin*

**Malherbe**, **François de** (1555–1628).   One of the great regularizers of the French **language** at the beginning of the Classical period, this Norman poet reacted against the wilder lexical and stylistic experiments of the Renaissance and early Baroque periods by stipulating that clarity and order must be paramount in writing.   His "rules" were only loosely codified during his lifetime, but were passed on to followers like Racan and Maynard and eventually institutionalized by the **Academy** and by later theorists such as Vaugelas and the abbé d'Aubignac.

Generally, Molière followed Malherbe's rules in his verses, seeking rich rhymes when possible and avoiding such practices as enjambment and neologisms based on Greek and Latin roots.   However, the playwright countered the thrust of Malherbe's "reforms" in one important way: while Malherbe insisted on the purification of literary language, initiating a trend theat would result in *préciosité*, Molière did not shy away from using many terms taken from the commoners' vocabulary, even bringing in coarse and everyday language when necessary to the essence of his scenes.   We know from the satirical passages of *Les Précieuses ridicules* and *Les Femmes savantes* what he thought of over-refined attempts to confine the French language. Indeed, it may be that his experiments in prose were designed to break free of many of the constraints that Malherbe and his followers had successfully placed on poetry of all kinds.

Molière disagreed with Malherbe in one other significant area, that of philosophy. The older poet had been a staunch Stoic, promoting the damping down of the emotions to such an extent that in many cases it undermined his own lyrical enterprise. His most famous poems advocate, in particular, a Stoical mastery over grief for lost loved ones. Molière's verses to La Mothe Le Vayer on the death of his son contradict this program of emotional abnegation, urging the griever to let **nature** take its course as a proper catharsis for feelings that cannot be smothered without dangerous results.

While never attacking the lofty and acknowledged status of linguistic authorities like Malherbe, he does not hesitate to poke fun at them in the name of practical values. In *Les Femmes savantes*, **Chrysale** concedes that Malherbe and **Guez de Balzac** might have been great authorities on language, but that they would be useless in his kitchen, where he wanted the **servants** to concentrate on a good dinner rather than on intellectual subjects.

**Malta**. The Mediterranean fortress island still defended against the **Turks** in Molière's time by the military order of the Knights of Malta. **Jodelet** claims in *Les Précieuses ridicules* that his friend **Mascarille** has commanded a regiment of cavalry in the **galleys** of Malta, a very laughable blunder.

**Marais Theater**. The second of seventeenth–century **Paris's** resident French theaters was established in a tennis court in the newly developed Marais neighborhood just in time to greet **Pierre Corneille's** greatest plays, in which its troupe, led by the outstanding tragedian Mondory, excelled. By Molière's time, the Marais had declined and even gone out of business for brief periods in the 1650s. Its strongest points were the veteran comic **Jodelet**, whom Molière soon lured to his own company, and **machine plays**. Despite professional rivalry, there were many close ties between Molière and his actors and the personnel of the Marais.

*See* Wilma Deierkauf–Holsboer, *Le Théâtre du Marais 1629–1673*, 2 vols. (Paris: Nizet, 1954–1958).

**Maréchaussée**. *See* **Marshals of France**.

*Mariage forcé, Le (Marriage by Compulsion)*. Performed originally in January 1664, *Le Mariage forcé* enjoyed a rather surprising popularity among Molière's *comédies–ballets*. Along with an elite corps of dancers and singers, the King himself performed in the court production, dancing the part of a **Gypsy**. This early version was published by **Robert Ballard**, who handled all the royal music. It contains a summary of the action of the play, but not the text. This was published later, in 1668, by **Ribou**. It had been slightly revised to include the new date in **Géronimo's** lines in scene 1, and had been transposed from three acts to one, with some of the more lavish musical and dancing interludes eliminated or curtailed.

The rather thin plot of the play concerns the intention of the fifty–two–year–old merchant **Sganarelle** to abandon his bachelorhood and marry. Though he questions his old friend Géronimo about the wisdom of doing so, he quickly reveals he has already committed himself to **Dorimène's** daughter, whom he hopes will provide good conjugal entertainment and numerous offspring. Géronimo surpresses his skeptical feelings about this and decides to take part in the inevitable confusion that is to result. When Sganarelle speaks directly with his wife–to–be, outlining the sexual demands he plans to make on her, she responds by assuring him that as long as he grants her absolute freedom and plenty of **money**, she doesn't care what he demands, for she wants to use the **marriage** to compensate for her dreary girlhood by living an extravagant life. Faced with the virtual certitude of cuckoldry, Sganarelle backs away from his earlier enthusiasm and searches desperately for authority that will confirm his new stance, first from Géronimo, then from the **Aristotelian** philosopher **Pancrace** and the **Pyrrhonian** philosopher **Marphurius**, then from two Gypsy fortune–tellers. After overhearing more plotting between Dorimène and her lover **Lycaste**, he confronts the girl's father, **Alcantor**, and tells him he regrets his decision. Alcantor summons his son **Alcidas**, who **politely** offers to cut Sganarelle's throat and then just as politely **beats** him until he agrees to the wedding.

Apart from Sganarelle's sentimental yearning for a family and Dorimène's very frank and materialistic explanation of her motives, there is little character development in the play, nor is there much in the way of topical comedy, other than the twin portraits of the pedants, each stuck in the pattern of his own system. Perhaps the very absence of controversy is the one thing that stood in favor of the comedy, both for the public and for Molière's troupe. The good memories it evoked at **court** must have made it welcome there. In fact, the play and the musical accompaniments are so cleverly intertwined in the original version that it is a shame they could not be produced well on the Parisian stage and that the public never saw this work in its full form.

*See* Anthony Ciccone, "Structure of Communication and the Comic in Molière's *Le Mariage forcé*," *Neophilologus* 66 (1982), 43–48.

**Mariane** (*L'Avare*). She appears at the beginning of the play to be a destitute, but charming and compassionate girl, caring for her ailing mother. She has caught **Cléante's** attention and won his heart before the beginning of the play. In the meantime, the professional matchmaker **Frosine** has been conspiring to wed her to **Harpagon**, using the famous "negative dowry" argument by which she would save the miser a fortune by spending so little. She demonstrates considerable sophistication when invited to Harpagon's house, whispering aside, "What a face!" and "What an **animal**!" She feels moral qualms about negotiating for **marriage** with this obviously unsuitable prospect, but shows a gift for elegant badinage with his more attractive son and his sister. In the recognition scene of Act V, she tells her woeful tale of shipwreck, **slavery**, and flight as she embraces her long–lost father (**Anselme**) and brother (**Valère**). Anselme and his full purse guarantee her marriage with Cléante, despite Harpagon's almost unending exactions.

**Mariane** (*Tartuffe*). **Orgon's** daughter is the paragon of filial modesty and obedience, and it almost destroys her. Her innocence likens her to **Agnès**, but in this play it is both a positive and a negative feature. On one level, it seems almost genetically related to her father's credulousness and submission in regard to **religious** values. Having played an incidental role in the opening scenes, she next appears at the beginning of Act II, where her father presents her rather brutally with the *fait accompli* of engagement to **Tartuffe**. Her confusion is perhaps justified, all the more so since she had expected her uncle to win some concessions from her father in their conversation. She is still reeling from the shock of this bombshell when **Dorine** barrages her with questions and taunts about her mild reaction to Orgon. Thus, she is psychologically on edge when **Valère** also arrives and appears to question her intentions. The groundwork for the **lovers' spite** scene has been well laid by the playwright and Mariane works it to perfection, right down to the quavering hesitations to part when the moment comes, and the stubborn retrenchments as soon as an opportunity for reconciliation opens up. She and Valère are perfect foils for each other. Unlike him, she is able to draw some strength from the adventure. When she next confronts her father, she makes a truly impassioned stand for her liberty, offering up all of her personal wealth (she is the forced heir of her mother's dowry, along with **Damis**), if only her father will not compel her to wed against her will. Orgon is almost swayed by her emotional speech, but she spoils her case by mentioning retirement to a **convent**, which awakens Orgon's religious mania and restores Tartuffe as prime directive. With Damis sent away, **Cléante** exhausted, and Dorine daunted, Mariane is unable to carry on the battle against bigotry, and along with the others, she places her future in **Elmire's** hands. If this daughter seems like too much of a shrinking violet, one must remember that her lover, Valère, is less vigorous and inventive than his counterparts in *L'École des femmes*, *Le Bourgeois gentilhomme*, *L'Avare*, or *Les Femmes savantes*. The original was probably played by **Mlle. De Brie**.

**Marinette** (*Dépit amoureux*). This **servant** girl is **Gros–René's** sweetheart, a naïve counterpart to her slow–witted partner, and the two share a scene of **lovers' spite** that parallels that of their master and mistress. Like Gros–René, she does display the ability to use some elements of upper–class **language**, such as "ruminate" and little **Latin** phrases. She has received some Parisian pins and a cheap pair of scissors as tokens of his **love**, and in Act I, with a little hinting, she gets a **ring** as a reward from **Éraste**. Her good humor helps her reconcile quickly in the servants' version of the lovers' quarrel. In the denouement, she quickly rebuffs **Mascarille's** attempts at flirtation (she claims that henceforth any man that sends sweet talk her way will be firing blanks) and reassures Gros–René that she will be a proper wife and tell him everything that happens.

**Marolles, Michel de, abbé de Villeloin** (1600–1681). Seventeenth–century intellectual and Classical scholar who translated and edited **Plautus**. Molière used his edition in preparing *Amphitryon* and *L'Avare*. Marolles was an example of a writer who was able to earn a tidy sum of 5,000 or 6,000 *livres* per year from his works. He also gathered a remarkable collection of engravings that he sold to **Colbert** in 1667. Nevertheless, his translations were the butt of many jokes in the literary community.

**Marotte** (*Les Précieuses ridicules*). This **servant** to **Cathos** and **Magdelon** angers her mistresses by her commonness and her mispronunciation of important *précieux* buzzwords and titles.

**Marotte, Mlle.** *See* **Ragueneau, Marie.**

**Marphurius** (*Le Mariage forcé*). Marphurius is a **Pyrrhonian**, or extreme skeptic, whom **Sganarelle** consults in scene 5 of the play. After giving Sganarelle a brief taste of the notion of appearances, which was important to all skeptics and especially so to **Pierre Gassendi**, Marphurius does listen to Sganarelle's question, which the **Aristotelian Pancrace** had failed to do. However, he responds only in curt, non–committal formulas, such as "Maybe" and "I don't know" and "It's not impossible." Asked if the **marriage** should take place or not, he replies, "One or the other," "According to circumstances," and "Whatever falls out." When he washes his hands of the affair, Sganarelle **beats** him, then wittily turns his own short answers against him in a game of railing rhymes. Sganarelle concludes, "It's impossible to get a positive word out of that man!" The role was played by **Du Croisy.**

**Marquis** (*La Critique de l'École des femmes*). This ridiculous aristocrat who pushes his way onstage and attacks Molière's play with silly arguments phrased in awkward terms is more repugnant than his average counterpart. Both **Élise** and **Uranie** make it clear that they find him distasteful, although the latter does extend him her hospitality. He is mainly notable for his mannerism of repetition, a sign that he is lacking in sound arguments. At the end of the play he is literally at a loss for words and can do nothing but sing inane tunes. Molière took this role himself.

**Marriage.** Though the goal of almost all comic plots, marriage itself could not be shown onstage in seventeenth–century France, because of its sacramental nature and the ban on all **religious** rites imposed by the notions of *bienséances*. Thus, the accomplishment of marriage was represented through synecdoche, by the signing of the marriage contract, although even this ceremony is more often alluded to than actually shown. This was considered convincing, since the French legal system placed a great deal of importance on the contractual nature of marriage and because the sums included in dowries often involved whole family fortunes. Even relatively poor **peasants** seldom could afford to forgo some modest legal agreement, though it might be drawn up and witnessed by a humble *tabellion*, as in some of the genre paintings by Le Nain, instead of a highly regarded **bourgeois notary**. **Engagement** was part of the legal process of marriage (*see* Engagement).

There was considerable controversy between the Church and state over the ultimate marriage authority, as well as over permission to marry. French legal authorities insisted that the Church respect their stipulation that parental permission was necessary before minors could legally marry, and the age of majority was in most areas well into the twenties. Thus, the marriage between **Octave** and **Hyacinte** in *Les Fourberies de Scapin* would not hold up to French legal standards, even if it had been based, as **Scapin** dishonestly pretends, on a case of *flagrante delicto*. On the other hand, the Church argued that the state should forbid parents from compelling their **children** to marry for mere financial reasons, insisting that individual consent from the couple was also a prerequisite. This did not stop some parents from "commanding" their children to marry, as **Monsieur Jourdain** attempts to do. His daughter **Lucile** reminds him that there is no legal way a parent can compel a child to marry against her will. Only an idiot like **Thomas Diafoirus** in *Le Malade imaginaire* would defend the idea of forced marriage. He does so by citing "the ancients" (he has in mind the Spartans) who abducted their brides from the house of the parent (II, 6). **Béline**, in the same play, argues against forced marriage, but only because she has designs of her own on the dowry money. **Oronte** is actually led to believe he has forced his daughter to marry the "sensible" **Éraste** at the end of *Monsieur de Pourceaugnac*, but in fact he has been maneuvered into that choice by the youngsters. Both Church and state authorities were equally stern against bigamy, which, as the chorus reminds Monsieur de Pourceaugnac, was a hanging offense and possible grounds for excommunication, as well. The notary in *Les Femmes savantes* makes a similar observation. Nevertheless, secret marriage was not infrequently mentioned in plays, as in *Dépit amoureux*, where **Ascagne** manages to wed **Valère** while disguised as **Lucile**. Even if Ascagne were not a minor (as she surely is), such an arrangement would be of dubious value before either civil or religious authorities, since it involved deception.

In bourgeois circles, marriages were often arranged for largely commercial reasons by the families of young couples. **Gorgibus** rails at the girls in *Les Précieuses ridicules* for rejecting the perfect suitors he has sent their way, "I know their families and I know their wealth!" It is not impossible that the young Molière himself came under such pressure before he joined the theater. **Géronte** uses a similar logic in *Le Médecin malgré lui* to reject the love match between **Lucinde** and **Léandre** in favor of one with more definite financial benefits. It is only the convenient demise of an uncle that allows him to accept Léandre at the conclusion of the play. But at other times, the wealth factor seems to play against the manic desires of the paterfamilias. In *Le Malade imaginaire*, **Toinette** criticizes her master for wanting to waste a fine dowry on a medical man, "What, sir, can you have made such outlandish plans, and with all the wealth you possess would you marry your daughter to a **doctor**?" (I, 5).

Noble families could be just as blind to the pleasure factor as bourgeois clans. It was a common, if often hushed–up, practice for aristocratic families to "fertilize their lands" by marrying a son to a rich bourgeoise endowed with a huge dowry. While this type of female hypergamy was accepted and widely condoned as a practical necessity, the opposite phenomenon of a noble daughter "marrying down" with a rich male commoner was not. One obvious reason for this was that **nobility** mainly was passed down from the father. Another was that males ordinarily brought a much smaller financial contribution to the contract table. In any case, the **Sotenvilles** are quite unconventional when they marry their daughter to **George Dandin**. Despite the fact that, in the country, rich "laboureurs" who owned much livestock, equipment, and land were superior to both regular farmers and impoverished gentry, or "**hobereaux**," the irregularity of such a union would be cause for exclusion and shunning by true noble society. Angélique makes a very frank and logical assessment of the stupidity of such arrangements (II, 2) that throws the blame for ensuing infidelities back from the passive wife to the greedy parents and inconsiderate husbands who broker them. It is a matter–of–fact indictment of the callous system that continued to force women to accept husbands to whom they would never freely give themselves, and all the more subversive because it calls the bluff of Church and state in deliberately overlooking the physical and moral coercion.

Yet, financial considerations could affect the choice of people who were entirely beyond the power of coercion. In *Le Bourgeois gentilhomme*, **Dorimène** is a widow and hence free to make a love match if she desires, but she agrees to marry Dorante out of a sense of *reconnaissance* or gratitude mixed with obligation, since she does not want him driven into poverty by the cost of courting her. She never makes a sentimental **avowal** and explains her acceptance in strictly sensible terms. One assumes that much of the same thinking also affects the widow **Célimène**, who admits to **Alceste** that she encourages the visits of people like **Oronte** and **Acaste** because they serve her financial and legal interests. She seems impervious to sentimental commitments, and when she does agree to marry Alceste on her own conditions late in the play, it is strictly to save her reputation, and she phrases her acceptance is such a way as to avoid the implication of emotional surrender.

Financial motives were not the only ones that led to a marriage of convenience in Molière's comedies. In the case of Sganarelle and Martine in *Le Médecin malgré lui*, the husband indicates that he found a rude surprise on his wedding night (she was no longer a virgin) and that she had cozened him to the altar for secret reasons (she was already pregnant). No wonder their union is less than blissful. Interestingly enough, this same motive has never, to my knowledge, been put forward as a possible explanation for Molière's marriage with **Armande Béjart**; perhaps he was less of a lecherous old **Arnolphe** than has been supposed, and more of a family friend stepping in to cover a dangerous situation. Surely Armande Béjart's later behavior would be in line with juvenile indiscretions.

Elopement as a prelude to marriage was a dangerous step. Without the benefit of any formalities, it could be the equivalent of rape — a capital offense. Nevertheless, it was not unknown, and the safest expedient in such cases was for the eloped couple to return posthaste to the girl's family and get permission for what had become a *fait accompli*. This is what happens in *L'École des maris* and *Le Médecin malgré lui*, and what seems to have happened to **Done Elvire** in *Dom Juan* (though in her case the abduction from a **convent** entailed special dangers). In most cases, the families had little choice but to give their blessing in order to avoid scandal.

The romantic theory of marriage based on mutual attractiveness and the biological imperative has, surprisingly, few advocates other than love–smitten young couples. One exception is **Jacqueline**, the nursemaid in *Le Médecin malgré lui*. Though unhappily married herself, she remains a believer in romantic love and tries to persuade her master with her tale of the young lovers Simonette and Robin, separated by the greedy father Pierre and his fat friend Thomas merely because the latter had an acre more of vineyard. Her allusion to a husband as the best "poultice" to apply to a love–starved young woman is laughably appropriate. In similar fashion, **Alcmène** and **Cléanthis**, the innocent women of *Amphitryon* see romantic love as an inseparable part of marriage and fail to understand the weird reluctance of their spouses. But **Amphitryon** and **Sosie** are less concerned with enjoying the benefits of conjugal life than with avoiding its unattractive prospect of cuckoldry. For **Jupiter** also, marriage in itself is a negative factor whose only positive aspect is the fiery enthusiasm of young love. The god feels, as do **Sosie** and his double **Mercury**, that the familiarity of marriage eventually stifles love and that, moreover, conjugal duty removes much of the significance of conquest and glory from the sexual act (I, 3 and 4). Jupiter's solution, to foist off all the troubles of marriage on the shoulders of the guilty husband, while giving credit for all its joys to the "hidden" lover, makes little sense to Alcmène because, unlike the men, she is not concerned with any incongruity. *Les Amants magnifiques* highlights an unusual situation in which a mother has given her daughter complete freedom of choice in marriage in order to arrange a match based solely on love, if desired. **Aristione** reminds the unctuous **Iphicrate** that no amount of flattery to the mother will alter the daughter's liberty in this matter. If **Ériphile** seems to be taking her time making the desired choice, it is because she has yet to coax out an **avowal** from the man she has secretly chosen, the distinguished but overly modest general **Sostrate**.

Age of marriage was a factor often emerging in comedy. On the one hand, early teenage marriage was strongly discouraged as indulgent to the senses and contrary to the dowry customs prevailing at all social levels. Men especially did not generally wed until they were well into their twenties, or even later. On the other hand, late marriages were also discouraged, both on the grounds that they were unlikely to engender domestic happiness and that they were not likely to result in fertile, financially stable couples. In the cases where preponderant wealth threatened to overcome this ecclesiastical and lay policy, the greybeard who married was likely to be shamed with a shivaree organized by his disapproving neighbors. There are several mentions of this practice in such works as *Le Mariage forcé*.

From the point of view of the *précieuses*, all marriages, regardless of the factors of finance, romance, or age, were to be avoided. They only approved of platonic love, removed from any type of physical consideration or contact. These prejudices are first encountered in *Les Précieuses ridicules* and later in *Les Femmes savantes*, where **Armande** makes fun of her younger sister's interest in marriage and accuses her of having a "downstairs mind." Those who indulged in physical pleasures were considered not only lower class, but barely human, since they were concerned with the "**animal** part" of existence rather than the realm of ideas. **Henriette** reminds her sister that marriage is the only honorable foundation for procreation, without which little **philosophers** cannot come into the world. But since Armande fears sex and childbirth, she also scorns **children**, referring to them as rodents (marmots). Much of the rest of the play is devoted to the practical instead of theoretic problems of marriage, but **Clitandre** takes time in Act IV to explain to Armande his own position. He appreciates her idealism, but points out that unfortunately he has a body as well as a mind and must take measures to satisfy it as well. He humorously wonders how, if marriage is so vile, it can be so fashionable. At the opening of the following act, Henriette questions how **Trissotin**, a man of ideas, can be interested is such a concrete thing as a dowry. To this, and to further questions regarding Henriette's loyalty to Clitandre, he responds with a kind of casuistry, questioning her attachment to one man, but defending his own proliferation of poetic "loves" as products of the intelligence rather than the heart. In the long run, it is useless to discuss the subject with him, since he is, at heart, interested only in exploiting Henriette: "In order to consummate such a charming vow, / Provided that I have you, it doesn't matter how." This is the cynical reality Molière exposes beneath the high–flown **language** of Neoplatonism.

**Marshals' Guard** (*Le Misanthrope*). **Basque** describes the uniform of this royal officer before the man appears on stage in Act II, scene 6 to summon **Alceste** before the **Marshals** on account of his quarrel with **Oronte**. He explicitly states his mission and emphasizes Alceste's obligation to obey.

**Marshals of France**. This select group of **noblemen** was appointed by the King, usually from among his relatives and most faithful courtiers. They were charged with important military duties in time of war, but were not completely inactive in time of peace, when they were often called upon to supervise certain domestic **police** affairs, including, from **Richelieu's** time onward, the royal prohibition against **dueling**. The five Marshals had a detachment of soldiers at their disposal, and if they caught wind of an impending combat among members of the **court**, these guards were sent to summon the parties before their court. Owing to power directly delegated from the throne, they possessed the authority to order the combatants to reconcile with each other. All but the most fanatical swordsman would find in this command the perfect excuse to avoid bloodshed while maintaining their honor intact. Any who opposed the Marshals risked a *lettre de cachet* that could send him into prison or exile. In *Le Misanthrope*, the description of a man clad in uniform with long pleated tails and a short gilded jacket (II, 5) signifies the arrival of one of the Marshals' guard. The man, who appears in the next scene, confirms that he has been sent by his masters to bring **Alceste** before the court, in hopes of mediating his worsening dispute with **Oronte**. True to form, Alceste refuses to budge from his critical stance on Oronte's verses. Only grudgingly does he follow the guard to the meeting. We later learn from **Philinte's** account of the scene (IV, 1) that he persisted even in the face of cajoling and threatening from the Marshals. Never before had their august assembly been stymied by such a foolish quarrel. In the end, the best Alceste could offer was to wish he had never been obliged to say such bad things about the poetry. With a quick, contrived embrace the Marshals sent the quarrelers on their separate ways, hoping for the best. It is clear that Alceste comes very close, albeit comically, to the capital crime of *lèse majesté* by almost refusing to obey the King's delegated authority. Perhaps it is the sheer bravery of this gesture that **Éliante** admires, something very rare in an age more fit for fawning. But by placing Alceste in this delicate situation, Molière is skillfully wielding the double–edged sword of subversion, placing his flawed, would–be hero in dangerous opposition to the might of royalty.

**Martial.** This first–century master of the **Latin** epigram, familiar to any decent student in Molière's time, is mistaken in *La Comtesse d'Escarbagnas* first for a popular Parisian glove–maker (by the **Countess**), then for the Louis XIII–era dramatist André Maréchal, who had collaborated with the **Illustre Théâtre** (by **Thibaudier**).

**Martine** (*Les Femmes savantes*). Almost certainly this character was played by **Mlle. Beauval,** who had taken **Madeleine Béjart's** old roles, rather than by the anonymous **servant** alluded to in a 1723 article that has long been held sacrosanct. Like other Beauval roles, Martine is an uppity servant. She is salty and very down–to–earth, equally unable to understand or to tolerate the ridiculous affectations of her mistresses. She moans about the powerlessness of servants in the first act, after she had been dismissed, and **Chrysale** can do little to save her. Nevertheless, her comical misunderstandings of the learned ladies' inflated **language** puncture their pretensions. When she returns to support her employer in the final act, she unchains her tongue and produces a laughable hodge–podge of ideas that contain much common sense, despite her endorsement of illiteracy and wife **beating**. In fact, her speeches parallel those of Chrysale. Earlier in the play, he had said he wanted women who were unconcerned with poetic niceties and lunar exploration, but competent cooks and seamstresses. Martine wants a man who is uninterested in the life of the mind and "knows not what is A or B and wants no other book but me."

**Martine** (*Le Médecin malgré lui*). **Sganarelle's** wife both opens and closes the play on a somewhat acrid note. In their opening argument, she accuses him of being unworthy of her, despite his raising the possibility that she might have accepted him as a husband out of convenience, being that she is already pregnant. She graphically describes how his alcoholism has deprived them of every stick of furniture in the household, down to the very bed they had slept in. She scarcely backs down when he threatens her with a violent **beating**, barraging him with insults until he lets fly his stick. Though he cajoles her into forgiving him in the second scene, she vows under her breath for vengeance. After a short monologue, she finds an apt occasion when **Valère** and **Lucas** approach, inventing for their benefit the tall tale of Sganarelle being a brilliant **doctor** who will only admit to his talents if he is beaten. However, she leaves before she can witness the effectiveness of her scheme, only reappearing in the closing scenes. Here, she mildly regrets her husband's impending demise, chiding him for dying in front of "all these people" and wishing she had had him lay in another cord of wood before he left the world.

**Mascarille** (*Dépit amoureux*). This role, created for and by Molière himself, is far different from the one in *L'Étourdi*. It opens with an example of verbal virtuosity similar to what was encountered in the earlier play. When **Gros–René** asks him where he has come from, where he is going, and whether he is staying, Mascarille replies he is not coming from anywhere because he hasn't been anywhere, he is not going anywhere because he is standing still, and he is not staying because he is about to leave. When he gives an untimely indication of **Valère's** secret **marriage**, he is the first of many Molière characters to try to get out of a spot by saying, "I'm not saying that!" As his conversations with **Albert** become more heated and later break down into the rhetorical battle style known as stichomythia, Mascarille begins to lose his composure. He is ready to threaten suicide, but his master insists that he stay alive to help him fight for his honor. From Act IV onward, Mascarille becomes more and more of a jibbering coward, citing ominous **dreams** of broken eggs and unstrung pearls and mouthing phrases such as "one dies only once and it's for such a long time!" He is reluctant to approach Albert's house because "it smells like sticks over there" (he fears he will be **beaten**). He is afraid to dispute his master openly and instead engages in a soliloquy at the beginning of Act V, where he plays the role of himself and his interlocutor, somewhat as **Sosie** will do in *Amphitryon*. The object of this verbal exercise is defense of "I whom am so dear to myself." He does manage to admit to Valère that he is useless at affairs of honor: "At table, count me as four, but count me as nothing if we have to fight." When invited to **duel** with Gros–René over the hand of **Marinette**, he objects, "My blood is doing just fine inside my body." Final attempts at chiding Gros–René as a complacent husband are parried by him and Marinette. This Mascarille starts out as a reflection of the "emperor of tricksters" in *L'Étourdi*, only to collapse into a figure more like his successor, Sganarelle, a man who shrinks from every serious encounter and survives by luck rather than ingenuity.

**Mascarille** (*L'Étourdi*). Played by Molière, this scheming valet makes his debut in this five–act comedy, where he describes himself as "the emperor of tricksters." Some authorities feel the character was originally **masked**, based on the name and on documentary evidence, but illustrations show Molière without one. Mascarille claims to enjoy the challenge of trickery for itself, rather than its financial rewards. However, besides whatever remuneration he gets from **Lélie**, he has accepted **money** from **Hippolyte** to drive **Léandre** back into her arms, and he also pretends to go into Léandre's service in Acts II and III. Throughout the play, his principal goal remains to obtain **Célie** for Lélie, however it may be done. The play mentions at least ten schemes spread over the play's five acts: three in the first, one in the fourth, and two in each of the others. Two of the plots involve outright purchase of the **slave** girl with others' funds — **Pandolphe's** and **Anselme's** in Act I and Léandre's in Act II. One involves outright robbery (of Anselme in Act I). Several require approach through assumed identities: those of a fortune–seeker in Act I, of an **Armenian** (by Lélie) in Act IV, and a **Swiss** innkeeper in Act V. One, in Act II, involves slander (of the character of Célie to Léandre). At least twice he pretends to betray his master, once to his father and once to his rival. Two plans revolve around more or less direct abduction: that of Célie by masquerade in Act III and that of **Andrès** by **police**, recounted at the beginning of Act V. Perhaps the most elaborate is the **feigned death** of Pandolphe in Act II, which almost constitutes a sketch in itself. In all of these encounters, Mascarille gives evidence of his verve and his verbal inventiveness, even when it requires him to cover his master's errors as an Armenian or to pass himself off as a speaker of Swiss **German**. He also shows much sarcasm when deriding Lélie's untimely tinkering with the schemes or his out–of–place heroics. He continually becomes angry and threatens to leave his master, only to quickly devise another scheme. When Lélie finally drops his last defenses and becomes despondent toward the end of the play, Mascarille shakes him out of it and gets back to the job of trickery. Brief bouts of petulance aside, he is a constantly optimistic figure who manages to stay one step ahead of any punishment by swaying with the currents when necessary. He is not above taking a stick to Lélie (whose poor performance really does deserve some punishment in Act IV), if it means sparing his own hide. His most interesting psychological trait may be the anxiety he feels as Lélie tries to play his part in the plots; he compares himself to a bowler feeling every little bounce and slip of the ball as it rolls toward its target. After Anselme agrees he has just the thing at home to satisfy Mascarille's itch for **marriage** at the end of the play, the valet manages to grasp the opportunity of having the last word, wishing sarcastically that heaven will give all the men **children** of whom they are the fathers.

**Mascarille** (*Les Précieuses ridicules*). Described in the first scene by his master **La Grange** as a clever but very ambitious valet, Mascarille's arrival onstage is certainly one of the most ostentatious and ridiculous in French Classical theater. He has himself brought into **Gorgibus's** house in a **sedan chair**, instead of being let out at the door. Bedecked with ribbons and lace beyond all bounds of good taste, he is the picture of the *petit marquis* who will serve as the butt of most subsequent sartorial humor in Molière's canon. Confronted by the two sturdy chair porters, who resent his slaps and failure to pay, he quickly quails and gives proof of servile poltroonery. His speech before the girls is a faithful imitation of the senseless banter of vapid courtiers, full of fashion terms and exaggerated claims. For example, he claims to know every verse that is composed in **Paris** and to be the author of no fewer than 200 sonnets, 200 songs, 400 epigrams, and 1,000 madrigals, not counting enigmas or **portraits**. Having exhausted those petty genres, he goes on to discuss *impromptus* and gives as an example a silly amorous quatrain ending in "Stop thief!" repeated four times. After showing off the various parts of his foppish **costume**, he greets his counterpart, the masquerading **Viscount Jodelet**, in what must have been a magic moment in seventeenth–century comedy, with the greatest surviving comic of the *farceur* tradition embracing the initiator of the new, naturalistic comic style. The two continue to vie for the girls' attention, vamping it up with laughable war stories (commanding a cavalry regiment on the **Malta galleys**, etc.) and showing off their "wounds" — which is curtailed when Mascarille wants to open his pants to show a "wicked scar." They decide to entertain the girls with **music and dancing**, with Mascarille prancing about and Jodelet, who was actually to die within months, complaining, "Whoa! Don't play the tune so fast! I'm just getting over an illness!" This ends in scene 13 with the entrance of their masters, who **beat** them first and then strip them of their finery right in front of the girls. Half–clothed and embarrassed, the two valets slip away a few steps ahead of the musicians, who have not been paid for their concert.

To the previous avatars of Mascarille, the emperor of trickery, this one adds the element of social presumption, which seems a natural extention of the character's comic exuberance. Having wracked his brains in the service of sighing, sometimes blockheaded, young masters, the intelligent valet strikes out for himself and proves to be a mere *demi–habile* among the upper classes. This sense of usurpation paves the way for the advent of **Sganarelle** in *Le Cocu imaginaire*, for Sganarelle is always slightly over–reaching the limits of his competency. This Mascarille also reaches forward in time, emerging from the characterized valet role that had existed in some form for ages past into the timely, satirical garb of the ridiculous marquis. He truly "finds himself" in this foppish attire and brings his humor into a totally current frame of expression.

**Masks.** Molière was the first major French comic actor to perform without any kind of mask, even face–obscuring paint. He thus broke from the heritage of French and **Italian farce**, following the example of **Scaramouche**. Furthermore, he seems to have imposed this naturalistic aesthetic on his whole company and on all the parts he created. The use of the expressive human face marked a huge step in the development of comedy and made it possible for Molière's works to cross over easily into all existing European dramatic traditions. When masks do appear, it is in the context of masquerades, thus reserving a more particular role for that type of activity. In the major comedies, the concept of the mask is equated with that of deception, thus linking with the great seventeenth–century theme of appearance versus reality. This context assigns an evil value to the mask, since the honest man supposedly would not need to dissimulate. Thus, **Alceste** says of his commoner opponent in the lawsuit, "Through his mask I can see the traitor plainly" (I, 1). Of course, *Le*

*Misanthrope* goes on to show that masks may nevertheless be necessary to protect both the masker and the onlooker from a reality too harsh to deal with. *Le Bourgeois gentilhomme* and *Le Malade imaginaire* demonstrate that benign masks can be the only means of affecting happiness in a universe blocked by blind authority.

**Masks** (*L'Étourdi*). The list of dramatis personae calls for two masked groups that appear in carnival scenes in the play.

**Masks (dancing characters in *Les Fâcheux*).** A group of masked mummers appears at the end of the play and is chased off by a group of dancing **Swiss** guards armed with halberds.

**Masquerade.** *See* **Carnival**.

**Mathurine** (*Dom Juan*). This **peasant** woman has been seduced by the protagonist and has accepted his **marriage** offer even before he encounters **Charlotte** in Act II, scene 2. She appears two scenes later to lay claim to her fiancé, whom she spies in the arms of her village rival. **Dom Juan** manages to keep the two women separated by a lot of clever footwork and simultaneous reassurances, knowing that their rural habits will help him to hide the truth of his duplicity. By encouraging both Charlotte and Mathurine to persist in their most dearly held **dreams**, he encourages each to believe in him. The part was played originally by **Madeleine Béjart**.
    *See also* **Peasants**.

**Matthieu, Pierre** (1563–1621). A lawyer and author of devotional *Tablettes de la vie et de la mort, ou Quatrains de la vanité du monde* that were still popular in Molière's time. They are mentioned in **Sorel's** burlesque *Berger extravagant* and in *Sganarelle*. Matthieu served as royal historiographer to both Henri IV and Louis XIII.

**Mazarin, Cardinal Jules (born Giulio Mazarini,** 1602-1661**).** Born in relative obscurity in the Abruzzi province of Italy, this clever schemer became one of the most fabulously successful adventurers to cross the Alps and establish himself in France. He first rose to prominence through service in the armed forces of the Papacy. Though he had no ecclesiastical training, he was hastily given holy orders and transferred from the military to the diplomatic corps. There he rose through the ranks until he was named in 1634 as papal *nuncio* to the court of **Louis XIII**. Ingratiating himself with **Anne of Austria** and **Richelieu**, he executed another whirlwind change of habit in 1636, passing from the papal side to that of the French. Richelieu saw to it that he was naturalized in 1639 and rewarded with a cardinal's cap in 1642, though he had never served as a priest or said a Mass. These necessary steps were performed only hours before his investiture as cardinal, a rather comic scene where the roguish Mazarin, barely tonsured, mumbled **Latin** phrases fed to him by a prompter, which he scarcely understood.  Though he replaced Richelieu and pursued his predecessor's foreign policies with success, obtaining important concessions from the Austrian and Spanish Hapsbourgs at the end of the Thirty Years War, he failed to gain popularity in France.  Reviled for his greed and corruption, and rumored to have seduced the Queen Mother, he was mainly responsible for provoking the Fronde revolts of 1648 to 1652.   A renowned art collector and bibliophile, Mazarin briefly served as a casual **patron** to Molière after the playwright's return to **Paris**, but not to the extent that he favored **Pierre Corneille**.   Following Mazarin's death, Molière's troupe profited by the  acquisition of the Cardinal's theater in what became the **Palais-Royal**.

*Médecin malgré lui, Le (The Doctor Despite Himself)*.  This three–act prose comedy was first performed in August 1666 and was on the shelves of the booksellers by the end of the year.   One reason for this remarkably quick conversion to print was the fact that the story line was so well known.  It traces back to the medieval *fabliau, Le Vilain mire*.  As in that tale, a woodcutter is betrayed by his wife to some men searching for a **doctor**, under the ludicrous pretext that he will only admit to his medical talents if he is soundly **beaten**. Like the original, **Sganarelle** easily cures the young patient, who was not really ill but only lovelorn.  In the course of this cure, he takes advantages of other opportunities for adventure.  Molière slightly changes the setting and register of the play, which had originally involved a princess and prince, placing the intrigue in a thoroughly **bourgeois** framework.  In fact, this play is merely the final avatar of a drama that the troupe had previously presented under the title of *Le Fagotier (The Woodcutter)*.  The earlier version was presumably a shorter comic companion piece used to lighten up the tragic **repertory** of their early years.
      The first act opens on a domestic argument between the drunken Sganarelle and his dissatisfied wife, **Martine**, who combine to rebuff the peace offerings brokered by their intruding neighbor, **Monsieur Robert**.  Once her husband and the nosy neighbor have departed, Martine vows revenge for the **beating** she has taken from Sganarelle.  She takes advantage of the approach of **Valère** and **Lucas, servants** searching for a doctor for their mistress, to tell them that her husband is just the man they need, but will only admit to it if they beat him up. The emissaries try kind words first, but then revert to Martine's advice, which elicits a quick agreement from Sganarelle.  As soon as they mention the possibility of a rich payment, however, the woodcutter decides to come along very willingly, hopeful that his glib tongue and a few years service with a real doctor may earn him some easy cash.  Much discussed by **Géronte** and his servants before his grand entry, Sganarelle arrives spouting false knowledge and immediately turns the table on his client, beating him with a stick and forcing him to admit he is not a doctor, either.  He then engages in prolonged flirtations with **Jacqueline** while her husband tries to separate them.  Next comes a ridiculous examination, where Sganarelle and **Lucinde** converse in pantomime about her desire for a husband.  He tosses around his bits of schoolboy **Latin**

and apprentice's anatomy with abandon, knowing that Géronte knows nothing of either. After promising a nocturnal rendezvous with Jacqueline, Sganarelle comically solicits payment from the old man and seconds later obtains a bribe from **Léandre**, Lucinde's sweetheart, who longs to carry her away. The opening of the final act sees Sganarelle approving Léandre's **apothecary disguise**. He then meets the peasants **Thibaut** and **Perrin**, who pay him for a cure for their beloved Perrette. Dispensing much nonsense, Sganarelle gives them a bit of old cheese that he says contains "gold, coral, pearls, and a great deal more precious things," before cynically telling them to bury the lady as well as they can if she should die. His tryst with Jacqueline is overheard by Lucas. Using a pantomime of an enema to tell Géronte that Léandre is a pharmacist, he leaves the assistant with Lucinde, meanwhile beguiling the father with more medical cock and bull stories. Even after Lucinde "recovers" the use of her tongue and shares her desire to marry Léandre, old Géronte will not relent on his opposition, so Sganarelle sends the couple into the garden to take the air, but in reality so that they can elope. After more stalling, the trick is made known, and Lucas gleefully accuses Sganarelle of being the mastermind. For a short while, he seems to be doomed to punishment. Even his wife is not too unhappy to see him go. However, Léandre's return spares him this fate, as Géronte makes the best of a bad situation by granting his blessing.

Not surprisingly, this is one of the most purely farcical of Molière's works, along with *Les Fourberies de Scapin*. It makes ample use of the entire register of gestural **lazzi** and verbal and situational humor, lacking only the musical dimension of the **comedy–ballet**. It is the last of the plays to feature Sganarelle as a character, and his final bow shows him using his nerve and bluster to triumph over the limitations of his existence. *Le Médecin malgré lui* was a solid success; though used mainly as a companion piece with repertory, it almost always improved receipts when it reappeared on the program.

*Médecin volant, Le (The Flying Doctor)*. Like *La Jalousie du Barbouillé*, this one–act **farcical** comedy is based on a manuscript found by **Jean–Baptiste Rousseau** and eventually published in 1819 by Viollet–le–Duc. It appears to have been written early in Molière's career when he was touring in southern France. **La Grange's** register records twelve performances between 1659 and 1664. The subject was a common one in the *commedia dell'arte*, including the **Italian** troupe that was resident in **Paris** during Molière's lifetime. After Molière had brought the tradition into the French theater, his rivals in the **Marais** and the **Hôtel de Bourgogne** hastened to mount productions as well, the latter based on a verse text by **Edmé Boursault** that would be published in 1665. The "flying" in the title refers not only to **Sganarelle's** speedy changes of identity, but also to the fact that he leaps several times from a window in order to make **Gorgibus** believe he is actually two separate brothers, one a valet and the other a physician. Gorgibus gets so caught up in this whirlwind deception, as he tries to reconcile the two estranged "brothers," that he allows his daughter **Lucile** to run away with her lover **Valère**. Although the dialogue of the play's sixteen scenes depends overmuch on macaronic hodgepodge speeches generated by Sganarelle and the **Lawyer**, it is less coarse than that of *La Jalousie du Barbouillé* and shows some progress toward the style of Molière's Italianate plays. The design of the scenes is still very primitive, allowing for a minimal development of character, and the ending is unconvincingly abrupt and optimistic. Notwithstanding this, the "flying doctor" sight gag would be re-employed by Molière with great success in *Le Malade imaginiare* by **Toinette** (III, 8–11).

**Medicine.** *See* **Doctors and Medicine**.

*Mélicerte*. This unfinished two–act "heroical pastoral comedy" was apparently Molière's first contribution to the **Ballet des Muses**, where it occupied the third *entrée* position during the month of December 1666. It was replaced at the beginning of January, following the birth of the young prince, by the *Pastorale comique*. Supposedly, the feud between **Armande Béjart** and **Baron** was the cause of this abrupt change.

The play is set in the valley of **Tempe** in **Thessaly** and all the characters are **shepherds** or herdsmen of some degree. The opening of the play is rather unique in that the first two scenes consist entirely of stichomythia, mirrored replies of equal meter by the various characters. This sustained stylistic element suggests that Molière might have envisioned the play originally as a kind of poetic tour de force. He also incorporates a passage of tender *stances* when **Myrtil** is addressing the sparrow he has captured.

In the opening scene, two shepherds, **Acante** and **Tyrène**, complain about their rejection by two **shepherdesses**, **Daphné** and **Éroxène**, who refuse to divulge their secrets to the men. Left alone, the ladies quickly reach a different understanding, showing each other lockets containing their true love's **portrait**. Remarkably, the lockets are exactly alike and both contain the miniature of Myrtil, a youth of very precocious character and attractiveness. The artist, **Atis**, seems to have made a nice living reproducing this line of **jewelry**. Both women agree to approach **Lycarsis**, the boy's father, in hopes of arranging a **marriage**, with the loser stepping quietly aside. Meanwhile, Lycarsis himself appears, in company of **Mopse** and **Nicandre**, two countrymen who are eager for the news that he refuses to pass on freely. When his greed causes them to lose interest, he stupidly blurts out the details of the prince's arrival, punishing them for what they "don't know." The pair of ladies accosts the old man, who seems very pleased with their interest in his son, and offers to take the less fortunate of them for his own bride. Yet, he leaves the choice up to Myrtil, who soon arrives and addresses a very gallant little poem to the sparrow he has captured as a pet for **Mélicerte**, his own sweetheart. He rejects the two ladies with great consideration for their pride and tells them of his choice, which infuriates his father. Myrtil's evocation of the **philosophy** of **nature** merely adds fuel to the fire, and the father storms out after his son, comically reminding the ladies that he will answer for him "body for body" in any case.

The second act opens with Mélicerte unhappily receiving news of the double proposal from her confidante **Corinne**. After a self–denying monologue,

was a step up in the **bourgeois** hierarchy to be a merchant, but **Monsieur Jourdain** is not proud of his father's designation as such. **Covielle** sarcastically agrees with him, saying, "Him, a merchant! That's pure slander, since he never was one; all that he did was to be very helpful and very generous, and since he was very knowledgeable about cloth, he went around collecting it here and there, had it brought to his house, and gave it to his friends in exchange for a little **money**" (IV, 3). Of course, Jourdain aspired to the status of gentleman, and he was smart enough to know that any type of trade was forbidden to members of the nobility.

**Mercury (*Amphitryon*).** Mercury is a glib and fanciful, but also somewhat sadistic, god, a henchman of **Jupiter** who delights in tormenting humans. His conversation with **Night** in the prologue demonstrates his cynicism about heaven and earth, which goes as far as forcing Night to comply through gossiping about her secrets. The way he toys with **Sosie** (I, 2) recalls **Dom Juan** and **Sganarelle**. He confounds the **slave** by relating all the details of his life and of the mission on which he has been sent. By the same token, he knows just how to infuriate **Cléanthis**, deflating her hopes of romance and insulting her even for remaining faithful to Sosie. Next, it is **Amphitryon's** turn to be Mercury's plaything (III, 2), for when the general knocks at his own door, the **god** locks him out. This scene recalls similar ones in *La Jalousie du Barbouillé* and *L'École des femmes* and prefigures the final act of *George Dandin*. The rage of a man locked out of his own house parallels the inner rage Amphitryon feels at being denied his own identity and the marital treasures he feels are due to him alone. In Mercury's final apparition, he sheds the ugly human form that he has reluctantly worn and ascends into the heavens, leaving the mortals to sort out the trouble he has caused. Sosie is perhaps right to compare Mercury repeatedly with a **devil** or demon, for this impish version of the "hidden god" disappears rather than take any responsibility for the lives he has afflicted. Whether the part was played by **La Thorillière**, **Du Croisy**, or **Hubert** is unknown.

**Méré, Antoine Gombaud, chevalier de** (1607–1684). Remembered as the theoretician of **politeness** and *honnêteté*, this aristocrat had begun to air his ideas in **salons** even before the publication of his popular *Conversations* in 1668. Few of the concepts in Méré's loosely constructed "code" were original, for manuals of politeness had been circulating for nearly a century by the 1660s. His contribution was to synthesize existing notions, bind them into a system of other–directed pleasure, and popularize them as the ultimate product of civilization in **Louis XIV's** reign. He further refined his theory of *honnête* behavior after Molière's death. The ideas expressed by **Philinte** at the beginning of *Le Misanthrope* coincide in many ways with those of Méré, but spring from a more **skeptical** background. Philinte feels that politeness is a form of social **armor**, necessary to avoid confrontations caused by human imperfections; he is suspicious of internalized *honnêteté*, which threatens to leave a naïve individual open to exploitation and abuse.

**Messages.**  **Philaminte** and **Chrysale** receive two different kinds of messages in *Les Femmes savantes*, one a calumny about **Trissotin** from **Vadius**, claiming that he has plagiarized many ancient authors, the other a pair of forged **letters** brought by **Ariste**, which seem to indicate financial ruin for the family on the basis of a contrary legal decision and a joint bankruptcy in **Lyon**. The **Viscount** receives a message in *La Comtesse d'Escarbagnas* that the feud between his parents and **Julie's** family is solved and that he can now go forward with his **marriage** plans.

*See also* **Letters.**

**Messina.**  City in **Sicily** on the strait between the island and Calabria. It is the setting of *L'Étourdi.*

**Métaphraste (*Dépit amoureux*).**  A pedant, he is tutor to the young **Ascagne.** He spews bits of **Greek** and **Latin** at every occasion, though he is scarcely a better conversationalist when he is confined to French, since he insists on interrupting and on having his say. His rationale for this loquacity is that a quiet fool is indistinguishable from a silent savant. **Quintilian**, **Cicero**, and **Vergil** are among those he cites. Exasperated at his wordiness, **Albert** finally gets rid of him by ringing a bell in his ears.

**Mignard, Pierre** (1612–1695).  Painter of **portraits**, frescoes, and **religious** works. His brother, Nicolas, had his atelier in the same building in **Avignon** where Molière's acting company performed in 1655, and it is possible that Pierre met Molière there on his way back from the Academy of **Rome**. Mignard and Molière had, by several accounts, a close and durable friendship. It was manifested on one hand by Mignard's superb oil portrait of Molière in the costume of Julius Caesar, undeniably our best image of the author, and on the other by Molière's poetic tribute to Mignard's ceiling paintings in the dome of the Val de Grace chapel. As a rival to **Charles Le Brun**, **Louis XIV's** favorite painter and the supervisor of all artistic decoration at **Versailles**, Mignard was considered an outsider, and Molière's poem takes on a rather anti–establishment air. Mignard's association with Molière's troupe was not limited to artistic matters. He was closely involved with the financial affairs of **Madeleine Béjart**, some of which also concerned the playwright, and probably used Madeleine as a model for some of his mythological and religious figures. The friendship between the families apparently went beyond one generation, since Mignard's daughter, Catherine–Marguerite, served as godmother for Molière's second son, **Pierre–Jean–Baptiste–Armand Poquelin**, in 1672.

*Misanthrope, Le, ou l'Atrabilaire amoureux.*  What many now regard as Molière's greatest comedy, and perhaps the greatest comedy ever written, originally appeared during the theatrical lull of summer in 1666 before a most "ordinary" Parisian audience at the **Palais Royal Theater**. The five–act verse play had been years in the making. Molière had been reworking certain scenes since the failure of *Dom Garcie de Navarre* and may have finished the two great sequences of the first act by 1664. It is ironic that such a gem would be presented to the world in such a modest setting, and with only modest receipts, while the **court** swooned and doled out fortunes for relative trifles like *Mélicerte*. Unique because it is the only one of Molière's *grandes comédies* to unfold in an exclusively aristocratic setting, *Le Misanthrope* immediately attracted the praise of the anonymous author of the **Lettre sur la comédie du Misanthrope**, presumably **Donneau de Visé**, and the master critic **Boileau**, who in his *Art poétique* would rank it as the most sublime comedy of the age.

The opening of the play is one of drama's greatest dialogues, involving a discussion of the nature of friendship between **Alceste** and **Philinte**. Fuming and pouting because Philinte has bestowed marks of friendship on a casual acquaintance, Alceste exposes the whole panoply of his wrath against humanity, which Philinte answers with a justification of civility in all its seventeenth–century splendor. In the course of this conversation, much development takes place: the spectator learns of Alceste's infatuation with the coquettish widow **Célimène**, Philinte's efforts on behalf of her undervalued cousin **Éliante**, and the potentially disastrous lawsuit that looms over Alceste's fortune that he deliberately neglects, in order to provide grist for his misanthropic mill. The pair of gentlemen is then confronted by a poetaster, in the person of **Oronte**, who ignores Alceste's warnings about his implacable literary standards and insists that they hear and judge a sonnet he has just written. As Oronte excessively glosses his trivial verses, Philinte utters satisfying but empty praise, while Alceste bursts out in insulting condemnation. Making laughably inadequate attempts to cushion the shock of his disapproval, Alceste delivers such a resounding rejection of Oronte's work that the versifier becomes outraged and threatens serious revenge.

The second act finds Alceste in direct confrontation with Célimène, who quickly proves as slippery as an eel in her ability to wriggle free of the misanthrope's ultimatum over a declaration of **love**. She scolds him playfully for his moral highhandedness and taunts him by inviting in the sort of rival he deplores — a foppish, flighty marquis loaded with gossip from the **court**. **Acaste** and **Clitandre** quickly manifest the very faults that Alceste had just described in them, as they engage Célimène in a game of verbal **portraits** that invites her to skewer all the people she knows with wittily derogatory sketches of their behavior and character. Unable to tolerate this sort of *médisance* for very long, Alceste faces off against the "laughers," accusing them of hypocrisy and decadence, though they point out that he is simply following his contrarian habits of disagreeing with whatever opinions prevail at the time. Just as a wise intervention from Éliante threatens to turn the dialogue in a more edifying direction, the arrival of a guard from the **Marshals of France**, summoning Alceste to discuss his argument with Oronte, breaks off the engagement and sets the pattern of interruption and deferral by pests that likens this play to *Les Fâcheux*.

The opening of the third act finds Acaste and Clitandre fatuously comparing notes to see which one has greater proof of preferment by Célimène. Even these social butterflies are not so different from Alceste or Oronte in their desire to obtain something from the hostess. Each hoping to outdo the other, they beat a quick retreat when the disgusting prude **Arsinoé** disembarks from her **carriage**. This lady has come with no more lofty purpose than embarrassing Célimène and gloating about how she has spread scandalous rumors about her among her circle of ultra–religious friends. But, rising to the challenge as always, Célimène merely turns the bigot's own words back upon her, explicitly showing how the aging lady uses faith as a vulgar **mask** to cover the flickering flame of her lust. Cut to the quick, Arsinoé predicts that Célimène may soon find herself in a similar situation and denies any **jealousy** toward the popular flirt. But Célimène makes her point and at the same time ends the bothersome interview by foisting off Arsinoé on the recently returned Alceste. Indeed, Arsinoé does little to conceal her interest in Alceste's attentions, as she crudely offers him wealth, political power, and aid with his lawsuit, if only he turns to her from Célimène. To his credit, he rebuffs her **flattery** and her offers until she tempts him with one irresistible morsel, a **letter** she has intercepted that will prove Célimène's unfaithfulness to him. The act closes as Alceste departs to read it.

At the beginning of the fourth act, Philinte delivers the account of Alceste's meeting with the Marshals that the misanthrope himself was prevented from making. It portrays the subject in all his stubbornness resisting the delegated authority of the Marshals and requiring commands from the King himself. Alceste only allowed for the flimsiest reconciliation with Oronte, refusing to change his opinion about the petty verses at the heart of the quarrel. Philinte goes on to press his plan for a **marriage** between Éliante and Alceste, but the two are just beginning to talk of their own mutual emotions when Alceste comes storming into the room, bellowing for revenge and brandishing the guilty letter. Éliante wisely rejects his offer to her to become his rebound bride, knowing that it will take more than this incident to shake the man's passion for her cousin. The next scene, where Alceste confronts Célimene with the evidence, proves Éliante right, for the flirt handles her enraged suitor like a skillful bullfighter, deflecting the fury of his charges into the illusion of his own imagination by barely suggesting the idea that he might be wrong, rather than offering a point–by–point defense. Alceste soon comes to doubt his heated accusations and is reduced to groveling and begging Célimène to supply an excuse for his continuing to love her. When he is almost reduced to complete abjection, the action is once again interrupted by an outside agent, this time the valet **Du Bois**, who has come from Alceste's home with dire tales of legal calamity.

The final act opens with a tirade from Alceste, who has apparently lost his suit and is preparing to abandon **polite** society and retreat into the countryside to live alone, despite Philinte's reassurances that all is not lost and the appeals have not been exhausted. It is clear Alceste needs only a pretext for breaking off all his relationships. Before he can accost Célimène, he witnesses Oronte pressing her to give exactly the same kind of definitive declaration that he seeks, and he joins his enemy in demanding an explanation. No female aid is forthcoming from Éliante this time, for she, too, desires to know the truth. But before Célimène can manage to utter an elaborate enough lie to satisfy the growing audience, Acaste and Clitandre return with documentary proof of their own.

They have exchanged letters from the lady and found that she despises all her suitors equally, lambasting them in pen and ink even more devastatingly than in speech. Having heard his shameful portrait, each man departs to seek revenge, with the exception of Alceste. He tells Célimène of his long–cherished fantasy of saving her from ruin so that she will be totally dependent on him and obligated to him forever, inviting her to share the rehabilitation offered by his flight from Paris and its vices. She, in turn, tries to negotiate a settlement that would allow her to stay in her beloved capital and pursue her interests without interruption — an alternative that Alceste cannot contemplate. Philinte and Éliante, who have managed to pledge mutual love in the midst of this chaos, hasten off as the curtain falls, eager to try once again to save the misanthrope from his own nature.

The superb **language** of the play, its subtle technical mastery, the surprising timeliness of its manners and the timelessness of the virtues and vices involved, all join to make this comedy a masterpiece. Each of the individual characters, down to the **servants**, marks a high point in Molière's theatrical creativity and is the result of years of experimentation and development. Though based on the syncopation of interruption, its lines have a curious rhythmic quality and a degree of inter–relatedness that provide an almost musical sense of movement in a play where not a note was actually sounded. Though it is not completely devoid of **lazzi** or **farcical** elements, these have been so largely replaced and confined that one sees *Le Misanthrope* as having attained zero degrees of buffoonery and owing its existence entirely to a new, refined type of dialogue. Yet the speeches here are typically Moliéresque, pithy and paradoxical, full of ideas in the heat of battle and contention. The effect is far from the froth and badinage that would inherit the late seventeenth–century stage and culminate in Marivaux's playful banter. It is no accident that detractors of Molière, from the ultra–orthodox clerics of **Louis XIV's** reign to **Rousseau**, knew that if they were to topple Molière, they would have to find a weakness in *Le Misanthrope*. But rave as they would about the play's moral interpretations, they could not begin to duplicate its artistic magic, and it has withstood all attempts of destruction or imitation.

Bibliography: *Le Misanthrope*, ed. Gustave Rudler (Oxford: Blackwell, 1947); *Le Misanthrope*, ed. Jonathan Mallinson (London: Bristol Classical Press, 1996); *Le Misanthrope*, ed. David Whitton (Glasgow: University of Glasgow Press, 1991); René Jaskinski, *Molière et le Misanthrope* (Paris: Colin, 1951); H. Gaston Hall, "The Literary Context of Molière's *Le Misanthrope*," *Studi francesi* 14 (1970), 20–38; Christian Biet, "La Veuve et l'idéal du mari absolu: Célimène et Alceste," *Cahiers du dix–septième* 7 (1997), 215–226; Richard E. Goodkin, "Between Genders, between Genres: Célimène's Letter to Alceste in Molière's *Le Misanthrope*," *Romanic Review* 85 (1994), 553–572; David Shaw, "Legal Elements in *Le Misanthrope*," *Nottingham French Studies* 38 (1999), 1–11; Marie–Odile Sweetser, "Théâtre du monde et monde du théâtre: *Le Misanthrope*," *Le Nouveau Moliériste* 3 (1996–97), 57–71.

**Molière** (*L'Impromptu de Versailles*).  Molière portrays himself in the frame play as an energetic but somewhat panicky director, calling the roll of his troupe to assemble them for rehearsal, constantly fretting about their not being ready with their lines, apprehensive about the command performance that is about to start.  He tries to keep his colleagues on the subject at hand, but succumbs to **Mlle. de Brie's** requests for information about his planned "comedy of comedians" and then gets so caught up in the spirit that he lampoons five of the **Hôtel de Bourgogne's** stars.  After marshaling his personnel for the play–within–the–play, he is totally attentive to their performance, so much so that he again jumps into the action, leaving his own ridiculous marquis character to deliver one of **Brécourt's** speeches.  Returning to the "real" Molière at the behest of **Madeleine Béjart**, who cannot so easily dismiss the invective heaped on him by his enemies, he convincingly shows a lack of hatred and a reasonable concern for his family's privacy and his company's prosperity.  However, the repeated summons from royal **servants** in the final scenes turn him into a dithering mess, and he seems so genuinely upset with the King's postponement that one senses he must have gone through similar experiences in "real life."

**Molière — Life.** *See* **Poquelin, Jean–Baptiste.**

**Molière Children.** *See* **Poquelin.**

**Molière, Mlle. de.** *See* **Béjart, Armande.**

**Molière, Mlle.** (*L'Impromptu de Versailles*).  **Armande Béjart's** role in both the frame play and the play–within–the–play is quite intriguing.  The frame play shows her far more silent and perhaps submissive than the senior women.  When she does try to get a word in edgewise, her husband tells her, "Shut up, wife, you are stupid!"  She then chides him for changing so soon from a solicitous suitor to a jaded husband, who takes her for granted.  Resigned to her role as Élise, a witty but playful woman, she teases **Mlle. Du Parc** on her appearance, then joins in the general assault on Molière by the **marquis** and their friends.  Interestingly, when the company leaves off the play–within–the–play to sympathize with Molière over the slurs to his person, Armande Béjart has nothing to say, leaving the conversation to her elders, **Madeleine** and **Mlle. de Brie**.  This portrayal shows us a lighter side of Armande Béjart than we are usually accustomed to seeing and suggests that at this stage of her career she was still considered as somewhat of a child, even though her husband/director grants her considerable free rein on stage.

**Molière d'Essertines.**  A minor novelist of the early 1600s.
    *See also* **Polyxène**.

**Money.**  The nondecimal monetary system under the *ancien régime* was not unlike that of Britain in some respects.  The basic unit of the *livre* or pound was subdivided into twenty *sols* (like shillings), which in turn were subdivided into twelve *deniers* (like pence). Coins did not necessarily match single units within the system, and their value could vary depending on royal decree. The most commonly mentioned French coin, the golden *louis*, was usually worth about ten *livres*, sometimes ranging toward twelve. **Monsieur Jourdain's** excellent accounting assures us that at the time of *Le Bourgeois gentilhomme* the *louis* was worth exactly eleven *livres,* providing that he is not including any interest, of course. The same was true of the Spanish *pistole*, which was in regular practical use because Spain had a much bigger gold supply from its New World mines than any other European power. Descending in value, there were *écus* of gold (worth about five *livres*) and silver (worth about three), the latter being much more common by Molière's time. Below this, most commonly circulated coins were made of bronze or an alloy and were worth less than one *livre*. The "quatre pièces tapées et cinq sols en doubles" mentioned by **Pierrot** as a wager in *Dom Juan* were worth only half a *livre*, though the little hoard would count thirty–four coins. There was a general shortage of currency, so many transactions took place on credit, often guaranteed by several parties, or by letter of credit. Failure of any link in this system of inter–depending debts could obviously have a domino effect, so bankruptcy was greatly feared and despised. With yearly family income from the lower **bourgeoisie** on down averaging 1,000 *livres* or less, any sum in excess of 100 *livres* could be considerable and even smaller amounts could mean a great deal for **peasants** or **servants**. The latter groups generally had very few coins in their possession and hoarded what they had to pay taxes or obtain other necessities. Furthermore, coins were often unscrupulously shaven or clipped to remove precious bits of metal, making it necessary to weigh them to ascertain their full value. Given the seriousness with which money was considered, one can readily understand the ridiculousness of **Bélise's** suggestion in *Les Femmes savantes* that **Henriette's** dowry be calculated in ancient minas and talents instead of *livres*.

**Monologue.** French term for a speech made by a lone character on stage.
   *See also* **Soliloquy**.

**Monsieur.** This title was reserved in the Bourbon **court** for the King's younger brother. In Molière's case, it referred to Philippe, Duke of Orléans and Chartres (1640–1701), who was his troupe's official patron from 1658 until the King claimed them himself, in 1665. In a rather tongue–in–cheek letter, Molière dedicates *L'École des maris* to his **patron**, excusing himself for offering such a mere "bagatelle." It may be worth noting in this regard that the troupe's wages of 300 *livres* per actor had not been regularly paid. Monsieur is said to have come to the troupe's aid following the demolition of the **Petit–Bourbon** theater in the fall of 1660, when he intervened to help obtain the Palais Royal Theater for them. His first wife, **Henrietta of England**, was also a fan and ordered a number of private performances, as did his second, the **Princess Palatine**. Philippe made the mistake of distinguishing himself in military leadership during the 1677 campaigns, which led to his being removed from any official duties by his **jealous** brother, who consigned him to a drone's existence at **Versailles**.

*Monsieur de Pourceaugnac*. *Monsieur de Pourceaugnac* was first presented October 6, 1669, at the royal château of **Chambord**, as a **hunting**–season entertainment for the **court**. The *livret* distributed at its première entitled the work *Le Divertissement de Chambord, mêlé de Comédie, de Musique & d'Entrées de Ballet*. It contained more extensive comic scenes integrating **musical and danced** expression than any of Molière's and **Lully's** previous collaborations. As such it constitutes a high point of the rapidly developing **comedy–ballet** genre, a major attraction in itself and a large advance in the direction of the genre's final masterpieces, *Le Bourgeois gentilhomme* and *Le Malade imaginaire*.

Reception both at court and in **Paris** (beginning November 15, paired on this occasion with *Le Sicilien*) was highly enthusiastic. Writing of the work's premiere, *La Gazette* praised its comic, musical, and danced constituents as "so well harmonized that one cannot imagine anything more agreeable," its sets as superb, and the overall effect as magnificent. In his "Lettre en vers à Madame" **Robinet** wrote of the novelty and magnificence of a "genre gaillard et follet" that delighted its royal audience. During the work's Parisian performances he praised Molière's achievement further: all was "Worthy of his genius rare, / Well–crafted, decked, beyond compare, / With many a new wonder." The latter remark appears to recognize Molière's constant reaching for new dramatic achievements. The work had a highly successful, exclusive run from its second performance (November 17) until the following January, when it was replaced by *Tartuffe*. It remained popular, being staged twenty–nine more times during the two remaining years of Molière's lifetime and eventually becoming a Mardi Gras tradition at the **Comédie–Française**.

*Monsieur de Pourceaugnac*'s title character is a provincial **nobleman** who arrives in Paris from his native **Limoges** in order to collect a bride, **Julie**, promised to him by her father, **Oronte**. Julie, who until recently was betrothed to her desired suitor **Éraste**, has other ideas. With Julie's consent Éraste calls on a pair of intriguers, **Sbrigani** and **Nérine**, to disrupt Oronte's and Pourceaugnac's plans. The conspiracy planned and executed furnishes much of the action of the play; with Sbrigani as its principal dramaturge, the play–within–the–play consisting of the tricks played on Pourceaugnac and Oronte may be considered to overwhelm its outer frame, the Limousin's voyage. In this highly individual dramatic construction, comic illusion first conquers, then helps to refashion reality.

According to both Robinet and **Grimarest**, there may have been an original model for the character of Pourceaugnac. Several candidates have been proposed, but none with convincing evidence. Provincial nobles as a group were in any case an easy target for ridicule both in Paris and at court, as the **Sotenvilles** of *George Dandin* (1668) had just recently exemplified. The crown's attempts to root out *faux nobles* during this period also lent piquant actuality to Pourceaugnac's dubious claim to **gentilhomme** (hereditary noble) status.

Various theatrical sources for the tricks played on Pourceaugnac and Oronte have been adduced, among them **Scarron's** play *Le Marquis ridicule* and the *commedia dell'arte* scenarios *Pulcinello burlato* (*Pulcinello Tricked*) and *Policinella pazzo per forza* (*Pulcinella Forced into Craziness*). Scarron's comedy and the first of the Pulcinella scenarios feature accusations of the protagonist having abandoned women with **children**. The second scenario stages a provincial Pulcinella whose **marriage** plans are undone by trickery, including being declared incurably insane before his intended father–in–law. The latter gag is found also in **Plautus's** *Menœchmi*. As always however in the mature Molière, the playwright reworks any preexisting elements into a strikingly new dramatic synthesis, amplified in the case of *Pourceaugnac* through the large presence of music and dance.

The *livret* distributed at the first performance contains stage directions indicating that Éraste leads a large group of voices and orchestral instruments in a serenade. Its lyrics clearly state major themes of what will come, especially in the lines "Quand deux cœurs s'aiment bien, Tout le reste n'est rien." Reciprocal **love** will conquer any attempt to oppose it, including tyrannical parents' strictures. Four ballet entries then figure a loose thematic succession of authority and harmony (two dance masters, then two pages), discord (four spectators dance a sword fight), and re–establishment of order (by two **Swiss** guards), leading to a dance of all participants. The discord–harmony opposition will be developed through comic dialogue and stage business, then further through **music and dance**. Dancing swordsmen and Swiss guards will reappear as Éraste and Sbrigani in effect "choreograph" each step of Pourceaugnac's Parisian experiences. The music and dance, at once more impressive and more obscure to Pourceaugnac than words alone, are integral to building the dramatic impact of his experiences.

The first act presents Julie's plight and fears, Éraste's assurances that Pourceaugnac's design will fail, and Nérine's and Sbrigani's pride in their cunning stratagems. Both Nérine and Sbrigani, who has already spied on Monsieur de Pourceaugnac, whet the audience's curiosity concerning Pourceaugnac's **nature**. His entrance immediately thereafter, in extravagant clothes of lurid colors, makes him visually memorable, while his confused anger at offstage laughter — he is the object of ridicule by unseen Parisians — confirms Sbrigani's judgment that his mind is of the dimmest. Sbrigani immediately feigns friendship for his prey. As Pourceaugnac takes Sbrigani for his one true friend in a strange city, Sbrigani is not just in control of the traps he will spring on the hapless Limousin, but also in a position to shape Pourceaugnac's beliefs and reactions. Although Sbrigani masterminds the entire affair, Pourceaugnac clings from start to finish to the illusion that his "friend" is loyally aiding him to deal rationally with the bizarre mores of Parisians.

Éraste and Sbrigani proceed to send the hapless Pourceaugnac down an obstacle course, each hurdle more bizarre, unsettling, and — so Pourceaugnac believes — more dangerous, until he believes that he must flee for his life. After astounding Pourceaugnac with his apparently intimate knowledge of the Limousin's family, Éraste, a second "friend," recommends him to a **doctor,** forewarned by Éraste that he will have to treat a mentally troubled patient who should not be allowed to escape. The doctor and a colleague interview him at great length, interspersing their questions with long disquisitions in authentic but highly convoluted medical jargon. They soon find confirmation of the "patient's" allegedly aberrant state, since he protests their questions and even denies being ill (I, 8). In order to lift his spirits out of the dangerously unstable melancholy that they diagnose, they prescribe a cure of music and dance.

Pourceaugnac's response, "Les gens de ce pays–ci sont–ils insensés?" leads into the first *intermède*, an even more absurd confrontation in which two "grotesque doctors" sing to Pourceaugnac in **Italian** their advice that he sing, dance, laugh, and imbibe. When an **apothecary** wishes to further the cure by cleansing his intestines, Pourceaugnac runs offstage with his hat clapped to his backside, returning to his chair only to take flight again with the chair in place of the hat as he is pursued by a whole company of apothecary, doctors, and dancing swordsmen, all menacing him with syringes. Capped by its dancing and the vibrant song "Piglia–lo sù" ("Take It Quickly"), the *intermède* is a stellar example of Molière's and Lully's increasing ability to sustain extended, wildly exhilarating comic scenes with music and dance that develop a joyful atmosphere that, while building directly on comic plot considerations, also goes well beyond them.

Act II opens as Sbrigani encourages the first doctor to recapture and treat the escaped patient to the doctor's full satisfaction, with handsome remuneration promised. At Sbrigani's urging the doctor convinces Oronte of Pourceaugnac's medical unfitness for marriage. Since the doctor now considers that Pourceaugnac and his illness are his personal property, he even threatens to treat Oronte if the patient is not recovered. Although the doctor's greed and lust for power are obvious, Oronte protests only mildly, bemused at the doctor's *belle raison.*

The more Sbrigani multiplies his tricks, the less Pourceaugnac understands. Although he can see that he is falsely accused, he never discerns the game behind the stratagems, which convince him that all of Paris — save his "friend" — is against him. Thanks to Sbrigani's preparations, when Oronte and Pourceaugnac meet for the first time, they are quick to insult each other (II, 5). By act's end, Pourceaugnac is reduced to begging to be examined by a **lawyer** in order to prove his lack of legal knowledge (practicing as a lawyer would be incompatible with the status of *gentilhomme*, which Pourceaugnac claims). Pourceaugnac's boundless gullibility clearly afforded Molière occasion for superbly acted variations on shock, frustration, incomprehension, and fear; both his and Lully's performances (the latter as a singing lawyer, eventually as Pourceaugnac also) remained memorable for decades.

In the second *intermède*, singing lawyers inform Pourceaugnac in absurdly incongruous counterpoint that his crime of polygamy is punishable by hanging. Shaken more than ever, the lawyer from Limoges believes that he must **disguise** himself to escape Paris. Act III finds the still–bearded Pourceaugnac attired in woman's dress in order to elude the guards he fears at the gates of the city. Sbrigani has Pourceaugnac "saved" from arrest only after the extraction of a large bribe. The lawyer exits with the bailiff whom he has just bribed and who promises to place him "in safety." Sbrigani convinces Oronte that Pourceaugnac has kidnapped Julie but that Éraste has valiantly rescued her. While Julie feigns love for Pourceaugnac alone, her father expresses his gratitude to Éraste by ordering Julie to marry him. Love thus conquers parental tyranny, with neither father nor unwanted suitor remotely the wiser. **Masked** revelers who are conveniently in the vicinity dance and sing a final scene of rejoicing: "Ne songeons qu'à nous réjouir: La grande affaire est le plaisir." Music and dance thus initiate, intervene repeatedly in, and end the work, always linked to the comic workings but extending comic action into a realm of joyously irrational festivity. As Sbrigani's tricks pour into the void of Pourceaugnac's ever–more–improbable incomprehension, comic action is used to destroy virtually all sense of normality: the doctors' belief in their own normality, for instance, is revealed to be just as farcical as Pourceaugnac's similar belief. The work's comic destruction simultaneously creates a dramatic place for other, joyfully festive energies. These latter qualities are of a largely grotesque nature until the finale, as in the dances with syringes of the first *intermède* or the pair of lawyers singing in wildly contrasted vocal parts of the mortal consequences of polygamy. The already bewildered Pourceaugnac is even more mystified and shaken by these interludes. Dramatically, they seal his illusion–bound isolation; but they also convert Sbrigani's and Éraste's comic "machines" and "batteries" into the instrument of a higher level of coherence. Monsieur de Pourceaugnac's comic destruction will be in part effected by music and dance, in part celebrated by these arts. Expressed through the finale's music, the work's nearest equivalent to a moral, "When all for mirth assemble/ The wisest men resemble/ Those who best play the fool," makes, at the end, eminently joyful sense.

Bibliography: Claude Abraham, "Illusion and Reality in *Monsieur de Pourceaugnac*," *Romance Notes* 16.3 (Spring 1975), 641–646; Jean–Marie Apostolidès, "Le diable à Paris. L'ignoble entrée de Pourceaugnac," *L'Esprit et la lettre: mélanges offerts à Jules Brody*, ed. Louis van Delft (Tübingen: Narr, 1991), 69–84; Stephen H. Fleck, "The Play of Illusions in *Monsieur de Pourceaugnac*," in *Car demeure l'amitié*, ed. Francis Assaf and Andrew H. Wallis, Biblio 17 (102) (Paris: Papers on French Seventeenth–Century Literature, 1997), 51–61; Fausta Garavini, "La fantaisie verbale et le mimétisme dialectal dans le théâtre de Molière: A propos de Monsieur de Pourceaugnac," *Revue d'Histoire Littéraire de la France* 72 (1972), 806–820; Robert Kenny, "Molière's Tower of Babel: Monsieur de Pourceaugnac and the Confusion of Tongues," *Nottingham French Studies* 33.1 (Spring 1994), 59–70; Jacqueline Marty, "Quelques emprunts de Molière au Théâtre de Béziers: Le Canevas de Monsieur de Pourceaugnac," *Revue des Langues Romanes* 81 (1975), 43–66; Edith J. Potter, "Problems of Knowing in *Momsieur de Pourceaugnac*," *Romance Notes* 17 (1976), 38–43.

*Stephen H. Fleck*

**Montauban.** A city in southern France that heroically survived a siege by the armies of the Duke de Luynes in 1621. The noble forces that had been raised by the royal armies behaved shamefully, abandoning the fighting when sickness broke out in the camp. **Monsieur de Sotenville** foolishly boasts of his father's participation in this disaster.

**Montauzier or Montausier, Charles de Sainte–Maure, Marquis and later Duc de** (1610–1690). This important **court** figure was husband of the famous beauty Julie d'Angennes, the pride of the Hôtel de **Rambouillet**. For her he composed the verses called "La Guirlande de Julie," which were widely respected for their lyrical quality at the time. **Louis XIV** made him governor to the young **dauphin**, a potentially powerful post that he filled badly. On the basis of his prickly personality, he was suggested by some, including **Boileau**, to be the model for Molière's character of **Alceste**. If so, it must have been a very distant imitation, for the figures offer more dissimilarity than agreement. Boileau's letter with the suggestion dates from 1706, and other critics have voiced the opinion that Boileau himself was a model!

See Denis Lopez, *La Plume et l'épée: Montausier (1610–1690)*, Biblio 17 (Tübingen: G. Narr, 1987).

**Montespan, Françoise–Anthenaïs de Rochechouart, marquise de** (1640–1709). Endowed with the legendary wit of the Mortemar family, this lady of the **court** became **Louis XIV's** second official mistress by the beginning of 1668 and bore him seven children, who were later legitimized as royal heirs. Her coming to power is often supposed to be shown in *Amphitryon*. The real Marquis of Montespan did not behave as well as the **Greek** husband, however, and was eventually banned from the court for demanding too much **money** for sitting idly by while the King enjoyed his wife's pleasures. He is further rumored to have struck her and even to have initiated legal proceedings. Between moments of repentance, Madame de Montespan enjoyed great influence at court until the late 1670s, when she fell to some degree from favor. She generally favored **Racine** over Molière.

See Jean–Christian Petitfils, *Madame de Montespan* (Paris: Fayard, 1988).

**Montfleury (stage name of Zacharie Jacob).** This rotund tragedian of the **Hôtel de Bourgogne** troupe took such umbrage at Molière's remarks in *Les Précieuses ridicules* and *La Critique de l'Ecole des femmes* that he wrote a *placet* to the King accusing Molière of incest and adultery in his relationships with the **Béjart** family. Declining an ad hominem response, Molière ridiculed his elephantine stage appearance and his stilted declamation (particularly his role in **Corneille's** *Nicomède*) in *L'Impromptu de Versailles*.

**Montfleury fils (nom de plume of Antoine Jacob,** 1639–1685). Son of a tragic actor of the **Hôtel de Bourgogne** whose bombastic style Molière mocked in the *Impromptu de Versailles*, Montfleury responded with the satirical play *L'Impromptu de l'Hôtel de Condé* (1663), which is mainly interesting as invective and lacked both the ingenuity and the metatheatrical boldness of the former play. Notwithstanding his continued hostility to Molière, Montfleury attempted to copy his treatment of cuckoldry in *L'École des jaloux* (1662) and the development of the *comédie–ballet* in *Le Mari sans femme* (1664). Other works drawing on Molière are *L'École des filles* (1665), *Le Femme juge et partie* (1668), *Le Procès de la femme juge et partie* (1669), *Le Gentilhomme de la Beauce* (1670) and *La Fille capitaine* (1671).

**Montpellier.** The major city of eastern Languedoc and one of the sites of parliamentary meetings in the seventeenth century. The troupe of **Charles Dufresne** probably spent much of the winter of 1653–54 in the city, as shown by an act where Molière served as godfather to a child of some friends.

See Claude Alberge, *Le Voyage de Molière en Languedoc, 1647–1657* (Montpellier: Presses du Languedoc, 1988); C. E. J. Caldicott, "Les Séjours de Molière en Languedoc," *Revue d'Histoire Littéraire de la France* 87 (1987), 994–1014.

**Montpensier, Anne–Marie–Louise d'Orléans, duchesse de** (1627–1693). Daughter of Gaston d'Orléans (Louis XIII's brother) and thus first cousin to the younger **Louis XIV**, this princess was one of the richest individuals in France. As a punishment for her role in the Fronde revolts, when she sided briefly against the royal family's forces, she was exiled throughout much of her adulthood to her Burgundian estate of Saint–Fargeau. The King vetoed many prospects for her **marriage**. Thus, she was also known as La Grande Mademoiselle. She eventually became enamored of the flashy **court** figure Lauzun, many years her junior and a possible model of Molière's ridiculous marquis, but was only permitted the most pathetic of relationships. Segrais served as her literary creature and sometime ghost writer.

See Jean Garapon, *La Grande Mademoiselle* (Geneva: Droz, 1989).

**Moors.** These nonspeaking characters appear in *Le Sicilien*, where they are involved in the **senator's** masquerade at the conclusion of the play. Originally, they were members of the royal dance company, and Molière may have employed the same people for the **Paris** production. **Gypsies** "dressed as Moors" also figure in the second *intermède* of *Le Malade imaginaire*, where they perform a mixture of songs and dances.

**Mopse** (*Mélicerte*). Mélicerte's putative uncle appears in only one scene, where he and his friend **Nicandre** try to pry news from the reluctant **Lycarsis**. Lycarsis goes to find him after reconciling with his son (II, 5), and we learn at the end of the play that Mopse's relationship with Bélise, Mélicerte's mother, has been called into question.

**Moreto, Augustin** (1618–1669). Madrid playwright whose *Distain versus Distain* served as a source for *La Princesse d'Élide*.

See also **Spanish Influences**.

**Morin, Jean–Baptiste** (1583–1656). An infamous **astrological** charlatan and professor of mathematics whose adventures were well known long after the time of Molière. He may have served as a model for **Anaxarque** in *Les Amants magnifiques*.

**Moron** (*La Princesse d'Élide*). The fool Moron is one of Molière's most interesting and demanding parts in some ways, for though it involves little depth of character, it imposes interesting conditions of physical comedy. For instance, the actor has only one scene in which to change out of the **Lyciscas costume** before he appears as Moron in the first act. He makes his entry at full gallop, chased offstage by a wild boar, at which he continues to cringe throughout his scene with **Euryale**, as he delivers a burlesque account of his **hunting** heroics. Though the prince chides him for failing to show more bravery, Moron replies that he would rather be a live coward than a dead hero, composing mock epitaphs to prove his point. He explains to the prince why he has not carried out his mission of talking with the **Princess**, professing a loyalty that is based on more than mere servitude, for he claims to be the bastard son of Euryale's royal father.

When Euryale and **Arbate** go off to discuss strategy, Moron stays behind to conduct "a little conversation with the rocks and the trees" about his love for **Philis**. After reciting a hilarious poem about how beautiful she looks milking a cow, he plays at echoes in the woods. However, what he took for an echo turns out to be another wild beast, this time a **bear** that grasps him in its paws. The cowardly clown cajoles the bear with outlandish **noble** titles and praises its "pretty nose, darling little mouth . . . gorgeous little claws." He is saved by a troupe of huntsmen who kill the bear and dance around its carcass as Moron, turned brave once again, batters it with blows.

In the second act, he encourages the Princess to give up her harsh ways by confiding that he himself is in **love** and in the ensuing third *intermède*, it is once again he who carries the action. He accosts Philis, only to have her criticize his "jabbering" and condemn him to shut up. Thus silenced, he professes love to her through amorous mimed **lazzi**. When he breaks the rule by speaking again, she stalks off to join her musical boyfriend **Tircis**. Moron then enlists a well–tuned **Satyr** to give him singing lessons. After a couple of numbers, he mistakes the note "fa" for the insult "fat" (idiot) and gets into a fight with his teacher, danced to the music of the royal violins.

In the next act Moron congratulates Euryale on his perverse strategy of inciting the Princess's interest through feigned indifference, and then, speaking with her, he repeats the lie and exaggerates it by adding: "He's the most vainglorious little knave you've ever seen. As he sees it, there's no one in the world who's his equal, and the Earth itself is not worthy to bear him on its surface." The increasingly desperate Princess begs his intercession at the end of the act, but he continues in the same vein, alleging that Euryale is implacable. Pressing his own interests, he intrudes on Philis and Tircis in the fourth *intermède*, trying to best the singer with a foolish ditty of his own. When the object of his love says she wishes he'd be willing to die for her, he pretends to comply, as Tircis eggs him on, but has the last laugh himself. His main contribution to the last two acts is a funny line comparing the Princess, who would spitefully prevent Euryale from marrying **Aglante**, to the proverbial dog in the manger.

**Mummers**. See **Carnival**.

**Music and Dance**. Thirteen of Molière's plays — more than a third of the total — and six of the last eight contain music and dance, "two arts which are closely linked together" (*Le Bourgeois gentilhomme* I.2): *Les Fâcheux* (1661); *Le Mariage forcé* (1664); *La Princesse d'Élide* (1664); *L'Amour médecin* (1665); *La Pastorale comique* (1667); *Le Sicilien* (1667); *George Dandin* (1668); *Monsieur de Pourceaugnac (*1669*); Les Amants magnifiques* (1670); *Le Bourgeois gentilhomme (*1670*); Psyché* (1671); *La Comtesse d'Escarbagnas (*1671, part of the *Ballet des Ballets); and Le Malade imaginaire* (1673). This is hardly surprising in a century that prized dance to such a great degree as not only a form of entertainment, exercise and preparation for swordsmanship but also as an exterior manifestation of internal worth and of universal harmony. **Monsieur Jourdain** begins his social "ascent" with dancing lessons, and it was as Mme. de Clèves and M. de Nemours began to dance — alone, before the entire court — that there arose "murmurs of admiration" from the spectators.

Molière's stated goal in creating *Les Fâcheux*, once it was decided that the small number of available dancers made it necessary to separate the entrées of Beauchamps's ballet by acts of his comedy, was "to have ballet and comedy be one and the same thing." Molière describes this "sewing together" of comedy and ballet as a novelty, but in reality it was a "mélange" that was new only in the limited domain of French comedy, since such mixtures were common in **Italian** comedy and opera as well as in French **court** ballet. Indeed, beginning with *Le Ballet comique de la Reine* in 1581, there had been a variety of experiments with means of making ballets more than a loosely connected series of entrées, and in the early 1660s the man who had the most expertise in this area, as well as considerable experience with Italian comedy and opera, was the "other" Baptiste, **Jean–Baptiste Lully**.

Lully's contribution to *Les Fâcheux* was limited to the courante sung in Act I scene 3 by **Lysandre**, who intends to have Lully help him with the instrumental parts. When the real collaboration between the two Jean–Baptistes began with *Le Mariage forcé* in 1664, Lully had ten years of experience at combining music and dance with comedy. His efforts had been in both of the two directions that would dominate the debate about the presence of music and dance on the theatrical stage: (1) creating a structure into which musical and balletic set pieces could be integrated and (2) creating scenes — often pastoral —in which all or part of the dialogue is sung. With hindsight, one can see Lully preferring the latter, moving toward opera and away from Molière, but the first direction was the one that produced the most memorable results in his collaboration with Molière.

*Le Mariage forcé* is an example of the first of these two directions. The ballet scenes take place between scenes of the comedy, but they do help advance the plot as, for example, **Sganarelle** consults **gypsies** and a **magician** about his upcoming **marriage**. It is important to remember that dance was so popular, especially at court, that the work was described by contemporaries as a "ballet mixed with comedy," and when the work was taken to Paris in February it was with its "ornements" of music, dance, and elaborate **costumes**. These were, however, omitted when the work was printed in 1668, making it almost impossible for the reader to have an idea of the work as it was originally conceived. (Molière would comment on this problem in the *Avertissement* to *L'Amour médecin*.)

Their next collaboration, *La Princesse d'Élide*, contains examples of the second direction. The first five *intermèdes* contain a mixture of spoken and sung lines, along with dance, and they often feature characters from the comedy, such as the **Princess**, **Moron**, and **Philis**. The music and dance still come at the end of the acts, but they do not necessarily introduce characters that could be found in any court ballet, such as the Gypsies and the magician in *Le Mariage forcé* (the **bear** and the **hunters** in the second *intermède* would be an exception). It is an important step toward the mature **comedy–ballets** (and Lully's later operas), as if Lully were pushing Molière in new directions.

*L'Amour médecin* is more like earlier comedy–ballets, with a sung prologue and dancing and singing after each act, related to the plot of the comedy but not featuring important characters from it. The importance of the combination of the arts, however, is underlined by Molière's *Au lecteur*, where he insists on the importance of the *jeu de théâtre*, the beauty of the singing, the skill of the dancers, and the music of the "incomparable Mr. Lully," as well as in the desire of comedy, music, and ballet, expressed in the prologue, to unite "to give pleasure to the greatest king in the world."

The two works on which Lully collaborated with Molière for the third entrée of the *Ballet des Muses* (1667) offer an example of both directions, a "comedy mixed with music" and a "ballet mixed with comedy." *La Pastorale comique*, which replaced the completely spoken *Mélicerte*, contains several scenes in which the main characters sing some of their lines, whereas *Le Sicilien* is more like *Le Mariage forcé* and *L'Amour médecin*: **Hali** introduces musical interludes that advance the action. Molière's text, with its numerous *vers blancs*, seems to take special advantage of the musical qualities of **language** that are more prevalent in the comedy–ballets than in his other works (with the exception of unusual passages such as the opening lines of *L'Avare*).

*George Dandin* seems much more disparate, containing a pastoral and a comedy in parallel with each other rather than a comedy with *intermèdes*. Indeed, the **Gazette** describes the comedy as "mixed with the entr'actes of another type of comedy with music and ballets." However, Félibien, writing about the 1664 fête that is another important aspect of the context of *George Dandin*, wrote that the two comedies were "so closely linked to a single subject that they form a single work and represent only one action." The true feelings and artificial setting of the pastoral illuminate the selfish characters and true–to–

life setting of the latter, while the concluding celebration puts things into perspective and looks forward to *Le Bourgeois gentilhomme* and *Le Malade imaginaire*.

Like these last two masterpieces, it is difficult to imagine *Monsieur de Pourceaugnac* without its music and dance. They remain in the *intermèdes*, as in *Le Sicilien*, but like **Monsieur Jourdain, Pourceaugnac** is forced to play a role in a "comédie" organized by other actors in the comedy, and it is he who requests the two **lawyers** who perform the *intermède* at the end of Act II. The lines Molière gave them are certainly comic in themselves, but how much more so when one hears them sung at the same time.

With *Les Amants magnifiques* (1670), Lully and Molière returned to the world of **galanterie** for a *divertissement* "composed of all those the theatre can offer." One could say that Molière is definitely at the service of Lully here, creating a structure to tie together extensive passages of music and dance that last longer than the spoken comedy, but he is also helping Lully master the art of creating long scenes in which the dialogue is sung. Opera, in which everything is sung, is not far away, nor is the break between Lully and Molière.

In *Le Bourgeois gentilhomme*, Lully and Molière's last comedy–ballet (which the *Gazette* described as a "ballet . . . accompagné de comédie"), music, dance, and comedy are so well integrated that M. Jourdain would not be the unforgettable character he is without his efforts at learning the indispensable arts of music and dance. It is not only the performance of music and dance — which remain in *intermèdes* — but the presence of representatives of these arts in the lives of Parisian bourgeois and nobles that makes the integration of comedy, music, and dance so successful. Nor could the major themes of appearances, communication, alienation, and internationality be understood in proper perspective without the concluding **Ballet des nations**.

*Psyché* (1671) is unique in several ways: a *tragédie–ballet* rather than a *comédie–ballet*, it incorporates the elaborate machinery that was such an important part of Baroque spectacle. The collaboration of **Corneille**, the famous author of two machine plays, and **Quinault**, Lully's future librettist, underscores how *Psyché* looks back toward an established tradition and forward toward a new genre. Lully contributed an Italian lament, as he had to several ballets, and music and dance are still relegated to the *intermèdes*, but the third and fifth in particular would not be out of place in a *tragédie lyrique*. With the break between Lully and Molière not far away, it is tempting to see in this hybrid, collaborative effort a sign of strain in their relationship, of debate about the direction musical theater should take.

*La Comtesse d'Escarbagnas* (1671) is not a comedy–ballet but part of the structure created by Molièreto tie together the various elements of Le Ballet des ballets, which contained excerpts from earlier Molière–Lully works and from Lully's entr'actes for Corneille's *Œdipe*. In this sense it is much like the 1672 *Les Fêtes de l'Amour et de Bacchus*, except that in the latter work Lully was collaborating with Quinault while using Molière's texts.

The team of the "deux Baptistes" had split, and Molière's last comedy–ballet would be with **Charpentier**, who also provided new music for the revival of *Le Mariage forcé* along with *La Comtesse d'Escarbagnas* in July 1672, as well as for revivals of various Molière plays until 1685. *Le Malade imaginaire* uses music and dance in a remarkable variety of ways. The first version began with a prologue glorifying the King, much like those of Lully's operas. The impromptu opera is essential to the plot, and the final ceremony is the actual denouement rather than a concluding ballet. The second *intermède* is more like the artificially introduced scenes of earlier Molière–Lully comedy–ballets, and the first seems to have as its role less the advancement of the plot than to the use of the old usurer **Polichinelle** to make fun of the avaricious Lully and the Italian comedians with whom he had collaborated and to poke ridicule at opera with its "mode de parler en musique." If Molière had ever been tempted to abandon a conception of musical comedy that kept music and dance separate from the spoken text, it was too late now that Lully had a monopoly on any type of theater that was completely set to music.

Occasionally, Molière would employ a song alone in a limited role in his comedies, without applying the full panoply of a comedy–ballet production. For instance, in *Le Médecin malgré lui*, Sganarelle sings a little tune ("Qu'ils sont doux, bouteille jolie") to his wine flask. **Alceste's** "perfect poem" in *Le Misanthrope*, "Si le roi me donnait Paris," actually accompanied a popular melody of several decades past, and he may have sung the words rather than simply speaking them. **Sosie** sings a bit to give himself courage in the second scene of *Amphitryon*, but his words trail off as **Mercury** lets his frightening voice be heard. **Clitidas** pretends to be singing a ditty to himself in order to approach **Ériphile** without alarming her in *Les Amants magnifiques*. One can only imagine what Molière's own voice was like and what laughable qualities he may have given to these songs.

Selected Bibliography: Claude Abraham, *On the Structure of Molière's Comédies–Ballets*, Biblio 17, no.19 (Paris/Seattle/Tübingen: PFSCL, 1984); James Anthony, *French Baroque Music from Beaujoyeulx to Rameau*, rev. and exp. ed. (1974; reprint Portland, OR: Amadeus Press, 1997); Sstephen H. Fleck, *Comic Creation in Molière's Comedy–Ballets*, Biblio 17 no. 88, (Paris/Seattle/Tübingen: PFSCL, 1995); Charles Mazouer, *Molière et ses comédies–ballets* (Paris: Klincksieck, 1993).

*See also* **Charpentier; Corneille, Pierre; Lully; Quinault, Philippe**.

*Buford Norman*

**Music Master (*Le Bourgeois gentilhomme*).** In the first act, this artist defends his service to a philistine like **Monsieur Jourdain** on practical grounds. The fool "has discrimination in his purse," and his ample payments support the everyday needs of musicians as they pursue their more cerebral interests and prepare works that will eventually please the true *cognoscenti*. He has to defend the recital of his star pupil with the blockheaded Jourdain, who maintains he is paying for the music of a teacher and not a student. Jourdain little realizes that a proud master would never permit his follower to perform unless he had the greatest confidence in his ability. In a dispute with the **Dancing Master** over which of their disciplines is best, he quickly jumps to the defense of music on the basis that it is the source of harmony, and harmony is necessary for the successful organization of all human activity.    He joins his colleague in defending the performing arts against the martial arts when the **Fencing Master** tries to lord it over both of them.  The spectacle of the little Music Master taking on a fully armed swordsman with his conductor's baton must have been a hilarious one on stage.  The role was undoubtedly taken by one of the chief vocal musicians of the King's entourage.  Could it have been handled originally by **Lully** himself?

**Music Master's Student (*Le Bourgeois gentilhomme*).**  This nonspeaking part is limited to performing a fashionable song.

**Musicians.**    While vocal and instrumental musicians were usually confined to the margins of the **theater** or to the musical intervals of **comedy–ballets**, they occasionally take a more direct and active role in the plays.  Though designated as "dog–handlers" in *La Princesse d'Élide,* the singers Estival, Don, and Blondel appear in the first *intermède* to try to rouse **Lyciscas** from his sleep and begin the **hunt**.  Another group of houndsmen, composed of the dancers Paysan, Chicanneau, Noblet, Pesant, Bonard, and La Pierre, perform a dance while blowing on their hunting horns.  They appear to be joined by various other musicians who compose the orchestra during this prelude.  The same groups appear in the pastoral finale, joined by six specialists on the harpsichord and double lute: Anglebert, Richard, Itier, La Barre the younger, Tissu, and Le Moine.  In *Le Sicilien*, three singers accompany **Hali** in the opening two scenes, presenting a vocal serenade to **Isidore**.  They do not reappear after the third scene.  Musicians are a massive presence in *Psyché*, where no fewer than 300 of them are lifted into the skies by **machines** in the finale of the **Tuileries** production.  Though Molière's troupe advertised the same musicians for the Palais Royal Theater production, it appears that the overall number was substantially reduced.  Moreover, it is known that some of the singers, who were used to performing only in a kind of screened booth, quibbled about appearing onstage and had to be given more **money** or replaced.  The great singer Mlle. Hilaire, who had often performed with the troupe, was such a casualty.  Some of the other singers who appeared were the ladies de Rieux, Desfronteaux, and Messieurs Langeais, Gillet, Oudot, Jannot, de La Grille, Gaye, Le Gros, Hédouin, Beaumont, Rebel, Serignan, Le Maire, Rossignol, Bernard, Deschamps, Bony, Morel, Bomaviel, Miracle, Thierry, Matthieu, Perchot, Pierrot, and Renier, as well as the brothers Gignan and the Piesche family. The most complete list of instrumental collaborators is given in the booklet for the Tuileries production of *Psyché*.

*See also* **Music and Dance; Shepherds and Shepherdesses**.

**Musicians (*Monsieur de Pourceaugnac*).**    Two **Italian** vocal musicians in fantastic **costumes** sing a comic song for the protagonist according to the prescriptions of his doctors in Act I, scene 10, in order to put him in a better mood for the enemas that are about to come.  They have no lines in French.

**Myrtil** (*Mélicerte*). This precocious lad, said by his father to be barely out of toyland and already attracting numerous female admirers, is said to have been played by Molière's protégé, **Baron**. At the time of production, Baron was only thirteen. Nevertheless, he must have been an accomplished actor already, as he successfully delivered Myrtil's very adult, sophisticated lines. Myrtil rejects the advances of **Daphné** and **Éroxène** with careful diplomacy and consideration for their feelings, while presenting his own **love** for **Mélicerte** with passionate conviction that wins over his crusty old father. Presenting a pet sparrow to his sweetheart, he launches into an ornate, gallant speech, but thoughtfully inquires into her feelings when he perceives she is upset with something. He handles his own suit with as much wisdom and maturity as he had shown in previous scenes. However, he becomes quite upset himself when he learns in the final scene that Mélicerte has been designated by the King as the bride of an important person. The legendary quarrel between Baron and **Armande Béjart** is seen as the usual explanation for cutting short the play's run and leaving it unfinished. Baron is said to have left the troupe in something of a huff after receiving a slap from Armande.

# N

**Nancy.** Capital of Lorraine, which was still technically an imperial fief independent of the King of France until 1766. **Monsieur de Sotenville** mentions having taken part in the siege of Nancy in 1635, a dark moment in French military history, when the feudal **nobility** mobilized by Louis XIII distinguished themselves only by their ineptitude and cowardice.

**Nantes.** Chief city of lower Brittany, near the mouth of the Loire River. In the autumn of 1645, Molière and the **Béjarts**, fleeing the collapse of the **Illustre Théâtre** and the prospect of debtor's prison, went to Nantes to join with the troupe of **Charles Dufresne**. The spring of 1648 saw the return of the players to this city for several weeks.

**Nanteuil (stage name of Denis Clerselier** fl. 1660–1675). Nanteuil was an actor and perhaps director of a wandering troupe that sometimes styled itself the Queen's Players, but usually seems to have performed in the Low Countries. He sought the patronage of the Prince of Orange and the princes of Brunswick and Lunenburg, publishing his works in Germany and at The Hague. Profoundly influenced by Molière's comedies, he attempted to integrate elements of them into such works as *L'Amour sentinelle* (*Love on Watch*), *Les Brouilleries nocturnes* (*Night–time Confusions*), *Le Comte de Roquefeuilles* (all 1669); *La Conquête de Brunswick*, *Le Campagnard dupé* (both 1671); *La Fille viceroy* (*The Viceroy Wench*, 1672); *L'Amante invisible* (*The Invisible Lover*, 1673), *and L'Héritier imaginaire* (*The Imaginary Heir*, 1674). Nanteuil's works are interesting in that they show his emulation of the free verse used in *Amphitryon*.

**Naples**. In *L'Étourdi*, the family of **Trufaldin** (alias Zanobio Ruberti) is split up by a revolt in their native Naples. Also, the home of the d'Alburcy clan in *L'Avare* (**Anselme, Valère, Mariane**, and her invalid mother). There had been a popular uprising led by a fisherman in 1647 that roughly corresponds to the troubles cited in Act V of the play, which forced the family to flee the city by sea. It is, in addition, the setting of *Les Fourberies de Scapin*.

**Narbonne**. One of the chief cities of Languedoc. The wandering players led by **Charles Dufresne** and including Molière performed there during the winters of 1649–1651.

**Nassau, Maurice de** (1567–1625). Son of William I of Nassau and successor to him as Staathouder of the Netherlands, this Protestant prince was reported to be an arch materialist, saying on his deathbed that he believed only that two and two was four and that four and four was eight. This comment is attributed to the protagonist of *Dom Juan* by Molière, a sign not only of iconoclasm, but of lack of originality on the part of the rake.

**Nature**. It is **Horace** in *L'École des femmes*, who first proclaims the supremacy of Nature in Molière's plays. He marvels at Nature's great influence as a teacher who is able to empower her mortal students to break the bonds of ignorance and achieve their destinies. Speaking of Nature's effects on **Agnès**, he does not realize that her impact has been no less remarkable upon himself. The **Quarrel of the School for Wives** afforded the dramatist further opportunities to examine Nature. His constant effort is to characterize his enemies' behavior and opinions as equally unnatural. This is as true for the **salon** conversation in the *Critique de l'École des femmes* as for the impersonations of bombastic tragedians in *L'Impromptu de Versailles*. Again in the *Tartuffe* affair, he promised never to step away from Nature's guidance in composing his plays. One would expect nothing less for an admirer of **Lucretius**, for the Roman **philosopher** repeatedly stresses the fact that Nature affects men in ways their intellect cannot imagine or anticipate, following a logic of her own that outstrips the logic of schools or individuals. It is often theorized that by the mid–1660s Molière had already read parts of his translation of Lucretius in Parisian gatherings, thus staking out his own skeptical position in the Republic of Letters. **Béralde** takes up this Lucretian thinking in *Le Malade imaginaire* when he describes the comprehension of the human body, "The motors of our machines are a mystery which until now has totally escaped man's understanding and . . . Nature has placed before our eyes veils too thick to penetrate" (III, 3).

Molière's generally optimistic faith in Nature to arrange a happy ending in the world does not extend to human nature. From *Le Misanthrope* and *Dom Juan* onward, one encounters warning after warning about the fundamental atavism of man, which can only be kept in check by effective social institutions. The rejection of such institutions by protagonists such as **Alceste** and **Dom Juan**, sometimes for reasons that appear appealing, raises the troubling possibility that the capacity of humans to find happiness despite themselves may be questionable. In *Amphitryon*, the usually reliable behavior of Nature seems to go haywire as time is disrupted and identities doubled by decree of the gods. **Sosie** trusts human nature to give him the appropriate traits for a slave: gluttony, cowardice, and a taste for self–preservation. Everyone trusts nature to supply him with a unique identity. When impossible betrayals seem to have taken place, **Amphitryon** can only conclude that these things "surpass nature" (II, 2) and objective witnesses such as **Naucrates** quickly come to the same conclusion (III, 4). However, strange as the events seem, the general cannot bring himself to think that the unnatural could intrude in the realm of **marriage** or disrupt the understanding between husband and wife (III, 1), thus following many other Molière characters who seem to believe that some special laws of science and philosophy must apply to the institution of marriage. While the general wants to take up arms against the unnatural, his countryman urges caution, embracing the skeptical position that things that seem inexplicable may only be so because of problems of perspective.

Molière's **doctors** constitute an example of how institutions can rise and flourish that are contrary to the power of Nature. The medical profession tries to channel natural rhythms through the artificial and often twisted conduits of its theory. They become enraged when patients die contrary to their orders or survive in spite of their ministrations. Their favorite therapy, the enema, is little more than an effort to empty bodies of their very nature, to inject them with a newer, more "healthy" being. **Argan's** internalization of this medical mentality represents one of the greatest possible dangers for humanity. Like **Monsieur Jourdain**, who deemed Nature's methods for conferring nobility unacceptable, Argan espouses a radical attempt to reprogram the world according to his own principles. **Toinette's** mocking prescriptions of self–mutilation can only partly convince Argan of his own malignancy. The medical diploma ceremony is like a vaccine made from the dead outward forms of the "unnatural" mutation that is meant to kill it within the body of the host. As Dom Juan had threatened to use Nature against Nature, Toinette and Béralde propose to use the Unnatural against the Unnatural. It is a very deep finesse for a skeptic habituated to doubt, but it is the only sort of weapon within his reach.

**Naucrates** (*Amphitryon*). One of two **Thebans** summoned by **Jupiter** to join in his feast (III, 4), Naucrates is the more talkative of the pair. He intercedes to stop the general from harming **Sosie**, whom he mistook for his double, **Mercury**. He also expresses amazement at the appearance of the two **Amphitryons**, one of them the disguised Jupiter. The prodigious sight causes him and **Polidas** to suspend their judgment, which makes Amphitryon go in search of new allies.

**Neighbors** (*Les Précieuses ridicules*). The stage directions to the play are incomplete, but the neighbors apparently arrive with **Lucile** in scene 12, since **Magdelon** specifically uses the plural in addressing some ladies who have been sent for to swell the ranks at a dance provided by the disguised valets.

**Nérine** (*Les Fourberies de Scapin*). This nurse who has been in charge of **Géronte's** daughter in **Tarento** appears only from Actt III, scene7 onward, and only has lines in the first of her scenes. She asks her master's pardon for having allowed his daughter to marry and reunites him with **Hyacinte**. Until this moment, she has known him under his alias as **Pandolphe**.

**Nérine** (*Monsieur de Pourceaugnac*). Played presumably by **Mlle. Beauval**, this female conspirator is somewhere between the go–betweens of the **Frosine** type and the male trickster. **Sbrigani** credits her with a past history of **gambling** scams, embezzlement, fraud, and perjury. She presumably coaches **Julie** on how to play the part of the love–crazed bride. She also performs her own number, **disguised** physically and verbally as a woman of **Picardy** whom **Pourceaugnac** has seduced and abandoned, after fathering a small **child**. Nérine must also be the one who has rounded up the three bogus children sent to embrace the startled Limousin. The major part of her role is done in dialect, which Mlle. Beauval, as a wandering player, may have picked up in the northern provinces. She marks a new dimension in female casting and character building for Molière, who might, had he had time, have constructed a true "femme d'industrie" as a protagonist in some play. As it is, the opportunity devolved to **Dancourt** and Regnard, who were able to create female tricksters as central characters.

**Neufvillenaine, or possibly Neufvillevaine.** Little–known author of notes on *Sganarelle* that allowed **Ribou** to publish a pirated version and probably to commission the second–rate imitation by **F. Doneau**, *Les Amours d'Alcippe ou la Cocue imaginaire*.

**Nicandre** (*Mélicerte*). This older **shepherd** is a crony of **Mopse** and **Lycarsis**. Along with the former, he tries to learn Lycarsis's precious news in the first act. They finally learn everything by threatening to leave. In the final scene, Nicandre is seeking Mélicerte to impart the news that the King has chosen her a husband, which makes **Myrtil** wildly unhappy.

**Nicole** (*Le Bourgeois gentilhomme*). The role of the irrepressible **servant** gave **Mlle. Beauval** a chance to display her strongest dramatic talents, including her peals of **laughter**. As soon as she comes onstage, she bursts out in a reaction of hilarity at **Monsieur Jourdain's** gawdy, unfashionable clothes. She continues to blurt out her feelings and opinions at any point in the play where she can, injecting a dose of practical wisdom from the lower classes. Her **"duel"** with Jourdain is another of the play's strongest moments of comic action, for without any training in fencing or the "demonstrative reasoning" that Jourdain has enjoyed, she soundly thrashes her clumsy master. The scene contains a larger metaphor relating to the unsuccessful schooling in the fine arts that Jourdain had purchased. Molière clearly implies that no form of pedagogy can replace what **Nature** has denied to the pupil. Education can awaken or quicken only those talents that are inherently present. She joins her mistress **Lucile** in the double

**lovers' spite** scene, cajoling the valet **Covielle** as Lucile attempts to speak with **Cléonte**. It is the sensible Nicole who discovers the origin of the misunderstanding in a slight the men had suffered earlier in the day, and she immediately offers a very convincing explanation for the women's apparent lack of attention. Without generating much action in the plot, she continues to assist the lovers' plots through the course of the play and is rewarded in the end with permission to marry Covielle. Her role marks an important step in the feminization of the servant roles in Molière's career and also in the creation of a more naturalistic and positive image of the domestic in an age when most writers could only conjure up the hackneyed visages of the drunkard, the coward, the confidante, or the trickster.

**Night (*Amphitryon*)**. Night appears in the prologue with **Mercury** and seems to relish the opportunity to talk with the glib deity. After some badinage and an expository speech, he asks her to delay her departure, so as to give **Jupiter** a few extra moments to spend with **Alcmène**. She lightly criticizes the god's many metamorphoses and frets over the "fine job" he has given her, but accedes to Mercury's request when he seems ready to reveal too many divine secrets to the public. She is seated in her chariot drawn by black horses, which is moved by **machines** across or above the stage. She does not reappear after Mercurey orders her to move on (I, 3).

**Nobility**. According to medieval theory, the nobility formed the second estate of France, below the clergy and above the common people, and were equal among themselves, the King being considered the first among nobles. In reality the situation was more complicated, and anyone alluding to the latter equality was likely to draw the ire of the vain **Louis XIV**. By the seventeenth century, the development of the *société d'états*, or society of conditions, had created a hierarchy within the nobility, separating **court** from country and warrior from royal **servant**. The nobility had ceased to participate as a body in royal military campaigns and life at court had grown so expensive that country nobles were increasingly isolated on their shrinking and debt–riddled estates, while court nobles gaily contributed to the spiraling luxury standards in all phases of life and benefited increasingly from royal handouts to do so. The court itself was soon dominated by relatives of the King, the princes of the blood royal, and an entourage of favorites and sycophants. This was, of course, just what the Bourbon kings wanted, since they were tired of aristocrats raising armed forces and warring amongst themselves or with the central government, as they had done during the religious wars and the Fronde. Since the late Middle Ages, the kings had used ennoblement as a way of paying for the increasing number of state servants they required, especially for the **parlements** and the royal finance apparatus. Instead of paying high salaries, the kings made the officers pay for the offices. These *nobles de robe* were inferior, in principle, to their counterparts in the *noblesse d'épée*, but they were often richer. In addition, they could transform their personal nobility into a hereditary form by paying a small annual fee and continuing the office in the family for three generations after which, office or not, the descendants were considered noblemen. At times of particular need, the crown also sold outright letters of nobility to those willing to pay, but often revoked them later. The anxiety over nobility was exacerbated in Louis XIV's time not only by the huge financial needs of sword and robe nobles alike, but by their efforts to close the spigots of social mobility that had during previous generations allowed relatively large groups to climb the social ladder. Thus arose the concern about usurpation and the institution of royal commissions of investigation, sent into the provinces to challenge all claims to nobility and require irrefutable proofs.

One person who could probably not pass muster in such a *recherche de noblesse* is **George Dandin**, who frets that "nobility in itself is fine, a considerable achievement, but it is accompanied by too many unfortunate details." His play contains a brief primer on forms of noble address, for **Monsieur de Sotenville** reminds his son–in–law that it is impolite to refer to a noble by a term of relation or by his family name in his presence. Simply "Monsieur," "Madame," and "Mademoiselle" were the correct forms in direct conversation. Thus, Dandin is obliged not only to address his wife with the formal "vous," but also to call her "Madame" because she is noble by birth, whereas he has recently (and perhaps even illegally) been ennobled by some other means.

There is also in this play a reference to the rather unusual practice of "nobility through the womb," wherein a person born to a non–noble father and a noble mother would inherit the woman's higher status. This form of ennoblement had a legal status only in certain parts of the County of Champagne where it had been implanted by medieval tradition and was still upheld by Louis XIV's commissions. **Madame de Sotenville** claims that George's children will thus be gentlepersons, which is technically correct, since George's acquired nobility, even if genuine, would affect only himself. Only the third generation of an ordinary ennobled family could make a claim to being a gentleman, and then only under certain conditions.

Another noble with a dubious claim is **Monsieur de Pourceaugnac**. His claim to being "a gentleman who has studied **law**" is oxymoronic, since the legal profession was closed to aristocrats. He also reveals that his family is filled with relatively low–level royal officers of the courts and the tax administration. His pretensions seem to rest on nothing firmer than do **Arnolphe's**. Equally suspect is the **Countess of Escarbagnas**. The best she can do to prove her husband's antecedents is to show that he had a pack of mutts he called **hunting** dogs and took the title of "count" in all the contracts he signed. In fact, she seems close to the Sotenvilles and the whole class of impoverished rural nobles, since she cannot even afford wax **candles**. Without **money** to lead a noble lifestyle, she might well be considered guilty of derogation from her station, and banished from the rolls.

While nobility itself was considered to be invariable, at least on the hereditary level, there did exist a hierarchy of ranks and titles. These were considered to be tied to the lands and fiefs held, rather than to the nature of the person who held them. The principal ranks that mattered in seventeenth–century

France were, in descending order: prince, duke, marquis, and count. Lower ranks such as baron and squire were considered to be so debased as to be insignificant, which added to the anxieties provoked by the *recherches*. There were also distinctions in protocol, the most obvious being in terms of address, where "Votre majesté" was followed by "Votre Altesse," "Votre excellence," "Votre Grandeur," "Monseigneur," and "Monsieur" (the possessives being used mainly in writing).

Nobility could be lost, either through derogatory activity on the part of the noble, notably any kind of commerce other than a few excepted fields, or through criminal activity of a type resulting in derogatory punishment, such as hanging. **Dom Juan**, a confirmed polygamist, falls into the latter field. Even if he has married most of the victims of his seduction, an ancient principle of common law held that "Il n'y a si bon mariage qu'une corde ne rompt" ("No marriage is so good it cannot be broken by a rope"). In other words, conviction of rape, bigamy, or other capital crimes over–rode any protections under subsequent marriage and nullified the ceremony itself. **Dom Louis**, the father of the rake, delivers a long tirade on the duties of a nobleman, which amounted to simply preserving the family honor and handing it on as unsullied as when one inherited it. While the ideal of nobility is incorruptible, the noble who lives ignobly shows himself unworthy of his estate and loses his right to its prerogatives. Theory held that this derogation lay in the act itself, the sentence of a sovereign court merely serving to give public notice of that which the unworthy individual had done to himself. Thus, by becoming a "great lord, awful man," Dom Juan turns himself into a walking oxymoron and loses his rights. Dom Louis merely emphasizes the shame of such a situation when he says he would make more of a laborer's son who was an honest man than a monarch who acted like his son. The matter had been a subject of great current interest ever since the days of **Richelieu**, who encouraged discussion of derogation as part of his campaign to curtail dueling and to subdue the rebellious elements of the aristocracy. Louis XIV's *recherches de noblesse* merely stimulated this already thriving debate.

If there is a character in Molière's plays who represents the exaggeration of nobility, it is **Alceste** in *Le Misanthrope*. His over–emphasis on his own noble honor and honesty creates the dynamic tension that runs through much of the play. He is not completely alone, since **Célimène's** clique also contains the preening courtiers **Acaste** and **Clitandre**, who seem in some ways to relate to the upstart foppish marquis figure of other Molière plays, but boast without lying about their attendance at important royal functions. They dress and act like caricatures of nobles, but contrary to expectation, they are actual aristocrats rather than complete fakes. Then, too, there is the figure of Géralde, one of the targets of Célimène's gossip, a man who hobnobs only with the most exclusive people and speaks ostentatiously of his horses, his carriages, and his pack of hounds. Géralde invites mockery by addressing all his fellow nobles with the familiar pronoun and avoiding the safer honorific of "Monsieur," but despite these foibles he is a genuine member of the upper class. Alceste stands on the pinnacle of his noble privilege, deriding his lower–class opponent in his lawsuit, and defying any but the King's direct orders in the matter of his quarrel with **Oronte**. He wants people (and especially Célimène) to recognize and worship his quality without having to earn respect through social gestures of the type **Philinte** advocates. Indeed, he speaks much and sometimes convincingly about virtue, but his failure to assert it through the course of the play puts the entire structure of noble quality at risk and leads to the play's ambiguous ending. It is ironic that this comedy, which incarnates noble behavior in a more accurate and naturalistic manner than any other of the century, also places the very foundations of nobility in question.

**Notaries**. Under the French monarchy, and even today, French notaries are far more important persons in the legal world than their American equivalents. Responsible for all property transactions in the civil **law** sector, they are much closer to some English solicitors and combine the functions of accountant and fiduciary. Their main function in French comedy was to draw up the **marriage** contract, record of which would later be kept in their study's files. This happy work was not always appreciated, as in the case of **Sganarelle** in *Le Médecin malgré lui*, who curses the notary that drew up his contract. Nevertheless, most of Molière's characters and spectators persistently depended on their notaries. For instance, when **Scapin** tells **Argante** of how **Octave** was supposedly married by constraint to **Hyacinte**, the old man tells him that the boy should have run to a notary to make a deposition immediately. From the scrupulous notary in *L'École des femmes* to the evil **Bonnefoy** in *Le Malade imaginaire*, Molière's notaries run the gamut of human nature.

**Notary (*L'Amour médecin*)**. This character arrives at the conclusion of the play. **Sganarelle** has been told he is merely a **doctor's** assistant masquerading as a notary. Thus, when he asks the **bourgeois** to sign a contract for a 60,000 *livre* dowry for **Lucinde**, Sganarelle willingly goes along, only realizing later that he has been gulled.

**Notary (*L'École des femmes*)**. Appearing only in Act IV, scene 2, the notary is part of an extended misunderstanding scene, where he believes he is discussing the **marriage** contract with **Arnolphe**, who in fact is soliloquizing on his woes. In professional fashion, he deploys his knowledge of Parisian common **law** to suggest legitimate ways of overcoming **Agnès's** lack of dowry in order to provide for her future security in case of the future husband's death. In a forced heirship system where the concept of community property did not really exist, this was a very understandable concern. If Molière, as several accounts tell, actually did study law, this was a chance for him to dust off his old property law notes and show that he wasn't sleeping in class. When Arnolphe awakes to the presence of the notary, an angry quarrel ensues, and the notary departs with an insult for his client.

**Notary (*L'École des maris*)**. Present onstage along with the **Commissioner** from Act III, scene 4 until the end of the play, this figure has only one line, pointing out that he is a "royal notary," thus able to exercise his office anywhere in the realm of France. He draws up a **marriage** contract that **Ariste** is urged to sign, supposedly to allow **Léonor** to marry a young man, but actually authorizing the marriage of **Isabelle** and **Valère**. **Sganarelle's** co–signature thus takes on the character of the main party, while Ariste's drops to that of a witness to the proceedings.

**Notary (*Les Femmes savantes*).** Brought in to draw up a **marriage** contract in the final act, this functionary is harassed by **Philaminte**, who wants him to drop all his courtroom terminology, and **Bélise**, who demands that he convert the dowry into the monetary system of ancient times. He is stopped dead in his tracks when the parents of the bride insist on two different husbands, one too many for the *coutume de Paris*, as he points out. Presumably, he can finish his document once **Ariste's** ruse has driven **Trissotin** from the field. The role may have been played by **Beauval** or **de Brie**.

**Notary (*Le Malade imaginaire*).** *See* **Bonnefoy**.

**Novels.** Fiction is almost always associated with flighty and unrealistic ideas in Molière's plays. In *Les Précieuses ridicules*, novels by **Mademoiselle de Scudéry**, **Gomberville**, and **Molière d'Essertines** are mentioned. Indeed, the affected girls in that play see novels as a metaphor for life and ask that they be allowed to complete the remaining chapters of their Parisian adventure before they are compelled to marry. It is true that **marriage** is usually delayed by thousands and thousands of pages in the novels themselves. The female lead in *Sganarelle* is described as having her nose too often in *Clélie* and too little in her own affairs. However, Molière himself is said to have borrowed the basis for *Mélicerte* from an episode in Scudéry's *Grand Cyrus*. **Béralde** in *Le Malade imaginaire* likens medicine to a novel.

# O

***Observations sur une comédie de Molière intitulée Le Festin de Pierre***
(***Obsevations on a Comedy by Molière entitled* The Feast of Stone**). This
pamphlet published in 1665 by Nicolas Pépingué of **Paris** systematically attacks
Molière's play with charges of gross impiety, even heres. The author,
designated B.A.Sr.D.R., is presumed to be an obscure lawyer named
**Rochemont,** who seems to be closely tied to the **Company of the Holy
Sacrament.** He denies that Molière possesses even the gifts of old farce actors
such as **Turlupin, Gautier–Garguille,** the **Capitan,** and Gros Guillaume. He
implies that the dramatist turned to timely matters to compensate for this lack of
talent, but that he obeyed evil motivation by attacking **religion,** committing four
different types of impiety in the course of ***Dom Juan.*** Strangely, he suggests
that this **satanic** bent is somehow allied to avarice. Also citing ***Tartuffe,*** the
author dwells on the idea that Molière is diabolical in intent and effect. He
implies that the King, reputed to be the defender of Christianity, can only defend
his reputation by executing Molière. This pamphlet elicited two more in favor
of Molière, the ***Réponse aux Observations*** and the ***Lettre sur les Observations.***

**Occasional Poetry.** *See* **Lyric and Occasional Poetry.**

**Octave (***Les Fourberies de Scapin***).** The son of **Argante** and lover of
**Zerbinette** is a typically callow youth who has succumbed to the charms of a
**Gypsy slave** girl. He enlists **Scapin's** help, since his own **servant Silvestre** is a
dim–witted poltroon. Since he has always been close to Scapin's master,
**Léandre,** and is about to unwittingly become his brother–in–law, this proximity
comes naturally. Other than in the opening scene, where he forces along
Silvestre's halting conversation, and the closing one, where he almost refuses to

marry his beloved through confusion, he is for the most part a "straight man" to the trickster. The part was probably played by **La Grange** or **Baron**.

**Offices.** The unrestrained appetite for royal, provincial, and even municipal offices that characterized early modern France is easily explained by the fact that offices were the steppingstones to eventual **nobility**. Of course, nearly all such offices were bought and sold, not only from the crown, but also from individual office holders. The price of even minor offices often far exceeded any guaranteed income, but the contacts and social prestige that could be acquired were priceless. Therefore, entire family fortunes were often put into play for the purchase of a particularly important office. Only the highest offices in the *parlements* and other "sovereign courts," such as those that dealt with finances and taxes, entailed personal nobility for the office holder. But office–holding families rarely **married** except with others of their kind, so each family was eager to establish a foothold in this **bourgeois** hierarchy and to make an advance whenever possible. For example, the purchase by the **Poquelin family** of the office of *tapissier et valet de chambre du roi* probably represented no particular direct financial advantage. However, it brought precious contacts with the royal family and the nobility who were the best customers for furnishings of all kinds. It also ensured the best quality apprentices and a powerful standing in the merchant community of **Paris**. It allowed the holder to consider himself a member of the royal household, no matter how distant. Finally, it transferred fairly easily to family heirs, thus in effect multiplying itself. It was easier for office holders to acquire certain other advantages in the campaign toward nobility, including permission to purchase fiefs. These, in turn, allowed one to take a noble–sounding name, such as that of Charles Varlet, **sieur de La Grange**. Being a fief–owning "seigneur" or "sieur" was the next best thing to inheriting nobility, and was actually easier to document sometimes in the courts of the *recherches de la noblesse*, whose judges were invariably *nobles de robe* themselves. Once acquired through higher office, personal nobility easily converted to hereditary nobility through holding an ennobling office for three generations and paying the small "Paulette" tax in the meantime. Even *nobles d'épée* were not immune from the office–holding frenzy, since by **Louis XIV's** time, many of the more desirable commands in the army and navy had become entirely venal. The need for large sums of capital placed hereditary nobles in the position of having to marry for **money** or to put their futures in the hands of bankers.

Many of Molière's characters refer to themselves with titles such as "sieur," including La Grange and **Du Croisy** in *Les Précieuses ridicules*. However, the only one explicitly identified as an *officier* is **Orgon** in *Tartuffe*. His family's comments about the good service he had provided for the crown during the "late troubles," or the Fronde **revolts**, can only mean that he was an officer of some standing, probably a *parlementaire*. Those strata were notable for their strong religious connections, such as those between **Lamoignon** and the ultra–Catholic **Company of the Holy Sacrament**. Many Parisian *parlementaires* were in fact disloyal to the King during the Fronde, just as Orgon's exiled friend Argan appears to have been. **Dufresne**'s theater company was based during the Fronde in **Bordeaux**, where the dramatist might have been able to observe the roles played by *officiers* in the local uprising known as the *Ormée*. Several of Molière's characters, such as **Chrysalde** in *L'École des femmes* and **Madame Jourdain** in *Le Bourgeois gentilhomme* voice some distrust toward the rush for upward mobility, and *Tartuffe* may contain some element of criticism from the lower rungs of the office–holding structure to their more privileged colleagues.

Despite the well–known path leading from offices to nobility, usurpation was a common phenomenon. **Arnolphe, George Dandin, Pourceaugnac,** and **Monsieur Jourdain** are all guilty of claiming noble prerogatives without passing through the system of offices or of jumping stages in the ennobling process. The gradual nature of this process receives a powerful endorsement from **Cléonte** in *Le Bourgeois gentilhomme*.

*Ombre de Molière, L' (Molière's Ghost).* A play written and produced immediately after Molière's death by **Brécourt** and the players of the **Hôtel de Bourgogne**. It was both a testament to Molière's greatness by a former associate and a shrewd financial move by the rival company, hoping to cash in on the demise of their nemesis. It was doubtlessly aided by the fact that, following Easter 1673, some of Molière's longtime colleagues left the **King's Troupe** and defected to the opposition, bringing their old roles and **costumes** with them. The play is little more than a review or skit in which Molière's **ghost** is tried in the afterlife and confronted by many of his characters, especially those with scores to settle against the author. However, far from a **satire**, the play upholds Molière's glory and exonerates him of all satirical faults and practices. It was published in the 1674 collected edition along with *Le Malade imaginaire*.

**Opera.** *Le Malade imaginaire* contains one of the few references to the growing vogue of opera when **Cléante**, disguised as a **music master**, tells **Argan** that he and **Angélique** are going to perform a duet from a recent opera, while in reality they simply make up lines to describe their emotions to each other.

*See also* **Lully; Music and Dance.**

**Operator** (*L'Amour médecin*). This *opérateur* is a snake–oil salesman who hawks his cure–all in public. Sganarelle spends thirty *sols* to buy a bottle of his brew for curing **Lucinde**. Luckily, she never has to ingest the stuff. Such barkers were common in **Paris** and in the French countryside and often had a show that helped attract attention to their wares.

**Orante** (*Les Fâcheux*). Along with **Clymène**, this lady accosts **Éraste** in Act II with the demand that he must arbitrate their dispute on a question of **love**: whether the **jealous** man makes a better lover than the tolerant man. Orante favors the latter, concluding, "As for me, I prefer lovers inspired by respect, /

And their submission testifies better to our control over them." The female casting of the play is debatable, but this quarrel seems to take up previous discussions in *L'École des maris* and *Dom Garcie de Navarre* and may well have involved the same pair of actresses.

**Orgon** (*Tartuffe*). Though not the title role of the play, this was certainly one of Molière's deepest parts and greatest challenges onstage. Orgon is important even in his absence, for it is clear that the family's light–heartedness in the first act is a result of his being away in the country. News of his return causes a sudden reversal: his brother–in–law springs into matchmaking action, his wife retires to the boudoir to await him on her own ground, and his **children** scatter. His subsequent interview with **Cléante** demonstrates the reason for this odd behavior. Orgon gives ample evidence of his obsession with **Tartuffe** and his disregard for the well–being of his "loved ones," for he disregards news of his children and his ailing wife, returning always to the subject of his overfed and over–indulged minion. It is clear that Orgon has succumbed to the charlatan's bogus brand of **religious** devotion, but actually Orgon only got what he was already seeking. He had been on the outlook for a Tartuffe, an ostentatious bigot who could act more outrageously pious than Orgon himself dared, and his parasite fit the bill. Orgon's self–delusion is just as strong, perhaps even stronger, than Tartuffe's guile. He is already an utterly selfish true believer before he encounters the fake and simply follows through until **Elmire** presents him with an unacceptable self–image. This is the reason **Damis's** denunciation fails, while Elmire's succeeds. Damis foolishly allowed his father to stay in the role of the powerful judge, able to mete out punishment or mercy. Naturally, Tartuffe appealed in a particularly skillful way to the option of mercy and this tickled Orgon's vanity enough to succeed. Elmire presented Orgon with proof of his own foolish image as a cuckold. Try as he might to ignore it, the husband could not avoid rejecting this horrible image in the end. Orgon's plight is so interesting because in many ways he represents a mainstream Catholic of **Louis XIV's** time. His frequent attendance at Mass and communion was fashionable. His desire for a *directeur de conscience* was in keeping with current mores. His quest for an antidote to the futility and noise of social intercourse was a common theme in secular as well as religious literature. He could even quote Scripture for authority, though selectively and inappropriately. The distance between his superficial righteousness and his more profound corruption becomes more evident in the final acts, when he becomes desperate and violent in the face of Tartuffe's continued success. He even fails in large degree to sympathize with his own mother when she presents him with the mirror image of his earlier credulity and blockheadedness. Orgon is a much more fallen soul than he thinks in his most pious meditations. Even when his perversity has cost him almost everything, he still needs the example of *hommes de bien* like Cléante and **Valère** to steer him toward actions that are not self–destructive or dangerous to his family. In Orgon, Molière portrays a bigot who nearly gets what he deserved, and whose deliverance through the agency of a godlike king is nothing short of providential.

***Orlando furioso***.  Epic romance by the **Italian** poet Ariosto, implicitly cited in Act V, scene 1 of ***Dépit amoureux*** by the sniveling coward **Mascarille**, who admits in his monologic conversation with his master that he is neither a Roland nor a Ferragu.

**Ormin** (***Les Fâcheux***).   Appearing in Act III, scene 3, this gentleman denounces the recently departed **Caritidès** as a crackpot and charlatan, but then tries to involve **Éraste** in an even stranger scheme than his predecessor, that of turning all the cities of the realm into seaports.  Just as Caritidès's fascination with inscriptions awkwardly prefigures an actual priority of **Louis XIV**, Ormin's canal–building plans differ from official policy in scope rather than in nature.  Canals spread all over the countryside for the next century and a half, giving France perhaps the most complete water access after Holland and giving rise to the subculture of the barge men.  They also turned many unlikely places, such as **Dijon**, into major inland ports.  Thus, while mocking the tactics of the *donneurs d'avis* who assailed the **court** with all manner of self–serving schemes, Molière targets areas that would actually develop in the years ahead.  Despite the sweeping scope of Ormin's petition, he shows us the real state of his finances at the end of the scene when he asks to borrow the trifling sum of two *pistoles* (twenty *livres*) from Éraste.

**Oronte** (***L'École des femmes***).  Father of **Horace** and ostensibly an old friend of **Arnolphe**, Oronte addresses a **letter** to his colleague in the first act, introducing his son and apparently asking for a line of credit.  We know that Oronte has vague **marriage** plans for his son that preclude the relationship with **Agnès**, but this seems to be merely a conventional offstage threat until Act V, scene 6, when a frantic Horace announces that his father has arrived in town and intends to impose his wedding plans on the boy.  As befits the character of an old pantaloon, Oronte's first words are ironic, for he remarks, "How full of tenderness is this embrace!" when the evil Arnolphe clasps him to his breast.  Through most of the denouement, Oronte's lines are cut off by the intriguing Arnolphe, or else express amazement at the precipitation of his actions and his failure to discuss the wedding plans.  In stichomythic alternation with his local counterpart, **Chrysalde**, Oronte unveils the long–hidden identity of Agnès as **Henrique's** daughter and the coincidence of her impending marriage with Horace.  When Arnolphe stalks offstage in an inchoate huff, Oronte voices the audience's thoughts by asking, "Why is he rushing off without saying a word?"

**Oronte** (***Le Misanthrope***).  Less flighty than **Acaste** and **Clitandre**, just as well connected as **Arsinoé**, and far more malicious than **Célimène**, Oronte is an interesting figure of a **noble**, almost unparalleled in Molière's work.  He approaches Alceste and **Philinte** in the first act of the play in order to obtain praise for his poetry.  Though rhetorically correct, Oronte's sonnet is lacking in originality and substance, flaws made all the more obvious by the poet's superfluous commentary that precedes and interrupts the reading.  Of course, his audience reacts typically, with Philinte dishing out large helpings of empty approval and Alceste erupting in outspoken condemnation. Oronte is understandably hurt by this reaction, but the depth of his spite is not explained simply by damaged artistic pride. One must understand his deeper motivations. He, too, after all, is a suitor of Célimène, and a much more formidable one than the silly marquis. The fact that he is seeking Alceste's death, which the **Marshals** discover, is proof of the seriousness of his pique. The Marshals' involvement in the affair speaks to his high **court** standing, for they did not intervene in trivial matters. He is a powerful enough personality to affect the outcome of Célimène's legal problems. His own intellectual standing is so considerable that he feels Alceste's backing is essential, and he insists on reading his sonnet even when the misanthrope warns him of a likely negative outcome. "The man with the vest," as Célimène calls him in her purloined **letter**, is more than just a failed man of letters. He is a thinly disguised bully, both in his first act reading and in his final act confrontation with Célimène. Philinte emphasizes that he is not to be trusted or ignored, and his plottings against Alceste bear this out. Beneath his elegant exterior beats a heart bent on ambition and vengeance, a desire to use others as his pawns. It is not known which actor took the role in the original production.

**Oronte (*Monsieur de Pourceaugnac*).** This pompous paterfamilias may have been portrayed originally by **La Thorillière**. He has broken his word to **Éraste** and arranged an **engagement** between his daughter **Julie** and **Monsieur de Pourceaugnac** before the action commences. This has been done sight unseen, reportedly on the basis of a difference of several thousand *livres* in wealth. The credulous burgher is soon made to regret his breach of faith, however, for Éraste convinces him that Pourceaugnac is mad, syphilitic, and indebted. Thus, the second act greeting scene between the groom and the father of the bride becomes a shouting match. Oronte is just as easy to trick in the third act, where **Sbrigani** alarms him about the alleged elopement of Julie and Éraste pretends to bring the runaway reluctantly back to her father. As the straight man in this comic return scene, Oronte is immobilized by fear and embarrassment, which allows the two youngsters to play their roles to the hilt. He becomes convinced that the only way to save the lusty Julie from a life of shame is to put her into the reasonable hands of Éraste. Oronte even counts himself lucky to pour more of his **money** into the dowry to seal a deal he thinks is in his own favor. The role is less stylized than many similar ones in the canon. In a play filled with exotic and fantasy elements, Oronte serves as a kind of anchor to establish verisimilitude and sympathy with the audience.

**Orphise (*Les Fâcheux*).** **Éraste's** sweetheart, and the ward of **Damis**, she is a fleeting presence during the play. In the first act, she appears on the arm of another man and pretends not to recognize her suitor. In the second, she displays **jealousy** when she finds him in the company of **Orante** and **Clymène**, who had accosted him so that he would arbitrate their quarrel over, of all things, jealousy. Orphise's pique is a twist on the theme, since the other two ladies were concerned only about male jealousy. Appearing with a torch at the end of the play, she rapidly consents to marriage when she learns that Damis intends to give her to Éraste out of gratitude.

# P

**Paladin.** **Covielle** uses the term to describe to **Monsieur Jourdain** the knightly importance of a *mamamouchi* in the **Turkish** Empire. It is, of course, out of place, since the paladins were legendary Christian knights, said to have accompanied Charlemagne and to have performed other deeds of importance in days of yore. Though the title of *mamamouchi* is completely fictitious, the Ottoman emperor did surround himself with an elite corps of **janissaries,** who were not unlike the paladins of medieval romance in their personal devotion and military prowess.

**Palais Royal.** The **theater** where Molière's troupe and their **Italian** neighbors moved when the **Petit–Bourbon** was razed in 1658 was located not far from the site of today's **Comédie–Française Theater.** As the name indicates, it was part of the building complex designed for **Richelieu** that had been passed on to his successor Mazarin and then to the royal family. The theater itself had originally been designed for opera productions, in which Richelieu himself dabbled. It had been out of use for some time when the troupes were moved and had to undergo extensive remodeling. This was repeated on a grander scale and at a cost of many thousands of *livres* during the Lenten break of 1671 in order to facilitate the production of *Psyché*, which required elaborate **machines.** The theater had the advantage of having been designed for spectacle rather than as a tennis court, as most other theater rooms had begun. In fact, it probably had much better acoustics than the **Tuileries** theater, which **Le Vau** had designed very badly on that account. Obviously, it was a great blow when the troupe was again forced out of the Palais Royal Theater after Molière's death, for despite the nearly equal conditions at the Guénégaud Theater, its location was far inferior to the centrally situated Palais Royal Theater.

**Pan.** In *Mélicerte*, **Lycarsis** mentions the festival of this goat–footed divinity as the most sacred in **Thessaly**, and he later blesses the two ladies who visit him to ask for his son's hand in **marriage** by asking Pan to give them worthy husbands. Pan reappears with a group of fauns in the original prologue to *Le Malade imaginaire*, where he joins Flora in exhorting the rural folk to praise **Louis XIV**, who had recently returned from the wars in Holland.

**Pancrace (*Le Mariage forcé*).** Played by **Brécourt** originally, and probably thereafter by **Hubert**, this **Aristotelian philosopher** is the source of much **laughter** in his one scene with **Sganarelle**. The **bourgeois** has come to consult him about **marriage**, but the pedant cannot free his mind from a trifling dispute with a colleague over whether one should refer to the "form" or the "figure" of a hat. He never really manages to listen to Sganarelle, repeatedly coming back to his dispute, spewing out macaronic **Latin**, and reeling off a list of possible **languages** they may converse in, similar to the list proposed by Panurge when he appears in **Rabelais's** *Pantagruel*. When he does begin to speak, it is at a breakneck pace and at the same time as his interlocutor, who pushes him back into his house and barricades him inside, concluding, "They warned me that his Master Aristotle was nothing but a gas bag!"

**Pandolphe (*L'Étourdi*).** Father to the blundering **Lélie**, Pandolphe appears near the end of Act I, where **Mascarille** pretends to share his critical attitude toward Lélie's pursuit of a **slave** girl. The valet then persuades Pandolphe to arrange a proxy sale of the girl to **Anselme**, in order to cut off the son's access, but an offstage error by Lélie squelches this plan while Mascarille is talking with **Hippolyte**. In Act II, Pandolphe is "killed off" — at least in rumor — by the clever **servant**. Actually, he was lured away to a country house with a fabulous story that workmen there had uncovered buried treasure. In the interval, Mascarille has wrapped up a bunch of sheets to simulate a corpse, and manages to fool Anselme into advancing Lélie a large sum for funeral expenses. Of course, the **money**, part of what Anselme owed Pandolphe, would really have been used to buy **Célie**. The reappearance of Pandolphe's "**ghost**" is an amusing sequence, part of a long tradition of "walking dead" scenes in seventeenth–century French comedy. There are several more allusions to Pandolphe's unquenched anger, particularly toward Mascarille, but he only appears at the end of the play to facilitate the multiple **marriages** of the young couples.

**Pandolphe (*Les Fourberies de Scapin*).** Alias used by **Géronte** when dealing with his second family in **Tarento**.

**Pantomime.** Molière attached great importance to gestural comedy, but "dumb shows" of the Shakespearean sort are quite rare in his comedy. Molière does mention it explicitly in *Les Amants magnifiques*, where the incomparable Beauchamp, together with Saint–André and Favier, perform a pantomime that was almost certainly done to music. Occasional mute exchanges take place by way of signs in *Le Malade imaginaire* and *Monsieur de Pourceaugnac*.

**Parfaict Brothers**. Eighteenth–century **theater** aficionados François and Claude Parfaict devoted over twenty years of research to their annals of dramatic life. Their fifteen volumes on the French theater cover the period from its inception through 1749, while the volume on the **Italian** players ends in 1697, when they were sent home by **Louis XIV**. These books constitute an important source for research on Molière and his times.

**Paris**. Molière was born and brought up in central Paris, in the neighborhood of the great marketplace of Les Halles. He was educated there, perhaps at the **Collège de Clermont**, and seems to have spent almost his entire life within the city walls until the failure of the **Illustre Théâtre** and his subsequent unsolved debts forced him to leave. Upon his return in 1658, the first of his plays to specifically mention Paris is *Les Précieuses ridicules*, where **Magdelon** refers to it as "a great bureau of marvels, the center of good taste, of fine wit and of *galanterie*." **Mascarille** agrees that "outside of Paris there is little salvation for **polite** society." Magdelon's comment about the "bureau of marvels" may refer to **Théophraste Renaudot's** employment agency, which also served as a sort of news service for the metropolis.

In *L'École des maris*, **Valère**, while trying to engage **Sganarelle** in polite conversation, says that Paris offers its denizens a hundred pleasures that are unmatched elsewhere, and adds that the provinces are bleak in comparison. This fairly conventional statement takes on a new light when considered in relation to the playwright's long peregrinations through the southern provinces with **Charles Dufresne's** troupe.

*La Critique de l'École des femmes* mentions not only the **Louvre** (still a royal residence in Molière's time) and the dramatist's own theater at the **Palais Royal**, but also Les Halles and the Place Maubert, bourgeois neighborhoods that **Élise** cites as centers of bad **language**. She uses as an example a bad pun on the term "voir de bon oeil" (to look kindly on someone), where it has the double meaning of "voir de Boneuil," a village several miles from Paris.

In *L'Amour médecin*, which is specifically set in the capital, **Doctor Tomès** talks of his wearying rounds in the city; "from the Arsenal to the Faubourg Saint–Germain . . . down to the Marais . . . to the porte Saint–Honoré . . . to the Faubourg Saint–Jacques . . . to the porte de Richelieu . . . to here . . . to the Place Royale." Sganarelle mentions the Saint–Laurent Fair, located just outside the city, as a place where he may buy his daughter some furniture. *Le Malade imaginaire* is also situated in Paris and makes devastating mention of its obsolete medical faculty.

*Le Misanthrope*, *L'Avare*, and *Monsieur de Pourceagnac* also are all specifically set in Paris. **Alceste's** favorite song, "Si le Roi m'avait donné / Paris, sa grand'ville," is a popular ditty the playwright remembered from his **childhood**. *Le Bourgeois gentilhomme* specifies that the Jourdains' home is in an upper–bourgeois neighborhood and that the fathers of both **Monsieur** and

**Madame Jourdain** plied their draper trade near the Porte Saint–Innocent. One of the mob of booklet–buyers in the first sequence of the ballet that follows the play strikes a note even closer to home when she describes herself as "the pride of the streets near the Palais–Royal." *Les Femmes savantes* mentions Les Halles, the Palais de Justice, the **Cours la Reine** (also cited in **Les Fâcheux**), and the many boudoirs and **gambling** halls of the capital.

It must be remembered that Molière's Paris was much more compact than today. There were cultivated fields beyond the Bastille in the east and the **Tuileries** Palace in the west, and Montmartre was crowned by a group of windmills that ground the local wheat, instead of serving as site for girlie shows. **Auteuil**, Villejuif, Aubervilliers, and even Chaillot were country villages, well beyond the suburbs. In typical seventeenth–century fashion, when Molière speaks of *la cour et la ville*, he is not speaking geographically, but rather socially, for the city metonymically represented its bourgeois inhabitants.

**Parlement.** Unlike the English Parliament, the French *parlements* were both regional legislative bodies and high courts. Their members, from *président* on down, had paid for their offices and considered themselves to be magistrates and **noblemen**. In fact, the expensive offices tended to stay so steadily in families that in no time their individual noble prerogatives became hereditary, thus creating the *noblesse de robe*. The Parlement de Paris was the most powerful in the land, its jurisdiction extending over much of the northern half of the country. Molière had troubles with it. In his youth, he fled its boundaries to save himself from debtor's prison on account of the failure of the **Illustre Théâtre**. In his maturity, its leader, **Lamoignon**, issued a crippling ban on *Tartuffe* and backed up the Devout Party in its attacks on the dramatist. The one man in Molière's plays who seems to have the status of a *parlementaire*, **Orgon** in *Tartuffe*, is certainly susceptible to the worst of such **religious** influences.

**Pascal, Blaise** (1623–1662). Brilliant mathematician, scientist, **philosopher**, and theologian. Molière and Pascal were both resident in **Paris** only from 1658 to the latter's death four years later. Furthermore, Pascal's austere views and lifestyle seem to have little in common with the **theater** and the artistic life Molière espoused. Molière's own forays into philosophy were far distant from Pascal's, on the **libertine** and skeptical fringe of accepted thought. Yet Molière seems curiously to have borrowed a great deal from the theologian. No matter what he thought of the dour **Jansenists**, he certainly could have read the *Lettres provinciales* and admired their laceration of Jesuit duplicity and authoritarianism. The fact that these letters remained unattributed for quite some time makes it unlikely Molière knew exactly who the author was. There are echoes of the eighth letter in *L'Avare*, where **Harpagon's** loan schemes are suspiciously close to the underhanded tactics of the Mohatra Contract lampooned by Pascal. **La Flèche** has lines in the same play that recall the sixth *Provinciale* and its discussion of the justification of theft by **servants**, including the tale of Jean of Alba. There are further similarities that even suggest Molière may have been familiar with manuscripts of parts of the *Pensées* circulated after

Pascal's death. For example, in *Le Malade imaginaire*, **Angélique's** declaration that "a daughter's duty has its limits, and neither **law** nor **reason** extend it to cover everything" recalls the famous saying, "The heart has its reasons that reason doesn't comprehend." Few critics can share René Jasinski's unrestrained enthusiasm for a Jansenist strain in Molière's work. But it is worthwhile to remember that one of Molière's own sisters was a strictly cloistered Visitandine nun and that, for an officially excommunicated actor, he made numerous trips to the baptismal font with **children** of friends and associates. Thus, without being an overt *dévot*, Molière may well have had a taste for some **religious** works, as did most of his contemporaries, whose libraries were largely dominated by such books. The moral aphorisms that are sprinkled through the *Pensées* could have touched Molière as much as they did others of his generation. Thus, even if one does not look to Jansenism as a pat explanation for Alceste's condemnation of the world, it is certainly worthwhile to note the many areas where the thoughts of Pascal and Molière converge.

**Pasqualigo, Luigi.** Author of the **Italian** comedy *Fedele*, which was translated into French by **Larivey** in 1611 and may have furnished several lines for *Les Femmes savantes*.

*Pastorale comique.* This play, whose text has not been preserved, figured in the third *entrée* of the **Ballet des Muses** spectacle in 1666–67 and seems to have replaced the unfinished *Mélicerte* from January 5, 1667, onward. The only remnant is a summary apparently written by Molière himself for the official festival guidebook, containing some of the verses penned by the playwright. Molière played the role of the "rich cattleman" **Lycas**. There is little more in the summary that gives a clue to the significance of his riches, but one senses an element that will reappear in *George Dandin*, the **satire** of the "laboureur" bumpkin. However, it is obvious that Lycas loves below his level rather than above, for his sweetheart is a mere **shepherdess**. He also has a helper in this play, the **shepherd Coridon**, played by **La Grange**, whose role seems to have been a bit like **Philinte** in that he acts as a confidant, advocate, and peacemaker. Lycas's rivalry with his colleague **Filène** spurs a challenge, but the **duel** is broken up by a party of country folk. When both suitors discover that they are rejected, they are about to cross blades and finish off their mutual suffering, when a lively young shepherd played by the dancer Blondel tells them: "Ah! What folly to leave this life for a beauty by whom one is spurned!" The action ends in a **Spanish** musical number with guitars, castanets, and a dancing **Gypsy**. Only Molière, La Grange, and **Mlle. de Brie** seem to have represented the troupe in this one–act piece, the rest of the roles being taken by members of the royal dance ensemble.

**Patronage.** Having profited from the patronage of both the **Duke of Épernon** and the **Prince of Conti** in his days as a wandering player, Molière understood the importance of having a financial and political protector when the troupe came back to **Paris** in 1658. It is said that **Louis XIV** "gave" them to his

younger brother, Philippe. But it is unlikely that this association was made
without a good deal of preparation by Molière and his Parisian contacts.
**Monsieur** was one of the best patrons the troupe could have selected. He was
youthful, pleasure loving, and married to a sophisticated, cosmopolitan woman
who loved comedy. Moreover, he was almost as close to the royal person as one
could come, guaranteeing a certain amount of consideration should luck turn
bad. He gave just the kind of support needed when the troupe found their home
at the **Petit–Bourbon** theater fall under the wrecking bar, and helped them
relocate to the excellent alternative of the Palais Royal Theater, close to his own
Parisian apartments. Next to Louis XIV, he remained the most important patron
of the group, ordering command performances of many plays both in Paris and
in such country locations as his estate at Villecôterets. No wonder **La Grange**
notes in his journal that even after the King took the troupe under his own wing
and awarded a royal pension, they explicitly asked Monsieur for his ongoing
protection and favor. (He did continue: the troupe's last visit during Molière's
lifetime was to Monsieur's estate at Saint–Cloud.) If Philippe had not managed
regularly to pay the pension that had originally been promised to his players, this
is perhaps a predictable if not inexcusable fault, since he was notorious for
letting **money** slip through his hands and for going begging to his royal brother.

The shift from Monsieur's household to the King's marked a decisive
departure in many ways for Molière and his companions. In the early years,
they made numerous private performances, or "visits," as La Grange calls them,
not only to Parisian residences of officers such as **Fouquet**, Le Tellier, and
**Colbert**, but also to the aristocratic townhouses of the **Richelieu** and
**Rambouillet** families, Cardinal Mazarin, the Dukes of Beaufort, Roquelaure,
Mercoeur, and Nevers, the Count of Soissons, the **Marshals** of Aumont, **La
Meilleraye** and **Grammont**, and to estates in the Île de France. These visits
testify to the widespread support for the troupe and its new forms of comedy.
They also put the lie to some anecdotes about Molière's enemies: for instance,
one finds among the list of patrons the **Marquis de la Feuillade**, who according
to one unfounded account attacked the dramatist and disfigured his face.

Following the royal appropriation of the troupe, which took place at **Saint–
Germain–en–Laye** on August 8, 1665, the King would almost monopolize
patronage, calling his players away on some occasions for months at a time.
Private visits declined from an average of over a dozen a year to a mere handful;
they were mainly limited to the highest levels of the **nobility**, including "peers
of the blood royal" such as the **Prince of Condé**. They became less and less
frequent (in 1666–67 there was only one visit, but it was an extended royal affair
of over two months and was compensated with a hefty fee of 12,000 *livres*). A
notable exception was the period in 1669 right after the successful release of
*Tartuffe* from the bans that had hampered it for five long years. The careful
record of *Tartuffe* productions kept by **La Grange** allows us to revisit and
correct some notable errors about the play, such as John Cairncross's theory of a
primitive but complete three–act version. The actor's register precisely records
the first two visiting performances as being "the first three acts" in an ink and
hand that are clearly contemporaneous with the production and not an

afterthought. For the visit when the play was first performed in its entirety, he notes *Tartuffe* "in five acts," indicating that the text was now complete, as well as revised according to the information in the **Placets** and in the *Lettre sur l'Imposteur*. Thereafter, there is no mention of the number of acts, even though the content was again revised before the 1669 version hit the boards.

One exception to the dwindling of patrons after 1665 was the Prince of Condé. This aging hero, Louis XIV's close cousin, could not be called into question for sharing the talents of the royal company. His favor of the troupe, especially during the *Tartuffe* affair, confirms his reputation as a superior and liberal intellect. As much may also be said for his close friend, the **Princess Palatine**, who co–sponsored some visits. It is said that Condé's presence at the Palais Royal on the afternoon of February 17, 1673, was one reason Molière allegedly ignored pleas by **Armande Béjart** and **Baron** to call off the performance during which he suffered a fatal attack. Molière's numerous statements in the *Impromptu de Versailles* and elsewhere give ample proof of the fact that he took the links of patronage very seriously.

**Pauper** (*Dom Juan*). This character, called **Francisque** in some versions of the text, appears only in one extremely controversial scene, which was partially cut as early as the second performance on February 17, 1665. In Act III, **Dom Juan** and **Sganarelle** have been walking through a forest in **disguise**, and the valet has just fallen on his face in an effort to **reason** with his master, when they encounter a pauper and ask directions of him. He readily points the way out of the forest and warns them against robbers in the area, then asks for alms, explaining that he has lived a hermit's life in the woods for ten years and has no income but what passing travelers give him. Dom Juan taunts him, saying that he should pray for a new suit of clothes, and asking how he could be in want if he communicates with heaven all day long. The section that caused so much scandal begins when the pauper admits he often has not a crumb to eat, and Dom Juan offers him a *louis d'or* if he will blaspheme. The pauper would willingly take the **money**, but refuses to swear, even when the aristocrat taunts him with the glittering coin. Sganarelle further spurs him on to "go ahead and swear a little — there's no harm in it." Nevertheless, the hermit stands his ground and says he would rather die of hunger than compromise his principles. At that point Dom Juan relents and hands him the coin "for the love of humanity," but many productions of the play in the twentieth century have called for the pauper to turn away without taking the tainted alms. The **nobleman** is then distracted by a nearby combat that he joins, unwittingly saving the life of **Elvire's** brother, **Dom Carlos**. It may be argued that the pauper represents the incorruptibility of the truly devout, an idea reiterated by Molière and his supporters in the face of ecclesiastical criticism. Even those who would see Dom Juan as an avatar of liberty, equality, and fraternity must admit that his insistence on blasphemy is gratuitously nasty and that it does not succeed in altering the ideas or behavior of the pauper. However one considers the scene, it constitutes yet another of the unequal "exchanges" that take place in the play, where Dom Juan always gets something for nothing (in this case, directions and a bit of sardonic entertainment). The pauper scene was maintained in its original in the **Amsterdam**, Brussels, and **Berlin** editions, while the reading and acting versions of the play remained mutilated. Only from the nineteenth–century Auger edition onward was the full **language** restored.

**Peasants**. Molière is not miserly in his representation of the rural lower classes. **Alain** and **Georgette**, **Lubin** and **Claudine**, and **Perrin** and **Thibaut** take the form of characters fresh from the earth, endowed with the thought and speech patterns that prevailed within a few miles of the walls of the capital and stretched over the extent of the land. The most extensive sequence involving peasants is in *Dom Juan*, where **Pierrot** and his friend Fat Lucas save the protagonist and his valet from drowning, only to unleash the seducer among the women of the village. As with other peasants, Pierrot and Fat Lucas are typically simple, amusing each other by throwing clods of earth back and forth before they notice the figures in the sea, then placing tiny bets on whether or not the creatures are human. To Pierrot, the bronze pocket change of "quatre pièces tapées et cinq sols en doubles," something like four quarters and two bits worth of nickels, represents a considerable sum of wealth and a manly wager. Having performed this little social rite, the brave lads take to the waves and save the skins of the two "city fellers." The peasants are foolish and good–hearted, like the anecdotal farmer who stopped **Louis XIV's carriage** to offer him his very best bunch of carrots, ignorant of the fact that snickering courtiers never lowered themselves to consume roots.

Pierrot is amazed at their wardrobe of costly and impractical garments. His girlfriend **Charlotte** sees the scene differently, for the newcomers represent the exotic realm beyond the sound of the parish bells, a Neverland that French peasants seldom saw. Charlotte has heard the call of the road and wishes to put the village life behind her, to become something better. That is why she refuses to engage in the roughhousing that her fiancé demands, for she does not wish to resort to the bucolic jokes that her neighbor Fat Thomassine plays on her lover Robin. She quickly falls for Dom Juan, as **Mathurine** already has done, for he represents her fairy tale image of a white knight who will whisk her away to the life of a princess. She genuinely thinks she is doing Pierrot a good deed by offering to give him the butter–and–cheese trade for her mansion, in exchange for renouncing his rights of engagement to her hand.

Pierrot's recriminations against the interloping seducer boldly express the ire of the rural French against the big–city manipulators who are always eager to descend on their hamlets and pillage all that is best. It is worth remembering that peasants were at the mercy of aristocratic **hunters**, who could trample their fields, local lords who could oppress them with time–consuming work projects or *corvées*, and in some remote regions even insist on the medieval *droit du seigneur* that allowed them to sleep first with every bride in the parish. Pierrot is too scared and too sensible to confront the skilled swordsman directly (and a good thing, too!), but he at least can air the frustrations of the peasantry by telling him to go back to town to abuse his own class of women and leave theirs alone.

Dom Juan proceeds to teach an object lesson in how to "manage" the country folk when he is confronted by both of the women to whom he has promised **marriage**. Aware that village spats are the daily bread of life in the provinces, he carefully separates the two girls, knowing that only a few hints of complicity will be enough to keep his hopes alive, while envy will stoke their rivalry and blind them to the truth that they have both been deceived. He knows that, like monkeys trapped with a coconut, they will hold on to their unusable prize forever, rather than loosening their fists and saving themselves. The prospect of marriage is the handful of rice that will allow him to have his way with them. However the city dweller conceives of cultural differences with the hayseeds, he will always turn them to his own advantage. Perhaps he is doing them a favor by giving such a short interval of time, a single day, for further news from him when he departs. In forty–eight hours, the two women may have worked out how to abandon their illusions and return to village reality, instead of being long beguiled by promises without foundation.

**Peasants (*Monsieur de Pourceaugnac*).** A farmer and his wife consult with the First **Doctor** in this play before the arrival of **Pourceaugnac**. They complain that the remedies so far suggested have failed to alleviate their mother's many symptoms. The physician decides to change from bleeding to purging and then, if necessary, to mineral baths, determined to find a protocol in which she can expire in orderly fashion. This consultation reminds the reader of similar scenes in *Dom Juan* and *Le Médecin malgré lui*.

**Pellisson, Paul (1624–1693).** Author of popular, though wan, **occasional poetry** and constant companion of **Mlle. de Scudéry** (despite a face horribly disfigured by smallpox), Pellisson's main link to Molière came through the production of *Les Fâcheux*. Pellisson had become a kind of literary secretary to **Fouquet** and had a major role in organizing the celebrations at **Vaux–le–Vicomte** where Molière's play was first produced before the King. It was he who penned the verses spoken by the Water Nymph (played by **Madeleine Béjart**) that served as prelude to the comedy. After Fouquet's disgrace, Pellisson was imprisoned for quite a long period, but eventually gained royal favor and shook off the shame of his earlier associations.

**Peneus.** A stream in the vale of **Tempe** mentioned by **Mélicerte** as the place where her mother **Bélise** cautioned her against the pleasures of young **love**, rather as Madame de Chartres did to the Princess of Cleves in La Fayette's novel. **Ériphile** mentions the Peneus's banks in *Les Amants magnifiques*.

**Péréfixe, Hardouin de Beaumont de (1605–1670).** This preceptor to the young **Louis XIV** and royal confessor became in 1662 the fourth archbishop of **Paris**, though his appointment was not confirmed by the Pope until 1664. He was an ally of the **Queen Mother** and the Devout Party. As such, he issued a ban on the public performance of *Tartuffe* or *L'Imposteur* in 1665, excommunicating anyone in the diocese who saw it. His main campaign, however, was against the nuns of Port–Royal–des–Champs and their **Jansenist** allies. Having failed to persuade them to renounce their views by signing his *formulaire*, he used canon **law** to exile sixteen of the leaders of the **convent** and took unusually harsh measures against the others, all to little effect.

**Pernelle, Madame** (*Tartuffe*). **Orgon's** mother is a stubborn old battle–axe, exactly the sort of "dragon of virtue" that **Elmire** refuses to be. She understandably resents the fact that Elmire has supplanted her late daughter in Orgon's house. Moreover, she shares her son's propensity for piety. Her disdain for fine clothes and worldly entertainment is perhaps due to a generational gap, since she represents the first generation of personal **nobility**, acquired through purchase of **office**. Previous to that momentous acquisition, she grew up and spent her life as a *bonne bourgeoise* and would prefer that the family stay on her level. Her **religious** ideas are founded on superstition and prejudice rather than on sound biblical knowledge and learning, as her references to the "Evil Spirit" and "tower of **Babylon**" prove. Though she professes Christian values, she is as quick to anger as the rest of her bloodline, and she slaps her poor maid **Flipote** for tarrying at Orgon's doorway. Her mulishness is evident when she persists in defending Tartuffe as a good Christian even though her own son gives powerful testimony against him. When the arrival of **Monsieur Loyal** gives such concrete proof of villainy that she can no longer resist, she simply appears astounded, saying, "I'm all discombobulated and feel as though I've fallen from the clouds!" The role was originally taken by **Hubert**, who made a minor specialty of old lady's parts. He had joined the troupe only a few weeks before the first performance at the *Plaisirs de l'Île enchantée*, but the memorization of such a short part was well within the scope of an actor who was already a veteran of the theater of the **Marais**.

**Perrault, Claude** (1613–1688). Architect whose eastern façade of the **Louvre** necessitated the destruction of the **Petit–Bourbon** theater and the relocation of Molière's troupe and the **Italians** to the Palais Royal Theater in 1660. His younger brother Charles (1628–1703) became a major writer, but the salient works of his career only emerged after Molière's death. Like Claude and another brother, Pierre, he joined the entourage of **Colbert** after having originally sought favor with **Fouquet**. Although the youthful Charles showed a propensity for burlesque humor, he also flirted with the *précieux* movement and thus remained outside Molière's circle, if not opposed to it. Another of his friends was Molière's dramatic rival **Quinault**. He would side with Quinault in minor literary disputes that placed him in opposition to **Boileau**. Their competition would eventually take on larger proportions in the Quarrel of the Ancients and the Moderns, a dispute over the nature of literary excellence that would extend from the 1680s through the turn of the century. Charles Perrault is primarily remembered for his historical poem, "The Century of Louis the Great," his *Parallels of the Ancients and the Moderns,* and his *Tales,* which collected many of the classic fairy tales, presumably from the oral tradition, and set them into print for the first time.

**Perrin** (*Le Médecin malgré lui*). Perrin and his father **Thibaut, peasants,** approach **Sganarelle** in Act III, scene 2 to seek a remedy for their mother and wife, Perette, who is afflicted with *hydropisie,* an internal swelling due to edema of one or more of the vital organs. Perrin recognizes Sganarelle's gestural demand for **money,** while his father ignores it as he describes the symptoms. Though he has a definite country accent, his speech seems free of the malapropisms that characterize Thibaut. The part may have been played by one of the actors' **children,** since it requires only a few lines and one scene on stage.

**Pests.** From the time of *Les Fâcheux* on through the rest of his career, Molière makes ample use of pests, both as a plot device and as a means of introducing timely **satirical** elements. *Le Misanthrope* is notably built around a series of delays that **Alceste** suffers from such pests as **Oronte, Arsinoé, Acaste, Clitandre,** and **Dubois,** who never cease to interrupt his quest for an **avowal** on the part of **Célimène. Iphicrate** in *Les Amants magnifiques* explains in the first scene that he considers the rival princes, with their unending series of entertainments and feasts, to be nothing more than crowned pests. The **Viscount** in *La Comtesse d'Escarbagnas* explains to the peeved **Julie** that he has been detained by a pest in the form of a provincial busybody. The man would not stop bothering him with comments about world affairs drawn from the *Gazette de Hollande.* **Politeness** made it difficult for people to get rid of pests, for it was unseemly to ask them directly to leave. On the other hand, the best comment a civil person could elicit is that he or she was never *fâcheux* or *importun.*

**Petit–Bourbon.** A building close to or adjoining the east wall of the **Louvre** that contained a **theater** assigned to Molière upon his return to **Paris** in 1658. The **Italian** players also used the theater, but the troupes alternated, with the Italians taking the "regular" theater days (Tuesday, Thursday, and Saturday) and Molière taking the others. When the building was hurriedly condemned in autumn of 1660 in preparation for work to begin on **Perrault's** new east façade, Molière's troupe quickly had to request a new home. They were given the theater in the **Palais Royal,** which had formerly belonged to **Richelieu** and then Mazarin — an excellent facility actually designed as a theater, but in need of some renovation.

*Petit Coucher.* A royal ceremony involving the King's going to bed. The *grand coucher,* held first, involved a huge crowd of aristocrats who pressed against the balustrade and wished His Majesty good night. Only the most intimate members of the **court** were permitted at the *petit coucher*, which took place entirely behind the railing, after the King had concluded most of the evening's business. In *Les Précieuses ridicules*, **Mascarille** claims to be going to the *petit coucher* at the **Louvre**, a statement that would appear suspect to anyone but the young ladies in the play.

**Pézenas**. Small city in eastern Languedoc near **Montpellier** where Molière and his troupe, led by **Charles Dufresne**, performed in 1650–51 and 1655–56. They probably passed through in 1653–54, as well, since they performed during that season at the nearby estate of the **Prince de Conti**, La Grange des Prés. Conti's secretary, **Sarasin**, died there in 1654, his head crushed by a blow from a pair of fireplace tongs wielded by his employer. Conti reportedly offered the job of the defunct poet to Molière, who wisely opted to continue his stage career. Despite its size, Pézenas served as a **parliamentary** seat for the province, though some of this activity was undoubtedly shared with the much larger city of Montpellier. In *Monsieur de Pourceaugnac*, **Lucette**, the false **Gascon** woman, claims that everyone in Pézenas came to her **marriage** with the protagonist.

**Philaminte (***Les Femmes savantes***)**. **Hubert** was cast as this **philosophical** battle–axe who bullies her husband and daughters at every opportunity, having launched herself on a quest for intellectual world dominion. Having cowed **Chrysale** into submission, she seems to have assumed him to be the least of creatures and to have adopted that which he despises most by way of adverse reaction. She is capable of waiting quietly while men have their say and then deflating them with a single comment or observation. Like **Armande** and **Bélise**, she seems to have sublimated whatever sex drive she once had into the intellectual sphere; together with them she swoons over **Trissotin's** poetry and rushes to lock lips with **Vadius** for the sake of his **Greek**. Her expressed desire "to put a little learning into **Henriette**" by means of **Trissotin** seems a bit crude, but is simply one step on the road to power that she sees unfolding before her. If she seems to change so abruptly at the end of the play, it is because Trissotin commits a virtual act of *lèse–majesté* by abandoning her in her apparent need. Such grand treason calls for a singular punishment, and Henriette simply serves as a vehicle for her to show her spite toward the poet. Despite the panoply of knowledge she sets forth, she is in most ways as mechanical a character as **Madame Pernelle**. Nevertheless, a number of Parisian women who dabbled in the sciences or other learned areas have been identified as possible "models" for Philaminte.

**Philinte (***Le Misanthrope***)**. **Alceste's** best friend clings to him tenaciously, no matter how brusque or even insulting the misanthrope's comments can be. In the first scene of the play, Alceste belittles Philinte to the point of implicitly comparing him to a dubious **noble**, whose status depends on his virtuous friend. He likens Philinte's esteem to that of a prostitute. Philinte, however, maintains his reasonable composure in the face of all this abuse and continually tries to enlighten Alceste to the inappropriateness, and even the danger, of his desire for universal sincerity. He tries to discourage his reluctant friend from "tilting at the world in general," but to little avail. Nevertheless, it would be a mistake to see Philinte as the unmitigated spokesman for Molière's private views. After all, he goes so far as to question the wisdom of trying to correct the manners of the age, calling it "a folly second to none," whereas the playwright would evoke the doctrine of *castigat ridendo mores* in his petitions to the King on **Tartuffe**. Rather than an omniscient *raisonneur*, it is more accurate to see Philinte as a polar opposite to Alceste, just as subject to flaws as his counterpart. Philinte himself suggests this relationship when he cites their resemblance to the two brothers in *L'École des maris*. If Alceste is overly critical of humanity, Philinte is overly indulgent. He lavishes comically superfluous praise on **Oronte's** mediocre sonnet. In trying to arrange a match between Alceste and **Éliante**, he almost forgets to tell the lady that he is in **love** with her himself. In fact, Alceste has adjusted so well to Philinte's chiding that the latter has become to some extent a "co–dependent" of misanthropy, indirectly supporting Alceste's exaggerated behavior. Yet one must admit that Philinte is the perfect model of *honnêteté*, the doctrine of other–directed social **politeness** developed by the **Chevalier de Méré** and other experts of civility. It is hard to think harshly of a **gentleman** who always puts his fellows before himself. There is, though, an irony in this self–abnegation, since it springs from a fundamental pessimism that Philinte only rarely exposes. In his deepest recesses, he views mankind as a race of wild beasts, predators, and scavengers always ready to betray their savage nature. His ability to maintain an *honnête* exterior is thus partly motivated by deep–seated fear, not too distant from the superstition of failure that haunts his friend. Philinte proves himself an obliging judge of poetry, a hale–fellow–well–met at **Célimène's salon**, an amusing raconteur, a well–intentioned matchmaker, and ultimately a successful suitor in his own right. To the very end, he is able to lay down his achievements, and perhaps his sanity, in order to try to reintegrate Alceste into a world whose assimilation the latter perversely resists. In this sense, his quest is ultimately just as quixotic as that of **Sganarelle** in *Dom Juan*, for in this play it is Molière who dreams of far–off worlds (deserted, instead of inhabited by sex–starved women), while good **La Grange** trots after him, trying in vain to connect him to reality.

**Philis** (*La Princesse d'Élide*). Played originally by **Madeleine Béjart**, this character doubles as a **servant** to the **Princess** and the **love** interest of the fool **Moron**. She prefers the melodious **Tircis** to the raucous jester, and she doesn't hesitate to tell him to his face in the third *intermède*, where he accosts her, or in the fourth, where he interrupts her serenade. She apparently goes too far by asking him to die for her, though, for he turns the matter into a joke at her expense and nevermore professes any interest in her. Along with **Clymène**, Philis provides the musical entertainment for the fifth *intermède*, singing a song of consolation to the Princess whose words actually conflict with her resistance to love, exacerbating her distress. It is Philis, appropriately, who announces the arrival of the musical **shepherds** at the conclusion of the play, initiating the sixth *intermède*.

**Philosophy**. Although Molière was claimed as a precursor by the philosophers of the Enlightenment, he left no original philosophical works, and even his translation of **Lucretius** has not come down to us. Philosophy was a standard part of the liberal education Molière received, especially the **Aristotelian** branch that was officially endorsed by the Church in association with scholasticism. Molière seems to have reacted rather negatively to this curriculum, if one is to judge by the plays. He almost certainly knew of the works of the great essayist, Montaigne, and through him of the doctrines of Stoicism that informed so much of Renaissance thought. However, Molière does not seem to have received very strong doses of either the Stoical ethic of self–denial or the effusions of Renaissance Neoplatonism so influential on previous generations. Likewise, much of **Descartes's** thought seems to have left him unimpressed, since he mocks Cartesian physics in *Les Femmes savantes*. There are numerous echoes of the *Discourse on Method*, especially the common–sensical beginning sections of the work, but this had become commonplace by the mid–seventeenth century. Characters who try to apply pure rationality without prudent reflection, such as **Arnolphe**, **Alceste**, and **Orgon**, are rudely punished for their rashness. **Monsieur Jourdain** employs a **Philosophy Teacher** to try to gain a veneer of learning. When the Teacher asks him what branch of philosophy he would like to study, Jourdain rejects logic (which the Teacher managed to muddle badly), morals (because he intends to act immorally), and physics (because it seems to be a hodge–podge to him), settling eventually on spelling! **Scapin** advocates the philosophy of pessimism, especially for fathers with **children**. Instead Molière seems most marked by **skeptical** philosophy. A long anecdotal tradition had him studying under **Gassendi** at the **Collège de Clermont**, but this is impossible, since the latter did not start teaching there until after Molière's departure for the provinces. Even skepticism, moreover, is examined critically. In such texts as *Le Mariage forcé*, we find abstract skepticism (**Pyrrhonism**) and abstract Aristotelianism balanced against each other and both rejected, in the persons of **Pancrace** and **Marphurius**, the equally impractical philosophers. In general, Molière seems to have applied the skeptical line inherited from Sextus Empiricus, Gassendi, and **La Mothe Le Vayer** very tacitly and to have seasoned it with doses of Epicurean thought from Lucretius and his followers.

Les Femmes savantes* shows us a veritable panoply of philosophies, for the learned ladies seek to absorb all the existing systems. **Trissotin** professes a preference for Aristotle's peripatetic school, **Philaminte** likes **Plato**, and **Armande** prefers the **Epicureans**, but when **Bélise** mentions that she feels Descartes has found just the right notion of physics, with his atoms suspended in "subtle matter" instead of floating in a vacuum, everyone readily agrees. Ironically, Molière mocks the Cartesian theories of magnetism, vortices (a dim apprehension of electron theory), and planetary orbits, all of which ultimately proved true. But then, no one looks to Molière for explanations of physics. Philaminte later mentions that she greatly admires the Stoics, who would seem to fit her temperament quite well.

An interesting passage touches on philosophy in *Les Amants magnifiques*, where **Sostrate** blames his distrust of **astrology** on his own materialism. He says that his own senses are too crude or limited to apprehend and believe in the subtle demonstrations of astrological influence that others claim to see. However, he evokes recent developments in astronomy to argue against the existence of such influences across the vast reaches of space that separate earth from other heavenly bodies. This was a rather daring statement to make in a Catholic country so soon after Galileo's torture and persecution for professing the same theories. Sostrate lumps astrology together with alchemy, necromancy, and other forms of superstition among what he pejoratively calls the "curious sciences."

The practical, empirical Sostrate would probably agree with Philinte when the latter states that civility is nothing more than philosophy put into action. What use is it to study the nature of virtue, argues the gentleman in *Le Misanthrope* (V, 1), if it does not serve to counter the inherent weaknesses and defects of human nature? Unlike Boethius, who sees philosophy as a kind of ideal retreat from injustice and vice, Philinte views it as an active social force that only realizes its potential when it is engaged in the interplay between right and wrong.

*See also* **Aristotle; Skepticism**.

*See* Andrew Calder, "Molière's Aristotelian Pedants," *Seventeenth–Century French Studies* 12 (1990), 65–75.

**Philosophy Teacher (*Le Bourgeois gentilhomme*).** It is thought that **Du Croisy** may have played this poor pedagogue, who has undertaken the thankless task of trying to civilize **Monsieur Jourdain**. He arrives as an apparent peacemaker in the quarrel between the other teachers over which discipline is superior, but after spouting words of wisdom and restraint, he thoughtlessly throws himself into the fray in an effort to uphold his own domain. Naturally, he comes off the worst of the four, battered on all sides and injured by the stings of insult. He is far from the perfect thinker. His own cowardice makes him think only of avenging himself with epigrams rather than blows. As he tries to explain the curriculum to Jourdain he makes a frightful hash of the realm of logic and, as Jourdain observes, a confusing hodge–podge of physics. Spelling, the pupil's ultimate choice, is probably more within his competence. Even at this fundamental level, however, he is hardly effective. He wastes most of his lesson telling Jourdain what he already knows, namely how to pronounce a few vowels. Equally obvious is his revelation that his pupil speaks in prose. His efforts at rewording Jourdain's compliment to **Dorimène** are equally flat–footed and ridiculous, for he contorts the phrase into some unrecognizable versions before stating finally that the first was the best. If he comes off looking like the worst of Jourdain's teachers, it is not only because he lacks force or agility, but also because he falls back into the long–established category of pedants who are doomed to mutter their fractured **Latin** and to blather strange explanations for everything.

**Phoebus Apollo.** This **Greek** god of the dawn is blasphemed by **Sosie** in the first act of *Amphitryon*, where the **slave** remarks that the deity must have had too much to drink the previous night, since he seems unnaturally late in rising with his sunbeams.

*See also* **Apollo**.

**Pibrac, Guy du Four de** (1529–1586). Author of devotional *Quatrains* recommended in burlesque fashion in **Charles Sorel's** *Le Berger extravagant* and by **Gorgibus** in *Sganarelle*. These poems were extremely well known and were reedited countless times.

**Picardy**. The region of northeastern France closest to the Flemish border. **Nérine** pretends to be a woman of Picardy in the second act of *Monsieur de Pourceaugnac*, where she accuses him of abandoning her and her **children**. The main characteristics of her pronunciation are the reduction of diphthongs to single closed vowels, the domination of the nasal "in" sound over other nasals (as in modern Québecois), and the interchange of "sh," "s," and "k" consonants under some circumstances. She mentions that their "**marriage**" took place in Saint–Quentin.

**Pichou, Claude** (ca. 1597–1631). Author of a number of rather under–appreciated comedies that influenced Molière. **Gros–René** briefly refers to *Les Folies de Cardenio* in his diatribe against women in *Dépit amoureux*. Pichou's brief writing career was cut short by an assassination.

**Pierrot (***Dom Juan***)**. Though he saves **Dom Juan** and **Sganarelle** from the waves, this **peasant** is rewarded by the seduction of his fiancée.

**Pirates**. A staple ingredient of ancient **Greek** romance and comedy, pirates were always abducting people and separating families, though they performed the occasional rescue as well. Imaginary pirates figure in the plots of *Les Amants magnifiques* and *Les Fourberies de Scapin*.

*Placets au Roi (Petitions to the King)*. These three short documents are usually published along with *Tartuffe*, which concerns them all. The first, written in 1664, sprung from Molière's desire to defend himself against the libels published in the priest **Pierre Roullé's** pamphlet, "Le Roi glorieux de ce monde" ("The Glorious King of this World"). Molière begins with a brief exposition of his theory of comedy, based on the device *castigat ridendo mores* (loosely translated: cure social ills through ridicule). He presents his reasons for attacking hypocrisy as a vicious practice, his care in distinguishing real from false **religious** devotion, and his disappointment that the Devout had influenced the King to ban public performances of *Tartuffe*. The dramatist explicitly credits the King with a personal approval of the play and its matter, and reiterates his willingness to obey the royal command. Molière then goes on to relate his shock at seeing **Roullé's** libels, several of which he repeats almost word for word. It is unclear whether the protection implored by Molière was ever really given, for there is no documentation on action against Roullé.

However, one can scarcely imagine that the publication of the *placet* was permitted without some kind of intervention, however subtle, having been made.

The second *placet* originated in 1667, following the unique performance of the second version of the play, *L'Imposteur*, and its ban by **Lamoignon**, the president of the **Parlement** of **Paris**. Molière gives several details of the kinds of modifications he made in his original play, both in the **costume** of the villain (now called **Panulphe**) and in the wording. He implies that he was following royal suggestions in making these changes. Nevertheless, he explains, the "cabal" that had organized in 1664 once again made its influence felt, this time by recruiting many "truly devout" voices to its cause through trickery. Included is Molière's argument that the reason for the rabid response from his enemies is that his plays attack hypocrisy, which they practice and cherish, unlike other plays that only attack religion itself, about which they care nothing. This implicitly cites an exchange between the King and the great **Duke de Condé** that he will repeat in his preface to *Tartuffe*. He again asks the monarch for help, ending his argument by a hint that if such attacks continue, he may refrain from composing any more comedies for the King's pleasure. Molière respectfully excused himself from bothering the King about this affair while he was busy with military affairs at the siege of Lille. The matter was important enough that he dispatched **La Grange** and **La Thorillière** to deliver the petition in person, at considerable expense of **money** and time to the troupe. La Grange's biography of Molière attached to the 1682 collected works edition explains that Louis promised to set the entire matter straight when he returned from his wars.

The very brief and jocular third petition, written in 1669 on the very day of the premiere of the final version of *Tartuffe*, is ostensibly a request for a canonicate on behalf of his doctor, Mauvillain. Actually, the author profited from this occasion to thank the King for keeping his promise that was made after the second *placet*. He laughingly asks that the monarch now give him the chance to reconcile with the medical world, as he had done with the spiritual.

**Plaisirs de l'Isle enchantée, Les (*The Pleasures of the Enchanted Isle*).** The first of **Louis XIV's** great **court** festivals to be held at **Versailles**, from May 7 to May 13, 1664. According to the official account, a "little army" of artisans, actors, dancers, and musicians collaborated on the entertainment, which, unlike the earlier urban festivals, was put on for the exclusive benefit of 600 invited guests. Vigarini, the **Italian** designer of theatrical **machines**, constructed the elaborate sets; **Lully** composed the music; **Benserade** and Perigny composed the verses declaimed in the course of the "games"; and Molière and his troupe supplied the dramatic entertainments.

The festival's title was derived from a famous episode of Ludovico Ariosto's Italian epic, the *Orlando furioso* (1516), which had inspired earlier court entertainments. In that episode (cantos 6–8 and 10), the knight Ruggiero succumbs to the spells of the alluring sorceress Alcina, and becomes a prisoner of love at her island court. Charged by Louis XIV with devising a unifying theme for the festival, the **duc de Saint–Aignan**, a courtier proud of his cultivation, had used the Alcina story as a sketchy plot, explaining the provenance of the various *plaisirs* the court was to witness. Thus, a *livret* or program distributed to spectators explained that Ruggiero, now dubbed Roger, had originally devised a series of Apollonian games in honor of Alcine. The sorceress had then called for the current reenactment in honor of Queen Maria–Theresa. As the *livret* implied, the festivities were dedicated to the Queen and Queen Mother, each of whom was honored during the entertainments by a verse encomium. However, since the King himself played the role of the enamored Roger, many courtiers perceived the praise of Alcine as a veiled tribute to the royal mistress, **Louise de La Vallière**.

The festivities opened with a ceremonial procession, in which Louis XIV appeared on horseback as Roger, followed by his knights, court nobles representing characters from the *Orlando furioso*. Each horseman was preceded by a page bearing a shield inscribed with his device. The king's device was a jeweled sun, accompanied by the words "Nec cesso, nec erro," likening the king's diligence to that of the sun, which neither rests nor strays from its course. Several of the knights' devices — a sunflower, for example, or an eagle soaring sunward — prolonged the solar theme, foreshadowing the nobles' imminent reduction to the role of royal satellites. Bringing up the rear of the procession was a chariot bearing Apollo and the four ages of history, played by **La Grange** and other members of Molière's troupe. The procession paused in formation before the royal box while Apollo and the ages made speeches lauding the Queen, as the author of a new golden age. Roger and his knights then participated in a "course de bague," competing to drive their lances through a suspended ring. After a display of skill, the king withdrew, leaving his knights to contest the prize, eventually won by the marquis de La Vallière, brother of Louise.

The day concluded with a sumptuous banquet. The various courses, a gift from the four seasons, were brought in by forty–eight waiters, **costumed** as members of the retinues of the seasons. The seasons themselves rode in on a horse, an elephant, a camel, and a bear, and were again played by members of Molière's troupe. **Pan** and **Diana**, played by Molière and **Madeleine Béjart**, then made a spectacular entrance, seated on one of Vigarini's **machines**, a tree–shaded mountain that appeared to be "borne on air." Following formal presentation speeches by the seasons, Pan, and Diana, the royal family and the principal ladies of the court took their places at a semi–circular table. They consumed the meal, lit by "infinite" numbers of **candles**, to the accompaniment of several dozen musicians, while Roger's knights stood gallantly by.

The second and third "days" were in fact held at night, thanks to equally extravagant illuminations. The second day was devoted to Molière's *La Princesse d'Elide*, commissioned for the festival and staged in an outdoor **theater** erected especially for the occasion. The third day depicted the end of Alcine's enchantments and thus the liberation of Roger and his knights. The **court** was seated at the edge of a circular reflecting pool, containing three artificial islands. Alcine and two attendants, played by three members of Molière's troupe — **Mlles. Du Parc**, **de Brie**, and **Molière** — appeared from behind the central island, mounted on a sea monster and two whales. The three approached the water's edge, directly opposite the royal box, where Alcine delivered a speech honoring the devotion to France of **Anne of Austria**, the Queen Mother. They then retired to the island palace, whose façade opened to reveal giants and dwarves. The ensuing ballet depicted skirmishes between Alcine's grotesque defenders and the captive knights. In the final entry, the fairy Melissa gave Roger, this time played by an actor, the magical **ring** that put an end to Alcine's enchantments. Her gesture precipitated the palace's destruction in a spectacular display of fireworks.

Although this finale concluded the activities directly related to the enchanted island theme, four more days of entertainment followed. These included additional tournaments, a lottery, described as His Majesty's gallant tribute to the ladies of the court, and three more plays by Molière. *Les Fâcheux* was presented on the fifth day of the festival, the original three–act version of *Le Tartuffe* premiered on the sixth, and *Le Mariage forcé* occupied the seventh and final day. The prominence of Molière and his players throughout the seven days of the festival was a striking mark of royal favor, noticed by contemporaries.

The festival, clearly intended to increase the stature of King and court, was well publicized. The May 21 edition of the *Gazette* carried an account of the festivities, and Marigny quickly published his own *Relation*. An official narrative, illustrated by the beautiful engravings of Israël Silvestre and augmented with supplementary verses accompanying the knights' devices, was published later in 1664, in both a limited in–folio edition and a duodecimo edition for more popular consumption. Its numerous reprintings included another in–folio edition in 1673. Louis XIV sent copies of the account to other European courts, thus using the entertainments to enhance his court's prestige abroad as well as at home.

*See* Marie–Christine Moine, *Les Fêtes à la Cour du Roi Soleil: 1653–1715* (Paris: Fernand Lanore, 1984).

*Kathleen Wine*

**Plato.** The great fourth–century B.C. idealist **philosopher** is much admired in **Philaminte's** circle, where his *Republic*, with its qualified call for female education, serves as a model for their academy. Predictably, he is a particular favorite of the ethereal **Bélise**, but **Armande** is also imbued with the principles of Neoplatonic love made popular during the Renaissance by such poets as Pontus du Tyard and vulgarized in **Mlle. de Scudéry's** novels.

**Plautus.** Famous comic author of ancient **Rome**. Molière loosely based his *L'Avare* on Plautus's *Aulularia*. Actually, Molière seems to have mainly relied on the edition by the **abbé de Marolles** (1658), which was accompanied by a translation and a supplement by the Renaissance scholar **Urceus Codrus** that filled in the gaps of Plautus's incomplete text and invented the name **Harpagon**. The same is true for *Amphitryon*, which seems to owe much to Marolles. There are further echoes of Plautus scattered through several other comedies.

**Plays–within–a–play**. These are numerous in Molière's works and fall into two types: identified plays and metatheatrical occurrences. The former are common in the context of the **comedy–ballet**, where some element of **music or dance** is usually involved. The latter are equally standard, occurring whenever any sustained deception is attempted. The adoption of a false identity or a pretense of death or abduction is a frequent motif. To take only *Le Malade imaginaire* as an example, one finds **Argan's** "play" at being ill, **Béline's** acting the faithful wife, **Louison's feigned death** to avoid spanking, **Toinette's** impersonation of a **doctor**, Argan's feigned death to test Béline's loyalty, and the medical masquerade in the conclusion. In *Les Amants magnifiques*, one of the most explicit deceivers, the **astrologer Anaxarque**, describes how he has constructed a little **machine play** involving the false apparition of **Venus** within the larger context of the romantic plot line. Molière arranges these nested performances to facilitate the suspension of disbelief among the characters he creates as well as between himself and the audience. Thus, his entire canon takes its place in the great Renaissance–Baroque metaphor of the world as a stage, which played such a great role in the works of Shakespeare, Calderon, **Pierre Corneille**, and other writers.

**Plutarch**. **Latin** translations of this first–century **Greek** biographer are known to have been among the most popular secular reading matter in seventeenth–century France, but **Chrysale** can think of no better use for the monstrous tome than to press his collars.

**Poetry.** *See* **La Gloire du Val de Grâce**; **Lyric and Occasional Poetry**; *Remerciement au Roi*.

**Poisson, Raymond** (1630–1690). Known on stage as Crispin, this comic wore a stylized black–and–white **servant** costume with **Spanish** features and favored the approach of the traditional *gracioso* of Golden Age drama. Recruited by the **Hôtel de Bourgogne** as a comic rival to Molière, he launched into the battle early with *Lubin* (1660), a crude and **farcical** offering, but soon learned to emulate Molière's **satirical** qualities with *Le Baron de la Crasse* (1661), a short and still very rough piece, but remarkably popular for its characterization of an unsophisticated country **noble** who visits the **court**. The **Sotenvilles** and **Pourceaugnac** can trace part of their genealogy to the Baron. Poisson's subsequent plays improved some in style, but drew mainly on the increasing popularity of the Crispin persona. They include *Le Fou raisonnable* (1663); *L'Après–soupé des auberges* (*Late Night at the Inns,* 1664); *Les Faux Moscovites* and *Le Poète basque* (both 1668); *Les Femmes coquettes* (1670); and *La Hollande malade* (1672). In tragedy, Poisson went by the name Belleroche.

**Poitou**. The region around Poitiers in western France. In the fifth entry of the **Ballet des Nations** that followed *Le Bourgeois gentilhomme*, singers, dancers, and musicians in **costumes** of the area execute two minuets.  This music on flutes and oboes was presumably based on regional airs as well.

*Polexandre*.  A lengthy novel by **Gomberville** that provides the name for a valet in *Les Précieuses ridicules*.

**Police**.  Guardians of the peace appear in both comic and serious guise in the works of Molière.  The playwright was well acquainted with them, after all, having been on both sides of the **law**, as a student and a convict in debtor's prison.  Their first mention is in *L'Étourdi*, where an account is given of **Mascarille's** attempt to kidnap **Andrès**, his master's rival.  An *exempt* and some deputy sergeants have been bribed to arrest the supposed **Gypsy** on trumped–up charges, but **Lélie** blunders in and vouches for the detainee on his good appearance.  When the officers failed to release their prey, the blockhead drew sword and challenged them and since, according to **Ergaste**, such men ordinarily fear for their lives, they took flight and abandoned Andrès, acting much more like the Keystone Cops than the Three Musketeers.  An equally funny police incident occurs in the first comedy–ballet interlude in *Le Malade imaginaire*, where **Polichinelle's** discharge of a firearm brings him face to face with the town watch.  This corrupt bunch of "archers" first asks for a large bribe and, failing that, imposes a penance of finger snaps to the nose and blows from a stick.  Not before enduring these cadenced and musical indignities does Polichinelle beat a retreat.  Two police sergeants accompany the lawyers whom **Monsieur de Pourceaugnac** tries to consult, but their only purpose is to perform a dance with two nimble prosecutors at the end of the second–act interval.  Later, an *exempt* and two archers come to the aid of the protagonist when he is physically assaulted while **disguised** as a woman.  However, they are part of **Éraste's** plot and immediately recognize Pourceaugnac as a "wanted man."  When **Sbrigani** mentions the possibility of a "fix" with the help of a few coins, the *exempt* sends his men away and agrees to escort the culprit to a safe distance in exchange for the contents of his purse.  The winks of recognition exchanged by Sbrigani and the *exempt* are not feigned.  According to **Nérine**, the trickster has already risked conviction for felony at least twenty times in previous brushes with the law.  She mentions the punishments of **galley** duty and branding on the shoulder that were reserved for serious criminals.  He does her the honor, in turn, of mentioning the numerous swindles, embezzlements, and perjuries in which she has distinguished herself — any of which would have justified long–term confinement or deportation, at the least.

    *Les Fourberies de Scapin* alludes to a more serious encounter with the police.  **Scapin** tells **Silvestre** that he has had a brush with the law and fared so badly that he has made up his mind to have nothing more to do with police and courts.  Later, when Silvestre begs not to be involved with anything illegal, Scapin tells him jokingly that "three or four years in the galleys, more or less, never did a body any harm" (I, 5).  Old **Géronte** has greater respect for the police and wants them called out when his son is supposed to have been taken away by **Turks**, until Scapin reminds him that they have no jurisdiction at sea.

An *exempt* armed with his white rod of authority appears most notably in **Tartuffe**, supposedly to arrest **Orgon**, but actually to convey the hypocrite to jail and to deliver the splendid speech of praise to the all–knowing judicial powers of **Louis XIV**. As *sergeant–à–verge* in the same play, **Monsieur Loyal** shows the other side of the police, the corrupt and vicious side. Fortunately, he is outranked by the *exempt*, who often enforced direct royal orders, such as *lettres de cachet*, while the *sergeant* was an officer of the local jurisdiction. A still higher level of policeman appears in *Le Misanthrope*, where a guard of the *maréchaussée* summons **Alceste** to appear before the **Marshals of France**. The peacetime duties of the Marshals included supervising the King's *gendarmes*, who ruled the highways, and preventing **duels** among the country's **gentlemen**. They answered directly to the crown and their edicts carried full royal authority, which is why Alceste's recalcitrance in their regard bears an almost rebellious stamp. The rank and file of the police force was made up of simple archers (who no longer carried bows) and *suisses*, who were hired to keep the watch, apprehend common criminals, and patrol the cities.

*See also* **Commissioner**.

**Polichinelle (interludes of *Le Malade imaginaire*).** **Toinette** describes Polichinelle as an elderly usurer who is wooing her. She wants to use him to deliver a **message** about **Angélique** to **Cléante**. Before she can ask, though, he tries to organize a serenade under her window, first giving a *récitatif* and then singing in **Italian**. He is answered by an old lady who appears above, presumably not Toinette, but then interrupted by a group of violins. After firing a gun in rage, he is arrested by the archers, who demand a bribe, unless he is to undergo physical punishment. He winds up paying the bribe as well as being **beaten**. He is not heard from again after the interval, for Cléante arrives on his own, garbed in his music master's **disguise**. The character and his **costume** probably came from the stock background of the **commedia dell'arte**.

**Polidas (*Amphitryon*).** One of the first pair of **Theban** citizens called by **Jupiter** to join in his feast, he has little to say other than a few sparse interjections in favor of the threatened **Sosie** and an expression of bewilderment at the appearance of a second **Amphitryon**.

**Polidore (*Dépit amoureux*).** Father of **Valère**, he seems to be a **polite** and relatively mild–mannered foil to **Albert**, with whom he shares a most amusing misunderstanding scene (III, 4). Each man comes seeking pardon from the other, Polidore for his son's apparent seduction of **Lucile** and Albert for his trick with **Ascagne's** identity. They outdo each other in forgiveness without realizing exactly what it is they are forgiving. Polidore appreciates the verve and nerve of his new daughter–in–law Ascagne–Dorothée and joins in the fun as she taunts him with the prospect of a **duel** in the final act. He has apparently found a ready solution to the issue of the inheritance that stood between Ascagne and Valère.

**Politeness**. More than just a ritual that was taken for granted, politeness was the mainstay of the seventeenth–century doctrine of *honnêteté*, promulgated by the **Chevalier de Meré** and others. It went beyond mere etiquette to involve a creative expression of social concerns. Experts in politeness used it as an important tool, even a weapon, in order to garner the attention and esteem of their fellow citizens. In *L'École des maris*, **Valère** greets **Sganarelle** with an elaborate mixture of bows and reverences as he tries to make his acquaintance, with the ulterior motive of wooing his ward, **Isabelle** (I, 3). Sganarelle's brusque rejection of these showy overtures constituted a series of *lazzi*, or gestural gags, that must have been most amusing to the public. This uneven exchange is reversed and renewed later in the play (II, 2), when Sganarelle abruptly accosts Valère in the street and then refuses several polite offers by the young man (entering his house, taking a seat), almost bringing his visit to a standstill. A similar bowing sequence unfolds in *Le Sicilien* between **Hali** and **Dom Pèdre**. Perhaps the clumsiest man with a bow in the Molière canon is **Monsieur Jourdain**, who has to ask his **Dance Master** how to execute a proper bow to greet a marquise. When he actually has to greet **Dorimène**, he awkwardly demands that she back up, so that he can complete the complicated four–step reverence he was taught earlier in the play. He learned the steps, only to spoil them by his lack of grace and verbal politeness. On the other hand, the graceful reverences that **Horace** and **Agnès** offer each other lead them to fall in **love** even without being able to articulate a single sentence. There can be no clearer proof of the power of politeness than their first meeting, recounted by the naïve young lady to her tormentor, **Arnolphe**.

Seating etiquette was also a primary element of politeness. Whether one sat in an armchair, a regular chair, or on a stool, or indeed sat at all, was determined by the relative ranks of those in the company. **Cathos** and **Magdelon** in *Les Précieuses ridicules* are impolitely slow in ordering seats for the suitors **La Grange** and **Du Croisy**. They then fail to use the right kind for their putative **noble** guests. **Célimène**, a true noble, manages to seat her visitors more properly as soon as they arrive. In *Le Malade imaginaire*, **Argan** keeps to his armchair on account of his illness but orders seats for **Thomas Diafoirus** and his father. **Dom Juan's** insistence that his creditor **Monsieur Dimanche** sit in an armchair in his presence constitutes, on the other hand, a strange breach of etiquette that the **money**–lender is loath to accept. He later tries the same trick on his angry father. The **Countess of Escarbagnas** manages to make the ritual of seating into an act of impoliteness. First she engages in a prolonged shouting match with her **servants** in order to bring in the chairs. Then she overdoes the act of actually sitting down to the point that she and **Julie** almost do not succeed in doing it. Then, when **Thibaudet** visits, she makes a point of making him sit in a folding chair to emphasize his social inferiority to her. **Philaminte** also has trouble with chair etiquette. When her lackey **L'Épine** comes into the room with an overload of chairs, he has a pratfall. Philaminte and **Bélise** shout at him, asking him if he knows about gravity, to which he replies, "I did notice it, Madame, once I was on the ground" (III, 2). When **Monsieur de Pourceaugnac** is installed at the **Doctor's** house, which he believes to be an inn, he is cordially seated, but the attendants who bring out the chairs seem to be swathed in medical black. This causes the Limousin to comment, "For such a young man, what lugubrious servants!"

Hats were another important item of etiquette. Custom demanded that they be doffed in the presence of ladies and persons to whom one owed respect. Servants sometimes neglected to do this, leading to comical sight gags such as those between **Harpagon** and **Maître Jacques** in *L'Avare*. Argan gives a medical excuse for remaining covered with his bonnet, while Sganarelle invokes no lesser an authority than **Aristotle** to do so in *Le Médecin malgré lui*.

Verbal politeness, of course, was not to be overlooked. The greeting had to be made in correct form, beginning with the form of address appropriate to the interlocutor. **George Dandin** can never manage this correctly, since he insists on referring to his wife and the **Sotenvilles** by their terms of relation rather than the noble "Monsieur" or "Madame" they were entitled to. **Thomas Diafoirus** cannot even figure out whom he should address first without the aid of his father. This must run in the family, since the older **doctor** cannot greet Argan without a collision of words and phrases. Though Thomas's little speeches are awkwardly ornate, he spoils the impression further by blurting out crude terms such as "Baiserai–je?" (literally, "Shall I kiss her?" — but the same word was also used for the sexual act) and by pointedly contradicting **Angélique** instead of offering a suitor's praise and submission.

Flattery was an element of politeness that was easily exaggerated, especially through a desire to gull the listener. **Sbrigani** ingratiates himself to Pourceaugnac through a shower of positive adjectives (sophisticated, likeable, gracious, kind, majestic, candid, cordial). All of these he attributes to a single outward glance that told him the secrets of the interloper's personality. Similarly, in *Le Bourgeois gentilhomme*, the **tailors'** four **apprentices** beg for tips by bombarding Monsieur Jourdain with outlandishly inflated honorifics, going from *mon gentilhomme*, through *Monseigneur* and *Votre Grandeur* almost to *Votre Altesse*, which was reserved for princes of the blood royal holding the rank of duke and peer. **Dorante** enters Jourdain's residence with another flurry of flattering compliments, though not so out of scale as those of the underlings. He quickly produces the desired reaction of vanity in Jourdain, but **Madame Jourdain** sees through his fine **language** and comments, "That one knows how to scratch him where it itches!" The "two gentlemen" then create an embarrassing scene over whether to take off their hats out of respect or keep them on because of "equality."

Politeness was not so much a virtue as a series of codes that could be learned and then abused. **Dom Juan** proves this with his twisted application of *préséance* that is meant to disarm his creditors and his elders. This preoccupation has passed to his **servant**, who is clearly fascinated by the codes of civility, although he has not managed to master them. One of the main attractions of **tobacco**, as Sganarelle explains to **Gusman** in the opening scene, is that it is the means of polite intercourse: "One learns with tobacco to be a truly civil fellow. Don't you see that as soon as you take a pinch, you begin to get along wonderfully with everyone? Wherever you are, classy people are overjoyed to offer it back and forth to each other. They don't even wait for you to ask, and they anticipate your every desire. Thus, it's true that tobacco inspires good breeding and virtue in everyone who uses it" (I, 1). Molière's point in this speech is that tobacco is one thing that permits politeness to become a mere commodity, rather than a moral exercise. The world will always be full of Sganarelles who look for the simplest possible representation of virtue and mistake that sign for the real thing.

The strained nature of politeness as a cover for evil intentions is most obvious in Act III, scene 4 of *Le Misanthrope*, where **Célimène** and **Arsinoé** trade barbs thinly disguised by the apparatus of polite speech. Arsinoé calls her hostess nothing less than a loose woman and a gold digger, luring men into her web in order to exploit them. Célimène repays this "kindness" by showing Arsinoé to be a bigot who has adopted the sham of **religious** devotion because she is no longer able to play the coquette. The fierce hatred that underlies their carefully crafted phrases lies at the opposite side of the spectrum of politeness from the ingenuous bows exchanged by Horace and Agnès.

**Polyxène. Magdelon**, in *Les Précieuses ridicules*, wants her father and others to use this name she has chosen from the novels she has read to replace her own. Ironically, the most well known novelistic Polyxène was the heroine of a story by **Molière d'Essertines**, from whom the dramatist may have copied his own stage name. In a further bit of irony, Molière probably derived the name of the character **Alceste** from that same novel, where it occurs in a rare, masculine context.

**Poquelin, Esprit–Madeleine** (1665–1723). Born on August 4, 1665, she was the only one of Molière's three **children** to survive to adulthood, her two brothers dying in infancy. Her godparents were **Madeleine Béjart** and her long–time companion, the Count of Modena, whose names were conferred on her. At the age of six, she participated in the production of *Psyché*. Friends of Molière assembled after his death to look after her interests, even after her mother remarried with **Guérin**. She was married in 1705 to one Claude de Rachel–Montalant.

**Poquelin, Jean–Baptiste** (1622–1673). Despite the efforts of the nineteenth–century Moliéristes and more professional scholars from Jal to Madeleine Jurgens and Elizabeth Maxfield–Miller, all too little is known of Molière's life. We have summarized his childhood in the **Poquelin Family** entry, and his adventures with the **Illustre Théâtre** under that heading. The young man who took the stage name Molière was apparently in most respects a typical Parisian **bourgeois**, distinguished only by his good humanistic studies, his knowledge of the fragility of family happiness, and his zest for the **theater**. The **Mignard portrait**, done soon after he returned to **Paris**, but perhaps sketched first at an even earlier period, shows him with a longish face and nose, dark hair, somewhat sallow skin, prominent eyes and lips, a wide mouth, and a contemplative expression. Several witnesses testify that he had some kind of speech impediment, variously described as a hiccup or vocal tic, that hampered him in serious roles. However, he was able to turn it to his advantage in comedy, as almost all great comics do with some feature of their body or physiognomy. We now know that his break from his relatives was neither as definitive nor as simple as was long supposed. Whether his years on the road in the western and southern provinces included red–hot romance with **Madeleine Béjart** or other females of the troupe is much more conjectural than most biographers, eager for a hearty subject, would like to admit. What is certain about the road years is that Molière rose steadily in the profession and was entrusted with more and more important work by **Dufresne** and his colleagues. He became the *harangueur* or spokesman for the troupe, which involved **monologues** to warm up the rowdy audience or calm them sufficiently to listen to the plays. Soon he was made a financial representative, as his signature on legal documents attests. While in **Bordeaux**, he may have witnessed the political upheaval of the *Ormée* uprising during the Fronde **revolts**. By the mid–1650s, as he was sharpening his pen to write his first intrigue comedies, he fell in with the **Prince de Conti** in Languedoc. This young **libertine** was not exactly the classmate that **La Grange** and **Vivot** make him out to be, but as *anciens élèves* of the **Collège de Clermont** brought by fate to the distant South, the two must have found mutual comfort and support in their friendship. However, Molière was wise enough to distance himself diplomatically from the prince after the latter slew his secretary in a fit of anger and proposed that the playwright take his place. Whether or not the anecdote of the murder is completely true, such a close, personal dependency would not be in keeping with Molière's need for independence. More to his taste was the friendship of the brothers Mignard, painters with a similarly deep commitment to art. Despite the hostility of the powerful and recently converted Conti, Molière seems to have engineered his return to Paris with organizational genius, arranging for patronage connections to the King and Monsieur and engaging a group of important, rising players to his company at just the right time.

Much suggests that Virginia Scott's biography, *Molière: A Theatrical Life*, is aptly named, for once reinstalled in the capital, Molière continued to live in buildings, streets, and neighborhoods filled with fellow actors. He was a regular feature at christenings in Saint–Germain–l'Auxerrois, the actors' church. When he married, it was with **Armande–Grésinde Béjart**, a child of the Dufresne troupe. He probably spent the better part of his life in the theaters, rehearsing and producing his own comedies and sitting in the audience to watch his competition on the off–days. Beginning as early as 1663, he had several bouts with illness that are represented by fallow periods in **La Grange's** register. Biographers and medical authorities have suggested various causes, from stomach ulcers to tuberculosis and other disorders. None kept him away from the stage for very long. Perhaps the most dramatic thing in his life was the play he was working on at the moment; each had its own little drama and these are described under the various play headings.

It is clear that among Molière's personal friends were a number of freethinkers and **skeptics** such as **Chapelle**, **Bernier**, and the young **abbé La Mothe Le Vayer**. Probably **Boileau**, too, figured in the group, before ambition threw him into the stuffy, conservative salon of **Lamoignon**. However, the more dependable evidence shows him enjoying free moments at the leafy country house at **Auteuil** with these companions, rather than engaging in extended orgies at the **White Cross Tavern**, as many an early legend claimed. The sheer demand of his work took most of his concentration. Perhaps too much so. It is difficult to deny the almost unanimous testimony about trouble in his marriage with Armande, especially after the death of their first son in 1664. Did Molière encourage his downcast, postpartum wife to enjoy social diversions, as **Ariste** of *L'École des maris* might have done? Or did he fume helplessly like **George Dandin** while his spouse sampled the pleasures of younger and more *galant* lovers? Or was the truth somewhere in between? This detail must remain unknown, and we can only speculate on his inner struggles as he battled with the separate rigors of disease and bigotry.

Out of the disappointments of marriage bed and infant's empty cradle and the clamor and vitriol of the **Quarrel of the School for Wives** and the *Tartuffe* and *Dom Juan* affairs, as well as the deception of young **Racine**, arose a remarkable artistic career advancing on four separate fronts. Without completely abandoning the **farce** traditions that had fueled his early career, Molière had virtually invented the comedy of character, the comedy of manners, and the **comedy–ballet**. Efforts by the authors associated with the **Hôtel de Bourgogne** or the **Marais** to emulate his methods only showed the immense distance he had already opened up on the pack that followed him. Well before the long–awaited release of *Tartuffe* in 1669, he had already carved his name on the stones of theater history and ensured that comedy would never again be the same after Molière. Almost before the applause died down at the **Palais Royal**, his works were shipped all over Europe, pirated in **Dutch** copies, or translated in fresh ink into **English**, Dutch, and **German**. Wealth and fame did not bring him any respite; driven by his tremendous sentiment of duty toward his company, he outdid himself in ever newer creations, confounding his imitators by turning from one apparently perfected formula to an entirely different comic mix with almost each mature production.

The great Molière remained the trusty bourgeois. Caring for the surviving members of his siblings' families, he eventually knit together his own household. Not long after his daughter had grown old enough to take the stage for the first time in *Psyché*, he and Armande tried a third time at parenthood, only to see baby Pierre perish less than a month after birth. It would be his orphaned nephew namesake who would carry on the Poquelin family name, rather than his own sons. This blow coincided with the last treasonous coup of Molière's career, **Lully's** grabbing of the privilege for the great **operatic** enterprise the two had planned together. Advocates of the Florentine genius give a variety of different excuses for his sudden change of plans. Nevertheless, Molière's ability to put his theatrical plans back on schedule with the help of **Charpentier's** musical ability shows that he was able to cooperate even under the most adverse circumstances. Lully was certainly not a vital ingredient of Molière's success, even in the **comedy–ballet** format. Collaborators had fallen away before, such as Racine and **Boileau**. Molière seems seldom to have been subject to bitterness. Several times before he had even turned enemies into allies, as in the cases of **Ribou**, **Donneau de Visé**, and **Pierre Corneille**. If Molière was alone at this stage of his career, it was not because he had failed his friends, nor because he was preoccupied with failure, ill health, cuckoldry, or conceit. He had simply moved to an artistic level where he did not depend on specific partners or artistic support, for he had outdistanced nearly everyone in terms of innovation and imagination. He had become the Einstein of comedy. In both artistic and biographic terms, *Le Malade imaginaire* represents as great a triumph as his early successes, as *Le Misanthrope*, or as *Dom Juan*.

In retrospect, it is easy to state that Molière died at the summit of his abilities, but could the world have expected more if he had lived? Certainly Lully's betrayal was accompanied and made possible by some degree of cooling on the part of **Louis XIV**. The desperate and meager nature of his funeral is proof, for Armande had appealed directly to the crown for some help with the obdurate religious authorities of Paris. Judging by the resounding financial success of Molière's last nonroyal projects and by the near–sainthood that was conferred upon him anecdotally after his death, Paris would not have abandoned its favorite theatrical son, no matter what the King did. The survival of the Hôtel Guénégaud troupe and then the **Comédie–Française**, despite massive royal mismanagement, attests to this commitment. Would Molière have honorably retired to Auteuil, like the failing Shakespeare to Stratford, or would he have imitated crusty old Jean Poquelin, who refused to leave the furniture business even when he had outlived his heir, Molière's brother Jean? We must be content that he achieved all that he did in his shortened life, for it was more than many other devoted professionals could do for hundreds of years to come.

**Poquelin, Louis**. Molière's first son was baptized on February 28, 1664, though he was born on the 19 of the previous month. He might have already demonstrated frail health, for he would die on November 10. His parents may have been reluctant to expose the child to the winter air and the rigors of christening. Another possible reason for the delay may have been arrangements with the child's royal godparents. Young Louis was named after the King, who was represented as godfather by the Duc de Créqui. **Madame** was the godmother, by proxy of her lady in waiting, the Maréchale du Plessis, a member of the **Richelieu** family.

**Poquelin, Pierre–Jean–Baptiste–Armand**. Born on September 15, 1672, Molière's second male child came into the world at a time when his parents may have been recently reconciled after several years of acrimony, if one is to believe a number of anecdotal tales. The union of both parents' names in the child's seems to point to such a hopeful rapprochement. As with his older brother Louis, he was not baptized right away, for his christening had to wait until October 1. In his case, however, the delay cannot be associated with eminent godparents, for he was held at the font by Boileau's brother, Pierre de Puymorin, and Mignard's daughter, Catherine–Marguerite. Placing their third child under the aegis of the intellectual community and of intimate family connections, Molière and Armande may have meant to eschew some of their respective ambitions and social illusions. Alas, little Pierre would not survive another fortnight. He died on October 11.

**Poquelin Family**. Molière's father, Jean Poquelin, and his mother, Marie Cressé, were married April 27, 1621. They came from neighboring families that had both been involved in the cloth trade and related commerce for several generations, tracing back to the time when they had migrated to **Paris** from nearby Beauvais. Their dowry amounted to just a couple of thousand *livres*, typical of the middle levels of the **bourgeoisie** of the time, and the household would make do with a single maid. **Jean–Baptiste**, their first son, was born shortly before his christening on January 15 of the following year in their home at the corner of the rue Saint–Honoré and the rue des Vieilles–Étuves in the center of the Right Bank of Paris. This home was called the "House of the Apes" because of a decorative carving that adorned the exterior. The couple would go on to have five other children: Louis (christened January 6, 1623), Jean (christened October 1, 1624), Marie (christened August 10, 1625), Nicolas (christened July 13, 1627), and Marie–Madeleine (christened June 13, 1628). Louis and Marie would die as infants. The younger of the surviving brothers, Jean, would receive the family office from his older sibling when Jean–Baptiste left to become an actor, but would predecease him. Madeleine would marry in 1651 with another upholsterer, André Boudet. In the meantime, the father's business as *maître tapissier* prospered. It involved not only the carpet trade, as the name would suggest, but also the manufacturing, maintenance, sale, and storage of all sorts of furniture. With the help of family funds, he acquired in 1631 the office of *tapissier ordinaire et valet de chambre du roi*. This royal appointment required him to see to the upkeep and transport of the royal furniture through a third of the year, with two other *tapissiers* serving consecutively for the remaining months. Since the furniture had to be transported frequently from one palace to another as the royal family moved about, the work necessitated continual contact with the **court**, albeit at a very modest level. Even as virtual **servants**, however, they were proud to be part of the king's household. Besides lucrative military contracts, the position also provided excellent contacts with the **nobility**, always in search of luxurious items for their lodgings.

At the age of eleven, the boy who would become Molière lost his mother. His paternal grandfather had long ago passed away and his paternal grandmother seems to have preferred other offspring to Jean–Baptiste, but the family retained strong ties with the Cressés, who may have helped care for the youngsters. After a year's mourning, his father remarried with Catherine Fleurette, a long–time neighbor. Jean Poquelin's brother Martin would soon marry Catherine's sister Marguerite. The new Poquelin couple soon produced children of their own: Catherine–Espérance (christened March 15, 1634) and an unnamed infant (buried April 9, 1635). The young stepmother would die the following year, perhaps due to complications of pregnancy, and her husband would never remarry. Uncle Martin had died in the interval, and other members of the family had numerous financial worries. Nevertheless, Jean–Baptiste had a fine education and would soon attend classes as a day student at the elite **Collège de Clermont**, where he would share the back rows with over a thousand other aspiring young bourgeois, while a smaller number of nobility clustered in front, a gilded rail separating them from their inferiors.

At the same time, Jean–Baptiste must have spent considerable time by the side of his father and several apprentices, learning the upholsterer's trade. He had barely passed the minimum age of fifteen when his father had him sworn into the guild as a *maître tapissier* and entered officially as heir to the **office** his father held. Royal records show that Jean–Baptiste actually appeared on the rolls of active *tapissiers du roi* in 1637, but it is unclear how long he served, or in what capacity. His studies at the Collège de Clermont would normally have continued until about the summer of 1639. Anecdotes about his accompanying the royal entourage at the time of the King's voyage to Languedoc in 1642 may be quite true. However, the persistent stories of Jean–Baptiste studying **law** must be taken with a grain of salt. There is no documentary evidence of his ever enrolling, studying, obtaining a degree, or practicing at the bar; the best testimony for such classes is the thorough command of legal terms and customs in his works. By June 1643, we do know that Jean–Baptiste was living on his own and deeply involved in the formation of the **Illustre Théâtre** and the adventures that followed its formation. The family had moved away from the childhood "House of the Apes," inhabiting a former rental property under the pillars of the great market of Les Halles, the "House with the Picture of Saint Christopher." In 1644, amid all these departures from the world in which he grew up, he took the actor's name of Molière and separated himself to some degree from the family, probably to distance them from his debts and scandalous status, rather than through any bad feelings. On the contrary, his father Jean continued to lend financial help from time to time, and there are several suggestions that he stayed in contact with his Aunt Adrienne and his half–sister Catherine, who entered the Convent of the Visitation at Montargis, founded by a pious family ancestor. Partly through apprentices and other contacts, Jean–Baptiste seems to have remained in contact with his father and brother during his long years wandering the southern provinces. In 1654, Molière's father, having earlier settled a portion of the family inheritance on his younger son Jean, signed over to this young man the Parisian portion of the family business and the title to the "House with the Picture of Saint Christopher," retaining only his functions as a royal officer. Jean married in January 1656, after which his father mainly lived elsewhere. Soon after his return to Paris, Molière stood as godfather to Jean's infant son, another Jean–Baptiste Poquelin, who would become a lawyer. But a year later, in 1660, brother Jean would suddenly die, before the birth of his second child, Agnès. Molière would also serve as godfather to his sister Madeleine's third child, Madeleine–Grésinde, in 1663 (the

Boudet's second son had already been named after his uncle). Molière would join with Madeleine's husband (as representative of their sons' inheritance) and Jean's widow, Marie Maillard, all joint owners of the "House with the Picture of Saint–Christopher," to rent it to a couple named Bélier in 1669. In 1664, Molière undertook to set up an orphan named Jean Rondeau as apprentice *tapissier* to his father, who was now engaged in a consortium with two other upholsterers and living in the rue de la Comtesse d'Artois. But when the elder Jean Poquelin died in February 1669, he had been living for two years in the rue du Cygne. The death inventory documents passed the next year list Madeleine as deceased, though it is unknown exactly how much earlier she had passed away. This left Molière as the lone survivor of his siblings, except for the nun Catherine, who had been largely raised by her maternal grandmother. He would continue to work with his sister–in–law and brother–in–law to provide for the next generation of Poquelins and Boudets, sometimes lending money to André Boudet when need arose.

Molière's own household would also be stalked by death and the needs of orphaned survivors. His own wife, **Armande–Grésinde Béjart**, was the posthumous child of the elder Joseph **Béjart**, raised in the traveling troupe by her mother, her aunts **Madeleine** and **Geneviève**, and her uncles Joseph and the pugnacious **Louis**.

*See also* **Poquelin, Jean–Baptiste**.

**Porters (*Les Précieuses ridicules*).** Specifically, these porters carry a **sedan chair**, in which **Mascarille** makes his ridiculous entrance in scene 7. Of course, sedan chairs were not usually carried into the house, but dropped their passengers at the door or under a porte–cochère. The unusual demands of Mascarille make the porters even more eager to get their fare. Thus, when Mascarille at first "stiffs" them, then slaps one of them, they protest that his quality doesn't pay for their dinner, and take the sticks from the supports of their chair, preparing to **beat** him. This causes him to open his purse and babble an overly wordy apology.

**Porters (*Les Fourberies de Scapin*).** Nonspeaking roles in the final scene, where they carry in **Scapin** on his stretcher.

***Portrait du peintre, Le (The Painter's Portrait)*.** An invective comedy presented at the **Hôtel de Bourgogne** in 1663 as part of the **Quarrel of the School for Wives**. Under the name of **Edmé Boursault**, it may have involved contributions from other writers and even actors of the company, if we are to believe the character of **Monsieur Lycidas** in *L'Impromptu de Versailles*. It raised against Molière the same scurrilous accusation of incest that **Montfleury's placet** to the King contained, as well as numerous other ad hominem criticisms. The King may have commanded Molière to respond to the attacks onstage, but the result was the *Impromptu*, where the dramatist refuses to give Boursault the publicity he craves by personifying him.

**Portraits.** Miniature portraits were often set in lockets as love tokens. (*See Sganarelle, Mélicerte,* and **Jewelry**.) Portraits of a purely verbal nature were also important, for they became a popular **salon** game among the *précieuses* and other circles. Unlike the effusive, hyperbolic portraits of **Mlle. de Scudéry** and her friends, the ones fashioned by **Célimène** and her clique in the famous "portrait scene" of *Le Misanthrope* (II, 4) are vicious and reductive. Verbal portraits soon found their way into literature, and Célimène's are no exception. The **letters** that **Acaste** and **Clitandre** make public in the final act differ little in style from the ones she lavished upon her listeners earlier. However the context is different. While the intimacy of the clique promised protection for those in the role of listener, the more restricted role of the epistolary correspondent is violated by the contradictory writings and, at the same time, shows the falseness of strictly oral security. Molière precociously demonstrates the fault lines in Classical description by lampooning the vogue of both verbal and written portraits.

**Posiclès** (*Amphitryon*). The general brings in Posiclès and **Argatiphontidas** as witnesses when his first pair are so stunned by **Jupiter's** successful impersonation that they can no longer tell which **Amphitryon** is real. Posicles differs from his fellow **Theban** in his more cautious, **skeptical** approach to the dilemma, whereas Argatiphontidas wants to settle the matter quickly at sword's point.

*Pourceaugnac, Monsieur de.* For the play, *see* **Monsieur de Pourceaugnac**.

**Pourceaugnac, Monsieur de** (*Monsieur de Pourceaugnac*). This **lawyer** from **Limoges** is certainly Molière's most well rounded provincial bumpkin and was one of his most memorable single roles as an actor. He made a strong impression from the moment of his entrance, dressed in a wild **costume** of clashing rainbow colors and shouting derision at unseen individuals in the wings and the audience who dared to **laugh** at him. Out of place from the beginning, he has a habit, like **George Dandin**, of speaking to himself or to no one in particular. He is credulous enough to be taken in by **Éraste** and **Sbrigani**, who approach him with tales of old acquaintances and floods of flattery. We follow him as he becomes increasingly enraged at the **Doctors** who touch him, probe him, and analyze him, when all he expected was to get room and board in their house. As they go on to certify his **madness**, to prescribe a shower of enemas, and to pursue him around the stage with their syringes, he becomes more and more pathetic and risible. Like **Alceste** and other Molière maniacs, he experiences the frustrations of being told he is wrong when he knows he is right, of having his most intimate convictions challenged by outsiders, of helplessly looking on and then fleeing when the world around him seems to have lost all hold on truth.

Pourceaugnac is a character who is searching desperately for an exit almost as soon as he appears onstage. He is not granted his escape until he has endured every imaginable indignity. No sooner does he shake off the anal fixations of his medical advisors than he must deal with another false image of the self. Éraste has already poisoned **Oronte's** mind with rumors that Pourceaugnac is crazy, afflicted with venereal diseases, and hopelessly in debt. For his part, he has learned from Sbrigani that his intended bride is a noted harlot. Thus, his odd greeting scene with the prospective father–in–law, where the two men are wary of each other from the outset and practically snarl with hostility after only a few words (II, 5). **Julie's** hot–blooded embraces seem to confirm what the Limousin had been told, while Oronte also sees his worst fears confirmed. Pourceaugnac has not even had a chance to recover from this surprise when he is confronted by two false wives and three false **children**, arriving supposedly from the far corners of the kingdom to accuse him of bigamy and abandonment. No wonder he exclaims, "Around here, it seems to rain wives and enemas!" (II, 10).

Even in matters legal, where he should enjoy an advantage because of his training, Pourceaugnac is so off balance that he can never manage a response. To preserve his façade of **nobility**, he consults Parisian **lawyers**, who can only sing about how fit he is for hanging. Instead of becoming more himself, he has to **disguise** himself in most outlandish fashion as a woman. The female identity becomes sticky, however, as it leads a pair of over–sexed **Swiss** guards to try to drag him away to bed. Even the **police** patrol that rescues him proves hostile, as they threaten to arrest him if he does not produce a large enough bribe. Spattered and disinfected, insulted and slandered, manhandled and nearly raped, penniless and without identity, Pourceaugnac is only too glad to bid goodbye to **Paris**. Like other bumpkins such as **Poisson's** Baron de la Crasse, he comes to harm in the capital and is chased back to the unfashionable realm where he belongs. His closest analogy in the canon is perhaps **Sosie**, for like the **Greek slave**, he is denied his very being for what seems to him no good reason at all. But in trying to conquer the big city, he has transgressed a dividing line as strong as that between noble and commoner, that of the central locus of taste and the outside darkness where beauty and pleasure do not exist. The fact that he is also trying to pass as an aristocrat only confirms and accentuates his provincial baseness. Could the Molière who escaped debt and honed his skills south of the Loire really be so cruel to those on the periphery of the French kingdom? In returning to Paris did he revive parochial prejudices that had ripened in the shadows of Les Halles? Molière was not the first to write a bumpkin satire and, in fact, was a latecomer to the subgenre. It may be argued that he was only giving his **court** spectators what they desperately wanted, a thrilling rush of superiority that was especially significant during the **hunting** season in the vicinity of **Chambord**, a strange environment fraught with additional anxieties and worries. Perhaps the very cruelty of Pourceaugnac's treatment, coupled with the scurrilous efficiency of his destroyers, invites the possibility of self–criticism, at least with the Parisian component of his audience. If a few citizens of the capital were perceptive enough to realize that one really ought not to act as inhospitably as Éraste or Oronte, certainly anyone from beyond the Loire would have taken notes on how to avoid acting like Pourceaugnac.

***Précieuses ridicules, Les* (*The Affected Young Ladies*).** This one–act **farce** in prose was first presented by Molière on November 18, 1659, following his troupe's production of **Corneille's** *Cinna*. Composed just after Molière's definitive return to **Paris**, *Les Précieuses* was an immediate success and marked the beginning of Molière's career as an author. Many of Molière's innovations are already evident in *Les Précieuses*, specifically the social comedy created using characters from everyday life which became his hallmark. Although very popular, *Les Précieuses* was suspended briefly twice because some of Molière's worldly public were blind to the **satire** and saw only an unflattering mirror of **salons** and *préciosité*. Even today *Les Précieuses* is often viewed as a sourcebook on *préciosité* instead of as a deforming satire.

In *Les Précieuses,* a **bourgeois**, **Gorgibus**, seeks to marry off his daughter **Magdelon** and niece **Cathos**. Two gentlemen arrive to court them and are rebuffed because Cathos and Magdelon, as confirmed *précieuses*, require suitors to follow a strict protocol gleaned from salon literature. Insulted, the young men take vengeance by dressing their valets up as false aristocrats with ways that conform to the *précieuses'* laws. When the true identity of these false "gentlemen" they admire is revealed, the young women are totally humiliated. The play ends with Gorgibus's exhortation that all the literature responsible for the girls' folly be thrown to the **devil**.

*Les Précieuses* contains a satirical catalog of the characteristics associated with *préciosité*. Molière's preface reveals his awareness that he is treading a fine line between amusing the influential salon public and insulting them. Though this work was first published by **Ribou** without the author's permission, Molière republished the play himself in 1660, but with this explanatory preface designed to appease the salon *précieuses*. He states that "true" *précieuses* would be wrong to see themselves in these ridiculous provincial imitations, and thus should not be offended.

Molière's claim to be mocking a provincial version of *préciosité* is problematic, given that the play clearly satirizes *préciosité* as a movement, especially the literature it inspired and created, its use of **language**, and one of the principal women associated with *préciosité*, the novelist **Madeleine de Scudéry**. Under Molière's pen, *préciosité* becomes a disease affecting the minds and tongues of women. The "fault" Molière highlights in *Les Précieuses* is women's desire to govern and thus escape the submissive roles allotted them by society. This desire takes the form of determining social conventions around **marriage**, manners, and language, three actions associated with *préciosité*. Since the literature produced by and for *précieuses* is responsible for the disorder in Gorgibus's house, Molière criticizes in particular writers such as Scudéry who produced such works, as well as the salon public who supported them.

*Les Précieuses ridicules* is Molière's first truly personal work in which he posits a new relationship between **theater** and real life. Perhaps more than any other work, *Les Précieuses*, along with his later *Femmes savantes*, is responsible for society's collective memory of *préciosité* and especially its negative connotation. If this early farce is still appreciated in spite of a context that is totally foreign to today's audience, as the more than 1,500 productions of it at the **Comédie–Française** would suggest, it is because Molière exploits an eternal source of comedy, the chaotic world resulting from people who refuse to conform to society's "**reasonable**" expectations.

See *Les Précieuses ridicules*, ed. Micheline Cuénin (Geneva: Droz, 1973); *Les Précieuses ridicules*, ed. David Shaw (London: Grant and Cutler, 1986); *Les Précieuses ridicules*, ed. Bronnie Treloar (London: Arnold, 1970); Martha Houle, "Plots and Plausibilities in *Les Précieuses ridicules*," *Cahiers du dix–septième* 2 (1988), 123–131.

*Faith E. Beasley*

**Préciosité.** *Préciosité* refers most often to a literary and social phenomenon in mid–seventeenth–century France associated with the **salon** movement. Women who frequented the salons were often referred to collectively as *précieuses*. Most historians locate the *précieuse* period as 1654–1660, but many argue that it started much earlier with **Rambouillet's** salon in the 1630s. *Préciosité* and *précieuse* are terms that resisted and still elude precise and impartial definitions. Much of what we know of *préciosité* is in fact drawn from the movement's **satirists**, especially **de Pure** and Molière. Prior to the mid–1650s, however, *précieuse* was used as a complimentary term describing a woman who wished to distinguish herself from the ordinary, although it was not used by salon women to describe themselves.

It is precisely the notion of distinction that best characterizes *préciosité*. The *Dictionnaire_Historique de la langue française* defines a *précieuse* as "a woman with a refined sensibility who adopts a different, uncommon way of living and speaking." Many salon participants interrogated women's place in society. The *précieuse* came to be associated with a rejection of **marriage** and its attendant role of providing heirs. Many *salonnières* advocated education, believing it would lead to greater freedom for women. The principal salon activities identified with and eventually criticized as *préciosité* included carefully woven conversations on subjects such as emotions, literature, and even **Descartes's philosophy**. Salon women prized friendship over **love** and passion, as is illustrated by the famous "Carte de Tendre" developed in Scudéry's salon. Many of these themes were further explored in the **novels** written in and around the salons, often penned by the *salonnières* themselves, the two most famous writers being **Scudéry** and Lafayette.

A second characteristic of the salons, and thus *préciosité*, is the desire for refined, elegant, and purified language. Vulgar, common terms were rejected in favor of a descriptive and precise vocabulary and style, often characterized by superlatives. This style is particularly evident in the poetry emanating from the salons, that of **Voiture** being the quintessential example. In addition to distinguishing themselves as writers — novels, literary **portraits**, and poetry being their genres of predilection — salon women were also known as literary critics who judged their contemporaries' works according to the criteria of "good taste" and "*bienséance*" or **propriety** as opposed to the rules defined by the traditional intellectual elite.

The drive toward linguistic, literary, and social distinction inspired critics, many of whom in the late 1650s viewed this desire for distinction as simply affectation. Thanks to satirists such as de Pure and Molière, the terms *précieuse* and *préciosité* came to connote prudes, coquettes, and women who ineptly tried to become learned. Some critics argue that the backlash resulting in the negative connotation of *préciosité* was primarily directed against those who carried the phenomenon too far. Others argue that the satire should be interpreted as an attempt to control an early feminist movement. Whatever the position taken, the vehemence of these satires attests to the fact that *préciosité* had a profound effect on the classical literary field, as well as on the social fabric of the Old Regime.

*Faith E. Beasley*

**Princess (*La Princesse d'Élide*).**  This role, played originally by **Armande Béjart,** is interesting chiefly as a study in perverse psychology and paradoxical effect.  She resembles the famous Classical figure of Hippolytus in the beginning of the play, since she has renounced **love** in favor of vigorous pursuits like **hunting,** and prefers forests to palaces.  Though she tries to assume the place of *meneur du jeu*, controlling the course of the action by preempting her father's speeches in favor of **marriage**, she quickly falls into **Euryale's** trap, demonstrating pique at his indifference to her and vowing to try to seduce him for punishment.  She attempts to establish an interesting double standard in Act III by saying that it is proper for females to avoid love, but fitting for males to engage in it.  When the Prince cleverly parries this argument, she reveals the depth of her contrariness: "His pride confounds me so that I am drowned in spite and no longer feel myself."  Outmaneuvered at every point in her guessing games with Euryale, she struggles in her grand soliloquy (IV, 6) with the hidden enemy, bidding it to take physical form as even the most fearsome beast, so that she can slay it.  But by this time she has been reduced to much the same level as Chimène in **Pierre Corneille's** *Le Cid*, acting and arguing in spite of herself. When she tries to block Euryale's threatened marriage with **Aglante** in the final act, she finds herself in a similarly compromised position, obliged to lie that she hates the Prince because he scorned her good looks, and confused when her father offers her the alternative of marrying him herself.  Her final plea for more time to reflect and adjust to her fate echoes Corneille's famous heroine.

**Princess Palatine, Charlotte–Élisabeth of Bavaria** (1652–1722).  The second wife of **Monsieur**, this lady was generally referred to by the above title to distinguish her from **Henrietta of England**, her predecessor and much beloved **Madame**.  Her acquaintance with Molière dated from the time of the **marriage** in December 1671, since the **Ballet des Ballets** held in honor of the event contained the premiere of *La Comtesse d'Escarbagnas*.  The Princess was a very intelligent and sometimes irreverent member of the **court** and a particular friend of the great **Condé**, whom she joined in supporting Molière during their brief overlapping interval in **Paris**.

*Princesse d'Élide, La* (*The Princess of Elis*).   A "comédie galante" first performed at **Versailles** on May 8, 1664, during the royal festival, *Les Plaisirs de l'île enchantée*, for which Molière composed it.  The five–act play begins in verse, but switches abruptly to prose in the second act.  A notice inserted at that point (II, 1, 366) explains that the time limits imposed by the royal commission obliged Molière to abandon his plan of composing all five acts in verse and to abbreviate several scenes.

The play is courtly rather than comic in inspiration.  The Prince d'Elide, recognizing his daughter's aversion to **love** and **marriage**, invites neighboring princes to participate in a series of games, hoping that one of them may win her affections.  One of those suitors, **Euryale**, shares the princess's temperament.  However, although he has long been impervious to her beauty, he is captivated by her prideful "disdain" for her suitors.  He eventually wins the princess's heart by feigning an indifference as haughty as her own.  This slender plot is considerably enlivened by the presence of the princess's buffoon **Moron**, played by Molière.

Moron especially shines in the play's six *intermèdes*, in which critics have seen a reflection by Molière on the character of his art, expanded by his collaboration with **Lully**.  The four *intermèdes* interspersed between the acts offer a comic counterpoint to the courtly plot.  Moron's antics include an attempt to learn singing from a **satyr** (*Third intermède*, scene 2) and an unsuccessful performance of an air by Lully (*Fourth intermède*, scene 2).  The much admired prologue brilliantly combines the poetic and comic themes of the work.  Moron especially shines in the play's six *intermèdes*, in which the playwright's words merge with dance and Lully's music.  Aurore's poetic address to the audience gives way to Molière as the sleepy valet **Lycisas**, who resists in spoken prose the singers' efforts to rouse him. The concluding ballet featured a **theatrical machine**: a tree bearing sixteen musicians dressed as fauns, which emerged from the stage floor.

Molière adapted the plot from **Moreto's Spanish** comedy, "El Desden con el Desden" (1654), replacing the Spanish characters and setting with **Greek** ones.  The princess's relationship to the Spanish heroine Diana is covertly acknowledged when she is compared to the goddess **Diane**, devoted only to the hunt (Act I, lines 71–72).  In Molière's hands, nonetheless, this plot takes on a distinctively French flavour.  The princess's pronouncements sound like those of a Parisian *précieuse*: "Shouldn't you blush to have promoted a passion that is only a mistake, a weakness, and a scandal, whose disorders clash so repugnantly with the good name of our fair sex?"  The *intermède*" on the other hand, are drawn from the pastoral, a genre traditionally devoted to love.  Molière seems particularly to have recalled the famous pastoral drama *Il pastor fido* (1590), by the Italian poet Guarini.  The audience, in any event, would have been amused by his pastiches of such well–worn conventions of pastoral drama and romance as the lover's interrogation of Echo or his suicidal tendency.

*La Princesse d'Elide* was intimately tied to the royal festival for which it was written. When published in the seventeenth century, it was always ensconced within the official narrative of Les Plaisirs de l'île enchantée. This context considerably enriches the play, revealing how skillfully Molière handled his assignment as court dramatist, coordinating his derivative materials with the frame and turning his play into a mirror of the young **court** at play. Much as Roger (**Louis XIV**) was supposed to have conceived the festival's entertainments as a reenactment of Apollonian games, so does Molière's plot involve games in Elide (the country of the Olympiad). After repeated echos of the festal frame, the play concludes as the fictive Greek court, like its French counterpart, sits down to be entertained by the final *intermède*. Throughout, Molière exploits an ambiguity in the festival as a whole, which was dedicated to the Queen, but which many saw as a tribute to the royal mistress **Louise de La Vallière**, the Alcine who had charmed the young monarch. Depicting the daughter of a prince who will eventually marry her royal suitor, *La Princesse d'Elide* could pass muster as a tribute to the Queen. But the heroine's abilities as huntress and horsewoman simultaneously evoked La Vallière. Moreover, most commentators view the play's opening dialogue, in which Euryale's preceptor sees in his charge's inclination to love the mark of a "finished prince" (Act I, line 44), as an homage to the enamored Louis XIV.

The play was staged in an elaborate outdoor theater constructed for the occasion. Israël Silvestre's engraving of the performance famously depicts the first row of spectators from the rear. The king sits in the center, perfectly placed to appreciate the perspective stage. The engraving also depicts the links between the play and the festival at large, as well as the participation of the other spectators. Thus, the theater's walls and proscenium arch are painted with greenery, bringing the festival's setting in the gardens of Versailles into the theater. Out of the trees peer faces turned toward the stage, emphasizing the presence of the entire court, entranced along with the King by Alcine's enchantments. The stage seems to project the scene into the audience, while the actors' elegant contemporary **costumes** recall those of the spectators, and the long rows of hedges prolong the greenery on the theater's walls.

Molière's troupe would later perform *La Princesse d'Elide* for the court, at **Fontainebleau** in July of 1664 and at **Saint–Germain** in 1669. The play's only public performances were at the Palais Royal Theater between November 9, 1664, and January 4, 1665. Revived in the late seventeenth and early eighteenth centuries, the play was last performed in 1745.

*Kathleen Wine*

**Promé, Pierre**. Parisian printer involved with the publication of *Les Femmes savantes* in 1672.

**Proprieties**. Early in the seventeenth century, a system of theatrical proprieties (*bienséances*) developed as part of the regularization of drama. One set of prohibitions protected against acts of violence or indecency. Combats, rapes, and bloody deaths were not to take place onstage. At the time of **Pierre**

**Corneille's** *Le Cid*, the limits of these proscriptions, which were never formally codified, were still being worked out. The instances of a slap that takes place on stage, swords that are at least partly drawn, and a man who appears in a lady's room with the bloody weapon that had slain her father were considered by some to be beyond the point of tolerance. But this was already a big change from the era of Alexandre Hardy, when stranglings, poisonings, stabbings, and even rapes were known to be depicted onstage. Apart from visual decency, a further extension of these proprieties applied to **language**. Indecent words or expressions were not permitted. This presented some difficulties in comedy, where certain kinds of jokes were inevitable. Molière tested the limits of these conventions in **Monsieur de Pourceaugnac**, where a couple of **Swiss** guards make very indecent proposals to the protagonist when he is **disguised** as a lady. He may have gotten away with this because of the fact that the provocative words were spoken in a kind of dialect by non–French characters. But a vocabulary of permitted terms gradually evolved and maintained its unwritten authority. For example, "courtisan" was permitted, but "putain" was usually not, though both words mean "whore." By the same token, "tétin" (nipple) was allowed, while "sein" (breast) was generally replaced through metonymy by "gorge" (throat). "Cul" (anus) was permitted when figurative, but not when literal. The private parts could only be alluded to by rather oblique wordings. Molière mainly stirred controversy in this area when he wrote *L'École des femmes*, which contains some obviously equivocal jokes about female body parts, even though they are never named, as in the famous scene where **Agnès** confesses that she lost "le — ." **Arnolphe** and the audience assume the missing word is "pucelage" (maidenhead) until she explains innocently that the lost item was only a ribbon. After answering his critics and defending his drama, Molière went on with more or less the same kind of humor.

Another set of proprieties protected things that were sacred: God, priests, and sacraments were not to be presented in the theater. For some time, biblical plays were granted an exception, provided they confined themselves to the Old Testament and its figures. Thus, **Pierre Du Ryer's** *Saül* can show the Witch of Endor and the **ghost** of the prophet Samuel with impunity, but mystery plays showing the Passion had been banned since the turn of the century on the grounds that they risked polluting sacred material with vulgar elements. Once again, *L'École des femmes* ruffled many feathers by the **religious** language Arnolphe uses to justify his authority, which contains references to **convents**, nuns, and hell. The Maxims of Marriage he has Agnès recite were extremely close in terminology to some real devotional literature commonly used by spiritual **directors**. But his biggest controversy erupted over the 1664 *Tartuffe*, which not only increased the volume and range of religious terminology, but dressed the villain in garb almost identical to that of a priest. Molière mitigated both **costume** and **language** in his second version of the play, *The Impostor*. However, the final 1669 production actually returned somewhat to the original in some ways.

Molière's brinksmanship with the proprieties was remarkably adroit and he avoided many problems in life through the protection of **Louis XIV**. However, he was posthumously attacked time and again, especially after the King underwent a pious conversion in the 1680s. Major ecclesiastical figures such as **Bourdaloue** and **Bossuet** lashed out at his immorality and impiety. It mattered little to them that the comedies written after Molière's death were generally much more cynical in their depiction of morality and religion. Their charges would be taken up during the Enlightenment by opportunistic authors such as **Riccoboni** and **J.–J. Rousseau**, who adopted a holier–than–Molière attitude to further their own religious and political agendas.

**Proverbs.** English readers and spectators are not always able to appreciate how Molière tapped the rich store of proverbial sayings available to his audience. Only when a character like **Sganarelle** in *Dom Juan* cites a well–known fable to say "the pitcher can only go to the well so many times before it breaks" (V, 2) does one appreciate the appeal to folk wisdom. When the earthy **Martine** says, "They tell the truth when they say that a man who wants to drown his dog accuses it of being rabid" (*Les Femmes savantes*, II, 5), one can easily infer that she is drawing on age–old speech patterns of her rural origins. As in these two examples, Molière mainly puts proverbs in the mouths of **servants, peasants**, and unrepentant **bourgeois**. He does not abuse the practice, however, as some of his rivals did, but judiciously selects a few pithy remarks per play to give color to the characters who need it. These well–chosen morsels supply just the right tone, as one would expect from the "fresco" approach he advocates to artistic creation in *La Gloire du Val de Grâce*.

*Psyché*. This five–act free verse **comedy–ballet** was actually a super–spectacular beyond the scope of earlier entertainments. It was commissioned for the neglected **Tuileries Theater** because **Louis XIV** wanted to make use of some splendid scenery of the underworld left behind from the **opera** *Ercole amante*. The theme of **Cupid** and Psyche, originally from Apuleius's *Golden Ass* and recently redone as a ballet by **Bensserade** and as a novel by **La Fontaine**, thus suggested itself. The Tuileries Theater was equipped with elaborate stage **machinery** designed by the great Italian machinist Vigarani, which permitted special effects on a scale never before contemplated, including the elevation into the sky of 300 musicians in the finale. Given a firm deadline, Molière was able to finish versifying only the first act and the first two scenes of Acts II and III. He hired **Pierre Corneille** to finish the rest "in a fortnight," while **Lully** and **Quinault** handled the **music** and libretto and Beauchamp's dancing corps was mobilized for the choreography. Several grand performances were given in the Tuileries, beginning on January 17, 1671 (meanwhile, the troupe continued to perform *Bérénice* and *Le Bourgeois gentilhomme* in a very successful alternation at their own theater). The great success of this first production led to plans for refurbishing the Palais Royal Theater and resuming performances there after the Lenten break. By July the arrangements and rehearsals were completed and the first performance took place on the July 24. It was an overwhelming triumph that only added to the prosperity the troupe had enjoyed ever since *Tartuffe* was finally allowed onstage. Of course, some reduction in the sheer manpower involved was necessary, for even with new machines the Palais Royal Theater could not manage the huge groups of entertainers present for the Tuileries version. Publication followed not much later, since there was little fear that a rival troupe could steal the show on account of its prohibitive expense.

The plot is extremely simple and follows well–established lines. In the first act, Psyche's **jealous** sisters **Aglaure** and **Cidippe** bemoan their sibling's greater success with males, then try to waylay a pair of princes who have come to visit her. The princes jointly propose to Psyche, who **politely** refuses them and tries to steer them toward her ill–mannered sisters, to no avail. Then **Lycas** arrives with a terrible **message** that the oracle has decreed Psyche must be sacrificed, which causes the sisters' spirits to rise considerably.

The beginning of the second act shows Psyche taking leave of her royal father, whose thoughts on her **childhood** and complaints against the injustice of the gods are quite interesting and unique. Corneille followed Molière's plans for the rest of the act by having the sisters visit next, gloating over their triumph, then the princes, who try fruitlessly to save Psyche, before she is eventually carried off, not by a monster, but by a **zephyr** sent by Cupid, who has fallen in love with the victim.

Molière's beginning to the third act features the zephyr, which he played himself, conversing with Cupid in a kind of banter that recalls *Amphitryon*. Corneille adds scenes where Cupid introduces himself incognito to his captive, arranges a visit from her sisters, and confesses his passion. The envious sisters arrive in Act IV and take advantage of Psyche's innocence before they are whisked away by the zephyr. Psyche presses Cupid to reveal his identity, but when she finally forces him to do so, he departs in a huff and the palace changes into a wilderness where the princess tries to drown herself. The local **river god** takes her into custody and hands her over to **Venus**, who takes her into the underworld for the final act. There she retrieves a mysterious box for the goddess and meets the **ghosts** of her two princely suitors, who have in the meantime succumbed to their grief. She opens the box and faints, setting off a supernatural row between Cupid and his mother, which is only appeased by the approach of **Jupiter**, who gives Psyche to Cupid to be his heavenly bride.

The success of the production can be explained entirely by the spectacular effects, which were prized by the audience. Though scholars and lovers of Molière tend to place little importance on the work today, it is significant as the playwright's nearest approach to operatic form. It carries forward his experiments in free verse, leaving us to regret that he was not able to go further with this medium. It also contributed to some degree to the upcoming quarrels between Molière and Lully, who seems to have resented the lack of recognition and remuneration that he got from his contribution to the project. One can understand that he feared being cut out of the rosy future of the Paris opera and decided to act first to ensure that he would have the lion's share. An interesting sidelight is that the production involved many **children** of the cast, including Molière's daughter **Esprit–Madeleine**, and gave some of them their first opportunities on stage.

*See* Philip Wadsworth, "The Composition of Psyché," *Rice University Studies* 53.4 (1967), 69–76.

**Psyche (*Psyche*).** Played by **Armande Béjart**, the part of the heroine gives ample opportunity to show off her verbal as well as physical charms. Though she is naïve as a judge of human and divine nature, Psyche is engaging and perfectly **polite**. Her dealings with the princes in the first act show that she can find dignified ways to reject unwanted suitors, using their own outstanding qualities of friendship as a basis for her negative judgment. In conversation with her father in the second act, she shows filial tenderness, but is less successful in her efforts to have him stop grieving and railing against the gods. This is perhaps because his passion is much stronger than hers, for she mainly raises Stoical arguments that he easily smashes, sounding much like Molière himself in his poetic advice to **La Mothe Le Vayer** when the **philosopher** lost his son.

**Pure, Michel, abbé de** (1620–1680). This polygraph was the author of a number of light works about the "**précieux**" movement, some of which may have served as sources for Molière's *Les Précieuses ridicules*, but others of which certainly postdate it. He seems to have been an intimate of the **Corneille** family, to judge by his correspondence with **Thomas**.

**Purgon, Monsieur (*Le Malade imaginaire*).** **Argan's** personal physician, like the **apothecary Fleurant**, is much talked about during the course of the play, but appears only in one scene (III, 5). Enraged at the fact that one of his prescriptions has not been followed (**Béralde** had just chased away Fleurant with the help of one of his own enemas), Purgon declares Argan guilty of treason against the Faculty of Medicine. He tears up the act transferring his wealth to his nephew (this was to have been the husband's dower for **marriage** with **Angélique**) and whines about the miraculous cures he was to have brought the patient. Then he pronounces a terrible curse of indigestion leading to upset stomach, leading to digestive malfunction, leading to diarrhea, leading to bloody dysentery, leading to total organic breakdown, and finally death. Neither **Diafoirus** nor the fake **doctor** impersonated by **Toinette** confirms Purgon's diagnosis of liver trouble, and the latter overturns all his dietary prescriptions. Though visible for only a short time, Purgon is one of the more formidable medical scarecrows raised by Molière, who may have thought too many lines would spoil the effect. The part may have been doubled with **Monsieur Bonnefoy**, perhaps by **Du Croisy** or **Hubert**.

**Pyrrhonians.** *See* **Skepticism.**

**Pythian Games.** These sacred contests are mentioned in *Les Amants magnifiques*, where they are supposedly taking place in **Thessaly**. In fact, they were held every four years at **Delphi**, in Phocia, since they were dedicated to **Apollo's** Pythian oracle, located there.

# Q

**Quarrel of the School for Wives**. Almost at soon as *L'École des femmes* premiered on December 26, 1662, ink began to flow in great quantities both in criticism and in praise of the box–office success. **Donneau de Visé**, who let his critical shotgun blast in many directions, advanced a number of objections to the play in his *Zélinde, ou la critique de l'École des femmes*, some of which he had formulated earlier against Molière in his *Nouvelles nouvelles*. Molière effectively countered the aesthetic complaints against his play in *La Critique de l'École des femmes*. While most of Donneau's barbs were of a nit–picking and textual nature, **Edmé Boursault** savaged Molière's personal life as well in *Le Portrait du peintre*, going beyond the charge of cuckoldry to those of adultery and incest. In sexual terms, the playwright's enemies felt he was damned if he did and damned if he didn't! These libelous charges could have been answered in kind, as some of the characters urge in *L'Impromptu de Versailles*. However, Molière used the latter play to achieve success on a very different plane, striking a definitive blow against the instigators in the **Hôtel de Bourgogne** by parodying their bloated tragic acting styles, while dismissing Boursault as unworthy even of his contempt. At this point, both royal and public favor weighed in heavily on Molière's side, with the King adding him to the crown's stipend list and the impartial chronicler **Robinet** issuing unqualified praise in his *Panégyrique de l'École des femmes*. Literary support, too, came in the form of poetic tributes from **Boileau** and his circle and the comedy *La Guerre comique, ou la Défense de l'École des femmes*, by Philippe La Croix. In this short play the gods themselves discuss Molière's masterpiece and pronounce it good. Molière's opponents persisted with **Antoine Montfleury's** *Impromptu de l'Hôtel de Condé* and Donneau's *Vengeance des marquis*. But the effect of these writings was negligible and Donneau himself soon switched sides and began writing for the **Palais–Royal**. By Easter of 1664, the controversy was dying down. Death soon removed other enemies, such as Montfleury's actor father, who had gone so far as to petition the King regarding

Molière's alleged sexual crimes. The trials and tribulations of *Tartuffe* also foreshortened the quarrel, bringing more sinister forces than the inkwell into play.

See also *Lettre sur la comédie de l'Imposteur*; **Roullé**.

**Queen Mother.** *See* **Anne of Austria.**

**Quinault, Paul** (1635–1688). Author at first of comedies, tragicomedies, and tragedies, this rival of Molière would come to emulate him in some of his later works and eventually to distinguish himself in the newly developed domain of **opera**. Quinault adapted **Beltrame's** *L'Inavvertito* at about the same time as Molière, calling his play *L'Amant indiscret ou le Maître étourdi*. It reached the printer several years before Molière's work, in 1656, which probably meant that the actors had released the text since it had fulfilled its useful stage life. Quinault's *La Comédie sans comédie* (1654) is noted as an interesting metatheatrical text of the time. His best comedy, *La Mére coquette ou les amants brouillés* (produced in 1665, published the next year) owes much to the style of Molière, but was produced by the **Hôtel de Bourgogne** in competition with **Donneau de Visé's** play by the same name that was on the bill of the **Palais–Royal**. Donneau claimed that Quinault had copied his play, and the chronicler **Robinet** seemed to agree. Though Molière gave Quinault the place of librettist for all the singing passages of *Psyché* except the prologue, Quinault seems not to have been one of his inner circle, if one is to judge from the rather savage criticism that **Boileau** unleashed on him from time to time. His association with **Lully** in the French opera after 1671 confirms this disharmony.

**Quinet, Gabriel.** One of the leading theatrical printers in **Paris** and publisher of Molière's *L'Étourdi* and *Dépit amoureux* (1663), *L'École des maris*, and the **"Remerciement au Roi."** He was part of the eight–printer coalition that published *L'École des femmes* and *La Critique de l'École des femmes*.

**Quintilian.** Among the Classical authors cited by the pedant **Métaphraste** in his conversation with **Albert** in *Dépit amoureux*, Act II.

# R

**Rabelais, François** (ca. 1490–1553). The author of *Gargantua* and *Pantagruel* was not exactly required schoolboy reading in the seventeenth century, but Molière must have enjoyed these "naughty," challenging epics, all the more so because they paralleled his own comical and skeptical tendencies. Rabelaisian spirit abounds in the more **farcical** scenes of Molière's comedies, but is nowhere more prominent than in *Le Mariage forcé*. Here, **Sganarelle's** quest for affirmation of his **marriage** plans, by earthly or supernatural means, recalls the theme of the *Tiers Livre*, where Panurge seeks the same vain reassurance and gets the same reply: marry if you will, but forsake guarantees against cuckoldry if you do. The connection to Panurge is made more explicit in Sganarelle's interview with **Pancrace**. The latter asks the burgher which **language** he would like to converse in, and reels off a litany of most European and some Oriental tongues. This recalls the scene in *Pantagruel* where Panurge first appears, bidding good day in virtually every known language (and a few imaginary ones) before settling into French. Molière also mentions Panurge specifically, along with Pantagruel, in the first scene of *L'École des femmes*, where **Chrysalde** compares his conversation with **Arnolphe** to a passage from Rabelais. The *Quart Livre* may have given Molière the idea for **Chrysale** in *Les Femmes savantes* to press his collars in the pages of an immense book. Also, the name of the **Pyrrhonian philosopher**, **Marphurius**, may have come from Rabelais. Along with the *Satire Ménippée*, Rabelais was part of the late medieval literature that linked Molière's comedy back to that of the urban classes of the Middle Ages.

**Racine, Jean** (1639–1699). Born in northeastern France in La Ferté–Milon, Racine was orphaned at a young age and spent much of his formative period in the **Jansenist** model schools at Port–Royal des Champs, where he was imbued with **Greek** literature. The combination of Jansenism's grim doctrines of persistent original sin and the Euripidean outlook on fatal passion combined to form the backbone of the tragedies for which he would later become famous.

He must have felt a dramatic vocation at an early age, for it was over this issue that he broke with Port–Royal and its moralism, when the Jansenist Nicole blamed the **theater** for much of the age's depravity. Ecclesiastical relatives packed Racine off to Uzès, in the remote Cévennes region of the south, but after several months there he abandoned the idea of a place in the Church and began leading the life of a playboy in **Paris**.

Successfully seeking royal favor by addressing encomiastic verses to the crown, Racine also prevailed on Parisian connections with **La Fontaine** and **Boileau** to gain an introduction to Molière. At this stage, Molière was casting about to find a steady tragic author for his troupe, without much luck. Even established poets such as Boyer and **Corneille** did not seem to be able to come up with a major success. Thus, the leader was happy to encounter a talented young drama lover eager to try his pen in the tragic genre. His first effort, *La Thébaïde ou les frères ennemis,* debuted in the slack period of June 1664, but the troupe made every effort to maintain it, keeping it onstage for over a dozen public performances, plus prestigious private visits before the King and **Monsieur**. Though they had been for years the object of much criticism for their lack of tragic expertise, Molière and his companions did all they could to nurture the new talent. They eagerly accepted his *Alexandre le grand* the next year and gave it a wonderful opportunity for a premiere on December 4 in the prime pre–Christmas season. When they learned, after seven fairly successful performances (four of them in the range of 1,000 *livres* for the house), that Racine had taken the unprecedented step of giving the script to the rival **Hôtel de Bourgogne**, it was a bitter blow. He had not even given notice to Molière's company, so they had to learn of the defection when the competition put up their posters. There was little compensation in dividing up among the players the author's share that would have gone to Racine, about 500 *livres*. Molière's troupe continued to show the same play, with much diminished receipts, for three more performances, until an event came that — perhaps mercifully — ended the head–to–head competition. The death of the **Queen Mother** brought a halt to all spectacles and the mourning period lasted well into February. The troupe managed to eke out what would normally have been the most remunerative part of the year by reviving *L'Amour médecin* and filling in with **repertory** pieces. During the Lenten break, their major tragic actress, **Mlle. Du Parc**, left them and followed Racine to the Hôtel de Bourgogne, probably for personal as well as professional reasons.

From Easter of 1666 onward, the relations between Racine and Molière formed part of the larger adversarial struggle between the two major French theater companies. It is to the credit of both dramatists that they did not enter into a direct personal feud over the *Alexandre* affair. When the Palais Royal troupe challenged Racine's *Andromaque*, it was through the intermediary of **Subligny's** *Folle Querelle*, and when Racine responded, it was by composing in 1668 *Les Plaideurs,* in an attempt to wrest the comic crown from his former colleagues. Perhaps the most direct confrontation came in 1671, when Racine's *Bérénice* was pitted against Corneille's *Tite et Bérénice*. But participating in this "Battle of the Tragic Titans" was simply good business sense on the part of

Molière's troupe. They could not afford to let such a good play fall into the hands of the **Marais**, and *Tite et Bérénice* was a solid box office success despite the critical palms that went to Racine. It is ironic that when Racine was beset by the opposition of his enemies to *Phèdre* in 1677, Boileau wrote him a consoling poetic epistle that evoked Molière's perseverence in the face of trouble. Boileau argued that great geniuses are not truly recognized until after they die, but that during their lifetime they are attacked by all sorts of petty men. He urged Racine, fruitlessly as it turned out, to pay no attention to the detractors. Less persistent than Molière, Racine ceased writing for the public theater after *Phèdre*.

Following Molière's death, it is well known that Racine went on to some of his most sublime artistic triumphs and his bitterest professional defeats. However, it may be argued that his semi–retirement from the stage had less to do with the Cabale's defeat of *Phèdre* than with his own ascension to the dignities of academician and royal historiographer. This, combined with other changes in his personal life, demanded a distancing from the "vile" world of the professional theater. He would indulge his last creative urges by composing his biblical plays *Athalie* and *Esther* for the girls of the Saint–Cyr school.

The Racine bibliography is immense, but two relatively recent sources that act as good points of departure are Alain Niderst, *Les Tragédies de Racine, diversité et unité* (1975) and Odette de Mourgues, *Racine, or the Triumph of Relevance* (1967).

**Raguenau, Marie** (1639–1720). Daughter of a poetry–loving pastry cook, this actress specialized in lively **servant** roles. Her father had joined Molière's troupe in **Lyon** in 1654, but died the same year. Marie and her mother stayed with the troupe, helping to operate the box office. At first, she only acted occasionally. One of her early roles with the troupe may have been that of **Marotte** in *Les Précieuses ridicules,* since that was also her nickname. Another might have been the mute part of **Flipote** in *Tartuffe*. In 1671, she played one of **Psyche's jealous** sisters, perhaps the less voluble **Cidippe**. In December of the same year she premiered in the title role of *La Comtesse d'Escarbagnas*, a part of considerable **satirical** depth and interest. She married **La Grange** in 1672, thus obtaining a handsome, familiar, and moderately rich husband. Though she was then taken into the troupe as a partner, she received only a partial share in view of her relatively limited acting skills. Nevertheless, she continued to act alongside La Grange through the eras of the Palais Royal Theater, the Hôtel Guénégaud, and the **Comédie–Française**, retiring only after his death, at Eastertide of 1692.

*Raisonneur*. Beginning in the Enlightenment, there has been a strong tendency to identify certain individual characters in Molière's theater as "reasoners" who speak with the voice of the author himself. While it is true that some characters are given passages reflecting a reasoned view that is clearly given approval by the playwright, and presumably the audience as well, one should not assume that these viewpoints are universally valid and applicable in all circumstances. Drama is, after all, a polyphonic medium and truth emerges contextually from the dialogues of all characters taken together, not from a single discourse isolated from the text. Let us consider **Chrysalde** in *L'École des femmes* as an example. When he criticizes **Arnolphe's** odd attitudes on **marriage**, his obsession with cuckoldry, and his projects for usurpation, he is speaking not only on his own account, but for all the other townspeople that Arnolphe is trying to bully. His opinion then carries the added weight of collective censure that Arnolphe is foolish to ignore. When he talks about the possible positive aspects of cuckoldry, he is obviously operating on more private and hypothetical ground. He becomes a comic opposite to Arnolphe, underestimating cuckoldry as much as his partner overrates it, and thus not a voice of unadulterated reason, but an individual voice with its individual faults.

Some of Molière's most successful "reasoners" evince approbation from the public by defending the interests of the family. **Cléante** in *Tartuffe* and **Béralde** in *Le Malade imaginaire* are notable in this regard. However, it is also worthwhile to note that they are often less than effective, especially when they try to reason on abstract and universal terms. As good as their arguments may sound to the audience, it is reasonable to assume that they cannot overcome the universalist tendencies of the maniac interlocutors, who literally believe that the world revolves around their pet ideas. **La Fontaine** and **La Rochefoucauld** would make the same point in their respective genres, that abstract reason is useless when self–interest presents a powerful contrary force.

It is not the numbers onstage that determine a character's collective stance, but rather his ability to evoke a larger constituency out in the audience. Thus, in *La Critique de l'École des femmes* Molière's defenders are quite outnumbered, but they are able to identify with much larger bodies of spectators, while the playwright's enemies isolate themselves in their foolish ideas. In *Le Misanthrope*, **Alceste** is able to challenge the laughers of **Célimène's salon** by pointing out their selfishness and their inability to sustain their gossip in public. **Clitandre** is almost all alone in *Les Femmes savantes* when he defends the **court** against **Philaminte's** clique, but his strength lay beyond the border of the stage, where the spectators identified with his opinions.

To conclude, one may say that just as Molière rejected the effectiveness of philosophical systems that operate in the realm of total abstraction, he tends to reject reason, no matter how appealing and well constructed, if it does not cohere to a given set of needs and situations. The strongest reasoners are those who strike a collective chord and thus relate to the widest possible mentality.

**Rambouillet**. A prominent noble family of seventeenth–century **Paris** that took their name from a *marquisat* and maintained a fine townhouse or *hôtel* where a great literary **salon** assembled. The glory years of the Hôtel de Rambouillet were slightly before Molière's time, when occasional poets outdid themselves to celebrate the charms of the noted beauty Julie d'Angennes, daughter of the marquis. She eventually married the **Duke of Montauzier**, who had wooed her with poetry. Anecdotes claim that Molière was angry at **Cotin** and **Ménage**

because they told the Rambouillet circle that Montauzier was the model for **Alceste**. This is supposedly the reason he **satirized** them so personally in *Les Femmes savantes*.    Another daughter, Angélique–Clarisse, married the Count of Grignan, and it was this lady who is said to have served as a model for Molière's *précieuses*. If so, it did not prevent the marquis and his family from commissioning several visits from the troupe.

**Reason**.    Along with **Nature**, Reason was a key element in Molière's comic formula. However, he was not a simple rationalist, nor did he follow **Descartes** as far as believing that Reason alone could be trusted to supply an answer for every dilemma.   In fact, the most Cartesian figures in Molière's theater may well be figures such as **Arnolphe**, **Alceste**, and **Monsieur Jourdain**, who have a rigid sense of reason rooted in their own selfish desires and wish to impose it on the world around them.  By always forging ahead in their chosen direction, they do not ever find their way to their sought–after goal, but only manage to isolate themselves and cede the social terrain to wiser and more adaptive personalities. For other characters, such as **Sganarelle** in *Le Mariage forcé*, reason comes too late to influence the critical choices in life.   Clearly such *ex post facto* reason is as good as none at all.   Molière seems to favor a kind of reason that is kept in balance with personal and collective tastes.   Wisest is the man who can direct his reason to that which would be best for his own circumstances. Unfortunately, as **Alceste** points out, reason is not strong enough to guide taste absolutely or to overcome strong and perverse urges that often spring from human nature itself. If reason cannot always set the course, it can still, however, affect the outcome of life's voyage by allowing adaptation.   In this sense, Molière's notion of reason approaches the doctrines of **politeness** and *honnêteté*, providing an other–directed framework that facilitates human intercourse and mitigates the flights of sincerity.

Remembering that Molière is primarily **skeptical** in his thought, one should expect that his reason would be closely linked with doubt.  It often works in a negative sense, searching out what is unreasonable and avoiding it.  Unreason is usually associated with some form of eccentricity or extremism that refuses to recognize the limits Nature places on all living things.   Thus, we see the importance of **Philinte's** formula for the entire Molière canon: "Perfect reason flees all extremity / And tempers wisdom with sobriety."

**Récit**.  French term for a speech recounting action that takes place offstage. This is often necessary in order to preserve the **unities** or the **proprieties**.  For example, **Philinte** delivers a piquant *récit* of **Alceste's** visit to the **Marshals'** court at the beginning of Act IV of *Le Misanthrope* because French standards would not allow this scene to be shown onstage.   **Orgon** recounts his first encounter with **Tartuffe** in church because it was impossible to represent a holy place in the theater.   On the other hand, some *récits* are simply elements of dramatic style, such as the ones given by **Horace** in *L'École des femmes*, which have great comic weight as retrospective accounts but would not have been very funny if presented directly in the action.

**Relative of Sganarelle (*Sganarelle*).** The minor character appears only for a moment, to cast doubt on the veracity of Sganarelle's claims to cuckoldry.

**Religion.** In principle, Molière's theater was separated from the orthodox Catholicism of **Louis XIV's** France in several ways. The laws of propriety prohibited theaters from showing religious ceremonies or people, such as priests, onstage. Thus such rites as funerals or **marriages** were banned, though the latter could be represented by the obligatory civil ceremonies of the marriage contract passed before a notary. By Molière's time, even plays based on saints or on the Old Testament had become rather rare, though they were still a staple of the previous generation. **Racine** would write his religious plays for private performance at the royal girls' school. Actors themselves were officially excommunicated *en bloc* by virtue of their profession. This did not prevent them from attending church under their civil identities or having their children baptized. St. Germain–l'Auxerrois was even considered the actors' church. Molière's own family was apparently quite regular in its observances. An aunt was in the **Convent** of the Annunciation at Langres and one of his sisters became a Visitandine nun.

The problem of religion in his plays first arises in *L'École des femmes*. **Arnolphe** employs a vocabulary strewn with religious terms, had **Agnès** schooled in stupidity in a convent, makes her study the devotional Maxims of Marriage, and refers at length to women's physical pleasure as a mortal sin. Combined with the jokes about the "it" that **Horace** took from Agnès, the "cream tart" she mentions in the basket game, and "babies conceived by the ear," this produced a risqué mixture of off–color humor and mockery of overly serious piety that set the Devout Party's teeth on edge. The latter were not an official, well–organized group, but rather a variety of interests in **court** and in town that included both Ultramontains, loyal mainly to the Pope, and Gallicans, who saw the King as the head of the French Church. Within the ranks of the Devout, there existed, however, the remains of some far more organized structures, such as the clandestine, ultra–orthodox **Company of the Holy Sacrament.** These people were to play a pivotal role in the **Quarrel of the School for Wives** and in the *Tartuffe* affair, persecuting Molière every chance they got. The latter play exacerbated tensions because in its earliest version Tartuffe was dressed in quasi–clerical attire, the so–called little collar that designated men who had taken religious orders. Tartuffe's exploitation of the shield of piety and his ostentatious practices of self–flagellation, of distributing the holy water, and of mystical prayer, struck at the very heart of Devout identity. His message that the physical world is a mere dung–hill paraphrases many devotional texts, such as the *Imitation of Jesus Christ* that **Pierre Corneille** translated. They were especially injured by **Cléante's** denunciation of "this plaster façade of bogus zeal, / These bold–faced hypocrites, these market–place saints" and by his specific mention of their slanderous plots and vengeful conspiracies. Tartuffe's own words constantly come so close to conventional religious discourse as to create uncomfortable questions. His attempts to seduce **Elmire** are larded with the terms of Jesuit casuistry, with its excuses for sin and its subtle conflation of worldly and spiritual interests.  The same language resurfaces in his discussion with Cléante, where he deviously refuses to comply with the interests of the family.  On the other hand, he was equally clever at parroting the discourse of more rigorous approaches, as his mock confession in the third act shows.  So it was no accident that the Devout Party used its control of both the Parlement and the Diocese of Paris to ban the play, even after Molière abandoned the offensive costumes and emended some of the dialogue.  It was largely in vain that Molière sought to place himself under the wing of such personalities as the papal legate, Cardinal Chigi.

As the *Tartuffe* affair dragged on over several years, Molière no doubt grew exasperated at his opponents and struck back repeatedly.  In *Dom Juan*, he seemed to some to use his materialistic protagonist to strike at all that was holy and his bumbling sidekick **Sganarelle** to ridicule all who were credulous enough to believe in the power of heaven.  **Dom Juan's** immersion into the fires of hell in the last act were not enough to overcome the shock of the "pauper scene," where he entices a holy hermit to blaspheme in exchange for gold.  Having professed a doctrine of materialism early in the play, the protagonist turns in the fifth act to a hypocritical masquerade in order to escape from responsibility for his misdeeds.  He gives a detailed and cynical explanation of his tactics, showing how he will use the machinery of the Devout Party to disable anyone who slights him or questions his motives.  Even Sganarelle's concluding cry for his wages seems to place into question the whole apparatus of the wages of sin.  Again, in *Le Misanthrope*, Molière takes a swipe at the Devouts in the person of **Arsinoé**, the falsely pious playgirl–turned–prude who offers to use her religious "machine" at court to advance Alceste's interests in exchange for his amorous attentions.

Molière's own works are not without allusions to the Bible.  Some of the discussion of hypocrisy in *Tartuffe* draws on Philippians, Philinte's formula for "sober wisdom" echoes Romans and **Henriette's** words about different personalities having different gifts recalls the same epistle.  It is interesting that Henriette's critique of her sister's celibacy is religious as well as practical: by failing to marry, she will keep new little philosophers from coming into the world.

Louis XIV's approval of the public performance for *Tartuffe* in 1669 seemed to have settled the religious controversies, and was accompanied by an avoidance on the part of the playwright of further topics that would challenge the **proprieties**.  There are only passing references to religious topics in most of the later plays, but the 1682 edition of the *mamamouchi* ceremony in *Le Bourgeois gentilhomme* contains some interesting elements under cover of **comedy–ballet** fantasy.  As the fake Muslims interrogate their neophyte, they ask him a series of questions on his faith: has he ever been an Anabaptist, a Zwinglian, a Copt, a Hussite, a pagan, a Lutheran, a Puritan, or a Brahmin?  Among the list of known religions, there are several that, in **Rabelaisian** fashion, appear to be totally imaginary; no one has successfully identified "Morists, Fronists, Moffins, or Zurins."  Perhaps these bizarre "faiths" serve to distract attention from the fact that the ceremony bore a certain resemblance to a number of rites in various existing Catholic orders. Certainly the equation between Christian followers of Zwingli, Huss, Luther, or Calvin and non–Christian pagans or Brahmins smacks of the orthodoxy tests that were being applied rigorously by the Counter–Reformation. It is interesting that this language does not seem to have been used in the original version played before the court at **Chambord**, but only in the one presented to the urban audience of the Palais Royal Theater.

However, if Molière seems to have avoided or hidden religious references in the later plays, the events of Molière's death and burial show that the opposition was merely biding its time. Despite his royal protection and evidence of a deathbed conversion witnessed by two nuns, the dramatist was allowed burial in sacred ground only with a small ceremony and at night. It is possible that his bones, which were not longer in the same spot when the revolutionary government authorized reinterment in the Pantheon, were removed from their resting place in the Cemetery of Saint–Josephe soon after the funeral.

***Remerciement au Roi.*** Shortly after receiving one of the annual royal stipends accorded to writers on the advice of the critique of **Jean Chapelain**, Molière addressed verses of thanks to the King. Chapelain's notes had praised the dramatist's mastery of natural comic sense, his judicious inventiveness, and his healthy worldview (but with a warning to avoid vulgarity if he wished to stay on the stipend list!). Barely over 100 lines in length, the witty poem was such a success that it was published soon after composition in a small "plaquette." Molière chose as his form free verse in stanzas of uneven length, and he handled the format as easily as **La Fontaine** or **Boileau**. The poem is based on the conceit of the writer bidding his Muse to deliver thanks to the King and sending him (this Muse is apparently masculine) on a realistic itinerary to the royal waking ceremony at the **Louvre** palace. Elaborate instructions are given, first for dressing the Muse as a ridiculous marquis, complete with plumed hat, wig, huge collar, tiny jacket, and a cloak slung over the back with a fashionable ribbon. Next come details for the proper petty aristocratic behavior: the Muse is to comb his hair as he walks all the way down the corridor of the guardroom, loudly greeting even the most distant acquaintance, then scratch on the door. But if the crowd is too dense, he is to jump on a chair and cry out his name so the doorman will know he is waiting. If the doorman doesn't answer, he is to elbow his way to the doorway and jam himself so tightly in it that he cannot help but slip in if someone else is admitted.

Next, the Muse is to jostle for a place close to the King's bedroom chair or find a spot where he can waylay the passing monarch to deliver his praise. As for the praise itself, Molière dispatches it with a few quick lines, urging his messenger "to promise much — you Muses are so good at that! / For like your chatty sisters, / Your mouth will certainly not prove deficient." However, Molière warns his Muse that he must not expect a long audience with this busy

King: "As soon as you open your lips / To speak of gift and magnanimity / He will know in a flash what you mean / And gently forming a smile / That never fails to charm all hearts / Off he'll fly swift as an arrow. / But never worry / Your compliment's delivered." The genius of the poem lies in its attitude, exhibiting just the right amount of confidence and intimacy with the royal **patron**. By allowing the royal sense of generosity to "fill in the blanks," as it were, the poet avoids the trite, overstated language that such poems usually contain. At the same time, he transforms the poem into a miniature comedy, aping the manners of the obsequious courtiers who flock to the royal chambers each morning. While answering the demands of patronage, it also demonstrates the active powers of Molière's naturalistic aesthetic.

**Repertory**. The performance of plays by other authors was obviously the major activity of Molière's troupe upon their arrival in **Paris**, since he had so far completed only *L'Étourdi* and *Dépit amoureux*, unless we count a batch of **farces** whose authorship is contestable and that he considered, more or less, as works in progress. From 1659, when our records begin, through 1669, when repertory performance temporarily ceased, both the number of plays in repertory and the number of authors used gradually decreased. Not surprisingly, the reduction came mainly among the plays least frequently performed. But even as the overall quantity of repertory was decreasing, the number of performances of plays in repertory actually had a tendency to increase somewhat. This practice was obviously more convenient for the actors, who did not need to burden their memory with the extensive number of parts their predecessors had to deal with. It also reflected the troupe's new image of itself, not as a sort of theatrical library as old troupes had been, but as a group with a special mission and a well–defined sense of the new type of drama they advocated. (Plays premiered by Molière's troupe are not included in this section, but are discussed under their various authors.)

Throughout Molière's productive period in Paris, **Pierre Corneille's** plays topped the repertory list. We know that the troupe's first royal performance involved Corneille's political tragedy, *Nicomède*, accompanied by a farce. For the 1659–60 year, seven of the twenty–two plays listed by **La Grange** belong to Corneille: *Héraclius, Rodogune, Cinna, Le Menteur, La Mort de Pompée, Le Cid*, and *Horace*. There were tides in the troupe's taste for Corneille's work. *Héraclius*, which was one of the favored texts through 1663, disappears from the list and gives way to *Sertorius* from 1663 on. The Corneille texts with the longest legs, besides *Sertorius*, were *Rodogune* and *Le Menteur*. *Nicomède* reappeared from 1660 through 1662.

Just as important as Corneille's plays, and perhaps more so in terms of numbers of performances, were three plays from the pen of **Paul Scarron**: *Jodelet maître et valet, L'Héritier ridicule*, and *Dom Japhet d'Arménie*. These held their own with Corneille's works until the 1666–67 year, when they were dropped from the repertory. The first of them, of course, involved the great comic **Jodelet**. Its continuance a considerable time after his death is most interesting: one wonders, for instance, whether the role was played with

Jodelet's signature pancake makeup and which actor took it. The obvious person would be Molière, who usually eschewed excessive face paint. He must have considered it a thrill, however, to impersonate the very comic who may have inspired his own choice of careers years before. The second play, while not quite as timely as Molière's own works in its treatment of the social topic of succession, was nonetheless seminal in its approach of the topic, and may have been a starting point for many of Molière's own experiments with **satire**. *Dom Japhet* was the kind of theatrical hybrid, neither comedy nor tragedy nor traditional tragicomedy, that fascinated Molière and drove him to compose *Dom Garcie de Navarre*. Like *L'Héritier*, it bore a kind of naturalistic stamp that coincided with his basic interests.

Another author represented in the repertory is Molière's distant relative, **Tristan L'Hermite**. *La Mort de Crispe* and *Mariane* were both performed in the 1659–60 year and dropped subsequently. However, while the former play, which had premiered with the **Illustre Théâtre** long before, was not revived, the latter, a famous biblical piece known to all for its outcry against tyranny, reappeared periodically from 1662 to 1667. The fact that the troupe was willing to take up the lofty verses of Tristan so far into their Parisian period shows that criticism did not make them entirely abandon their aspiration to traditional tragic greatness as easily as some critics have inferred.

**Pierre Du Ryer**, like Tristan L'Hermite, had been associated with the Illustre Théâtre. His *Scévole* was another of the plays purchased by the ill–fated group that was still on the boards in 1659–60. In some ways, the role of Scévole is not unlike that of César in *La Mort de Pompée,* which Molière favored so much that he sat for **Mignard's** portrait in that **costume**. Both are essentially "tragic seconds," overshadowed through much of the play by Pompée and Porsenne, respectively, but both are victorious in the end. During the same year, the troupe also gave one performance of Du Ryer's *Alcionée*, another heroic tragedy. The subsequent disappearance of these works from the repertory may have had much to do with the death of Du Ryer, whose prestige as an academician and translator, outliving his dramatic output, faded quickly after his passing.

**Jean Rotrou** was the only other dramatist with multiple plays in the troupe's repertory. His well–respected tragedy *Venceslas* appeared at intervals for several years. *La Soeur,* a refined comedy performed five times in 1662–63, contributed to the **Turkish** elements in *Le Bourgeois gentilhomme*.

Of the authors represented in the repertory by a single play, the names of **Desmarets de Saint–Sorlin**, Guérin du Bouscal, and **Thomas Corneille** stand out. Desmarets's *Les Visionnaires* was an old comic standby that influenced many of Molière's own texts. Similarly, Guérin's *Sanche Pansa,* which allowed Molière to play the role of the famous sidekick, linked his theater to the multi–faceted universe of Quixote. What Molière admired in *Dom Bertrand de Cigarral* was certainly not its author, for Molière and his friend **Boileau** seem to have found nothing very sympathetic in Thomas Corneille and to have spared no occasion to make fun of him. However, the play was a solid theatrical success and, like Scarron's *Dom Japhet*, a genre–bender calling for an acting style far different from declamation tragedy. Other single plays in the repertory included **Boisrobert's** often–performed *La Folle Gageure,* Gillet de la Tessonnerie's ground–breaking bumpkin satire *Le Campagnard,* **Gabriel Gilbert's machine play** *Endymion,* Pousset de Montauban's *Félicie,* and *Jodelet prince,* another of that comic's early triumphs.

Additionally, there were a number of farces and dramatic tidbits in the repertory that were probably adapted by Molière from existing material. *La Jalousie de Gros–René* was almost certainly a version of what is now known as *La Jalousie du Barbouillé.* The same is probably true about **Gorgibus dans le sac,** a forerunner to *Les Fourberies de Scapin,* and *Le Fagotier,* an early avatar of *Le Médecin malgré lui.* It has been suggested that *Le Docteur pédant* and *Le Grand Benêt de fils aussi sot que son père* may have contained the germs of *Le Malade imaginaire.* However, *Le Grand Benêt* was originally applied to a bumpkin and was likely composed by the actor **Brécourt,** which would suggest it did not have medical themes at all. On *Gros–René écolier, Plan–plan, Les Indes, La Pallas, Le Geolier de soi–même,* and *La Farce de la cassaque,* we can only speculate. A few entries in **La Grange's** register speak only of "a farce" or "a dance" or "a pastoral." *L'Accouchée ou l'embarras de Godard,* performed nineteen times from 1667 to 1669, has been attributed to **Donneau de Visé,** but this seems unlikely, since all of Donneau's works that were new were clearly designated by La Grange, including some less successful ones. *Le Fin lourdaud,* performed thirty times in the last three years of Molière's career, has been interpreted by some as an early version of the **Diafoirus** sequences in *Le Malade imaginaire,* but this is also subject to considerable doubt. It was, with *Sertorius,* virtually the only repertory element during this stage of the troupe's history.

Some of the changes among the plays may have been due to the actors available, since Molière's best tragedian, **La Thorillière,** did not join the troupe until June of 1662. The departure of the best female tragic lead, **Mlle. Du Parc,** in May of 1667 must have certainly restricted the choices available to the troupe. **Madeleine Béjart** was certainly skilled as a tragic thespian, but her age would limit the kind of roles she could accept. Some critics thought that by the late 1660s she was long past resemblance to **Venus** or other figures of beauty. She seems to have stopped taking new parts when **Mlle. Beauval** joined the troupe, and her brother Louis's parts must have been taken over by **Baron** and **Beauval.** **Armande Béjart** was probably unschooled in the skills of tragic acting. That left only **Mlle. de Brie,** and later **Mlle. Beauval** and **Mlle. La Grange,** all of whom were essentially comediennes. In general, it can be summed up that the tremendous influence of the repertory on Molière and his company has been largely overlooked, except in terms of direct source quotations, and that it may offer substantial insights into the development of both actors and comic material.

***Réponse aux Observations touchant le Festin de Pierre de Monsieur de Molière.*** Pamphlet published in 1665 by **Gabriel Quinet** that supports Molière against the charges of impiety brought in the *Observations.* The unknown author, who claims to be previously unpublished, says that the *Observations* betray too much passion to be objective. Stating that they deform the concept of comedy, using **Dom Juan** to attack comedy in general, the author refutes the points of the *Observations* one by one. He deplores the fact that they "make war in fox fashion," instead of confronting the issues sincerely.

**Retz, Jean–François–Paul de Gondi, Cardinal de** (1613–1679). This churchman was most famous for his political ambitions, which drove him to play a major part in the Fronde **revolts** of 1648–1652, when he was coadjutor archbishop of **Paris**. Although he won a cardinal's hat by his intrigues, he also was imprisoned, escaped, fled the country, and appealed his case at Rome. He returned to France in 1662 under conditions amounting to internal exile. **Madame de Sévigné** was a great friend, and she records engaging Molière to read *Les Femmes savantes* to the ailing prelate.

**Revolts.** There were several uprisings of various kinds during Molière's life that may have informed his social ideas during his career. Though it took place slightly before his time, he may as a boy have heard discussion of the revolt of the Va–nu–pieds in Normandy, a fairly typical peasant uprising or *jacquerie*, involving an outburst of ill–focused violence followed by a brutal armed repression. In 1627–28, the Protestant municipal revolt in La Rochelle must have elicited some attention in **Paris**, one of the most ardently Catholic cities in the kingdom. It was conquered through siege and starvation by **Richelieu**, and was used as a pretext for the cancellation of many Protestant rights guaranteed by the Edict of Nantes. During the period between 1648 and 1652, Molière was away from Paris and missed many of the historical events of the Fronde, including the **Grande Mademoiselle's** role in opposing the royal armies. The Fronde was actually a confusing series of overlapping and intertwining revolts and military actions, involving sedition by both the *parlementaires* and the **nobility** for quite different reasons. **Condé** was one of the leaders of the aristocratic wing, and he actually left France to enter the service of Spain for a while because of bitter feelings over the outcome. One common concern, shared by many non–Frondeurs as well, was opposition to the regency of Cardinal Mazarin. The Regent was vilified in a torrent of satirical *mazarinades* that accused him of defrauding the treasury, exercising undue influence over the **Queen Mother**, and even being her lover. However, Molière had a good chance to study the effects of a major revolt in the Bordelaise branch of the Fronde, which was called the Ormée. This local uprising combined bourgeois and noble grievances with those of the common people of **Bordeaux**, and even featured some calls for democracy. There were further bloody repercussions of the Fronde in Provence, and Molière may have learned of them when his troupe passed through **Avignon**. The only character openly associated with the Fronde in Molière's works is **Orgon**. His family states that he has done remarkably good service to the King during the "late troubles." In fact, *parlementaires* who stayed loyal to **Louis XIV** were well rewarded afterwards, while those who revolted or took part in traumatic events like the house arrest of the royal family were dealt with severely. Such is the case of Orgon's friend Argan, who has left his chest of important papers (deeds? political documents? letters of nobility? financial records?) in Orgon's care. Argan did not reckon that Orgon's latent sense of guilt would cause him to hand this "hot potato" directly into the hands of **Tartuffe**, who could hold it more safely. By the way, it is never explained by the Exempt at the end of the play whether His Majesty had seen the contents of the chest, whether it would be returned, or whether this had any bearing on Orgon's pardon.

**Ribou, Jean.** A publisher of dramatic texts in Paris. Although Ribou appears to have tried to pirate the texts of *Les Précieuses ridicules* and *Sganarelle*, as well as commissioning one **F. Doneau** to pen a pale imitation of the latter, Molière apparently reconciled with him after legal action had been taken and consented to his involvement with publishing several subsequent plays, including an authorized *Sganarelle, Le Mariage forcé, Tartuffe, Le Misanthrope, Le Médecin malgré lui, Le Sicilien, Amphitryon, George Dandin, Monsieur de Pourceaugnac* and *L'Avare*.

**Richelieu, Armand–Jean Duplessis, Cardinal de** (1585–1642). Mentioned in the *Observations sur le Festin de Pierre* as an authority for the condemnation of evil in the theater. Richelieu's nephew and nieces were important members of the **court** of **Louis XIV**, one of whom proxied for **Henrietta of England** as godmother for Molière's first son, Louis. The family ordered some private performances by Molière's troupe.

**Rings.** These were important tokens of **love**, preliminaries to **marriage**, or very often, rich gifts for services rendered. In *Dépit amoureux*, **Éraste** gives **Marinette** a ring from his own finger to reward her for helping him woo her mistress **Lucile**. At the conclusion of *L'Amour médecin*, **Clitandre** gives a wedding band with jewels to his beloved **Lucinde**, explaining (presumably to **Sganarelle**, who thinks the scene is a deception) that it is a starry ring that will protect her from mental illness. **Géronimo**, Sganarelle's friend and advisor in *Le Mariage forcé*, returns to the stage in scene 3 to suggest that the husband–to–be should consult a jeweler he knows regarding the purchase of a beautiful diamond wedding band. It is possible that he feels that if he cannot prevent Sganarelle's marriage, he might as well profit from a fat commission. In *L'Avare*, **Cléante** uses a ring as a gauge of love, but it still is tainted with deception, since he almost tears it off his father's hand to present it to the lady. **Harpagon** is only partly mollified by Cléante's explanation that the gift is in his name, for he never would have parted with such a valuable object in the service of **love**. **Monsieur de Pourceaugnac** uses a ring to bribe **Sbrigani** into revealing a secret about his intended bride. Sbrigani planned to leak the false information anyway, but he cleverly showed reluctance until he could extract more from his victim. The damaging information that **Julie** is a lascivious wench further plays into **Éraste's** plot to foil the marriage. In the third act of *Le Bourgeois gentilhomme* we learn that **Monsieur Jourdain** has already given a diamond ring to **Dorimène**, or believes he has, for **Dorante** has presented the ring on his own behalf. Even if Dorante had not tainted the ring with his dishonesty, Jourdain already had, for it was an adulterous, rather than an innocent, gift.

**River God** (*Psyche*). This character, played by **De Brie**, does not appear in any of the scenes written by Molière, but only in Act IV (penned by Corneille), where he prevents the heroine from drowning herself after **Cupid's** departure and then hands her over to **Venus**.

**Robbers**. While Parisian crooks were fairly common in comedies by Molière's rivals, he only features professional thieves in *Dom Juan*, where a gang of highway robbers attacks **Dom Carlos**. The protagonist rushes offstage to help disperse the brigands.

**Robert, Monsieur** (*Le Médecin malgré lui*). This **bourgeois** neighbor intervenes to break up a fight between **Sganarelle** and his **wife** (I, 2). The latter pushes him across the stage, saying that she prefers to be **beaten** and it is none of his business. When he changes his tune and consents to the violence, the husband bullies him and states that he chooses not to beat his wife. The part, which consists almost entirely of retreat and agreement, may well have been doubled with that of **Thibaut**, who appears only later in the play.

**Robinet**. Man of letters who took over the writing of the *Gazette* or *Muse historique* from **Loret**.

**Rochemont**. A name mentioned as the identity of the "B.A.S.D.R." who wrote the *Observations sur le Festin de Pierre*. The author describes himself as a **lawyer**.

*Roman de Renart* (*or Renard*). The medieval cycle of French verse stories involving **animal** figures. Originally based on the *Isopets*, Old French versions of Aesop's *Fables*, the cycle grew into many branches from the twelfth to the fifteenth centuries. The later additions tended to be thinly veiled satires of late medieval life, usually with strong anticlerical elements. In *Monsieur de Pourceaugnac*, **Éraste** fools the protagonist with a trick used by Renart the fox on Chanticleer the rooster. Starting with vague bits of information that could apply to any family or place, Renart convinces the fowl that he is a relative, though it is actually Chanticleer who unwittingly reveals most of the lineage. Similarly, Éraste gets Pourceaugnac to divulge details about **Limoges** and his family, convincing the visitor that he is an intimate friend of the family. Disguised as a Levantine traveler, **Covielle** uses a very similar brand of deception to approach **Monsieur Jourdain** in *Le Bourgeois gentilhomme* (IV, 3). Of course, the only detail necessary to gain Jourdain's confidence was the statement that his father was a gentleman.

**Rome.** Sganarelle and **Géronimo**, in the first scene of *Le Mariage forcé*, recall that they have spent eight years together in the **Italian** metropolis, presumably engaged in commerce. **Chrysale** also recalls his salad days there with **Clitandre's** father, when they sowed their wild oats among the Roman ladies and became the talk of the town. Rome is mentioned in passing in *Le Bourgeois gentilhomme*, where **Covielle** closes the dialogue of the play proper by observing that if anyone can find a bigger fool than **Jourdain**, he will make a pilgrimage to the holy city. There is no evidence that Molière himself ever visited Rome, or any other part of Italy, but he may have heard extensive descriptions of it from **Lully**, **Scaramouche**, and **Mignard**.

**Rosimond (stage name of Claude de La Rose**, d. 1686). This actor was a prominent member of touring troupes before being engaged by Molière's colleagues to take his parts after he died. Rosimond was already an author as well as an actor, having imitated Molière in *Le Duel Fantasque* (*The Crazy Duel*, 1668); *L'Avocat sans étude* (*The Lawyer without an Office*), *Le Nouveau Festin de Pierre* (both 1670); *La Dupe amoureuse* (*The Bamboozled Mistress*), *Les Trompeurs trompés* (*The Tricksters Tricked*, both 1671); and *Les Qui pro quo* (*The Mix–ups*, 1673). Rosimond continued on with the troupe as it moved to the Hôtel Guénégaud and then became the **Comédie–Française**. He was a full member when he died in October 1686.

**Rotrou, Jean de** (1609–1650). French dramatist of the generation of **Pierre Corneille**. One of his tragedies, *Venceslas* (1647), was an important element of the repertory of Molière's troupe. Though performed less frequently, his comedy *La Sœur* contributed some dramaturgical and linguistic elements to the **Turkish** scenes in *Le Bourgeois gentilhomme*, as well as the Turkish kidnapping in *Les Fourberies de Scapin*. Rotrou was a paragon of poetic regularity with a restrained sense of humor and a very baroque taste for striking tragic effects.

**Rouen.** In 1658, Molière and his troupe gave a number of performances in Rouen before heading upriver to **Paris**. Here they may have met the **Corneille** brothers, the city's leading literary lights and the authors of much of the troupe's **repertory**. They may have even let it be understood that they would take up residence in the city, which would explain why Molière had to take "secret trips" to Paris (the **language** is that of **La Grange** and **Vivot**). At least the luggage belonging to the troupe, if not the actors themselves, made the trip upstream in **Cardin Gorgibus's** riverboat.

**Roullé, Pierre.** Parisian curate who wrote the vehemently anti–Molière pamphlet *Le Roi glorieux de ce monde*. Roullé pointedly calls Molière a "demon dressed in human flesh" and rather high–handedly demands that **Louis XIV** do his Catholic duty by executing the unholy playwright. The pamphlet, published early in August 1664, belonged ostensibly to the *Tartuffe* affair, but may also be linked to ongoing persecution of Molière by the **Company of the Holy Sacrament**.

**Rousseau, Jean–Baptiste** (1671–1741). Certainly the greatest lyric poet of the eighteenth century until the advent of André Chénier, this child of the Parisian merchant bourgeoisie lived mainly abroad after 1711, when he was exiled for supposedly maligning the crown. He is important to Molière studies as the discoverer of the texts of *La Jalousie du Barbouillé* and *Le Médecin volant*. They were described by Voltaire and well known in the intellectual community by the end of the 1730s. Originally scheduled to appear in the 1734 Prault edition of Molière's "complete" works, they were not actually published until nearly 100 years later by the antiquarian Viollet–le–duc. Rousseau himself felt the text was not really that of Molière, but a sort of copy that was meant to serve as a loose basis for *commedia dell'arte*–style improvisations.

**Rousseau, Jean–Jacques** (1712–1778). Rousseau showed little specific interest in Molière until around 1758. His sudden interest in the dramatist at that point stems from a series of coincidences in his private needs and logistics. Always on the edge of wearing out his welcome wherever he happened to roost, Rousseau thought he might soon be expelled from France. After enjoying the fruits of Parisian civilization, he hoped to facilitate his return to sober, Calvinist Switzerland as a refugee from those who were enraged by his unpredictable disloyalties. At the same time, the *Encyclopédie* had just published the volume with D'Alembert's article on Geneva. Though Genevans themselves showed little reaction to the mathematician's largely positive assessment, Rousseau tried to create an issue in order to ingratiate himself to the Swiss authorities. D'Alembert's only quibble with the Helvetians was that their city lacked a **theater**, which, he claimed, would give the inhabitants a school of manners to give them the polish that they lacked. Rousseau pounced on this point in his *Lettre à D'Alembert sur les spectacles*. Picking up the argument against the dangers of civilization already laid out in his two *Discourses*, he claimed that Geneva was best protected by avoiding all theatrical productions. To prove his thesis, he set out to show that the best of all comedies, *Le Misanthrope*, was also the most dangerous of all plays, since it ridiculed virtue (in the form of **Alceste's** vaunted **sincerity**) and rewarded vice (in the form of **Philinte's politeness**, reinterpreted as dissimulation). His analysis of Molière's play, which reveals more about Jean–Jacques's paranoia than about comedy, occupies only a small part of the *Lettre*. By greatly foreshortening his study, he seeks to assimilate Philinte to **Célimène** and her circle of laughers, transforming him into a spokesman for the values of **Acaste, Clitandre**, and **Oronte**. He typifies their attitude as that of the popular Enlightenment boogie man, the *petit maître* so persistently attacked by **Voltaire** and his allies. As Philinte is painted over into a cat's paw of the evil aristocracy, Alceste, though the haughtiest character in

Molière's play, is refitted as a voice of the common man, craving the kind of putative "plain speaking" and false intimacy dished out by Jean–Jacques. Naturally, he has little so say about the character of **Éliante**, who provides important polyphonic relief to the debate on sincerity.     As with almost everything Rousseau wrote, the *Lettre* had a widespread influence far beyond its objective merit. **Fabre d'Eglantine's** mawkish drama, *Le Philinte de Molière*, is a direct response to Rousseau's call for a revision of the *grand siècle* in the light of Revolutionary class conflict. It may be considered in many ways to be the first work of the Socialist Realism proclaimed over a century later by Stalin's stable of propagandists.

*See* Pierre Force, "What Is a Man Worth? Ethics and Economics in Molière and Rousseau," *Romanic Review* 80 (1989), 18–29; Monique Wagner, *Molière and the Age of the Enlightenment* (Banbury: Voltaire Foundation, 1973).

# S

**Sabine** (*Le Médecin volant*). The complicitous cousin of **Lucile**, Sabine helps her communicate with her lover, **Valère**, and fool her father, **Gorgibus**.

**Sabir.** A trade language consisting of elements of **Italian**, French, Arabic, and other languages, used in the Levant in Molière's time. Passages in Sabir are spoken by the **Turks** in *Le Sicilien* and *Le Bourgeois gentilhomme*. In the latter play, the pseudo–Turkish in the prose text is imaginary, while the language in the *mamamouchi* ceremony, which was sung, is passable Sabir. Molière may have learned about the language during his provincial years or from his friend **Bernier**, a famous Oriental traveler.

**Saint–Aignan, François–Honorat de Beauvilliers, Duke of** (1607–1687). In an early equivalent to the vanity press, this nobleman and self–styled comic author paid a substantial sum to Molière's troupe in early 1664 to produce his mediocre comedy, *Bradamante ridicule*. It ran for only eight performances. However, the production undoubtedly had more to do with theatrical politics than aesthetics. Saint–Aignan was a well–known **patron** and protector to writers and may already have aided Molière in his capacity as governor of Touraine. More importantly, Saint–Aignan was organizer of **Louis XIV's** royal entertainments, and thus an important ally of the playwright. His son became Duke of Beauvilliers and preceptor to the young Duke of Burgundy, one of the royal **children** whom Louis XIV would outlive.

**Sainte–Beuve, Charles–Augustin** (1804–1869). The most prominent literary critic of the Romantic period, Sainte–Beuve devoted to Molière one of his best-known "Literary Portraits," which was composed for an 1835 edition of Molière's plays. In it, he corrects some of the errors that had persisted in

Molière biographies from **Grimarest** onward, notably those concerning his birthplace and his **marriage** with **Armande Béjart**. Sainte–Beuve drew upon research by the police commissioner and early Moliériste Beffara in making these corrections. However, he let stand other errors and even revived some of the picturesque anecdotes that **Voltaire** had stricken on the basis of unreliability. Aside from biography, Sainte–Beuve's assessment of Molière's poetic qualities and his genius of composition is by far the best ever done until his time, and in many ways is still outstanding. He also laid to rest the search for keys to Molière's work that had always wasted critical effort and focused attention away from the plays themselves. He did tend to reinforce, however, the Romantic image of a melancholy, contemplative Molière, forced to live alone with his precious but heavy burden of knowledge on the human condition. In *Port–Royal* (1840–1869), especially chapters 15 and 16 of the third section, Sainte–Beuve makes many insightful remarks about the affinity between Molière's works and **Pascal's**.

**Saint–Germain–en–Laye**. Village immediately west of Paris and site of a residence often used by the royal family during Molière's time. Only one wing of the original structure survives today. Molière's troupe was often called there during **Louis XIV's** reign for command performances, including those of *L'Avare* and *George Dandin* in the autumn of 1668. Even more impressive were the **Ballet des Muses** entertainments that were held from the beginning of December 1666 to mid–February 1667 and included, at various points, *Mélicerte, Pastorale comique*, and *Le Sicilien*. In February 1670, the castle also saw five performances of the "royal diversion" that was later to be renamed *Les Amants magnifiques*. Seven performances of the **Ballet des Ballets** were given there in December 1671 and January 1672 in order to celebrate the remarriage of **Monsieur** with the **Princess Palatine**. *La Comtesse d'Escarbagnas* was the main novelty of this entertainment.

**Saint Louis**. When **Madame Jourdain** asks her husband if he thinks his family is "descended from Saint Louis' rib," she is referring to the popular medieval king, Louis IX, still referred to as "Good King Louis" by Parisians of the seventeenth century. Of course, few in the **nobility** of the Bourbon **court**, much less in the Parisian **bourgeoisie**, could trace their antecedents to the blood of this great Capetian monarch and crusader.

**Saint–Quentin**. This important crossroads town in southern Picardy is mentioned by **Nérine** in *Monsieur de Pourceaugnac* as the supposed site of her **marriage** to the protagonist.

**Sambix, Jean**. A Franco–German printer in Cologne who issued a 1674 imprint of *Le Malade imaginaire* based on a transcribed text. Sambix maintained, and rightfully so, that his edition was far more accurate than the one printed in Holland, supposedly by **Daniel Elzevier**. Whether his motives were mainly private or were coordinated with the players of the **Hôtel de Bourgogne** (who were only prevented from acting the promising play until it was printed, and who included in their number **La Thorillière**, the second **Argan**) is unknown.

**Sancho Panza.** Molière was well acquainted with the Quixote saga and staged at least two plays based on it: Guérin de Bouscal's *Gouvernance de Sanche Pança* and **Madeleine Béjart's** less successful *Don Quichotte*. He probably played Sancho in each of them and incorporated much of this figure into his **Sganarelle** in *Dom Juan*. There are further echoes of Cervantes's novel in *Le Bourgeois gentilhomme*.

**Sarasin** or **Sarrazin, Jean–François** (1605–1654). Society poet and favorite of the **Précieuses**, he became secretary to the **prince de Conti**, who killed him with tongs from a fireplace and offered the job to Molière.

**Sardanapalus.** Debauched Assyrian emperor to whom **Dom Juan** is compared by **Sganarelle**.

**Satan.** Molière's monomaniacs frequently evoke Satan or satanic influence as a reason for the failure of their schemes. The earliest to do so was Sganarelle in the final act of *L'École des maris*. **Arnolphe** also cites Satan as an inspirer of female liberation. He believes that cuckoldry can only result, in his case, from some "malignant influence," calling the old lady whom **Horace** uses as a go–between with **Agnès** an "agent of Satan." In *Le Misanthrope*, Alceste evidently thinks bad poetry comes from the same source, for he mutters that **Oronte** (or perhaps his fellow critic **Philinte**) is a "devil's poisoner." Like Arnolphe, he fears some vague form of supernatural evil at work in the universe, for he tells **Célimène** that despite her deception "my stars told me what I most had to fear" (IV, 3). Of course, it was considered dangerous to name Satan directly, lest he decide to appear, so many references are indirect. In **peasant** oaths, this usually took the form of a deformation, such as "le gueble" in *Le Médecin malgré lui*. Other times Satan is mentioned in **proverbial** form, such as **Lubin's** expression about "the devil times four" in *George Dandin*. Under the sobriquet of the "Evil Spirit," Satan figures prominently in *Tartuffe*, where **Mme. Pernelle** declares that parties, balls, and social events are his inventions. Of course, there are many references to lesser devils and she–devils. In *Dom Juan*, **Sganarelle** seems more concerned with petty demons, such as *le moine bourru*, a bogeyman of popular tales. This does not prevent him from calling his master a devil during his discussion with **Gusman**. He later asks the rake if he believes in hell or the devil, provoking only laughter. The closest thing to true supernatural evil in the comedies is the sadistic activity of **Mercury** in *Amphitryon*, which **Sosie** aptly compares to that of a devil or demon on a number of occasions. Molière himself was called a "devil dressed in flesh" by some of his ecclesiastical enemies.

**Satire**. Molière does not mention satire as a dramatic form in his *placets* or elsewhere in discussing dramatic literature. He does mention it as a poetic genre in *Le Bourgeois gentilhomme*, where the **Philosophy Teacher** menaces his enemies with a satire in the manner of **Juvenal**. **Boileau's** *Satires* were, of course, well known to Molière and represented his audience's notion of the word. It is also in this sense that **Alceste** mentions satire in *Le Misanthrope* when he tells **Célimène**, "The laughers are with you! It's enough to say, / Madame, that they can push their satire all the way" (II, 4).

**Satyr** (*La Princesse d'Élide*). The musical satyr appears only in the second part of the third *intermède*, where he tries to teach **Moron** to sing, only to end in a fight when the fool mistakes the note "fa" for an insult ("fat" or idiot). The role was probably played by one of the King's chorus.
*See also* **Musicians**.

**Sbrigani** (*Monsieur de Pourceaugnac*). One of the few valet tricksters not played by Molière himself, Sbrigani was apparently created for the versatile **Du Croisy**. He is as glib as **Mascarille** or **Scapin**, but with a bit more cruelty, as he quickly shows by responding to **Nérine's** incriminating information about his past with a more thorough review of various felonies. He greets **Pourceaugnac** with a smothering dose of flattery that lasts throughout the play, so much so that the protagonist's ironic parting words are, "Adieu! That's the only honest man I've encountered in this city" (III, 5). We see much of his obsequious commiseration with the victim and relatively little of his vaunted conspiratorial talents, but he assures the spectators in an aside, "I'm keeping an eye on everything and it's not going badly at all. We'll wear out our country bumpkin so completely that, my faith, he'll have to take to his heels" (II, 9). He is just as effective with **Oronte**, convincing him in just a few words that Pourceaugnac has eloped with his daughter. Unlike Mascarille, he undertakes his trickery strictly out of desire for gain, and though we do not witness his reward at the end of the play, one must assume it could only be counted in pieces of gold.

**Scaramouche (stage name of Tiberio Fiorilli**, 1608–1694). The Neapolitan leader of the **Italian** players in **Paris** during Molière's career, Scaramouche was himself an immensely popular comedian who developed a style distinct from other *commedia dell'arte* stock figures and from the traditional French **farce** actors. Most notable was his abandonment of the **mask** in favor of the expressive use of the human face. To increase the effect of his expressions, Scaramouche wore moustaches that drooped around the corners of his mouth and a very thin and short goatee. One can readily see in this arrangement the source of Molière's famous "parenthetical moustaches." Scaramouche's natural features (large eyes and eyebrows and a long nose) further accentuated his facial movements. Molière enjoyed a similar physiognomy; his somewhat more rounded face had the added advantage of a very large mouth and relatively large lips. By most accounts, Molière developed a close relationship with Scaramouche and his colleagues during their years sharing the same theater. It is certain that Scaramouche's acting style had a tremendous influence on Molière's, leading him to do away with masking and maximize the comic aspects of the human face. Many of the pejorative writings against Molière described him as Scaramouche's ape. One engraving in particular is labeled "Scaramouche teaching and Molière studying." It shows the two actors, aided by mirrors, **grimacing** in identical ways. Scaramouche's **costume** also contributed to that of Molière's **Sganarelle**. It consisted of a beret–style hat, a ruffled "strawberry" collar, and a short cape over conventional valet clothing, all in black and white. Molière's Sganarelle clothing generally differed from this in its bright colors, much smaller hat, larger collar, and even shorter cape. Unlike Scaramouche's simple attire, Sganarelle's generally features a good amount of ribbon and sometimes embroidery, reflecting his greater social pretensions. By 1665, Scaramouche and his costume had become such a fixture in the theatrical scene that his likeness appeared in the form of several dancers involved in the ballet scenes of *L'Amour médecin*. Molière pays a verbal homage to him in *Le Sicilien* when **Hali** compares the darkness of a moonless night to Scaramouche's costume: "Tonight the skies are dressed as Scaramouche, and I don't see a single star that pokes his nose out" (scene 1).

**Scarron, Paul** (1610–1660). Comic poet, novelist, and playwright. Dwarfish and deformed by chronic rheumatism and other maladies, Scarron was not above begging for royal subsidies and insisted on calling himself "the Queen's invalid." Nevertheless, he managed to produce an impressive array of works, including the popular *Virgile travesti*, which set a standard in the burlesque genre, the *Roman comique*, which pictured the life of an itinerant troupe not unlike Molière's provincial players, and such well–known plays as *Dom Japhet d'Arménie* and *Jodelet maître et valet*, the latter setting a precedent for Molière's development of **servant** characters. Both plays were staples of Molière's **repertory**, along with the comedy of *L'Héritier ridicule*. One of his shorter works of fiction, "La Précaution inutile" ("The Useless Precaution") surely influenced the plot of *L'École des femmes*. Oddly enough, his wife survived him and became Madame de Maintenon, **Louis XIV's** mistress and secret second wife.

**Scatological Humor.** The French **farce** tradition had relied heavily on this vulgar type of humor, but Molière uses it very sparingly. In *Dom Juan*, after **Sganarelle** has hidden in the bushes while his master engaged in mortal combat, he explains his absence by implying that his fear caused him to relieve himself. He tries to blame this attack of bowel–loosening fear on the effect of his **doctor's disguise**, but his master replies, "At least cover your cowardice with a more seemly excuse" (III, 5). In *Le Malade imaginaire*, **Argan** explains to **Béline** that **Toinette's** pestering makes him defecate from rage.

**Scudéry, Madeleine de** (1607–1701). She was the author of several major adventure novels that helped propel the movement of *préciosité* into public prominence. *Artamène, ou le grand Cyrus* (1649–53) was set in ancient Persia, but actually constituted a *roman à clef* featuring the great **Condé** as Cyrus and various members of Scudéry's own entourage as well as **court** figures. *Clélie* (1654–60), purporting to give an amorous history of the overthrow of the Tarquins and rise of the Roman republic, is likewise a vehicle for barely hidden character **portraits**, discussions about the extreme refinement of **love** and **language**, and elaborate games with words and romantic gestures. Although her name is not mentioned in the play, she was the obvious target of *Les Précieuses ridicules*. The frontispiece illustrations accompanying the 1682 edition of the play show the affected girls wearing a profusion of velvet beauty marks all over their faces, which may have been a further allusion, since Madeleine was notoriously ugly and made use of the cosmetics to cover her numerous pock marks. The text does refer not only to *Artamène*, which the unschooled **Marotte** laughingly calls "le grand Cyre," but also to its heroine Mandane and its famous Map of Tenderness, as well as to Clélie and her lover Aronce. Mademoiselle de Scudéry's cohorts were not particularly influential, and there is no record of her launching a major counterattack against Molière in the literary world. However, Molière himself appears to have paid her at least a silent tribute, if we are to believe that *Mélicerte's* plot is based on an episode in the Cyrus saga.

**Secchi, Nicolo.** Venetian playwright and author of *L'Interesse* (1585), which served as a major source for *Dépit amoureux*.

**Sedan Chairs.** These were still popular forms of conveyance for upper–class people in early modern Europe, carriages not becoming widespread until the beginning of the eighteenth century. They allowed the rider a certain degree of privacy and protected him or her from the filth that filled the streets and ruined clothes and footwear. Disguised as a marquis, **Mascarille** arrives in a sedan chair in *Les Précieuses ridicules* and takes the unusual step of being carried right into the girls' rooms instead of being dropped off before the door. When the porters ask for payment, he slaps one of them, but the threat of a **beating** with the chair's carrying sticks quickly makes him adopt a different tone. He tells the porters to wait for him below and take him later to the King's *petit coucher* ceremony at the **Louvre** palace, where a carriage would be more or less *de rigueur*. **Acaste** in *Le Misanthrope* has a slightly different complaint, for he says that the loquacious Damon has kept him an hour out in the sun when he craved the shady comfort of his sedan chair.

**Self–references.** Molière was not above alluding specifically to his own works in his writings. One such moment comes in the first scene of *Le Misanthrope*, when **Philinte** compares himself and **Alceste** to the brothers in *L'École des maris*. *La Critique de l'École des femmes* is, of course, a sustained self–reference. **Monsieur de Pourceaugnac**, having patiently kept silent while his **doctors** discuss his case of insanity, finally blurts out, "Sirs, I have been listening to you now for an hour; are we acting out a comedy here?" (I, 8). *La Comtesse d'Escarbagnas* contains two self–references, first an allusion to

*Psyché* by the Countess, then a tirade by **Harpin**, who wishes he were in a public **theater** so that he could denounce the Countess's double–dealing to everyone. Molière returns to his own subject in *Le Malade imaginaire* (III, 3), where **Argan** rails against the impertinence of Molière's attacks on the medical profession. When **Béralde** points out that they are not the only targets of his pen, Argan fantasizes about the playwright dying without the help of doctors, who shout from afar, "Go ahead and croak! That will teach you to make fun of the Faculty of Medicine!" Béralde adds that it would be better for Molière to stay clear of physicians, since he is too ill to withstand most of their remedies. Perhaps there is no better way in comedy to support one's points than by placing their critique in the mouths of characters who are ridiculous or dysfunctional. One can hardly blame Molière for using this form of advertising, since he was one of the few comic authors of the period who could point with pride to the entire range of his own works, instead of always hoping to get a better reaction from something new.

**Senator (*Le Sicilien*).** **Du Croisy** is listed in the guidebook to the **Ballet des Muses** as the actor who filled this role. It was originally listed as a "magistrate" and changed to senator in the version that accompanied the printed text. Perhaps Molière imagined that Sicily had the same form of government as Venice. In any case, the person is meant to be rather like a French **parliamentary** magistrate, who was both a legislator and a judge. Thus it is to him that **Dom Pèdre** goes in the last scene when he wishes to set the **law** on the young people who have just eloped from his home. But like a French magistrate, this **Italian** has pleasure on his mind more often than lawsuits, for he has just organized a masquerade and can think of nothing else. Their conversation is a drawn–out misunderstanding until Dom Pèdre finally gives up and lets the mummers take over the stage with their festivities.

**Sercy, Charles de.** One of the coalition of printers and booksellers in **Paris** to whom Molière sold publication rights for his plays. Sercy was involved with such texts as *L'École des maris*. He was part of the eight–printer coalition that published *L'École des femmes* and *La Critique de l'École des femmes*, holding the royal privilege himself for the latter play. Sercy also published the somewhat premature 1664 edition of Molière's works that included the **"Remerciement au Roi."**

**Servant (*La Princesse d'Élide*).** This role, played by the wage–actor Prévost, does not have any lines and hence is not listed in the text. It is unclear when he came onstage and whom he accompanied.

**Servants.** A ubiquitous part of the seventeenth–century social world, servants are also present in most of Molière's plays. Whereas some of the manuals of the day call for extensive communities of servants in each household, and even in some cases for servants serving other servants, many of Molière's households seem to make do with minimal help. **Orgon** has a single **lady's maid** for his wife and daughter, **Célimène's salon** manages with a single **Basque**, and **Philaminte's** busy house has only the old maid **Martine**. On the contrary, the people who seem least likely to support a horde of domestics seem to have them. **Harpagon** has a small army of servants and **Dom Pèdre** calls out the names of nine lackeys alone to defend the house from intruders. **Monsieur de Pourceaugnac, disguised** as a lady of quality and giving a performance of how such a person would act, calls out repeatedly for his "little lackey" to help him into his **carriage**. Whereas **Alceste** and **Dom Juan** appear to manage with a single valet, **Mascarille** calls out for several imaginary ones in *Les Précieuses ridicules*. Trying to hide from the police in *Le Malade imaginaire*, **Polichinelle** calls for "Champagne, Poitevin, Picard, Basque, Breton!" It was common practice simply to address lackeys by the province of their origin, since they were quite numerous and expendable.

In Molière's later plays, servants become somewhat more strident in discussing their own problems and feelings. Both **La Flèche** and **Maître Jacques** in *L'Avare* become spokesmen for their class, pointing out that Harpagon's wealth means nothing for them if it is withheld from them, and demanding some recognition for minimal dignity. But La Flèche addresses most of his comments "to his hat" and **Valère** represses Maître Jacques's claims with some violence, indicating that however much the author acknowledged the consciousness of servants, he did not hold out great hope for their self–expression. **Sosie** makes a similar point in *Amphitryon*. Lucidly, he gives his master the choice of hearing pleasant lies or unpleasant truths, knowing that when the latter are called for, a **beating** will not be long in following. When Amphitryon dismisses his unlikely but true account of encountering his double, Sosie remarks that whatever inferior folk say will be branded as nonsense, while the same words become wisdom in the mouths of the overlords. Capable of using sophisticated terms, such as "incongruity" and "conference," he nevertheless acknowledges that the stereotypical qualities of gluttony and cowardice suit the servant imperative of survival. The dismissed cook Martine laments in *Les Femmes savantes* that "service to others is no insurance policy." The cause of her removal was not one of the common ones, such as breaking crockery, cracking a mirror, failing to watch over the silver service, or committing some sexual offense. Instead, she has merely broken some of **Vaugelas's** new grammar rules.

**Love** among the servant class is quite frequent in Molière's plays, but must be conducted on a very limited budget. **Gros–René** and **Marinette** mention their little gifts of ribbons, pins, and pocket knives in *Dépit amoureux*. In *Le Bourgeois gentilhomme*, **Covielle** has courted his **Nicole** not with sonnets and serenades, but with evenings helping in the kitchen, turning the spit by the fire or fetching buckets full of water from the well.

Masters were considered to be responsible for their domestics' moral as well as physical well–being. **Chrysale** complains at length about how his wife's policies have ruined their servants' work ethic. They worry about what is going on on Mars, Venus, or Saturn instead of taking care of the chamber pots. They burn the roast while reading books and fail to serve the wine because their minds are on poetry. When **L'Épine** falls with a load of chairs, the ladies try to teach him about gravity instead of giving him more practical instruction. In short, Chrysale has servants who do not serve. Perhaps this is to be expected in a house where reasoning has banished reason.

On the other hand, **Mercury** shows how bad servants can be, frustrating and reversing **Amphitryon's** notions of his own natural superiority over all underlings. **Clitidas**, another **Greek** figure who is not exactly a servant, nevertheless exhibits an expected servant behavior in his cowardice, as he runs from a boar that is threatening **Aristione**. Earlier he had contrasted his thinking with that of the brave but lovelorn **Sostrate**, saying, "I am not of your disposition and I know that for me the sight of a single Gaul, sword in hand, would make me tremble more than fifty pairs of the most beautiful eyes in the world" (I, 1). The profusion of servants, real or imagined, usually badly organized and badly treated, is a sign of social pathology in Molière's comedies, rather than an attempt naturalistically to portray the society of the times.

**Seventeenth–Century Criticism** (1658–1715). Clearly, the most pertinent contemporary analysis of Molière's works is to be found in the anonymous **letters** about *Le Misanthrope, Dom Juan*, and *Tartuffe*, as well as in the polemical literature of the **Quarrel of the School for Wives**. Molière received brief but important statements of support from **Boileau, La Fontaine**, and, more indirectly, **La Bruyère** and **Madame de Sévigné**. Boileau's partial change of heart in his "Art poétique," where he praised the playwright again as the heir of **Terence**, but flouted him for reverting occasionally to "low" comedy of the **farcical** tradition, was to remain a critical benchmark for centuries. Following the dramatist's death, religious authorities who had been held in check somewhat by **Louis XIV's** support for Molière unleashed their venomous attacks with full force. He was denounced as a fountain of immorality in **Bourdaloue's** sermons and in **Bossuet's** *Maximes et réflexions sur la comédie* (1694). Molière's lowly status as a comedian and his discretion about his private affairs contributed in no small part to a great many errors that sprang up regarding his biography, errors which, owing to their age, took on a spurious air of authority that has only recently been properly challenged. **Gédéon Tallemant des Réaux**, the author of the sprightly but naughty character sketches called the *Historiettes*, treated Molière only in a virtual footnote to his discussion of **Madeleine Béjart**. He erroneously said that the playwright had been studying at the Sorbonne (the school of theology) when he became enamored of the beautiful actress, though most sources agree that if Molière had any university education at all, it was in **law**. Tallemant also stated that Molière married Madeleine herself, instead of her younger sister **Armande**. He capped off this **portrait** by summarily judging Molière to be a mediocre actor. While the biography by **La Grange** and **Vivot** that accompanied the 1682 collected works seems even today to present a mainly accurate view of Molière's life, **Grimarest's** 1705 biography followed the trend established by *La Fameuse comédienne* in proliferating flimsy anecdotes gathered from self–interested or unreliable sources. For lack of better material, early biographers such as Pierre

Bayle attached undue importance to the anecdotes. However, Bayle did manage in his *Dictionnaire* and in the *Nouvelles de la République des Lettres*, both written in the editorial safety of the Netherlands, to begin developing a **philosophical** slant on Molière's works. This tendency to interpret the playwright as a legitimate moral voice was carried forward by the churchman and academician Fénelon in his *Dialogues des morts* and other writings. Fénelon's own position of protest in the Quietist controversy helped engage Molière in the current of radical thought leading into the Enlightenment.

**Sévigné, Marie de Rabutin–Chantal, marquise de** (1626–1696). This famous epistolary artist referred occasionally to Molière throughout her correspondence. In the early 1670s, performances of Molière's plays, from *Le Tartuffe* to *Les Femmes Savantes*, were significant social and cultural events mentioned by Mme. de Sévigné as part of her accounts of daily life (2.18.71; 8.12.71; 3.1.72; 3.9.72; 8.30.75). She had also attended the premiere of *George Dandin* at the **Grand Divertissement Royal de Versailles** (1668). The marquise particularly appreciated *Le Tartuffe,* and she referred to the eponymous character and the play's comic situations in a number of her letters (12.1.64; 7.5.71; 8.12.71; 3.9.72; 9.3.77; 1.3.80; 4.12.80; 8.6.80; 1.26.83; 8.5.84). Commenting on the trial of **Nicolas Fouquet**, Sévigné invoked the character Tartuffe to denounce and satirize the conduct of Pierre Séguier, who was presiding over the trial: "I am absolutely disappointed that I was not the one who coined the phrase about *the metamorphosis of Pierrot into Tartuffe.* This was such a natural observation that if I had as much wit as you believe me to, I would have found it at the tip of my tongue" (12.1.64). In observing the social and political circumstances of her times, Sévigné developed a distinct appreciation for the Moliéresque: "It's too bad Molière is dead; he would have written a good **farce** about what's going on at the Hôtel de Bellièvre" (7.10.75); "It would be quite a farce if I told you everything said and done by this Mirepoix, but since he is so detestable and since Molière, who would have done wonders with his character, is dead, I will say no more" (8.26.75); "I hope that this story will prevent in the future that kind of usurpation and will correct it, as Molière corrected so many ridiculous practices" (6.19.95). Perhaps the most common topic that caused Sévigné to refer to Molière was medicine and, as Sévigné grew older, medical problems: "It is true that lately everyone speaks only of their health : 'How are you feeling ? How are you feeling ?' And yet they know nothing of the scientific side of our most important needs: study, my daughter, instruct yourself, and you will need no further license than to wear a **doctor's** robe, as they do in [*Le Malade imaginaire*]" (11.24.79). *L'Amour médecin, Le Malade imaginaire,* and *Le Médecin malgré lui* thus constituted perhaps the most significant part of the marquise's ongoing interest in Molière (4.10.71 ; 9.13.71 ; 10.20.75 ; 10.23.75 ; 7.1.76 ; 7.6.76 ; 9.16.76 ; 11.24.79 ; 5.18.80 ; 7.24.80 ; 10.16.80 ; 3.10.87 ; 7.13.89 ; 9.14.89). While Molière's plays helped the marquise to find humor in the behavior of others, she drew on Molière also to cultivate a sense of humor about herself, as when she described to her daughter the process of taking the waters at Vichy: "By now all the baths and showers at Vichy have soaped me up so completely that I feel nothing ill can be in my body and you can say as they do in the comedy: 'My mother is not impure'" [*Le médecin malgré lui,* 3.2] (7.1.76).

*Roland Racevskis*

**Sganarelle** (*L'Amour médecin*). In this text, Sganarelle is clearly a **bourgeois** who seems on equal terms with his neighbors, a goldsmith and an upholsterer. He exposes the multiple faces of his character in the very first scene. Lamenting the absence of his dead wife, he quotes ridiculous **proverbs** ("He who has land, has war, and one misfortune never comes without another!") and asks for advice on how to cure his speechless daughter. But having listened to the craftsmen, a local lady, and his niece, he shrewdly detects the self–interest in each one's words and discards them. He then speaks to his daughter with a mixture of maudlin sympathy and annoyance. When he finally hits upon the cause of her disorder, the lack of a husband, she nods energetically, but he pretends not to see, just as, in the following scene, he pretends not to hear when **Lisette** reiterates eight times that it is a husband that is lacking. In scene 5, after congratulating himself on not acknowledging **Lucinde's** desires, he protests against the custom of dowries: "Has man ever seen anything so tyrannical as this custom that fathers are subject to? Anything more annoying and ridiculous than amassing wealth with strenuous work and raising a daughter with much care and tenderness, only to give up both into the hands of a man who has no connection to us?" Just as he had paid no attention to Lisette's insistent cries a few moments earlier, she then makes him ask again and again before relating a false tale of Lucinde's **fainting** and depression. Having summoned a quartet of **doctors**, he tries to hush Lisette's disrespectful jibes. But he grows impatient and distrustful himself, first with the argument between **Tomès** and **Des Fonandrès** and then with the contrasting but empty speeches of **Macroton** and **Bahys**. He winds up mocking the latter two, before rushing to buy a bottle of *orviétan* cure–all from a street vendor. By the time he returns to the stage, Lisette has sent the doctors packing and replaced them with the **disguised Clitandre**. Sganarelle obligingly dances for joy at her news and succumbs to all explanations offered, even for the most bizarre behavior, such as taking his daughter's pulse through his own wrist. Genuinely pleased at his daughter's progress, he goes along with signing the "mock" **marriage** contract, setting the dowry at a generous 60,000 *livres*. Only after the couple has absconded during the dancing does he realize with outrage that he has been tricked. Like many other versions of Sganarelle, this one demonstrates both cleverness and gullibility. He is shrewd when his own illusions are not at stake, but helpless when people tell him what he longs to hear. Irascible one moment and nearly tender the next, he shows the instability and mood swings governing human nature, and proves the concept that man can be very rational except when his vanity blinds him.

**Sganarelle** (*Dom Juan*). It makes sense to pay special attention to the characters played by Molière in the original productions of the plays. In the case of *Dom Juan, Molière* played the role of Sganarelle, seemingly a traditional comic **servant**: a mere clownish, cowardly, grotesque foil for his master. Certainly, it is Sganarelle who keeps the play close to the comic register, but it is on **Dom Juan** that most serious critical commentary has concentrated. Careful examination of the play reveals, however, that it is Sganarelle who defines the major issues explored by this play. Moreover, Sganarelle stands in for both Molière himself and the spectator.

*Dom Juan*'s first scene is a conversation between Sganarelle and **Gusman**, who has come to see Dom Juan on behalf of the latter's recently abandoned wife, **Done Elvire**. Insofar as we are ambivalent about Dom Juan, Sganarelle is our reflection in the play. The servant is both impressed and frightened, fascinated and horrified, by his master's resolute rebelliousness. In this scene, Sganarelle immediately establishes the play's central theme of corrupted exchange and informs Gusman that Done Elvire will be badly repaid for her **love**. In fact, Sganarelle's first speech places the issue of exchange in the context of the circulation of commodities and the reduction of social relations to empty gestures. Sganarelle opens the play with a "praise of **tobacco**." Tobacco, of course, was a new commodity in early modern Europe, and one that came to Europe as a result of the conquest of the New World. In general, tobacco is an excellent symbol for the changes in European society in the early modern period: erosion of personal accountability, greater mobility of all kinds, increasingly competitive relationships, greater emphasis on self–interest, and weakening kinship ties, for example. Sganarelle indicates that relations among members of high society, and, indeed, virtue itself, are now defined by exchanges of tobacco.

This opening prepares us well to see the play's full implications. As Sganarelle mimics and describes it, the passing around of tobacco is a trivialized form of exchange; giving and receiving small quantities of a luxury commodity are described by Sganarelle as being the principal occupation of the social elite. This amounts to an exchange of mere gestures without real substance or ethical significance. In mimicking the gestures of those who give and receive tobacco, Sganarelle represents the ambitions for social mobility that are encouraged by the reduction of high status to empty, trivial gestures and the exchange of flattery without social commitment or mutual benefit. This speech prepares the way for Dom Juan's purely semiotic performance of "**nobility**" and the self–interested gullibility that marks the desire and ambition with which others respond to him. The exchange of commodities and flattering gestures is becoming a self–propagating mania, a kind of contagion.

Sganarelle points out Dom Juan's exploitation of others' social ambition and the leveling effect of such ambition. He implies that his master levels the classes by being willing to marry, indiscriminately, women of the nobility, the **bourgeoisie**, and even the **peasantry**. Sganarelle also brings up the issues of place and mobility, saying that his master's desire moves endlessly from one false attachment to another, refusing to stay in one place or to be tied down by any commitment.

In his first conversation with Dom Juan, in Act I, scene 2, Sganarelle gives a detailed description of his master's clothing. To avoid being punished for expressing disapproval of Dom Juan, Sganarelle pretends that it is to and about another that he is speaking. This passage is both an indication of the tyrannical power underlying Dom Juan's "rationalism" and a suggestion that his **costume** makes him a mere copy of what is fashionable. It also shows Sganarelle in a position much like that of Molière as a critic of the powerful in his society. Perhaps Sganarelle, like Molière, is forced to pretend to be less acute and more of a buffoon than he really is in order to communicate at all in a context dominated by power. Sganarelle explicitly brings **language** and communication to the play's thematic center when he says that Dom Juan has the advantage in communicative exchanges because he speaks like a book. Dom Juan's speaking like a book resembles his dressing like a picture, and it places him in the same category as **Trissotin, Tartuffe**, and the learned ladies. Speaking like a book, of course, implies both authoritativeness and unwillingness to listen to responses. Sganarelle also draws our attention to Dom Juan's lack of real spontaneity and originality by saying that the nobleman speaks as if he had memorized his arguments.

In Act II, scene 2, we see Dom Juan apply his communicative method to Sganarelle and the peasant woman, **Charlotte**. Here, we understand that the twin pillars of Dom Juan's technique of dominance are bookish, seductive eloquence and the threat of force. At the beginning of the scene, Sganarelle begins to reproach his master, but, perceiving the latter's menacing look, he immediately expresses subservience. So, the seduction of Charlotte through the use of what we recognize as gallant clichés is framed by Dom Juan's silencing of any speech that he finds challenging. Again, Sganarelle's being troubled by Dom Juan's behavior reminds us of Molière, and the nobleman's repression of inconvenient speech reminds us of the banning of Molière's *Tartuffe*. Dom Juan's impressiveness thus depends on his power and his monopoly of prestigious, bookish language. Charlotte will not be allowed to hear any alternative discourse or any critical commentary on what Dom Juan says. It has been argued that rationalism's elaborate and arcane discursive codes overwhelm those who are unprepared to think, speak, and, especially, write abstractly. Rationalism's contempt for "superstition" has a class dimension, since rationalism, being a skill acquired and exercised in institutions to which access is limited, tends to work against the interests of the poor. Modern systems of communication place what is defined as valid knowledge beyond the reach of popular speech, just as Dom Juan's bookish dialect disqualifies or intimidates dissenters. This scene is one of the play's clearest suggestions that Dom Juan's "rationalism" is itself a kind of superstition that is buttressed by threats, not legitimated by dialogic exchange.

So, for all of his buffoonery, Sganarelle is the means whereby a number of serious issues are brought into the play and to our attention. The play ends with Sganarelle crying for the **wages** he will never receive, since Dom Juan has been consumed by the fires of hell. Like Molière and his troupe, with *Tartuffe* banned, Sganarelle is the victim of corrupted exchange: his "reward" for trying to moderate his master's abuses is to be deprived of his livelihood.

Larry W. Riggs

**Sganarelle** (*L'École des maris*).  The **bourgeois** Sganarelle of this play appears to be perhaps a bit better off financially than his counterpart in *Le Cocu imaginaire*, since he is implicitly able to afford worldly entertainment such as plays and balls, which he denies, however, to his ward Isabelle.  In a parallel movement of economy, he eschews the **courtly** dress of his elder brother, **Ariste**, in favor of more ordinary, modest garments, even though he may be "dressing down" in doing so.  He explains in the first act that he wants no open *jabot*, but a nice, tight jacket to keep his stomach warm, his own hair (rather than a wig) to shelter his head, and roomy shoes to accommodate his feet. Although he defends his own choice in clothes under the principle that all men are entitled to their own tastes, he mercilessly lambastes his brother as an outdated fop.  However, in criticizing Ariste's educational methods, Sganarelle paints them with the colors of vice, while identifying his own motives as moral and holy.  In Act I, he rejects **Valère's** neighborly advances with nearly monosyllabic abruptness, but in the following act, he accosts the young man in a way that strains the demands of **politeness**.  But Valère is more than willing to put up with this lack of protocol in view of the fact that Sganarelle has unwittingly assumed the role of go–between messenger to the two young lovers. This stupidity clashes with his own sense of control, for he asserts, "Girls are nothing more than what we make them be."  As for Valère, Sganarelle feels so superior to him that he can even afford the boy a bit of sympathy at having such a powerful rival as himself.  If he is vain enough to believe Valère's fake concessions, Sganarelle is also mean enough to try to take advantage of his brother's supposed state of cuckoldry.  Ironically, it is this streak of ill–will that causes his own downfall, since all the provisions for **Léonor's** elopement are actually employed by **Isabelle** and her beau.  Like earlier avatars, this Sganarelle is ultimately the victim of his own useless precautions, especially since it is he, rather than the youngsters, who contrives to get the courts mixed up in authorizing the elopement through a **marriage** contract.  This untimely recourse to justice will have several repercussions throughout the career of Sganarelle and similar comic types of Molière's theater.  So will his renunciation of the fair, but devious, sex in the final scene, where he declares, "With all my heart I give it to the **Devil**!"

**Sganarelle** (*Le Mariage forcé*).  At fifty–two years of age, the Sganarelle we meet in this play is older than his counterparts.  His periods of residence, apparently as a merchant, in **Rome**, **England**, and Holland also qualify him as a member of a higher **bourgeois** stratum.  His sentimental desire to forsake a bachelor's life and embark on the seas of matrimony, both to fulfill his physical urges and to surround himself with a flock of offspring, is also unique in the history of this feckless character.  Elements that make him similar to other Sganarelles are his mutability and pusillanimity.  If anything, this figure is even more of a poltroon than the others, since he neglects to confront **Dorimène** directly over her plans to violate the **marriage** vows openly. He only raises the matter with the greatest circumspection before her father, **Alcantor**. When confronted by **Alcidas**, he offers no defense at all. In the ballet version, this behavior is paralleled by his cowering before the very demons he has asked the **magician** to conjure. Like **Rabelais's** Panurge, he seeks to ascertain in advance if he is liable to be a cuckold or not. He does not pursue the matter as far as Rabelais's character, not does he ever reach the obvious conclusive answer: that the only way to avoid the possibility is to shun marriage in the first place. The only moments when he seems to be in control of events are in his reactions to the two **philosophers**, especially **Marphurius**. While he had only managed to barricade **Pancrace** back in his house, he attacks the **Pyrrhonian** in a more active manner, **beating** him and then turning Marphurius's pleas back with the very same **language** of indetermination that the philosopher had lavished on him.

**Sganarelle** (*Le Médecin malgré lui*). The final in the series of Sganarelle characters in Molière's comedies, this figure lacks the **philosophical** implications of his namesake in *Dom Juan*. However, he compensates for this by boldly embracing the lighthearted humor prevalent in the **farce** and by projecting his always overblown ego successfully onto his little world. The author injects into this main character the usual doses of pretentiousness that accompany Sganarelle, for he vamps up his part with much macaronic **Latin** and many incredible diagnoses. Moreover, as soon as he is delivered by **Lucas** and **Valère** to the household of **Géronte**, he develops his own libidinous interest in the buxom nursemaid, **Jacqueline**. He shows how light on his feet and swift of hand he can be in trying to fondle Jacqueline's breasts under the nose of her husband. The effect is closer to the triumphant personality of **Mascarille**, "emperor of the tricksters," than to many of his namesakes. Like Dom Juan's valet, he is also ready to accept **money** from any source, soliciting a bribe from **Léandre** to **costume** him as an **apothecary** in order to elope with **Lucinde**, and taking advantage of the gullible farmhands **Thibaut** and **Perrin**. Though **Martine** accuses him of being a drunkard, he never approaches the abject and brutal stupidity of **Le Barbouillé** or other stage alcoholics of the age. Instead he passes off his tippling as a form of medication, approaching the image of Frans Hals's subjects in their merry self–indulgence. As a woodcutter, he is situated at the dead bottom of the bourgeoisie, for this is a profession without craft or shop, unincorporated and lacking apprentices. Furthermore, this Sganarelle has fallen even farther by squandering the training he got in a **doctor's** practice and the money that his wife's dowry brought. Yet he refuses to surrender or even to acknowledge any real disadvantage. It is as though he has prophesied his own comment at the end of the play: "Medicine has escaped by the skin of its teeth!" There is a bit of a **Rabelaisian** quality about this character as well; though it is a pity the play does not permit room for further development, this Sganarelle shows proof that Molière did not emerge from his worldly trials bowed and bloodied, as some critics assumed, but just as jovially subversive as ever. Thus, he can blithely pardon his wife for her trick for the high state into which it has raised him, but his parting words warn her that she will henceforth have to learn to live with a much more respectable man than before, and one whose powers are not so easily scoffed at.

**Sganarelle** (*Le Médecin volant*). He appears here as a wily valet attached to **Valère**. Given Molière's use of the name as a stock character, the role was almost certainly played by Molière himself while the troupe was in **Paris**. It is possible that prior to 1660, when the playwright created the play also known as *Le Cocu imaginaire*, the character may have had a different name. In his vivacity and poise, this Sganarelle actually is closer to **Mascarille** than to the other Sganarelle figures in later plays. In order to provide a screen for his master's wooing of **Lucile**, Sganarelle **disguises** himself as a **doctor** who spouts nonsense laced with macaronic **Latin** and **Greek** . Then, to further confuse **Gorgibus**, he convinces the old man that the doctor and the valet are feuding brothers. With rapid change of **costume**, he alternates between the two identities, leaping in and out the window of the house onstage in order to stay ahead of his dupe. When **Gros–René** espies this trick and tries to reveal it, Sganarelle mystifies both him and Gorgibus by making a sort of puppet out of the doctor's clothes and his own elbow, appearing to be two men at once. The ease with which this Sganarelle slips into the medical personality foreshadows later impersonations in *Dom Juan* and *Le Médecin malgré lui*.

**Sganarelle** (*Sganarelle, ou le Cocu imaginaire*). Described in the dramatis personae as a "**bourgeois** de **Paris**" and husband to an unnamed woman. This Sganarelle combines the qualities of cowardice and presumption developed in **Mascarille** with a middle–class identity and an obsession with **jealousy**. His **language** is rather coarse, characterized by **animal** metaphors and strange oaths (by Beelzebub!). When he comes upon the fainted **Célie** in scene 3, he tries to revive her and manages to fondle her breasts and nearly kiss her in the process. Seeing this, his wife quickly assumes that he is having an affair with the girl, which would explain his recent lack of affection in the conjugal chamber. On the other hand, when Sganarelle returns to find his wife in possession of **Lélie's** locket **portrait**, he assumes it is she who has "treated herself to the ragout of a lover." Husband and wife argue over the bauble, trading accusations of infidelity and drunkenness. Having recovered the portrait and meeting Lélie in the street, he tells the disconcerted young man that the lady from whom he got the locket is his wife. He also complains of his cuckoldry to one of his wife's relatives, but the man is skeptical. Just when Sganarelle has settled down and considered he was imagining his troubles, he spots Lélie (who had, in turn, **fainted**) on his doorstep with his wife. This causes him to think of revenge and physical punishment, but he leaves off these thoughts and decides it is safer to share his shame with the first person to come by, who happens to be Célie. Having told her enough to send her off in a fit of pique, he ponders the possibility of direct revenge again, but the prospect of a confrontation scares him: "When I have played the hero and received, for my troubles, some low blow that runs me through the belly, and word of my demise spreads through the town, tell me, my honor, will you be any better off for it?" He is also plagued by fear of the **police** and the courts. However, despite the feeling that he himself has done no wrong, he turns again to thoughts of vengeance. When he reappears in scene 21, he is wearing an antique set of **armor** and prepared to fight with Lélie. But when the young man arrives, in a rather peaceful mood, Sganarelle's courage abandons him. Trying to pump up his resolve, he instead **beats** himself into submission without Lélie having to lay a hand on him. As the denouement unfolds and all misunderstandings come to light, he stands by in befuddlement. Speaking the play's last words, he warns the audience never to trust anything.

***Sganarelle, ou le Cocu imaginaire* (*The Imaginary Cuckold*).** First performed in December 1658 at the **Petit–Bourbon** theater and published in 1660. The text was at first pirated by **Ribou**, on the basis of detailed descriptions obtained from **Neufvillenaine**. Following legal proceedings on the part of Molière that included an arrangement over the pirated copies, Ribou was apparently allowed to enter into the coalition of booksellers that produced the authorized editions. Ribou also seems to have instigated or encouraged the composition of a stale imitation by one **F. Doneau** entitled *Les Amours d'Alcippe ou La Cocue imaginaire*. Set in **Paris**, the one–act play seems in some aspects to mark a retrogression after the success of the highly original *Précieuses ridicules*. Its topical elements are almost nonexistent and most of the characters are highly conventional. The meager plot is moved forward by devices that were almost immemorial. We never even see the lovers' main obstacle figure, **Villebrequin's** son Valère, who is represented only by the verbal image of a pile of ducats. Sganarelle's **language**, though picturesque, is by no means as surprisingly naturalistic nor as effectively modern as in the earlier play. Even the denouement is disappointingly foreshortened, and lacks the verve and imagination of some of its forerunners. Yet in other ways it marks a new departure for the author. It was composed in twelve–syllable couplets at a time when almost no one–act plays were honored by that usually noble form. Furthermore, its central character and eponym embodies a fusion of many characteristics of the former Molière persona, **Mascarille**, with a **bourgeois** identity that permits totally new associations that were never open to the valets of one–act comedy. Sganarelle's combination of **jealousy** and cowardice, conformity and outrageous individualism paves the way for many of the playwright's manic protagonists of the years to come. Even his tan–colored outfit sets the pattern for more realistic attire that will be carried forward by **Arnolphe** and **Orgon**. When the loving couple, **Célie** and **Lélie**, run afoul of Sganarelle and his **wife**, each is soon led to believe that the other has been unfaithful with his or her petty bourgeois counterpart. This protracted set of misunderstandings is achieved through the means of a lost **portrait** and the misinterpretation of several overseen incidents, as well as through Sganarelle's untimely broadcasts about his cheating wife. Sganarelle's efforts to restore his putative honor while dressed in a suit of rusty **armor** and **beating** himself on the head and body to summon his courage are the most broadly comic moments of the play. We see a protagonist locked in a syndrome of failure that will serve many more developed contexts in the great comedies. Célie and Lélie uncover their mutual errors without the recourse of an interesting sequence of **lovers' spite**, and Villebrequin's abrupt news of his son's secret **marriage** furnishes an all–too–pat ending for the action. The play remained part of the standard fare of Molière's troupe throughout his life. There seems to be a good deal of disagreement over its initial reception, with some anecdotal claims of great success balanced by rather disappointing receipts indicated in **La Grange's** register. It is possible that, in their haste to capitalize on the trendiness indicated by *Les Précieuses ridicules*, some over–eager intellectuals were mistaken about the nature of this comedy. Molière, however, labored under no such false expectations. It was in his next one–act play, *L'École des maris*, that he would achieve the synthesis of Sganarelle's pliable character and the timely **satire** of manners initiated in his little prose masterpiece. *Sganarelle*, however, nudged out the later play as the most popular production during Molière's lifetime, being played 122 times by the time of the author's death.

**Shepherds and Shepherdesses.** In *La Princesse d'Élide,* shepherds and shepherdesses appear outside the body of the play itself, in the sixth *intermède.* One group of four men and two women, composed of Masters Le Gros, Estival, Don, and Blondel, and Mistresses de La Barre and Hilaire, sang and danced. An all–male octet, made up of Chicanneau, Du Pron, Noblet, La Pierre, Balthazard, Magny, Arnald, and Bonard, confined themselves to dance, with the latter four representing women. It is assumed that their costumes were Grecian, since they are described as "heroical" shepherds. Everyone in *Pastorale comique* is, in fact, a shepherd or shepherdess, but there are two unnamed ones that demand separate listing in the dramatis personae. They are the lively young shepherd who persuades **Lycas** and **Filène** to abandon their self–destructive **dueling** in the fourteenth scene and the one who presents Filène's challenge to Lycas in the fifth. They were played, respectively, by the royal dancers Blondel and Chasteau–Neuf. The original prologue of *Le Malade imaginaire* called for a troupe of male and female flock tenders, the former led by Tircis and Dorilas and the latter by Climène and Daphné. They perform a number of airs and dances dedicated to the King's recent military campaigns. **Lully's** intrigues caused a severe reduction in the prologue, for the second version contains only one singing shepherdess, surrounded by several fauns and other mythical creatures.

*Sicilien, Le, ou l'Amour peintre*. This one–act comedy was added to the **Ballet des Muses** as a fourteenth *entrée* in February 1667, but owing to Molière's subsequent illness, it was not presented to the **Parisian** audience until June, when it doubled on the bill with **Corneille's** new tragedy, *Attila*. It had middling success, probably because the commercial stage setting removed some of the costly original trappings that surrounded it in the ballet. It is unusual in many ways, for it uses only two actresses and three main actors, though the rest of the troupe probably filled some of the unnamed and mute supporting parts. Molière's role as **Dom Pèdre** is somewhat more restrained than usual, no doubt in consideration of his physical weakness. Though other plays of Molière's smuggle suitors into a house in medical **disguise**, this is the only one to use that of the painter to facilitate romance. It is a clever concept and may owe something to Molière's friendship with **Mignard**. Molière himself was popularly known as "The Painter," both for the realism of his parts and for the contemplation that he lavished on French society. The exotic setting in **Sicily** allowed for exotic elements in both **costumes** and **music**, adding to the fun of the production.

As the action opens, **Hali** the **Turkish slave** is waiting with some musicians for **Adraste** and his lackeys to give a serenade to the captive **Isidore**. Following some expository discussion and jokes about music, the serenade takes place. It awakens the grouchy Dom Pèdre, who overhears some of the conspiring between Hali and Adraste and calls out his army of **servants**. With this foray finished, Hali crawls out of his hiding place and vows to Adraste that he will spare nothing in finding a way to approach the young lady. In the meantime, Isidore frankly discusses her girlish desires with Dom Pèdre and criticizes his futile **jealousy**. Hali then reappears in **disguise** with four other slaves and tries to land a musical job in the Sicilian's household. Dom Pèdre hates their song and drives them off, but not before the uncovered Hali can promise more and better trickery to come. His master reappears and announces his painter friend has given him an introduction that will allow him to say sweet nothings to Isidore while painting her **portrait**. He manages to dismiss his liberties with her as French customs and exchanges much banter with her, while Hali, dressed as a **Spaniard**, distracts Dom Pèdre with talk of a **duel**. Following Adraste's departure, Dom Pèdre barely has time to express his exasperation with the painter before the trap is sprung, and **Climène** arrives seeking sanctuary from an imaginary bloodthirsty husband. Adopting the role of mediator, Dom Pèdre seeks to mollify the apparently angry Adraste, while the girls change clothes. Isidore is rushed out of the house under the guise of the battered wife, while Climène stays on for a bit to gloat over the success of the plotters. Dom Pèdre finds himself with no recourse other than the **law**, but his attempts to interest a sybaritic **senator** in his case are all in vain and the play concludes with an outbreak of **carnival** mirth.

Though the play contains some elements of the **comedy–ballet** style, with two musical interludes and a finale of song and dance, it does not feature the regular pauses that usually characterize that genre. Its Turkish elements foreshadow *Le Bourgeois gentilhomme*, while some other details hark back to the early **Mascarille** comedies. As with *Le Médecin malgré lui*, it displays a lightheartedness that contradicts notions of an increasingly morose Molière. The fact that he was able ironically to place rebellious words against wifely claustration in the mouth of his own wife leads one to suspect that he was not as afflicted with cuckoldry as some critics may imagine. The text was published by **Ribou** in 1668.

*See* Claude Abraham, *On the Structure of Molière's Comédies–Ballets*, Biblio 17 (Tübingen: Gunther Narr, 1984).

**Sicily**. The setting of *L'Étourdi, Dom Juan*, and *Le Sicilien*, Sicily was still under **Spanish** control in Molière's time and would stay that way until the Risorgimento.

**Sincerity**. This was generally considered to be a virtue in Molière's time, as long as it was kept in balance with other values. The emphasis in the doctrines of *honnêteté* on pleasing one's companions precluded too much frankness. Like most other virtues, its practice depended on the context and on the audience. Virtues were like spices, to be balanced rather than added indiscriminately.

The spokesman for sincerity in *Les Femmes savantes* is **Clitandre**. He is not afraid to explain his passion for **Henriette**, even in front of her jealous sister, though he takes some care to mitigate his resentfulness toward her for not responding to his devotion (I, 2). He later expands on this explanation, telling her that his physical nature simply could not stand the demands of her platonic ideals. Clitandre's advocacy of sincerity is balanced by the repeated claims to sincerity on the part of Molière's most duplicitous characters. For instance, in *Monsieur de Pourceaugnac*, **Sbrigani**, a hardened criminal and professional liar, manages to convince the protagonist that he is sincere, merely by telling him so. Perhaps this appeal works because the beleaguered traveler, like **Orgon** observing **Tartuffe's** elaborate aping of Christian piety in the church, cannot imagine someone presenting a false front under such serious circumstances. **Dom Juan**, the most accomplished liar in Molière's works, makes frequent claims to total sincerity. He tells **Elvire**, "I must admit, Madame, that I lack the art to dissimulate and that I have a sincere heart" (I, 3). Later, he uses similar language in his proposal to **Charlotte**. Such caveats merely enforce Molière's implicit warnings that sincerity itself, like any other virtue, is subject to counterfeiting.

**Skepticism**. The school of **philosophy** featuring as its main component doubt, rather than either authoritative dogma or method (**Aristotelianism**) or pure rationalism (**Cartesianism**), was the approach favored by Molière. It was usually referred to pejoratively as rank **Pyrrhonism** in his day. However, Molière's attitude seems further from the extreme rejection of epistemological certitude associated with true Pyrrhonians than the measured skepticism passed down through Sextus Empiricus to **Pierre Gassendi** and a variety of contemporary Parisian thinkers, including Molière's friend **La Mothe Le Vayer**. It is extremely unlikely that Molière could have studied directly with Gassendi, as was long believed, since he would have graduated from the **Collège de Clermont** before the philosopher arrived in **Paris** from his native Digne. However, the playwright could well have gotten excellent accounts of his teachings from **Chapelle**, La Mothe, or another friend, **Bernier**, whose translations from **Latin** into French did much to popularize Gassendi's abstruse ideas.

A key element of this moderate branch of skepticism was the notion of appearances. This concept allowed the philosopher to deal with ideas or phenomena that seemed to be real and true but might not be. The emphasis shifted from the inherent properties of the things themselves to the interpretation and reliability of the subject's senses and intellect. By the same token, the truth–seeming of things prevented philosophy from dissolving into a purely idealistic pursuit, divorced from physical reality. The skeptic accepts a thing's capacity to be real without necessarily conceding that it necessarily is. All phenomena must therefore pass through the filter of doubt. Doubt demands within a reasonable framework that things present some proof of their truth before truth is acknowledged. Doubt applies not only to the external thing–ness being examined, but to the process of examining itself, demanding a certain accountability from the senses and intellect involved. **Sostrate** in *Les Amants magnifiques* gives an admirable example of the skeptical method at work when he responds to **Anaxarque's** question about whether he believes in **astrology**. Anxious not to offend his sweetheart's mother, who accepts astrology on faith, he first ascribes his doubtful stance to his mind's own inability to deal with the mysterious method of the pseudoscience, or "science curieuse," as he deems it. But growing more bold, he turns the epistemological tables on Anaxarque and asks the astrologer how he can account for the alleged strength of astral powers when the latest scientific experiments have established the immense distances between the stars and earth. This double–edged skepticism begins to approach eighteenth–century empiricism and the development of a scientific method of inquiry.

Another clever skeptic is **Cléante** of *Tartuffe*, who does not dismiss the possibility that **Orgon's** faith can be real, but applies doubt as to whether it actually is or not. Accepting the likelihood of apparent faith in the truly devout, he asks if **Tartuffe's** ideas and behavior are congruent with those of holy folk. Orgon has been guilty of accepting appearances uncritically and does not want to acknowledge the likelihood of his being wrong. He affirms that faith is entirely essential and impossible to verify by external means. As long as he clings to this stance, Cléante cannot break through to win any comparativist concessions from the true believer. But of course the real target of Cléante's argument is not his brother–in–law, but rather the audience in the theater, who are certainly reluctant to identify with Orgon's self–satisfied faith. The more obdurate Orgon proves to be, the more willing is the spectator to acknowledge the kind of doubt advocated by Cléante.

**Slaves.** Slave characters, especially captive girls, were a stock feature in ancient theater that persisted in seventeenth–century France, thanks to the influence of the **Italian** *commedia sostenuta*, among other factors. Slavery provided a ready obstacle to **marriage** for virtually any situation. In almost all cases, it is clear that the slavery involves Europeans, or at least Caucasians, who have generally been captured at sea by Mediterranean **pirates**. The case of Cervantes proves that such stories were not at all uncommon in early modern Europe. **Célie**, in *L'Étourdi*, is one such captive, having been sold to **Trufaldin** by **Gypsies**. In

*Le Sicilien*, **Hali** is a **Turkish** slave serving a French master, **Adraste**, and **Isidore** is a **Greek** slave who has been emancipated but is still kept under close guard by **Dom Pèdre**. He intends to force her to marry him, which she denounces as an even more shameful type of servitude: "What should I owe you if you change my slavery into another even more harsh? If you never allow me to enjoy liberty, and wear me down, as you are wont to do, with continual confinement?" (scene 7). Hali sets forth a more comic view of slavery in his song, "Chiribirida ouch alla!" where he offers his many services: "Me make good grub, / Me get up early morning, / Me make boil kettle. / You no buy me?" (scene 8). **Sosie** and **Cléanthis** in *Amphitryon* are technically slaves, but their words and behavior are actually closer to contemporary *servants*. This serves to show all the more strongly that slaves were for Molière a vehicle for the exotic in comedy, a sign for a greater suspension of disbelief than he would ordinarily demand of the audience. French ships were already involved to some degree in the African slave trade by the time of Molière, but this did not influence the French theater. It was far closer to literary convention and far more convenient simply to have white slaves appear onstage.

**Slaves** (*Le Sicilien*). There are a number of other slaves in the play, but these four unnamed characters are specifically those who join with **Hali** in scene 8 to sing the ditty, "Chiribirida ouch alla!" in order to gain admittance to **Dom Pèdre's** household and send **messages** to **Isidore**. The other slaves, who are also supposed to be **Turks**, take to their heels more quickly than Hali at the end of the scene.

**Slavonians.** **Albert** facetiously mentions this ethnic group along with **Albanians** and **Greeks** in his conversation with the pedant **Métaphraste** in *Dépit amoureux*. Seventeenth–century geographers frequently used the term Slavonia to refer to the entire Balkan territory that was recently comprised by Yugoslavia and Hungary. In reality, the area contained a great ethnic and religious diversity.

**Smallpox.** *See* **Doctors and Medicine**.

**Soldiers.** Molière was no lover of professional soldiers, probably because they caused continual problems at the Palais Royal Theater, where they insisted on entering without paying because they were in the King's service. There are records of legal action taken by Molière against them, and even of armed brawls and injuries in the **theater** itself. The only time soldiers are mentioned is in *Les Fourberies de Scapin*, where the trickster tells **Géronte** that **Hyacinte's** mythical brother has sent soldiers from his company to search for the old man, spreading out by platoons into the streets of **Naples**.

**Soliloquy.** The French term for this type of lonely speech is "**monologue**," and they are frequent and well used in Molière's comedies. **Arnolphe** and **George Dandin** are among the most notable soliloquizers, but some of the **Sganarelles**

and **Monsieur de Pourceaugnac** also dabble in this type of set piece. So does **Sosie** near the beginning of *Amphitryon*, as he rehearses what is supposed to be a *récit* of his master's great victory in battle. **Argan's** accounting scene at the beginning of *Le Malade imaginaire* is another unusual and masterful soliloquy. Finally, one cannot forget **Harpagon's** raving about his lost strongbox. Molière takes care to adapt his soliloquies to the particular obsessions of his characters and to use the speeches to reveal a great deal about the deranged or defective processes of the characters' minds.

**Somaize, Antoine Baudeau, sieur de** (1630–ca. 1685). Man of letters attached to the entourage of the **Grande Mademoiselle, Mlle. de Montpensier**. Somaize was involved in the affair of the pirated edition of *Les Précieuses ridicules*. After **Ribou's** privilege to print the play was revoked and barred from the register of the Company of Booksellers (January 12, 1660), Somaize obtained a *privilège* to publish the same play, set into verse. The edition was finished on April 12, and contained a vicious attack on Molière. According to Deierkauf–Holsboer, he had already penned another play, *Les Véritables Prétieuses*, that proceeds in the same vein. In the preface, Somaize accuses Molière of stealing material from the **abbé de Pure**, the **Italian** players (especially *Le Médecin volant*), and the old farce actor, **Guillot–Gorju**. Somaize claims that Molière bought from Guillot–Gorju's widow a book of his memoirs and bases all his plays on them. Not surprisingly, the affair led to a **lawsuit** and settlement. Somaize continued to exploit the "**précieux**" phenomenon with "keys" (indexes identifying the real–life counterparts of characters in popular *romans à clef*) and other trifling works, such as *Le Procès des Prétieuses* (*The Précieuses on Trial*), where a **nobleman** from Le Mans brings suit to stop the movement of *préciosité*. By this time, he had given up trying to claim credit for Molière's coup. **Gabriel Gilbert's** *La Vraie et la Fausse Précieuse*, which was staged at the Palais Royal Theater, may have been an attempt to refute Somaize, but given that author's lack of conviction, it was more likely yet another comic swipe at affectation in general.

**Sorel, Charles** (1600–1674). Comic novelist whose *Berger extravagant* (1627–1628) may have influenced some of **Gorgibus's** comments on devotional literature in *Sganarelle*. A 1622 story from *Le Palais d'Angélie*, "Olynthie," probably inspired part of the plot for *L'Amour médecin*. Sorel also wrote a continuation of **Molière d'Essertines'** *Polyxène*, where he added to his forerunner's figure of **Alceste** another called **Philinte**. Sorel has Alceste engage in further quarrels and **jealous** confrontations with his nemesis Cloryman, who seriously wounds him in a **duel**.

**Sosie** (*Amphitryon*). Played by Molière, this character combines elements of the traditional **Sosie** portrayed by **Plautus** and **Rotrou** with aspects of other memorable **servants**, such as **Sancho Panza** and **Dom Juan's** valet, **Sganarelle**. He displays the gluttony and cowardice expected of such figures and even ascribes them to **Nature**: "Nature, in forming us, followed her fancy, /

Making us follow different inclinations: / Some find thrills exposing themselves to danger, / But I delight in self–preservation" (II, 1). For instance, he admits to **Mercury** that during the **Thebans'** battle, he had taken refuge in a tent and attacked a large ham and a bottle of **wine**. When faced with two **Amphitryons** at once, he chooses the one who offers a feast instead of the real one. He repeatedly quails before the threat of a **beating**, be it by Mercury or the general. Yet, as he explains, his kind is interested in surviving, and he shows more resiliency than Amphitryon when it comes to dealing with the unpleasant truth of his doubleness. His opening **monologue** is one of the most memorable in the canon, as he rehearses the speech he is to give **Alcmène**, substituting a lantern (symbol of prostitutes) for his "chaste" mistress. He uses parts of his body to represent the Theban host whose battle plans he describes, only to shrink in terror when Mercury approaches: "The army corps is scared!" (I, 1). He comes to accept Mercury's impersonation with Sancho–like fatalism: "Your blows have not brought me metamorphosis, / And all the change I find in things / Is that I am Sosie beaten up" (I, 2). It is a form of reverse usurpation that he is unused to, and so is the audience. It is also a subtle send–up of the fragility of **Cartesian** rationalism: "As far as I'm concerned, he is already Sosie by force; / He may be me by reason as well. / Yet when I touch myself and call to mind my life / It seems to me that I am myself." Sosie finds it is hard to preserve the self when one is not sure what it is. The *cogito* that seemed so sure is itself part of a shifting desert of appearances that can disconnect and overwhelm the mind. Sosie realizes this quite early, knowing he must give to Amphitryon a report that will seem like nonsense and cannot be believed. When the general rejects the faithful account simply because of Sosie's social station, the servant agrees ironically with the master: "All words are foolishness / Coming from a man without clout, / But put them in the mouth of an aristocrat / And they become exquisite wisdom" (II, 1). Following his master's spiteful scene with Alcmène, Sosie fearfully interrogates **Cléanthis** to see if he, too, has been cuckolded, coaxing out her account by alleging that drink has clouded his memory of the previous night. When he finds that Mercury rejected her, he whoops for joy, but she angrily counters that she ought to find a lover, just to spite him. Sosie avoids this topic and later attempts a fuller reconciliation, but gives up when she proves obstinate. Tricked by the false Amphitryon into summoning officers for a feast, Sosie finds his real master more enraged than ever, since Mercury has in the meantime played the disobedient and insolent servant to the hilt. He only avoids a sound thrashing because **Jupiter** arrives to astound his look–alike, who departs in search of better testimony to his identity. The final act sees him relax in the role of a sarcastic commentator, where he is very comfortable, since his attempts to **reason** a truce with Mercury fall on deaf ears. Sosie's surprisingly large and sophisticated vocabulary, added to a store of folk wisdom and adages, lends itself to this occupation, with quips like "Master Jupiter certainly knows how to sweeten the medicine!" For want of gods or mortals in charge of their wits, he actually becomes the **meneur du jeu** at the end of the play, sending the awestruck Thebans home, assured they will not say the wrong thing about the royal family's delicate condition. Sosie is an engaging character, battered, slapped, reviled, stripped of everything, but never defeated; he cowers, he dodges, but he always lands back on his feet. Unfettered by concerns of honor, he can learn from his mistakes and adjust to the changing, absurd world he inhabits.

**Sostrate (*Les Amants magnifiques*).** This general is supposed to have shown great merit in defeating **Brennus** and the **Gauls** during their 279 B.C. invasion of **Greece**. He is modest about this merit and absolutely secretive about his **love** for the princess **Ériphile**. So well covered are his emotions, which are known only to the jester **Clitidas**, that he is suggested as an arbitrator by **Aristione**, who is unsuccessfully asking her daughter to choose a husband. Though he attempts to shirk off this responsibility, he is also approached by **Iphicrate** and **Timoclès**, who do not see him as a rival. When he agrees to ask Ériphile for her decision, she too attempts to make him the arbitrator, and he is only saved by the beginning of another round of entertainment. He succeeds at his secrecy mainly because, as he had told Clitidas, he realized from the outset that the love would remain unrequited because of Ériphile's high station. Living only to die without divulging his passion, he is surprised and delighted to learn from Ériphile in Act IV that she has long held the same feelings for him, even if she intends to do nothing about them, for fear of losing her reputation and honor. He exits lightheartedly, prepared to expire after having obtained the one benefit life could offer him, but comes upon Aristione menaced by a ferocious boar, and earns Ériphile's hand by slaying it. His most interesting speeches concern his reasons for hiding his love and his opinions about **astrology**. Sostrate approaches the latter very much from the standpoint of learned **skepticism** that Molière favored. He professes no prejudice against it, but objects that his own senses are too blunt to see its effects, thus causing him to doubt (III, 1). He groups astrology in the category of "curious sciences," along with alchemy, magnetism, black and white witchcraft, and occult healing and dismisses them all as too subtle and insubstantial for his belief. He then turns one science against the other and mentions recent astronomical discoveries and calculations, saying that the tremendous distances of other heavenly bodies from the earth prevent their influencing life on this planet. Thus, while representing an extreme and almost excessive delicacy of sentiment, Sostrate stands as a Grecian "honnête homme," employing **reason** within the bounds of civility. The part was almost certainly played, like that of other young male leads, by **La Grange**.

**Sotenville, Madame de (*George Dandin*).** Tradition has it that **Hubert**, specialist in impersonating old ladies, played this foolish member of the impoverished rural aristocracy. The illustration by **Brissart** and **Sauvé** shows her ridiculously dressed with a profusion of petticoats and beauty spots, all out of place. We can readily believe her claim that she comes from a long line of women about whom nobody has said anything in centuries. These **satirical** elements must have severely undercut the lessons in courtesy that she doles out to her son–in–law, especially in the first act. Like her husband, she insists on the honor they have done **Dandin** by allowing him to marry into their family. She incarnates a dying caste, bedazzled by its own empty honors.

**Sotenville, Monsieur de (*George Dandin*).** His name means "foolish in town," but we hardly need to set him in a town to see how foolish he is. His own introduction to a fellow member of the gentry, when he boasts of his ancestors' roles in various military disasters and invites his neighbor to hunt the noble hare, is enough to confirm him as a total bumpkin. One must not forget, however, that his appearance matched his words, as we find from the **Brissart** and **Sauvé** engraving in the 1682 collected edition, where he wears a medieval–looking helmet and hauberk, like some scarecrow looming out of the thirteenth century. The excuses and humiliations that he forces on his son–in–law are real enough, however. Roger Planchon's film version of the play makes him still more violent, as he personally administers **beatings** to **Dandin**. That version also makes him the commander of a remote coastal fortress, a minor cog in the Bourbon machine of central authority. This clashes fiercely with Molière's insistence on making him an excluded figure, a *pharmakos* of failed **nobility** such as one finds in many other contemporary plays. Thus did the **court** nobility enhance its otherwise dubious prestige in maligning those who were nobly born, but too poor to maintain the lavish lifestyle that was evolving. If it is true that **La Thorillière** played **Lubin**, then one supposes **Du Croisy** must have taken this role, although common sense suggests the latter. La Thorillière's gaunt frame and stiff deportment seems better suited to Sotenville and Du Croisy's rubicund visage and rounder form to the **peasant**. But both were, after all, accomplished actors, and could certainly play against character.

**Spaniards.** Spanish characters were common on the early modern French stage, despite the fact that Spain and France were at war for much of the first half of the seventeenth century. Spanish plays were repeatedly adapted by writers such as **Corneille** and **Boisrobert,** and eventually by Molière himself. Often Spanish characters were pejorative, as in the case of **Capitan** Matamore. In *L'Étourdi*, the **letter** that **Lélie** has written under the name of Dom Pedro de Guzman is accepted with **skepticism** by **Trufaldin**, who says that people of the Spanish nation do not merit much faith. The Spanish identity of **Dom Garcie de Navarre** may have greatly detracted from the impression Molière wanted to create with the character. **Dom Pèdre** in *Le Sicilien* appears more Spanish than **Italian**; indeed, the Spanish remained overlords of the island until the mid– nineteenth century. Three Spanish singers and six Spanish dancers contribute the music and choreography of their country to the **Ballet des Nations** at the end of *Le Bourgeois gentilhomme*.

**Spanish Influences.** Like many French playwrights of his time, Molière was steeped in the theatrical traditions of many nations, but the impact of Spanish theater on his work has often been neglected. Where and how Molière first began his study of dramatic works from the Iberian peninsula is uncertain. Spanish texts were popular in France during Molière's time, thus explaining the extensive collection of Spanish *comedias* in his library. Moreover, his travels in the French provinces (1643–1659) and subsequent return to the capital may have afforded him a unique opportunity to see a live, Spanish performance.

The European success of Cervantes's *Don Quixote* (Part I, 1605, and Part II, 1615) and the prolonged military and political conflicts between France and Spain initiated a period of competition and emulation that was still strong during Molière's time. The teaching of Spanish in France was prevalent and, along with **Greek, Latin,** and **Italian,** formed a sort of "linguistic quadrivium" among the educated tiers of French society. Many in Molière's literary circle read Spanish texts in the original or enjoyed the ample translations available. Interest in Spanish theater was also high among other French dramatists. Of the plays written between **Jean Rotrou's** first imitation of a Spanish work (*La Bague de l'oubli,* based on Lope de Vega's *La Sortija del olvido*) around 1628 and Molière's death in 1673, approximately seventy–two have been identified as imitations of Spanish texts.

Molière may have actually seen works from south of the Pyrenees either during his time in the provinces or upon returning to **Paris.** Although their success varied, itinerant Spanish theatrical troupes visited France periodically throughout the seventeenth century. As early as 1604, Spanish actors performed in several French cities including the capital. **Anne of Austria** brought a troupe of Spanish actors with her to Paris in the fall of 1613 after her **marriage** to Louis XIII, but they did not fare well with the French public. Paris held the same fate for a Spanish troupe five years later, as well as Francisco Lopez's entourage in 1625.

Nonetheless, Molière's 1658 return to Paris afforded him the best opportunity to see live Spanish theater. After **Louis XIV** married the Spanish Maria–Teresa in 1660, the Spanish queen brought with her a group of actors from her homeland. **La Grange** alludes to their brief appearance and lack of success. The French playwright even had the opportunity to work with Spanish actors at **Saint–Germain–en–Laye** during the production of *Mélicerte,* put on to mark the end of mourning for the King's Spanish mother, who had died in 1666.

Although it is difficult to pinpoint a chronological timetable for Molière's contact with Spanish actors or live Spanish drama, his textual and thematic borrowings are evident. In a general sense, Molière learns from and reinvigorates many Baroque elements found in Spanish theater of the early seventeenth century, especially when dealing with the individual/society conflict. The Spanish *comedia* is replete with examples of individuals refusing the identity roles assigned to them in order to escape a distasteful fate. Yet their experimentation with new identities is cut short when the protagonists orchestrating a particular ruse overcome the obstacle(s) or attain the goal desired. The characters usually have no problem distinguishing between the temporary persona and their usual identity.

In contrast, Molière's protagonists really believe their imaginary identities to be genuine while all those around the protagonists clearly see the identities as false. The main difference from the *comedia* is one of belief. The protagonists of the Spanish theater generally realize the persona they project to the rest of society is false, so there is no explicit identity crisis. But Molière's theater depicts characters who have full faith in their improbable identities from the outset and struggle to force society to recognize them as well — a situation that has serious repercussions for the hierarchical system in which Molière lives.

Molière's most direct influence from Spanish theater can be traced to **Agustín Moreto's** *El Desdén con el desdén* (1654), largely acknowledged as the model for *La Princesse d'Élide* (1664). Molière began his version in verse, but had to finish it in prose to meet the deadline for the May 1664 festivities at **Versailles**, supposedly in honor of the King's Spanish mother and wife. The similarities between these works provide good evidence that Molière possessed an advanced knowledge of Spanish, since no French translation of Moreto's play existed at the time.

Both works tell the story of much sought after maidens who have spurned men and **love** in favor of other pursuits. The women remain unmoved by the numerous paramours who propose marriage until one suitor in each play demonstrates a veneer as indifferent to love as that of the women. While this eventually leads Moreto's heroine to declare her love, Molière's princess stops just short of committing herself to marriage. In addition to plot similarities, some scenes from Molière (II, 4; II, 5; IV, 1; IV, 4; IV, 5) resemble closely the organization and content of those in Moreto (vv. 755–1030; 1240–1380; 2315–2506; 2567–2626; 2525–2552, respectively). Even more striking are those fragments from Molière (vv. 75–80; II, 4; IV, 1; IV, 4) that seem at least partially translated from Moreto's original (vv. 253–262; 768–812; 2318–2506; 2570–2626, respectively). Such compelling textual similitude has led some critics to conclude Molière may have even used a manuscript copy of Moreto's work.

**Tirso de Molina**, a pseudonym for Fray Gabriel Téllez, is most famous for bringing to life the Don Juan legend in *El Burlador de Sevilla* (1616–20, ca. 1625?). Although Molière, like most European playwrights of the time, was familiar with the myth of the Spanish nobleman, it is not at all certain that he knew of Tirso's original when writing *Dom Juan*. The French playwright was probably more familiar with two Italian versions based on Tirso's work: **Giacinto Cicognini's** *Il convitato di pietra*, which probably existed as early as 1632, and another by **Giliberto**, staged by the Italians in the same building where Molière worked. He undoubtedly knew of two French works of the same name, *Le Festin de pierre*, by **Villiers** (1660) and **Dorimon** (1659).

While Molière's and Tirso's versions share several scenes (the shipwreck, the seduction of the fisherwomen, confrontation with the father, the statue coming to dinner, Don Juan's divine punishment), there are significant differences as well. Although Molière's Dom Juan tries to be as brazen as his Spanish predecessor in violating social and **religious** codes, his story is really a string of failures. Unlike Tirso's protagonist, Molière's hero falls short of seducing any woman during the course of the play and is equally unsuccessful in getting the poor man to swear (III, 2). Seemingly resigned to the fact that his identity as a great seducer will not be confirmed by society, Dom Juan sees that he can actually be a greater threat by becoming a hypocrite that is accepted by the community, a clear signal that society is crumbling from within. It is in this internal, societal strife, that we see Tirso's most striking (albeit, indirect) influence on Molière. By openly disobeying what are believed to be the **laws** of God and of the community, Tirso's Don Juan runs the risk of revealing society to itself and, thus, cannot be permitted to continue. The same is true for Molière's Dom Juan, for allowing him to live as a hypocrite would be proof that society helps create, and indeed rewards, false identities.

*El Burlador de Sevilla* is not the only Tirsian work that may have figured prominently in *Dom Juan* and other Molière plays. The title character of *Marta la piadosa* (1614–15) invokes the same pretext as Dom Juan (an oath to God) to explain why she cannot marry. Marta says to Gomez she would break a divine vow in marrying him (vv. 949–952) and Dom Juan uses a similar excuse when **Dom Carlos** demands that the trickster marry his sister (V, 3). For general characterization, Molière may have modeled **Célimène** of *Le Misanthrope* on Marta, as both heroines share a cleverness and astuteness in manipulating the collective imagination to generate alternate identities for themselves.

By far the most prolific of the seventeenth–century Spanish playwrights, Félix Lope de Vega Carpio had a profound and enduring impact on European dramatists of the age. Molière was certainly well aware of Lope's prodigious production (of which only a fraction is known today) and was inspired by the Spaniard's repertoire for some of his own works. Generally, one can see how the energy and verve of Lope's characters infused Molière's creations, but cases of a more direct influence are also evident. The idea of an ignorant, awkward woman made clever and elegant after falling in love is the basic premise of both Lope's *La Dama boba* (1613) and Molière's *L'École des femmes*. However, this plot device was rather common in Molière's day and may have come from numerous sources. Nonetheless, some scenes from Lope's work — the cat giving birth, Finea's inability to comprehend metaphoric **language**, and her naïve confessions to her father of enjoying a young man's embrace — find their echo in Molière's **Agnès**. She promptly informs **Arnolphe** the cat has died, takes literally the old woman's words that she has injured **Horace**, her young suitor, and readily admits to Arnolphe that she enjoys her time with the young man. In another scene, Agnès may be imitating Finea when she hides Horace from Arnolphe in her armoire, since her Spanish predecessor does much the same by hiding Laurencio from her father in the attic after the old man has ordered Laurencio's expulsion from the house. In addition, Laurencio's verses on love's role throughout history and its influence on Finea's sudden change could have served as Molière's model for Horace's speech on how love has brought about such a metamorphosis in Agnès.

Traces of *La Dama boba* are also apparent in *Le Bourgeois gentilhomme*. Both works feature a parade of teachers who try to instruct their slow–learning students in the fine arts. Finea's *maestros* provide not only a point of comparison with **Jourdain's *maîtres***, but also introduce the notion of changing identity through a knowledge of the fine arts. Even their failures share common traits. Finea's inability to learn the alphabet and predilection for instruments of strong sound are reminiscent of M. Jourdain's phonetics lesson and his taste for the trumpet.

Other indications of Lope's influence can be found in Molière. Although most critics agree the principal Spanish source of Molière's *L'École des maris* was **Antonio de Hurtado's** *El Marido hace mujer* (1643), Lope's contributions are clear. In *La Discreta enamorada* (1653), Lope, probably borrowing from **Boccaccio**, tells the story of a man who unwittingly sabotages his own plan to marry a younger lady while simultaneously facilitating the amorous ambitions of his rival to wed the same woman. This mirrors closely the plot lines of both *L'École des maris* and *L'Avare*. The latter contains a scene (III, 7) that evokes a part of *La Discreta enamorada* (II, 14–15) in which a father and son are rivals for the hand of a young lady. In these scenes, the sons give not–so–veiled compliments to the ladies and the fathers react jealously, although Molière's **Harpagon** does not seem as sharp as Lope's Bernardo in picking up the double-entendre of the compliment. Molière may also have depended on Lope's *El Entremés del marqués de Alfarache* (1644) for the scene with **Monsieur Dimanche** in *Dom Juan*. Much like Molière's hero, Lope's title character kills his guest with kindness in order to avoid payment. He even offers him a seat and inquires about his wife, as does the French trickster. No French translation or adaptation of this *entremés* was known to exist during Molière's time.

Ruiz de Alarcón's role in the development of Molière's dramaturgy can be evaluated, at best, as indirect. The Spanish playwright's work, *La Verdad sospechosa* (1619–1622?), was adapted, and in some places, translated, by **Pierre Corneille** for *Le Menteur* (1643). Near the time Molière first staged *Dom Juan*, his troupe had already presented Corneille's play with great success. In fact, three actors from his troupe (Molière, **La Grange**, and **Louis Béjart**) played the valet, son, and father roles from *Le Menteur* (Cliton, Dorante, Géronte) and *Dom Juan* (Sganarelle, Dom Juan, Dom Louis), respectively. Thus, not only Molière, but also his troupe, was familiar with the interpersonal dynamics first put in motion by Alarcón's valet, son, and father trio (Tristán, García, Beltrán).

The most convincing case for Alarcón's work filtering through Corneille and into Molière's *Dom Juan* can be made by examining the paternal admonitions directed at the sons. Alarcón's Beltrán (vv. 1396–1399), Corneille's Géronte (vv. 1501–1512), and Molière's Dom Louis (IV, 4) all question their sons' notion that noble rank is simply inherited and that subsequent nefarious actions do not jeopardize that status. The idea that noble lineage represents an obligation to prove oneself worthy of noble ancestors, clearly expressed by Beltrán (vv. 1405–1411, 1424–1427) and Dom Louis (IV, 4), is seemingly absent in Corneille's *Le Menteur*. Nonetheless, most critics agree this single example is insufficient to claim any direct adaptation of Alarcón by Molière.

Bibliography: Antoine Adam, *Histoire de la littérature française au XVIIe siècle*, Tomes I–III (Paris: Domat, 1948); Claude Bourqui, *Les Sources de Molière* (Paris: SEDES, 1999); Alexandre Cioranescu, *Le Masque et le visage: Du baroque espagnol au classicisme français* (Genève: Droz, 1983); James F.

Gaines, *"Le Menteur* and *Dom Juan*: A Case of Theatrical and Literary Adaptation," *Romance Quarterly* 32 (1985), 245–254; Thomas P. Finn, *Molière's Spanish Connection: Seventeenth–Century Spanish Theatrical Influence on Imaginary Identity in Molière* (New York: Peter Lang, 2001); Édouard Fournier, *L'Espagne et ses comédiens en France au XVIIe siècle* (Paris: Revue des provinces, 1864); Françoise Labarre, *Jouer la comedia: le théâtre du siècle d'Or sur la scène française du XVIIe siècle à nos jours*, ed. Marc Vitse, Françoise Labarre, and Maïté Mir (Toulouse: Centre de promotion de la recherche scientifique, Université de Toulouse–Le Mirail, 1993); Gustave Lanson, *Etudes sur les rapports de la littérature française et de la littérature espagnole au XVIIe siècle (1600–1660)*, (Paris: n.p., 1896); E. Martinenche, *Molière et le théâtre espagnol* (Paris: Hachette, 1906); Jean Robert, "La bibliothèque d'un grand seigneur en Gascogne au XVIIe siècle," *XVIIe siècle* 117 (1978), 56–69; idem, "Théâtre et musique dans les châteaux d'Aquitaine et de Languedoc," *XVIIe siècle* 118–119 (1978), 37–56.

*Thomas P. Finn*

**Spectre (*Dom Juan*).** This figure of a veiled woman appears in the final act to warn **Dom Juan** that his destruction is at hand. When he grows angry and strikes at it with his sword, it assumes the shape of Father **Time** with his scythe and flies away. It was one of the **machine** effects of the play.

**Straparola, Giovanni** (ca. 1485–ca. 1557). Venetian writer remembered chiefly for his collection of tales, *Le piacevoli notti*, published 1550–1553. They were rapidly translated into French and other languages. Molière may have known several of the tales, especially one that contains a sack **beating** not unlike the ones in *Gorgibus dans le sac* and *Les Fourberies de Scapin*.

**Subligny, Adrien Thomas Perdou de.** This minor theater author almost certainly contributed *La Critique d'Andromaque*, also known under its alternate title *La Folle Querell*. However, this spoof, which premiered in May 1668 and never achieved much success, was not credited to the author in **La Grange's** register. His later and only slightly more popular work, *Le Desespoir extravagant*, was listed as his work. He was also credited with various works more commonly assigned to **Baron** or **Madame de Villedieu**, including the novel, *Aventure ou Mémoires d'Henriette–Sylvie de Molière* (1672), which has nothing to do with Molière the dramatist or his family. Some have averred that Subligny was a **lawyer**.

*Suivante.* See **Lady's Maid**.

**Sumptuary Laws.** There is much discussion of **costume** and the appropriateness of social taste in Molière's plays, but one of the rather rare references to sumptuary laws themselves takes place in Act II, scene 6 of *L'École des maris*. Here, **Sganarelle** praises the King for issuing the ordinances, but interprets them in a unique way. Rather than considering their usefulness in maintaining separation between the various social distinctions, Sganarelle imputes to them the purpose of saving husbands from spending too much on their wives. Comically, he wishes the King had banned cuckoldry along with fancy adornments. He says he plans to buy an offprint of the law and have it read at the dinner table, a most unusual form of promulgation.

**Superstition.** *See* **Satan**.

**Swiss.** Molière several times creates characters who are portrayed as real or false Swiss people, generally with a **German** accent that reverses "p's" and "b's," as well as "t's" and "d's," reshuffles vowels, and plays havoc with grammar. One such person in the Swiss lodging house operator played by **Mascarille** in the final act of *L'Étourdi*. The impersonation is quite ingenious, for the valet even used his dialect to deflect suspicion. When accused of really being Mascarille, he replies righteously that he is not a "maquerelle" (pimp), never having sold a woman or a girl. A ballet entry of Swiss guards with halberds appears at the end of *Les Fâcheux* to chase away all the **masked** mummers who have invaded the stage. **Scapin** impersonates a Swiss guard as one of the ruffians who is supposed to be **beating Géronte** while the latter is hiding in a sack. A couple of real examples of this type make an appearance in *Monsieur de Pourceaugnac*, where they accost the **disguised** protagonist and try to take him to bed. Later, a different and more musical *Suisse* takes part in the crowded booklet–vending scene in the **Ballet des Nations**. The **Countess of Escarbagnas** boasts of having a Swiss guard to serve as doorman, but in view of her habit of re–labeling humbler things, he is probably an ill–clad lackey, fresh off the Dordogne farm.

**Swiss (*Monsieur de Pourceaugnac*).** The two Swiss guards in this play are off–duty and looking for excitement when they encounter **Pourceaugnac** in woman's clothing. They are either so sex–starved or so drunk that they make a number of indecent propositions to her, and even start to pull her back and forth between them, before "her" cries for help summon the **police** and cause the Swiss to flee.

**Swordplay.** *See* **Duels and Dueling; Weapons**.

**Syphilis.** *See* **Doctors and Medicine**.

# T

**Tabarin**.  A **farce** actor of the generation before Molière, Tabarin regularly performed on the Pont–Neuf in **Paris**.  His often vulgar little plays were printed posthumously and may have contributed some elements to *Les Fourberies de Scapin*, as **Boileau** suggested.

**Tarento**.  Port in Pullia in southern Italy mentioned in *Les Fourberies de Scapin*.  **Géronte**–Pandolphe has raised his second family there.

**Tartuffe (*Tartuffe*)**.  The eponymous character in one of Molière's greatest plays, Tartuffe is the most famous *faux dévot* in seventeenth–century French theater.  Although its origin is difficult to determine precisely, the name evokes the image of an unscrupulous person bent upon deceiving others.  In Old French, *truffe* or *truffle* had the sense of deceit, deception, and fraud, and the **Italian** *tartuffo* had a similar meaning.  The infinitive *truffer* meant to deceive.  Literary historians have pointed out that the name of Molière's character bears a certain phonetic resemblance to that of the hypocrite, Montufar, in **Scarron's** *Les Hypocrites*.  This work may have been a literary source of the play by Molière; he certainly knew Scarron's writings.  Like Tartuffe, Montufar makes a great public show of devoutness, attempting to deflect the justified attacks on his false piety by telling his accusers that he is an unworthy sinner and prostrating himself at their feet.  Molière had also read Aretino's *Lo Ipocrito*, whose principal character ostentatiously exhibits his piety and worms his way into his victim's family.

In addition to such literary sources, Molière had only to look around him to find people who might readily have served as models for Tartuffe.  During the seventeenth century, there was no dearth of *directeurs de conscience*.  These laymen reported to no religious authority but took it upon themselves to counsel others on matters of **religion** and morals. Molière must certainly have been familiar with the stories about Crétenet, one such *directeur* active in **Lyon**. Inhabitants of the city protested vociferously against this barber–surgeon. Among the faults with which they charged him were his inordinate ambition and extreme bigotry. In the rue Saint–Thomas–du–Louvre, where Molière lived after 1664, there occured an incident similar to events in *Le Tartuffe* and mentioned by **Tallemant des Réaux** in his *Historiettes*. The abbé de Sainte-Croix, Charpy, seduced a certain Madame Patrocle right under the nose of her husband. Not surprisingly, many of Molière's contemporaries believed that the character of Tartuffe was based on someone the author actually had heard about or knew. It seems more likely that the figure of the hypocrite was an amalgam derived from Molière's readings and broad experience.

The nature of Tartuffe's relationship to the Church was at the heart of much of the heated debate about the play. His **costume** provided an explicit sign of his connection to the Church and changed in an important way between the 1664 and 1667 versions of the play. The 1667 *placet*, written in response to the play's having been banned a second time, explains that the hypocrite's costume has been modified to portray him as an "homme du monde" who now has "a small hat, long hair, a wide collar, a sword, and lace on his clothing." Presumably, then, in 1664, Tartuffe wore a "petit collet," as would have been typical of a *dévot* attached, probably in some minor way, to the Church. Molière introduced the new costume to remove some of the sting felt by those opposed to the play's being performed. They, however, continued to see in Tartuffe a dangerous mockery of piety or, as Molière thought, of themselves.

Tartuffe does not appear onstage until the second scene of the third act, but the audience knows early on what kind of character to expect and what he will look like. He is the very picture of corpulence and physical well–being: "Tartuffe? He's as well as can be, / Florid, fat, rubicund and as hungry as three" (I, 1). Lusty, determined, and clever, Tartuffe also has about him the air of a physically unsavory, disgusting creature. **Mariane's** understandable horror at the thought of **marriage** to Tartuffe results in part from revulsion at his appearance. When she shrinks before the necessity of standing up to her father's plan to marry her to the hypocrite, **Dorine** reminds her of what awaits her in marriage: "Tartuffe's the man for you! He'll clasp you to his chest, / You'll be tartuffified before you can protest" (II, 3). This thought alone brings Mariane to the brink of despair.

Dorine and the members of **Orgon's** family recognize that Tartuffe's supposed piety is nothing more than a **mask**, an empty appearance of devoutness. He is a hypocrite in the etymological sense of that word, an actor who plays his role wearing a mask. What Tartuffe really wants has nothing to do with religious piety. As **Damis** tells his grandmother, **Madame Pernelle**, Tartuffe has come into the household to "enslave our home in a tyrant's power" (I, 1). Dorine seconds this unfavorable opinion when she says that Tartuffe has so misunderstood his place as to "oppose everyone and play at being master" (I, 1). Tartuffe wants the power to control others.

Cunning though he be, Tartuffe has a coarse nature. Orgon had first met him in church begging for alms. The impostor's lack of refinement makes the true motivation of his every gesture self–evident. **La Bruyère's** portrait in his *Caractères* of the *faux dévot*, Onuphre, is a direct response to Molière's character. Unlike Tartuffe, Onuphre plays his role to perfection. He would never, for example, confound the **language** of religious devotion and that of **love**, as Tartuffe does to hilarious effect in his attempted seduction of Orgon's wife, **Elmire**. Onuphre's imitation of piety is convincing, while only Orgon and his mother could possibly be tricked by Tartuffe.

Tartuffe has often been referred to by critics as a parasite, an intruder into the firmly established **bourgeois** order of Orgon's family, and that he certainly is. Like a virus that spreads uncontrollably, Tartuffe has an impact on everyone with whom he comes into contact. The play's plot centers on the breakdown of order brought about by Tartuffe's actions and the restoration of that order by his expulsion from the household. But Tartuffe differs from the normal parasite in that Orgon invites him into his home and insists that he remain there even after Damis has told his father about Tartuffe's attempt to seduce Elmire. If Orgon is duped by Tartuffe — and he is — he also needs the hypocrite and uses his presence as a means to exert mastery over his family. Orgon and Tartuffe have their false piety in common. They share as well another, more insidious characteristic, a will to power that ultimately turns them into bitter rivals.

Tartuffe represents much that the comic author found wrong in seventeenth–century French society. Hypocrisy, above all, was for Molière as reprehensible as it was prevalent, especially when it became a tool for limiting the personal freedom of others. It was also extremely dangerous, for, as *Le Tartuffe* demonstrates, it was capable of threatening the very foundation of the social order, the family. But the play is not just about its eponymous character nor is he its protagonist. Not insignificantly, Molière cast himself in the role of Orgon. Tartuffe could not succeed without the active cooperation, indeed the collusion, of Orgon. Molière's genius was to recognize this and dramatize it in one of his most curious and memorable couples. Tartuffe is a brilliant creation and may, in fact, be Molière's most famous character. His name has long since entered the French language. And yet, it is difficult to think of him without calling to mind Orgon. Tartuffe and Orgon repeatedly address each other as "brother." *Le Tartuffe* is about this classic pair of characters, the rivalry that will make of them enemy brothers, and the way the perversity of their relationship extends beyond themselves to menace the entire social order.

*Michael S. Koppisch*

***Tartuffe, Le, ou l'Imposteur*.** Even before its first performance, at the **court of Versailles** on May 12, 1664, the penultimate day of **Louis XIV's** lavish festival, the *Plaisirs de l'île enchantée*, members of the **Company of the Holy Sacrament** fiercely attacked *Le Tartuffe ou l'imposteur*. This inauspicious first response to what would become one of Molière's most successful plays turned out to be a harbinger of events to come in the work's troubled early history. Between 1664 and 1669, when *Le Tartuffe* was finally presented in the five–act version known today, his opponents, offended by the broadly drawn portrait of a hypocrite who bore a marked resemblance to some of them, besieged Molière and lobbied successfully to have the play banned. Charged with defaming true **religious** piety, he parried their every thrust and in the end carried the day. His victory was both a triumph for the theater and a stunning blow against the *cabale des dévots* that had dogged him at every turn.

Conceived in 1627 by Henri de Levis, Duc de Ventadour, the Compagnie du Saint–Sacrement, the most imposing organization in the *cabale*, brought together a group of mostly lay collaborators who engaged in charitable works running the gamut from offering assistance to the poor to missionary activities and giving succor to **galley slaves**. The company's ranks included many men of substantial wealth and influence. Members of the family of **Nicolas Fouquet**, *surintendant des finances* under Mazarin, were associated with the society, as were Molière's former patron, the **Prince de Conti**, and Vincent de Paul, founder of the Lazarists and the Sisters of Charity. In addition to good works, the **Company of the Holy Sacrament** championed some of the harshest measures of the Counter–Reformation and took upon itself the role of policing moral behavior. Its members, for example, would report to husbands the amorous adventures of their errant wives. Such meddling in the affairs of citizens made trouble primarily for those most immediately concerned, but the real power of the company lay in its considerable political clout. The high moral dudgeon of its members seriously annoyed Louis XIV. Their pro–papal, pro–**Spanish** stance led him to ban the company after the death of his ailing mother, **Anne of Austria**, a *dévote* with great sympathy for its goals.

Molière never published the first version of *Le Tartuffe*, nor has any text of it survived. Much speculation has therefore surrounded it. Certainly, the original performance had three acts, and the hypocrite was named Tartuffe, but whether the play performed on May 12, 1664 was a finished piece or a work in progress yet to be completed remains unclear. Citing conflicting documentation from the period, scholars have argued both sides of this question. One may point out, however, that the entry in **La Grange's** Register is very similar to that for the two acts of *Mélicerte*, a play as yet unfinished when presented. In either case, just which of the final version's five acts were performed in 1664 is in doubt. Many commentators believe that the first three acts of today's text constituted the first *Tartuffe*. The British critic, John Cairncross, has proposed something quite different: in its first performance of *Le Tartuffe*, Molière's troupe played today's acts I, III, and IV.

Whatever the presentation at Versailles that day, reaction to it was swift and, for Molière and his company, crushing. Less than a week after its first performance, *Le Tartuffe* was banned by the King. The Queen Mother had been scandalized by the play, and the archbishop of **Paris, Hardouin de Péréfixe**, as well as the Premier Président du **Parlement, Guillaume de Lamoignon**, opposed it. Molière's initial defense of his work came in a *Placet au roi* that he wrote to respond to the diatribe of **Pierre Roullé**, a curate in the parish of Saint–Barthélemy. In his polemical *Le Roi glorieux au monde*, Roullé called Molière "a man, or rather a demon dressed in flesh and clothed as a man, and the most outrageously impious libertine who has ever appeared in centuries." He also suggested that Molière be burned at the stake, whose fire would serve as a forerunner for what the dramatist would surely suffer in hell. Quoting to the King this description of himself, Molière contends that the function of comedy is to "correct people while entertaining them." He can imagine nothing more beneficial than to "attack the vices of these times through ludicrous depictions." In his denunciation of hypocrites, he has taken care to distinguish between the truly pious and those who merely ape them. He reminds the King that despite having banned *Le Tartuffe*, His Majesty had found nothing particularly objectionable in the comedy itself and that a number of prelates, including the papal legate, Cardinal Chigi, had actually given the play their nod of approval. Molière attributes Louis's ban more to "the sensitivities of your mind in matters of religion" than to anything scandalous in the play itself. It is true that the King seems to have appreciated the play and must have known that even though he had banned it, *Le Tartuffe* was given a number of private readings for such figures as the **Grand Condé**. Moreover, in August 1665, Louis XIV named Molière's company the "**Troupe du Roi**," thus taking over from his brother the role of its royal **patron**. Molière had good reason to express his confidence in the King's judgment, which he does in the *placet's* final lines.

On August 5, 1667, Molière produced a second version of his play at the Palais Royal Theater. The work now had five acts and a new title, *L'Imposteur*. The hypocrite's name was changed to Panulphe. Louis XIV was away from Paris with his army at the time, but he had probably made some verbal comment to Molière that the dramatist interpreted as permission to perform *L'Imposteur*. Be that as it may, Lamoignon, who in the King's absence had the authority to do so, immediately banned the play again, and on August 11, the archbishop of Paris issued a strongly worded condemnation of it. Péréfixe forbade the faithful in his diocese, under pain of excommunication, to perform, read, or attend readings of the play. Molière appealed personally to Lamoignon, but to no avail. He then dispatched two of his actors, **La Thorillière** and **La Grange**, to the King's encampment at **Lille**. They carried with them a second *placet* in which Molière explained that he had, in this new version of his play, introduced certain "adoucissements." Among these was giving Panulphe a **costume** less likely to be confused with the dress of a cleric. Still, he complains, his attackers, those "famous models of the **portrait** I would paint," remain relentless in their assault against him while paying no attention to flagrantly antireligious works by other writers. Molière will rightly argue in his preface that he had taken care to "carefully distinguish between the character of the hypocrite and that of the truly righteous man," and in the *placet*, he insists that what his opponents resent about *L'Imposteur* is not that it is dangerous to religion or genuine devoutness but rather that it puts those very people onstage for all to see and makes them a laughingstock. Molière will have to stop writing comedy if these "tartuffes," as he calls them, continue to have the upper hand. The King let stand the ban but agreed to reexamine the case upon his return to Paris.

Several weeks after the only performance of *L'Imposteur*, a *Lettre sur la comédie de l'Imposteur* was published in defense of the play. Its author is unknown, but the precision and detail with which he describes the play's performance suggest, at the very least, the possibility of some collaboration with Molière. The letter's tone communicates a confidence that the play will eventually be performed again in public, as indeed it was on February 5, 1669 in a final version now entitled *Le Tartuffe*. If the *Lettre* is to be trusted, *Le Tartuffe* was very close to *L'Imposteur*. It was an immense success and continues to this day to be widely read and presented on stage.

The story it tells is simple. Tartuffe, an unctuous *faux dévot*, has insinuated himself into the comfortable bourgeois household of **Orgon**, who, having witnessed the hypocrite's fervent displays of piety in church, has been so completely taken in that he invites the impostor home with him. Once installed in Orgon's residence, Tartuffe tries to lord it over the entire family. Aside from the paterfamilias himself, only Orgon's mother, **Madame Pernelle**, is fooled. All the other family members see Tartuffe as the parasitic intruder he is. Impervious to the rational arguments against his infatuation offered by his brother–in–law, **Cléante**, Orgon has decided to marry his daughter, **Mariane**, to Tartuffe, despite his earlier pledge to allow her to wed her beloved **Valère**. Tartuffe's only mistake is to try to seduce **Elmire**, Orgon's wife. Elmire feigns interest in the hypocrite in order to dissuade him from marrying Mariane. The ensuing seduction scene is interrupted by a shocked, infuriated **Damis**, Orgon's son, who proceeds to inform his father of the horror that he has just witnessed. Incredulous, Orgon turns to Tartuffe, who admits to being a miserable sinner without owning up to the attempted seduction. Duped again and now enraged by what he believes to be Damis's false accusation of the holy man, Orgon banishes his son, disowns him, and makes over his estate to Tartuffe. In an attempt to prevent the **marriage** of Mariane to Tartuffe and to prove to her husband the hypocrite's treachery, Elmire convinces Orgon to watch from under a table as she allows Tartuffe to try once more to seduce her. After far too much hesitation, Orgon finally emerges from his hiding place and insists that Tartuffe leave, only to be reminded that Tartuffe now owns the property. The day is saved by the **Exempt**, who arrives as the representative of an omniscient, all–powerful Louis XIV. Tartuffe is arrested for a series of crimes committed before he met Orgon, and the property is restored to Orgon, who now declares that Mariane and Valère shall marry.

That Tartuffe comes dangerously close to carrying the day and is defeated not by a counterbalancing religious force but rather by the King probably added grist to the mill of Molière's opponents, for if good triumphs in the end, the victory belongs not to true piety but to secular and social imperatives.

*Le Tartuffe* is organized around two groups of characters: Tartuffe and his acolytes — the impostor's servant, Laurent, who speaks not a word, Madame Pernelle, and Orgon — and, on the other side, everyone else. In the latter group, Cléante most nearly approximates a kind of ideal. His approach to life is at once rational and pragmatic. He sees through Tartuffe and understands that Orgon's credulity has turned his brother–in–law into a dupe, and a ridiculous one at that. Orgon's fault, in Cléante's view, is his failure to draw a clean distinction between hypocrisy and piety. To mistake the mask Tartuffe wears for the real

Tartuffe is to "confuse appearance with reality" (I, 5). Cléante's counsel sounds very much like **Descartes's** definition of "bon sens," the capacity to distinguish between truth and falsehood. While denying that he is in any way "libertin," Cléante leans in his thinking toward the **philosophical** rather than toward the religious. The moral guide he proposes is that of the "honnête homme," not that of the fellow traveler of the Compagnie du Saint–Sacrament.

Orgon's family and their servant, **Dorine**, share Cléante's mistrust of Tartuffe. In this, they are obviously correct, but their motives are complicated. Damis loves Valère's sister and has, therefore, a vested interest in Orgon's honoring his commitment to Mariane and her lover. Damis has also been displaced in his father's attention — and his estate — by Tartuffe. This can only stir up the son's hatred for the intruder and intensify Damis's desire to force his father to see Tartuffe for what he really is. For Mariane and Valère, Tartuffe not only exemplifies religious hypocrisy and tyranny over the family, but he is also the obstacle to their marriage and future happiness. The reactions of Orgon's children reflect their sense of what is right, their own personal needs, and their relationship with their father.

Elmire is Orgon's second wife and the sympathetic stepmother of his children. Madame Pernelle accuses her of being a spendthrift, dressing like a princess, and setting a generally bad example for Orgon's children. Given the nature of the accuser and Elmire's behavior in the play, none of this impugns her character. The author of the *Lettre sur la comédie de l'Imposteur* speaks of Elmire as "a truly upright woman who knows her duties perfectly well and satisfies them scrupulously." She tells her husband that she is amazed by his "blindness" and "strange weakness" for the hypocrite (IV, 3). She is determined to disabuse him of his wrong–headed opinion of Tartuffe. Sensing the impostor's attraction to her, Elmire uses it to protect Mariane and to save Orgon from his own folly. In both instances, she must place herself in a potentially compromising situation with the ruthless Tartuffe, whose presence always represents a danger. Elmire's virtue, needless to say, remains intact.

Only Orgon and his mother allow themselves to be seduced by Tartuffe's patently false piety. Madame Pernelle has from the outset convinced herself that he is "a righteous man who must be heard" (I, 1). Even after Orgon has seen Tartuffe in action with Elmire, Madame Pernelle refuses to believe that her idol has fallen. Appearances often deceive, she tells her son: "One should not always judge by what one sees" (V, 3). Orgon's obstinacy equals hers until he becomes an eyewitness to the impostor's perversity and hears Tartuffe tell Elmire that her husband is "just between us, a man with a ring in his nose" (IV, 5). The desire of these characters to control the family helps explain their devotion to Tartuffe. Although Madame Pernelle and Orgon are duped by Tartuffe, they also use him as a cudgel against others. Madame Pernelle defends Tartuffe's authority because she experiences it vicariously, and Orgon imposes his will on a recalcitrant family by forcing the hypocrite upon them. Being oblivious to the truth about Tartuffe becomes both convenient and necessary for Orgon, as there develops between the two men a mutual need. Tartuffe is the play's eponymous character, but Orgon, whose role was performed by Molière, is no less crucial to its action. Orgon and Tartuffe are, until the denouement, an inseparable couple.

The complexity of the relationship emerges gradually but plainly in a series of telling scenes. In the first act, Orgon returns home, inquires of Dorine about the state of affairs in his household, and quickly reveals that he cares only about Tartuffe. Each time the servant describes a symptom of the malady suffered by Elmire, Orgon responds, "Et Tartuffe?" and to Dorine's descriptions of the scoundrel's hearty appetite and splendid good health, Orgon exclaims, "The poor fellow!" (I, 4). In the next scene, he describes for Cléante how he met Tartuffe in church and was overwhelmed by him. Although he appears to be little more than a mindless dupe of the wily Tartuffe, Orgon demonstrates by certain of his comments that his predilection for the hypocrite is not so simple. Tartuffe, he tells Cléante, "teaches me not to care for anything" (I, 5). In the presence of Tartuffe, Orgon divests himself of all feelings of attachment to his family and sees them as pawns to be manipulated for his own purposes. When Damis confronts Orgon with the truth about Tartuffe (III, 6) and the impostor threatens to leave the household, Orgon will have none of it: "No, you shall stay! My life depends on it!" (III, 7). Here Orgon admits his dependence on Tartuffe and shows his own willfulness. He may be tricked by Tartuffe, but he also insists that Tartuffe stay put as proof of the domination he as father still exercises over his family. Finally, that Orgon hesitates to come out from under the table where he is hiding as Tartuffe makes advances to Elmire indicates that the demise of his hero represents for Orgon a loss of power that he cannot easily relinquish. What seems to incite Orgon's belated reaction is Tartuffe's deprecating remark about leading his victim around by the nose. The possibility of Elmire's being dishonored is a secondary concern. Orgon has been a willing dupe. He and Tartuffe call each other "brother." While each seeks to control the other, they establish a fraternity defined by a common purpose: both plot to dominate the members of the family and become master of the entire household.

As in much of Molière's theater, the servant in *Le Tartuffe* plays a significant role. Dorine appears in the first scene and despite the hectoring of Madame Pernelle, draws a portrait of Tartuffe that prepares the audience for his eventual appearance in the third act: "His whole act is nothing but hypocrisy, believe me!" (I, 1). Dorine's good sense and perceptiveness lead her to realize what Tartuffe is up to and where his weakness lies — "Elmire holds some sway over his heart" (III, 1). Her understanding of Tartuffe's vulnerability suggests the importance of her part in the work. In the second act, which has been criticized as insubstantial and unnecessary, Dorine resolves a lovers' spat between Mariane and Valère, who has heard about Orgon's plan to give his daughter to Tartuffe and is angry that she has not resisted more vehemently. Dorine's intervention reunites the couple, thereby undermining Tartuffe's prospects.

The denouement of *Le Tartuffe*, in which a representative of the King appears as a *deus ex machina* to bring about a happy ending, has seemed to many critics facile and contrived. With this conclusion to his play, Molière sings the praises of a king with whom he was understandably pleased and who is known to have been susceptible to such flattery. The Exempt, who comes to announce the arrest of Tartuffe and the pardon of Orgon for a minor bit of collaboration in the Fronde, portrays Louis XIV as "a Prince who hates fraud and whose eyes pierce into the very hearts of his people" (V, 7), a prince who can never, therefore, be taken in by a Tartuffe. Whether or not this end satisfies all audiences, it does restore to the household and to the lives of its members the good order that had been threatened by the introduction of Tartuffe into Orgon's family. One senses, however, that order will hold sway only temporarily, for Orgon, although chastened by what has happened, undergoes no fundamental change. And Molière undoubtedly knows that there will be other Tartuffes to replace the one whom the King is about to jail.

   Bibliography: *Tartuffe*, ed. J.–P. Collinet (Paris: Gallimard, 1985); *Tartuffe*, ed. H. Gaston Hall, 2nd ed. (London: Arnold, 1979); *Tartuffe*, ed. Richard Parish (London: Bristol Classical Press, 1994); John Cairncross, *New Light on Molière* (Geneva: Droz, 1956); James F. Gaines and Michael S. Koppisch, eds., *Approaches to Teaching Molière's Tartuffe and Other Plays* (New York: Modern Language Association, 1995); J. L. Kasparek, *Molière's Tartuffe and the Traditions of Roman Satire* (Chapel Hill: University of North Carolina Press, 1977); Herman P. Salomon, *Tartuffe devant l'opinion française* (Paris: PUF, 1962); Jacques Scherer, *Structures de Tartuffe* (Paris: SEDES, 1966).

*Michael S. Koppisch*

**Tempe**.   A valley in **Thessaly**, mythological home of **shepherds and shepherdesses**, which is the scene of *Mélicerte* and *Les Amants magnifiques*.

**Terence**.   This great **Roman** comic playwright of the second century B.C. was, according to **La Grange** and **Vivot**, young Molière's favorite author while he was at school. If Molière usually preferred to emulate the rowdier **Plautus**, it was perhaps because Terence had already been heavily worked over by the Renaissance humanists and left little room for originality. Indeed, in *Les Femmes savantes*, **Vadius** reports to **Philaminte** that **Trissotin** had already plagiarized Terence. However, Molière did turn to the more refined poet for *Les Fourberies de Scapin*, when he looked to *Phormio* and other Terentian originals for the basis of his plot.

**Theaters**.   Generally, Parisian theaters of the seventeenth century were converted tennis courts: long, narrow buildings that were open to the weather by louvers under the roof. Conversion involved adding a narrow, raised stage; several rows of bleacher–like seating against the walls, called the amphitheater; and some loges built into the upper parts of the walls over the stage. Large chandeliers directly above the stage provided lighting. These are the types of modifications made by the **Illustre Théâtre** company to the two tennis courts that they had converted consecutively in 1641 and 1642. The fact that the buildings were not closed to the weather meant that during the winter theater season they could be quite cold, and it was the extraordinary cold wave of that winter that doomed the Illustre Théâtre more than the quality of its acting or its texts. During most of Molière's career, there were three other resident troupes in Paris. The oldest played in the **Hôtel de Bourgogne**, a building originally converted in the sixteenth century for the performance of mystery plays. This troupe, which went by the name of the King's Comedians or Great Comedians, was proud of its seniority. The junior French troupe performed at the Théâtre du **Marais** and were simply known by the latter word. It was this group, led by the great Mondory, which had brought **Corneille's** tragic tetralogy to the stage in the 1630s and 1640s. **Italian** players were also present, performing *commedia dell'arte* scenarios in their own language. When Molière returned to **Paris**, they were led by the great **Scaramouche** and used the theater in the **Petit–Bourbon** that Molière and his comrades were allowed to share. The Italians moved along with Molière's players in 1660 when the Petit–Bourbon was razed to make room for **Claude Perrault's** new east façade of the **Louvre**. Their new quarters in the Palais Royal Theater offered distinct advantages, since the theater had actually been designed for drama and **opera** by **Cardinal Richelieu**.

In *Les Fâcheux*, Act I, scene 1, **Éraste** gives a lengthy description of his afternoon at the theater with a pest who flouts the conventions of good behavior. After buying a seat on the stage, a practice that cash–seeking companies regrettably condoned, this **nobleman** makes a spectacle of himself by planting himself in the very middle of it — literally in the "king's place." He goes on to create further distraction by speaking loudly with all his acquaintances, speaking the lines before the actors do, and then leaving the theater before the last act is finished. **Acaste** adds to this description of impertinent playgoers in *Le Misanthrope*, where he boasts to **Clitandre** of attending all the newest shows, and making lots of noise every time the audience says, "Ah!" (III, 1). One can imagine the effect of such lines upon the contemporary audience, who could point to a dozen such individuals in their own midst as they hooted with joy.

*See also* **Audience**; **Groundlings**; **Machine Plays**.

**Thebes**. Capital of ancient Boeotia, this city was the setting of *Amphitryon*.

**Théocle (***La Princesse d'Élide***)**. **Du Croisy** originally played this prince of Pylos, comrade of **Aristomène** and, like him, spurned suitor to the hand of the **Princess**. He arrives onstage at the beginning of Act II to voice a few lines of disappointment and again at the end of the play, silently, to accept **marriage** with either **Aglante** or **Cynthie**.

**Theocritus**. This Syracusan poet of the third century B.C. is one of the ancients that **Trissotin** is accused by **Vadius** of plagiarizing. His pastoral idylls were admired as masterpieces, even by those who did not have access to the original **Greek**.

**Thessaly**. A region of **Greece** in the northeast part of the peninsula that in ancient times was sparsely inhabited and relatively undeveloped. The rural paradise of the Vale of **Tempe** is located there. In *Amphitryon*, Molière mistakenly places **Thebes** in this province, alluding to the powers of its

**magicians**. Thebes was actually to the south, in Boeotia. He commits another geographic error by placing the **Pythian Games** in Thessaly in *Les Amants magnifiques*. Dedicated to Apollo and named after the famous Pythian oracle, those athletic contests were actually held every four years at the temple site of **Delphi**, which is in Phocis. The association probably came through the character of **Sostrate**, who is supposed to have defeated **Brennus** and the **Gauls** in their invasion of Greece in 279 B.C. According to the legend, Brennus was defeated by a local force at Delphi and pursued to the region of Thermopylae, which is in Thessaly. Molière again mentions the magic of Thessaly in *Psyché*, where her sisters wonder whether it may be the source of her attractiveness.

**Thibaudier, Monsieur (*La Comtesse d'Escarbagnas*)**. The ludicrous nature of this role, played by **Du Croisy**, is "telegraphed" onstage in the form of a gift and **love letter** even before the person arrives. It is not just the pears that this lawyer sends to the Countess but the awkward manner in which he puns on them that makes him laughable. He goes on to present verses that are equally half–baked. Upon hearing the first oddly metered stanza of short lines, the **Viscount** sarcastically exclaims, "After that, I am lost!" The second offering starts off a bit less haltingly, but still relies on flattery of the Countess's pretensions, and ends with a disastrous metaphor involving a tiger. Thibaudier is only slightly less inadequate when he stays within his legal jargon, for his efforts to be "the lawyer of my flaming love" simply pollute the conventions of love with legalese.

**Thibaut (*Le Médecin malgré lui*)**. Appearing only in Act III, scene 2, with his little son **Perrin**, this **peasant** character speaks not only with a thick accent, like **Lubin**, but also forms numerous malapropisms as he describes his wife's symptoms to **Sganarelle**. He confounds *hypocrisie* with *hydropisie*, *sériosités* with *sérosités*, *syncoles* with *syncopes*, *conversions* with *convulsions*, and so forth. Sganarelle refuses to understand him until some payment is made. When Perrin gives him a couple of coins he says the boy is much clearer than his father. This role could very well have been doubled with that of **Monsieur Robert** in Act I, both being played perhaps by **De Brie**.

**Thierry, Denis II** (ca. 1620–1712). Parisian printer who, along with **Barbin**, published the 1674 collected edition of Molière's works. **Trabouillet** joined the pair when they added *Le Malade imaginaire* in the eighth volume, followed by **Brécourt's** testimonial *L'Ombre de Molière*. Thierry, who became a syndic of the printers' guild in 1671, was **Boileau's** regular publisher.

**Time**. In Act V, scene 4 of *Dom Juan*, the veiled female **spectre** that appears to warn the protagonist of his imminent destruction transforms when he tries to run it through with his sword. It becomes a figure of Time holding his scythe and flies off. Rather than the conventional image of Father Time, many productions depict this figure as the Grim Reaper, an even more appropriate companion for the rake.

**Timoclès (*Les Amants magnifiques*).** This prince is far more taciturn than his rival **Iphicrate** and apparently places his faith in his singers and dancers when it comes to wooing the princess. The effort seems misplaced, for she seems less impressed by the non–stop series of concerts and **ballets** than any other character in the play. In other respects, Timoclès is a mirror of his fellow prince, flattering and bribing the same intermediaries, though less well, and readily agreeing to the use of **astrology** to pick a husband for **Ériphile**. He is no more successful than Iphicrate when it comes to speaking privately with the princess, but he accompanies his counterpart in the final scene, where they bitterly complain after the fact that **Aristione** has accepted a son–in–law of lower standing than themselves. They both make vague threats to her, which she adroitly deflects, trying to interest them in the games to come.

**Tircis (*La Princesse d'Élide*).** This unlisted character appears with **Philis** at the end of Act III and apparently waits in the wings with her while **Moron** and the Princess finish their conversation. During the fourth *intermède* he sings to his beloved in the conventional pastoral manner of the age. Moron offers a little ditty that cannot compete with Tircis's polished melodies, and when the fool talks of committing suicide out of desperation, Tircis encourages him in song: "Take heart, Moron! Die promptly / As a thoughtful lover should!" Pretending to stab himself, Moron mocks Tircis, but Philis asks him to accompany her to Echo Point, where they can continue their serenade. The musical part was probably taken by one of the singers listed in the sixth *intermède*, either Le Gros, Estival, Don, or Blondel.

**Tirso de Molina, Gabriel Tellez, alias** (ca. 1583–1648). Spanish playwright of the late Golden Age whose *Burlador de Sevilla*, the original Don Juan play, was to have a huge impact on Molière and other French Classical playwrights. However, Molière borrowed mainly from the two previous French versions of the story by **Dorimond** and **Villiers**, as well as from lost **Italian** scenarios. A more obscure play, *La Vengeance de Tamar*, has been suggested as a source for some of the medical conversation in *L'Amour médecin*, although there is little documentary evidence for this.

*See also* **Spanish Influences**.

**Tobacco.** Already a rage in Holland and **England**, tobacco was gradually gaining a foothold in France in Molière's time. **Sganarelle** discusses its alleged benefits for the mind in the first scene of *Dom Juan*. He is obviously talking about snuff, rather than smoking tobacco. There was considerable medical controversy over the herb at the time, some **doctors** considering it poisonous and others lauding its positive effects on the brain, the respiratory system (!), and other bodily and mental functions.

**Toinette (*Le Malade imaginaire*).** One of the sauciest and most energetic of female **servants** in Molière's comedies, she is more a general factotum than a mere maid in **Argan's** household, where she has to care for a flirtatious second wife, a hypochondriac master, a fashionable young lady, and a mere child of six years. She is onstage almost continually, from the second scene, where she appears in answer to Argan's frantic bell ringing, to the medical masquerade that ends the play. Her first lines, where she moans about hitting her head while running to help her master, underline the sarcastic counterpoint that she provides throughout the dialogue. It is she who characterizes **Fleurant** and **Purgon** before they even appear as grotesque sniffers of chamber pots and experts on excrement, deriving their living from the wastes of people's bowels. Later, she does the same for **Diafoirus** and his son, summing up the pair even before they set foot onstage. Argan no sooner introduces his plans to trade **Angélique** in **marriage** for a live-in **doctor** than Toinette launches a massive verbal counterattack, correctly predicting her master's maudlin sentimentality when it comes to actually hurting his daughters. She acts as a confidante and a prop to Angélique's morale and an accessory to all plans to thwart the Diafoirus marriage and to promote **Cléante's** cause instead. Her performance as a **disguised** doctor in Act III recalls the **farce** of *Le Médecin volant*, because she has to run back and forth, convincing Argan that she is two people at once and that the uncanny resemblance between her and the physician is strictly a coincidence. Her repetition of "the lungs" as the cause of all of Argan's problems, her counter-prescription of a diet of hearty meats and full-bodied **wine**, and her parting suggestion that Argan amputate an arm and gouge out an eye, the latter deriving from a surprisingly serious biblical context, are all memorable details of her medical **satire**. She can successfully ape the submissive servant, however, when she is dealing with the malicious **Béline**, who never guesses that she is faithful to Argan and his family. The role was a real tour de force for **Mlle. Beauval** and the key to much of her future success in the French theater. It also neatly sums up the increasing trend of the feminization of the domestic staff in Molière's theater, as she emerges to become the equal of a **Mascarille** or a **Sganarelle**.

**Tomès** (*L'Amour médecin*). This **doctor**, an ardent proponent of bleeding as a universal remedy, was probably based on **D'Aquin**, Molière's landlord and court physician.

**Toulouse**. Major city of the upper Garonne valley. **Charles Dufrense's** wandering troupe of actors, including Molière and the **Béjarts**, performed there in the spring of 1649.

**Trabouillet**. Parisian printer who joined **Barbin** and **Thierry** in publishing the final volume of the 1674 edition of Molière's collected works.

**Trissotin** (*Les Femmes savantes*). Ridiculous savant and poet, based on the model of the **abbé Cotin**. Like Tartuffe, he is much discussed before he arrives onstage. His opening scene proves the dysfunction that he threatens to bring to the household, for all the usual roles are reversed. Instead of handing out compliments, he is on the receiving end; instead of acting like a male, he assumes a kind of female identity, comparing the poem he reads to a baby he will have in **Philaminte's** salon. Like **Oronte** in *Le Misanthrope*, he introduces his stupid poems (taken from the actual works of Cotin) with excessive self–interruptions. The arrival of **Vadius** prompts him to engage in a passage of stichomythia, where each man matches the other's compliments line for line. However, as soon as Vadius pronounces a negative opinion of the octosyllabic sonnet about Urania's fever, he initiates a mirror sequence, where the two match each other insult for insult. His stream of insipid comments fits him neatly into the dialogue of the circle of women, but a discussion with **Clitandre** shows how badly **Trissotin** fares in conversation with a man. Clitandre has the better of the *bons mots*, showing paradoxically how in this case much science has produced a great idiot. A few lines later, he calls the poet an ignorant idiot, which Trissotin tries to dismiss on the grounds of redundancy, but Clitandre avers that there is an even closer relationship between the words "idiot" and "pedant." When Trissotin attacks the tastes and generosity of the **court**, Clitandre delivers a shattering defense of both, implicitly justifying Cotin's removal from the royal pension lists. Trissotin later gives evidence of a certain moral casuistry, for when **Henriette** tries to disengage herself from his clutches, he fights her arguments with one pretext after another, but finally admits that he just wants to enjoy her body, cost what it may. Just as unctuously, he quickly cuts and runs when it appears that Philaminte's family has lost all its **money**, for his lust is seasoned with gold and without that ingredient he will not stay for the meal. Trissotin is perhaps a slightly less deadly parasite than Tartuffe, since he does not seek right away to drain the entire family of its lifeblood, but he operates in much the same fashion. In this play, though, there is no defense of "real intellect," as there is of "real devotion" in the earlier comedy. Perhaps Molière felt that the play itself is a demonstration of real intellect in action, and therefore needs no reasoning spokesman in the text. Still, there is the impression that Trissotin would have been a more interesting figure in some ways if he had a little less of Cotin and a little more of the idealized intellectual parasite in him, so that a clearer distinction could be drawn in favor of his true opposite. **La Thorillière** was first cast in the role.

**Trivelin.** Stock character of the *commedia dell'arte*, Trivelin is mentioned in the preface to *Les Précieuses ridicules*, along with the **Capitan** and the **Doctor**, as comic figures at whom the soldiers, savants, magistrates, and princes of the real world should take no offense, no matter what they poke fun at onstage. In *L'Amour médecin*, a group of figures **costumed** as Trivelins dance with **Scaramouche** figures in the second entr'acte.

**Troupe du Roi.** *See* **King's Troupe**.

**Trufaldin** (*L'Etourdi*). An elderly man, Trufaldin has bought **Célie**, and apparently some others including **Andrès**, from a wandering troupe of **Gypsies** who promise him that she will be richly ransomed by her family. Several attempts to approach her are made by her suitors, **Lélie** and **Léandre**. In the first act, **Mascarille** gains entrance by pretending to consult Célie's Gypsy fortune–telling powers for his master. Trufaldin consents, provided she refrain from using any black magic. Later, both young men attempt to elope with her during masquerades, only to end in failure. Lélie stupidly unmasks his own agent, Mascarille, and Léandre receives the contents of a chamber pot on his head, courtesy of Trufaldin. In the fourth act, having learned that Trufaldin is actually a former Neapolitan named Zanobio Ruberti, whose son has been lost during his studies, Mascarille dresses up Lélie as an **Armenian** and gains access to the house with bizarre tales of foreign encounters. Trufaldin's grasp of geography and his perceptive powers eventually cause the plot to fail, with a little help from his godchild Jeannette. Trufaldin finally finds out the truth about his **children** in Act V, when he and Andrès interrupt a fight between two old hags, only to discover that they are the real and false guardians of Ruberti's daughter Célie and that Andrès is his long–lost son. He rapidly agrees to an arrangement with **Pandolphe** whereby Lélie weds Célie and Andrès weds a conveniently single daughter. Trufaldin appears to be almost as greedy as **Anselme**, since he is eager to realize his profit on the purchase of the **slave** girl. Beyond this, there is little but the obligatory outpouring of sentiment in the recognition scene to distinguish him from the stock figure of the comic pantaloon.

**Tuileries.** The Tuileries Palace was originally a separate part of the **Louvre**, eventually to be connected by the long gallery along the Seine. It contained a sumptuous **theater** designed by **Le Vau** that was capable of accommodating 7,000 spectators. This room was mainly used for staging **Italian operas**, since it was equipped with all the necessary facilities for stage **machinery**. Thus, it was well suited for the first court performance of *Amphitryon* on January 16, 1668, and for the premiere of *Psyché* in 1671.

**Tunis.** In *L'Étourdi*, **Mascarille** instructed **Lélie** to identify **Tunis** as the city where he (the "**Armenian**") had encountered **Trufaldin's** lost son. Unfortunately, Lélie blurts out "Turin" instead.

**Turin.** The city that **Lélie**, disguised as an **Armenian**, mistakenly specifies as the place where he met **Trufaldin's** lost son in *L'Étourdi*. Trufaldin knows enough geography to recognize immediately that Turin is in Piemonte, but **Mascarille** tries to explain away the error by saying that a unique phenomenon in the Armenian **language** causes them to pronounce "nis" as "rin."

**Turkey and Turks.** In *L'Étourdi*, **Mascarille** instructs **Lélie**, dressed as an **Armenian**, to tell **Trufaldin** that he has met his lost son in **Turkey** or **Barbary**, "It's all the same." Actually the vague geography of this scheme to approach **Célie** helps lead to its collapse, when the young man confuses **Tunis** with **Turin**. In *L'École des maris*, **Lisette** compares **jealous** men to barbarous Turks, who keep their women cooped up in a harem and incur the wrath of God for doing so. Turks were also popularly associated with **piracy** and **slavery**, so it is natural that **Scapin** blames them for abducting **Léandre** in their infamous **galley** as a pretext for collecting "ransom" from **Géronte**.

**Hali**, the slave in *Le Sicilien*, is a Turk who dresses the part, for in the **Brissart** and **Sauvé** engraving included in the 1682 collected edition, he is shown with a strange pointed hat and a long oriental robe with odd shoes. He introduces other Turkish slaves who are **musicians**, and together they sing an exotic song, "Chiribirida ouch alla," that is largely in the trade **language Sabir**, rather than in actual Turkish. Though he introduces many of the visual and linguistic effects that will be taken up in *Le Bourgeois gentilhomme*, this "real" Turk is closer to **Mascarille** in that he takes pride in his trickery. Hali's verve and silliness was not considered typical of his nation, as Turks were credited with great fortitude. **Monsieur Diafoirus** tells **Argan** in *Le Malade imaginaire* that his son is "strong as a Turk" in his opinions (II, 5). **Sganarelle** calls his master a Turk in *Dom Juan*, apparently referring both to his stubbornness and his heterodoxy.

The Turkish element is most prominent in *Le Bourgeois gentilhomme*. It is well known that the genesis of this play had much to do with a failed diplomatic mission between the Ottoman Empire and the French **court** earlier in the year 1670. **Louis XIV** made the mistake of trying to dazzle the ambassador with his riches, having most of the royal jewels sewn into a diamond–studded formal suit for his audience. The ambassador, a vain and somewhat inexperienced diplomat, took umbrage and said his master's horses wore more jewels for their daily parade. For his part, Molière makes no reference to the diplomatic mission, but confines himself to borrowing a few elements from **Rotrou's** *La Sœur* and incorporating the masquerade closely into his text, which is principally concerned with **bourgeois** usurpation. **Jourdain** only becomes aware of Turkey when the **disguised Covielle** dangles the prospect of an ennobling ceremony before his nose. Turkey's only importance throughout the conclusion of the play is as a source of **nobility** through the fantastical title of *mamamouchi*, which Jourdain believes he has acquired. Though a Turkish expert, the chevalier d'Arvieux, was placed at the disposal of Molière and **Lully** as they concocted their entertainment, it lacks actual Turkish **language** (the foreign words are either imaginary or Levantine Sabir) or customs (the clothes and manners involved are merely exotic stylizations). If Jourdain is lured with promise of alliance to the son of the Grand Turk, it is probably because, below the highest levels, foreign nobility did not really mean much in seventeenth–century France, as Molière's friend the Count of Modena could testify. Turkey was only good for a laugh in the play, which was quite in keeping with royal policy, since in the long run Louis had no intention of abandoning an alliance that could cause so much trouble for his Austrian enemies.

**Turlupin.** One of the **farce** players of the **Hôtel de Bourgogne** whose career peaked during Molière's **childhood**. He is among the *farceurs* to whom Molière is negatively compared in the *Observations on the Festin de Pierre*. The author of that booklet praises Turlupin for his ad lib jokes, aimed to appeal to the whims of the audience.

**Tyrène** (*Mélicerte*).   He is a double for **Acante** and joins him in wooing unsuccessfully the **shepherdesses Daphné** and **Éroxène** (I, 1).   He also accompanies his friend to confront **Myrtil** with their displeasure (II, 6), rejoicing to learn that Myrtil loves elsewhere.  This is thoroughly conventional portrayal of the sad **shepherd**, perhaps by **Du Croisy**.

# U

**Unities.** By Molière's time, the **Aristotelian**–Horatian unities of time, place, and action had become firmly implanted in the French theater through the influence of the **Academy** and such theorists as the abbé d'Aubignac. Molière observes them scrupulously in almost all of his plays. The unity of time decreed that the play should take place within the imaginary span of twenty–four hours, which could be stretched somewhat to include a day and parts of two adjoining nights or a night and parts of two adjoining days. The unity of place demanded a specific locus of all action in the scenes: if not a specific room, public place, or area, at least adjacent parts of a single building or, at very worst, places in the same town. In terms of action, the unities forbade independent subplots. A corollary of this added that all scenes within an act be joined, preferably by at least one character staying on stage from one scene to another, or at very least the departing actors referring to the arriving ones, or vice versa. Molière's one great sin against the unities was in the multiple settings of *Dom Juan*. However, it might be argued, had Molière taken to defending his plays as vocally as **Corneille** did, the tradition of this play absolutely demanded such multiplicity. As it is, Molière takes some care to knit things together, combining the original seaside elements from **Tirso de Molina** with **peasant** elements from the **Italian** scenario. Thus it may be said that Acts I and II take place near the same body of water, Act III in an adjoining wooded area, Act IV at a property of Dom Juan's within walking distance of the **Commander's** statue, and Act V somewhere not far from the spot seen in Act IV. From a certain point of view, all the events may even have transpired within the span of a single, very busy day.

**Uranie (*La Critique de l'École des femmes*).** This hospitable intellectual opens her **salon** to a variety of characters. Though she favors Molière's art, she generally plays a moderate role in the discussion, unlike her lively and playful cousin. She is the one who proposes that the entire scene should be dramatized by Molière himself at the close of the play. Either **Mlle. De Brie** or **Madeleine Béjart** probably played the part, more likely the latter, since the former seems strangely out of touch with recent events of the troupe when she speaks in *L'Impromptu de Versailles*.

**Urceus Codrus (alias Antonio Urceo,** fl. 1446–1450). Noted Renaissance teacher and humanist scholar who wrote a supplement to **Plautus's** *Aulularia*, filling in the lost scenes. The **abbé de Marolles** included the supplement in his 1658 edition.

# V

**Vadius** (*Les Femmes savantes*).  This scholar, much admired and fondled for his knowledge of **Greek**, was probably played by the versatile **Du Croisy**.  Vadius pretends to be too modest to read his verses in **Philaminte's salon**, but then hands out copies instead.  After trading niceties line for line with **Trissotin** on his arrival, he fires salvo after salvo of insults at his departure.  At a safe range, he sends a vitriolic **letter** to Philaminte accusing her favorite of pillaging the great Classical authors.  Gilles **Ménage**, the apparent model for the character, is not subjected to quite so damning a dose of criticism as **Cotin**, since his own poems are not dissected on stage.

**Valère** (*L'Avare*).  He has saved the life of **Harpagon's** daughter **Élise** before the play opens and is "slumming" in the guise of an *intendant* or supervisor in the miser's house in order to be close to his **love**.  He most notably enters into conflict with the "cook/coachman" **Maître Jacques**, arguing over household provisions and other items of "labor relations."  When Jacques challenges him, he soundly routs the commoner.  Jacques gets his revenge by fingering Valère as the thief of the strongbox in the final act.  This gives way to the famous misunderstanding scene, where Valère, unaware of the robbery that has taken place because he was seeing to a pig butchering, confesses his passion, causing Harpagon to think that those erotic thoughts were attached to his **money**.  The recognition scene in the denouement restores his lost father (**Anselme**, aka Dom Thomas d'Alburcy), sister (**Mariane**), and inheritance, enabling him to marry Élise.

**Valère** (*Dépit amoureux*).  He is **Polidore's** son and **Mascarille's** master.  Valère merely laughs off **Éraste's** inquiries about the progress of his suit for the hand of **Lucile**, for he thinks he is already secretly married to the girl, having enjoyed several trysts under cover of night. Little does he know that his partner was actually **Ascagne–Dorothée**, who had fallen in **love** with him when her sister seemed to spurn him. Under cover of her male **disguise**, she teases him about her feelings for him in the first act. His attempt to present his compliments to his "bride" are met with a strong rebuff. Hostilities grow between Valère and Lucile's family, though Éraste, confident of his place after the lovers' quarrel, removes himself from the possible combat that is looming. Valère's attempts to enlist the help of Mascarille give rise to much moaning and poltroonery on the part of the **servant**. When finally confronted with Lucile's champion Ascagne (much to the amusement of Polidore, who is in on the joke), Valère is mystified until true identities are revealed. This part is not as interesting as that of the obsessively **jealous** but sentimental Éraste, calling merely for gracious **politeness**, a bit of desperation, and a good deal of bewilderment.

**Valère** (*L'École des maris*). **Isabelle's** lover. He describes his rival Sganarelle as a savage, a brute, and a hateful Argus. Having tried in vain in Act One, scene three to strike up a friendship with Sganarelle, he explains in the following scene that he has trailed Isabelle like a shadow for months, without being able to enjoy a moment's confidential conversation or to find out how she feels about him. Valère is all the more surprised, then, when Sganarelle accosts him and demands a discussion in the middle of the street. The awkward *quid pro quo* that ensues over the proper etiquette for a discussion prefigures **Dom Juan's** encounter with **Monsieur Dimanche**. He is pleased to learn, however, that Isabelle has chosen none other than her guardian to deliver an indirect **message** of **love**, though Sganarelle scarcely realizes the real meaning of what he is saying. A few scenes later, Valère receives a box with a love **letter**, again via Sganarelle, which Isabelle sends him in the guise of a returned gift. The young man obliges by returning a verbal bouquet of his own, once again using Sganarelle as the unwitting messenger. By the same means, he receives Isabelle's plans for an elopement, using the identity of her sister **Léonor** to cover her tracks. Having performed this, Valère is content to say little for the rest of the play and to consent to a general reconciliation. This personification of the figure of Valère as young lover is beginning to turn away from the crass seducer toward the more *honnête*, if still ingenious characters that we see in later plays, such as *Tartuffe* and *L'Avare*.

**Valère** (*La Jalousie du Barbouillé*). Presumably an adulterous seducer, Valère flirts with Le **Barbouillé's** wife **Angélique** and accepts an assignation, but then disappears from the action.

**Valère** (*Le Médecin malgré lui*). This is the only Valère in Molière's theater who does not have a **love** interest. He is described as a "domestique" (**servant**) of **Géronte**, but also wears a sword and a rather fancy outfit. This is a bit unusual, even if one remembers that the *fabliau* original for Géronte was a prince. At any rate, he would qualify as a "gentleman attendant" at the very least, thus raising Géronte's status to a considerable height. Valère appears in the first act with **Lucas**, searching for a physician who can cure Géronte's daughter. The pair contrasts remarkably, with Lucas dressing and speaking like a **peasant** and Valère like a person of quality. They administer a **beating** to make Sganarelle admit to being a **doctor**, then convey him, at the beginning of Act Two, to Géronte's house to effect his cure of the sick girl. Unlike Lucas, Valère is absent from the third act. Could this part have been played, as other Valères seem to have been, by La Grange? There is no reason to doubt it, since *L'Avare* and *Le Bourgeois gentilhomme* feature other lovers beside La Grange. In terms of stage presence and importance, the roles of Valère and **Léandre**, **Lucinde's** lover, are about equal.

**Valère** (*Le Médecin volant*). Lover of **Gorgibus's** daughter, **Lucile**. He is skeptical about his valet's deceptive talents, but later praises them profusely. He disappears at the end of scene thirteen and apparently absconds with Lucile, but reappears with her in the last scene and asks successfully for forgiveness.

**Valère** (*Tartuffe*). Less enterprising than **Horace** or many other Valères in the Molière canon, this character is absent through the first, third, and fourth acts. His contribution to Act Two is the extended **lovers' spite** scene with **Mariane**. Emotionally volatile, Valère has rushed to Mariane for reassurance at the first rumor that she might not marry him. Finding her confused and upset, he hands her an ultimatum instead of allowing her to recollect herself. This starts the prideful tennis game of exchanged rebuffs, followed by parallel hesitations, as the two cannot bear to tear themselves away from each other, even in the midst of argument. **Dorine** must use a lot of verbal wheedling and some physical displacement to put the two back together. Valère is a perfect incarnation of the nuances of emotion that string themselves together in such spats. His second appearance, in Act Five, adds a dimension of courage and generosity to his character. He has learned that **Orgon** is in dire straits, which prompts him to place his purse and his **carriage** at the disposal of the defeated judge. This certainly serves the purpose of establishing his worthiness as a son–in–law, but in practical terms it comes too late to forestall **Tartuffe's** final maneuvers. He is a concrete, spontaneous counterpart to the abstract, meditative **Cléante**, neither of whom is truly capable of restraining the powers of bigotry.

**Vaugelas, Claude Favre de** (1585–1650). Great grammarian and **academician** whose *Remarks on the French Language* were a landmark in scholarship. **Philaminte's** circle places such importance on his rules that she fires **servants** who break them, but neither her husband nor the cook has great regard for him. Molière does not satirize Vaugelas himself, who would have been the first to point out that his rules were never meant to apply to the **language** of the rural hearth or the city kitchen.

**Vaux–le–Vicomte.** Splendid country house and estate created by Le Vau, Le Nôtre, and **Le Brun** at the orders of Nicolas **Fouquet**, superintendant of finance. The celebrations held there on August 17, 1661 entailed the first production of

*Les Fâcheux*. However, it was not the first of Molière's work for Fouquet. In October 1660, Molière and his troupe found themselves forced into a three–month hiatus. Their theater in the **Petit Bourbon** was being demolished for the expansion of the **Louvre's** Cour Carré, and renovations were required before they could take over the theater promised them in the **Palais Royal**. Fortunately for the troupe's finances, the actors were invited to perform during this period in private homes. According to **La Grange's** Register, one of these productions took place at the residence of the Superintendent, where the troupe acted both *L'Étourdi* and *Le Cocu imaginaire* for which they were liberally rewarded.

Fouquet's generosity to Molière was not surprising, since by 1660 he was well–known in **Paris** as a man of taste and culture and as a bounteous **patron** of artists and writers. Two years earlier, for example, Fouquet had, with a liberal stipend, persuaded **Pierre Corneille** to write his *Oedipe* after an absence of seven years from the theater. About the same time Fouquet's beneficence had attached, among others, the poets **La Fontaine** and **Pellisson** to his service. In addition, the construction which Fouquet had begun at his property Vaux–le–Vicomte in 1656 was providing lucrative work for a number of artists and artisans. This property, which Fouquet had acquired much earlier, in 1641, consisted of an old manor house and its surrounding property some forty kilometers southeast of Paris. Most importantly for its new owner, however, this domain established him as a member of the landed **nobility**.

Born in 1615 into a family of the robe nobility, one that had ennobled itself through judicial service in the **Parlement**, Nicolas was already an office–holder himself by the age of twenty. Then, after his **marriage** in 1640 and the death of his father the same year, Nicolas decided to invest the funds from his wife's substantial dowry and from his father's estate in property that might further enhance his noble status. The very year that he bought Vaux, Fouquet's wife died; nevertheless, he continued adding to his land holdings there. Meanwhile, he continued a steady advance in his career of service to the state, allying himself with the King and Cardinal Mazarin, Louis's first minister, during the Fronde and becoming procureur général, essentially the King's representative to the Paris Parlement, in 1650. A second marriage in 1651 preceeded his being named in 1653 Superintendent of Finances. This post, which Fouquet had to share with Abel Servien until the latter's death in 1659, called on its incumbents to provide financial resources for the crown. Using their personal credit to obtain **money** to be lent at interest to the state, Fouquet and Servien were able to amass great fortunes for themselves.

To reassure his creditors with outward signs of great wealth, as well as to satisfy his own passion for beauty, Fouquet began a program of property acquisition and building shortly after being named Superintendent. By 1654 he had built and sumptuously decorated a house and garden at Saint–Mandé, near his protector Mazarin at **Vincennes**. Nevertheless, by 1656 Fouquet had turned his attention to Vaux–le–Vicomte, where he planned to replace the old house with a magnificent château to be set in the midst of a monumental formal garden. To design this dwelling, Fouquet chose the architect Louis Le Vau, who had already made a name for himself in Paris with the plans for several private mansions on the Île Saint–Louis and who had in 1654 replaced Jacques Lemercier as the King's architect at the Louvre and **Tuileries**. André Le Nôtre, the son and grandson of landscape gardeners associated with the royal Tuileries Gardens, was put in charge of creating the park. Young Charles Le Brun, a painter whom Fouquet had already employed at Saint–Mandé, was assigned responsibility for the interior decoration of the château from ceiling paintings to furniture.

Work on Fouquet's country home proceeded rapidly, and news of the vast undertaking soon brought distinguished visitors to the building site: Mazarin in June 1659; the King, his mother, and his brother in July 1659; and the King again, this time with his new bride, Marie–Thérèse of Spain in July 1660. On each occasion the visitors were provided with a tour of the unfinished house and grounds and with a splendid meal. As the work at Vaux neared completion in 1661, however, Fouquet was able to offer an even more elaborate entertainment to the Queen of England, widow of Charles I, her daughter, and her son–in–law, the King's brother, during a visit on July 12 of that year. In addition to the usual tour and meal, Fouquet furnished these visitors with a theatrical interlude for which he called upon Molière. In the Chambre des Muses of the new château, the company performed for the Superintendent's royal guests Molière's new comedy, *L'École des maris*, first presented in Paris only two and a half weeks earlier. During this summer of 1661, Fouquet had the highest hopes for the advancement of his career; for in March, Mazarin had died, and the Superintendent believed that the young Louis XIV would soon call upon him to replace the cardinal as first minister. In the context of this lofty political dream, then, Fouquet invited the court to a lavish entertainment at Vaux, ostensibly to honor the King, but also to mark the minister's own apotheosis as builder and patron of the arts.

Thus, early in the evening of August 17, 1661, Louis XIV, his mother, his brother and sister–in–law, and the leading figures of the court, with the exception of the Queen who was pregnant and not up to traveling, arrived at Vaux–le–Vicomte after a three–hour journey from neighboring **Fontainebleau**. The structure that greeted the royal guests as they passed by the elegant outbuildings and arrived in the court of honor was a compact limestone palace with high–pitched slate roofs covering symmetrical pavilions and surrounded by an ornamental moat. After touring the interior, the visitors moved through a two–story oval salon before exiting into the garden where they could turn back and admire the structure's majestic dome and lantern. Then, directing their gaze along the main axis of the garden, they beheld a perspective of symmetrically–placed flower gardens, clipped hedges, ornamental pools, fountains, and statuary. As they penetrated further into the park, they took delight in the sight and sound of water: a vast number of fountains, a balustrade of low–rising water jets on either side of the central pathway, a cascade roaring beside a broad canal, and a massive jet spraying water some five meters high.

It was to this magnificent garden, then, that the royal visitors returned after nightfall for a theatrical entertainment, once again provided by Molière and his actors. For this special evening Fouquet had requested a new play, which the playwright had raced to produce in the space of two weeks. Since Fouquet also wanted a **ballet**, the musical artists involved, Pierre Beauchamps and Jean–Baptiste **Lulli**, had agreed with Molière that the dances should occur during the interludes of Molière's play and should be as thematically linked to his text as possible. Consequently, when the distinguished group assembled at the garden's *grille d'eau*, they witnessed the premiere of Molière's first **comedy–ballet**, *Les Fâcheux*.

A bit less than three weeks later, on September 5, 1661, Fouquet, having been convoked by his monarch to **Nantes**, was arrested on the King's orders. The charges against him were the theft of public funds and *lèse–majesté*. Although it is unlikely that Fouquet's entertainment for the King was directly responsible for his arrest, the lavish expenditures so evident at Vaux–le–Vicomte could only have served to confirm long–standing suspicions of embezzlement, which had been spurred vigorously by his rival for the King's favor, Jean–Baptiste **Colbert**. The charge of *lèse–majesté*, more serious still, was based on Fouquet's activities at another of his properties, Belle–Île, along the Atlantic coast of Brittany. What Fouquet had most likely intended there as preparations for a maritime and commercial enterprise designed to encourage France's colonial expansion, Louis saw as preparations for sedition and rebellion.

The trial was sensational, and Fouquet's self–defense was formidable and showed the Superintendent to be essentially innocent of both charges. Political forces won out, however; and when the lengthy trial ended in December 1664, Fouquet was found guilty of questionable financial practices and sentenced to banishment for life. Louis XIV, still highly suspicious of his former minister and disappointed that the court had not condemned him to death, changed this sentence to life imprisonment in the fortress of Pignerol, located across the Alps in territory that today is a part of Italy. Here in a dismal cell, far from family and friends and allowed virtually no communication with the outside world, Fouquet languished until his death in March 1680.

But even before his trial had concluded, Fouquet may have felt some satisfaction in realizing that the splendor that was Vaux–le–Vicomte in that summer of 1661 was being recreated at **Versailles** by the very artists who had brought Vaux into being. Then, in May 1664, when Molière and his actors participated in the festivities inaugurating Versailles and its gardens and especially when they performed once again, but for Louis's guests this time, *Les Fâcheux*, it was evident that Louis XIV's imitation of Fouquet was complete. Politics may have irrevocably separated the monarch and his minister, but in matters of taste they were as one!

*William O. Goode*

**Venice.** The locale where **Andrès** spent some of his "lost years" in *L'Étourdi*.

**Venus (*Les Amants magnifiques*).** It is amusing to note that in the dramatis personae this character is specified to be a "false Venus," in case one may have mistaken her for the real one. This fake deity emerges, accompanied by four little **cupids**, in a **machine** from a grotto that **Aristione** and **Ériphile** are passing (IV, 2). In verse, she delivers the remarkably clear prophecy that Ériphile should marry the man who saves her mother's life. As soon as the women run off to offer thanks at the nearest temple, **Anaxarque** the **astrologer** explains to his son that he has contrived the whole scene at no small expense of time and **money**, hoping to gain a lasting grasp on the royal family. According to Anaxarque's plan, the prophecy is supposed to be fulfilled by **Iphicrate**, who will deliver Aristione from some hired **"pirates,"** but **Sostrate** makes the scheme backfire by preempting this and saving the princess from a boar. It is unknown whether the original actress merely provided a voice for the mechanical apparition or actually emerged in person. In any case, Molière shows remarkably little respect for the love goddess and her influence.

**Venus** (*Psyché*). The only scene from Molière's pen in which Venus appears is the prologue, where she answers the pleas of the sylvan spirits with bitter complaints over the fact that **Psyche** is considered more beautiful than her. Thus she peevishly sets in motion the demand for a sacrifice that will bring Psyche and **Cupid** together. The role was played by **Mlle de Brie**.

**Vergil.** See **Virgil.**

**Verisimilitude.** The doctrine of *vraisemblance* or verisimilitude held that realism was less important in drama that the presentation of events as they could likely happen. This tended to squeeze out many of the extraordinary elements that had appeared in the baroque theater of the turn of the century. Even in *Dom Juan*, which necessarily preserves some of the trappings of **Tirso de Molina's** original, such as the statue that comes to life and the divine punishment of the offender, Molière tends to try to bring events within the realm of the French imagination in order to conform to this idea.

**Versailles.** Royal **hunting** lodge located about 15 miles southwest of **Paris**, which **Louis XIV** began in Molière's time to transform into the monumental palace that stands there today. Following **Fouquet's** famous feast at his newly finished estate at **Vaux–le–Vicomte**, Louis engaged the same trio of builders, the architect Le Vau, the landscape architect Le Nôtre, and the painter **Le Brun**, to construct an even more magnificent residence for his personal use. By 1664, the King began organizing splendid spectacles at Versailles, incorporating parts of the gardens into the theme of the entertainment. As part of the festival of **The Pleasures of the Enchanted Island**, *Tartuffe* was presented there in its earliest form, as well as *L'Amour médecin* in 1665. The **Grand Divertissement Royal de Versailles** made strategic use of the gardens, statues, fountains, and other elements to form a fairyland background for the plays presented there in 1668, including *George Dandin*. In July,1674, it was the site of a reprise of *Le Malade imaginaire* for the **court**, with the entire apparatus of the original prologue and musical accompaniment that had been trimmed shortly after Molière's death by **Lully's** intriguing. One must assume that the reduction from six singers and twelve musicians to two and six, respectively, affected not only the opulent introduction, but also the conclusion, which in the booklet calls for no fewer than 47 people on stage in the medical ceremony spectacle. The King had not yet seen the now famous play, and it was impossible for Lully to impose his prerogatives in the face of the royal will. From the beginning, the construction of Versailles went hand in hand with the development of the *comédie–ballet* as an art–form, since the overwhelming baroque effect created by a multimedia performance was well suited to the political ends of the monarch in making Versailles a means for implementing absolutism and subjecting the **nobility** and all other elements of the country to his will.

**Verse Forms.** As Molière has **Monsieur Jourdain** learn, all writing is either prose or verse, and he was equally adept at both when it came to comedy. Molière used only two forms of verse: the twelve–syllable rhymed couplet known as the *alexandrin* and a type of rhymed and metered free verse very similar to that employed by **La Fontaine** in the *Fables*. The latter was generally confined to songs or quasi–lyrical passages in the works, such as **Mélicerte's** verses to his caged sparrow. The exception was *Amphitryon*, which is free verse throughout.

*Vilain mire, Le (The Peasant Doctor)*. A medieval rhymed tale, or *fabliau*, that provided the essential story for *Le Médecin malgré lui*. Whether Molière adapted an existing **farce** version or a more literary source is a matter of conjecture, for the story had spread widely through European folklore and letters by the seventeenth century, migrating from its original late Old French to many different vernaculars.

**Villebrequin (*La Jalousie du Barbouillé*).** The few lines given to this minor character concern his attempts to make peace during the arguments that constitute much of the play. The name is also mentioned in *Le Médecin volant* as a disagreeable suitor of **Lucile**, but he never appears on stage. Villebrequin appears to have been a stock character in comedies for the actor **De Brie**.

**Villebrequin (*Sganarelle*).** Father to **Valère**, who never appears on stage. **Villebrequin** has arranged for his rich son to marry **Célie**, the daughter of **Gorgibus**, but he appears in the final scene to ruefully announce that his son is already secretly married and that Gorgibus must make other arrangements.

**Villiers (tragic stage name of Claude Deschamps, 1600–?).** This actor and occasional author, whose comic stage name was Philippin, was attached for years to the Hôtel de Bourgogne troupe, as was his wife, Marguerite Béguin. He is noteworthy as the author of a **Don Juan** play (*Dom Juan, ou l'Athée foudroyé*) that, along with those of **Dorimond** and the **Italians**, influenced Molière's *Dom Juan, ou le Festin de Pierre*. He also tried his hand at some light comedies, such as *L'Apothicaire dévalisé* (*The Robbed Druggist*, 1659), *Les Ramonneurs* (*The Chimneysweeps*, 1660) and *Les Costeaux* (*The Gluttons*,

1664), but without much success. In *L'Impromptu de Versailles, Molière* mocked his tragic performance as Iphicrate in **Corneille's** *Oedipe*. Villiers may have replied as early as 1663 in the *Réponse à L'Impromptu de Versailles*, though this text is also attributed to **Donneau de Visé**. He is also often given credit for the anonymous *Critique de Tartuffe* (1669), though it had little effect on the success of Molière's masterpiece. By 1671, Villiers and his wife had disappeared from the roster of the Hôtel de Bourgogne, and one might presume that they had been pensioned, as was wont in that troupe.

However, an unusual note in La Grange's register specifies that from April 28 to August 11, 1672, a certain Villiers was engaged as a "gagiste," or share-less wage–actor, with Molière's troupe. La Grange's lack of qualifiers suggests that it might indeed have been the famous Villiers who had joined the junior troupe and then left abruptly under odd circumstances. If this is the case, it can only be a matter of speculation whether he had broken up on bad terms with the Great Comedians or was experiencing health problems. It is more likely that this Villiers was actually Claude Deschamps's son, who by 1680 was a member of the Hôtel de Bourgogne when it fused with the Hôtel Guénégaud to form the **Comédie–Française** and continued with that company through the end of the century. This Villiers was married to Catherine Raisin. Their son Grandvallon and their daughter Anne, later Mlle Dufey, also became members of the French company. It can only be a mystery why Molière would engage one of his most unspoken enemies, or that man's son, as a part of his troupe.

**Vincennes**. The Château de Vincennes is usually associated in our century with the last use of the guillotine to decapitate criminals. However, in Molière's time, it was still a princely residence, often occupied by Cardinal Mazarin, and a number of command performances took place there, especially in the years before **Versailles** began to be habitable. Molière no doubt knew the place as well as he did the **Louvre** and **Saint–Germain–en–Laye**, since like them it was part of the royal upholsterer's itinerary that he and his father had plied.

**Violinists (*Les Précieuses ridicules*)**. These minor characters appear only at the end of the play, from scene 12 onward, where they play a few tunes and then demand their wages from **Gorgibus**, who chases them out of his house with blows.

**Virgil**. The great first century B.C. poet of **Rome** is cited by **Métaphraste** in the second act of *Dépit amoureux*. **Trissotin** compliments **Vadius** by saying his eclogues are better that Virgil's, but Vadius later accuses him of copying the great Roman.

**Viscount (*La Comtesse d'Escarbagnas*)**. La Grange did not wear himself out with this role. The longest speech concerns a pest who delayed his interview with his beloved **Julie**. He gives an extensive enough **portrait** of the provincial gossipmonger in question, an avid reader and devotee of the **Gazette de Hollande**, to entertain her and assuage her irritation. He offers her a poem that is not addressed to her (though he quickly patches it up) and is probably not his own work. His extreme reluctance to hand her the written version and his cautions about the dangers of leaving written evidence suggest that he pillaged the fairly decent verses in some popular collection. Nevertheless, he has sacrificed himself by pretending to woo the detestable **Countess** in order to approach Julie, whose family is at odds with his. His wit is certainly superior to the provincial yokels who are his rivals, **Thibaudier** and **Harpin**. Apart from the first scene, when he is alone with Julie, he is limited mainly to a few sarcastic remarks about the Countess, played by the woman who would soon become his wife, **Marie Raguenau.**

**Viscount Jodelet** (*Les Précieuses ridicules).* See **Jodelet**.

*Visionnaires, Les* **(*Deluded by Visions*)**. A 1637 comedy by **Desmarets de Saint-Sorlin** that contributed much to Molière's theater. The "visionaries" in the title are insane or delusional, suffering from a warped view of the universe that springs from the bizarre personal identities their imagination has constructed. In the spirit of the Renaissance fools' play, a series different extravagant personalities is presented: one is a *miles gloriosus*, one believes himself rich beyond description, another thinks she is irresistible to any man who sets eyes on her, etc. The play was an important part of Molière's **repertory**, which meant that lines familiar to his actors could be lifted or paraphrased easily into new plays. The overall "review" format influenced the structure of *Les Fâcheux*, while the character of the lady who believes all men love her was adapted for **Bélise** of *Les Femmes savantes*.

**Vivot.** This obscure collaborator helped La Grange with the 1682 collected edition of Molière's works and perhaps with the biographical material as well. All that is known of him is that he was apparently an art dealer and collector living in **Paris**, with a shop in the rue de l'Arbre Sec. A 1670 sonnet by Pinchenes, Vincent **Voiture's** nephew, mentions him as a patron of the arts and a friend of the engraver François **Chauveau**, the painter François **Mignard**, **Pierre Corneille**, Jean **Racine** and (surprisingly) the abbé **Cotin**. The variant spelling of the name of Vinot is an error.

**Voiture, Vincent** (1597–1648). This man of letters was a habitué of the Hôtel de **Rambouillet**, and some have seen him as its poetic ambassador to the rest of France, in charge of promulgating its ideas about the refinement of **language** and verse. Most of his own output was of the light, occasional variety. He was also a member of the **Academy**. Some have seen him as a model for **Vadius** in *Les Femmes savantes*.

**Voltaire, pen name of François–Marie Arouet** (1694–1778). In his youthful correspondance, Voltaire was often rather disparaging ofMolière, even calling him "dull." He mentioned him as a mere derivative of the court of the Bourbon king in *Le Siècle de Louis XIV* and omitted him shockingly from *Le Temple du*

*Goût*. But he became more interested in the comic genius for awhile during the 1730's, when he was trying to interest a publisher in an edition of his plays. Voltaire completed synopses of many of the plays and a life of the author, but the editor's job went to an obscure rival, La Serre.    Making the best of his labor, Voltaire eventually published the biography, and it became a standard ingredient in many editions until, and even after, the great "Grands Ecrivains" edition by Despois and Menard. His "Life of Molière" draws heavily on both La Grange and **Grimarest**. However, it explicitly rejects most of what the latter had to say about **Chapelle** (almost half the book) because his own sources pronounced it worthless.    Voltaire also noted the existence of the farces, *La Jalousie du Barbouillé* and *Le Médecin volant*, which had been discovered in manuscript in the two decades since Grimarest's work.    On the negative side, Voltaire fabricated a good deal of material to fill in the blank years in Molière's life.    For instance, he claimed that Molière and his father had an adversarial relationship, old **Poquelin** having supposedly blocked the young man's education.    Voltaire started the legend that Molière had personally studied for five years with **Gassendi**, enjoying a virtual private arrangement with the master skeptic, even though Gassendi did not come to **Paris** until almost the moment when Molière left with the remnants of the **Illustre Théâtre**. He scrambled some of the information about Molière's life in the provinces, claiming for instance that *Les Précieuses ridicules* was composed in the mid–1650's while the group was still far from Paris.    Most damning of all in some ways, he affirmed that Molière had married not **Madeleine Béjart's** sister, but her daughter, and that thus there was some suspicion of truth behind the incest accusations leveled by **Montfleury** against his rival. Because of the tremendous authority placed in almost anything Voltaire said, many of these errors continued to persist, even when good evidence to the contrary had been exposed. For instance, long after Beffara had discovered the **marriage** certificate for Molière and Armande Béjart stating the latter's identity, many critics held out for years that Voltaire was right. The same is true even today regarding his alleged relationship with Gassendi.    Another less troublesome aspect of Voltaire's "Life" was that he placed Molière squarely in the **philosophic** tradition, claiming him as a predecessor for the struggle for rights that would go on during the century.

# W

**Wages.** Although many **servants** and workers, like Sganarelle in *Dom Juan*, appear to have worked for little more than room and board, we do get an interesting glimpse into the scale of wages for seventeenth–century workers in *George Dandin*, where the peasant **Lubin** reveals that his usual wage is 10 sols a day, or half a livre. Since this is a day wage, and discounting 52 Sundays and holidays (almost 40 days a year under the old regime), that would make a yearly income of about 130 livres. Thus the fact that he has left off his ordinary work, accepting "three gold pieces" (either gold *écus* or *louis*, thus 15 or 30 livres) to deliver messages for **Clitandre** is quite understandable — it represents more than a month of wages. The readiness to accept solid cash was understandable in view of the fact that many workers and servants couldn't recover their wages. Sganarelle's claim is doomed by the fact that death cancelled all debts under Old Regime law.

**Weapons.** Besides the frequently mentioned swords that the **nobility** was entitled to carry, the walking sticks of the **bourgeoisie**, and the occasional halberd carried by a member of the watch, weapons are seldom mentioned in the plays. An exception is *Dom Juan*, where the protagonist, among the extravagant arrangements ordered for **Monsieur Dimanche**, calls for **servants** armed with torches and muskets to accompany the moneylender home. In *Le Sicilien*, **Dom Pèdre**, in order to chase off unwanted suitors from his house, calls forth a veritable arsenal: "Quickly, my sword, my shield, my halberd, my pistols, my muskets, my carbines! Hurry! Quick! Kill! No quarter!" (scene 4). In *Le Malade imaginaire*, **Polichinelle** fires what is variously described as a "mousqueton" or a pistol, but it was probably closer to an obsolete blunderbuss, if we are to judge by the comic effect produced. A slightly more exotic weapon is the **Turkish** scimitar or *sciabbola* mentioned in the mamamouchi ceremony of *Le Bourgeois gentilhomme*.

**White Cross Tavern**. The Croix Blanche was a famous drinking place frequented by all the most notorious **libertines** and freethinkers of **Paris**. Because **Chapelle** was a regular customer, it was assumed by many that Molière must also have been one. There is no documentary evidence to back this up, nor are there any allusions to this particular establishment in the plays. Moreover, the playwright was far too productive to be a sot, so his visits, if any, must have been merely occasional.

**Wife of Sganarelle** (*Sganarelle*). She appears to be an emotional woman of the *petite ou moyenne* **bourgeoisie**, who quickly sympathizes when she finds the swooning **Lélie** and fantasizes over the locket she finds on the ground after **Célie's faint**. She does not hesitate to call her own husband a drunk or an "old hide." Yet she complains that he has not been very affectionate in bed.

**Wills and Testaments**. **Argan** wishes in *Le Malade imaginaire* to write his will so as to benefit his second wife **Béline** and show his gratitude for her doting behavior. He is not pleased to learn from **Bonnefoy** that common law provided for forced inheritance by **children** and that parents could not arrange for a community property regime in the **Paris** jurisdiction. When **Argante** expresses the desire to disinherit **Octave** in *Les Fourberies de Scapin*, the trickster attempts to argue him out of it by denial. *See* **Law**; **Notary.**

**Wine**. From the very beginning of Molière's theatrical career, wine plays an important role. It is certainly the main interest of the protagonist in *La Jalousie du Barbouillé*. But from that play onward, Molière departs from the traditions of his rivals and makes wine most significant by its absence or moderation. He did not want to produce just another generation of drunken comic figures, such as had dominated the Parisian stage through much of the 1640's and 1650's. Mascarille has little time for wine, and Sganarelle, though often complaining of a dry throat, is seldom able to quench his thirst, other than a few quick gulps in *Dom Juan* and a quiet moment with his bottle in *Le Médecin malgré lui* that is interrupted by abrupt **beatings**. **Scapin** admits to absconding with a cask of Spanish wine, presumably sherry, from his master's cellar, but this escapade with his friends is quickly forgotten. **George Dandin** is able to drown the indignities of unsuccessful usurpation and manifest cuckoldry in wine, but only after the action of the play itself has ended. Similarly, the two rejected **Satyrs** at the conclusion of *Les Amants magnifiques* seek liquid consolation. Wine is frequently mentioned as an indispensable ingredient of good living and civility, especially in fashionable *cadeaux* of the type **Dorante** organizes in *Le Bourgeois gentilhomme*.

**Writing**. Writing of both prose and verses occupies a considerable place in Molière's work, but is mainly confined to the learned and the aristocratic. Even as highly placed a person as **Monsieur Jourdain** possesses rudimentary writing skills at best, since he needs help with his spelling and doesn't even realize that he has been "speaking in prose." Most of the **servant** and **peasant** classes were illiterate, even **Alceste's servant** in *Le Misanthrope*, who cannot read the papers sent to his master. However, some managed to achieve a degree of self–taught literacy. **Lubin** in *George Dandin* boasts that, although he cannot decipher cursive, he can recognize printed letters and read signs. Writing was still evolving in Molière's time, with the **Academy** just beginning to issue edicts regularizing such things as punctuation and spelling. However, it had not evolved as far as **Cléante** claims in *Le Malade imaginaire*, where he tricks **Argan** by telling him that a new form of musical notation contains the words as well as the melody (II, 5). Writing was held to be so powerful a medium that it could convey with accuracy not only objective truth but also real impressions of personality. **Clitandre** tells **Henriette** in *Les Femmes savantes* that long before he met **Trissotin**, he had read his works and formed such a thorough picture of him that when he finally encountered him in a crowded assembly, he spotted him right away. But if writing can reveal much, it is no substitute for virtue itself. The **Philosophy Teacher** in *Le Bourgeois gentilhomme* appears ridiculous when he tries to seek vengeance from a **beating** by replying in print. Molière himself made it a point to avoid spilling ink in fruitless literary squabbles. Instead of writing libels and defamatory **letters**, he limited his written ripostes to jokes in the plays that would increase the receipts for the Palais Royal Theater.

# Z

**Zanni**. Traditional comic figures from the *commedia dell'arte*, they were generally associated with particular geographic regions, such as Bergamo, Milan, or Bologna.

**Zephir** (*Psyché*). Molière's role as **Cupid's** helper is unique in that it is so limited. He appears only in a few scenes, one of them a singing interlude. His **language** resembles the banter of *Amphitryon*, but he is very unlike the harried **Sosie**, having actually less at stake than almost any subordinate in a Molière comedy. In some ways he resembles **Clitidas**, but he is more active and powerful at times, especially when he uses the **machines** to make people come and go from Cupid's palace. But as a divine henchman, he has none of the sadistic peskiness of **Mercury**. In all, it gave Molière just enough presence, without placing on him any exorbitant demands of voice or energy.

**Zerbinette** (*Les Fourberies de Scapin*). This **Gypsy slave** girl, with whom **Léandre** falls in **love**, has an overwhelming form of **laughter** that reveals her identity as the actress **Mlle Beauval**. She demonstrates this trait in her conversation with **Géronte**, where she recounts all the particulars of his infamous bag incident to his face, laughing hysterically all the time. Despite this characteristic, Zerbinette has become very dear to **Hyacinte**, who begs her father to allow her to stay with them, regardless of the apparent impropriety, since **Léandre** is in **love** with her. She is soon after revealed by an identifying bracelet to be **Argante's** long–lost daughter, which gives her the standing needed to wed her admirer.

# Bibliography

## EDITIONS

Fabre d'Eglantine, Philippe–François–Nazaire. *Le Philinte de Molière*. Ed. Judith K. Proud. Exeter: University. of Exeter Press, 1995.

Grimarest, Jean–Léonor Le Gallois de. *La Vie de Monsieur de Molière*. Ed. Georges Mongrédien. Paris: CNRS, 1955.

Hubert, André. *Registre*. Ed. Sylvie Chevalley. *Revue d'Histoire du Théâtre* 25 (1973), 1–132, 147–195.

La Grange, Charles Varlet de. *Registre*. Ed. Burt Young and Grace Philpott Young. 2 vols. Paris: Droz, 1947. Reprint. Geneva: Slatkine, 1977. 2 vols. In 1.

———. *Registre*. Ed. Sylvie Chevalley. Paris: Minkoff, 1972.

La Mothe Le Vayer, François de. *Lettre sur la comédie de l'Imposteur*. Ed. Robert McBride. Durham, UK: University of Durham Press, 1994.

*La Querelle de L'École des femmes, comédies de Jean Donneau de Visé, Edme Boursault, Charles Robinet, A. J. Montfleury, Jean Chevalier, Philippe de la Croix*. Ed. Georges Mongrédien. 2 vols. Paris: Nizet, 1971.

Molière. *L'Avare*. Ed. P. J. Yarrow. London: University of London Press, 1958.

———. *Le Bourgeois gentilhomme*. Ed. H. Gaston Hall. London: University of London Press, 1966.

———. *Le Docteur amoureux*. Ed. P. Lerat. Paris: Nizet, 1973.

———. *Dom Juan ou le Festin de Pierre*. Ed. W. D. Howarth. Oxford: Blackwell, 1975.

———. *L'École des femmes* and *La Critique de l'École des femmes*. Ed. W. D. Howarth. Oxford: Blackwell, 1963.

———. *Les Femmes savantes*. Ed. H. Gaston Hall. Oxford: Clarendon, 1974.

———. *Le Festin de Pierre (Dom Juan). Édition critique du texte d'Amsterdam (1683)*. Ed. Joan DeJean. Geneva: Droz, 1999.

———. *Les Fourberies de Scapin*. Ed. John T. Stoker. London: University of London Press, 1971.

————. *Le Malade imaginaire.* Ed. Peter Nurse. Oxford: Clarendon, 1965.

————. *Le Misanthrope.* Ed. Gustave Rudler. Oxford: Blackwell, 1972.

————. *Œuvres.* Ed. Charles Varlet de La Grange and Vivot. 8 vols. Paris: Thierry, Barbin and Trabouillet, 1682.

————. *Œuvres complètes.* Ed. E. Despois and P. Menard. 13 vols. Paris: Hachette, 1873–1900.

————. *Œuvres complètes.* Ed. Georges Couton. 2 Vols. Paris: Gllimard, 1971.

————. *Les Précieuses ridicules. Documents contemporains. Lexique du vocabulaire précieux.* Ed. Micheline Cuénin. Paris: Minard, 1973; Geneva: Droz, 1973.

*Recueil des textes et documents relatifs à Molière.* Ed. Georges Mongrédien. 2nd ed. 2 vols. Paris: CNRS, 1973.

## CRITICAL STUDIES

Abraham, Claude. *On the Structures of Molière's Comédies–Ballets.* Biblio 17. Tübingen: G. Narr, 1984.

*Actes des Journées internationales Molière (Paris, 18–21 juin 1973). Revue d'Histoire du Théâtre* 26 (1973), 3–216.

Adam, Antoine. *Histoire de la littérature française au XVIIe siècle.* Vol. 3. Paris: Del Duca, 1954.

Albanese, Ralph Jr. "Argent et réification dans *l'Avare.*" *L'Esprit Créateur* 21,3 (1981), 35–50.

————. *Le Dynamisme de la peur chez Molière.* University, MS: University Monographs, 1976.

————. "Hypocrisie et dramaturgie dans *Dom Juan.*" *Le Nouveau Moliériste* 2 (1995), 123–143.

————. *Molière à l'école républicaine.* Saratoga, CA: Anma Libri, 1992.

Albert–Galtier, Alexandre. "Un Comédien en colère: masques et grimaces de Molière dans la Querelle de *l'École des femmes.*" *Cahiers du dix–septième* 7 (2000), 91–104.

*Alceste et l'absolutisme: essais de dramaturgie sur* le Misanthrope. Ed. J.–P. Vincent. Paris: Galilée, 1977.

Apostolidès, Jean–Marie. *Le Roi–machine, spectacle et politique au temps de Louis XIV.* Paris: Minuit, 1981.

Attinger, Gustave. *L'Esprit de la commedia dell'arte dans le théâtre français.* 2nd ed. Neufchâtel: La Baconnière, 1950.

Bamforth, Stephen, ed. *Molière. Proceedings of the Nottingham Molière Conference.* Nottingham: University of Nottingham, 1994.

Baschera, Marco. *Théâtralité dans l'œuvre de Molière.* Tübingen: G. Narr, 1998.

Bénichou, Paul. *Morales du grand siècle.* 2nd ed. Paris: Gallimard, 1980.

Bourqui, Claude. *Polémique et stratégies dans le Dom Juan de Molière.* Biblio 17. Tübingen: G. Narr, 1992.

Bray, René *Molière, homme de théâtre.* Paris: Mercure de France, 1954.

Brody, Jules. "*Dom Juan* and *Le Misanthrope,* or the Esthetics of Individualism in Molière." *PMLA* 84 (1969), 559–576.

Cairncross, John, ed. *L'Humanité de Molière.* Paris: Nizet, 1988.

————. *Molière bourgeois et libertin.* Paris: Nizet, 1963.

————. *New Light on Molière.* Geneva: Droz, 1956.

Calder, Andrew. "Molière, Plautus, and Terence, and the Renaissance Theories of Comedy." *New Comparison* (1987), 19–32.

————. *Molière. The Theory and Practice of Comedy.* London: Athlone, 1993.

Caldicott, C.E.J. *La Carrière de Molière: entre protecteurs et éditeurs*. Amsterdam: Rodopi, 1998.

———. "Les Séjours de Molière au Languedoc." *Revue d'Histoire Littéraire de la France* 87 (1987), 994–1014.

Carmody, Jim. *Rereading Molière: Mise en scène from Antoine to Vitez*. Ann Arbor: University of Michigan Press, 1993.

Chartier, Roger. "George Dandin ou la leçon de civilité." *Revue d'Histoire Littéraire de la France* 96 (1996), 475–482.

———. "George Dandin ou le social en représentation." *Annales–HSS* 49 (1994), 277–309.

Chevalley, Sylvie. *Molière en son temps*. Paris: Minkoff, 1973.

———. *Molière, sa vie, son œuvre*. Paris: F. Birr, 1984.

Chill, E. S. "Tartuffe, Religion, and Courtly Culture." *French Historical Studies* 3 (1963), 151–183.

Christout, M.–F. *Le Ballet de Cour*. Paris: Picard, 1967.

Ciccone, Anthony A. *The Comedy of Language: Four Farces by Molière*. Potomac, MD: UPA, 1980.

Collinet, Jean–Pierre. *Lectures de Molière*. Paris: A. Colin, 1974.

Conesa, Gabriel. *Le Dialogue moliéresque*. Paris: PUF, 1983.

———. "*Le Misanthrope* ou les limites de l'aristotélisme." *Littératures classiques* 38 (1999), 19–29.

Corvin, M. *Molière et les metteurs en scène d'aujourd'hui*. Lyon: Presses Universitaires de Lyon, 1985.

Dandrey, Patrick. *Le Cas Argan: Molière et la maladie imaginaire*. Paris: Klincksieck, 1993.

———. Dom Juan *ou le critique de la raison comique*. Paris: Champion, 1993.

———. *La Médecine et la maladie dans le théâtre de Molière*. 2 vols. Paris: Klincksieck, 1998.

———. *Molière ou l'esthétique du ridicule*. Paris: Klincksieck, 1992.

Daniel, George B., ed. *Molière Studies to Commemorate the Tercentenary of His Death*. Special issue of *Romance Notes* 15, suppl. 1 (1973), 1–187.

Defaux, Gérard. *Molière ou les métamorphoses du comique*. 2nd ed. Paris: Klincksieck, 1992.

Descotes, Maurice. *Les Grands Rôles du théâtre de Molière*. 2nd ed. Paris: PUF, 1976.

Dock, Stephen Varick. *Costume and Fashion in the Plays of Jean–Baptiste Poquelin Molière: A Seventeenth–Century Perspective*. Geneva: Slatkine, 1992.

Duchêne, Roger. *Molière*. Paris: Fayard, 1998.

Emelina, Jean. "Les comiques de Molière." *Littératures classiques* 38 (1999), 102–115.

———. *Les Valets et les servantes dans le théâtre comique en France de 1610 à 1710*. Grenoble: Presses Universitaires de Grenoble, 1985.

Eustis, Alvin. *Molière as Ironic Contemplator*. Paris: Mouton, 1973.

Fargher, Robert. "Molière and His Reasoners." In *Studies of French Literature Presented to H. R. Lawton*. Manchester, UK: Manchester University Press, 1968. Pp. 105–120.

Fellows, Otis. *French Opinion of Molière (1800–1850)*. Providence: Brown University Press, 1937.

Fernandez, Ramon. *Molière, ou l'essence du génie comique*. New ed. Paris: Grasset, 1979. Trans. by Wilson Follett as *Molière: The Man Seen through the Plays*. New York: Hill and Wang, 1958.

Finn, Thomas. *Molière's Spanish Connection*. New York: Peter Lang, 2001.

Fleck, Stephen H. *Music, Dance, and Laughter. Comic Creation in Molière's Comédy–Ballets.* Biblio 17. Tübingen: G. Narr, 1995.

Force, Pierre. *Molière ou le prix des choses.* Paris: Nathan, 1994.

Forestier, Georges. *Esthétique de l'identité dans le théâtre français (1550–1680).* Geneva: Droz, 1988.

——. *Molière en toutes lettres.* Paris: Bordas, 1990.

——. *Le Théâtre dans le théâtre sur la scène française du XVIIe siècle.* Geneva: Droz, 1981.

Gaines, James F., and Michael C. Koppisch, eds. *Approaches to Teaching Molière's* Tartuffe *and Other Plays.* New York: Modern Language Association of America, 1995.

——. "*Caractères,* Superstition and Paradoxes in *Le Misanthrope.* In *Alteratives: Studies in Honor of Jean Alter.* Lexington, KY: French Forum, 1993. Pp. 72–84.

——. "L'Éveil des sentiments et le paradoxe de la conscience." *French Review* 41 (1997), 407–415.

——. "Le Malade imaginaire et le paradoxe de la mort." In *Le Labyrinthe de Versailles,* ed. Martine Debaisieux. Amsterdam: Rodopi, 1998. Pp. 73–84.

——. *Social Structures in Molière's Theater.* Columbus: Ohio State University Press, 1984.

——. "*Tartuffe* et les paradoxes de la foi." *Dix–septième Siècle* 180 (1993), 537–549.

Garapon, Robert. *Le Dernier Molière.* Paris: SEDES, 1977.

Gendarme de Bévotte, Georges. *Le Festin de Pierre avant Molière.* Paris: Cornély, 1907.

Gethner, Perry. "Challenges to Royal Authority in French Classical Comedy." *Seventeenth–Century French Studies* 21 (1999), 85–90.

Goldschmidt, Georges–Arthur. *Molière ou la liberté mis à nu.* Paris: Julliard: 1973.

Goode, William O. "Reflections in a Bourgeois Eye: Noble Essence in *Le Bourgeois gentilhomme.*" *Romance Notes* 39 (1999), 163–171.

Gossman, Lionel. *Men and Masks: A Study of Molière.* Baltimore: Johns Hopkins University Press, 1963.

Grimm, Jürgen. *Molière en son temps.* Biblio 17. Tübingen: G. Narr, 1993.

Guicharnaud, Jacques, ed. *Molière: A Collection of Critical Essays.* Englewood Cliffs, NJ: Prentice–Hall, 1964.

——. *Molière, une aventure théâtrale.* Paris: Gallimard, 1963.

Guichemerre, Roger. *La Comédie avant Molière, 1640–1660.* Paris: A. Colin, 1972.

Gutwirth, Marcel. "Dom Garcie de Navarre et le Misanthrope, de la comédie héroïque au comique du héros." *PMLA* 83 (1968), 188–196.

——. *Molière ou l'invention comique.* Paris: Minard, 1966.

——. "Insaisissable Alcmène." *Le Nouveau Moliériste* 2 (1995), 229–245.

——. "Tartuffe and the Mysteries." *PMLA* 92 (1977), 33–40.

Hall, H. Gaston. *Comedy in Context: Essays on Molière.* Jackson: University Press of Mississippi, 1984.

——. "The Litarary Context of Molière's *Le Misanthrope.*" *Studi francesi* 14 (1970), 20–38.

——. *Molière: Tartuffe.* London: Arnold, 1960.

Herzel, Roger W. "The Décor of Molière's Stage: The Testimony of Brissart and Sauvé." *PMLA* 93 (1978), 925–954.

——. *The Original Casting of Molière's Plays.* Ann Arbor: UMI Research Press, 1981.

Hilgar, Marie–France. *Onze Mises en scène parisiennes du théâtre de Molière (1989–1994).* Biblio 17. Tübingen: G. Narr, 1997.

Hope, Quentin. "Molière's Curtain Lines." *French Studies* 26 (1972), 143–155.
———. "The Scene of Greeting in Molière." *Romanic Review* 50 (1959), 241–254.
Horville, Robert. *Dom Juan de Molière: une dramaturgie de la rupture.* Paris: Larousse, 1972.
Howarth, W. D. *Molière. A Playwright and His Audience.* Cambridge, UK: Cambridge University Press, 1982.
Howarth, W. D., and Merlin Thomas, eds. *Molière: Stage and Study, Essays in Honour of W. G. Moore.* Oxford: Clarendon, 1975.
Hubert, Judd. *Molière and the Comedy of Intellect.* Berkeley: University of California Press, 1962.
Jasinski, René. *Molière.* Paris: Hatier, 1969.
———. *Molière et le Misanthrope.* Paris: Nizet, 1951.
Johnson, Roger, Jr., Guy T. Trail, and Editha S. Newman, eds. *Molière and the Commonwealth of Letters: Patrimony and Posterity.* Jackson, MS: University Press of Mississippi, 1975.
Jurgens, Madeleine. "L'Aventure de l'Illustre Théâtre." *Revue d'Histoire Littéraire de la France* 72 (1972), 976–1006.
Jurgens, Madeleine, and Elizabeth Maxfield–Miller. *Cent Ans de recherches sur Molière.* Paris: SEVPEN, 1963.
Kasparek, J. L. *Molière's Tartuffe and the Traditions of Roman Satire.* Chapel Hill: University of North Carolina Press, 1977.
Kern, Edith. "*L'École des femmes* and the Spirit of Farce." *L'Esprit Créateur* 13 (1973), 220–228.
Knutson, Harold C. *Molière: An Archetypal Approach.* Toronto: University of Toronto Press, 1976.
———. "Molière's *Raisonneur*: A Critical Assessment." *Œuvres et critiques* 1 (1976), 129–131.
———. *The Triumph of Wit.* Columbus: Ohio State University Press, 1988.
———. "*Vraisemblance* and Molière's Comedies." *PFSCL* 4 (1977), 39–50.
Koppisch, Michael S. "Désordre et sacrifice dans *Geroge Dandin*." *Travaux de Littérature* 9 (1996), 75–86.
Lancaster, Henry C. *History of French Dramatic Literature in the Seventeenth Century.* 9 vols. Baltimore: Johns Hopkins University Press, 1929–1942.
Lanson, Gustave. "Molière et la farce." In *Essais de méthode, de critique et d'histoie littéraire*, ed. Henri Peyre. Paris: Hachette, 1965.
Lawrence, Francis. *Molière: The Comedy of Unreason.* New Orleans: Tulane University Press, 1968.
———. "*Tartuffe*: A Question of *Honnête* Behavior." *Romance Notes* 15, suppl. 1 (1974), 134–144.
Lebègue, Raymond. *Études sur le théâtre français.* 2 vols. Paris: Nizet, 1977–1978.
Magné, Bernard. "*L'École des femmes*, ou la conquête de la parole." *Revue des Sciences Humaines*, no. 145 (1972), 125–140.
Mallinson, G. J. *Molière; L'Avare.* London: Grant and Cutler, 1988.
Martinenche, Ernest. *Molière et le théâtre espagnol.* Paris: Hachette, 1906.
Mazouer, Charles. "Les Défenseurs ecclésiastiques de Molière." *Le Nouveau Moliériste* 2 (1995), 57–67.
———. *Molière et ses comédies-ballets.* Paris: Klincksieck, 1993.
———. *Le Personnage du naïf dans le théâtre comique du Moyen Age à Marivaux.* Paris: Klincksieck, 1979.
McAuley, Gay. "Language and Theater in *Le Malade Imaginaire*." *Australian Journal of French Studies* 11 (1974), 4–18.

McBride, Robert. *The Skeptical Vision of Molière*. London: Macmillan, 1977.

————. *The Triumph of Ballet in Molière's Theatre*. Lampeted, Wales: Edwin Mellon Press, 1992.

Mélèse, Pierre. *Le Théâtre et le public à Paris sous Louis XIV, 1659–1715*. Paris: Droz, 1934.

Michaut, Gustave. *Les Débuts de Molière*. Paris: Hachette, 1923. Reprint. Geneva: Slatkine, 1968.

————. *La Jeunesse de Molière*. Paris: Hachette, 1922. Reprint. Geneva: Slatkine, 1968.

————. *Les Luttes de Molière*. Paris: Hachette, 1925. Reprint. Geneva: Slatkine, 1968.

Millespierres, François. *La Vie quotidienne des médecins au temps de Molière*. Paris: Hachette, 1964.

*Molière*. Spec. issue of *Cahiers de l'Association d'Études françaises* 16 (1964), 181–303.

*Molière*. Spec. issue of *L'Esprit Créateur* 6 (1966), 127–216.

*Molière*. Spec. issue of *L'Esprit Créateur* 36 (1996), 1–209.

*Molière*. Spec. issue of *Revue d'Histoire Littéraire de la France* 72 (1972), 769–1003.

Molino, Jean. "Les Nœuds de la matière: l'unité des *Femmes savantes*." *Dix–Septième Siècle*, no. 113 (1976), 23–47.

Mongrédien, Georges. *Dictionnaire biographique des comédiens français au XVIIe siècle*. Paris: CNRS, 1961.

————. *La Vie quotidienne des comédiens au temps de Molière*. Paris: Hachette, 1966.

Moore, Will G. *Molière, a New Criticism*. 2nd ed. Oxford: Clarendon, 1964

Morel, Jacques. "Molière ou la dramaturgie de l'honnêteté." *Information littéraire* 15 (1963), 185–191.

Mornet, Daniel. *Molière*. Paris: Boivin, 1943.

Muratore, Mary J. "Theatrical Conversion in Molière's *Dom Juan*." *Nottingham French Studies* 34,2 (1995), 1–9.

Nelson, Robert J. "*L'Impromptu de Versailles* Reconsidered." *French Studies* 11 (1957), 305–311.

Norman, Larry F. *The Public Mirror: Molière and the Social Commerce of Depiction*. Chicago: University of Chicago Press, 1999.

Nurse, Peter H. *Molière and the Comic Spirit*. Geneva: Droz, 1991.

Pellisson, Maurice. *Comédies–ballets de Molière*. 2nd ed. Paris: Eds. D'Aujourd'hui, 1976.

Poulaille, Henry. *Corneille sous le masque de Molière*. Paris: Grasset, 1957.

Rey–Flaud, Bernadette. *Molière et la farce*. Paris: Droz, 1996.

Riggs, Larry. "Molière, Paranoia and the Presence of Absence." *Cahiers du dix–septième* 6 (1992), 195–211.

————. *Molière and Plurality. Decomposition of the Classical Self*. New York: Peter Lang, 1989.

Romero, Laurence. *Molière: Traditions in Criticism, 1900–1970*. Chapel Hill: University of North Carolina Press, 1974.

Ronzeaud, Pierre, ed. *Molière des* Fourberies de Scapin *au* Malade imaginaire. Spec. issue of *Littératures classiques* (January 1993).

Saintonge, Paul, and R. W. Christ. *Fifty Years of Molière Studies. A Bibliography*. Baltimore: Johns Hopkins University Press, 1942.

Salomon, Herman P. *Tartuffe devant l'opinion française*. Paris: PUF, 1962.

Scherer, Jacques. *La Dramaturgie classique en France*. Paris: Nizet, 1950.

Schlossmann, Beryl. "Transports of Love: Desire, Image, and the Object in Molière's *Dom Juan*." *Modern Language Notes* 111 (1996), 918–937.

Scott, Virginia. *The Commedia dell'arte in Paris, 1644–1697.* Charlottesville: University of Virginia Press, 1990.

———. *Molière. A Theatrical Life.* Cambridge, UK: Cambridge University Press, 2000.

Sells, A. Lytton. "Molière and La Mothe Le Vayer." *Modern Language Review* 28 (1933), 352–357, 444–455.

Simon, Alfred. *Molière par lui-même.* Paris: Seuil, 1957.

Steinberger, Deborah. "Molière and the Domestication of French Comedy: Public and Private Space in *L'École des femmes.*" *Cahiers du dix-septième* 6,2 (1992), 131–139.

Sweetser, Marie-Odile. "Hypocrisie et dramaturgie chez Molière." *PFSCL* 16 (1989), 95–109.

———. "Naissance fortuite et fortunée d'un nouveau genre: *Les Fâcheux.*" In *Car demeure l'amitié: Mélanges offerts à Claude Abraham.* Biblio 17. Tübingen: G. Narr, 1997. Pp. 87–98.

———. "La Nature et le naturel: le cas d'Agnès." In *Thèmes et genres littéraires aux XVIIe et XVIIIe siècles. Mélanges en l'honneur de Jacques Truchet.* Paris: PUF, 1992. Pp. 443–449.

———. "Structure et signification du *Misanthrope.*" *French Review* 49 (1976), 505–513.

Tobin, Ronald W. "Civilité et convivialité dans *Le Misanthrope* et ses suites." *Le Nouveau Moliériste* 4–5 (1998/99), 145–168.

———. *Tarte à la crème: Comedy and Gastronomy in Molière's Theater.* Columbus: Ohio State University Press, 1990.

Treloar, Bonnie. *Molière. Les Précieuses ridicules.* London: Arnold, 1970.

Truchet, Jacques, ed. *Thématique de Molière.* Paris: SEDES, 1985.

Vedel, Valdemar. *Deux Classiques français vus par un critique étranger.* Trans. E. Cornet. Paris: Champion, 1935.

Vernet, Max. *Molière: côté jardin, côté cour.* Paris: Nizet, 1991.

*Visages de Molière.* Special issue of *Œuvres et critiques* 6,1 (1981).

Wadsworth, Philip A. "The Composition of *Psyché.*" *Rice University Studies* 53,4 (1967), 69–76.

———. *Molière and the Italian Theatrical Tradition.* 2nd ed. Birmingham, AL: Summa, 1987.

Wagner, Monique. *Molière and the Age of Enlightenment.* Banbury: Voltaire Foundation, 1973.

Waterson, Karolyn. *Molière et l'autorité.* Lexington, KY: French Forum, 1976.

Watson, H. "Sainte-Beuve's Molière: A Romantic Hamlet." *French Review* 38 (1965), 606–618.

Wilcox, John. *The Relation of Molière to Restoration Comedy.* New York: Columbia University Press, 1938.

Wolfe, Kathryn W. "Contesting Authority in Molière's *Tartuffe.*" *Cahiers du dix-septième* 6,2 (1992), 140–151.

# Index

# About the
# Editor and Contributors

JAMES F. GAINES is chair of Modern Foreign Languages and Professor of French at Mary Washington College. Prior to joining the faculty at Mary Washington, he taught for more than twenty years at Southeastern Louisiana University, where he was awarded the President's Award for Excellence in Research. He is the author of *Social Structures in Molière's Theater* and has worked with Michael S. Koppisch to edit *Approaches to Teaching Tartuffe and Other Plays by Molière*. His other books include *Pierre Du Ryer and His Tragedies: From Envy to Liberation*, a critical edition of Du Ryer's tragedy *Lucrece* prepared in collaboration with Perry Gethner, and a volume in progress on Molière and paradox. In addition, he has written over fifty articles on such early modern authors as Pierre Corneille, Jean de la Bruyère, Blaise Pascal, Jean de la Fontaine, and Madame de Lafayette. He served for over a decade as General Editor of the *Sociocriticism* monograph series published by Peter Lang. With his late wife, Josephine A. Roberts, he collaborated on a number of projects dealing with early modern comparative literature.

RALPH ALBANESE, JR is chair of Modern Foreign Languages and Literatures at the University of Memphis and Professor of French. His Molière scholarship includes *Le dynamisme de la peur chez Molière: Une Analyse socio-culturelle de Dom Juan, Tartuffe, et L'École des femmes* (Romance Monograph Series, 1976) and *Molière à l'école républicaine: De la critique universitaire aux manuels scolaires (1870-1914)* (Anma Libri, 1992), as well as dozens of articles on individual plays. He is also the author of *Initiation aux problèmes socioculturels au dix-septième siècle* and the soon-to-appear *La Fontaine à l'école républicaine: Du poète universel au classique scolaire* (EMF Critique). He has also written widely on Corneille, Racine, and other French Classical dramatists.

FAITH E. BEASLEY is associate professor of French at Dartmouth College. She is a specialist in women's literature in the French Classical period. Along with *Revising Memory: Women's Fiction and Memoirs in Seventeenth-Century France* (1990), she has edited *Approaches to Teaching La Princesse de Clèves* (1998, with Katharine Ann Jensen). She has written articles on Madame de Lafayette, Madame de Sévigné, Madame de Villedieu, and other writers.

THOMAS P. FINN is assistant professor of French at Ohio Northern University. His research interests in the relationship between French and Spanish theatrical traditions in the early modern period and the theories of comedy that emanated from them have resulted in *Molière's Spanish Connection: Seventeenth-Century Spanish Theatrical Influence on Imaginary Identity in Molière* (Peter Lang Publishers, 2001) and numerous articles on related subjects.

STEPHEN H. FLECK teaches French at California State University, Long Beach. He has published on various seventeenth-century topics, especially comic, musical, and festive aspects of Molière's theater; Racinian language and speech act theory; and the intersections of music, drama, and literature in the early modern period.

PERRY GETHNER is professor of French at Oklahoma State University and head of the Department of Foreign Languages and Literatures. He has edited a ground-breaking multi-volume collection of plays by seventeenth- and eighteenth-century French women dramatists, as well as critical editions of plays by Rotrou. He has collaborated with James Gaines on the critical edition of Pierre Du Ryer's tragedy *Lucrece*. As a translator, he has made available to English-speaking audiences versions of early modern plays relating to women writers and Biblical topics. He is the author of over forty articles on the history of the seventeenth-century French theater, with special emphasis on genre studies and the conditions of theatrical presentation.

WILLIAM O. GOODE teaches in the Department of Romance Languages at the University of North Carolina–Greensboro. He served a distinguished term as a member of the main publication team of the *French Review*. In addition to a career of research on seventeenth-century dramaturgy, his more recent interest in the history of the city of Paris and its relationship to literature has led to the design of an online course, "Paris: Construire la ville/Écrire la ville," and to such articles as "Three French Queens and the Urban History of Paris" and "Molière au Bureau des Merveilles: Molière's Paris."

RICHARD E. GOODKIN is Professor of French at the University of Wisconsin–Madison. His books include: *The Symbolist Home and the Tragic Home: Mallarmé and Oedipus* (John Benjamins, 1984), *The Tragic Middle: Racine, Aristotle, Euripides* (University of Wisconsin Press, 1991), *Around Proust* (Princeton University Press, 1991), and *Birth Marks: The Tragedy of Primogeniture in Pierre Corneille, Thomas Corneille, and Jean Racine* (University of Pennsylvania Press, 2000). Besides numerous articles on early modern and modern French literature and a current project on the relations between the theater and the novel in early modern France, he has edited *Autour de Racine: Studies in Intertextuality* (Yale French Studies 76, 1989).

MICHAEL S. KOPPISCH is professor of French at Michigan State University. His books include *The Dissolution of Character: Changing Perspectives on La Bruyère's Caractères* and *Approaches to Teaching Molière's Tartuffe and Other Plays* (co-edited with James Gaines). He has written on a wide range of seventeenth-century topics and is currently preparing a book-length study on Molière's theater.

BUFORD NORMAN received his Ph.D. from Yale and taught at Iowa State University before moving to the University of South Carolina, where he holds the Jesse Chapman Alcorn Memorial chair as professor of Foreign Languages. His books include a study on Pascal, *Portraits of Thought* (Ohio State University Press, 1987), a critical edition of Quinault's libretti (Littératures classiques, 1999), and the soon-to-appear volume *Touched by the Graces: The Libretti of Philippe Quinault in the Context of French Classicism* (Summa, 2002). In addition, he has co-edited Quinault's *Alceste* and related texts and is currently writing a book on Racine and music. Other articles treat Cyrano, La Rochefoucauld, Nicole, and, of course, Molière.

ROLAND RACEVSKIS, assistant professor of French at the University of Iowa, is the author of *Time and Ways of Knowing: Molière, Sévigné, Lafayette*. He has published essays on French seventeenth-century narrative and theater and on the history of early modern sciences of measurement. He is currently preparing a book on the representation of thresholds in the secular tragedies of Racine.

LARRY W. RIGGS is professor of French and head of Modern Languages, Literatures, and Cultures at Butler University. His major publications include: *Molière and Plurality: Decomposition of the Classical Self,* and *Resistance to Culture in Molière, Flaubert, and Camus.* Currently, he is working on a book on Molière and the codes of modernity. His ongoing research interests are reflected in such recent articles as: "Monstres naisssants: Masculine Birth and Feminine Subversion in the Theatrum Mundi," "Delusions of Self-Fashioning: Moralisme as Critique of Modernity," and "A Note on the Intimations of Post-Modernism in *Manon Lescaut.*"

DAVID LEE RUBIN is professor emeritus of French at the University of Virginia and founding editor of *Continuum, EMF: Studies in Early Modern France*, and *EMF Critiques*. In addition, he is publisher of the Rockwood Press. A former Guggenheim Fellow and recipient of a Festschrift entitled *The Shape of Change*, he is the author of *Higher, Hidden Order, The Knot of Artifice,* and *A Pact with Silence*. He has edited or co-edited a score of books and his essays have appeared in such publications as *The New Princeton Encyclopedia of Poetry ad Poetics, Yale French Studies,* and *Comparative Literature*.

KATHLEEN WINE is associate professor of French at Dartmouth College. She is the author of *The Forgotten Goddess: Humanism and Absolutism in Honoré d'Urfé's* L'Astrée (Droz, 2000) and is co-editing *Theatrum Mundi: Essays in Honor of Ronald W. Tobin* (forthcoming from the Early Modern France series of Rockwood Press). Her interests in the early modern portrayal of women and in court festival have led to such recent articles as: "*Le Tartuffe* and *Les Plaisirs de l'Isle enchantée*: Flattery or Satire?," "Honored Guests: Wife and Mistress in *Les Plaisirs de l'Isle enchantée*," and "Romance and Novel in *La Princesse de Clèves*."